EVALUATING DEMOCRACY

EVALUATING DEMOCRACY
An Introduction to Political Science

JOE ALLMAN, UNIVERSITY OF OREGON AND WALT ANDERSON

GOODYEAR PUBLISHING COMPANY, INC.,
PACIFIC PALISADES, CALIFORNIA

GIFT

Library of Congress Cataloging in Publication Data

Allman, Joe, comp.
    Evaluating democracy.

    1. Democracy—Addresses, essays, lectures. I. Ander-
son, Walt, 1933–   joint comp.   II. Title.
JC423.A53   321.8   73-88138
ISBN 0-87620-281-4

Contents

Preface

The act of writing a book is a process of personal growth, whether the writer chooses it to be so or not. Frequently a writer sets out to write a book which will change other people and finds out, along the way, that it is changing him.

This has been our experience. When we started to write this book we knew, of course, that we were involving ourselves in a task of communication. As we explored the material more deeply, seeking to clarify and understand precisely what it was we were trying to communicate, we found ourselves developing a new perspective about the whole discipline of political science, and revising some of our assumptions about what it has been, is, and will become.

For one thing, we agreed at an early stage of the proceedings that we would try to do more than simply present a neutral and diffused survey of all the things that are ordinarily considered to be parts of the discipline; we agreed that we would focus on a central theme so as to convey some sense of the discipline's main purpose and direction. And the farther we journeyed into the heart of the discipline, the more apparent it became to us that its overriding concern—the single subject which most engages its energies—is democracy. This is, in a way, strikingly obvious. It is to be expected that an academic discipline taught and practiced within a democratic nation and in a world where democracy is praised (if not practiced) on all sides, would naturally have such a focus. This is especially true of a discipline which has opted to be empirical—to emphasize the study of what actually goes on in modern politics.

And although we were primarily concerned with contemporary political science, we definitely saw the behavioral era as a chapter in political study and not—as some of the champions of behavioralism would have it—the whole story. This conviction led us toward the classics, and we decided to include in the text a section dealing with some of the main themes of political philosophy in the past—especially where this would help us to understand how the modern mass democracies, the nation-states, came to be. This required us to take another look at the commonly-accepted distinction between "normative" and "empirical" theory, the idea that the ancient political philosophers occupied themselves mostly with thoughts about what should be, while the modern scientists of politics study only what is.

The more we thought about contemporary political science within the context of contemporary mass democracy, the more we became convinced that despite its empirical thrust, political science is essentially an evaluative pursuit. In fact we came to see that it is far more than that: it contains an ideology, a set of statements about how things are and about how things *should be* as they are. This ideology, which lies beneath the impersonal facade of pluralist theory, is discussed in Part Two of this book; the point we wish to make about it here is that it expresses the inevitable connection between political theory and the social order in which it is developed. Classical political theories—as we show in Part One—were products of their times; so is modern political science.

Perhaps the most challenging task of all was that of searching for some sense of where political science is headed. Ordinarily, it is the function of a textbook to present the current status of the discipline, a picture of the accepted work which has been done within the existing paradigm, and no more. We chose to violate this rule and to search for a vision of what might lie beyond the present boundaries. This arose in part from our dissatisfaction with the limitations of the view of politics and political science which has prevailed over the past decades: it seemed to us that the decision to criticize things as they are placed upon us a responsibility to say something about things as they may become. We were also impelled in this direction by the conviction—which grew as we went along—that a new paradigm of politics is already in the process of being created.

We describe this new paradigm as "developmental." Each of us had been moving in this direction in separately-published works.[1] But we had not previously employed the concept of human development as an ordering framework for political science or attempted to show how existing fields of political science, such as policy analysis, fit into a developmental perspective.

Lovers of consistency will find much to make them unhappy in this book. It contains three parts, each of which has its own kind of structure: Part One presents short readings in the context of historical background and exposition of the work of individual thinkers. Part Two presents longer readings in contemporary political science linked together by a critical essay about the present shape of the discipline. Part Three presents, with short introductory essays, a variety of readings aimed toward tracing the outlines of a developmental paradigm. In each case we have allowed the subject matter to dictate the structure rather than vice versa.

Acknowledgements: Al Goodyear first brought us together, over lunch in Pacific Palisades, to discuss this project. Clay Stratton, and later Dave Grady, provided the necessary editorial companionship along the way. We are grateful for the various contributions of Sue MacLaurin, Lee Massey, Nancy Tandberg, and Jane Hellesoe-Henon. And we especially wish to acknowledge, with affection and a touch of apologetic male chauvinism, the contributions of our wives, Judy Allman and Mauriça Anderson: they are responsible for much of the thinking that went into this book, and for a disproportionate amount of the hours of typing and editorial busywork that it consumed.

[1] Allman, *Creative Politics* (Goodyear, 1972); Anderson, *Politics and the New Humanism* (Goodyear, 1973).

EVALUATING DEMOCRACY

Part One
Toward Mass Democracy

The trend toward mass democracy is one of the salient facts of the political experience of Western society. It is, therefore, naturally a central theme of Western political analysis. To understand how mass democracies function— what they do, how they do it, who governs, who gets what and when and how—is the guiding purpose of the activity called political science.

This activity is an evaluative pursuit as well as an analytic one. It deals with such subjects as the composition of elites, the behavior of elected representatives, and the dynamics of competition among organized interest groups—subjects that are, essentially, different ways of asking: How democratic is a mass democracy? Or, put into a slightly different focus: How is a mass democracy democratic?

The nature and meaning of the modern effort to evaluate democracy can be seen most clearly, we believe, within a historical context: The institutional forms that modern democracies have inherited come down to us encumbered with a massive weight of ideology, tradition, folklore, and faith. To cut through all of these encumbrances and take a new, hard look at the reality of how democratic systems do, in fact, function has been the chief aim of the contemporary science of politics. This book is mainly about that enterprise, about political science as it has emerged in the United States during this century, and about how it deals with the heritage of democracy. But in order to further the understanding of modern democracies, we choose to present something of the heritage itself; therefore, we begin not with Arthur Bentley or C. S. Merriam, but with Plato and Aristotle.

Our method of presentation is not a summary of the "great ideas" of political philosophy, but rather an attempt to show that the ancient philosophers, like modern political scientists, have always been occupied with the political experience of their own times. Polybius used the concept of separation of powers as a way of explaining the apparent stability of the Roman Republic, and Montesquieu used the same concept as a way of showing how nation-states could guard against tyranny. In neither case was the writer indulging in an abstract philosophical discussion.

Our purpose in including historical material in the first part of this book is not only to point out the "relevance" of the classical political philosophers but also to provide a perspective from which to view the politics and the political science of our own time. In particular, we wish to call attention to the processes that brought the nation-states into existence; modern mass democracy is an institution that seeks to govern nations—large, egalitarian, industrialized, populous states—and in preparing to study mass democracy we should consider the origins of these kinds of societies. We are concerned, then, not only with the development of democracy, but with the revolutionary changes whereby the nations that had first consolidated their independence as monarchies, buttressed by ideas of sovereignty and divine right, became converted into political institutions with such features as written constitutions, elected representatives, and popular suffrage.

In the first three chapters of this section, we look first at the development of democracy in the Greek city-state; next, at the expansion of political space embodied in the Roman Empire and its successor, the Roman Catholic Church; and then at the growth of the national monarchies and at the philosophical concepts, such as sovereignty, that were used to legitimize that growth.

These chapters are not offered as a comprehensive introduction to Western political history or political philosophy. They present, rather, a review of material that gives perspective and coherence to a book about modern political science. Our perspective, then, is highly foreshortened; Chapter 4, "Revolution and Mass Society," is as long as the first three chapters combined. In Chapter 4, building upon material presented earlier, we survey some of the key revolutionary transitions of European and American governments, the development of classical democratic theory in the works of such writers as Locke and Rousseau, the foundations of modern conservatism and liberalism, and the first critiques of mass democracy: the line of thought that runs from Tocqueville through Marx and Weber to modern sociology and political science.

In the beginning of this book, we encounter democracy as an assortment of innovative practices used in governing a city-state with a population of less than a half million; later we look at it as the way of governing a nation of more than two hundred million inhabitants, with a much wider extension of voting rights.

It is, in a way, remarkable that the term "democracy" is used to describe such vastly different political orders. Yet, in spite of the enormous differences, there is a common purpose that can be seen to motivate the creation of both Athenian and modern democratic institutions. This purpose is to organize—to move toward more complex and diversified communities with wider boundaries, toward higher differentiation of roles and occupations, toward increased opportunities for choice and fulfillment—while retaining a significant measure of personal freedom and, for the individual, influence over governmental policy.

Any extension of political space poses a dilemma: As the state becomes greater, does the individual become less? Totalitarian societies offer one kind of answer; although the individual does indeed sacrifice some personal autonomy in such a society, there is as a reward the opportunity to bask in the reflected grandeur of the state, to consider oneself mighty because the state is mighty.

Democracy offers (or tries to offer) a greater reward, a gain of national power without a loss of personal power. The state may become mighty, but it remains fundamentally the instrument of its citizens, responsible to their will. Consider the words republic, *res publica,* a public thing; democracy, *demos kratein,* the people rule.

If and how the modern nation-state is a public thing, if and how the people rule—these are questions that political scientists ask in seeking to analyze and evaluate the processes of government. Underlying these are even more fundamental questions: Is democracy possible at all, and is it a good form of government? These issues, which are basic to the modern science of politics, were also basic to the political struggles and the political philosophy of the Athenian city-state.

1 Democracy in the City-State

THE RISE AND FALL OF ATHENS

Throughout a relatively brief and fairly tumultuous period of history, the Greeks of the city-state of Athens created a society that was not only more democratic in its political structure than any comparable state but was also politically and militarily strong, rich in material goods, and productive of art, drama, science, and philosophy. For a while—but only for a while—the Athenians made their experiment in self-government work; for a while the internal conflict among opposing classes was contained within the workings of the political system; and for a while the Athenians were sufficiently united and powerful to hold off all challenges from their external enemies. The strengths of the Athenian system have served for centuries as models for other democratic governments. Even its weaknesses have been productive to history, for they have set philosophers to work trying to understand what went wrong and trying to determine how people might build some kind of political order that would truly endure.

The Athenians moved slowly toward their democratic experiment. The city had the normal succession of semi-deified kings, in the years when it was barely a city at all and before its history was recorded in any way that is still available to us. Then, perhaps a thousand years before Christ, executive powers became vested primarily in the office of the *archon*, or governor. At first there was one *archon*, chosen for life. Later, the term of office was reduced to ten years; then to one year, with the powers divided among nine different *archons*. The *archons* were always chosen by and from among the wealthy landowners, and these wealthy men also provided the membership of the city's Senate, the body that met in the evenings on the hill called the Aereopagus. The wealthy class ruled; Athens under the *archons* was an oligarchy, not yet a democracy.

The Athenians had a growing body of legal tradition, the beginnings of a constitution, which was subject to periodic change and to drastic revision in times of crisis. Whenever the seams of the city's political order seemed about to burst apart, the Athenians would give unlimited power to some individual to frame a new legal system to hold it together. Thus, in the seventh century B.C., when the rise of the mercantile middle class was threatening other segments of the population, when the holdings of many of the landowners were being divided into small, debt-ridden farms, when the peace was being continually broken by murderous tribal feuds—the *archon* Draco was commissioned to organize a written code of laws. The Draconian code, which is best remembered for the harsh punishments it provided for minor crimes, did not do away with tribal conflict nor solve the city's severe economic problems. But it did slightly extend participation in government to some of the newly rich, and it gave the Athenians a written code of laws.

In the next century another lawmaker, Solon, was empowered to revise and codify the laws. Class conflict was still bitter, and radicals within the city were demanding a revolutionary redistribution of power and wealth. Solon, a wealthy merchant of aristocratic descent who was trusted by most of the competing factions, gave Athens a new constitution that not only reduced the level of strife but also moved the city a great step toward democracy. Debts were canceled, persons enslaved for indebtedness were set free, the value of currency was revised, and a new tax structure divided free Athenians of all tribes into various classes according to their wealth and property.

Solon distributed the governmental powers among three councils of varying size: the Senate of the Aereopagus, made up of members of the wealthiest class; a new Council of four hundred, composed of elected representatives of the four Athenian tribes; and an Assembly of all citizens, which revived the ancient institution of the *Ecclesia*, or town meeting. The Assembly was given the right to elect the *archons*, from members of the wealthiest class only, and to remove them from office. Solon also extended the right of participation in the judicial body, a jury of 600 members, to all free citizens.

The system that Solon created and set into motion seemed to be running fairly smoothly until a few years before his death—but then it was upset by the ambitions of Peisistratus, leader of the small farmers living in the hills surrounding the city; he gathered a body of armed men about him and seized control of the government. Peisistratus was overthrown twice but returned to power each time, maintaining his dictatorship until his death. Although he was an autocratic ruler, his reign was not a total disaster for the Solonian constitution but, in the opinion of some historians, was in fact an aid to its perpetuation. Peisistratus retained the Senate and the Council and the Assembly and the courts, and he allowed the *archons* to be elected as usual. He made relatively few changes in the Solonian legal code, which gained the strength of custom and tradition among Athenians during its years of use. When Peisistratus died his sons did not succeed in holding his power, and there was another period of warfare and revolution. When it was over the Athenians, under the leadership of Cleisthenes—a popular leader who was also a member of Athens' most noble family—established a new and still more democratic system.

Cleisthenes abolished the old tribal arrangement and set up a new system of ten tribes, a move that weakened the source of power of the aristocracy and also lessened regional rivalries, which had so often threatened the unity of the city-state. He also admitted freemen of foreign origin to full rights of citizenship, thus broadening popular support of the new order.

The Council, its membership enlarged to 500, became a more important governing body. It took over some of the powers of the Senate and exercized control over the business of the Assembly, somewhat as a legislative committee functions in the American Congress. The greatest innovation in the new Council was the way its members were chosen. They were not elected, but picked by lot; any citizen over the age of 30 had a chance of becoming a member of the city's most important deliberative body. If his name came up he would serve for a year, and later a rule was adopted forbidding any man to serve more than one term. This meant that almost every free Athenian citizen could expect to hold office, at some time in his life, as a member of the Council.

With the addition of the new citizens, the Assembly now had some 30,000 members. Partly because of its unwieldy size, and partly because of the loss of powers to the Council, the Assembly was not an effective deliberative body. But it did have one important new power to use as a check: At any time a quorum was present, the members of the Assembly could, by secret ballot, vote to send any Athenian into exile. This power was not used often, but it served as an effective restraint against the aspirations of some of the community's more powerful and restless men.

The new system retained the *archons,* but their power gradually became merely administrative. An increasingly influential group of public officers were the ten *strategoi,* or generals, one elected from each of the ten new tribes.

As Athens grew more democratic, it also grew more powerful. In the sixth and fifth centuries B.C. the Persian Empire made war against the city-states of Greece, and during the wars Greek leadership gradually passed to Athens. In two great contests, the land battle of Marathon and the sea battle of Salamis, Greeks led by Athenians defeated much larger Persian forces. When the Persian wars were over, Athens was clearly the first city in Greece. It consolidated this position in its domination of the Delian League, a defensive alliance of city-states, and gradually transformed the alliance into an empire.

This growth of power did not diminish the internal conflict among Athenian political factions. Even during the so-called "golden age," there was continual tension between the oligarchical or conservative groups, composed mainly of the wealthier citizens, and the democratic party, which included the poorer free citizens, middle-class merchants, and some aristocrats. Pericles, who emerged as the leader of the *demos* during the height of Athenian imperial power, was an aristocrat-turned-democrat in the same tradition as his ancestor Cleisthenes. He was elected repeatedly to the council of generals for nearly 30 years, and he gradually transformed the office of *strategos autokrator*, or chief general, into the most powerful position in the government.

Pericles' authority in some areas was virtually dictatorial, and yet in his era the democratic system flourished and became, in some ways, still more democratic. The participation of free citizens in government increased, as new offices of real power were filled by the method of choice by lot. This was, to Athenians, the truest exercise of democracy; it meant that any citizen, not merely the men with political ambitions or political followings, might become an important office-holder. Also, under Pericles' rule the eligibility for election to the office of *archon*, which was still a position of some prestige and influence, was extended to all free citizens instead of remaining the privilege solely of members of the wealthiest class.

Still, the Athenian system at its best was never a "complete" democracy. There was always the powerful presence of the *strategos autokrator* hovering over the city, and there were many limitations on the democratic process. It was indeed an exhilarating experience to be a citizen, eligible for membership in the Council and likely to be chosen for some important office—but not every Athenian was a citizen. Women had no part in the process, nor did males who had not come of age, nor did the thousands of slaves in the city, nor did freemen of foreign birth.[1] Perhaps as few as one-tenth of the 400,000 or so people in Athens and the nearby area actually enjoyed the rights of citizenship, and not all of them chose to attend Assembly meetings or to otherwise participate in government. Athens was more democratic than any state of its size and power had ever been, but much of the leisure its citizens enjoyed and could turn toward participation in government was paid for by the slaves who worked at the most unpleasant jobs, and much of its wealth was extracted from the tributary cities that were cowed by the might of the Athenian fleet.

Under Pericles, Athens was a city of unparalleled beauty and culture. Pericles commissioned artists and sculptors and architects, and he left such structures as the great temple of Athena, the Parthenon, as monuments to the creativity of his reign. Some of the greatest dramatists of all time—Sophocles and Euripides and the satirist Aristophanes—composed plays for the public festivals, and a host of philosophers taught and deliberated and searched for new insights into astronomy, mathematics, biology, medicine, and politics.

The Athenians were understandably proud of their city and its accomplishments. Pericles, in his famous funeral oration, praised the citizens for their "versatility and grace" and called Athens "the school of Hellas." Pericles seemed to have a sense of the place his city would occupy in history:

There are mighty monuments of our power which will make us the wonder of this and of succeeding ages. . . . For we have compelled every land and every sea to open a path for our valor, and have everywhere planted eternal memories of our friendship and of our enmity.[2]

And if the pride of Athenians is understandable, so is the resentment felt by other Greeks as the wealth and power of Athens and its empire grew.

Athens' chief rival was Sparta, the militaristic city-state whose leaders provided encouragement and support to opponents of democracy throughout Greece. The threat of Sparta to Athens was not merely that of an eternal enemy; it also echoed within Athenian politics, as some leaders of the oligarchical faction looked to Sparta as the possible solution to the threat of a continuing democratizing process that might eventually place all power in the hands of the lower classes.

Athens had other enemies: tributary city-states of the empire, and cities that resented the control of trade throughout the Aegean Sea by the Athenian fleet. Finally war broke out, precipitated by a rebellion in one of the subject cities, and Sparta—with the support of nearly all the other cities of Greece—moved against Athens. The Peloponnesian Wars lasted, with intermissions, for 27 years. During this long and incredibly destructive struggle, which is sometimes described by historians as the suicide of Greek culture, a plague

---

[1] Rights of citizenship were extended to residents of foreign birth in the time of Cleisthenes, but this dispensation was not granted to later generations of outsiders.

[2] Benjamin Jowett (trans.) *Thucydides*, I (Oxford: Clarendon Press, 1900), pp. 130–31.

broke out in Athens and thousands of people, including Pericles, died. The city was ruled by a series of erratic leaders and was weakened by military disasters abroad and revolutions within. Power shifted back and forth between oligarchic and democratic factions in one revolutionary coup after another; meanwhile, the last proud source of Athenian military strength, the fleet, was destroyed by Spartans in the Sea of Marmora. The victorious Spartan admiral Lysander then brought a naval blockade against the Athenian port, and Athens was forced to surrender. Lysander's victory led to the realization of the hopes of the oligarchs—a government controlled by the wealthy, with the support of Spartan military power.

The rule of the oligarchs under the Council of Thirty lasted only a year, but during that time thousands of leaders of the democratic faction were exiled or put to death. Another revolution restored the democracy, and the new democratic government proceeded to commit one of the most infamous acts of history: the trial and execution of Socrates, at the age of 70, for alleged nonrecognition of the official gods and corruption of the youth. The death of Socrates, in the year 399 B.C. is customarily used by historians to mark the end of the Golden Age. Thousands of Athenians, including many of the greatest, were dead from disease or war or civil conflict. The fleet was destroyed, many of the buildings of Athens and much of the surrounding farmland had been severely damaged by war, and the empire was gone.

Later in the fourth century B.C., Athens for a time seemed to be regaining its former power and prosperity, but it could not hold the leadership of Greece. The influence of the northern state of Macedonia was on the rise, first under Philip and then under his son Alexander. After being defeated by Philip's army, Athens became a member state of a Greek federation dominated by Macedonia. Athens retained some autonomy and a semblance of the old democratic system, but it was in a chaotic state, shaken again and again by internal class conflict and by repercussions from the military successes and failures of the Macedonian kings. Even after it had lost its wealth and power, Athens enjoyed a certain respect for its culture, its educational centers, and its democratic innovations; its place in the history of western civilization is legendary. But even the greatest admirers of the Golden Age have had to concede that the Athenian democracy lacked at least one thing: stability. The flowering of culture in Athens produced, among other things, two of history's greatest political philosophers, Plato and Aristotle. But ironically, and perhaps understandably, they were both extremely skeptical about democracy, and they applied themselves to a search for less erratic systems of government.

Plato

A few years after the short and bloody reign of the Council of Thirty, the restoration of democracy, and the subsequent execution of his teacher Socrates, Plato wrote of his reaction to the chaos within the Athenian state:

The result was that I, who had at first been full of eagerness for a public career, as I gazed upon the whirlpool of public life and saw the incessant movement of shifting currents, at last felt dizzy . . . and finally saw clearly in regard to all states now existing that without exception their system of government is bad. Their constitutions are almost beyond redemption except through some miraculous plan accompanied by good luck. Hence I was forced to say in praise of the correct philosophy that it affords a vantage-point from which we can discern in all cases what is just for communities and for individuals; and that accordingly the human race will not see better days until either the stock of those who rightly and genuinely follow philosophy acquire political authority, or else the class who have political control be led by some dispensation of providence to become real philosophers.[3]

The same idea is expressed in a famous passage in Plato's major political work, *The Republic,* when Socrates says that there can be "no rest from troubles," "unless either philosophers become kings in their countries or those who are now called kings and rulers come to be sufficiently inspired with a genuine desire for wisdom."[4]

Plato, who was 28 at the time of Socrates' death, immortalized his teacher in a series of works composed in the form of philosophical dialogues among Socrates and various friends and students. In the works that are mainly political—*The Republic, The Laws, and The Statesman*—and in parts of many of the other dialogues, Plato inquired into some of the basic problems of human social life, searching for

[3] Letter VII, 325d–326b, trans. L. A. Post

[4] F. M. Cornford (trans.) *The Republic of Plato* Oxford: Oxford University Press, 1945, p. 230

principles upon which a sound political system might be constructed. The sum of Plato's work is a heroic effort to create order out of the chaos and uncertainty of political life, by one supreme act of intellect. His work is also an indication of an important development in human imagination; people were beginning to see states as something more than manifestations of the incomprehensible will of nature and the gods. For Plato, the state was a living structure that could be shaped by human effort.

The Republic is an account of an attempt to find, through rational discussion, a set of working principles for a stable society. The ideal republic that Socrates and his friends create in their long conversation is, significantly, not a democratic state. Plato's misgivings about democracy come through clearly, and so does his lack of interest in the "versatility" so admired by Pericles. Citizens in the ideal state would not concern themselves with a multitude of activities but would be devoted to a single occupation; the division of labor was fundamental to Plato's view of a just and workable state.

Justice is one of the basic themes in *The Republic.* The book begins with a general discussion of the subject, and the whole exercise in state-creating that follows is explained as a way of getting at a basic understanding of justice by seeing it at work in society. Yet the justice that Plato expounds is not quite the same concept that we are familiar with today. As George H. Sabine has pointed out, the idea of justice employed in *The Republic:*

is at least as striking for what it omits as for what it includes. For it lacks the notion, connoted by the Latin word ius *and the English word right, of powers of voluntary action in the exercise of which a man will be protected by law and supported by the authority of the state. Lacking this conception Plato does not mean by justice, except remotely, the maintenance of public peace and order; at least, external order is but a small part of the harmony which makes the state. What the state provides its citizens is not so much freedom and protection as a life—all the opportunities for social interchange which make up the necessaries and the amenities of a civilized existence. It is true that in such a social life there are rights, just as there are duties, but they can hardly be said to belong in any particular sense to individuals. They are inherent rather in the services or functions that individuals perform. Resting as it does upon the principle that the state is created by*

mutual needs, the analysis runs necessarily in terms of services and not of powers.[5]

This interrelationship between social justice and the separation of labor leads naturally to an assertion that, just as shoes should be made by shoemakers and cloth by weavers, the job of ruling should be assigned to those whose only task is to rule. Socrates and his friends discuss this matter extensively, considering the qualities desirable in members of a ruling class and the way to educate them for their duties. *The Republic* is in part a treatise on education, outlining a process for training members of a "guardian" class to carry out their duties as defenders and rulers of the ideal state: how they would be selected, what subjects they would study at which stages of their lives, what subjects they should *not* study (Plato, a ready censor, felt that much of mythology and art should be deleted from the education of guardians), and how they would approach their duties as adults. Rulers, properly educated, should naturally prefer study to action, contemplation to the exercise of power.

Plato also advocated a form of communism, probably inspired in part by the example of the disciplined Spartan rulers, who denied themselves material goods. Members of the guardian class would own no property (ownership being a source of corruption) and would live together in barracks, eating from a common table. Even families would be held in common; women would be the equals of men in the duties of rulership, sex relations for the purpose of begetting children would be arranged by a committee, and children would be raised by the state. Thus, the guardians would be free from the distractions of family life and would be able to put their duties above all else.

The Republic stands as the first comprehensive attempt to look at the *whole* of a political society and to try to distill from its inner workings a set of principles that might lead to the creation of an ideal state. Other philosophers had talked about certain principles of politics, but Plato in *The Republic* was the first to look at the entire political system. His work foreshadows several later forms of political theory: "utopian" concepts of ideal states, descriptions of the structures and functions of institutions, and analyses

---

[5] George H. Sabine, *A History of Political Theory.* (3rd ed.; New York: Holt, Rinehart and Winston Inc., 1963), p. 55.

of social orders in terms of interworking systems and subsystems.

Plato's faith in expertise, his advocacy of rule by a select class of specially trained "guardians," has caused many modern political theorists to criticize him as being not merely anti-democratic, but totalitarian. Sheldon S. Wolin says, in Plato's defense:

Taken in the round, Plato's writings were not an unvarnished apologia for despotism, but a body of ideas with an unresolved contradiction. He was convinced that philosophy contained the saving knowledge that alone could bring happiness to society, yet he remained painfully aware that knowledge could only be translated into practice by the method he distrusted most, an act of power. Although he tried to resolve these two beliefs, in the idea of the philosopher-king, he remained distinctly apprehensive over any lesser arrangement. He knew too well the meaning of power.[6]

In his later writings, *The Statesman* and *The Laws*, Plato showed that his thinking about politics had undergone some transformations. *The Statesman* moved away from the single concept of an ideal state presented in *The Republic* toward a more sophisticated classification of various kinds of states: those ruled by one, those ruled by a few, and those ruled by the many. This was not an entirely new idea; Plato's main refinement of the system—and evidence of the changes in his own view of the workings of government—was a further classification into the good and bad forms of each system. The rule of one had its good form, the pure monarchy of a philosopher-king, and its bad form, tyranny. The rule of a few could take the form of aristocracy or oligarchy, and there could be moderate or extreme forms of democracy.

In *The Statesman* Plato placed greater emphasis on the role of law in the political system, a consideration he had virtually ignored in *The Republic*, and in his last work, *The Laws*, he advocated a political system whose stability would be guaranteed, not by the wisdom and expertise of its rulers, but by the perfection of its legal constitution. "Mankind," he wrote, "must either give themselves a law and regulate their lives by it, or live no better than the wildest of wild beasts, and that for the following reason: There is no man whose natural endowments will ensure that he shall both discern what is good for mankind as a community and invariably be both able and willing to put the good into practice when he has perceived it."

But even in *The Laws* Plato retained the view that the wisest men should have ultimate control. The political system he outlined was a "mixed" democracy, with a good deal of political participation by ordinary citizens but with ultimate power in the hands of a body called the Nocturnal Council, which could change the laws or the constitution at will. To the end, Plato remained deeply suspicious of the uncertainties and destructive possibilities of popular government.

PLATO ON THE ORIGINS OF JUSTICE

Socrates and some friends go to the Piraeus, the Athenian port, to attend a religious festival, visit the home of Cephalus, a wealthy citizen, and get into a philosophical conversation. Socrates (the narrator) is now discussing the idea of justice:

Justice, which is the subject of our enquiry, is, as you know, sometimes spoken of as the virtue of an individual, and sometimes as the virtue of a state.

True, Glaucon replied.

And is not a State larger than an individual?

It is.

Then in the State the quantity of justice is likely to be larger and more easily discernible. I propose therefore that we enquire into the nature of justice and injustice, first as they appear in the State.

That, he said, is an excellent proposal.

And if we imagine the State in process of creation, we shall see the justice and injustice of the State in process of creation also.

I dare say.

A State arises, as I conceive, out of the needs of mankind; no one is self-sufficing, but all of us have many wants. Can any other origin of a State be imagined?

There can be no other.

---

[6] Sheldon S. Wolin, *Politics and Vision* (Boston: Little, Brown, 1960), p. 67.

From *The Republic*, Book II, trans. Benjamin Jowett (Cleveland: The World Publishing Company, 1946), pp. 66-76. (Edited and abridged.)

Then, as we have many wants, and many persons are needed to supply them, one takes a helper for one purpose and another for another; and when these partners and helpers are gathered together in one habitation the body of inhabitants is termed a State.

True, he said.

And they exchange with one another, and one gives, and another receives, under the idea that the exchange will be for their good.

Very true.

Now the first and greatest of necessities is food, which is the condition of life and existence.

Certainly.

The second is a dwelling, and the third clothing and the like.

True.

And now let us see how our city will be able to supply this great demand: We may suppose that one man is a husbandman, another a builder, some one else a weaver—shall we add to them a shoemaker, or perhaps some other purveyor to our bodily wants?

Quite right.

The barest notion of a State must include four or five men.

Clearly.

And will you have a work better done when the workman has many occupations, or when he has only one?

When he has only one.

Then more than four citizens will be required; for the husbandman will not make his own plough or mattock, or other implements of agriculture, if they are to be good for anything. Neither will the builder make his tools—and he, too, needs many; and in the like manner the weaver and shoemaker.

True.

Then carpenters, and smiths, and many other artisans, will be sharers in our little State, which is already beginning to grow?

True.

Yet even if we add cowherds, shepherds, and other herdsmen, in order that our husbandmen may have oxen to plough with, and builders as well as husbandmen may have draught cattle, and curriers and weavers fleeces

and hides—still our State will not be very large.

That is true; yet neither will it be a very small State.

Then, again, there is the situation of the city—to find a place where nothing need be imported is well-nigh impossible.

Impossible.

Then we shall need merchants who will import the required supplies from another city and export the produce of our husbandmen and artisans in trade.

We shall.

And if merchandise is to be carried over the sea, skillful sailors will also be needed, and in considerable numbers?

Yes, in considerable numbers.

Then, again, within the city, how will they exchange their productions? To secure such an exchange was, as you will remember, one of our principal objects when we formed them into a society and constituted a State.

Clearly they will buy and sell.

Then they will need a market-place, and a money-token for purposes of exchange.

Certainly.

Suppose now that a husbandman, or an artisan, brings some production to market, and he comes at a time when there is no one to exchange with him—is he to leave his calling and sit idle in the market-place?

Not at all; he will find people there who, seeing the want, undertake the office of salesmen. In well-ordered states they are commonly those who are weakest in bodily strength.

This want, then, creates a class of retail-traders in our State.

Yes, he said.

And there is another class of servants, who are intellectually hardly on the level of companionship; still they have bodily strength for labor, which accordingly they sell, and are called, if I do not mistake, hirelings.

True.

Then hirelings will help to make up our population?

Yes.

And now, Adeimantus, is our State matured and

perfected?

I think so.

Where, then, is justice, and where is injustice, and in what part of the State did they spring up?

Probably in the dealings of these citizens with one another. I cannot imagine that they are more likely to be found anywhere else.

Let us then consider what will be their way of life, now that we have thus established them. Will they not produce corn, and wine, and clothes, and shoes, and build houses for themselves? And when they are housed, they will work; in summer commonly stripped and barefoot, but in winter substantially clothed and shod. They will feed on barley-meal and flour of wheat, baking and kneading them, making cakes and loaves.

But, said Glaucon, interposing, you have not given them a relish to their meal. You should give them the ordinary conveniences of life. People who are to be comfortable are accustomed to lie on sofas, and dine off tables, and they should have sweets and sauces in the modern style.

Then the question you would have me consider is, not only how a State, but how a luxurious state is created.

Certainly.

Then we must enlarge our borders, for the country which was enough to support the original healthy state will be too small now. A slice of our neighbors' land will be wanted, and they will want a slice of ours if, like ourselves, they exceed the limit of necessity.

That, Socrates, will be inevitable.

And so we shall go to war, Glaucon, shall we not?

Most certainly, he replied.

And our State must once more enlarge; and this time the enlargement will be nothing short of a whole army.

Very true, he said.

But is not war an art?

Certainly.

And an art requiring as much attention as shoemaking?

Quite true.

And the shoemaker was not allowed by us to be a husbandman, or a weaver, or a builder in order that we might have our shoes well made; to him and to every other worker was assigned one work. Now nothing can be more important than that the work of a soldier should be well done. But is war an art so easily acquired that a man may be a warrior who is also a husbandman, or shoemaker, or other artisan? How will he who takes up a shield or other implements of war become a good fighter all in a day? The higher the duties of the guardian, the more time, and skill, and art, and application will be needed by him.

No doubt, he replied.

Will he not also require natural aptitude for his calling?

Certainly.

Then it will be our duty to select, if we can, natures which are fitted for the task of guarding the city?

It will.

Is not the noble youth very like a well-bred dog in respect of guarding and watching?

What do you mean?

I mean that both of them ought to be quick to see, and swift to overtake the enemy when they see him; and strong, too, if when they have caught him, they have to fight with him.

All these qualities will certainly be required.

Your guardian must be brave?

Certainly.

And his soul is to be full of spirit?

Yes.

But are not these spirited natures apt to be savage with one another, and with everybody else?

A difficulty by no means easy to overcome, he replied.

Whereas, I said, they ought to be dangerous to their enemies and gentle to their friends; if not, they will destroy themselves. Would not he who is fitted to be a guardian, besides the spirited nature, need to have the qualities of a philosopher?

I do not apprehend your meaning.

The trait of which I am speaking, I replied, may be also seen in the dog and is remarkable in the animal. The dog, whenever he sees a stranger, is angry; when he sees an acquaintance, he welcomes him, although the one has never done him any harm nor the other any good. Your dog is a true philosopher.

Why?

Why, because he distinguishes the face of a friend and of an enemy only by the criterion of knowing and not knowing. And must not an animal be a lover of learning who determines what he likes and dislikes by the test of knowledge and ignorance?

Most assuredly.

And is not the love of learning the love of wisdom, which is philosophy?

They are the same, he replied.

And may we not say confidently of man also, that he who is likely to be gentle to his friends and acquaintances must by nature be a lover of wisdom and knowledge?

That we may safely affirm.

Then he who is to be a really good and noble guardian of the State will require to unite in himself philosophy and spirit and swiftness and strength.

Undoubtedly.

Then we have found the desired natures.

Aristotle

Aristotle, a native of the small outpost city of Stagira, came to Athens at the age of 18 and spent 20 years as a student of Plato at the Academy. After Plato's death he left Greece, served for a while as adviser to an Eastern prince, and in the year 343 B.C. entered the employment of Philip of Macedonia as tutor to the king's young son Alexander.

The relationship between one of history's foremost philosophers and the young Alexander the Great has excited the imaginations of writers for centuries, but in fact, little is known of what took place during Aristotle's years of residence in the Macedonian court. When Philip died in 336 B.C., Aristotle returned to Athens and founded his own philosophical school, the Lyceum. Over the next twelve years he set down one of the most comprehensive bodies of philosophical work ever produced by one man: systematic studies of art and drama and poetry, government and economics, language, physics and astronomy, biology, and ethics.

In *Politics,* his chief work on government, Aristotle drew heavily on the concepts and categories formulated by his teacher Plato. But he differed from Plato on many points, and his work grew out of a different view of the role of the political philosopher. He did not concern himself exclusively with the creation of an ideal state but also attempted to discover some principles for the government of existing states. "We should," he wrote, "consider not only what form of government is best, but also what is possible and what is easily attainable by all."[7]

The *Politics* includes a discussion of an ideal state, but it is a discussion that never quite comes to a conclusion; much of the treatise deals instead with problems that had been encountered by *actual* states in Greek history. Most contemporary scholars believe that the *Politics* was written over a long span of time, during which Aristotle became less interested in following Plato's style of philosophical speculation and more interested in analyzing the workings of real governments. One of his main projects with his students at the Lyceum had been collecting historical information on 158 different constitutions, and these findings form the basis of much of his discussion. Because of his emphasis on the collection and study of factual material, Aristotle is sometimes called the first political scientist. Plato's model of thought had been mathematical, a search for abstract ideals, but Aristotle's political theorizing seems to run more closely to the kind of work he had done in biology: the description and classification of actual types.

When Aristotle did talk of an ideal state he showed a clear preference for monarchy and/or aristocracy. He took issue with Plato about the idea of abolishing private property and the family, and he also defended the institution of slavery as natural. "That some should rule and others be ruled is a thing not only necessary, but expedient," he wrote. "From the hour of their birth, some are marked out for subjection, others for rule."[8] In Aristotle's ideal state there would be slaves, and the rights of citizenship would be limited to a fairly small class—warriors, rulers, and priests. These would not be separate occupational categories but different functions that the members of the ruling class would exercise at certain periods of life. The members of this class would also be the only landowners. Farmers, craftsmen, and traders would be excluded from citizenship. "Such a life is ignoble

[7] Aristotle *Politics,* IV, 1, trans. Benjamin Jowett.

[8] *ibid.,* I, 5.

and inimical to virtue," Aristotle said. "Leisure is necessary both for the development of virtue and the performance of political duties."[9] Like Plato, Aristotle saw education as a fundamental necessity for the perpetuation of an ideal state, and much of *Politics,* like *The Republic,* is a treatise on education for citizenship.

When Aristotle took up the question of justice, he distinguished between "distributive justice," or the parceling out of wealth and political power, and "remedial" justice, which involved matters of civil or criminal law. In distributive justice, he favored a distinction according to the merit of individuals; honors, wealth, and political offices would go in highest proportion to those of greatest virtue. But in the courts responsible for remedial justice, all persons would be regarded as equals.

In his classification of states, Aristotle followed the traditional idea of the three fundamental types—rule by one, rule by few, rule by many—and he also accepted Plato's pronouncement that there could be good and bad forms of each. But Aristotle further refined the concept into several sub-categories: five kinds of monarchy, three kinds of tyranny, four kinds of oligarchy, aristocracy, polity (a mixture of democracy and oligarchy), and four kinds of democracy. In his discussion of each form, he applied historical detail from his analyses of constitutions to show how different kinds of government actually came into being and how they functioned. From historical data, he compiled not only categories of states but also general rules about why some states maintained stability while others were ended or changed by revolution.

Although Aristotle's preferences obviously were in the direction of government by the highly qualified few, he cited a form of democracy as the best practicable (as opposed to ideal) kind of state. This kind of government, to which he gave the name "polity," would be not a pure democracy (which Aristotle considered to be the *worst* of all forms of government) but rather a combination of democracy and oligarchy, leaning heavily on the participation of the middle class as a source of balance and stability. Aristotle felt that such a system was workable and within the reach of any existing society.

Aristotle's historical researches were not simply com-

pilations of data. He was always guided by basic beliefs about the *purposes* of a state, which he felt were to satisfy social needs—"Man is by nature a political animal"—and to help people live a better life. Whenever Aristotle used the term "state," he meant an organized political community defined and arranged by a constitution. Aristotle took great interest in different kinds of legal constitutions, but his ideas of law and justice and organization were always closely linked to concerns about the health and well-being of members of the community. One modern scholar of political theory writes:

The parallel between sociopolitical health and personal health, both physical and mental, is a central theme in Aristotle's political analysis. . . . Eighteenth and nineteenth centuries tended to discard any such proposition, at least as Aristotle formulated it. But in the twentieth century we are not so sure. Will the constitution of a people (in Aristotle's sense) in part determine whether they are mentally healthy or not? Aristotle's "organic" account of the interdependence of individual and corporate health tends to take on a new meaning in an age when one out of every two beds in American hospitals is occupied by a mental patient. Can one, in other words, isolate the individual's well-being and integration from the well-being, justice and integration of the society?[10]

Aristotle's work was generally a more sophisticated system of political philosophizing than was Plato's, and it greatly influenced the thinkers who later concerned themselves with government. But Aristotle's thinking, although it was far more advanced than that of his predecessors in so many ways, still had one very important limitation: Almost all his discussion of forms of government had to do with the city-state. Ironically, while Aristotle was philosophizing about the politics of the city-state, his former pupil Alexander was trying to build an empire that would govern the entire world. Alexander died in the attempt, a year before Aristotle died in Euboea, to which he had been exiled by Athenians who distrusted him because of his former association with the young emperor. The Macedonian empire crumbled after Alexander's death, and soon the growing power of Rome began to dominate the Mediterranean world. The city-state was losing its importance as the basic unit of politi-

[9] *Ibid.,* VII. 9.

[10] Mulford Q. Sibley, *Political Ideas and Ideologies* (New York: Harper & Row, 1970), p. 105.

cal organization. New political philosophers would have to talk in terms of empire.

ARISTOTLE ON REVOLUTION

In considering how dissensions and political revolutions arise, we must first of all ascertain the beginnings and causes of them which affect constitutions generally. They may be said to be three in number; and we have now to give an outline of each. We want to know (1) what is the feeling? (2) what are the motives of those who make them? (3) whence arise political disturbances and quarrels? The universal and chief cause of this revolutionary feeling is the desire of equality, when men think that they are equal to others who have more than themselves; or, again, the desire of inequality and superiority, when conceiving themselves to be superior, they think that they have not more but the same or less than their inferiors (pretensions which may and may not be just). Inferiors revolt in order that they may be equal, and equals that they may be superior. Such is the state of mind which creates revolutions. The motives for making them are the desire of gain and honour, or the fear of dishonour and loss; the authors of them want to divert punishment or dishonour from themselves or their friends. Other causes are insolence, fear, excessive predominance, contempt, disproportionate increase in some part of the state; causes of another sort are election intrigues, carelessness, neglect about trifles, dissimilarity of elements.

What share insolence and avarice have in creating revolutions, and how they work, is plain enough. When the magistrates are insolent and grasping they conspire against one another and also against the constitution from which they derive their power, making their gains either at the expense of individuals or of the public. It is evident, again, what an influence honour exerts and how it is a cause of revolution. Men who are themselves dishonoured and who see others obtaining honours rise in rebellion; the honour or dishonour when undeserved is unjust; and just when awarded according

From *Politics*, Book V, trans. Benjamin Jowett. (Oxford: The Clarendon Press, 1885), pp. 147-59. (Edited and abridged.)

to merit. Again, superiority is a cause of revolution when one or more persons have a power which is too much for the state and the power of the government; this is a condition of affairs out of which there arises a monarchy, or a family oligarchy. And therefore, in some places, as at Athens and Argos, they have recourse to ostracism. But how much better to provide from the first that there should be no such preeminent individuals instead of letting them come into existence and then finding a remedy.

Another cause of revolution is fear. Either men have committed wrong and are afraid of punishment, or they are expecting to suffer wrong and are desirous of anticipating their enemy. Thus, at Rhodes the notables conspired against the people through fear of the suits that were brought against them. Contempt is also a cause of insurrection and revolution; for example, in oligarchies when those who have no share in the state are the majority, they revolt, because they think that they are the stronger. Or, again, in democracies, the rich despise the disorder and anarchy of the state.

Political revolutions also spring from a disproportionate increase in any part of the state. A state has many parts, of which some one may often grow imperceptibly; for example, the number of poor in democracies and in constitutional states. When the rich grow numerous or properties increase, the form of government changes into an oligarchy or a government of families. Forms of government also change, sometimes even without revolution, owing to election contests; or owing to carelessness, when disloyal persons are allowed to find their way into the highest offices—as at Oreum, where, upon the accession of Heracleodorus to office, the oligarchy was overthrown, and changed by him into a constitutional and democratical government.

Again, the revolution may be facilitated by the slightness of the change; I mean that a great change may sometimes slip into the constitution through neglect of a small matter; at Ambracia, for instance, the qualification for office, small at first, was eventually reduced to nothing. For the Ambraciots thought that a small qualification was much the same as none at all.

Another cause of revolution is difference of races which do not at once acquire a common spirit; for a state is not the growth of a day, any more than it grows out of a multitude brought together by accident. Hence the reception of strangers in colonies, either at the time of their foundation or afterwards, has generally produced revolution; for example, the Achaeans who joined the Troezenians in the foundation of Sybaris, becoming later the more numerous, expelled them.

Now, in oligarchies the masses make revolution under the idea that they are unjustly treated, because, as I said before, they are equals and have not an equal share, and in democracies the notables revolt, because they are not equals, and yet have only an equal share.

Again, the situation of cities is a cause of revolution when the country is not naturally adapted to preserve the unity of the state. For example, the Chytians at Clazomenae did not agree with the people of the island; at Athens too, the inhabitants of the Piraeus are more democratic than those who live in the city. For just as in war the impediment of a ditch, though ever so small, may break a regiment, so every cause of difference, however slight, makes a breach in a city. The greatest opposition is confessedly that of virtue and vice; next comes that of wealth and poverty; and there are other antagonistic elements, greater or less, of which one is this difference of place.

In revolutions the occasions may be trifling, but great interests are at stake. Even trifles are most important when they concern the rulers, as was the case of old at Syracuse; for the Syracusan constitution was once changed by a love-quarrel of two young men, who were in the government. The story is that while one of them was away from home his beloved was gained over by his companion, and he to revenge himself seduced the other's wife. They then drew the members of the ruling class into their quarrel and so split all the people into portions. We learn from this story that we should be on our guard against the beginnings of such evils, and should put an end to the quarrels of chiefs and mighty men.

Governments also change into oligarchy or into democracy or into a constitutional government because the magistrates, or some other section of the state, increase in power or renown. Thus at Athens the reputation gained by the court of the Areopagus, in the Persian War, seemed to tighten the reins of government. On the other hand, the victory of Salamis, which was gained by the common people who served in the fleet, and won for the Athenians the empire due to command of the sea, strengthened the democracy. And generally, it should be remembered that those who have secured power to the state, whether private citizens, or magistrates, or tribes, or any other part or section of the state, are apt to cause revolutions. For either envy of their greatness draws others into rebellion, or they themselves, in their pride of superiority, are unwilling to remain on a level with others.

Revolutions also break out when opposite parties—for example the rich and the people—are equally balanced, and there is little or no middle class; for, if either party were manifestly superior, the other would not risk an attack upon them. And, for this reason, those who are eminent in virtue, always a minority, usually do not stir up insurrections. Such are the beginnings and causes of the disturbances and revolutions to which every form of government is liable.

Revolutions are effected in two ways, by force and by fraud. Force may be applied either at the time of making the revolution or afterwards. Fraud, again, is of two kinds: (1) Sometimes the citizens are deceived into acquiescing in a change of government, and afterwards they are held in subjection against their will. This was what happened in the case of the Four Hundred, who deceived the people by telling them that the king would provide money for the war against the Lacedaemonians, and, having cheated the people, still endeavoured to retain the government. (2) In other cases, the people are persuaded at first, and afterwards, by a repetition of the persuasion, their goodwill and allegiance are retained. The revolutions which effect constitutions generally spring from the above-mentioned causes.

And now, taking each constitution separately, we must see what follows from the principles already laid down.

Revolutions in democracies are generally caused by the intemperance of demagogues, who either in their private capacity lay information against rich men until they compel them to combine (for a common danger unites even the bitterest enemies), or coming forward in public stir up the people against them. At Cos the democracy was overthrown because wicked demagogues arose, and the notables combined. The democracy at Heraclea was overthrown shortly after the foundation of the colony by the injustice of the demagogues, which drove out the notables, who came back in a body and put an end to the democracy. Much in the same manner the democracy at Megara was overturned; there the demagogues drove out many of the notables in order that they might be able to confiscate their property. At length the exiles, becoming numerous, returned, and, engaging and defeating the people, established the oligarchy.

Of old, the demagogue was also a general, and then democracies were changed into tyrannies. Most of the ancient tyrants were originally demagogues. They are not so now, but they were then; and the reason is that they were generals and not orators, for oratory had not yet come into fashion. Whereas in our day, when the art of rhetoric has made such progress, the orators lead the people, but their ignorance of military matters prevents them from usurping power; at any rate instances to the contrary are few and slight.

There are two patent causes of revolutions in oligarchies: (1) First, when the oligarchs oppress the people, for then anybody is good enough to be their champion, especially if he be himself a member of the oligarchy, as Lygdamis at Naxos, who afterwards came to be tyrant. But revolutions which commence outside the governing class may be further subdivided. Sometimes, when the government is very exclusive, the revolution is brought about by persons of the wealthy class who are excluded, as happened at Massalia and Istros and Heraclea, and other cities. (2) Of internal causes of revolutions in oligarchies one is the personal rivalry of the oligarchs, which leads them to play the demagogue. Now, the oligarchical demagogue is of two sorts: either (a) he practises upon the oligarchs themselves, or (b) the oligarchs may play the demagogue with the people. But an oligarchy which is at unity with itself is not easily destroyed from within; of this we may see an example at Pharsalus, for there, although the rulers are few in number, they govern a large city, because they have a good understanding among themselves.

Oligarchies, again, are overthrown when another oligarchy is created within the original one, that is to say, when the whole governing body is small and yet they do not all share in the highest offices. Thus at Elis the governing body was a small senate; and very few ever found their way into it, because the senators were only ninety in number and were elected for life and out of certain families in a manner similar to the Lacedaemonian elders. Oligarchy is liable to revolutions alike in war and in peace; in war because, not being able to trust the people, the oligarchs are compelled to hire mercenaries, and the general who is in command of them often ends in becoming a tyrant; or if there are more generals than one they make themselves into a company of tyrants. Sometimes the oligarchs, fearing this danger, give the people a share in the government because their services are necessary to them. And in time of peace, from mutual distrust, the two parties hand over the defense of the state to the army and to an arbiter between the two factions, who often ends the master of both.

We must remark generally, both of democracies and oligarchies, that they sometimes change, not into the opposite forms of government, but only into another variety of the same class; I mean to say, from those forms of democracy and oligarchy which are regulated by law into those which are arbitrary, and conversely.

2/The Search for World Community

THE CITY AND THE EMPIRE

The development of Rome parallels that of Athens in some ways: Rome was first a small city-state, ruled by kings, and then the monarchy gave way to a republican form of government, with elective magistrates. Rome emerged from a long military conflict, the Punic Wars with Carthage, in a new position of leadership and with the foundation of an empire. Although Rome never moved as far as did Athens along the road of democracy, it moved much farther along the road of empire. Rome's drive to govern the world was no help to those who wanted Roman citizens to be able to govern themselves.

The Roman republic—which began in approximately 509 B.C. with the overthrow of the Etruscan monarch, Tarquinus Superbus—underwent several constitutional changes in its two-and-a-half centuries of existence, but despite the continuing efforts of its common citizens, the Plebeians (plebs), and their leaders, the weight of governmental power remained always with the wealthy and wellborn. The most important magistrates were the consuls, and it was typical of the Romans, who had a continual (and well-grounded) fear of a possible return to monarchy, to keep two consuls in office at the same time. Every Roman politician aspired to the office and normally could expect to attain it only after years of experience in public and military affairs; this tended to limit the office to men who could afford a lifetime in politics. In the later years of the republic, plebs were theoretically eligible for the office, but in fact few plebs were elected to it, and those who were came from the more prosperous levels of their class.

When a consul had completed his term, he became a life member of the senate. By the third century B.C. the Roman republic had assumed its "classic" form, with three separate deliberative bodies—the senate, the *comita centuriata,* and *comita tributa.*

The *comita tributa,* the forum of the plebs, in 287 B.C. gained the power to elect the tribunes—officials who could observe the governmental process and veto decisions—and to approve laws passed by the senate; these were important and hard-won rights, but the *comita tributa* was manipulated by the patricians who held senate and magisterial offices.

The *comita centuriata,* a somewhat more exalted assembly, was composed of arms-bearing men organized through "centuries," or regiments, that were based on status and wealth. There was a proportional voting arrangement in the *comita centuriata* that granted heavy representation to smaller and wealthier classes. This military and aristocratic body elected the consuls and other major magistrates and, until it lost the right to the *comita tributa,* approved laws passed by the senate.

The senate, composed of patrician leaders and retired magistrates, was the greatest center of power in republican Rome. Where the magistrates held office for a year, the senators were members for life; they were men of wealth and status, who had spent their lives in public service. Will Durant writes:

Most of them had been magistrates, administrators, and commanders; some of them, as proconsuls, had ruled provinces as large as kingdoms; many of them came of families that had given statesmen or generals to Rome for hundreds of years. . . . When Cineas, the philosopher who had come to Rome as envoy of Pyrrhus (280), had heard the Senate's deliberations and observed its men, he reported to the new Alexander that here was no mere gathering of venal politicians, no haphazard council of mediocre minds, but in dignity and statesmanship veritably "an assemblage of kings."[1]

This assemblage was the decision-making center of Rome throughout the years of the republic, as the city led Italy in the century-long wars against Carthage and won an empire that stretched from Persia to the British Isles.

The Punic empire, built by descendants of the ancient Phoenician sailors who had traveled and traded around the Mediterranean, had as its capital the great city of Carthage in Northern Africa. It had colonies in Spain and also on islands near the Italian peninsula: Malta, Sardinia, Corsica and Sicily. Sicily, only a mile off the Italian coast, was the cause of the first war between Carthage and Rome; the war ended with Sicily a Roman province. The second Punic War almost brought about the destruction of Rome, when the young Carthaginian general Hannibal led his legendary invasion from Spain, across Gaul, over the Alps, and down into Italy. But Hannibal never entered Rome, and the Romans, fighting back under the leadership of Scipio, did invade Africa; the second Punic War ended with Rome stripping Carthage of her empire. The new colonies in Africa provided wheat to feed the growing urban population of Rome, and the mines of Spain helped to finance Rome's conquest of Greece and the remnants of the Macedonian empire. In the third Punic War the state of Carthage was utterly destroyed, and the city of Carthage was burned to the ground.

As Rome became the capital of an empire, it became the center of Western civilization's culture, trade, and commerce. Legions and laws went out to subdue and govern new colonies, art and philosophy were imported from Athens, and material goods were imported from every corner of the empire.

The wealth and power that flowed into Rome tended to concentrate in the ruling classes, and from the lower orders there were constant rumblings of rebellion. They surfaced in such disturbances as the slave uprising led by the gladiator Spartacus, the land-reform campaign of the Gracchi, the debt-cancellation revolt of Catiline. Revolutionaries usually met unhappy ends—Spartacus was cut to pieces on a battlefield, Tiberius and Caius Gracchus were both murdered, and Catiline was killed by Roman legions under the command of Cicero. The common citizens of Rome were granted greater rights of participation in the government from time to time, but the "democratic" concessions never brought about real redistribution of power; it remained with the wealthy, because the votes of citizens were openly bought and sold at election-time.

There was political conflict between conservative and democratic factions, but both sides were dominated by the military leaders who gained public attention from their adventures on behalf of the ever-growing empire. Julius Caesar, who did as much as any man to destroy Rome's last remaining pretenses to democracy, emerged as a leader of the democratic faction.

Caesar had worked his way up through a sequence of military and civil offices, had built a personal fortune, and had served a term as consul before he achieved his greatest military accomplishment: the victory over the Gauls that added what is now France to the provinces of Rome. As a victorious general who was identified with the democratic factions, Caesar had a sizable popular following in Rome; as governor of Gaul and commander of the legions in the north, he had an army of his own. When the senate, unable to get him to leave his office or to disband his personal army, gave dictatorial powers to his rival Pompey, Caesar and his legions crossed the Gallic boundary at the Rubicon, moved southward into Italy, and took control of Rome. In the ensuing civil war he defeated the armies of Pompey and forced the senate to vote him a dictatorship for ten years, which was later extended to life. Five months after his ten-year term had been extended to a life term, he was dead, murdered in the senate by a group of conspirators who knew that Caesar's power was the end of the republic and its aristocratic rule. But Caesar's death did not bring the republic back to life. There were more years of warfare, first between the would-be heirs of Caesar's power, his lieutenant Marc Anthony and his grandnephew Octavian; then between the aristocratic forces and an Anthony-Octavian alliance; then again between Anthony and Octavian. When the chaos was finally over, fourteen years after Caesar's death,

---

[1] Will Durant, *Caesar and Christ, The Story of Civilization* (New York: Simon and Schuster, 1944), III, p. 28. © 1944 by Will Durant. Reprinted by permission of Simon and Schuster.

Octavian became the first emperor of Rome.

Octavian, who was given the title Caesar Augustus by the senate, was a clever politician and a superb administrator. As he assumed the powers of a monarch, he retained the outward forms of republican government—he had himself repeatedly elected to various offices, he submitted measures to the senate for ratification, and he even proclaimed during his reign that the republic had been restored. The Mediterranean world that had been torn by war for so many years settled down to prosper under the *Pax Romana*—the peace of Rome, which had been imposed by the power of the emperor.

Roman citizenship was conferred, like an honorary title, on people from the provinces. Even for the citizen who lived in the capital, the experience of citizenship was far different from that of the Athenian—not the exhilarating sense of participation, but the reflected glow from the grandeur of the empire; certainly not a sense of community, but rather a sense of identification with a great and awesome legal institution. Even the aristocrats of Rome had little real power; they contented themselves with the trappings of it, such as participation in the empty rituals of senate debate, and enjoyed the enormous wealth that poured into the capital.

Under the reign of Augustus, Rome became a city of great buildings: temples, baths, enormous homes for the wealthy. Toward the end of his life, Augustus boasted that he had found a city of brick and had left it clothed in marble. But the comforts of Rome's buildings, like the wealth of its empire, were not equally enjoyed by all. According to Lewis Mumford, a present-day student of urban life:

The houses of the patricians, spacious, airy, sanitary, equipped with bathrooms and water closets, heated in winter by hypocausts, which carried hot air through chambers in the floors, were perhaps the most commodious and comfortable houses built for a temperate climate anywhere until the twentieth century; a triumph of domestic architecture. But the tenements of Rome easily take the prize for being the most crowded and insanitary buildings produced in Western Europe until the sixteenth century . . . poor in all the facilities that make for decent daily living, they were in addition so badly built and so high that they offered no means of safe exit from the frequent fires that occurred. And if their tenants escaped typhoid, typhus, fire, they might easily meet their death in the collapse

of the entire structure. . . .

These buildings and their people constituted the core of imperial Rome, and that core was rotten.[2]

For the common people of Rome, there were other consolations. Every person got his share of the grain that was shipped in from the various colonies, and, for entertainment, every person had access to the bloody spectacles of the arena. In the first century A.D., the satirist Juvenal said that the Roman people lived for two things only—bread and circuses.[3]

POLITICAL PHILOSOPHY IN THE ROMAN REPUBLIC

While political and economic leadership of the world was shifting to Rome, educational and philosophical leadership continued to reside in Greece. In the so-called Hellenistic period that followed the decline of Athenian power, several philosophical schools—Cynics, Stoics, Epicureans—flourished in Greece and also had followings in Rome. The literary style of almost all political philosophy written by Romans was heavily influenced by the Greek masters, especially Plato and Aristotle.

STOICISM

The Stoic school, founded in Athens in the third century B.C., reflected the gropings of political thinkers toward wider frames of reference, toward concepts of human community larger than the city-state. Stoicism had important influences in Rome—as a philosophy for its soldiers and politicians, as a basis for its newly-evolving system of laws, and, finally, as a foreshadowing of the idea of a universal church. We see in Stoicism an early attempt to create an idea of world community by an act of the intellect.

The Stoic philosophy, as originally enunciated by the school's founder, Chrysippus, had for its basic ethical ideal the life of disciplined and rational self-sufficiency. The Stoic was governed by will, intellect, and sense of duty, not by

---

[2] Lewis Mumford, *The City in History* (New York: Harcourt Brace Jovanovich, Inc., 1961) pp. 220-21. Published in Great Britain by Martin Secker & Warburg, Limited.

[3] Juvenal *Satire X*, (line 80).

urges toward passing pleasure. Rationality was a force of nature, the chief characteristic of a world-state in which all people and all gods were citizens. The natural law governed all, and the wise person, using "right reason," could discover and carry out the laws of nature. People might exclude themselves from participation in the world-state through their own foolishness, but potentially anyone—Athenian or foreigner, aristocrat or slave—could become a citizen of this universal community.

A later head of the Stoic school, Panaetius, migrated to Rome in the second century B.C. and acquired a considerable following among Roman aristocrats who wanted to absorb Athenian culture. Stoicism, somewhat modified in the teachings of Panaetius, became for the Romans an ethic of military discipline, public service, and self-control. We know that most Romans fell far short of the ideal, but there were also stern, hard-working, plain-living people such as Marcus Aurelius, who proved to the world that the Stoic philosophy could be a reality even for men of wealth and power.

The Stoic concepts of natural law and right reason provided useful theoretical underpinnings to the growing Roman legal system. With its population expanding and becoming more diverse in ethnic background, with its government extending to newly conquered colonies, Rome was developing a highly complicated and sophisticated body of laws and legal procedures. As Athens has found a place in history through its civic life, its art and poetry and philosophy, Rome stands as a monumental achievement of law and government. And part of the Roman practical accomplishment was undoubtedly based on the Athenian philosophical heritage; the idea that people could "discover" true laws of universal application was a helpful aid to empire-building.

Polybius

One important figure in the intellectual life of Republican Rome was the historian Polybius, a man of Greek birth, who was first brought to Rome as a political prisoner and then settled there, becoming a close friend of the Stoic philosopher Panaetius. Polybius had been a cavalry commander in his native Megalopolis and later served as a military adviser to the Romans during the third Punic War. He was present at the destruction of Carthage, and in his account of the event he says that the Roman general Scipio, as he watched the city perishing in flames, "burst into tears, and stood long reflecting on the inevitable change which awaits cities, nations, and dynasties, one and all, as it does every one of us men." Polybius' *Histories*, written in the later years of his life, are the oldest existing record of the rise of the Roman Empire and are also a significant body of political theory— an extensive commentary on the Roman constitution and an attempt to comprehend the transience of political power, which was so evident in the flames of Carthage.

Part of the importance of Polybius' works lies in the change from Athenian ways of thinking that they reflect. William Ebenstein writes:

Whereas Plato and Aristotle had studied political institutions in relation to the good life of the community and the individual—assuming a Greek world in which small, self-sufficient city-states existed side by side without a great deal of mutual interference—Polybius was the first to examine the institutional fabric of a state as the chief determining factor in the formation of national strength.[1]

Polybius used the concept of three different kinds of states—monarchy, aristocracy, and democracy—and developed it into a cyclical theory of history. He described how states first came into existence, passed through various phases represented by different forms of government, and eventually degenerated into anarchy and violence.

Both Plato and Aristotle had discussed the possibility of some kind of mixture of the three kinds of government; Aristotle had seen a balanced participation of the various social classes as the ideal form of polity. Polybius discussed the balance in slightly different terms, not so much an interaction of social classes as an institutionalized interworking of different legal structures. He saw the Roman republic, with its consuls, senate, and popular assemblies, as a successful example of mixed government—part monarchy, part aristocracy, part democracy. This kind of a system, with its ingenious balancing of forces and ambitions, could avoid the collapse that was the fate of other governments. The

[4] William Ebenstein, *Great Political Thinkers: Plato to the Present* (New York: Holt, Rinehart and Winston, 1951), p. 113.

mixture provided stability: "All remains *in status quo*," wrote Polybius, "because any aggressive impulse is sure to be checked."

In his analysis of the Roman constitution, Polybius anticipated the separation of powers and checks and balances, concepts that would be developed in a more sophisticated form by Montesquieu and later incorporated into the United States Constitution. Polybius was an influential thinker, even though he overstated his case: the Roman republic never ran quite as smoothly in reality as it did in his description, nor was it resistant to change; not long after Polybius' death, the mixed government of Rome was giving way to chaos and civil war, and was headed for dictatorship.

POLYBIUS ON THE ADVANTAGES OF A MIXED CONSTITUTION

I will now explain how each of the three parts of the state is enabled to counteract or cooperate with the others. The consul, when he leaves with his army, appears to have absolute authority in all matters necessary for carrying out his purpose; but in fact he needs the support of the people and the senate, and he is not able to bring his operations to a conclusion without them. For it is obvious that the legions require constant support and without the consent of the senate neither corn, clothing nor pay can be provided; so the commander's plans will come to nothing if the senate chooses to be negligent and obstructive. The senate can also determine whether or not a general can carry out his conceptions and designs to completion, since it has the power to either replace him when his year's term in office is completed or to retain him in command. And the processions they call triumphs, in which the generals bring the spectacle of their victories before the eyes of their fellow citizens, cannot be properly organized unless the senate consents and provides the necessary funds. As for the people it is essential that the consuls conciliate them, however far away from home they may be; for the people can ratify or annul terms of peace and treaties,

From *The Histories*, III trans. W. R. Paton (Cambridge: Howard University Press, 1923), vol. III. (Edited and abridged.)

and the consuls are obliged to account for their actions to them. So it is not safe for the consuls to neglect keeping in favor with both the senate and the people.

The senate, although it possesses great power, is obliged to pay attention to the commons in public affairs; it cannot carry out investigations into the most grave offenses against the state, those punishable by death, unless the *senatus consultum* is confirmed by the people. This is also the case in matters which involve the senate itself; if anyone introduces a law meant to deprive the senate of some of its traditional authority, it is the people alone who have the power of passing or rejecting any such measure. And if a single one of the tribunes interposes in any matter, the senate is unable to make a final decision and cannot even meet and hold sittings. And the tribunes are always obliged to act as the people decree and to pay every attention to their wishes. Thus, for all these reasons, the senate is afraid of the masses and must pay due attention to the popular will.

Similarly, the people must be submissive to the senate and respect its members both in public and in private. Throughout Italy vast numbers of contracts are given out for the construction and repair of public buildings, and also there are contracts involving navigable rivers, harbors, gardens, mines, and land. In all these matters involving management of public property, the senate is supreme. Also the judges in most civil trials, whether public or private, are appointed from the senate. So all citizens are at the mercy of the senate and look forward with alarm to the outcome of its decisions. In the same way citizens are reluctant to oppose the consuls, since all are under their authority when in the field.

Thus, each part of the state has the power of hampering the others or cooperating with them; so their union is adequate to all emergencies. It would be impossible to find a better political system than this.

Cicero

Cicero is probably the most eminent political philosopher Rome produced, but his work is mainly derived from the Greeks, in both style and content. Some of his writings borrowed the Socratic dialogue style from Plato, whom Cicero greatly admired, and he entitled two of his political works *The Republic* and *The Laws*. Many of his basic ideas are restatements of Stoic philosophy.

Although Cicero imitated Plato's literary style, he did not follow Plato's example in turning away from active political life; on the contrary, he was near the center of Roman governmental power and political intrigue through most of his adult life. He moved up through the ranks of office to a position of great influence, but finally, like so many other politicians of imperial Rome, came to a violent death.

Cicero came from Arpinum, a town a few miles from Rome. He served in the military, studied law, held the office of praetor (judge and law-court supervisor), and was elected consul in 63 B.C. The greatest challenge to his authority during his term as consul came from Cataline and the mob of commoners who were seeking debt cancellation and land reform. Cicero had four of the leaders strangled and called out the Roman legions to finish the job of putting down the incipient rebellion; he is said to have regarded this forceful action as the greatest accomplishment of his term in office. He later served as governor of the province of Cilicia, in Asia Minor, and was for many years an active member of the Roman senate.

For a busy man who was embroiled in legal work and politics, Cicero managed to leave behind him a prodigious amount of words. We have 57 of his orations, which are regarded as masterpieces of political invective; 864 letters, informal comments, and records of his private life—all written during his active years; and another vast library of political and philosophical books written during his retirement.

Although Cicero's work, for all its bulk, does not add up to a philosophical system comparable to that of Plato or Aristotle, his frame of reference is in some ways wider. The Greek philosophers had talked about government for Greeks, but Cicero talked about government for the entire human race. And although he professed to be a devout disciple of Plato, his political writings reflect a somewhat different concern: Cicero was not looking for philosopher-kings, but for stability through law. He defined the state, in fact, as a "community of law," echoing the ideas of the Stoics. He often expressed his conviction that laws need not be merely arbitrary pronouncements, but that true laws are rooted in nature and are capable of being reasoned out by the human mind.

This view of the source of the law also placed ultimate authority in the people; the republic, for Cicero, was an association among a number of people in basic agreement about law and justice. Cicero was writing at a time when the republican form of government in Rome was obviously about to topple, and his theories were in part an argument for the maintenance of the system. He agreed with Polybius about the cyclical rise and fall of governments, and about the advantages of the mixed constitution of the republic.

He managed to bring together many sources in his writings, although the differences between them were not always reconciled. Yet despite the contradictions in Cicero's work, his writings were widely read and, like those of Polybius, were highly influential on later thinkers. Cicero did not place much stress on theology, but his concept of the universal community was easily adapted by Christian philosophers into an idea of a universal church.

Although some of Cicero's ideas seem to be democratic, he was identified with the more conservative elements in the republic. His political life was, in a way, as full of unresolved contradiction as was his philosophical work. He made peace with Caesar when Caesar became dictator of Rome, and after Caesar's death he came out of retirement and made peace with Caesar's assassins. He sided with Octavian in the conflict between Octavian and Marc Anthony, but he had no chance to make peace with Anthony when the latter came to power in alliance with Octavian. Anthony's soldiers hunted Cicero down, murdered him, and brought his head to be hung up in the Roman Forum, where he had so often devastated his enemies with oratory.

CICERO ON NATURAL LAW

True law is right reason in conformity with nature; it is universal, unchangeable, and eternal; its commands urge us to duty, and its prohibitions restrain us from evil. The good respect its injunctions, and the wicked treat them with indifference. This true law cannot be

From *The Republic*, Book III, and *The Laws*, Book I, in Cicero *Treatises*, trans. C. D. Yonge (London: George Bell and Sons, 1887), pp. 360, 408. (Edited and abridged.)

contradicted by any other law; it is not right to try to alter it or repeal it. Neither the senate nor the people can give us any dispensation for not obeying this universal law of justice. It needs no other expositor and interpreter than our own conscience. Any person who disobeys this law flees from himself and denies his own human nature. And by doing so he will endure the severest penalties, even if he escapes the other evils which are usually called punishment.

Since nothing is better than reason, and since this is the common property of God and man, there is a certain natural and rational correspondence between divine nature and human nature. But for these two to have reason in common they must also have right reason in common. And since this right reason is what we call law, then men and gods must be considered as associated by law. Also, there must be a community of justice where there is a community of law. And thus the whole universe, gods and men, can be considered a community of law and justice.

THE EMPIRE AND THE CHURCH

Caesar Augustus, formerly Octavian, consolidated the boundaries of the Roman empire—in part by choosing not to extend them, as when he fortified the Danube and pulled Roman troops to the southern side of that border—and consolidated the power of the emperor with similarly cautious effectiveness: he extended his authority while denying its existence. He never took the risk of trying to become king; but the names and titles he did assume—especially Caesar, Augustus, and *imperator*—came to have their own meaning as titles of high office.

Augustus in his lifetime had chosen as his successor his son-in-law Tiberius; Tiberius, who was 55 when he came to power, proved to be a sensible and moderate ruler. The next two emperors, Caligula and Nero, were not. Caligula, overwhelmed by his own power and wealth, turned his reign into one long orgy. He bathed in perfume, once invited a race horse to dinner, squandered millions, engaged in sexual excesses that were unusual even for a Roman, and finally proclaimed himself to be a god. He was replaced by the elderly and incompetent Claudius, who was murdered by

his wife, Agrippina, and was succeeded by her son Nero. Nero, who wanted to be respected as an artist, gave public performances in the theaters. During his reign there was a great fire in Rome, and, according to legend, Nero amused himself by playing the lyre while thousands died in the crumbling tenements. Nero, too, had himself officially deified, and he, too, died a violent death.

Such were the ups and downs of Roman rule. The lines of succession were never clear. Sometimes power passed peacefully to a new emperor who had been chosen and trained by his predecessor; more often it passed violently, through murder or intrigue or warfare or political coup. Once, after the emperor Pertinax had been murdered by men of the Praetorian Guard, the leaders of the guard auctioned off the empire to the highest bidder—a wealthy senator named Didius Julianus, who held the throne until he was beheaded 66 days later. Some of the emperors were courageous leaders and wise administrators, whom any historian would rank among history's great statesmen, and others were monuments of human foolishness.

While emperors came and went, the vast legal machinery of the empire churned on. The emperors held enormous personal power and prestige, in their role at the apex of the social structure of the whole Western world, but still the empire was never governed by a single man. (If it had been, it would never have outlasted Caligula, who believed that he was regularly visited by a moon goddess.) Power and responsibility abroad were divided among various provincial governors, military commanders, and rulers of tributary kingdoms, Within Italy, the complex duties of running the state from day to day became the responsibility of a growing governmental bureaucracy; and throughout the empire, the flexible, complex, and ever-changing legal system provided its own network of social order.

Religion was another source of stability. Caligula was not the first Roman to become a public deity. Julius Caesar had been proclaimed a god by the senate after his death, and Augustus was posthumously proclaimed *divius Augustus;* the Romans felt it was a breech of etiquette only for Caligula to be proclaimed a god in his own lifetime. But that practice, too, later became customary. Many practical emperors, more interested in statesmanship than theology, allowed themselves to become officially deified for whatever added grandeur and legitimacy it might give them in the eyes of the people.

According to Gibbon, "the various modes of worship which prevailed in the Roman world were all considered by the people as equally true, by the philosopher as equally false, and by the magistrate as equally useful."[5] As people from all over the empire found their way to Rome, so did their religions; the capital became a carnival of cults. The official paganism of the state continued to be observed, but it was easy for most Romans to worship new gods along with the old.

In the early days of the empire the authorities were usually tolerant of new religions; the important question was whether or not they served the purposes of the state. But the growing sect of Christianity—one of the many foreign religions that found its way to Rome and began to win converts—was based on the idea of a universal church that demanded a higher loyalty than human emperors and human laws. By the time of Nero, Christianity had become enough of an annoyance to be made a capital offence; several Christian leaders were blamed for the great Roman fire and were executed for it. Some of the later emperors tolerated Christianity, but others persecuted Christians. The sect grew, and persecution seemed only to increase the loyalty of its members to their own—as opposed to Rome's—hierarchy. In the third century A.D. the emperor Diocletian launched a massive campaign to wipe out Christianity entirely; hundreds of Christians were killed, and thousands publicly recanted their faith. But when the persecution had finally run its course, Christianity was stronger than ever: It had the sympathy of many non-Christians, a legend of heroism and martyrdom, and the official toleration of the state. In the year 313 the Edict of Milan officially confirmed the legal status of Christianity, and ten years later Constantine, then emperor, declared himself a Christian.

By this time the empire was well along in the process of decentralization that would ultimately lead to its collapse. Diocletian had made his capital in Asia Minor, in the city of Nicomedia, while his co-emperor, Maximian, ruled the other half of the empire from Milan. Constantine built a new capital for himself on the ruins of Byzantium and made it his headquarters, although he also ordered the construction of many new buildings, including a number of churches in Rome. Similarly, later emperors recognized the status of Rome as the symbolic capital of the empire; but the truth was that a sort of centrifugal force was pulling the empire apart, diffusing its power to the peripheral capitals where provincial generals headquartered with their armies. Various arrangements of co-emperors reflected this division, and in the fourth century a division between eastern and western empires became final. The emperor Valerian ruled in the west, while his brother Valens ruled the other half of the empire from Constantinople.

Both parts of the empire were in an almost constant state of warfare with barbarian tribes. The Goths, whose land was on the other side of the Danube, the ancient boundary that had been fortified by Caesar Augustus, were themselves threatened by the incursions of other barbarian nomads to their north. There was a general movement across the Danube, and in 400 the Visigoths, led by Alaric, crossed the Alps into Italy. In 410, a landmark in any history of the empire, they entered Rome. By the end of the fifth century, there was a barbarian king of Italy, and the western half of the empire had come to an end. Barbarian rulers maintained a cautious coexistence with the emperors in Constantinople, while the Roman Catholic church increased in power—both political and spiritual—to become the main force for social stability in Italy.

THE EARLY CHRISTIAN PHILOSOPHERS

The New Testament tells that Christ, when asked by Pharisees if tribute should be paid to the Roman emperor, told one of them to produce a coin and see whose name and image were on it. They looked at a penny and answered that the name and image were Caesar's. "Therefore," said Christ, "render unto Caesar the things that are Caesar's; and unto God the things that are God's."[6]

The fact that such a question should arise, and that an answer to it should come down to us as a proverb, reflects a tremendous change in the nature of human consciousness and human loyalties since the times when—as in classical Athens—it was possible for the sense of citizenship to encompass home, occupation, social class, political allegiance, and religious faith. But the Roman Empire held hundreds of

[5] Edward Gibbon, *Decline and Fall of the Roman Empire* (ed. Dero A. Saunders) (New York: Viking Press, 1952), pp. 50–51.

[6] Matthew 22:21; Mark 12:17.

thousands of people who were officially citizens of Rome, although they had never seen the city and never would; within the city were thousands more who had come from all the corners of the empire and whose experience as citizens was transient and confusing. The armies that defended the empire against its enemies were filled, similarly, with men from all parts of the empire; soon the emperors themselves were men who had been born in distant provinces and had spent their lives on battlefields, everywhere but Rome. Rome never attempted to impose its official pagan religion on conquered provinces, and many Romans, both in the capital and abroad, became attracted to other faiths. The rise of Christianity, a religion intensely and increasingly attuned to its own inner sources of authority, caused the emergence of a fragmented kind of human consciousness and a new political problem—the question of the relationship between church and state (which still troubles us after 2,000 years).

During the early years of Christianity, the attitude of believers toward the state and its authority was deeply affected by the prevailing conviction that the Day of Judgment, which would bring an end to the worldly order of things, was near at hand. This conviction had waned by the third and fourth centuries, but there was still the sense of a higher loyalty. "Your citizenship, your magistracies, and the very nature of your *curia* is the Church of Christ," the African theologian Tertullian declared. "You are an alien in this world, and a citizen of the city of Jerusalem that is above."[7]

Much of Christian political thinking, then, was a search for the proper degree or form of participation in the affairs of the state. Some degree of disengagement from earthly and material power was the essence of early Christianity, but there was still a general recognition of the need to obey the laws and to deal with the authorities of the state. One factor in this recognition was the growing danger to all the empire from the barbarian forces beyond its borders.

The question of whether a Christian should serve in the army was an important one to early theologians, and most of them agreed that it was wrong to do so. Lactantius, another Christian philosopher, said: "When God prohibits killing . . . He warns us not to do even those things which are regarded as legal among men. And so it will not be lawful for a just man to serve as a soldier."[8] But as time

went on, the number of Christians serving in the Roman legions increased, and meanwhile the church and the state were drawing nearer together—a process that was tremendously accelerated by Constantine. A year after this emperor issued his edict of tolerance, the church enacted a canon threatening Christian soldiers with excommunication for discarding their weapons in time of peace; a century later, the government required that all soldiers be Christians.[9] The once-persecuted and foreign sect had now become the official religion of the Roman Empire. This meant that the defense of the empire against its enemies was the duty and interest of Christians. The success of Christianity brought a host of new philosophical problems; once it had been necessary for the church to figure out ways of relating to governmental authority, but now the church itself was beginning to *acquire* governmental authority. Futhermore, the enemies of Christianity could now blame the church for the successes and failures of the empire. When Rome was sacked by the Visigoths, less than 30 years after Christianity had won its official status, non-Christians argued that the new religion had sapped the power of the empire.[10] An attempt to refute these charges led to one of the monumental works of Christian theology, St. Augustine's *City of God.*

St. Augustine

Augustine, a convert to Christianity who had risen to the position of bishop of the North African city of Hippo, began writing *City of God* a few years after Alaric's invasion of the capital and finished the 22-volume work 13 years later. It was in part a defense of Christianity against paganism, but it was also an exposition of Augustine's thinking about worldly power, about the condition of humanity in the state of "the Fall" resulting from original sin, and about the prospects for happiness and political order on this earth. Augustine's work, written at a time when the empire was revealing its weakness and the church was consolidating its new strength, stands as a major piece of Christian political thinking, an indicator of the transition from the era of the Roman Empire to the Middle Ages.

[7] Tertullian *De Idolatria* 18, 19.

[8] Lactantius *Divinae Institutions,* VI, XX, 15-17.

[9] Mulford Q. Sibley, *Political Ideas and Ideologies* (New York: Harper & Row, 1970), pp. 176-77.

[10] Christianity was proclaimed the official religion, and paganism was prohibited, in 383 A.D.; Alaric entered Rome in 410.

Augustine's fundamental contribution to political-theological philosophy—the idea that there were coexisting cities of God and of the world—is an ambiguous blending of some of the more abstract notions of late Stoic thought with the obvious fact of the existence of two different institutions that claimed human loyalty: the church and the empire.

The later Roman Stoics had described the cosmos in terms of a series of concentric circles: the household innermost; then the city, which included all households; then the earthly community of the living, which included all cities; and beyond that the greater universal community of living people, the souls of the dead, and all the angels.

Augustine's writings borrowed this concentric image. He referred to the various centers of human life and discussed the possibilities of order at the domestic, civil, and spiritual levels—through obedience to the proper authorities at each level. He also described the existence on earth of two distinct "cities": the city of earth, and the city of God. The *civitas terrena* was distinguished by pride, striving, lust, and human conflict. The *civitas dei* was characterized by humility, faith, moderation, and obedience.

The city of earth and the city of God did not simply correspond to the empire and the church; the concepts were much more abstract than that, and Augustine nowhere gave absolutely clear criteria for identifying either city clearly with existing people or institutions. Rather, the idea of the two cities served as a way of distinguishing between conflicting sets of values, the worldly and the godly, and as an exposition of the difference between the damned and the saved. There was already a considerable amount of conflict within the church, and Augustine was by no means willing to have it be understood that membership in the church automatically conferred membership in the city of the elect of God. The *civitas dei* can only be equated with the church of some future time, "as it is destined to be when no wicked person shall be in her."[11]

In his description of the efforts of the city of earth's inhabitants, Augustine stressed the impermanence of empire. In this respect he was like many observers of world history, ancient and modern, who have tried to make some sense out of the all-too-obvious fact of the transience of political

orders. For Augustine, the collapse of empire was only a sign of the inevitable decay of any kind of worldly power, the condition of human life after the Fall. Men who hungered after power and wealth and glory might attain their goals, but their satisfaction would never be anything but imperfect and fleeting.

As for the power of the state and the necessity of obedience to it, Augustine recognized that the Christian's higher loyalty was always to God. But he did not advocate revolution, and repeatedly in his works he spoke of the virtue of obedience. Obedience to the proper authorities led to order and peace, and the good Christian should accept the things of earthly existence—even tyranny and injustice and slavery—as the will of God. Even slaves should remember that in the more enduring kingdom of God they are free, and give thanks for their lot. "The good man, even if he is a slave, is free; but the bad man, even if he reigns, is a slave."[12]

Augustine was pessimistic about the possibility that the state could ever be a true vehicle of Christianity, but he did not rule out this possibility entirely. His works included enough suggestions of the ways that the state might make at least some contributions to peace on earth to stand as a justification for the active participation of Christians in government and—more importantly—for the active intervention of the church in encouraging earthly rulers to live up to their Christian obligations. The final message of Augustine, which may explain his enormous influence during the Middle Ages, is one of the Christian's duty of obedience to *both* secular and religious authority.

ST. AUGUSTINE ON PEACE

Two cities have been formed by two loves: the earthly by the love of self, even to the contempt of God; the heavenly by the love of God, even to the contempt of self. The former glories in itself, the latter in God. In the one, the princes and the nations it subdues

[11] *City of God.* XX, 9.

[12] *Ibid.,* IV, 3.

From *The City of God* (trans. Marcus Dodds), in Vol. II of *A Select Library of the Nicene and Post-Nicene Fathers* (New York: Charles Scribners, 1889.) (Edited and abridged.)

are ruled by the love of ruling; in the other, the princes and the subjects serve one another in love, the latter obeying while the former take thought for all.

The earthly city has its good in this world, and rejoices in it with such joy as such things can afford. But it is not free of distresses: it is often divided against itself by litigations, wars, quarrels, and victories which are either life-destroying or short-lived. If, when it has conquered, it is inflated with pride, its victory is life-destroying; if it turns its thoughts upon the common casualties of our moral condition and is anxious rather than elated, this victory, though of a higher kind, is short-lived, for it cannot continue to rule over those whom it has subjugated. But the things which this city desires cannot justly be said to be evil; it desires earthly peace for the sake of enjoying earthly goods, and it makes war in order to attain to this peace.

The peace of body and soul is the well-ordered and harmonious life and health of the living creature. Peace between man and God is the well-ordered obedience of faith to eternal law. Peace between man and man is well-ordered concord. Domestic peace is the well-ordered concord between those of the family who rule and those who obey. Civil peace is a similar concord among the citizens. The peace of the celestial city is the perfectly ordered and harmonious enjoyment of God, and of one another in God. The peace of all things is the tranquility of order. Order is the distribution which allots things equal and unequal, each to its own place. And hence, though the miserable, insofar as they are such, do certainly not enjoy peace but are severed from that tranquility, nevertheless, inasmuch as they are deservedly and justly miserable, they are by their very misery connected with order.

Domestic peace is the well-ordered concord of those in the family who rule and those who obey. For they who care for the rest rule—the husband the wife, the parents the children, the masters the servants; and they who are cared for obey—the women their husbands, the children their parents, the servants their masters. But in the family of the just man who lives by faith and is as yet a pilgrim journeying on to the celestial city, even those who rule serve those whom they seem to command; for they rule not from a love of power, but from a sense of the duty they owe to others—not because they are proud of authority, but because they love mercy.

CHRISTENDOM

As the Roman Empire disintegrated into a complex of small feudal states and warring barbarian tribes, the church slowly took its place as the great unifying force in Europe. Christianity survived the attacks on it inspired by the barbarian invasion and continued to grow, both as a religious faith and as a political institution, through the long years of the Roman Empire's demise.

The end of the empire, like the end of the republic, was an unclear—perhaps in its time even invisible—transition. Careful adherence to the outer forms of the past sustained the impression, for a while, that no major change had taken place at all. Odoacer, the first barbarian king of Italy, placed an emperor on the throne in Rome, maintained the ceremonial meetings of the senate, and established friendly diplomatic relations with the eastern empire in Constantinople. Behind the façade, however, Italy was changing from a relatively urbanized, Rome-centered nation into a rural and decentralized area, its governments insecure at best and sometimes nonexistent. In the sixth century an invasion from Constantinople drove out the Goths and "reunited" the empire, but the war left much of Italy in ruins. In the war's aftermath, even the last vestige of Roman tradition, the senate, ceased to exist. Ferdinand Gregorovious, a medieval historian, wrote:

In the tempest of the Gothic war, the old life had disappeared forever. In the towns, burnt and deserted, only the ruins recalled a vanished prosperity. The Sybil's prophecy was fulfilled, and a deep night spread over the Latin world. In the darkness, there shone no light except the candles of the churches and the solitary lamp of a monk within his monastery.[13]

Later in the sixth century another barbarian tribe, the Lombards, moved into Italy, and for the next 200 years the peninsula was divided between the Lombard territories and those ruled from Constantinople through a representative

[13] Ferdinand Gregororious; *History of the City of Rome in the Middle Ages,* trans. Annie Hamilton (London: G. Bell, 1902), p 276.

called the exarch, whose headquarters was at Ravenna. In fact, both regimes were only loose aggregations of dukedoms and militarily governed counties. There was no really unified secular government in the land, and the strength of the popes in Rome grew in its absence.

This flourishing of the church was not caused simply by an opportunity to spread the faith unhindered by political restraints; it was also based on an increase in tangible wealth and worldly power. It had become customary for wealthy Christians to leave gifts of land to the church upon passing to their heavenly reward, and the papacy soon became the greatest landowner in all of Italy, master of more than 2,000 square miles of property on the mainland and on the islands of Corsica, Sicily, and Sardinia. Schools and monasteries were built, occasional mercenary armies were fielded to fight off incursions of barbarian tribes, and, as Lombardy and the eastern empire fought to maintain their shaky bases of power in the north, the church slowly transformed its landlordship into political sovereignty and made itself the ruling force in Rome.

The increase in wealth and political power aided—and was aided by—the spread of the Roman version of the Christian faith. The Lombards were converted to Roman Catholicism in the sixth century. The Franks, the first barbarian tribe to embrace the faith, were rapidly becoming the major power on the European continent. England was converted in 597 and, until the religion of Mohammed began to take hold, Roman Catholicism was also the prevailing faith in Spain and northern Africa.

In the eighth century, as the strength of the Franks increased and that of the eastern empire was shaken by the astonishing rise of Mohammedanism, the Roman church broke for good with Constantinople and formed a new alliance—a move that had great consequences for European history. Western Europe, once on the remote and barbarous outskirts of a culture dominated by Greece and Rome and Constantinople, was now becoming a power center of a new, Christianized political order.

The Franks, whose kingdom covered what is now Holland and Belgium as well as much of France and Germany, underwent a change of rule in 751 when Pepin le Bref, with the blessings of Rome, deposed the reigning king; shortly thereafter, Pepin led his armies into Italy to protect Rome from invasion by the Lombards, who were trying to extend their control over the entire peninsula. Pepin's son, Charlemagne, was anointed and crowned by Pope Leo on Christmas day of the year 800. Thus emerged one of history's more curious political institutions: the Holy Roman Empire.

Actually, Charlemagne's empire was rather short-lived. His descendants could not hold it together, and for a while, after the collapse of his kingdom, papal power declined in the absence of a protector beyond the Alps. But in the tenth century a new alliance was formed, and King Otto of Germany was crowned Holy Roman Emperor by Pope John XII, in return for military assistance to Rome.

The creation of a new empire may have been necessary for the church, but it meant that there were now two centers of power in Christendom, and much of medieval history is a map of the intricate and endless conflict that went on between them.

Voltaire, in the eighteenth century, was to describe the Holy Roman Empire as neither holy, nor Roman, nor an empire. In fact, The Holy Roman Emperor was usually a German prince. He would first be elected King of Germany, by the ruling lords of that country, and then would be crowned King of Italy by the Lombards; finally, if his relations with the pope were in good order and if politics among his feudal supporters did not make it too dangerous for him to leave his own country, he might journey to Rome to receive the imperial crown. Thereafter, he could look forward to a lifetime of conflict, either somewhere beyond the boundaries of his empire, or with the feudal lords who were nominally his vassals, or with the pope. In his dealings with the pope, he would always have to keep in mind the possibility that the church's ultimate weapon, excommunication, might be used against him. Excommunication of an emperor, which released his subjects from their vows of allegiance to him, always gave a host of ambitious or unhappy nobles a golden opportunity to rebel.

Although the church was the one institution that had a claim on all loyalties, it was itself far from united at any time. There were many clerics who resented control from Rome and who had greater ties to secular rulers, and there was competition for power within the church, which often became as bloody and violent as any struggle for a secular throne. In the confusion of feudal politics, a clear line was never drawn between church and state. Sometimes clerics sided with secular rulers against the pope, sometimes secular rulers sided with the pope against other rulers or other clerics. Sabine contends that in this era, church-state conflict as we think of it today did not exist:

There was, properly speaking, neither church nor state in the modern meaning of those terms. There was not one body of men who formed the state and one which formed the church, for all men were included in both. There was only a single Christian society, as St. Augustine had taught in his City of God, *and it included, at least for the eleventh century, the whole world. Under God this society had two heads, the pope and the emperor, two principles of authority, the spiritual rule of priests and the temporal rule of kings, and two hierarchies of governing officials, but there was no division between two bodies or societies. A controversy between these two hierarchies was in a legal sense jurisdictional, such as might arise between two officials of the same state.*[11]

But one of these jurisdictional conflicts was long enough in duration and bitter enough to begin the opening of the breech between church and state that would become so evident a few centuries later. This was the controversy over investiture, the power of secular rulers to choose men as bishops and invest them with the ring and crozier that symbolized the power of this office. The central issue, which was far from symbolic, was one of authority and loyalty, a question of whether bishops—who were usually powerful figures in medieval politics—should consider themselves to have been placed in office by their king or by the pope. This problem was a legal issue that kept scholars of canon law busy for years, and it was also a personal struggle between a powerful emperor, Henry IV, and a powerful pope, Gregory VII. During the struggle Gregory excommunicated the emperor twice, the emperor temporarily managed to depose the pope and replace him with another pope of his own choosing, and the issue was not resolved until after both antagonists had died. Finally, in 1122, it was agreed that the power of investiture of religious office lay with the pope.

The church was now near the height of its political power. In Italy it had direct governmental authority, which made it a kingdom in its own right. With the legal support of a spurious "donation" attributed to the Emperor Constan-

tine, the pope ruled a large territory stretching from Rome to Ravenna.[15] The church had well-established authority in the Holy Roman Empire and—by the time of the reign of Pope Innocent III in the thirteenth century—had obtained vows of allegiance from the eastern empire of Constantinople (conqured by crusaders) as well as from the rulers of southern Italy and Sicily, Aragon, Barcelona, Portugal, Provence, England, Norway, Sweden, Denmark, Bohemia, Bulgaria, Hungary, Croatia, Serbia, Poland, Kiev, Armenia, Jerusalem, and Athens.

Innocent III had assumed office with grandiose beliefs about the power of the pope: "The Lord Jesus Christ," he wrote, "has set up one ruler over all things as his universal vicar; and as all things in heaven, on earth, and in hell bow to the name of Christ, so should all obey Christ's vicar, so that there may be but one flock and one shepherd." The really remarkable thing about Innocent III was that he had the brilliance and the will to make the papacy, in his lifetime, very nearly the supreme authority in Christendom that he believed it ought to be. He was a skillful diplomat and an imperious ruler, and he intervened freely in the politics of kingdoms and the private lives of kings.

Naturally, during these centuries of conflict between kings and popes, there were conflicting theories of political authority. All parties claimed allegiance to the Christian faith, but there were differing opinions as to the precise manner in which God intended the people of His world to be ruled. Secular rulers often claimed that their authority came directly from God; the church generally agreed that earthly kings had a proper place in the divine order of things, but held that priests and popes held a somewhat higher place. This argument was expressed in the writings St. Thomas Aquinas.

St. Thomas Aquinas

The great accomplishment of Thomas Aquinas was giving to the medieval world a philosophy of an orderly and unified Christian society; more accurately, he gave it

---

[14] George H. Sabine, *A History of Political Theory,* (3rd ed., New York: Holt, Rinehart and Winston, Inc., 1963), pp. 225-26.

[15] The "donation of Constantine," recorded in a document fabricated in the eighth century, was based on a legend that the Emperor Constantine, having been cured of leprosy by Pope Sylvester, gave most of central Italy, including Rome, to the church. Falsity of the document was conceded by church officials in the fifteenth century.

a philosophy of an ordered Christian universe in which human laws and political institutions had a clearly defined role.

He was born in 1225, in the castle of the wealthy and noble Aquino family, and received his early education from Benedictine monks. At the age of 18 he joined the Dominican order and then spent several years studying in Paris and Cologne, with the eminent Aristotelian scholar Albertus Magnus.

Aristotle's works had not, in Thomas' time, been favorably received by the church. They were being translated into Latin and were widely read by scholars in the thirteenth century, but church authorities distrusted the rationalistic, scientific bent of Aristotle's thinking, and the study of his works was banned– apparently without great success–in the Christian universities at Oxford and Paris. The Greek philosopher who *was* revered and accepted was Plato, whose view of the nature of truth–considerably more mystical than that of Aristotle–had been reconciled to Christian theology in the writings of St. Augustine. Thomas performed a similar intellectual feat with the works of Aristotle. He blended Aristotelian logic with Christian dogma in his own writings, and in the process revolutionized the official philosophy of the church. Thomas' writings were condemned by the church in 1274, the year of his death, but in spite of the condemnation his works were read; a few years later the ban was lifted, and his philosophy was officially accepted as Christian teaching. In 1323 he was canonized, in the sixteenth century he was recognized as the equal of the great Fathers of the Latin church, in the nineteenth century his works were declared to be the official basis of Christian theology, and in the twentieth century Pope Pius X declared that the works of St. Thomas Aquinas were "not to be placed in the category of opinions capable of being debated one way or another."

Part of the reason for the acceptance of St. Thomas and, through him, of Aristotle, may be that the church *needed* a more comprehensive philosophical system in order to satisfy and maintain control over the intellectual activity that was growing in the new centers of learning in Western Europe. William Ebenstein sees the victory of Thomism as evidence of the "adaptability and high survival capacity" of the church:

As time went by, particularly from the eleventh century on, it became evident that theology was not enough, and that the challenge of budding humanism and secularism had to be met on its own ground. The adoption of Aristotle by the church, through St. Thomas, indicated its tremendous intellectual vitality and flexibility. In Aristotle the church found a systematic and encyclopedic body of thought, encompassing many disciplines and forming a coherent whole; it was moderate in temper and outlook, adaptable to changing circumstances, full of common sense, and timeless. Though it lacked the spark and brilliance of Plato's philosophy, it was rich in solidity and endurance, characteristics that are prosaic but that wear well under all conditions. To be born, the church needed Plato. To last, it needed Aristotle.[16]

Thomas' writings were not only impressively comprehensive in their scope; they also carried a rather awesome sense of certainty, which must have eased the way for their transformation into dogma. His chief work, the twenty-volume *Summa Theologica,* was written in the form of discussions of theological and moral questions, such as: "Whether Prudence is a Virtue Necessary to Man?", "Whether the Holy Ghost Proceeds from the Son?", "Whether Christ Suffered at a Suitable Time?", "Whether There Can Be Mortal Sin in Touches and Kisses?" After each question is stated, the "incorrect" answer is given in a series of "objections"; following this the correct answer is given, usually in the form of a scriptural quotation; then the authoritative citation is supplemented by logical argument; finally, each objection is individually demolished. The technique was a formidable performance that combined scriptural citation with logical argument, demonstrating Thomas' belief in the compatibility of faith with reason.

Thomas Aquinas touched on matters of politics in several parts of the *Summa Theologica,* and also in the shorter work, *On Kingship.* Wherever he discussed politics and society, it was always from a perspective on human society as an integral part of Creation, and all earthly institutions were seen as subordinate to the higher purposes of God. In this sense his thinking was similar to that of earlier Christian philosophers, such as St. Augustine. But where Augustine had viewed all government in a rather gloomy light, as a manifes-

[16] William Ebenstein, *Great Political Thinkers: Plato to the Present* (New York: Holt, Rinehart and Winston, 1951), pp. 216–17.

tation of the results of original sin and a condition of life after the Fall, with no prospect of lasting peace or satisfaction, Thomas revived the Aristotelian concept of humanity as a social and political animal who quite naturally sought fulfillment in the life of the community. This humanistic idea was reconciled to theology by the condition that every person's ultimate purpose, which community life should help to attain, was divine salvation.

We see in Thomas none of the distrust, even contempt, of secular authority that had marked the works of earlier Christian philosophers, especially those who wrote in the times when the church was still an outcast and its members were persecuted. Thomas was respectful of the wielders of earthly power, and he urged loyalty toward kings. One of the products of his vast and generally integrative philosophical system was the idea that the Christian citizen had a single loyalty, to a political order in which earthly and religious authorities occupied well-defined but not conflicting niches. Because the church was dedicated to a higher motive—the salvation of souls—and because its authority came directly from Christ, its role was naturally superior.

Thomas touched on the much-debated question of what a people might properly do when they find themselves subjected to the rule of an obvious tyrant, but he backed away from the position taken by John of Salisbury, another prominent medieval philosopher, who had argued that the killing of tyrants was justified. Thomas urged legal action and Christian forbearance in the case of excessive tyranny, and warned that revolutionary resistance to minor tyranny often leads to a worse tyranny, imposed by the leaders of the revolution (an argument that would be picked up centuries later by conservative modern theorists).

In discussing the various forms of government, he used the traditional classification of rule by the many, the few, or the one, expressing a clear preference for monarchy as the form most likely to produce unified, orderly, and peaceful government. He modified this, however, with touches of democracy and aristocracy—monarchs might be elected by the people, and they should appoint leading citizens to lower positions of authority.

One of Thomas' great synthesizing concepts—broad enough to encompass divine revelation, Aristotelian natural science, and political institutions—was his fourfold classification of laws. He described the ordering of the universe and everything in it according to four sets of principles: eternal law, the ultimate plan of creation, is beyond human comprehension. Natural Law, the manifestation of Eternal Law in actual created things, is accessible to human rationality. Divine Law is the authority of revelation, as in the Holy Scriptures—truth that is not so much discovered through the human reasoning powers as given directly by God. Human Law regulates the conditions of human behavior in societies; the enactment of such laws should always be a product of reason, and thus good Human Law is derived from Natural Law.

In general, the final effect of Thomas' work is not only integrative but hierarchical. He did not simply synthesize reason and revelation, divine authority and earthly power; he assigned them values of higher and lower. His view of the universe is one in which all things are ranked on a scale, above or below one another, and are always ultimately subordinate to God.

This kind of a hierarchical vision of creation was presented in a much more vivid and dramatic form not long after St. Thomas' time by the poet Dante, who in his *Divine Comedy* described the universe as a series of levels, which ascended upward through Paradise to the angels and God, and downward through the Inferno to demons and the Devil. Although Dante produced this vivid image of the hierarchical universe, he also wrote a political work, *On World-Government,* in which he argued that the power of kings comes directly from God (not via the pope), and that the church should exercise no temporal authority.

Almost at the same time as the finishing touches were being applied to the integrated, hierarchical medieval view of the universe, the picture was apparently beginning to crack. The weak spot in the picture, of course, was the obtrusive and divisive role of the church in European power politics. Even true believers were able to see that priests and popes were human beings who scrambled, often in most un-Christian ways, for political advantage. The church, even at the apex of its power, never had a firm grip on political authority, and soon its fortunes began to swing the other way, toward a limited and diminished position in which it would be more strictly confined to spiritual concerns.

ST. THOMAS AQUINAS ON THE PURPOSES OF SOCIETY

It is clear that the purpose of a community gathered together is to live virtuously. For men form a group in order to live fully, in a way that would not be possible if they were living alone, and the fullest life is the virtuous life. Therefore, the virtuous life is the object of human society.

This is proved by the fact that we regard as members of the community only those who contribute to the fullness of its social life. If men came together merely to exist, then we would have to regard animals and slaves as parts of the civil community. Or if they came together only to multiply wealth, then we would regard all who trade with one another as members of the same city. But it is only those who obey the same laws, and who are guided toward fullness of life by the same government, that we regard as members of the same community.

Now, through virtuous living, man is ordained to a still higher purpose, which is the enjoyment of God. Therefore, since the highest purpose of a society can be no different from that of the individual man, it is the ultimate end of a community to attain to the enjoyment of God through virtuous living.

If it were possible to attain this ultimate end through human power, then it would follow that it would be the duty of kings to guide men toward it.

The higher the end which a government serves, the higher is the government. It is always the one who is concerned with the highest end who directs those who carry out the things which are meant to help attain that end. For example, the captain, whose duty it is to navigate the ship, tells the shipbuilder how to construct a vessel which will suit his purpose; and the citizen who is to bear arms tells the blacksmith what kind of weapons to make. In the same way, since man does not achieve his purpose, which is the realization of God, by human power but rather by divine grace, therefore the guidance toward this end must come, not from a human government, but a divine one.

Consequently, government of this kind is the authority of that king who is not only a man, but also God, namely our Lord Jesus Christ. This is the government which was entrusted to Him and because of which he is called, in the Holy Scriptures, not only Priest, but King.

Thus, in order that spiritual things might be separated from earthly things, the ministry of this kingdom is entrusted not to the rulers of this earth, but to priests, and in particular to the chief priest, the successor of St. Peter, the Vicar of Christ, the Roman Pontiff. To him all the kings in Christendom should be subject, as they are to our Lord Jesus Christ Himself. For those who are concerned with the subordinate ends of life should be subject to him who is concerned with the ultimate end, and be directed by his commands.

From *On Kingship*, trans. Gerald P. Phelan, rev. p 1. Th. Eschmann (Toronto: Pontifical Institute of Mediaeval Studies, 1949), pp. 60–62. (Edited and abridged.)

3/The Power of Nations

In Dante's time political conflict in the cities of Italy was mainly channeled into the ongoing feud between the Guelfs and the Ghibellenes. The Guelfs were traditionally the supporters of the papacy, and the Ghibellenes were the supporters of the Holy Roman Empire. That conflict pervaded life in the Italian cities during the late medieval period, even though both the institutions represented by it were on the decline. The era of popes and emperors was passing, and Europe was coming increasingly under the domination of the rulers of the great nation-states.

One of these rulers, Philip IV of France, challenged the papacy early in the fourteenth century and brought it to a position from which it never fully recovered. Philip, who had been at war against England, was ordered by Pope Boniface VII to make peace; he not only continued the war, but taxed the French clergy in order to finance it. Boniface, seeking to assert his authority, issued a papal bull in which he claimed—in even stronger terms than had Innocent III—supremacy over secular rulers. Philip's reply was to send his men into Italy to arrest the pope. The attempt failed. But Boniface died soon afterward, and Philip managed to make a prisoner of the papacy itself: He had a French pope elected and moved the capital of the church to Avignon. For the next 68 years, a period described by church historians as the "Babylonian Captivity," the popes were closely supervised from the French throne.

During this period Henry VII of Germany announced his intention to cross the Alps to receive the crown of the Holy Roman Empire, and he was immediately hailed by the Ghibellenes as the precursor of a new era of Italian unity and power. "Rejoice, O Italy," Dante wrote:

Now will you be the envy of the whole world because your bridegroom, the comfort of the world and the glory of its people, the most merciful Henry, Divius, Augustus, Caesar, hastens to his wedding.[1]

Henry's wedding was not a success, however. He ran into problems in the feuding city-states of northern Italy, first; then when he reached Rome, he found church officials in confusion about who should conduct the coronation in the absence of a pope, and about where the ceremony should be held. Henry managed to receive the imperial crown, but he never succeeded in unifying Italy under an imperial rule. A few months after the coronation, while marching against Guelf opponents in Naples, he died—according to his followers, from a glass of poisoned sacramental wine. Actually, his brief reign was of little historical importance except as an indication that the Holy Roman Empire was not about to unite Italy, as its supporters hoped, into a new force that would be able to compete with the rising new powers of Europe.

Gradually, amid massive changes in the life and culture of Western society—the weakening political power of the church, the decline of the feudal nobility, the increase in trade, the slow but unmistakable altering of the ways people saw the world and felt the possibilities of their own lives within it—Europe was emerging from the medieval era and arranging itself into nation-states. In England, where feudalism had never been strongly entrenched, this change proceeded rapidly and was accompanied by the rise of Parliament as a balance to the powers of the national monarch. France

[1] *On World Government, or, De Monarchia,* trans. Herbert W. Schneider (New York: Liberal Arts Press, 1949), p. 87.

had greater difficulties in establishing its nationhood, but its monarchy became in time an awesomely powerful institution. Another powerful monarchy was that of Spain, which emerged as a third major European nation-state in the fifteenth century, with the marriage of Ferdinand of Aragon and Isabella of Castille. In the same year that these Spanish rulers drove the last of the Moors from their country, Columbus discovered the New World, which became a source of financing for Spain's conflicts with other European powers.

The church had moved its headquarters back to Rome in 1377, partly in an attempt to maintain control over the Papal States, but the move did not bring a return to the old days of political authority over secular rulers. Rather, it brought a transition into an even more ignoble period of church history, known as the "Great Schism." In 1378, on the death of Pope Gregory XI, who was French, the College of Cardinals assembled in the Vatican to elect his successor. Pressured by the threats of Roman nobles and intimidated by a rioting mob that was demanding an Italian pope, the cardinals elected the Archbishop of Bari, who took the title of Urban VI. A group of French cardinals left the city and, at a safe distance from the Roman tumult, elected another pope, a cardinal from Geneva, who took the title of Clement VII and re-established the capitol at Avignon. The whole Christian world was thus split into Urbanist and Clementine factions, and matters were further complicated when the College of Cardinals, seeking to end the conflict, met at Pisa in 1409 and elected a third pope, Alexander V, whose legitimacy was disputed by the incumbents of both Rome and Avignon.

The Great Schism was finally resolved eight years later, with the abdication or deposition of the three competing popes and the election of a new one, Martin V, a Roman; but the schism, and the cooperation among Christian leaders of many nationalities that ultimately ended it, gave great impetus to a movement for a moderate democratizing of church government. Spokesmen for the new movement wanted to establish a permanent council that, somewhat like the English Parliament, the French Estates-general, and the Spanish Cortes, would participate in the formulation of policy. The conciliar cause was ultimately outflanked by later popes, who managed to maintain the essentially monarchical nature of their office; but it produced a new burst of political theorizing, which argued that church authority required some basis of consent from the Christian community. This line of thinking, of course, did not die out with defeat of the conciliar movement; it would surface again with new strength at a later period. The other side of the argument also produced some political theorizing, which had, according to Mulford Sibley, a more immediate influence:

With the triumph of anticonciliarist conceptions in the Church, the foundations are laid for the development of the theory of the divine right of kings; for if the pope is indeed the direct agent of God, rather than an official of the community, why does not the same principle hold in secular affairs?[2]

Another consequence of the Great Schism and the Babylonian Captivity was the church's loss of control over the Papal States, and the drive of popes to maintain the monarchy within the church during the fifteenth century was paralleled by a continuing struggle to regain political power in central Italy.

The Italian peninsula had not been united under any effective central government for a thousand years, and it remained divided as other areas bonded together in national unity. The north was dominated by the city-states of Milan, Venice, and Florence, which were often at war with one another; in the central area were the Papal States, which the church was trying desperately to hold onto; in the south were the kingdoms of Sicily and Naples, both embroiled in complex dynastic politics involving the houses of Aragon and Anjou. Inevitably, the great powers of Europe began to intervene in Italy. Late in the fifteenth century a conflict among Naples, Milan, and Florence led to an invasion by Charles VIII of France; a few years later armies of both France and Spain entered Italy to settle another dispute, and the result of this expedition was that, by 1504, Spain controlled Naples and France held Milan. In 1527 a mob of German mercenaries in the service of Emperor Charles V entered Rome and began an orgy of rape, plunder, and murder that was far worse than the earlier barbarian invasions. Although Italy was entering into a new period of enormous artistic and intellectual creativity, the climate was one of political intrigue and constant insecurity, as kings

[2] Mulford Q. Sibley, *Political Ideas and Ideologies* (New York: Harper & Row, 1970), p. 284.

and popes and princes competed in ever-shifting patterns of political power, and the armies of mercenaries and foreign rulers marched across the Italian countryside.

THE ITALIAN RENAISSANCE

Although Italy lagged behind other parts of Europe in developing national unity, it was in the forefront of remarkable new intellectual developments, as people began to break free from medieval ways of living and thinking.

The Renaissance is customarily described as a rebirth of interest in classical philosophy and literature; it was that, but it was also much more. Plato was revered by scholars throughout the Middle Ages, and Aristotle was revived and given a new Christian respectability in the works of St. Thomas Aquinas; the difference was that, in the fifteenth century, many people no longer found it quite so necessary to reconcile the ideas of the Greeks and Romans with Christian doctrine. There was a new spirit of paganism in the land, which was evident even in the behavior of popes and bishops.

Although religion, the Christian religion, continued to be a great force during and after the period we know as the Renaissance, it began to occupy a somewhat more limited and bounded space. Increasingly, people came to regard certain subjects as simply not relevant to religion; the great medieval image of the hierarchical universe, in which all things occupied the places ordained for them by God, was giving way to a more compartmentalized structure. In ways that are very similar to the thought-habits of modern times, people of the Renaissance were able to profess religious beliefs while simultaneously thinking and acting without constant reference to them. The divine was "off there" and unknowable; separate from it was the daily life of human affairs.[3]

Thus freed from the sense of guilt and sin that had pervaded so much of medieval thought, the human spirit exuberantly channeled itself into celebration of the beauty of nature in painting and sculpture, into new humanistic philosophies that explored the enormous varieties and possibilities of experience, and into poetry and stories about the pleasures and intrigues of love. Akin to this was a reviving spirit of individualism; people of the Renaissance were full of personal ambition and were eager to achieve things in their own lifetimes, to create and be praised, and to enjoy the rewards of their abilities. "Italy," Jacob Burckhardt writes, "began to swarm with personalities."[4]

This secular and individualistic trend also had a dramatic impact on Italian politics, Personal ambitions and personal greeds were out in the open; mercenaries and soldiers of fortune and tyrants, large and small, warred and maneuvered for power and wealth. In the midst of this the popes of the church, no longer able to impose their wills on all the kings of Europe, busied themselves with trying to maintain their rule over central Italy. Such a political climate required a different sort of political philosophy, one more attuned to the daily realities of power and less concerned with the divine ordering of God's universe. This was the kind of theorizing that emerged in the work of a man who is sometimes called the first modern political scientist: Niccolo Machiavelli.

Niccolo Machiavelli

It is a curious fact that Machiavelli, who is best-known to the world as the author of a how-to-do-it book for despots, had a strong personal bias toward republicanism. Like many philosophers, he thought of a mixed constitutional government with power divided among prince, nobles, and the people as the best form, and in his *Discourses* he spoke approvingly of the ability of free people to defend their own liberty.[5] In his own political life he was closely identified—too closely for his own good, as it turned out—with the republican party of Florence.

Florence, nominally a republic, was one of the major city-states of northern Italy, and it was usually seething with internal struggle among the various groups—merchants, ar-

---

[3] Ernst Cassirer identifies the works of Nicholas Cusanus, one of the major theorists of the conciliar movement, as a key source of new concepts that separated the worldly from the divine. See Cassirer, *The Individual and the Cosmos in Renaissance Philosophy, trans. Mario Domandi (New York: Harper Torchbooks, 1963).*

[4] Jacob Burkhardt, *The Civilization of the Renaissance in Italy* ed. Irene Gordon (New York: The New American Library, 1960), p. 122.

[5] "When the people are intrusted with the care of any privilege or liberty, being less disposed to encroach upon it, they will of necessity take better care of it; and being unable to take it away themselves, will prevent others from doing so." Machiavelli, *The Prince and The Discourses*, trans. Christian E. Detmold (New York: Random House, Inc. 1940) p. 122.

tisans, aristocrats—who made up its fragile balance of power. During the fifteenth century a wealthy banking family, the Medici, began to assume a degree of political control that soon became, in everything but name, a monarchy. Cosimo de' Medici, maintaining the official status of private citizen, ruled the city and surrounded himself, meanwhile, with many of the greatest artists of the early Renaissance. After Cosimo's death, the city was dominated for some time by the zealous priest Savonarola; Florence was invaded by Charles VIII of France and then, after the people turned against Savonarola and burned him at the stake, the city was ruled by a republican government dominated by the mercantile classes.

Machiavelli, son of a Florentine lawyer, obtained a minor post in the new administration and spent the next 14 years in public service, representing Florence on several diplomatic missions to other parts of Italy. He spent some time in Rome and was particularly impressed by the career of Cesare Borgia, illegitimate son of Pope Alexander VI, who was then busy extending his father's control over the Papal States and enriching himself in the process.

In 1512 the republican interval ended and a new Medici, Lorenzo, became the ruler of Florence. Machiavelli was more than willing to continue to serve under the new regime, but was suspected of having anti-Medici loyalties. He was arrested, tortured, and then released. He went into exile and spent most of the remaining years of his life outside of Florence, writing and trying to get back into public life. *The Prince*, dedicated to Lorenzo de' Medici, was presented to him with a letter in which Machiavelli expressed the hope that "you will receive it with favor, knowing that it is not in my power to offer you a greater gift than that of enabling you to understand in a very short time all those things which I have learnt at the cost of privation and danger in the course of many years."[6] But Lorenzo apparently ignored the book, and Machiavelli never found his way back into the center of Florentine politics. He performed a few minor missions for the Medici and, in the final irony of his life, was denied a post by the new republican government that came to power a few months before his death.

The Prince was constructed as a study, based on observations taken from current politics and classical history, of techniques by which a ruler might win and maintain power. Machiavelli suggested to Lorenzo in his dedication that if His Highness would study the book he might attain to "that grandeur which fortune and your own merits presage for you," and it is quite obvious that Machiavelli hoped that Lorenzo, having been given the key to political and military success, would reward him with a position. But Machiavelli also had another and much greater goal, beyond his own and Lorenzo's political careers: the unification of Italy.

He was a shrewd observer of the history of his times, and he saw clearly that Italy, so divided by its own eternal squabbles, was at the mercy of foreign armies. The last chapter of *The Prince*, entitled "Exhortation to Liberate Italy from the Barbarians," called on Lorenzo to assume this greater task and, in the process, to cover himself with glory:

This opportunity must not, therefore, be allowed to pass, so that Italy may at length find her liberator. I cannot express the love with which he would be received in all those provinces which have suffered under these foreign invasions, with what thirst for vengeance, with what steadfast faith, with what love, with what grateful tears. What doors would be closed against him? What people would refuse him obedience? What envy could oppose him? What Italian would withhold allegiance?[7]

Machiavelli was above all else a pragmatic man, and, whatever personal preferences he may have had for a mixed or republican form of government, he clearly did not believe that Italy could be united except by the power and skill of a determined monarch. As Leo Strauss interprets Machiavelli's message:

To liberate Italy from the barbarians means to unify Italy, and to unify Italy means to conquer Italy. . . . The liberator of Italy cannot depend on the spontaneous following of all inhabitants of Italy. He must pursue a policy of iron and poison, of murder and treachery. He must not shrink from the extermination of princely families and the destruction of Italian republican cities whenever actions of this kind are conductive to his end. The liberation of Italy means a complete revolution. It requires first and above everything else a revolution in thinking about right and wrong. Italians have to learn that the patriotic end hallows every

---

[6] Machiavelli, *The Prince and The Discourses*, trans. Christian E. Detmold. (New York: Random House, Inc. 1940) p. 3.

[7] Ibid., p. 98.

means however much condemned by the most exalted traditions both philosophic and religious.[8]

Machiavelli's work did not produce a political revolution or the unification of Italy, but it did contribute immeasurably to a revolution in thought. The remarkable and radical thing about Machiavelli's work is the absence of theological concepts and traditional Christian morality. Machiavelli occasionally made passing references to God, but it is quite clear that he simply was not interested in theology; he was interested in the visible realities of politics. Furthermore, he was not looking for moral truths but for behavioral laws. St. Thomas Aquinas had concerned himself with deciding whether certain things were fundamentally, eternally good or evil; Machiavelli was trying to discover what things worked, and the things that worked he considered to be good. We can see this pragmatism in the chapter headings of his discourses, which have titles such as:

TO FOUND A NEW REPUBLIC, OR TO REFORM ENTIRELY THE OLD INSTITUTIONS OF AN EXISTING ONE, MUST BE THE WORK OF ONE MAN ONLY.

WHOSOEVER WISHES TO REFORM AN EXISTING GOVERNMENT IN A FREE STATE SHOULD AT LEAST PRESERVE THE SEMBLANGE OF THE OLD FORMS.

ROME BECAME GREAT BY RUINING HER NEIGHBORING CITIES, AND BY FREELY ADMITTING STRANGERS TO HER PRIVILEGES AND HONORS.

FORTRESSES ARE GENERALLY MORE INJURIOUS THAN USEFUL.

DECEIT IN THE CONDUCT OF WAR IS MERITORIOUS.

Machiavelli's indifference to moral considerations is sometimes described in terms of the modern concept of scientific detachment, but Machiavelli was not detached; he had definite personal commitments. He was committed to

[8] Leo Strauss, *Thoughts on Machiavelli* (Glencoe, Ill.: The Free Press, 1958), p. 67.

the liberation of Italy and to political stability in general, and he favored the strategies and tactics that would bring about those goals. He was fully aware of what the commonly held values were—honor, honesty, generosity, kindness, and so forth—and he believed that, so long as it was practical, people should act according to them. But whenever political ends made it necessary, people should be prepared to abandon traditional morality. Machiavelli, deeply involved in the politics of his time even during his years of exile from active participation, was advocating a reordering of priorities, in which tangible social goals would be placed above abstract personal morality. Thus, immorality became a kind of duty in the service of a higher cause, which was the state.

Machiavelli often employed the concepts of *fortuna* and *virtu*. *Fortuna* represented the uncontrollable in life, the luck or fate that, he believed, controlled about half of all human action. The other half could be controlled by people who had *virtu*—meaning will, energy, audacity, drive. He saw *virtu* as a necessary quality for princes, and also for peoples: When *virtu* was lacking in a people, tyranny was likely to be the result. But *virtu* in a people—and Machiavelli considered Rome in the era of the republic to be the best example of this quality—could lead to greatness. When *virtu* was a widespread and common quality, in other words, there was likely to be popular participation in government; when the quality was at a low ebb and could be found in only a few individuals, those individuals would of necessity become despotic rulers. Machiavelli had a rather low estimate of the general quality of people in his own time, and consequently his imagination was often caught up with thoughts of the fierce and audacious individual: "I certainly think that it is better to be impetuous than cautious," he wrote in *The Prince*, "for fortune is a woman, and it is necessary, if you wish to master her, to conquer her by force; and it can be seen that she lets herself be overcome by the bold rather than by those who proceed coldly."[9]

The idea of *fortuna,* the uncontrollable chance that governs some part of all human lives, was about as far as Machiavelli went in the direction of metaphysics. Usually when he spoke of the religion of his times, it was either to express his disgust at the hypocrisy of the leaders of the church or to discuss the political applications of religion. Thus, one of the chapters of the *Discourses* was entitled:

[9] Machiavelli, op. cit., p. 91.

HOW THE ROMANS AVAILED OF RELIGION TO PRE-SERVE ORDER IN THEIR CITY, AND TO CARRY OUT THEIR ENTERPRISES AND SUPPRESS DISTURBANCES.

It is not surprising, then, that Machiavelli's ideas became highly unpopular with the fathers of the Roman Catholic church. Machiavelli was relatively obscure throughout most of his lifetime, but after his death he became not only famous but notorious. His works were read by intellectuals and rulers, were cited as the justification for countless acts of political violence and dishonesty, were translated into dramas of power and royal intrigue by Elizabethan playwrights, and were so equated with cunning and evil that, as "Old Nick," Machiavelli eventually became roughly synonymous with the devil himself.[10] Then, as now, people were both fascinated and repulsed by his cool calculations of the usefulness of murder and deceit. His work was a forerunner of things to come in the way of justification for acts in the service of the state; it was also an accurate reflection of Renaissance politics. As Sibley has said:

Whether or not we adopt his moral and political generalizations as a whole, we can hardly deny that his insight into the politics of his time was remarkable. The man of the sixteenth century, says Machiavelli, had ceased to have roots; and because of his lack of anchorage, he found himself more able both to create and to destroy. His creativity sprang from the exhilaration he felt when he no longer deemed himself bound to the precedents of the immediate past; but his destructive capacity, too, arose from the same source. In both art and politics, the model was a man who ran roughshod over previous restraints in the quest for self-expression.[11]

MACHIAVELLI ON PUBLIC OPINION

I say that every prince must desire to be considered merciful and not cruel. He must, however, take care not to misuse this mercifulness. Cesare Borgia was considered cruel, but his cruelty had brought order to the Romagna, united it, and reduced it to peace and fealty. If this is considered well, it will be seen that he was really much more merciful than the Florentine people, who, to avoid the name of cruelty, allowed Pistoia to be destroyed. A prince, therefore, must not mind incurring the charge of cruelty for the purpose of keeping his subjects united and faithful; for, with a very few examples, he will be more merciful than those who, from excess of tenderness, allow disorders to arise, from whence spring bloodshed and rapine; for these as a rule injure the whole community, while the executions carried out by the prince injure only individuals. And of all princes, it is impossible for a new prince to escape the reputation of cruelty, new states being always full of dangers.

Nevertheless, he must be cautious in believing and acting, and must not be afraid of his own shadow, and must proceed in a temperate manner with prudence and humanity, so that too much confidence does not render him incautious, and too much diffidence does not render him intolerant.

From this arises the question whether it is better to be loved more than feared, or feared more than loved. The reply is, that one ought to be both feared and loved, but as it is difficult for the two to go together, it is much safer to be feared than loved, if one of the two has to be wanting. For it may be said of men in general that they are ungrateful, voluble, dissemblers, anxious to avoid danger, and covetous of gain; as long as you benefit them, they are entirely yours; they offer you their blood, their goods, their life, and their children, as I have before said, when the necessity is remote; but when it approaches, they revolt. And the prince who has relied solely on their words, without making other preparations, is ruined; for the friendship which is gained by purchase and not through grandeur and nobility of spirit is bought but not secured, and at a pinch is not to be expended in your service. And men have less scruple in offending one who makes himself loved than one who makes himself feared; for love is held by a chain of obligation which, men being selfish, is broken whenever it serves their purpose; but fear is maintained by a dread of punishment which never fails.

Still, a prince should make himself feared in such

[10] Edward Meyer, *Machiavelli and the Elizabethan Drama, Litterarhistorische Forschungen* (Weimar: Verlag Von Emil Felber, 1897), p. 93.

[11] Mulford Q. Sibley, op. cit., p. 307.

From *The Prince*, trans. Luigi Ricci, revised by E. R. P. Vincent (New York: The Modern Library, 1950), pp. 60-66. (Edited and abridged.)

a way that if he does not gain love, he at any rate avoids hatred; for fear and the absence of hatred may well go together, and will be always attained by one who abstains from interfering with the property of his citizens and subjects or with their women. And when he is obliged to take the life of anyone, let him do so when there is a proper justification and manifest reason for it; but above all he must abstain from taking the property of others, for men forget more easily the death of their father than the loss of their patrimony. Then also pretexts for seizing property are never wanting, and one who begins to live by rapine will always find some reason for taking the goods of others, whereas causes for taking life are rarer and more fleeting.

But when the prince is with his army and has a large number of soldiers under his control, then it is extremely necessary that he should not mind being thought cruel; for without this reputation, he could not keep an army united or disposed to any duty. Among the noteworthy actions of Hannibal is numbered this, that although he had an enormous army, composed of men of all nations and fighting in foreign countries, there never arose any dissension either among them or against the prince, either in good fortune or in bad. This could not be due to anything but his inhuman cruelty, which, together with his infinite other virtues, made him always venerated and terrible in the sight of his soldiers, and without it his other virtues would not have sufficed to produce that effect. Thoughtless writers admire on the one hand his actions, and on the other blame the principal cause of them.

I conclude, therefore, with regard to being feared and loved, that men love at their own free will, but fear at the will of the prince, and that a wise prince must rely on what is in his power and not on what is in the power of others, and he must only contrive to avoid incurring hatred, as has been explained.

How laudable it is for a prince to keep good faith and live with integrity, and not with astuteness, everyone knows. Still, the experience of our times shows those princes to have done great things who have had little regard for good faith, and have been able by astuteness to confuse men's brains, and who have ultimately overcome those who have made loyalty their foundation.

You must know, then, that there are two methods of fighting, the one by law, the other by force: the first method is often insufficient, one must have recourse to the second. It is therefore necessary for a prince to know well how to use both the beast and the man. A prince being thus obliged to know well how to act as a beast must imitate the fox and the lion, for the lion cannot protect himself from traps, and the fox cannot defend himself from wolves. One must therefore be a fox to recognize traps, and a lion to frighten wolves. Those that wish to be only lions do not understand this. Therefore, a prudent ruler ought not to keep faith when by so doing it would be against his interest, and when the reasons which made him bind himself no longer exist. If men were all good, this precept would not be a good one; but as they are bad, and would not observe their faith with you, so you are not bound to keep faith with them. Nor have legitimate grounds ever failed a prince who wished to show colorable excuse for the non-fulfillment of his promise. Of this, one could furnish an infinite number of modern examples, and show how many times peace has been broken, and how many promises rendered worthless, by the faithlessness of princes, and those that have been best able to imitate the fox have succeeded best. But it is necessary to be able to disguise this character well, and to be a great feigner and dissembler; and men are so simple and so ready to obey present necessities, that one who deceives will always find those who allow themselves to be deceived.

It is not, therefore, necessary for a prince to have all the good qualities, but it is very necessary to seem to have them. I would even be bold to say that to possess them and always to observe them is dangerous, but to appear to possess them is useful. Thus it is well to seem merciful, faithful, humane, sincere, religious, and also to be so; but you must have the mind so disposed that when it is needful to be otherwise you may be able to change to the opposite qualities. And it must be understood that a prince, and especially a new prince, cannot observe all those things which are considered good in men, being often obliged, in order to maintain the state, to act against faith, against charity, against humanity, and against religion. And, therefore, he must have a mind disposed to adapt itself according to the wind, and as the variations of fortune dictate, and, as I said before, not deviate from what is good, if possible, but be able to do evil if constrained.

A prince must take great care that nothing goes out of his mouth which is not full of the above-named five qualities, and, to see and hear him, he should seem to be all mercy, faith, integrity, humanity, and religion. And nothing is more necessary than to seem to have this last quality, for men in general judge more by the eyes than by the hands, for every one can see, but very few have to feel. Everybody sees what you appear to be, few feel what you are, and those few will not dare to oppose themselves to the many, who have the majesty of the state to defend them; and in the actions of men, and especially of princes, from which there is no appeal, the end justifies the means. Let a prince therefore aim at conquering and maintaining the state, and the means will always be judged honourable and praised by every one, for the vulgar is always taken by appearances and the issue of the event; and the world consists only of the vulgar, and the few who are not vulgar are isolated when the many have a rallying point in the prince.

REFORMERS AND SOVEREIGNS

When Niccolo Machiavelli visited Rome as an emissary of the republican government of Florence, he observed the worldliness of the Renaissance religious leaders, dismissed them as hypocrites, and concentrated his attention on the impressive if unscrupulous political operations of Cesare Borgia. When Martin Luther visited Rome a few years later, representing the Augustinian order of Germany, he had no eyes for politics—but he saw, and, according to Lutheran tradition, was deeply shocked by, the pagan immorality and corruption within the church. When he returned to Germany he became increasingly involved in protest against such actions as the open selling of indulgences. His opposition culminated in the famous Ninety-five Theses, which launched him into the leadership of a new and historically momentous drive for reformation of the church.

Luther was not by any means the first reformer. There had been others who saw clearly the corrupt practices and personal greed of church officials, and there had been other attempts, such as the conciliar movement, to bring the church more closely into line with Christian morality. But political developments and changing patterns of thought were making the church more vulnerable than it had been before, and the new attack that Luther began was to break it apart completely—with important consequences for European monarchs and for the institution of monarchy in general.

Luther was excommunicated, but Lutheranism spread through Germany, supported by believers who wanted a pure and reformed Christian community and by princes who wanted a basis for opposition to the authority of popes and emperors. Soon there were Lutheran as well as Catholic churches in Germany, a league of Catholic princes and a league of Lutheran princes. A war between the two factions was settled in 1555 in the Peace of Augsburg, which recognized the right of every German prince to decide which religion would be recognized in his own domain. Within each principality, citizens had the choice between conforming to the official religion or moving somewhere else.

The Peace of Augsburg recognized only Catholicism and Lutheranism, but this was a time of widespread religious upheaval, when many new sects were organizing, defying the authority of Rome, and struggling for political power. The Anabaptists, one of the most radical reformation groups, took over the government of Münster and held it for a few years, until the Catholic bishop returned in command of an army, recaptured the city, and had thousands of the revolutionaries tortured and executed. A few years later John Calvin, who had been a leader of the Protestant movement in France, began to gain control of the city of Geneva by more peaceful and gradual means. Geneva became a Protestant theocracy with Calvin as its political and religious dictator. In Scotland John Knox, an admirer of Calvin, led the Protestant opposition to the Catholic government of Mary, Queen of Scots.

The most severe political conflict during the Reformation era took place in France. The nation was predominantly Catholic, but the Huguenots (French Calvinists) were steadily growing in number in spite of severe repression and persecution, and inevitably the religious conflict became involved with the political aspirations of competing noble families. There were eight civil wars in France during the latter part of the sixteenth century; the so-called religious wars were a long and bloody struggle, marked by such episodes as the St. Bartholomew's Day Massacre. The massacre, which was actually several massacres, occurred during an interval of peace, when Paris was celebrating the marriage of the Catholic king's sister Margaret to the Protestant Henry Bourbon. The king's mother, Catherine, had several Protestant leaders murdered. Mobs took over from there, killing some two thousand Protestants in Paris and thousands more in the provinces. The event was cited by some observers as a good example of Machiavellian theory in action (Catherine was a Medici). It was praised by many Catholics and was celebrated by the pope with a special Mass.

There were, during this long struggle, three main political groupings in France: the Protestants, whose number included some of the nobility; the Catholic extremists, who favored complete extermination of Protestantism; and a moderate Catholic element called the *politiques,* who hoped for some kind of reconciliation and an end to civil war. Each of these groups was in some ways identified with personal political ambitions, but each of them also represented certain ideas and points of view about religion, revolution, and the nature of national unity. The Reformation started out as a conflict about morality within the church, but the involvement of the church with politics was so intense and pervasive that the conflict eventually forced people to take a new look at political authority itself.

POLITICAL THEORY OF THE REFORMATION

Although the Reformation eventually produced some revolutionary political ideas, its two great early leaders, Luther and Calvin, both preached obedience to legal authority.

Luther, whose political ideology was in some ways a throwback to St. Augustine, thought of people as living in a state of sin and scarcely worthy of good government at all: "The world is too wicked," he wrote, "and does not deserve to have many wise and pious princes." The duty of the Christian was to accept his lot, obey the rulers that God's will had ordained for him, and prepare himself for the life beyond. Luther, in his treatise entitled *Secular Authority: To What Extent It Should Be Obeyed,* quoted with approval the passage from the Book of Romans: "Let every soul be subject to power and authority, for there is no power but from God. The power that is everywhere is ordained by God. He who resists the power resists God's ordinance."[12] Luther's radicalism lay in his religious views: that all Christians were equal, that faith was a matter of personal conscience and not capable of being imposed by force, that each person's spiritual life was fundamentally a thing between oneself and God, and was not dependent on the help of popes and bishops.

Calvin's doctrines were quite similar to those of Luther. He did admit of the possibility of resistance to tyrannical rulers, but he was far from being an advocate of rebellion; in fact, Calvin's own rule over Geneva was fairly tyrannical, with a generous use of exile and execution to maintain the strict Christian morality he preached. In his writings he stressed humility, discipline, and obedience to law, and he did not share Luther's belief that faith could not be enforced. His ideology, like his activity in Geneva, was involved with a concept of a community of believers, with virtue embodied in and maintained by its various institutions. Calvin believed that Christians needed authorities to help them attain salvation, but he also believed that congregations should have the right to choose their own leaders. Although Calvin was more involved in politics than was Luther, both were mainly concerned not with politics but with religion. Christian philosophers had been teaching obedience to secular authority for more than a thousand years, a tradition that early reformers such as Luther and Calvin neither wanted to nor could upset overnight.

But the Reformation was to become a greater upheaval than its early leaders could possibly have realized, and the course of events soon forced many Protestants to assume a different political stance.

One important development was the Counter-Reformation, the church's own attempt to purify itself from within. Although a large part of Europe—including England, the Scandinavian countries, Switzerland, and most of Germany—had broken off from the Catholic church by the time the Counter-Reformation got underway, it prevented further losses, and it gave new strength and vitality to the church. The Council of Trent, which was the chief organizing force in the Counter-Reformation, issued recommendations that led to the elimination of much of the laxity and corruption among the clergy. While the church reformed, it also repressed its opposition wherever possible. Courts of Inquisi-

[12] Romans 13: 1–2.

tion were set up in Italy and Spain, where critics of the church and preachers of Protestant ideas were tried as heretics and silenced with torture and execution. Another facet of the Counter-Reformation was the emergence of a zealous new Catholic order, the Society of Jesus; the Jesuits, who characterized themselves as "soldiers of Christ," believed in strict obedience to the leadership and doctrines of the church, and they energetically worked against the spread of Protestantism. Dreaming of the return of the prodigal nation-states to the reformed church, the Jesuits brought forth a new body of political theory that managed to be both authoritarian and revolutionary. Robert Bellarmine, for example, conceded that the pope had no secular authority, but insisted that the pope was the spiritual head of the church and that his power derived from God. The power of kings, on the other hand, arose from the people, and a king therefore had no right to demand complete obedience from his subjects; furthermore, a king might be deposed by a pope, if he were guilty of heresy. A Spanish Jesuit writer, Juan de Mariana, went further than Bellarmine in this respect; Mariana described the sovereign's power in terms of a contract between himself and his subjects, and insisted on the right of the people to depose tyrants. When Henry III of France was assassinated by a Dominican monk, Mariana defended the act as justifiable tyrannicide.

Curiously, Protestant theorists were at the same time moving along an almost parallel route, toward a new and somewhat revolutionary view of secular authority.

The St. Bartholomew's Day Massacre, although praised by the pope and conservative Catholics in Italy and Spain, brought forth a torrent of tracts and protests from the shocked Huguenots. Probably the most important of these works was a book entitled *Vindiciae contra tyrannos*, published under the pseudonym Stephen Junius Brutus.[13] The *Vindiciae* contained, in an early and relatively conservative form, some of the basic ideas of what would later become democratic theory, including a somewhat complex idea of a social contract. This social contract was in reality two contracts. One was between God, on one hand, and the sovereign and people of a nation on the other; the second was between the sover-

eign and the people. In the first contract, the ruler and the ruled agreed to worship and obey God. In the second, the ruler and the ruled recognized their obligations to each other. In the event of a failure to live up to the obligations of the contract, God might impose punishment by causing the king to act against his people, or by causing the people to rise up against the king. We should understand, though, that the author of the *Vindiciae* was not an advocate of revolt by the masses. The Huguenots were led by elements of the French nobility, and the kind of resistance advocated in their philosophy was more coup than revolution.

Part of what made the Reformation a bitter political struggle as well as a religious struggle was the total absence from sixteenth-century thought of any idea of freedom of religion. Church and state were becoming increasingly identifiable as different entities, but it was still virtually impossible for most people to conceive of any social order in which the two might actually function separately from one another. The ultimate source of governmental authority was still thought to be God, and this assumption opened the door for arguments that authority should be shared in some degree by God's ministers. Conversely, it was generally understood that a ruler's duties included the enforcement of Christian morality, and this naturally meant protecting, perpetuating—and, inevitably, participating in the administration of—the church. So both Jesuits and Calvinists, caught up in an argument about which church should be established and how believers might justifiably overthrow a ruler who did not establish the right church, were dealing with similar ideas. Meanwhile, the power of national rulers continued to grow at the expense of both antagonists; the real victors in the battles of the Reformation were the kings, and one of the most important political concepts to come out of the long religious struggle in France was the idea of sovereignty. It emerged, significantly, from a member of the group called the *politiques*—the moderate Catholics who wanted the conflict resolved in the interests of national unity, who were more interested in maintaining a single France under a single king than in the question of how French citizens should worship.

Jean Bodin

At about the same time that the Huguenots were ex-

<hr>

[13] The book has been published in English translation as *A Defense of Liberty Against Tyrants*, ed. H. J. Laski (London: G. Bell, 1924). The actual identity of Junius Brutus has been a matter of much debate among scholars. See J. W. Allen, *History of Political Thought in Sixteenth Century* (London: Methuen, 1951).

pressing their reaction to the St. Bartholomew's Massacre in political tracts that edged cautiously toward ideas of government by consent and justifiable revolution, Jean Bodin was emerging as the spokesman for the *politiques*, with a concept that gave new strength to the image of the absolute monarch.

This concept was sovereignty, an abstraction that subtly transformed the monarchy-aristocracy-democracy system of classification of governments, which had been common currency of political philosophers since the time of the ancient Greeks. Sovereignty, which was for Bodin the thing that distinguished a state from an unorganized aggregation of families or individuals, meant power: the power to command, to judge, to make laws and enforce them. In every well-ordered state, Bodin argued, sovereignty had to exist somewhere; however, sovereignty did not reside in the same place in all states. In a monarchy, sovereignty was vested in a single ruler; in an aristocracy, in a few individuals; in a democracy, in the people. Furthermore, this sovereignty was not a thing that could be divided or given away. A prince might delegate authority by appointing someone to an office, a people might similarly delegate their authority by electing officials. But in neither case could this delegation be regarded as permanent or irrevocable; it could always be recovered by whoever, in that particular state, became sovereign.

Sovereignty was also absolute and unlimited. A sovereign ruler could make laws, and he could also violate them and change them. He was bound by the laws of God and nature, but by no human law whatever. It seemed to Bodin entirely illogical that a prince, possessing sovereignty, might legally impose limitations on himself when his own will was the source of the limitation.

Obviously, the concept of sovereignty as Bodin presented it was incompatible with the "mixed system" of government that had been the favorite of so many theorists in the past. If sovereignty were to be absolute, it could not be divided up among king, people, and aristocracy; it had to reside in one place, and there only. And, although Bodin's sovereignty was theoretically compatible with democracy, he did not in fact believe democracy to be workable. He considered the arguments in favor of it at rather great length in the final volume of his major work, the *Six Books of the Commonwealth*, and concluded that the disadvantages of democracy were far greater than the advantages. "A popular

state," he wrote, "is always the refuge of all disorderly spirits, rebels, traitors, outcasts, who encourage and help the lower orders to ruin the great." Many people, he thought, had high hopes for democracy, but he warned them that "unless its government is in the hands of wise and virtuous men, a popular government is the worst tyranny there is."

Bodin's discussions of the meaning and nature of sovereignty had a tendency to drift toward arguments for the supremacy of monarchy. In *Commonwealth* he argued that, although a collective sovereignty of some sort was imaginable, "in fact there is no true sovereignty unless there is some head of the state who can unite all."

The final essence of sovereignty, for Bodin, was the power to command, and he doubted that such a power could ever be effectively wielded by a multitude. The holder of sovereign power, as he saw it, had to be able to act with speed and certainty and to be answerable to no one for the consequences of his decisions.

But it would be a mistake to interpret Bodin's theories as simply an argument for the superiority of monarchy over democracy. They were also an argument for obedience to the king rather than rebellion of the Jesuit or Calvinist varieties, and for national unity as opposed to factionalism.

Although Bodin, like Machiavelli, ended his days in relative obscurity, the policy for which he and the *politiques* had fought, the reconciliation of Catholics and Huguenots under a strong national ruler, was eventually triumphant. Henry of Navarre, a Protestant, succeeded to the French throne as Henry IV in 1589, changed his religion in order to consolidate his support with the Catholic majority, and some years later issued the Edict of Nantes—providing France with an arrangement that, if something less than religious freedom, was closer to religious peace than anything that torn country had known for decades. The edict granted to the Huguenots the right to worship openly and to control their cities in southwestern France, and it cautiously recognized the right of noble Huguenot families to practice their religion privately elsewhere. The Edict of Nantes was, given the mood of the times, a triumph of religious toleration. (Although the Huguenots had further troubles with the Catholics later, under the administration of Cardinal Richlieu, the issue by then was not religion but the centralized authority of the French government.)

France was becoming, in the sixteenth and seventeenth

centuries, the archetype of the powerful national monarchy. Bodin's theories of sovereignty as absolute and perpetual power were merging with an ancient stream of thought, the argument that the king's power came directly from God, to form a new concept of monarchy: the divine right of Kings. This idea was as arrogant and all-embracing as the concept of the papacy that Thomas Acquinas and Innocent III had promulgated in the Middle Ages. Divine-right theory, a popular political doctrine that received considerable support from monarchs such as Louis XIV of France and James I of England, held that the king's power came to him directly from God, that kings were "the breathing images of God upon earth," that sovereignty was automatically passed on to a king's heirs, and that rebellion was justified in no case whatever.

The growing reverence for royal power was not a victory of monarchy over aristocracy or democracy, or even a victory of a theory of divine origin of authority over one of popular consent. It was, most of all, a sign of the consolidation of the nation-state. Through centuries of feudalism, power and allegiance had been spread ambiguously among lords and kings, kings and emperors, emperors and popes; now kings were in a position to claim full sovereign authority within the boundaries of their nations, and also to deny that any external authority—whether secular or religious—had any right to interfere in that nation's government. The king thus became the symbol and embodiment of nationhood, as expressed in the statement attributed to Louis XIV: "L'Etat, c'est moi" (I am the State). And we can see the importance of sovereignty as a concept for the defense of the inviolable nation-state in the fact that today, although few sovereign monarchs remain, the term sovereignty is still commonly employed in dialogues concerning the legal rights of nations.

JEAN BODIN ON SOVEREIGNTY

Sovereignty is the absolute and perpetual power contained in a state. The term needs to be carefully

Jean Bodin, "Six Books on the State," pp. 349–51, from *Great Political Thinkers: Plato to the Present*, Third Edition, by William Ebenstein. Copyright 1951, (c) 1956, 1960 by William Ebenstein. Edited and abridged by permission of Holt, Rinehard and Winston, Inc.

defined, because, although it is the distinguishing mark of a state and a fundamental requisite for any real understanding of the nature of politics, no jurist or political philosopher so far has attempted to define it.

I have described it as *perpetual:* Persons or groups of persons who are given power, even absolute power, for a period of time, are not sovereign rulers if, when that time expires, they become citizens again; they are only lieutenants of the sovereign ruler. The true sovereign ruler is always in possession of his power. This is why the law requires the governor of a province or the lieutenant of a prince to formally surrender his power at the end of his term of office. If it were otherwise, and the power given were sovereign, then the subordinate might command his prince—which is obviously absurd. However much power the sovereign may give, he always retains a certain amount of authority of his own, and may exercise this by intervening in various ways in the actions of his officials. Any authority extended by a sovereign can also be revoked, and the term of office may be made as long or as short as he desires.

By perpetual power we mean lasting for the lifetime of the person empowered. If a magistrate is elected for any specified time limit and continues to hold power after the end of his term, he does so either by consent or by force. If it is by force it is tyranny, but still the tyrant is a true sovereign. But if he remains in office by consent of the people he is not a sovereign; still less is he a sovereign if the term of office is not fixed at all, for in such a case he is only exercising a temporary commission which may at any time be revoked by the people.

If the people give him power absolutely and unconditionally, not temporarily nor in the form of a revocable commission, then the people have given up their sovereignty; this is no longer a popular government and the ruler must be recognized for what he is, a sovereign.

Let us now consider the meaning of the word *absolute:* The people or the aristocracy of a state can give to someone of their choice the sovereign and perpetual power to dispose of their property and persons, to govern the state, and to choose his own successor. This is a true gift, unconditional and irrevocable. If there are any conditions placed upon it, then the power given is not absolute.

The sovereign cannot in any way be bound by the commands of another, for he is the person who makes laws and amends or abrogates those already made. He is not bound by laws he has made previously, nor by laws made by his predecessors. One may be subject to laws made by another, but is is impossible for one to be bound by laws made by oneself. And thus a sovereign cannot be subject to his own laws. Just as, according to canon law, the pope cannot tie his own hands, so the sovereign cannot restrict himself, even if he chooses. This is why laws and ordinances conclude with the words, "because it has so pleased Us," indicating that the laws of a sovereign, even when they are founded on truth and right reason, nevertheless proceed from his own free will.

It is otherwise with the laws of God and nature. All the sovereign princes of the world are subject to natural and divine law, before which they must bow their heads in fear and reverence. These laws are the only limitations upon the true sovereign.

CIVIL WAR IN ENGLAND

England passed through the same historical experiences as the rest of Europe—a Renaissance, a Reformation, a consolidation of sovereign nationhood—but the timing of the process was different, and the outcome was a distinctly English political order.

The Renaissance came late to England; Reformation of a sort came early, and the causes of England's abrupt break with the Roman church were more political and economic than spiritual. There had been a long history of conflict with Rome over such matters as the king's appointment of bishops and control of the ecclesiastical courts, and many English were strongly anti-papal; then there was the matter of the wealth and vast amounts of land owned by the English church. When the occasion for a break with the pope finally came, as a result of the efforts of Henry VIII to divorce his wife in order to marry another who might give him a male heir, there was a considerable basis of support for it in English public opinion. And when Henry distributed much of the church's holdings among the nobles and

country gentry, he created a newly prosperous, landed aristocracy that had a vested interest in Protestantism. The Parliament passed several acts that facilitated the separation from Rome, and in 1534 passed the Act of Supremacy, which formally declared the king to be the head of the church in England.

There was a brief return to Catholicism under the reign of Mary Tudor, and then a more lasting re-establishment of the Church of England under Henry's other daughter, Queen Elizabeth I. Elizabeth had Parliament pass a new Act of Supremacy and establish a code of religious principles and a Book of Common Prayer, which were foundations of the new Church of England. She also lent a hand to the Protestant movement in Scotland by ordering the beheading of her cousin Mary, the stubbornly Catholic Queen of Scots. Mary, who was descended on her mother's side from the Guise family of France—leaders of that country's conservative Catholic faction—had done everything possible to keep Scotland from being won over by the fiery Protestant leadership of Calvin's friend John Knox. She was finally forced to abdicate and sought sanctuary in England, but she was still the center of political-religious conflict; Philip II of Spain was plotting to have her replace Elizabeth as Queen of England and hoped to restore all of Britain to Catholicism. Elizabeth learned of the plan and decided it was necessary to have her cousin beheaded; Philip then declared war on England. The defeat of the Spanish Armada by the English navy in that war began England's long era of global naval supremacy.

The Elizabethan Era was England's Renaissance, and the most brilliant expression of its spirit was in the plays of Shakespeare, which celebrated the myth of the king as dramatic hero, featuring the larger-than-life exploits of sovereigns and pretenders to thrones.

Elizabeth's successor was James I (son of the executed Mary, Queen of Scots), a tireless defender of the principles of the divine right of kings. James, a somewhat pedantic monarch, had serious trouble with the variety of religious minorities—ranging from Catholic to Puritan—who refused to conform to the principles of the Anglican church, and he also had some trouble with his Parliament.

The English Parliament was developing into a powerful political force, one that would soon be capable of changing England from an absolute to a limited monarchy. The comparable assemblies in Spain and France—the Cortes and the Estates-General, respectively—had for a variety of reasons failed to develop into bodies capable of achieving an effective degree of unity or of acting as truly *national* institutions. But the Parliament did develop along with England's nationhood. It cost money to run a national government, and the wealthy classes that were usually the object of the king's fund-raising efforts established with fair success the right of Parliament, which was their representative body, to levy taxes. Parliament, as it had evolved in the early seventeenth century, was hardly a democratic legislature; it more resembled what is called in one history a "committee of the ruling classes,"[14] but it was quickly becoming a body without whose cooperation the king could not govern the nation.

James I may have suspected this, but his whole life was dedicated to stubborn insistence on the absolute and God-given authority of the king. His son and successor, Charles I, was equally stubborn—and so was Parliament. The conflict between them led to civil war, to the execution of the king, and eventually to reconstitution of the English monarchy.

Religion was one factor in the escalation of the king-Parliament battle. The Reformation and the break with Rome had left England with an incredible variety of semi-organized religious groups, ranging from papal loyalists to strict Puritans. Queen Elizabeth's Thirty-nine Articles and Book of Common Prayer were designed for wide acceptance, and it had been her policy to accommodate all but the most extreme Catholics and reformers within the Church of England. The policy of James I, much more rigid, aimed at establishing greater religious conformity and consolidating the Anglican hierarchy as a support of the throne. Increasingly, the king became identified with the official High Church and the Parliament with Puritanism—the latter word being a rather general term, which applied to a variety of positions relating to simplicity in religious service, strictness in morality, and freedom from governmental control of church policy.

Charles I managed to get into trouble with Parliamentary leaders on the major issues, taxation and religion, and on several secondary issues as well. While waging war against Spain and France, he forced some of the wealthier

[14] Crane Brinton, John B. Christopher, Robert Lee Wolff, *A History of Civilization* (Englewood Cliffs N.J.: Prentice-Hall, 1960), I, 615.

aristocracy to lend money to the crown, and he also quartered troops in private homes at the expense of the owners. Parliament's response was the Petition of Right, a piece of legislation that became one of the models for the American Bill of Rights. The petition placed several significant limitations on the powers of the king: no taxation without the consent of Parliament, no quartering of troops in private homes, no imprisonment without a statement of charges and due process of law. Charles consented to the petition in order to get Parliament to authorize taxation, and then proceeded to exceed the authorization. Parliament passed new resolutions, opposing both the new taxes and the king's increasingly harsh religious policies. Charles dissolved the Parliament, had several of its leaders imprisoned, and governed for 11 years without calling another Parliament into session.

During this hiatus Charles tried to strengthen the High Church in Scotland, which meant purging that country of its strongly entrenched Presbyterianism. He embarked on a disastrous military campaign against the Scots, which ended with the Scottish army encamped in England and demanding an indemnity from the king. In order to raise money to pay the indemnity and rid England of the embarrassing presence of Scottish troops, Charles was forced to call another Parliament. Puritanism and the distrust of royal power were stronger now than ever, especially in the House of Commons, and the Parliament proceeded to pass a series of punitive and restrictive measures against the throne. Charles resorted to the tactic he had employed successfully against an unruly Parliament before—ordering the arrest of its leaders—but the result this time was civil war. The members of Parliament evaded arrest, while the House of Commons raised an army to defend itself against the king.

Many of the English nobles—those who became known as the "cavaliers"—rallied to the support of the throne, while Parliament came increasingly under the domination of its more radical element, the "Roundheads," a small group of Puritans led by Oliver Cromwell. In 1649, Parliament ordered the execution of the king and declared England to be a republic.

However, the Puritans who had established the republic were a minority, and clearly would be unable to maintain control if free elections were held. The government became a military dictatorship, with Cromwell exercising his considerable abilities as a general to wage successful wars against

Scotland, Ireland, Holland, and Spain. In 1653 Cromwell accepted the official title of Lord Protector of the Commonwealth, and he ruled England until his death five years later. His son Richard inherited the office of protector but was not strong enough to hold it; a more moderate group reconvened Parliament and voted to restore the monarchy by offering the throne to Charles' exiled son, who became King Charles II.

But the English monarchy would never again be what it had been under the Tudors. Charles II was king, but he was king at the invitation of Parliament and had had to accept certain of its conditions before returning to England to accept the throne. The days of religious controversy and stress between king and Parliament were far from over in England, and the monarchy was not yet the powerless symbol it has become in the twentieth century, but England was clearly moving away from absolutism, toward a more limited form of government.

Thomas Hobbes

The dubious distinction of being the first political scientist has been conferred on a number of philosophers: on Aristotle, because he collected and classified data about various kinds of states; on Machiavelli, because he brushed aside conventional morality and tried to deduce the principles of statecraft from the experience of history; and on Thomas Hobbes, because he constructed the first comprehensive political theory in the English language on a model of geometrical reasoning. "The skill of making, and maintaining, commonwealths," he believed, "consisteth in certain rules, as does arithmetic and geometry . . . which rules, neither poor men have the leisure, nor men that have had the leisure, have hitherto had the curiosity, or the method to find out."

Hobbes's chief work, *Leviathan*, described the principles by which people create political order out of natural chaos; the work itself, like so much of political theory, was the author's attempt to create order out of the chaos of his own times.

Hobbes lived through the era of the English Civil War, and most of his years were spent shuttling between England and France, never feeling entirely comfortable or safe in either place. He was educated at Oxford and employed as tutor by a noble English family. Hobbes visited the European continent for the first time on the "grand tour" with his employers, and was in Paris in 1610 when Henry IV, the Huguenot-turned-Catholic king, was assassinated. He was living in England when his first political treatise—a defense of the sovereign power of the king—was published; Hobbes's ideas tended toward absolutism, which made him the obvious enemy of the Roundhead cause, and he prudently left England before the Parliamentary radicals took control. In France he served for a time as tutor in mathematics to the exiled English prince, the future Charles II, and wrote *Leviathan*. *Leviathan* displeased Charles because, although it favored monarchy, its concept of sovereignty rested on an idea of contract among the people rather than on the divine-right doctrine that had been so persistently expounded by Charles' grandfather, James I. The book also made it dangerous for Hobbes to remain in Paris, because a large part of it, under the title of "The Kingdom of Darkness," was a denunciation of the Catholic church. He had to leave France but was permitted to take up residence in England again, after declaring his loyalty to Cromwell.

In the midst of this confusion, Hobbes discovered a sure source of truth: science. He lived in a time when the "new science" was making great advances, both theoretical and practical, and Descartes and Galileo were among his personal acquaintances. He became interested in geometry ("fell in love with it," according to one account[15]) when he was about 40, and much of his writing shows the geometric influence, the assumption that the truth about politics can be comprehended by abstract reasoning and the application of fundamental principles.[16]

In *Leviathan*, Hobbes analyzed the principles whereby people emerged from a savage and primitive condition—which he described as "the state of nature"—into an organized political body that was capable of maintaining internal peace and dealing with external enemies. His description of this emergence was not meant to be a historical account of what had actually, at some time, taken place; rather, it was a sequence of abstract logical propositions, in which

[15] Quoted by A. D. Lindsay in his introduction to *Leviathan* (New York: E. P. Dutton, 1914), p. viii.

[16] Hobbes's identification of geometrical reasoning with scientific method would be unacceptable to contemporary science, which puts a higher value on the experimental process and empirical verification of hypotheses, and tends to avoid reasoning from first principles. See Wolin, *Politics and Vision*, p. 251.

he tried to show how the laws of nature and the basic characteristics of human beings led inexorably to the creation of a powerful sovereign state.

Hobbes did not see human beings as inherently "political animals," but rather as solitary and predatory creatures. Neither did he believe that people differed significantly in their natural abilities. There was, he thought, a kind of natural equality, which helped to create conflict: "The weakest has strength enough to kill the strongest, either by secret machination, or by confederacy with others, that are in the same danger with himself." Thus, in the state of nature nobody was really secure, and the prevailing condition was one of war, with "every man against every man." But, although people might not have any deep inner drive toward an ordered social life, they had the wit to comprehend the danger of the situation and to change it. Each person—and Hobbes tended to view all social processes individualistically, in terms of the combined decisions of separate human beings—came to understand that the state of nature, the constant war, was not in his own self-interest and did not adequately serve his urge to stay alive and to seek glory. Using his reasoning ability, he deduced certain laws of nature (which were more guidelines of good sense than natural laws in the classical meaning of the term) and this understanding led him to enter into a social contract with others, in which he surrendered his natural right to take whatever he could get in return for a greater security. In Hobbes's philosophy, people do not enter into social relationships because they have outgrown their natural greed and brutality; they retain their essential nature, but use their intelligence to gain an enforced protection from the greed and brutality of others. The peace that ends the condition of perpetual war is a kind of armed truce, guaranteed by the might of the sovereign.

The social contract in Hobbes's writing was not between the people and the king. It was among the people, all of them—a covenant in which each individual, to get protection from all the others, agreed to surrender will and power to a sovereign who would keep the peace. The sovereign thus created was as powerful as all the people put together; to describe this mighty and massive political being, Hobbes used the name of the biblical monster Leviathan.

When Hobbes talked about this sovereign power, he generally referred to it as a "man or assembly of men," but, like Bodin, he believed that sovereign power could be more effectively wielded by a single person. He compared monarchy to representative assembly at some length and found several advantages to monarchy. For one thing, following a line of reasoning that might seem curious to moderns, monarchy united private with public interest: "The riches, power and honor of a monarch arise only from the riches, strength and reputation of his subjects. For no king can be rich, nor glorious, nor secure, whose subjects are either poor, or contemptible, or too weak through want or dissension to maintain a war against their enemies." Other advantages of monarchy included the monarch's ability to arrive at decisions through august and private consultations with chosen advisers, as contrasted with the emotional and wordy deliberations of assemblies, and—with obvious reference to recent English experience—the possibility of dissent in an assembly: "A monarch cannot disagree with himself, out of envy or interest, but an assembly may, and that to such a height that may produce civil war."

The kind of commonwealth that Hobbes believed was necessary to maintain order among people, and thus permit them to live fruitful lives, was clearly authoritarian, whether monarchical or not. There was a hint of future totalitarian ideology, in his insistence on the necessity of the submission of the will and power of citizens to the will and power of the sovereign. Once the contract had been made, the sovereign became the lawmaker for all, and his authority was absolute; Hobbes offered no justification for rebellion and no provision whereby the people, having conferred sovereignty, might take it back. There was only one loophole in the Leviathan-creating contract, but it was an important one: self-preservation. Hobbes did not see how it was possible that anyone could, legally or otherwise, "lay down the right of resisting them that assault him by force, to take away his life." He was not inclined to elaborate this into a theory of revolution, but many writers have reasoned from what he *did* say that, because each person enters into the social contract to preserve life and creates the sovereign authority for that purpose, the contract is no longer binding on an individual whose life or person is threatened by it.

Part of the complexity, and historical importance, of Hobbes's work lies in the fact that it is a defense of absolute monarchy, which contains within it the seeds of democratic theory. The origin of the state, for Hobbes, was to be found not in the mind of God but in the minds of people, fashioned by human ingenuity out of the awareness of human brutality: "By art is created that great Leviathan." Leo Strauss has cited the following two points among the key characteristics of Hobbes's philosophy:

The movement away from the idea of monarchy as the most natural *form of State to the idea of monarchy as the most perfect* artificial *State. . . .*

The movement away from the recognition of a superhuman *authority—whether of revelation based on Divine will or a natural order based on Divine reason—to a recognition of the exclusively* human *authority of the State.*[17]

So even in the works of Hobbes—conservative, authoritarian, monarchical—we can see signs of the drift toward a new way of thinking about politics. The idea that people—all people—create the state was for Hobbes the foundation of a defense of sovereignty; for others it would become a justification for nationalism, democracy, and revolution.

THOMAS HOBBES ON CREATING THE STATE

In the state of nature we find three principal causes of quarrel: competition, distrust, and glory. The first makes men invade for gain, the second for safety, and the third for reputation.

During the time men live without a common power to keep them all in awe, they are in that condition which is called war—every man against every man. War consists not only in battle but in the known disposition thereto, over any period of time when there is nothing to guarantee peace.

In such a condition of continuous war there is no place for industry, because the fruit thereof is uncertain; consequently there is no culture of the earth, no navigation or use of commodities that might be imported, no commodious building, no instruments of moving things that require great force, no knowledge of the face of the earth, no account of time, no arts, no letters, no society—and, worst of all, there is continual fear and the danger of violent death. The life of man is solitary, poor, nasty, brutish, and short. The notions of right and wrong, justice and injustice, have no place in the state of nature: There is no law where there is no common power, and there is no injustice where there is no law. Also there can be no property, no understanding of *mine* and *thine,* but only that which any man can get for himself, so long as he can keep it.

These are the ill conditions in which man is placed by nature. But it is possible for him to come out of it—partly because of his passions, and partly because of his reason.

The passions that incline men to peace are fear of death, desire of such things as are necessary to commodious living, and a hope by their industry to obtain them.

And reason suggests convenient articles of peace, upon which men may be drawn to agreement. These articles are precepts or general rules by which a man is forbidden to do that which is destructive of his life. It is a precept or general rule of reason *that every man ought to endeavor peace as far as he has hope of obtaining it, and when he cannot obtain it he may resort to war.* The first branch of this rule contains the first and fundamental law of nature, which is *to seek peace and follow it.* The second branch contains the sum of the right of nature, which is *to defend ourselves by all means we can.*

From this fundamental law of nature, by which men are commanded to seek peace, is derived this second law: *that, in order to obtain peace and self defense, people must be willing to lay down their natural right to all things, and that each man be contented with as much liberty to act against others as he would allow others against himself.* For as long as every man holds the right of doing anything he likes, all men are in the condition of war. But if other men will not lay down their rights also, then any man who did so alone would expose himself to prey. This is that law of the Gospel: *Whatsoever you require that others should do to you, that do ye to them.*

When a man lays down his right to anything, he divests himself of the liberty of hindering another from his enjoyment of the same right. And whenever a man

[17] Leo Strauss, *The Political Philosophy of Hobbes,* trans, Elsa M. Sinclair (Chicago: University of Chicago Press, 1952), p. 129. [Italics added.]

From *Leviathan,* Parts I and II. (Edited and abridged.)

transfers his right or renounces it, it is either in consideration of some right reciprocally transferred to himself, or for some other good he hopes for thereby. The final cause or design of men who naturally love liberty and domination over others, in the introduction of that restraint upon themselves in which we see them live in commonwealths, is the foresight of their own preservation and of a more contented life thereby; that is to say, of getting themselves out from that miserable condition which is consequent to the natural passions of men when there is no visible power to keep them in awe and tie them by fear of punishment to the performance of their covenants and observation of the laws of nature.

For the laws of nature, such as that of doing unto others as we would be done to, are contrary to the natural passions which carry us to partiality, pride, revenge, and the like. Everyone will obey these laws only when he has the will, and when he can do it safely. And covenants, without the sword, are but words and have no strength. If there be no greater power erected, man will and may rely on his own strength and art for caution against all other men. ·

The only way to erect such a common power, able to defend men from the invasion of foreigners and the injuries of one another and to enable them to live contentedly by their industry and the fruits of the earth, is to confer all their power and strength upon one man, or upon one assembly of men, that may reduce all their wills, by plurality of voices, unto one will—which is as much as to say, to appoint one man or assembly of men to act for them all, so that in things which concern the common peace and safety all will submit their wills to his will, and their judgments to his judgment. This is more than consent or concord; it is a real unity of them all, in one and the same person, made by covenant of every man with every man. It is as if every man should say to every man: *I authorize and give up my right of governing myself, to this man or to this assembly of men, on this condition, that thou give up thy right to him and authorize all his actions in like manner.* This done, the multitude so united into one person is called a Commonwealth, in Latin *civitas.* This is the creation of that great Leviathan, or rather, to speak more reverently, of that *mortal god* to which we owe, under the *immortal God,* our peace and defense. For by this authority, given him by every person in the commonwealth, he has the use of so much power and strength conferred on him that by terror thereof he is enabled to form the wills of them all, to obtain peace at home and mutual aid against their enemies abroad. And in him consists the essence of the commonwealth, which to define it is *one person, of whose acts a great multitude, by mutual covenants one with another, have made themselves every one the author, to the end he may use the strength and means of them all, as he shall think expedient, for their peace and common defense.*

And he that carries this person is called *Sovereign* and is said to have *sovereign power;* and every one else is his subject.

G. B. SELDEN.
ROAD ENGINE.

No. 549,160.   Patented Nov. 5, 1895.

4/Revolution and Mass Society

ENGLAND: THE MODIFIED MONARCHY

Late in the seventeenth century England went through another period of crisis, which completed its transition from absolute monarchy to parliamentary sovereignty. This conflict, like the one that had precipitated the English Civil War, started out as a power struggle with religious overtones and ended with a victory for Parliament.

Charles II, Hobbes's one-time mathematics pupil who had been invited to return from France to accept the English throne, ruled for 25 tense years. He lived extravagantly, had a number of conflicts with Parliament, and was mistrusted by many because of his friendliness toward Catholicism and France. When he died in 1685 he was succeeded by his brother James II, a Catholic.

By this time most of the English had become staunchly anti-Catholic, except for a small minority who still clung to the Roman religion. Protestantism had become something akin to patriotism, while Catholicism represented the sinister international machinations of the popes and the faith of England's two greatest enemies, France and Spain. So the position of James II as the Catholic king of an anti-Catholic nation was precarious at best. The people seemed inclined to tolerate James as long as his successor was Mary, his daughter by his first wife; Mary was solidly Protestant and so was her Dutch husband, William of Orange. But when James' second wife, a Catholic, gave birth to a son in 1688, it appeared likely that England would have a new dynasty of Catholic kings. To forestall this, Parliament offered the crown to William and Mary. James, who did not have enough support to launch another civil war, fled to France; his three-year reign was ended, and so was royal absolutism in England for all time. This transition is recorded in English history as the "Glorious Revolution."

The Bill of Rights, the new legal document by which Parliament conferred the crown on William and Mary, clearly established England as a limited and constitutional monarchy; in fact, it clearly established the supremacy of Parliament. It rendered the king unable to govern—to levy taxes or to raise an army—without the continuing support of Parliament, it established meaningful guarantees of free speech in political and religious matters, and it provided for the free election of members of Parliament.

The Glorious Revolution was a triumph of the English upper-middle classes. It established a government by a broadly based aristocracy, which acted through its elected representatives in Parliament and was protected by certain legal guarantees from the threat of an overly powerful monarch. But the system that it created would prove to be a flexible one; it would require only an extension of the right to vote, such as that provided in the Reform Laws of the nineteenth century, to widen the base and convert the system to a mass democracy.

Although the government that ruled England after the Glorious Revolution was a class government, it was liberal for its time, and its defenders began to express some strikingly new political ideas. One example is John Locke, whose writings in support of the new government became one of the fundamental sources of democratic theory.

John Locke

Although John Locke has been more-or-less appropriated by America—one scholar calls him "America's philosopher, our king in the only way a philosopher has ever been king of a great nation"[1]—he was very much a man of his own time and place. He was so involved in the politics of England that he had to leave it at one point; in fact, much of the historical debate about his work turns on the issue of whether he was a true political theorist of universal application or only the spokesman for seventeenth-century Whig ideology.

Locke's father had fought in the English Civil War on the Parliamentary side, and Locke, after completing his studies at Oxford, joined the service of Lord Ashley (later Earl of Shaftesbury), who was a leader of the anti-monarchical faction in English politics. England's political controversies were just beginning to be institutionalized in the form of two parties—the Tories, who tended to be identified with the interests of the throne, the landed nobility, and the High Church; and the Whigs, who were advocates of parliamentary supremacy, the upper-middle classes, and religious freedom. Locke, who had been trained in medicine, first served Shaftesbury as family physician, then as a general advisor. Shaftesbury led a conspiracy to prevent the Catholic James II from becoming king by placing Charles II's illegitimate son, the Duke of Monmouth, on the throne; when the plot failed, both Shaftesbury and Locke sought political exile in Holland. Locke did some of his most important writing in this period of exile, during the short reign of James II. He returned to England on the same boat with Mary, the new Protestant queen. His *Two Treatises of Government* were published in England after his return, and although Locke attempted to remain anonymous, it became generally known that he was the author. The treatises were widely read and praised, especially by English Whigs, who saw in them a powerful argument for the Glorious Revolution and all its principles.

The First Treatise was mainly a refutation of the doctrines of Sir Robert Filmer, a defender of the principle of divine right of kings. Filmer had written, in such works as *Patriarcha* (published in 1680), that no person is born free and that absolute monarchy is the natural form of government, based on descent from Adam and the Biblical patriarchs. Locke's arguments took him toward a diametrically opposite position: that all people are born free, and that the most natural form of government is a limited one based on the consent of the governed. In the Second Treatise, he developed these ideas into his own theory of how and why governments are created, what kinds of limitations should be imposed on them, and when they might justifiably be overthrown.

Locke used the concepts of the state of nature and the social contract, as had Hobbes, but gave them a different form; the state of nature described by Hobbes had been murderous and chaotic, but the state of nature in Locke's writing was—or, at least, could be—relatively peaceful. Part of the difference can be accounted for by different views of natural law: in the Hobbesian "state of nature," people had no real laws to restrain them and had only the harsh dictates of self-preservation to guide them toward a better social order; the people in Locke's account were subject to a much more broad and benign system of natural law, which was not too different from the universal community of right reason that had been described by Cicero and the Stoics before him. "The state of nature," Locke wrote, "has a law of all mankind, who will but consult it, that being all equal and independent, no one ought to harm another in his life, health, liberty or possessions." In this state of nature people lived as equals, each enjoying the property that came to him as a result of his labor, and each was rightfully entitled to take to himself the responsibility of punishing any person who transgressed the natural law. The state of nature as Locke saw it was not intolerable. It was only impractical.

Its impracticality lay in the danger of its lapsing into a state of war. War was not a perpetual state for Locke, as it had been for Hobbes. But there was always the possibility that, in the absence of clearly established laws and recognized judges to settle disputes, the natural peace might be broken by conflict—and that the conflict, once started, might continue indefinitely:

To avoid this state of war (wherein there is no appeal but to heaven, and wherein even the least difference is apt to end, where there is no authority to decide between the contenders) is one great

---

[1] Robert A. Goldwin. "John Locke," in *History of Political Philosophy*. ed. Leo Strauss and Joseph Cropsey (Chicago: Rand McNally, 1963). p. 467.

reason of men's putting themselves into society and quitting the state of nature. For where there is an authority, a power on earth, from which relief can be had by appeal, there the continuance of the state of war is excluded, and the controversy is decided by that power.[2]

The need for authority, for a more efficient and secure way of living within the fundamental natural law, led people to "enter into society"—that is, to create a state. The act of creation, the social contract, had two stages; in the first, the people unanimously agreed "to join and unite into a civil community for their comfortable, safe and peacable living one with another, in a secure enjoyment of their properties, and a greater security against any that are not of it." In creating the body politic, they agreed—as the second stage of the contract—that the majority of them should have "a right to act and conclude the rest."[3]

The newly formed body politic might then proceed to establish a legislative power, which would determine its form of government. Locke insisted on the importance of the legislative as the "supreme power" of the commonwealth. This power could be retained by the majority of the people, in which case the government was a democracy, or it could be delegated in a variety of ways—to an elected assembly, to an absolute monarch, or to various combinations. Locke admitted of many possibilities, but his preference for Parliament is evidenced in his tendency to discuss the legislative power most often and most favorably in terms of an elected assembly. Although Hobbes and Bodin and so many philosophers before them had launched into extensive discussions of the dangers and weaknesses of democracy, Locke turned instead to the perils of absolute monarchy. He found it to be "inconsistent with civil society," indeed, "no form of government at all," and as incapable of insuring peace and justice as the state of nature wherein every man could be his own judge. The weakness of absolute monarchy was in the absence of some established judge, other than the monarch, who could settle disputes. A sovereign not subject to some such authority, was outside of the political order; thus, in a sense, the state of nature still existed. This was essentially an argument for a separation of powers—a principle that, although fairly rudimentary in Locke's writing, would eventually become a fundamental concept of democratic theory and a technique widely applied for limiting the powers of government.

One of the most controversial passages in the Second Treatise—and undoubtedly one of the chief reasons why Locke thought it would be safer to keep its authorship anonymous—was the defense of revolution. Locke saw the social contract as a grant of power by the people according to explicit terms and limitations, which, if violated, rendered the contract invalid and released the people from their obligation to the government. He gave several examples of actions by which a monarch might violate, and thereby dissolve, the established government—and all of the examples had the sound of recent English history: setting up his own will in place of the laws of the society, hindering the legislative body from assembling, altering the means of electing legislators, or subjecting the people to a foreign power. In each of these cases, according to Locke's argument, the monarch's action dissolved the government. Thus, any action by the people to establish another government was not rebellion against authority but merely an attempt to re-establish order. Similarly, when the legislative body might violate its basic responsibility:

and either by ambition, fear, folly or corruption, endeavour to grasp themselves or put into the hands of any other an absolute power over the lives, liberties, and estates of the people, by this breach of trust they forfeit the power the people had put into their hands for quite contrary ends, and it devolves to the people; who have a right to resume their original liberty, and by the establishment of the new legislative . . . provide for their own safety and security, which is the end for which they are in society.[1]

Locke's justification of revolution was an integral element in his conception of society and politics; it was a way of thinking that tended to view society as natural, and politics as artificial and slightly suspect. Sheldon Wolin describes this view as a characteristic of the liberal tradition that Locke helped found:

[2] John Locke, *Second Treatise of Government.*

[3] The original contract requires the unanimous consent of all those who join the community; those who do not consent remain in the state of nature. See *Second Treatise,* Chapter VIII. This has often been criticized as one of the weaker links in Locke's system.

[4] Ibid.

Gradually society came to be conceived simultaneously as an entity distinct from political arrangements and as the shorthand symbol of all worthwhile human endeavor . . . these developments left little scope and less prestige for the political. The political became identified with a narrow set of institutions labelled "government," the harsh symbol of the coercion necessary to sustain orderly social transactions.[5]

Perhaps the most striking thing about Locke's work, in contrast to that of Hobbes, was its tremendous emphasis on *limiting* government. The two writers talked about many of the same things, using similar terms and agreeing on several points; yet in terms of fundamental values, the gulf between them was enormous. Hobbes was a theorist of sovereignty, a defender of absolute monarchy; Locke was a theorist of limited government and popular consent. It is hardly surprising, then, that Locke became a sort of ideological ancestor to the American Revolution. He was widely read by American statesmen, and his thinking about revolution is echoed in the Declaration of Independence, his thinking about the social contract in the preamble to the United States Constitution.

The concept of property was important in Locke's writings. Again and again, he stressed the enjoyment of property as a basic human drive, the protection of it as a main reason for creating governments. God had given the earth to humankind, and every person in the state of nature acquired property as a result of work. Locke saw it as equally natural that different people should acquire differing amounts of property, that money would be used as a system of exchange, and that eventually governments would come into existence as a way of protecting and regulating property rights. Consequently, a government that abused the property rights of its citizens was violating its most basic purpose for existence. This is where Locke's theories had a down-to-earth relevance for prosperous Whigs in their struggle to limit the powers—especially the taxing powers—of the English throne, and later for the propertied American colonists in their similar conflicts with the mother country.

It is easy for the modern reader to make the mistake of believing that Locke was more egalitarian and democratic than he actually was. Locke spoke of "the people" as the source of consent for the government, but nowhere did he argue that all people should participate equally in the rights of citizenship, and one scholar[6] has recently argued convincingly that Locke would have abhorred the idea of universal suffrage (which did not become a reality in England until the twentieth century, after a series of reform bills had, one step at a time, reduced the property qualifications for voting). In the state of nature, as Locke described it, everyone presumably had property; in seventeenth-century England everyone quite obviously did not—and Locke's ideas became mainly a defense for the rights of those who *did* have property. He was not in the line of thought with such early radical groups as the Diggers, who advocated equal sharing of property for all.

There was a similar restraint in Locke's advocacy of revolution. His treatment of the subject has a rational and reassuring sound; revolution, to Locke, was simply a reconstituting of legal government, after the previous authority had dissolved an existing contract by violating its constitutional limitations. Locke knew that revolution could be violent, that it could bring "blood, rapine and desolation" to a country—yet, in his discussions of it, we get an impression of the establishment of rightful government by the more responsible members of a society, rather than of a wild and massive outburst of anger against a repressive authority. This view is understandable; England had just gone through a peaceful revolution, and its example was a good reason to be confident that other nations could make similar transitions. Nobody, least of all the optimistic and victorious Whigs of seventeenth-century England, could have been expected to foresee that European society was just beginning a period of vast and violent upheaval.

JOHN LOCKE ON THE LIMITS OF POWER

Since the great end of men's entering into society is the enjoyment of their property in peace and safety, and the great instrument of that is the laws established

---

[5] Sheldon S. Wolin, *Politics and Vision* (Boston: Little, Brown, 1960), p. 291.

[6] C. B. Macpherson, *The Political Theory of Possessive Individualism* (New York: Oxford University Press, 1962), Chap. V.

[7] Universal manhood suffrage, 1918; suffrage for women, 1928.

From the *Second Treatise of Government*. Ch. XI. (1690). (Edited and abridged.)

in the society, it follows that the first and fundamental positive law of all commonwealths is the establishing of the legislative power; and the first and fundamental natural law—which is to govern even the legislative itself—is the preservation of the society and (as far as consistent with the public good) of every person in it. This legislative is the supreme power of the commonwealth, sacred and unalterable in the hands where the community have once placed it; no edict of anybody else can have the force and obligation of a law without the sanction from that legislative which the public has chosen and appointed. For without this the law could not have that which is necessary to its being a law: the consent of society. Nobody can have a power to make laws over the society but by society's own consent, and by the authority received from them. Therefore all obedience terminates in this supreme power and the laws which it enacts; and no oath to any power, foreign or domestic, can discharge any member from his obedience to the legislative. It is ridiculous to imagine that one can be tied ultimately to obey any power in the society which is not the supreme power.

Although the legislative power—whether placed in one person or in many—is the supreme power in every commonwealth, there are certain limits upon it:

First, it cannot be absolutely arbitrary over the lives and fortunes of the people. For it is but the joint power of every member of society given up to that person or assembly which is legislator; it can be no more than those persons had in a state of nature before they entered into society. For nobody can transfer to another more power than he has in himself; and nobody has an absolute arbitrary power over himself or over any other, to destroy his own life or to take away the life or property of another. The legislative power is thus limited to the public good of the society. It has no other end but preservation, and can never have a right to destroy, enslave, or deliberately impoverish the subjects. The law of nature—which is fundamentally the preservation of mankind—stands as an eternal rule to all men, legislators as well as others.

Secondly, it cannot assume power to rule by arbitrary decrees, but is bound to dispense justice by promulgated standing laws, and known authorized judges. The laws of nature being unwritten and found nowhere but in the minds of men, they who mistake or misapply it through passion or interest cannot easily be convinced of their mistake where there is no established judge; and he that has right on his side may not have force enough to defend himself from injuries. To avoid these inconveniences, which disorder men's properties in the state of nature, men unite into societies, in order to have the united strength of the whole society to secure and defend their properties, and may have standing rules by which every man may know what is his own. These laws are not to be varied in particular cases; they must apply equally to rich and poor, to the favorite at court and the countryman at his plough. When the laws are established and promulgated, the people may know their duty and be safe and secure within the law; and the rulers, too, may be kept within their due bounds and not be tempted by the power they have in their hands.

Thirdly, the supreme power cannot take from any man any part of his property without his own consent. The preservation of property is the end of government, for which men enter into society. Men have a right to the goods which by the law of their community are theirs, and nobody has a right to take their substance or any part of it from them without their own consent. Without this guarantee they have no property at all, for I have no property if another can by right take it from me when he pleases, against my consent. Hence, it is a mistake to think that the supreme or legislative power of any commonwealth can do what it will, and dispose of the estates of the subjects arbitrarily or take any part of them at pleasure. This is not so much to be feared in governments where the legislative consists wholly or in part in assemblies whose members, upon the dissolution of the assembly, are subjects under the common laws of their country. But in governments where the legislative is in one lasting assembly, always in being, or in one man as in absolute monarchies, there is danger that they will think themselves to have a distinct interest from the rest of the community and so will be apt to increase their own riches and power by taking what they think fit from the people. It is true that governments cannot be supported without great charge, and it is fitting that everyone who enjoys his share of the protection should pay his proportion for the maintenance of it. But still it must be with his own consent, that is, the consent of the majority, giving it either by themselves or through their chosen representatives. For if any one shall claim a power to levy taxes on the people by his own authority and without such consent, he thereby invades the fundamental law of property and subverts the end of government.

Fourthly, the legislative cannot transfer the power of making laws to any other hands; it is a delegated power from the people, and they who have it cannot pass it over to others. The people alone can appoint the form of the commonwealth, by constituting the legislative and appointing in whose hands it shall be. And when the people have said: We will submit to rules and be governed by laws made by such men and in such forms, nobody else can say other men shall make laws for them. Nor can the people be bound by any laws but such as are enacted by those whom they have chosen and authorized to make laws for them.

These are the bounds which the trust that is put in them by the society, and the law of God and nature, have set to the legislative power of every commonwealth, in all forms of government.

FRANCE: PRELUDES TO REVOLUTION

While England was making the transition to a limited form of government, France was at the height of its absolute monarchy. In the years since the end of the religious wars in France, the power of the central government had grown steadily. The wars themselves had somewhat weakened and decimated the French nobility, and afterward the first Bourbon king, Henry IV, had worked with some success to build a national government, until his reign was ended by assassination in 1610. The next real ruler of France was Louis XIII's chief minister, Cardinal Richelieu, who systematically built up a centrally controlled bureaucracy, whittled away at the power of the nobility, and deprived the Huguenots of the military fortifications that had been their bastions of regional and religious independence. Richelieu's successor, Cardinal Mazarin, ruled while the young Louis XIV was coming of age, and he, too, tried to unify France under

a single central regime. His greatest unifying accomplishment was the suppression of the Fronde rebellion (1648-1653), an attempt by a group of nobles—undoubtedly inspired by the examples of Cromwell and the English Parliament—to establish their right to participation in government. When Mazarin died, Louis XIV, aged 22, began his long period of personal rule. The reign of "The Sun King" or "The Grand Monarch" was a period of moderate national glory, tremendous destructiveness, great elegance, and oppressive government. Louis XIV saw his own powers in terms of the theory of divine right, and he reigned accordingly. He silenced public criticism through rigid censorship policies, reduced the functions of the nobility to the empty posturings of courtiers, and led France into a series of wars on both the European and American continents. Some of the wars were victorious, some were not; in either case they were expensive, and Louis' pursuit of national glory put the French people under a heavy burden of taxation. Those who paid the greatest price were not the landed nobles—whose estates were exempt from taxation—but the middle classes and the peasantry.

The next king, Louis XV, who reigned through the greater part of the eighteenth century (1715-1774), was at least as extravagant as Louis XIV had been. Although he was a powerful monarch and another firm believer in the divine right of kings to rule, he was irresolute and in some ways incapable of running a national government over which he had virtually unlimited authority. He is said to have remarked, "Aprés moi, le déluge," but that is the best indication we have that he was aware of what was happening to France; he made no consistent effort to stabilize the French economy or to deal with the vast inequities in the social and political orders.

Some of the sources of dissatisfaction among French intellectuals, the middle class, and the peasantry were: the king's military adventures, the extravagances of the nobility, the church, taxation, and royal absolutism. Louis XV's military escapades, notably the War of the Austrian Succession and the Seven Years' War, added nothing to France's international prestige and, in fact, resulted in the loss of important territorial holdings in America. The French nobles lived lives of glamorous extravagance either on their vast country estates or at the king's court, where they were maintained at public expense. Then there was the Catholic church, which owned nearly 10 percent of the land in France and enjoyed an enormous income from various tithes and fees; at this time there were approximately 130,000 members of the clergy in France, and most of the higher church offices were held by members of noble families. Taxes included a tax on land owned by peasants, income tax, poll tax, ecclesiastical tithes, various sales and excise taxes, customs fees, and the *corvée*, or forced labor required of farmers. The monarchy successfully resisted all attempts by the nobles and middle classes to win meaningful participation in government; the Estates-General, the French legislative body, did not meet for 175 years, from 1614 to 1789.

For all its decadence, the eighteenth century in France was a period of brilliant intellectual accomplishment. This is not contradictory; much of the intellectual effort of the times was directed toward social criticism, ridicule of the existing order, and the search for principles of human progress. French philosophers of the time tended to equate foolishness with the way things were run, and rationality with the discussion of how things might be run.

THE FRENCH ENLIGHTENMENT

The French Enlightenment, sometimes called the Age of Reason, was the product of a potent injection of English political ideas and scientific theory into the rather overheated atmosphere of eighteenth-century France. Some historians, who take their philosophy seriously, see this intellectual movement as one of the main causes of the revolution. Others doubt that France was simply "a healthy individual who fell upon the ground foaming at the mouth after drinking a cup of poison . . . philosophic doctrine,"[8] and they are more inclined to look at the social and economic pressures that were developing in the country. There is really no need to argue about whether the *philosophes* did or did not cause the revolution, when they so obviously—if unwittingly—contributed to it. It was unmistakably subversive for a group of people to advocate government according to principles of reason and to ridicule the church, in a country that was ruled by the personal whim of a rather stupid man who believed his power came from God.

The French Enlightenment actually had its beginnings in England: philosophically, in the work of Isaac Newton and John Locke; politically, in the governmental institutions and principles that emerged from the civil war and the Glorious Revolution.

Newton's work in physics—his discoveries, and the way in which he made them—created a kind of revolution of its own, a revolution in the way people felt about truth and knowledge. According to one historian:

Newton struck the imagination of his time, as Darwin did of his time, just because his important conclusions were arrived at by such commonplace methods. If the character of so intangible a thing as light could be discovered by playing with a prism, if, by looking through a telescope and doing a sum in mathematics, the force which held the planets could be identified with the force that made an apple fall to the ground, there seemed to be no end to what might be definitely known about the universe. Perhaps after all God moved in these clear ways to perform his wonders; and it must be that He had given man a mind ingeniously fitted to discover these ways. Newton, more than any man before him, so it seemed to the eighteenth century, banished mystery from the world. In his hands "Philosophy" came to be no more than a matter of observation and mathematics, an occupation which any intelligent person might in some measure pursue. . . .[9]

Thus, Newton's discoveries generated a tremendous feeling of power and potential, as if the deepest secrets of the universe were in the process of being revealed by the application of reason. The poet Alexander Pope may have been overstating the case somewhat, but he gave a true representation of the spirit of the time when he wrote:

Nature and Nature's laws lay hid in night:
Then God said, Let Newton be! and all was light.

Not far behind Newton as a shaper of the era was Locke. In his writings on the method of philosophy, especially in his *Essay Concerning Human Understanding*, he had argued persuasively for discipline and reason. He tried to show how confusion about problems often arose in the mind, through

---

[8] Kingsley Martin, *French Liberal Thought in the Eighteenth Century* (Boston: Little, Brown, 1929), p. 66.

[9] Carl Becker, *The Declaration of Independence* (New York: Harcourt, Brace, 1922), pp. 41–42.

unclear thinking, rather than in the inherent difficulty of the subject itself. An early empiricist, he advocated an approach based on the observation of events, as opposed to the abstract or geometrical model of reasoning from a priori principles.

In England the empirical method and the ideas of limited government that Locke had derived from it were well-suited to the prevailing intellectual climate of the times, and certainly to the Whigs who held the bulk of power. But it was possible for ideas that were respectable in England to be subversive in France, and the men who did the most to bring English thought to the continent are often inaccurately characterized as political radicals.

One man who became a great popularizer of English philosophy was Voltaire (Jean François Marie Arouet). He lived in England from 1726 to 1729, and returned full of a determination to lead his country toward reason and common sense. His *Letters on the English*, published a few years later, praised the new scientific method, and especially Locke:

Locke has developed human reason before men, as an excellent anatomist unfolds the mechanism of the human body. Aided everywhere by the torch of physics, he dares at times to affirm, but he also dares to doubt. Instead of collecting in one sweeping definition what we do not know, he explores by degrees what we desire to know.[10]

Voltaire was a dazzling and versatile writer, effective both as a propagandist for the cause of reason and as a satirist against pomposity and power and official dogma. One of his favorite targets was the Catholic church; by ridiculing its claims to a monopoly on truth through Biblical authority, he made it easier for others—scientists, philosophers, even common men—to dare to seek the truth from their own experience. Voltaire was no revolutionary; he was an aristocrat by temperament, and his idea of good government was rule by an enlightened despot. He never went so far as to argue that the common people could define and defend their own rights. But he did argue that all people *had* rights—the fundamental ones Locke had talked of, and a right to freedom of expression as well—and in time the phrase *les droits des hommes* would become a kind of battle-cry.

The other *philosophes* of the French Enlightenment were

[10] Voltaire, *Letters on the English.*

not revolutionaries, either, but neither were they philosophers in the classical meaning of the word. They were men of letters, and this fact explains something of their impact on French culture. Many of them, like Voltaire, wrote plays and poems and social satires as well as essays, and their essential message of progress, freedom, and reason managed to slip past the obstacle of official censorship—which was as badly run as the rest of the government—and reach a large public. The *Encyclopedia*, which started out as a rather staid scholarly venture, became, under the editorship of Denis Diderot, a spirited forum for Enlightenment thought—and one of the most widely read publications in the country.

The political thinking of the Enlightenment tended to flow along two different lines—either the natural-law approach or the utilitarian approach—but any differences were mainly theoretical: Both schools claimed descent from Locke, and both tended toward liberal political conclusions. The natural-law theorists, who were trying to scientifically update that classic philosophical concept, believed that the natural laws of human behavior could be observed and calculated, as Newton had done with the natural laws of physics; their thinking moved easily, if not always with the sure logic of physical science, from the concept of natural law to that of natural rights. Utilitarians, such as Helvetius and Holbach, approached the problem differently; instead of searching for universally applicable laws, they tried to work out principles of government on the basis of the happiness of the governed—the best policies being those that provided the most pleasure at the cost of the least pain. This early utilitarianism, which seemed eminently reasonable and free of abstractions and a priori principles, claimed descent from Locke's discussions of sense perceptions in the *Essay Concerning Human Understanding*.

Another Enlightenment writer whose work was influenced by observation of the English system was Charles-Louis de Secondat, Baron de la Brède et de Montesquieu. Montesquieu's first literary triumph was *Persian Letters*, a satire on politics and religion in France. When he visited England, a few years after Voltaire, he studied the works of Locke and observed English social and political conditions; back in France he set to work on a long and complex work of political theory, *The Spirit of the Laws*.

Montesquieu wanted to develop a science of politics,

and *The Spirit of the Laws* was an attempt to build a comprehensive classification of types of government and principles of law, based on the study of national character, climate, and soil conditions. That part of his work was not as scientific as he meant it to be, and it had little or no historical influence. But his discussion of the idea of separation of powers had a great impact on political thinking and has helped to shape the constitutions of many states and nations. In every government, Montesquieu argued, there were three kinds of power—legislative, executive, and judiciary—and separation of the three provided a built-in protection against tyranny:

When the legislative and executive powers are united in the same person, or in the same body of magistrates, there can be no liberty; because apprehensions may arise that the same monarch or body will enact tyrannical laws in order to carry them out in a tyrannical manner.

And there is no liberty unless the judicial power is separate from the legislative and the executive. If it is joined with the legislative the lives and liberty of the people would be subject to arbitrary control, for the judge would be the lawmaker. If it were joined to the executive power, the judge might behave with violence and oppression.

There would be an end to everything if the same man or body—whether of the nobles or of the people—should exercise those three powers: that of enacting laws, that of carrying them out; and that of trying the cases of individuals.[11]

Montesquieu was not, of course, the first philosopher to advocate separation of powers; the idea had been implicit in the "mixed government" recommended by Plato and Aristotle, and also in Polybius' explanation of the stability of the Roman republic. But the classification of legislative, executive, and judicial powers—although it was not entirely clear—provided a concept that seemed to be generally applicable; appearing, as it did, near the beginning of an era of constitution-writing, it placed Montesquieu's imprint on the formal structure of most Western governments.

In the later years of the eighteenth century, the mainstream of French thought seemed to turn away from the brisk rationalism of the *philosophes* toward a revival of interest in the emotional side of human experience. The man who was mainly responsible for this transition was Rousseau.

Jean Jacques Rousseau

An English writer, Lytton Strachey, once said of Rousseau that "he possessed one quality which cut him off from his contemporaries, which set an immense gulf betwixt him and them: he was modern."

Certainly Rousseau was different from his colleagues, especially his colleagues of the Enlightenment, in many ways: He had been born in Switzerland and was a foreigner, was something of an eccentric, was fiercely and self-consciously Bohemian, and was involved in an intensely personal way with his search for some understanding of how political organization could serve human needs. We have seen that other philosophers—Machiavelli, Hobbes, Bodin, Locke—were involved in the politics of their times, but Rousseau's involvement was deeper and more emotional, a commitment comparable to that sometimes seen in modern, quasi-religious, forms of patriotism and rebellion. Rousseau was also different because he combined his search for truth about society with a search for truth about himself. William Blanchard, in a recent psychological study of him, wrote:

Jean Jacques Rousseau sought to discover the relationship between personal candor and good government, opening the door to a new field of study. Recognizing that this task required an unusual moral courage, he declared himself ready and set out upon his venture. From a modern vantage point, with the insights into nature recently acquired, it is clear that he was not fully aware of the risks he faced. In his effort to shape the structure of the good society he came face to face with his own weakness. But his failure was never a complete rout. In his bold approach he overturned some of the sacred falsehoods of his age.[12]

More than anyone else, Rousseau was responsible for the transition of literary eras from the Age of Reason to the Age of Romanticism, and more than anyone else, he was revered as the patron saint of the French Revolution.

[11] *The Spirit of the Laws*, trans. Thomas Nugent (New York: Colonial Press, 1899), Vol I, pp. 151–52.

[12] William H. Blanchard, *Rousseau and the Spirit of Revolt* (Ann Arbor: University of Michigan Press, 1967), p. xi.

He undoubtedly contributed much to the growth of demo-cratic ideology, but it has been argued that in his desire to make the state the agent of human fulfillment, he helped the development of totalitarianism as well.[13]

Rousseau came to Paris in the 1740's, to seek his fortune as a writer and composer. He had grown up in Geneva, where the severe Protestantism of John Calvin still dictated personal and public morality, and then had spent several years wandering through Italy and France. His adventures during this period, including an affair with a Catholic widow named Madame de Warens, are described with characteristic frankness in his *Confessions*. He began to become prominent in Paris when he won an essay contest, sponsored by the academy of Dijon, with a discourse arguing that most of the "progress" of civilization was, in fact, a decline from the natural goodness of humankind—an idea that in various forms, was to be central to much of his later work.

Rousseau expressed his belief in naturalness in his personal life. At a time when styles were at their most elegant, he wore simple clothes of coarse material, which only added to his popularity and made him more desirable as an "attraction" at Parisian social functions. He turned increasingly to political philosophy, in the *Discourse on the Origin of Inequality* (1755), an *Encyclopedia* article on "Political Economy" (1758), and *The Social Contract* (1762). The *Discourse* dealt mainly with his ideas about people in the state of nature; in the *Encyclopedia* article and *The Social Contract*, he was more concerned about people in society, and in these two works he developed his theory of the general will.

The state of nature had become something of a staple of political philosophers by this time, but it was different things for different men. Hobbes had seen it as perpetual war, requiring a powerful sovereign to bring and maintain peace. Locke had seen it as an era of primitive common sense, maturing eventually into the more sophisticated common sense of limited government. For Rousseau, nature was a state of beautiful but dangerous freedom. He agreed with Hobbes about the importance of the instinct of self-preservation, and he recognized that there might sometimes be quick outbursts of violence, "perhaps mechanically and on the spot, as a dog will sometimes bite the stone which is thrown

at him." But he also believed in the human instinct of compassion: "a natural feeling, which, by moderating the violence of love of self in each individual, contributes to the preservation of the whole species." This instinct was so strong, Rousseau argued, that it had even managed to survive in modern civilization, where it was expressed in such "social virtues" as generosity, clemency, and humanity.

The original, or primitive, state of nature gave way to a second stage, society without government, a way of life that was in some ways idyllic but that would in time become more complex:

So long as men remained content with their rustic huts, so long as they were satisfied with clothes made of the skins of animals and sewn together with thorns and fishbones, adorned themselves only with feathers and shells, and continued to paint their bodies different colors, to improve and beautify their bows and arrows, and to make with sharp-edged stones fishing boats or clumsy musical instruments; in a word, so long as they undertook only what a single person could accomplish, and confined themselves to such arts as did not require the joint labour of several hands, they lived free, healthy, honest, and happy lives, so long as their nature allowed, and as they continued to enjoy the pleasures of mutual and independent intercourse. But from the moment one man began to stand in need of the help of another; from the moment it appeared advantageous to any one man to have enough provisions for two, equality disappeared, property was introduced, work became indispensable, and vast forests became smiling fields, which man had to water with the sweat of his brow, and where slavery and misery were soon seen to germinate and grow up with the crops.[11]

Work, property, the division of labor: these were the developments, the "progress," that would create greater inequality among individuals and make life in the unorganized society increasingly stressful, acquisitive, and dangerous, until finally there would be a move toward the formation of a political order. The move, as Rousseau saw it, would be initiated by the rich—who had the most to lose, and who would persuade others that some kind of formal govern-

---

[13] See Jacob Leib Talmon, *The Origins of Totalitarian Democracy*, (New York: Praeger, 1960).

[14] Jean Jacques Rousseau, "A Discourse on the Origin of Inequality," from the book *The Social Contract & Disclosures and Other Essays* by Jean Jacques Rousseau, pp. 243-44. Trans. and with an Intro. by G. D. H. Cole. Everyman's Library Edition. Published by E. P. Dutton & Co., Inc. (New York), and J. M. Dent & Sons Ltd. (London), and used with their permission.

ment was necessary to them all. Thus persuaded, "all ran headlong to their chains, in hopes of securing their liberty; for they had just wit enough to perceive the advantages of political institutions, without experience enough to enable them to foresee the dangers."

In this description of the division of labor as a fundamental factor in the political society, Rousseau's view resembled that of Plato. But where Plato had used occupational specializations as the building-blocks of an ideal state, Rousseau saw the whole process as a loss of natural simplicity, which created problems that could only be solved by establishing a government—with a consequent loss of freedom for individuals.

Rousseau's own opinion changed in the years after the publication of the above ideas in the *Discourse on the Origin of Inequality*. In the Discourse, he had emphasized the negative aspects of the transition as a kind of hoax played by the rich on the poor; in the *Social Contract*, he was more positive and optimistic about the advantages of life in an organized society.

In *The Social Contract* Rousseau revived the classical organic concept of political society; it became for him, as it had been for Aristotle, the vehicle for the greatest fulfillment of the lives of its members. But Rousseau added something new, a difficult—some say vague—idea that had a great impact on political thought: the "general will." The concept of the general will was, among other things, a response to the earlier philosophers who had argued that democracy was naturally prone to divisiveness, indecision, and lack of direction, because of the absence of a single unifying will. Rousseau argued that the state possessed a general will, which was the true and wise essence of the best interest of all its members, was the source of laws, and was the natural guide to the preservation of the society.

The general will was the fundamental concept of Rousseau's theory of popular sovereignty: the people, all of them together, possessed this essential truth, which was the natural basis of power. In the social contract, each individual voluntarily became subordinated to the will of the entire body; thus, in the political order each person had an active role as a citizen who was a part of the general will, and a passive role as a person who was subject to this will.

Further, this popular sovereignty could not be delegated. The people could delegate power, as in the election of officials, but the essential will, or sovereignty, remained always with the whole community. Similarly, Rousseau argued, the general will could not be divided; either there was one general will, for a whole people, or there was none at all.

The general will was obviously a democratic notion, but it was also, as so many of Rousseau's critics have pointed out, a most elusive democratic notion. The general will was not simply the will of the majority—it was not even necessarily the will of all the people, because there was always the possibility that the people might be confused by self-interest. The general will had to be right, to be the true sense of what was best for all. And it is an indication of Rousseau's vision of society as an organic whole that he often employed singular terms for it: the state was a "moral person," a "collective body," the "body politic." At the center of Rousseau's work was the belief that individuals might discover among themselves a natural unity that transcended the divisive force of individual selfishness. He had a vision of the state (which in his time was inevitably interpreted to mean the nation-state) as a community.

Rousseau's works were condemned by the French government, and to escape arrest he went into exile, first in Switzerland and then in England. He eventually returned to France, where he lived out the last ten years of his life without being arrested, and wrote his *Confessions;* he died in 1778.

His works became enormously important in certain phases of the French Revolution, not only as a source of theory for popular sovereignty, but also as a justification for revolutionary cliques who believed they had access to the general will.

One of the most fascinating things about Rousseau is the tremendous breadth of the points of view that have been in some way influenced by his ideas. He was cited as scripture by French revolutionaries, but was also a source for the great critic of the French Revolution, Edmund Burke. There is an early hint of Marxist theory in his view (in the *Discourse*) of the political order as a means of protecting the property of the rich, and some have interpreted his belief in the need for submission to the general will—especially the famous remark that individuals should be "forced to be free"—as an apology for totalitarianism.

All those things were indeed present, in rough form,

in Rousseau's work, and the fact that he has been interpreted in so many different ways cannot be explained simply in terms of the vagueness of his concepts. He was, it is true, often unclear and often contradictory—but he was struggling toward a rationale for mass democracy, a kind of governmental order that was still nonexistent and beyond his own capacity to visualize. He was also working, out of his own need as an alienated wanderer in a corrupt yet desirable society, toward some idea of the state as a source of gratification and satisfaction and meaning for its citizens. What Rousseau created was a mystique of democracy.

JEAN JACQUES ROUSSEAU ON THE GENERAL WILL

The essence of the social contract is reducible to the following terms:

"Each of us puts in common his person and his whole power under the supreme direction of the general will; and in return we receive every member as an indivisible part of the whole."

Forthwith, in place of the individual personalities of all the contracting parties, this act of association produces a moral and collective body, which is composed of as many members as the assembly has voices, and which receives from this same act its unity, its common self, its life, and its will. This public person, which is thus formed by the union of all the individual members, formerly took the name of *city*, and now takes that of *republic* or *body politic;* it is called by its members *State* when it is passive, *sovereign* when it is active, *power* when it is compared to similar bodies. The associates take collectively the name of *people*, and are called individually *citizens*, as participating in the sovereign power, and *subjects*, as subjected to the laws of the State.

We see from this formula that the act of association contains a reciprocal agreement between the public and the individuals, and that every individual, contracting so to speak with himself, is bound in a double relation: as a member of the sovereign he is bound to the individuals, and as a member of the State he is bound to the sovereign.

From *The Social Contract*, trans. Henry J. Tozer (London: George Allen & Unwin, 1909), pp. 110–124. (Edited and abridged.)

As soon as the multitude is thus united in one body, it is impossible to injure one of the members without attacking the body, still less to injure the body without the members feeling the effects. Thus, duty and interest alike oblige the two contracting parties to give mutual assistance.

Now, the sovereign, being formed only of the individuals that compose it, neither has nor can have any interest contrary to theirs; consequently the sovereign power needs no guarantee towards its subjects, because it is impossible that the body should wish to injure all its members; and we shall see hereafter that it can injure no one as an individual. The sovereign, for the simple reason that it is so, is always everything that it ought to be.

But this is not the case as regards the relation of subjects to the sovereign, which, in spite of the common interest, would have no security for the performance of their engagements unless it found some means to insure their fidelity.

Indeed, every individual may, as a man, have a particular will contrary to, or different from, the general will which he has as a citizen. His private interest may prompt him quite differently from the common interest; his naturally independent existence may make him regard what he owes to the common cause as a gratuitous contribution, whose loss will be less harmful to others than the payment will be burdensome to himself, and he might be willing to enjoy the rights of a citizen without being willing to fulfill the duties of a subject. The progress of such injustice would bring about the ruin of the body politic.

In order, then, that the social contract may not be a vain formula, it tacitly includes this agreement, which alone can give force to the others—that whoever refuses to obey the general will shall be constrained to do so by the whole body. This means nothing less than that he shall be forced to be free; for this is the condition which, uniting every citizen to his native land, protects him from all personal dependence. This insures the control and working of the political machine, and alone renders legitimate civil agreements which, without it, would be absurd and tyrannical and subject to the most enormous abuses.

It follows from all this that the general will is always right and always tends to the public advantage; but it does not follow that the resolutions of the people are always equally correct. Men always desire their own good, but do not always discern it; the people are never corrupted, but they are often deceived, and it is only then that they seem to will what is evil.

There is often a great deal of difference between the will of all and the general will; the latter regards only the common interest, while the former has regard to private interests, and is merely a sum of particular wills; but take away from these same wills the pluses and minuses which cancel one another, and the general will remains as the sum of the differences.

If the people came to a resolution, when adequately informed and without any communication among themselves, the general will would always result from the total of the small differences, and the resolution would always be good. But when factions are formed, to the detriment of the whole society, the will of each of these partial associations becomes general with reference to its members, and particular with reference to the State; it may then be said that there are no longer as many voters as there are men, but only as many voters as there are associations. The differences become less numerous and yield a less general result. Lastly, when one of these associations becomes so great that it dominates all the rest, you no longer have as a result a sum of small differences, but a single difference; there is then no longer a general will, and the opinion which prevails is only a particular opinion.

It is important, then, in order to have a clear declaration of the general will, that there should be no factions within the State, and that every citizen should express only his own opinion. But if there are partial associations, it is best to multiply their number and prevent them from being unequal. These are the only proper precautions for insuring that the general will may always be enlightened, and that the people may not be deceived.

REVOLUTIONS

The late eighteenth century was a time of change, when many transformations—some subtle and slow to mature, some explosive—were taking place, moving the world into the modern era of mass production and mass democracy. One such transformation, perhaps the most far-reaching of all, was the Industrial Revolution. It began almost imperceptibly, with new developments in England's economy, developments that increased the output of manufactured goods at lower prices, stimulating the growth of new markets at home and in the colonies. At the same time the distribution of population changed, as small holdings were consolidated into large farms, and a new class of landless workers migrated to the industrial towns. Historians dispute the exact time and nature of these beginnings, but it is clear that the changes that were taking place in England's economic system were a true revolution: they led England to a new kind of predominance in world politics and, in time, they profoundly affected the conditions of human life everywhere in the world.

The two great political revolutions of the eighteenth century—the American and the French—were in fact a closely interrelated series of events, which followed the peaceful internal transition in England, the intellectual ferment of the Enlightenment, and the martial adventures of the French monarchy. One of the indirect causes of the American Revolution was England's victory over Louis XVI's army in the Seven Years' War, which added the St. Lawrence and Mississippi valleys to English colonial possessions in 1763.

These new and largely unsettled territories had to be fortified and defended, and it seemed logical to the government in London that the costs should be borne by the colonists. Things might have gone differently if the English Whigs had been in control during this period, but England was going through a resurgence of royal power; George III was seeking to regain executive authority for the throne, and Tory leaders calling themselves "Friends of the King" were becoming dominant in Parliament. A similar political cleavage existed in America, but as the policies of the mother government became more severe, the party of colonists who opposed the king and his Tory supporters became larger and louder. The taxes and restrictions imposed by England fell most heavily on the business and professional classes, who roughly corresponded to the Whig elements in England, and in fact many English Whigs were sympathetic to the cause of the colonists.

King George's government attempted, for one thing, to revive and enforce the Navigation Acts, which would have meant an end to the smuggling trade that was an important segment of colonial business. New taxes, such as the stamp tax, placed additional expenses on merchants. Another policy strongly opposed by various business groups in the colonies was the decision to close the newly won western areas to immediate settlement; this ban conflicted with the plans and aspirations of prospective settlers, mer-

FROM LOCKE'S SECOND TREATISE OF GOVERNMENT

Man being born, as has been proved, with a title to perfect freedom and an uncontrolled enjoyment of all the rights and privileges of the law of nature, equally with any other man, or number of men in the world, hath by nature a power . . . to preserve his property, that is, his life, liberty and estate . . . .

men unite into societies that they may have the united strength of the whole society to secure and defend their properties . . .

Whensoever therefore the legislative shall . . . endeavor to grasp themselves, or put into the hands of any other, an absolute power over the lives, liberties, and estates of the people, by this breach of trust they forfeit the power the people had put into their hands for quite contrary ends, and it devolves to the people; who have a right to resume their original liberty, and by the establishment of a new legislative (such as they shall think fit), provide for their own safety and security . . . .

Great mistakes in the ruling part, many wrong and inconvenient laws, and all the slips of human frailty will be borne by the people without mutiny or murmur. But if a long train of abuses, prevarications, and artifices, all tending the same way, make the design visible to the people, and they cannot but feel what they lie under, and see whither they are going, 'tis not to be wondered that they should then rouse themselves, and endeavor to put the rule into such hands which may secure to them the ends for which government was at first erected . . . .

FROM THE DECLARATION OF INDEPENDENCE

We hold these truths to be self-evident, that all men are created equal; that they are endowed by their Creator with certain inalienable rights; that among these are life, liberty, and the pursuit of happiness.

That to secure these rights, governments are instituted among men, deriving their just powers from the consent of the governed;

that whenever any form of government becomes destructive of these ends, it is the right of the people to alter or to abolish it, and to institute a new government, laying its foundation on such principles, and organizing its powers in such form as to them shall seem most likely to effect their safety and happiness.

Prudence, indeed, will dictate that governments long established should not be changed for light and transient causes; and accordingly all experience hath shown, that mankind are more disposed to suffer, while evils are sufferable, than to right themselves by abolishing the forms to which they are accustomed. But when a long train of abuses and usurpation, pursuing invariably the same object, evinces a design to reduce them under absolute despotism, it is their right, it is their duty, to throw off such government, and to provide new guards for their further security.

chants, and land speculators.

The policies of the rather stiff-necked Tory administration increased colonial opposition, making more and more colonial leaders receptive to the ideas of the radicals who wanted to declare independence. The Declaration of Independence, drafted by Thomas Jefferson with the help of Benjamin Franklin and John Adams, was based mainly on the theoretical principles set down by the philosopher best-known to most of the educated colonists: John Locke. In terms of its practical effects, it blocked the possibility of reconciliation with England and opened the way for aid from France.

The declaration was one of the few victories for radicals in the internal politics of the colonies; as so many historians have pointed out, the American Revolution was not an uprising of the masses but a political transition engineered with a good deal of sophistication by a well-educated and prosperous elite. After independence had been won and an experiment with a loose confederation of states had run its course, a federal government was established by a Constitution that was, among other things: (1) an incorporation of many elements from the English historical experience, including the Bill of Rights; (2) a practical application of Enlightenment political ideas, such as Montesquieu's separation-of-powers doctrine; and (3) an effective provision for the needs of the financial classes represented by Alexander Hamilton. The new government that emerged from the American Revolution admirably protected and encouraged the development of banking, interstate commerce, and manufacturing; the men who assumed office in it were without exception men of property and education (George Washington was one of the richest men in the United States), and the voting qualifications set up by the various states restricted active participation in the democratic process to white male property owners and taxpayers. The new republican government was indeed an experiment, but not a wild one; it was an experiment in the application of recognized governmental principles by responsible and prosperous men.

During the Revolutionary War, dissatisfaction with the king and his administration increased in England; after the British surrender at Yorktown, Tory strength declined sharply, and the new Whig administration that came to power was much more willing to negotiate a generous peace treaty with the colonists. The Revolution also had important reper-

cussions in France; the French, having just lost an important segment of their North American territory to England, welcomed the opportunity to hand their colonial rivals a similar setback. In that respect, their aid to the American revolutionaries was a successful maneuver—England's loss as a result of the Revolution was at least as serious as the one France had suffered in the previous decade. But the cost of helping the Americans led the French government into a financial crisis, which in turn touched off the series of political upheavals known as the French Revolution.

With his government near bankruptcy, King Louis XVI convened an "assembly of notables" in 1787, asking the aristocracy to give its support to a series of economic reform measures—including increases in taxation—that might alleviate the crisis. The notables, hoping to use the crisis to win greater participation by the aristocracy in government, were surprisingly uncooperative, and in desperation the King decided to call into session the Estates-General, the national body that had been inactive since 1614.

It was a decision from which French monarchy never recovered. The meeting of the Estates-General brought together and gave voice to some of the most dissatisfied elements in the social order. Chief among these were representatives of the mercantile middle classes, which had grown in size and prosperity without any parallel advances in social and political status. Most historians see the aspirations of these middle classes as the chief pressure for revolutionary change. Will and Ariel Durant speak for this point of view:

The essential cause of the Revolution was the disparity between economic reality and political forms—between the importance of the bourgeoisie in the production and possession of wealth and its exclusion from governmental power. The upper middle class was conscious of its abilities and sensitive to its slights. It was galled by the social exclusiveness and insolence of the nobility—as when the brilliant Mme. Roland, invited to stay for dinner in an aristocratic home, found herself served in the servants' quarters. It saw the nobility milking the coffers of the state for extravagant expenditures and feasts while denying political or military office or promotion to those very men whose inventive enterprise had expanded the tax-yielding economy of France, and whose savings were now supporting the treasury. It saw the clergy absorbing a third of the nation's income in maintaining a theology that almost all educated Frenchmen considered medieval and infantile.

The middle classes did not wish to overthrow the monarchy, but they aspired to control it. They were far from desiring democracy, but they wanted a constitutional government in which the intelligence of all classes could be brought to bear upon legislation, administration, and policy.[15]

The Estates-General, in its traditional feudal form, consisted of three bodies, representing clergy, nobles, and commoners. The assembly that gathered at Versailles in 1789 consisted of 308 clergy, 285 nobles, and 621 commoners. The commoners, or Third Estate, were representatives of the middle classes; they were the most united of the three bodies, the most determined to bring about change, and after a few confusing weeks they emerged as the most powerful. At first they were at a disadvantage because the traditional structure of the Estates-General assigned a single vote to each body; that is, a measure passed by any two of the three units was considered to have been approved by the whole, and thus the clergy and nobles could out-vote the commoners. The Third Estate's aim was to have the three groups meet as a single body, with each member's vote counted equally, which would give the edge to the commoners and their allies among the liberal nobles and lower clergy.

After about six weeks of bickering, the king ordered the members of the Third Estate to give up their demand. Barred from entry to their regular meeting-place, the members of the Third Estate—now calling themselves the National Assembly—met on the king's tennis court and took an oath not to disband until they had given France a constitution.

King Louis finally granted the commoners' demand to combine the three houses into a single assembly, with each member holding an equal vote, but he continued to resist the pressure for a written constitution as the price for the new taxes he proposed. The king's attempts to repress the revolutionary activity in the Assembly provoked popular protest actions, especially in Paris, and on July 14 a Parisian mob captured the great prison, the Bastille.

The storming of the Bastille became a symbol of popular resistance to tyranny. The event itself was an uncertain victory; about a hundred lives were lost and seven prisoners—five criminals, two madmen—were set free. Yet the uprising immediately became legendary. Veterans of the Bastille appeared everywhere in France as revolutionary heroes, poems and songs and plays celebrated the people's victory, and stones of the old prison were sold throughout Europe as souvenirs. One result of the Bastille uprising that was real, rather than symbolic, was the king's decision to present himself to the people as a friend of the Assembly and its constitutional cause.

The Assembly, now functioning both as a legislative body and a constitutional convention, inaugurated sweeping social and economic reforms, stated its basic theoretical propositions in the Declaration of the Rights of Man, and in 1791 finally brought forth a constitution. The constitution reflected the essentially middle-class nature of that stage of the revolution. It created a one-house legislature, the Legislative Assembly, which was clearly the dominant governing body; it left some formal executive authority with the king, but delegated most executive powers to the Executive Council, a committee of the Assembly. There were two classes of citizenship, active and passive; active citizens, who had the right to vote, were adult property-owning males.

This Whiggish constitutional phase lasted scarcely a year, and then a combination of pressures—the intrigues of the nobles, the demands of the radicals, the meddling of pro-royalist forces in Austria and Prussia—pushed the revolution a step farther. It was already an international affair in many ways. There were German princes with hereditary claims to French estates, there were colonies of exiled French nobles in Austria and Prussia who conspired with foreign rulers, and there was a strong radical element within France that wanted a war to overthrow monarchies everywhere.

In 1792 an official declaration of war by the Legislative Assembly launched France into war with Austria and Prussia, and thus began a series of international conflicts that would involve most of the Western world.

In a war that had overtones of an ideological struggle between democracy and its enemies, the position of the French king was obviously difficult. King Louis XVI and Marie Antoinette had tried unsuccessfully to leave France in 1791, and it was becoming evident that they were prisoners in their own country. Shortly after the beginning of the war, the Duke of Brunswick, commander of the Austro-Prussian forces, declared that if any harm came to the king and

---

[15] Will and Ariel Durant, *Rousseau and Revolution* (New York: Simon & Schuster, 1967), p. 937. ©1967 by Will and Ariel Durant. Reprinted by permission of Simon & Schuster.

queen, captured French soldiers would be punished by him as traitors and Paris would be destroyed. This manifesto only increased anti-royalist sentiment, and in Paris there was an uprising against the king. In the midst of the rioting a radical group gained control of the Assembly, established universal manhood suffrage, and proclaimed an end to the monarchy and the constitution of 1791.

As revolutionary leaders struggled against their enemies, foreign and domestic, and sometimes among themselves, France passed through the tragic years known as "the Terror." There was a foretaste of what was to come in September of 1792, when thousands—perhaps as many as ten thousand—royalists and suspected royalists were killed by rioting mobs in Paris and elsewhere. In that same month a new governing body, the National Convention, was elected by universal suffrage. By now the government was no longer under the control of the middle-class elements who had banded together on the king's tennis court a few years earlier. It was seldom clear who, if anyone at all, did control the course of events in the bewildering internal politics of the Convention, but obviously the French Revolution had progressed far beyond the relatively mild upheavals in England and America.

Early in 1793 the radical faction in the Convention, then known as the Montagnards or Mountaineers (because members' seats were in high sections of the meeting hall), succeeded in getting the majority to vote. to execute the king, who had been tried before that body on charges of crimes against public liberty and national safety. The death of Louis XVI was the real beginning of the Terror. It set a conspicuous example for the use of execution as a solution to political complications, and it shocked much of Europe into united opposition to the French revolutionary regime—which in turn intensified the climate of fear and suspicion within France, as external enemies grew in strength and unity, and internal factions competed for leadership in the struggle to transform a divided and confused nation into a pure revolutionary community.

The new revolutionary government that was organized by the Convention included a judiciary body with extensive powers for trying "traitors, conspirators and anti-revolutionists," a national network of investigative bodies. and a powerful executive arm called the Committee of Public Safety. Although this inquisitorial machinery was ostensibly for the

purpose of dealing with enemies of the revolution, it soon became a weapon in the rivalry between the two main revolutionary factions, the Girondins and the Montagnards. In June of 1793 the Terror began in earnest, with the arrest and execution of 22 Girondin leaders. Power now rapidly concentrated in the hands of Montagnard leader Maximilien Robespierre and the Committee of Public Safety; the revolutionary government was, in fact, a dictatorship.

During the years of the Terror, some 20,000 people died on the guillotine; the victims were royalists, royalist sympathizers, and people who represented all shades of opposition to the ruling Montagnard clique. The Terror consumed some of the greatest leaders of the revolution, and in time it consumed the Terrorists as well; the remaining non-Montagnard members of the Convention rose up against the Committee of Public Safety in 1794, and Robespierre and about one hundred of his supporters were executed.

Throughout the Terror, French patriotism had risen to a kind of frenzy, and the revolutionary armies had won impressive victories over their enemies on the battlefields. After the overthrow of Robespierre and the establishment of a new constitution, which vested executive power in a five-member Directory, the war continued, and the common people of France found a new hero: a young general, Napoleon Bonaparte. Napoleon, who had been associated with the Montagnard rulers during the Terror and was briefly imprisoned after their fall, managed to ingratiate himself even more solidly with the new ruling clique; his marriage to Josephine Beuaharnais, former mistress of one of the Directors, led to his promotion to the rank of general at the age of 27. But Napoleon soon showed the world that he was capable of more than political intrigue; as commander of the French armies in Italy, he routed the Austrians in a display of brilliant and audacious generalship.

Napoleon's next campaign was an expedition to conquer Egypt and thereby end England's supremacy in the East. The Egyptian campaign foundered and Napoleon abandoned it; he returned to Paris to launch an even greater project—a coup d'état against the Directory itself. With the aid of two members of the Directory, the support of the army, and a fabricated radical plot against the government, Napoleon precipitated a crisis and offered himself as its solution. The Directory was abolished and replaced by a new government, which vested executive power in a triumvirate of consuls: Napoleon and his two supporters. This arrangement was soon formalized in a written constitution that established a limited republican government, with consuls elected for ten-year terms, and with the office of First Consul—held by Napoleon—clearly predominant in executive authority. In 1802, by a vote of the Senate and a popular plebescite, Napoleon was elected First Consul for life. He had already consolidated governmental power beyond even the absolutism of Louis XIV; in 1804 he took the final step and—again with the approval of the Senate and the people—was crowned Emperor of France.

The French Revolution did not end with the coronation of Napoleon (in many ways, it still has not ended), but for a time it seemed that France had exhausted its capacity for political innovation. In little more than a decade, the country had gone from absolute monarchy to limited monarchy, from limited monarchy to republic, from republic to mass democracy, and from there through several variations of government by clique, dictatorship, and anarchy. The revolution had cost thousands of lives and had sent the other nations of Europe into political upheaval from which they never fully recovered. It had produced several written constitutions, and had served as a kind of open laboratory for political transformation, which the rest of the world watched with awe and fascination. Few political events in history have so dominated the world's attention or produced such outpourings of words and emotions. At its beginnings, the revolution was a great inspiration for people with democratic sentiments. A Danish writer tells of how, one night after the news of the Fall of the Bastille had reached Copenhagen, his father gathered his sons about him and, crying with joy, told them that there had just begun a new era of opportunity for all, in which "poverty would vanish, the lowliest would begin the struggles of life on equal terms with the mightiest, with equal arms, on equal ground."[16]

The Revolution provided a focal point for the thoughts and actions of believers in democratic forms of government, and it pushed the monarchies of Europe into unprecedented cooperation. With its cult of loyalty to the nation as an organic community (everyone, even Louis XVI, had read Rousseau) it helped form the modern idea of patriotism.

It was a great consumer of ideas—hardly a political philosopher in history was left out of the speechmaking or neglected as a source of wisdom in the creation of new governmental arrangements—and it was also, of course, a powerful stimulus to later political thinking. Philosophers from the revolution onward could hardly ignore it, and most drew heavily on it as a source of human political experience.

Their task was made more difficult by history's refusal to give them a resting-place, a calm and permanent status quo from which to look back on a time of change. After Napoleon's reign there was a restoration of the Bourbon monarchy, then another revolution and another republic, then another Napoleon. Meanwhile, other revolutions spread like waves throughout the world. Historian E. J. Hobsbawm distinguishes three waves of revolution in the nineteenth century: first, the uprisings in Naples and Greece and Spain, between 1820 and 1824, which were followed by colonial revolutions against Spain and Portugal in the New World; next the upheavals of 1829–1834, which touched Ireland and several continental countries and produced the first Reform Law, extending the voting franchise in England; and then the outburst of 1848, which again involved France, as well as Italy and the German states.[17] By this time, the effects of the Industrial Revolution had also become apparent outside England, bringing still more changes. Change, not stability, had become the norm, and political philosophers were finding it necessary to formulate concepts and values capable of dealing not only with one change or two, but with the phenomenon of change itself.

Edmund Burke

One of the intellectual byproducts of the French revolution was a philosophy of conservatism. There had been other conservative philosophies before, of course—certainly the various concepts supporting the notion of the divine right of kings were that—but there had not been a need for a position to be taken about change itself. The foundations of modern conservatism were laid down by Edmund Burke, a busy English Whig parliamentarian who did not think of himself as a political philosopher or attempt to

---

[16] Quoted in Crane Brinton, *A Decade of Revolution* (New York: Harper, 1934), p. 66.

[17] *The Age of Revolution* (London: Weidenfeld and Nicholson, 1962), pp. 109–112.

formulate a system, but who lived through the time of the American and French revolutions and said what he thought about them.

Burke was not an aristocrat. He was born in Dublin, son of a middle-class Irish lawyer, and he became a member of Parliament at the age of 36 (then considered a rather late start for a political career), after a period of employment as private secretary to the Whig prime minister, Lord Rockingham. Nor was he particularly conservative according to the alignments of his times; he was ever a loyal Whig, and one of his early forays into political prominence was a pamphlet entitled *Thoughts on the Cause of the Present Discontents*, a defense of the powers and freedom of Parliament that appeared in 1770–the year that George III, with the help of Tory "friends of the king," was gaining new royal influence in the House of Commons.

As the Tories came to power, Burke became a leading opposition spokesman. He was especially critical of Tory policies toward the American colonies. In his speeches *On American Taxation* in 1774 and *On Conciliation with America* in 1775, he defended the liberties of the colonists–not on abstract grounds of natural law and human rights, a kind of thinking he distrusted, but on the basis of the nature of the colonists ("the true temper of their minds") and the kind of policy that ought reasonably to be used toward it. Of the character of Americans, he believed that "a love of freedom is the predominating feature which marks and distinguishes the whole: and as an ardent is always a jealous affection, your colonies become suspicious, restive, and untractable, whenever they see the least attempt to wrest from them by force, or shuffle from them by chicane, what they think is the only advantage worth living for."

This love of freedom, Burke thought, had grown up naturally in the social fiber of the colonies, resulting from the forms of representative government developed in the various legislatures, from a heritage of English political tradition, from the effects of Protestant religion in the north and social structure in the south, from education, and from the distance from the mother government.

Furthermore, the love of liberty tended to focus itself on one specific issue: taxation. "Liberty might be safe or might be endangered in twenty other particulars without their being much pleased or alarmed. Here they felt its pulse; and as they found that beat, they thought themselves sick

or sound." Along the same lines–not abstract principle, but practicality–Burke argued against the use of force: "It may subdue for a moment, but it does not remove the necessity of subduing again: and a nation is not governed which is perpetually to be conquered."

In his opposition to Tory policies against the rebelling American colonies, Burke spoke for the mainstream of Whig thought. It might naturally have been expected, then, that when the French Revolution began some fifteen years later, Burke would look favorably on it. To many English, Whigs especially, the early developments–the reluctance to submit to new taxation, the tennis-court oath, the move toward a written constitution–seemed to be an admirable continental version of their own Glorious Revolution. But Burke was, from the first, critical and suspicious of the happenings in France.

Burke had predicted such an event, 20 years earlier; in 1769 he had said: "Under such extreme straitness and distraction labors the whole of French finances, so far does their charge outrun their supply in every particular, that no man . . . who has considered their affairs with any degree of attention or information, but must hourly look for some extraordinary convulsion in that whole system; the effect of which on France, and even on all Europe, it is difficult to conjecture."[18]

When the convulsion finally came, Burke, who was then 60, had almost nothing good to say about it, and the rest of his life became one long campaign to dissuade the English from seeing this type of revolution as an acceptable means of political change. The greatest literary labor of his later years was the book *Reflections on the Revolution in France*, published in 1790, in which he argued that the French Revolution was a foolish and dangerous break in historical continuity. The French, he thought, had made the disastrous mistake of trying to create a new political order all at once, and on the basis of ideology. Their best prospect for bringing about political change, if it were necessary, would have been to retain as much of the current system as possible and build on it, using existing political institutions and social forms and the established religion wherever possible. Instead, Burke said, they had chosen to rely on the wild abstractions, the so-called "discoveries," of political theorists–he men-

[18] Edmund Burke, *Observations on the State of the Nation*, 1769.

tioned Rousseau, Voltaire, and Helvetius by name at one point, and at another referred in general terms to "the declamations and buffooneries of satirists" and "the polluted nonsense of their most licentious and giddy coffeehouses." Burke criticized not only the character of the revolution, but also the character of the revolutionaries; he described its leaders, with some accuracy, as being mainly provincial lawyers, who lacked breadth or depth of political experience.

Burke was naturally taken to task for inconsistency, in so strongly opposing the French Revolution when he had supported the American one, but there was actually a considerable continuity in the thinking that underlay the two different positions. The Americans, he believed, had developed a certain national character and social structure, and had obtained long experience in government in their various legislatures; the revised Tory taxation policies were an unwise attempt to tamper arbitrarily with what had become in fact an established political order in the colonies. The French, although possessing "in some parts the walls, and, in all, the foundations, of a noble and venerable castle," had neglected to preserve their heritage; their revolution was "a revolution of doctrine and theoretic dogma," and its leaders were a "college of armed fanatics."

The important thing, for Burke, was tradition. He was inclined to believe that any political system that had held up over time was demonstrably acceptable to a country, and the fact that people could live with it was more important than the abstract concept of the rights of man. The conventions that a society had developed over the course of time were the natural source of its laws and its political order. Thus, George Sabine argues, Burke's main political beliefs were at all times the same:

> . . . that political institutions form a vast and complicated system of prescriptive rights and customary observances, that these practices grow out of the past and adapt themselves in the present with no break in continuity, and that the tradition of the constitution and of society at large ought to be the object of a reverence akin to religion, because it forms the repository of a collective intelligence and civilization.[19]

Burke's stand on the French Revolution brought him into bitter conflict with members of his own party. It also brought him many new admirers; as time went on and the revolution progressed into the stage of the Terror, more and more people were persuaded of the rightness of his arguments. He died in 1797, and thus did not live to see how prophetic he had been in the closing pages of the Reflections, where he had written:

> In the weakness of one kind of authority, and in the fluctuation of all, the officers of an army will remain for some time mutinous and full of faction, until some popular general, who understands the art of conciliating the soldiery, and who possesses the true spirit of command, shall draw the eyes of all men upon himself. Armies will obey him on his personal account. But the moment in which that event shall happen, the person who really commands the army is your master; the master of your king, the master of your Assembly, the master of your whole republic. . . .

For all of Burke's professed dislike for abstract concepts, he employed many of them in his speeches and publications, and we can see in the body of his work a descent from some of Locke's ideas—especially the reverence for property—and also from Rousseau, of whom Burke disapproved. Like Rousseau, Burke saw society as a living, organic whole, and Rousseau's statement that people must be "forced to be free" is echoed in Burke's belief that "the restraints on men, as well as their liberties, are to be reckoned among their rights."

And, if the French Revolution had contributed something to the modern idea of patriotism, so did Burke in his opposition to it. The French had called for loyalty to la patrie; Burke called for loyalty to a body of traditions and working institutions, to a national history and an established social order. He set down a basic body of ideas that are still valued and quoted by American conservatives such as Russell Kirk, William Buckley, and Barry Goldwater. In addition, he did as much as any Englishman to articulate the philosophy of gradual change and of respect for traditional forms, which enabled that country, in the twentieth century, to venture into socialism without giving up monarchy.

---

[19] George H. Sabine, *A History of Political Theory.* (3rd ed.; New York: Holt, Rinehart and Winston Inc., 1963), p. 608.

EDMUND BURKE ON POLITICAL CHANGE

A state without the means of some change is without the means of its conservation. Without such means it might even risk the loss of that part of the constitution which it wished the most religiously to preserve. The two principles of conservation and correction operated strongly at the two critical periods of the English Restoration and Revolution. At both those periods the nation had lost the bond of union in their ancient edifice; they did not, however, dissolve the whole fabric. On the contrary, in both cases they regenerated the deficient part of the old constitution through the parts which were not impaired. They kept these old parts exactly as they were, that the part recovered might be suited to them.

A spirit of innovation is generally the result of a selfish temper and confined views. People will not look forward to posterity, who never look backward to their ancestors. Besides, the people of England well know that the idea of inheritance furnishes a sure principle of conservation, and a sure principle of transmission; without at all excluding a principle of improvement. In what we improve, we are never fully new; in what we retain, we are never wholly obsolete.

The science of constructing a commonwealth, or renovating it, or reforming it, is, like every other experimental science, not to be taught a priori. Nor can a short experience instruct us in that practical science, because the real effects of moral causes are not always immediate; that which in the first instance is prejudicial may be excellent in its remoter operation; and very plausible schemes, with very pleasing commencements, have often shameful and lamentable conclusions. The science of government being therefore a matter which requires experience, and even more experience than any person can gain in his whole life, however sagacious and observing he may be, it is with infinite caution that any man ought to venture to pull down an edifice which has answered in any tolerable degree for ages the common purposes of society, or to build it up again, without

From *Reflections on the Revolution in France* (1790). (Edited and abridged.)

having models and patterns of approved utility before his eyes.

To avoid the evils of inconstancy and versatility, which are ten thousand times worse than those of obstinacy and the blindest prejudice, we have consecrated the state, that no man should approach to look into its defects or corruptions but with due caution; that he should never dream of beginning its reformation by its subversion; that he should approach to the faults of the state as to the wounds of a father, with pious awe and trembling solicitude. By this wise prejudice we are taught to look with horror on those children of their country, who are prompt rashly to hack that aged parent in pieces, and put him into the kettle of magicians, in hopes that by their poisonous weeds, and wild incantations, they may regenerate the paternal constitution, and renovate their father's life.

Society is indeed a contract. Subordinate contracts for objects of mere occasional interest may be dissolved at pleasure—but the state ought not to be considered as nothing better than a partnership agreement in a trade of pepper and coffee, calico or tobacco, or some other such low concern, to be taken up for a little temporary interest, and to be dissolved by the fancy of the parties. It is to be looked on with other reference; because it is not a partnership in things subservient only to the gross animal existence of a temporary and perishable nature. It is a partnership in all science; a partnership in all art; a partnership in every virtue, and in all perfection. As the ends of such a partnership cannot be obtained in many generations, it becomes a partnership not only between those who are living, but between those who are living, those who are dead, and those who are yet to be born.

Rage and frenzy will pull down more in half an hour than prudence, deliberation, and foresight can build up in a hundred years. The errors and defects of old establishments are visible and palpable. It calls for little ability to point them out. The lazy but restless disposition, which loves sloth and hates quiet, directs the politicians, when they come to work to supply the place of what they have destroyed. To make everything the reverse of what they have seen is quite as easy as to destroy. No difficulties occur in what has never been tried. Criticism is almost baffled in discovering the defects of what has not existed; eager enthusiasm and cheating hope have a wide field, with little or no opposition.

At once to preserve and to reform is quite another thing. When the useful parts of an old establishment are kept, and what is superadded is fitted to what is retained, a vigorous mind, steady, perservering attention, various powers of comparison and combination, and an understanding fruitful in expedients, are to be exercised; they are to be exercised in continued conflict with the combined force of opposite vices: the obstinacy that rejects all improvement, and the levity that is fatigued and disgusted with everything of which it is in possession. But you may object—"A process of this kind is slow. It is not fit for an assembly which glories in performing in a few months the work of ages. Such a mode of reforming, possibly, might take up many years." Without question it might, and it ought. It is one of the excellences of a method in which time is among the assistants, that its operation is slow, and in some cases almost imperceptible. By a slow but well-sustained progress, the effect of each step is watched; the good or ill success of the first gives light to us in the second; and so, from light to light, we are conducted with safety through the whole series. We see that the parts of the system do not clash. The evils latent in the most promising contrivances are provided for as they arise. One advantage is as little as possible sacrificed to another. We compensate, we reconcile, we balance. We are enabled to unite into a consistent whole the various anomalies and contending principles that are found in the minds and affairs of men. From hence arises, not an excellence in simplicity, but one far superior, an excellence in composition. Where the great interests of mankind are concerned through a long succession of generations, that succession ought to be admitted into some share in the councils which are so deeply to affect them.

Alexis de Tocqueville

One of the favorite activities of nineteenth-century men of letters was visiting the United States, observing for a while, and then writing a book to regale civilized Europeans with accounts of the peculiarities of American behavior. Most literature of this genre was not especially memorable, but there is one such book—Alexis de Tocqueville's *Democracy in America*—that is still read and studied as a penetrating analysis of American society and democracy.

The young Frenchman's purpose in visiting America was not merely to take a look at native customs; Tocqueville was convinced that democracy was Europe's future, and he wanted to examine it firsthand:

It is not, then, merely to satisfy a legitimate curiosity that I have examined America; my wish has been to find there instruction by which we may ourselves profit. . . . In America I saw more than America; I sought there the image of democracy itself, with its inclinations, its character, its prejudices, and its passions, in order to learn what we have to fear or to hope from its progress.[20]

The America he visited in 1831–1832 was going through a major change that was in some ways more of a true revolution than the winning of independence from England had been. The Eastern aristocrats who had created and controlled the national government were being challenged by a variety of dissident political forces, and the conflict was changing the shape of many political institutions.

The most potent opposition to the dominant manufacturing and financial elites came from the states of the South and West. The West, in the early nineteenth century, meant the new states beyond the Alleghenies; these were steadily filling with settlers, and they practiced a more egalitarian form of government. The old states continued to hold onto various kinds of property qualifications for voting, but the new Western states were coming into the Union with universal white male suffrage. In 1828 Andrew Jackson, the hero of the "outs"—the workers, the small farmers, the old elites of the South, and the newly rich of the West—was elected President of the United States. The Jacksonian era brought in a host of changes: extensions of the voting franchise, rotation in office, appointment of political loyalists to government positions in the "spoils system," popular vote

[20] *Democracy in America*, trans. Henry Reeve (New Rochelle, N.Y.: Arlington House, 1966), Vol. I, pp. xlvi–xlvii.

on presidential electors, and nomination of presidential candidates in convention instead of by congressional caucus.

The Jacksonian era was not quite as clear a triumph of the common people as it is sometimes described. Jackson himself was a rich plantation owner, and the basic Jacksonian ideal seems to have been to allow a "natural" aristocracy of ability to compete with the entrenched aristocracy of wealth and social class—yet the drift of the times, with its relatively unpolished new leaders and the noisy hordes of new voters who carried them to power, was certainly egalitarian. This was the America to which Tocqueville came looking for an answer to the question: How does equality affect personal liberty? He hoped that, by knowing and understanding what was happening in America, the nations of Europe would be able to make democracy work. He did not argue that democracy was desirable; only that it was inevitable, and that the wise course of all civilization was to make the best of it:

I have not even pretended to judge whether the social revolution, which I believe to be irresistible, is advantageous or prejudicial to mankind. I have acknowledged this revolution as a fact already accomplished, or on the eve of its accomplishment; and I have selected the nation, from amongst those which have undergone it, in which its development has been the most peaceful and the most complete, in order to discern its natural consequences, and to find out, if possible, the means of rendering it profitable to mankind.[21]

Thus, *Democracy in America* was a kind of case study of democracy at work in one place at one period of time. As such, it was different from most of the discussions, from Plato onward, that had tended to speak of democracy as an abstract idea: Tocqueville was studying a specific experience.

The overwhelming reality of that experience, as he saw it, was equality: "Among the novel objects that attracted my attention during my stay in the United States," he wrote, "nothing struck me more forcibly than the general equality of condition among the people."

Although this process had proceeded furthest in America, it was not uniquely American; Tocqueville saw the history of all Western society, over a period of several centuries,

as one long march toward social equality. Among the things that had helped it along were the breaking-up of the feudal estates, the growth of towns, the invention of firearms and the printing press, the development of postal service, the spread of Protestantism, the new importance of finance and business, the development of nation-states and the attendant conflict between kings and nobles (the kings of France, he thought, had been great levelers), and the discovery of America. All of these things had contributed to the erosion of the rigid old class structures in which all people knew their exact places, and had brought in a new mass society in which class distinctions were shifting, unclear, and relatively unimportant.

But increasing equality did not necessarily mean increasing personal freedom, and Tocqueville thought it might even mean the reverse. In America he saw a new kind of tyranny: the tyranny of the majority. Any decision arrived at by the majority of the people had an overwhelming power over those in the minority. Dissent was rare. "I know of no country," he wrote, "in which there is so little true independence of mind and freedom of discussion as in America." The pressure against independence and freedom was not the official censorship of royal or clerical authority, but rather the weight of public opinion, the need to conform:

In America the majority raises very formidable barriers to the liberty of opinion; within these barriers an author may write whatever he pleases, but he will repent if he ever step beyond them. Not that he is exposed to the terrors of an auto-de-fe, but he is tormented by the slights and persecutions of daily obloquy. . . .[22]

What Tocqueville perceived was the enormous power that was available to an egalitarian, democratic society. Where so many of his contemporaries had seen democracy mainly in terms of the absence of older forms of power and had talked of it as a system of freedom, Tocqueville viewed it as a system of power.[23] Public opinion in an egalitarian society exerted power over the minds of individual members, and democratic government—drawing its strength from the majority—exerted power over individual citizens.

Tocqueville also came to the original conclusion that

[21] Ibid., p. xlvii.

[22] Robert A. Nisbet, *The Sociological Tradition* (New York: Basic Books, 1966).
[23] Ibid., p. 254.

there was a relationship between democracy and commercialism:

Men living in democratic times have many passions, but most of their passions either end in the love of riches or proceed from it. . . . When all the members of a community are independent of or indifferent to each other. the co-operation of each of them can be obtained only by paying for it; this infinitely multiplies the purposes to which wealth may be applied and increases its value. When the reverence that belonged to what is old has vanished, birth, condition and profession no longer distinguish men, or scarcely distinguish them; hardly anything but money remains to create strongly marked differences between them and to raise some of them above the common level.[24]

The above passage reflects Tocqueville's conviction that American society had no meaningful social classes. In their absence, the possession of money became one of the most important evidences of status: "The distinction originating in wealth is increased by the disappearance or diminution of all other distinctions." This was a more transient kind of status than that of hereditary nobility—an ambitious man could gain wealth in his own lifetime, and an unlucky or inept person born to wealth could lose it—but Tocqueville believed that a more permanent social stratification based on wealth might take form in America. He had described industrialization as one of the historical forces that had contributed to the growth of democratic equality, but he also saw that industrialization might in the course of time produce a new aristocracy—a manufacturing aristocracy.

This would come about in part through the debasement, the dehumanization, of the worker:

When a workman is unceasingly and exclusively engaged in the fabrication of one thing, he ultimately does his work with singular dexterity; but at the same time he loses the general faculty of applying his mind to the direction of his work. He every day becomes more adroit and less industrious; so that it may be said of him, that in proportion as the workman improves, the man is degraded. . . . He no longer belongs to himself, but to the calling he has chosen.[25]

[24] Ibid., p. 254.

[25] *Democracy in America*, Vol. 2 (London: Longmans, Green & Co., 1889), p. 144

The same process that debases the worker elevates the person who employs him:

Whereas the workman concentrates his faculties more and more upon the study of a single detail, the master surveys a more extensive whole, and the mind of the latter is enlarged in proportion as that of the former is narrowed. In a short time the one will require nothing but physical strength without intelligence; the other stands in need of science, and almost of genius, to ensure success. This man resembles more and more the administrator of a vast empire—that man, a brute. . . . Each of them fills the station which is made for him, and out of which he does not get: the one is continually, closely, and necessarily dependent upon the other, and seems as much born to obey as that other is to command. What is this but aristocracy?[26]

Although this was a kind of aristocracy, Tocqueville—who was himself descended from a noble family of Normandy—found it far inferior to the traditional sort. There was interdependence between the two classes, but it lacked the protective relationship wherein the master defended and cared for the workman. It was, Tocqueville thought, one of the harshest forms of aristocracy that had ever existed, and although its development had so far been quite limited, he warned against its future growth: "The friends of democracy should keep their eyes anxiously fixed in this direction; for if ever a permanent inequality of conditions and aristocracy again penetrate into the world, it may be predicted that this is the channel by which they will enter."

In general, he believed that there was small possibility of any future revolution in America. The general conditions of equality, the possession of property, and the general busyness of Americans all conspired against this—"Violent political passions have but little hold on those who have devoted all their faculties to the pursuit of their well being." Yet, there was a danger of intense political struggle if the new inequality should progress too far: "The political struggle will be restricted to those who have and those who have not; property will form the great field of battle." Another potential source of upheaval was a class that so far had not participated in the equalizing process he described: the slaves. Nor did he believe that ending slavery would eliminate the

[26] Ibid., p. 145.

danger of racial conflict:

I am obliged to confess that I do not regard the abolition of slavery as a means of warding off the struggle of the two races in the Southern states. The Negroes may long remain slaves without complaining; but if they are once raised to the level of freemen, they will soon revolt at being deprived of almost all their civil rights; and as they cannot become the equals of the whites, they will speedily show themselves as enemies.[27]

Tocqueville's predictions about future developments in democratic America were, on the whole, remarkably accurate, and modern readers are often amazed at such things as his speculation that America and Russia—then both second-rate powers—would emerge as the two dominant nations of world politics.

One of the most outstanding things about Tocqueville is the view he took of the nature of the changes that were then taking place in society. He talked not only about an Industrial Revolution, an American Revolution, a French Revolution, but also about a "social revolution" that included them all. In his writings he made no attempt to separate American economic life from American social and political life; the trend toward egalitarian, commercialized, industrialized mass democracy was, to him, all one process. The form of this process was not yet evident to Americans themselves, but Tocqueville saw it and took it to be not only the future of America but the norm of social change for Western civilization.

ALEXIS DE TOCQUEVILLE ON THE DESPOTISM OF EQUALITY

No sovereign ever lived in former ages so absolute or so powerful as to undertake to administer by his own agency, and without the assistance of intermediate powers, all the parts of a great empire: none ever attempted to subject all his subjects indiscriminately to strict uniformity of regulation, and personally to tutor

---

[27] *Democracy in America,* Vol. 1, p. 372.

From *Democracy in America,* vol. 2, pp. 288–92.

and direct every member of the community. The notion of such an undertaking never occurred to the human mind; and if any man had conceived it, the want of information, the imperfection of the administrative system, and, above all, the natural obstacles caused by the inequality of conditions, would speedily have checked the execution of so vast a design.

When the Roman emperors were at the height of their power, the different nations of the empire still preserved manners and customs of great diversity; although they were subject to the same monarch, most of the provinces were separately administered; they abounded in powerful and active municipalities; and although the whole government of the empire was centred in the hands of the emperor alone, and he always remained, in case of need, the supreme arbiter in all matters, yet the details of social life and private occupations lay for the most part beyond his control. The emperors possessed, it is true, an immense and unchecked power, which allowed them to gratify all their whimsical tastes, and to employ for that purpose the whole strength of the state. They frequently abused that power arbitrarily to deprive their subjects of property or of life: their tyranny was extremely onerous to the few, but it did not reach the many; it was fixed to some few main objects, and neglected the rest; it was violent, but its range was limited.

It would seem that, if despotism were to be established amongst the democratic nations of our days, it might assume a different character; it would be more extensive and more mild; it would degrade men without tormenting them. I do not question, that, in an age of instruction and equality like our own, sovereigns might more easily succeed in collecting all political power into their own hands, and might interfere more habitually and decidedly with the circle of private interests, than any sovereign of antiquity could ever do. But this same principle of equality which facilitates despotism, tempers its rigor. We have seen how the manners of society become more humane and gentle, in proportion as men become more equal and alike. When no member of the community has much power or much wealth, tyranny is, as it were, without opportunities and a field of action. As all fortunes are scanty, the passions of men are naturally circumscribed, their imagination moderates the sovereign himself, and checks within certain limits the inordinate stretch of his desires.

Independently of these reasons, drawn from the nature of the state of society itself, I might add many others arising from causes beyond my subject; but I shall keep within the limits I have laid down.

Democratic governments may become violent, and even cruel, at certain periods of extreme effervescence or of great danger; but these crises will be rare and brief. When I consider the petty passions of our contemporaries, the mildness of their manners, the extent of their education, the purity of their religion, the gentleness of their morality, their regular and industrious habits, and the restraint which they almost all observe in their vices no less than in their virtues, I have no fear that they will meet with tyrants in their rulers, but rather with guardians.

I think, then, that the species of oppression by which democratic nations are menaced is unlike anything which ever before existed in the world: our contemporaries will find no prototype of it in their memories. I seek in vain for an expression which will accurately convey the whole of the idea I have formed of it; the old words despotism and tyranny are inappropriate: the thing itself is new, and since I cannot name, I must attempt to define it.

I seek to trace the novel features under which despotism may appear in the world. The first thing that strikes the observation is an innumerable multitude of men, all equal and alike, incessantly endeavoring to procure the petty and paltry pleasures with which they glut their lives. Each of them, living apart, is as a stranger to the fate of all the rest—his children and his private friends constitute to him the whole of mankind; as for the rest of his fellow-citizens, he is close to them, but he sees them not; he touches them, but he feels them not; he exists but in himself and for himself alone; and if his kindred still remain to him, he may be said at any rate to have lost his country.

Above the race of men stands an immense and tutelary power, which takes upon itself alone to secure their gratifications, and to watch over their fate. That power is absolute, minute, regular, provident, and mild.

It would be like the authority of a parent, if, like that authority, its object was to prepare men for manhood; but it seeks, on the contrary, to keep them in perpetual childhood: it is well content that the people should rejoice, provided they think of nothing but rejoicing. For their happiness such a government willingly labors, but it chooses to be the sole agent and the only arbiter of that happiness; it provides for their security, foresees and supplies their necessities, facilitates their pleasures, manages their principal concerns, directs their industry, regulates the descent of property, and subdivides their inheritances: what remains, but to spare them all the care of thinking and all the trouble of living?

Thus, it every day renders the exercise of the free agency of man less useful and less frequent; it circumscribes the will within a narrower range, and gradually robs a man of all the uses of himself. The principle of equality has prepared men for these things; it has predisposed men to endure them, and oftentimes to look on them as benefits.

After having thus successively taken each member of the community in its powerful grasp, and fashioned him at will, the supreme power then extends its arm over the whole community. It covers the surface of society with a network of small complicated rules, minute and uniform, through which the most original minds and the most energetic characters cannot penetrate, to rise above the crowd. The will of man is not shattered, but softened, bent, and guided; men are seldom forced by it to act, but they are constantly restrained from acting: such a power does not destroy, but it prevents existence; it does not tyrannize, but it compresses, enervates, extinguishes, and stupefies a people, till each nation is reduced to be nothing better than a flock of timid and industrious animals, of which the government is the shepherd.

I have always thought that servitude of the regular, quiet, and gentle kind which I have just described might be combined more easily than is commonly believed with some of the outward forms of freedom, and that it might even establish itself under the wing of the sovereignty of the people.

Our contemporaries are constantly excited by two conflicting passions; they want to be led, and they wish to remain free: as they cannot destroy either the one or the other of these contrary propensities, they strive to satisfy them both at once. They devise a sole, tutelary, and all-powerful form of government, but elected by the people. They combine the principle of centralization and that of popular sovereignty; this gives them a respite: they console themselves for being in tutelage by the reflection that they have chosen their own guardians. Every man allows himself to be put in leading-strings, because he sees that it is not a person or a class of persons but the people at large, who hold the end of his chain.

By this system, the people shake off their state of dependence just long enough to select their master, and then relapse into it again. A great many persons at the present day are quite contented with this sort of compromise between administrative despotism and the sovereignty of the people; and they think they have done enough for the protection of individual freedom when they have surrendered it to the power of the nation at large.

ALEXIS DE TOCQUEVILLE ON DEMOCRATIC ARMIES

In democratic armies, all the soldiers may become officers, which makes the desire of promotion general, and immeasurably extends the bounds of military ambition. The officer, on his part, sees nothing which naturally and necessarily stops him at one grade more than at another; and each grade has immense importance in his eyes, because his rank in society almost always depends on his rank in the army. Amongst democratic nations, it often happens that an officer has no property but his pay, and no distinction but that of military honors: consequently, as often as his duties change his fortune changes, and he becomes, as it were, a new man. What was only an appendage to his position in aristocratic armies, has thus become the main point, the basis of his whole condition.

Under the old French monarchy, officers were always called by their titles of nobility; they are now

From *Democracy in America*, Vol. 2., pp. 242–44. (Edited and abridged.)

always called by the title of their military rank. This little change in the forms of language suffices to show that a great revolution has taken place in the constitution of society and in that of the army.

In democratic armies, the desire of advancement is almost universal: It is ardent, tenacious, perpetual; it is strengthened by all other desires, and only extinguished with life itself. But it is easy to see, that, of all armies in the world, those in which advancement must be slowest in time of peace are the armies of democratic countries. As the number of commissions is naturally limited, whilst the number of competitors is almost unlimited, and as the strict law of equality is over all alike, none can make rapid progress—many can make no progress at all. Thus, the desire of advancement is greater, and the opportunities of advancement fewer there than elsewhere. All the ambitious spirits of a democratic army are consequently ardently desirous of war, because war makes vacancies, and warrants the violation of that law of seniority which is the sole privilege natural to democracy.

We thus arrive at this singular consequence, that, of all armies, those most ardently desirous of war are democratic armies, and of all nations, those most fond of peace are democratic nations; and what makes these facts still more extraordinary is, that these contrary effects are produced at the same time by the principle of equality.

All the members of the community, being alike, constantly harbor the wish and discover the possibility of changing their condition and improving their welfare: this makes them fond of peace, which is favorable to industry, and allows every man to pursue his own little undertakings to their completion. On the other hand, this same equality makes soldiers dream of fields of battle, by increasing the value of military honors in the eyes of those who follow the profession of arms, and by rendering those honors accessible to all. In either case, the inquietude of the heart is the same, the taste for enjoyment as insatiable, the ambition of success as great—the means of gratifying it alone are different.

These opposite tendencies of the nation and the army expose democratic communities to great dangers. When a military spirit forsakes a people, the profession of arms immediately ceases to be held in honor, and military men fall to the lowest rank of the public servants: They are little esteemed, and no longer understood. The reverse of what takes place in aristocratic ages then occurs; the men who enter the army are no longer those of the highest, but of the lowest rank. Military ambition is only indulged when no other is possible. Hence arises a circle of cause and consequence from which it is difficult to escape: The best part of the nation shuns the military profession because that profession is not honored, and the profession is not honored because the best part of the nation has ceased to follow it.

It is then no matter of surprise that democratic armies are often restless, ill-tempered, and dissatisfied with their lot, although their physical condition is commonly far better, and their discipline less strict, than in other countries. The soldier feels that he occupies an inferior position, and his wounded pride either stimulates his taste for hostilities which would render his services necessary, or gives him a desire for revolution, during which he may hope to win by force of arms the political influence and personal importance now denied him.

The army, taken collectively, eventually forms a small nation by itself, where the mind is less enlarged, and habits are more rude, than in the nation at large. Now, this small uncivilized nation has arms in its possession, and alone knows how to use them; for, indeed, the pacific temper of the community increases the danger to which a democratic people is exposed from the military and turbulent spirit of the army. Nothing is so dangerous as an army amidst an unwarlike nation; the excessive love of the whole community for quiet continually puts the constitution at the mercy of the soldiery.

It may therefore be asserted, generally speaking, that, if democratic nations are naturally prone to peace from their interests and their propensities, they are constantly drawn to war and revolutions by their armies. Military revolutions, which are scarcely ever to be apprehended in aristocracies, are always to be dreaded amongst democratic nations. These perils must be reckoned amongst the most formidable which beset their future fate, and the attention of statesmen should be sedulously applied to find a remedy for the evil.

John Stuart Mill

When Tocqueville's *Democracy in America* was published in England, it had an immediate and rather curious success. It was taken up by leading conservatives, who liked the sound of the phrase "tyranny of the majority," and who saw the work as a warning to the world about the dangers of too much equality; but it was also praised by John Stuart Mill, who proceeded in his own writing to transform some of Tocqueville's ideas about personal freedom in mass society into concepts that are fundamental to modern liberalism.

Mill himself, the inheritor of a long tradition of liberal thought, was the product of a rather authoritarian upbringing, deliberately designed to train him to be a liberal philosopher. His father, James Mill, had been a disciple of Jeremy Bentham, the great theorist of English utilitarianism, and the elder Mill put his promising young son through a rigorous education that had him studying Greek at three and political economy at 13. The aim was to make J. S. Mill the next generation's great advocate of utilitarianism; it was mainly successful, although it did not work out precisely as James Mill had planned. John went through a severe emotional crisis when he was about 20, and in the process of recovering developed a taste for romantic poetry, which remained one of the great interests of his life. He continued in his writing to remain nominally faithful to utilitarian doctrine, but actually his own thinking took him considerably afield of the basic utilitarian formula of the greatest happiness for the greatest number. The work for which he is known best is in defense of the rights of the individual. Like Tocqueville, he feared the repressive possibilities of democracy, and although he was strongly in favor of the reform bills of 1832 and 1867, which extended the voting franchise in England well into the working classes, he never agreed with those who tended to equate egalitarianism with freedom. In his essay on Tocqueville he expressed his own fear of a new kind of authority that seemed to emerge in egalitarian societies—the authority of numbers: "The more perfectly each knows himself the equal of every single individual, the more insignificant and helpless he feels against the aggregate mass, and the more incredible it appears to him that the opinion of all the world can possibly be erroneous." He followed that observation of his own by quoting Tocqueville: "Faith in public opinion becomes . . . a species of religion, and the majority its prophet." This problem of how to preserve the integrity of the individual's right to think and speak freely in a mass society became one of Mill's main concerns; it was closely related to his conviction that the society could not long survive without such freedom, that the liberty of individuals to inquire, think, discuss, and dissent was the chief source of the vitality of the whole community.

In this respect, the kind of democracy that Mill hoped for—a state in which every opinion would be regarded as provisional and fallible, subject to modification in the light of experience and new data, and open always to the ideas of dissenters and heretics and lonely thinkers—was far different from Rousseau's concept of the unified state guided by the wisdom of the general will, its individual members "forced to be free" and to realize themselves in harmony with the organic whole.

The emphasis that both Tocqueville and Mill placed on public opinion was evidence of the growing tendency of political thinkers to make a distinction between society and government. The danger of political tyranny—of overt actions of repression by the legal institutions of the state—was real, but it was less insidious and less pervasive than the social tyranny that could enslave not merely the body but, as Mill put it, "the soul itself."

Mill's *On Liberty* (1859) argued the necessity and value of freedom, and offered a fundamental rule "to govern absolutely the dealings of society with the individual in the way of compulsion and control." The rule:

. . . *that the sole end for which mankind are warranted, individually or collectively, in interfering with the liberty of action of any of their number, is self-protection. The only purpose for which power can be rightfully exercised over any member of a civilized community, against his will, is to prevent harm to others. His own good, either physical or moral, is not a sufficient warrant. He cannot rightfully be compelled to do or forbear because it will be better for him to do so, because it will make him happier, because, in the opinions of others, to do so would be wise, or even right. These are good reasons for remonstrating with him, or*

reasoning with him, or persuading him, or entreating him, but not for compelling him, or visiting him with any evil, in case he do otherwise. To justify that, the conduct from which it is desired to deter him must be calculated to produce evil to some one else. The only part of the conduct of any one, for which he is amenable to society, is that which concerns others. In the part which merely concerns himself, his independence is, of right, absolute. Over himself, over his own body and mind, the individual is sovereign.

There were, it should be noted, some qualifications: Mill meant the rule to apply only in the case of adults, not to "those who are still in a state to require being taken care of by others," and he meant it to apply only to civilized nations, not to the "backward states of society." In the case of the latter, he spoke with the voice of the British empire, whose interests he had served for more than 30 years as an employee of the East India Company: "Despotism is a legitimate mode of government in dealing with barbarians, provided the end be their improvement, and the means justified by actually effecting that end." His principles of freedom were in response to, and designed for, developed democratic societies.

Although Mill does not shine forth from history as a leading defender of colonial peoples, he does stand as one of the few political thinkers of his or any other era who took note of the situation of one of the other great masses of people who had been left behind by democracy: women. Many of Mill's friends in English intellectual circles were friendly toward the growing women's suffrage movement, and in 1851 his wife, Harriet Taylor Mill (whose assistance and advice in much of his later work appears to have amounted to virtual collaboration[28]) published an essay of her own arguing the case for enfranchisement of women. A few years after her death Mill went to work on his *The Subjection of Women*, which was published in 1869; it was widely read in its own time, then ignored by most scholars of political philosophy for decades, and revived again in recent years as one of the classic arguments of women's liberation.

---

[28] See Alice S. Rossi, introduction to John Stuart Mill and Harriet Taylor Mill, *Essays on Sex Equality* (Chicago: University of Chicago Press, 1970).

In *The Subjection of Women,* Mill argued that civilization's massive march toward equality had completely bypassed the female sex, creating an enormous political and social anachronism:

The social subordination of women thus stands out an isolated fact in modern social institutions; a solitary breach of what has become their fundamental law; a single relic of an old world of thought and practice exploded in everything else. . . . [29]

Mill, whom an admirer once called the "saint of rationalism," attacked the issue on logical grounds: There was simply no empirical proof of an inherent deficiency in the character of women that could justify their being kept in a subordinate position. He called for greater equality in marriage, for greater opportunity for women to express themselves in social roles other than that of wife and mother, and for women to be given the right to vote. During the brief period that he served as a member of Parliament in the 1860s, he not only advocated extending suffrage to the working class but also introduced an amendment to the Reform Bill, which would have substituted the word "person" for the word "man." (The amendment, considered ridiculous by most of the gentlemen in the House of Commons, did not pass, but Mill did manage to win 73 votes in its favor.)

Mill believed that thinking citizens in a democracy had to keep putting their opinions to the test, shaping them in the light of other viewpoints and new data—and his own life work, taken as a whole, shows much of this kind of change and evolution; it does not stand as a single, monolithic set of ideas. We can see, for example, a concern for governmental reform (the main aim of the Benthamist utilitarian tradition), which was modified by—or perhaps was in conflict with—a growing desire for deeper changes in the social order. We can see a lifelong dedication to extension of suffrage, yet serious misgivings about the dangers to personal liberty that seemed to be inherent in mass democracy. In the sphere of economics, we can see a transition from classic laissez faire thinking to an interest in socialism. [30]

If Mill failed to resolve some of the conflicts in his thinking about democracy, it should be said in fairness to him that most democracies have not resolved them, either. The problem of individual freedom in mass society is still with us. Like Tocqueville, Mill recognized the problem and tried to confront it squarely. As an advocate of democracy, he was willing to take a hard look at the dangers along the way; he did not deceive himself that democracy necessarily produced community, and he seems to have been willing to accept alienation as part of the price of freedom. He belongs to a continuum of liberal-radical thought, which goes back to the *philosophes* of the Enlightenment and is still alive in our own time. And yet the individualism that he championed is also an important element in certain strains of modern conservative thought. Modern conservatives of the libertarian persuasion often quote him, and conservative critics of the modern welfare state would agree with Mill's concern for the individual:

A government cannot have too much of the kind of activity which does not impede, but aids and stimulates, individual exertion and development. The mischief begins when, instead of informing, advising, and, upon occasion, denouncing, it makes them work in fetters or bids them stand aside and does their work for them. The worth of a State, in the long run, is the worth of the individuals composing it. . . . A State which dwarfs its men, in order that they may be more docile instruments in its hands even for beneficial purposes, will find that with small men no great thing can really be accomplished; and that the perfection of machinery to which it has sacrificed everything, will in the end avail it nothing. . . . [31]

JOHN STUART MILL ON FREEDOM OF OPINION

The time, it is to be hoped, is gone by when any defense would be necessary of the "liberty of the press" as one of the securities against corrupt or tyrannical government. There is little danger of the law of England being put in force against political discussion, except during some temporary panic, when fear of insurrection drives ministers and judges from their propriety. Gener-

[29] John Stuart Mill, *The Subjection of Women.*

[30] Mill's *Chapters on Socialism,* published posthumously, advocated a rational, non-revolutionary assessment of the benefits of socialism through the establishment of experimental socialistic communities.

[31] Mill, *On Liberty* (1859).

From *On Liberty* (1859). (Edited and abridged.)

ally speaking it is not to be expected that, in constitutional countries, government will attempt to control the expression of opinion except when in doing so it makes itself the organ of the general intolerance of the public; we may suppose that such government is entirely at one with the people, and never thinks of exerting any power of coercion unless in agreement with what it conceives to be their voice.

But I deny the right of the people to exercise such coercion, either by themselves or by their government. The power itself is illegitimate. The best government has no more title to it than the worst. It is as noxious, or more noxious, when exerted in accordance with public opinion, than when in opposition to it. If all mankind minus one were of one opinion, and only one person were of the contrary opinion, mankind would be no more justified in silencing that one person than he, if he had the power, would be justified in silencing mankind.

The peculiar evil of silencing the expression of an opinion is that it is robbing the human race; posterity as well as the existing generation; those who dissent from the opinion still more than those who hold it. If the opinion is right they are deprived of the opportunity of exchanging error for truth; if wrong, they lose what is almost as great a benefit, the clearer perception and livelier impression of truth produced by its collision with error.

Those who desire to suppress an opinion of course deny its truth; but they are not infallible. They have no authority to decide the question for all mankind, and exclude every other person from the means of judging. To refuse a hearing to an opinion because they are sure that it is false, is to assume that *their* certainty is the same thing as *absolute* certainty. All silencing of discussion is an assumption of infallibility. If condemnation may be allowed to rest on this common argument, not the worse for being common.

While everyone knows himself to be fallible, few think it necessary to take any precautions against their own fallibility or admit the supposition that any opinion, of which they feel very certain, may be one of the examples of the error to which they acknowledge themselves to be liable. Absolute princes, or others who are accustomed to unlimited deference, usually feel this complete confidence in their own opinions on nearly all subjects. People who sometimes hear their opinions disputed place the same reliance on such of their opinions as are shared by all who surround them or to whom they habitually defer: in proportion to a man's want of confidence in his own solitary judgement, he usually places implicit trust in the infallibility of "the world" in general. And the world, to each individual, means the part of it with which he comes in contact; his party, his sect, his church, his class of society; the man to whom it means anything so comprehensive as his own country or his own age may be called by comparison almost liberal and large-minded.

Nor is his faith in this collective authority at all shaken by being aware that other ages, countries, sects, churches, classes, and parties have thought, and even now think, the exact reverse. It never troubles him that mere accident has decided which of these numerous worlds is the object of his reliance, and that the same causes which make him a Churchman in London would have made him a Buddhist or a Confucian in Peking. Yet it is evident that ages are no more infallible than individuals, every age having held many opinions which subsequent ages have deemed not only false but absurd.

It is strange that men should admit the validity of the arguments for free discussion but object to their being "pushed to an extreme," not seeing that unless the reasons are good for an extreme case they are not good for any case. Strange that they should imagine that they are not assuming infallibility when they acknowledge that there should be free discussion on all subjects which can possibly be *doubtful,* but think that some particular principle or doctrine should be forbidden to be questioned because it is *so certain,* that is, because *they are certain* that it is certain. To call any proposition certain is to assume that we ourselves, and those who agree with us, are the judges of certainty.

In the present age, which has been described as "destitute of faith, but terrified at scepticism"—in which people feel sure, not so much that their opinions are true, as that they should not know what to do without them—the claims of an opinion to be protected from public attack are rested not so much on its truth as on its importance to society. There are, it is alleged, certain beliefs, so useful, not to say indispensable to well-being, that it is as much the duty of governments to uphold those beliefs, as to protect any other of the interests of society. It is maintained that in a case of such necessity something less than infallibility may warrant governments to act on their own opinion, confirmed by the general opinion of mankind. It is also often argued, and still oftener thought, that none but bad men would desire to weaken these salutary beliefs, and that there can be nothing wrong in restraining bad men. This mode of thinking makes the justification of restraints on discussion not a question of the truth of doctrines, but of their usefulness; and flatters itself by that means to escape the responsibility of claiming to be an infallible judge of opinions. But those who thus satisfy themselves do not perceive that the assumption of infallibility is merely shifted from one point to another. The usefulness of an opinion is itself a matter of opinion; as disputable, as open to discussion and requiring discussion as much, as the opinion itself.

JOHN STUART MILL ON SEXUAL INEQUALITY

Standing on the ground of common sense and the constitution of the human mind, I deny that any one knows, or can know, the nature of the two sexes, as long as they have only been seen in their present relation to one another. If men had ever been found in society without women, or women without men, or if there had been a society of men and women in which the women were not under the control of the men, something might have been positively known about the mental and moral differences which may be inherent in the nature of each. What is now called the nature of women is an eminently artificial thing—the result of forced repression in some directions, unnatural stimulation in others. It may be asserted without scruple, that no other class of dependents have had their character so entirely

From *The Subjection of Women* (1869.)

distorted from its natural proportions by their relation with their masters; for, if conquered and slave races have been, in some respects, more forcibly repressed, whatever in them has not been crushed down by an iron heel has generally been let alone, and if left with any liberty of development, it has developed itself according to its own laws; but in the case of women, a hot-house and stove cultivation has always been carried on of some of the capabilities of their nature, for the benefit and pleasure of their masters. Then, because certain products of the general vital force sprout luxuriantly and reach a great development in this heated atmosphere and under this active nurture and watering, while other shoots from the same root, which are left outside in the wintry air, with ice purposely heaped all round them, have a stunted growth, and some are burnt off with fire and disappear; men, with that inability to recognise their own work which distinguishes the unanalytic mind, indolently believe that the tree grows of itself in the way they have made it grow, and that it would die if one half of it were not kept in a vapour bath and the other half in the snow.

G. W. F. Hegel

The conservative nationalistic tradition—a line of thought that can be traced through Machiavelli's belief in the necessity of national unity, Rousseau's romantic search for community, and Burke's reverence for established institutions—culminated in the work of Georg Wilhelm Friedrich Hegel, in the philosophy that is sometimes described as "the cult of the state."

Germany, Hegel's homeland (he was born in Stuttgart in 1770), was slow to take form as a single nation-state, although it did have a common language and a common culture. During the Napoleonic era there was a Confederation of the Rhine, in which several German states were combined under French control, and after Napoleon's defeat a German Confederation, with 37 member states, was created. This was a loose organization, made up mostly of small principalities and dominated by its two most powerful members, Austria and Prussia; its main source of unity was the common desire of German princes to perpetuate the institution of hereditary monarchy and to protect their subjects from exposure to revolutionary political ideas. As German nationalistic sentiments began to develop, they were usually expressed in authoritarian, rather than democratic, terms; it was assumed that the nation would have to be united under some powerful leader. At first Austria—whose chancellor, Prince Metternich, was guiding the monarchies of Europe in their campaign to restore the pre-revolutionary status quo—was the chief hope of the nationalists; later, attention began to shift toward Prussia, the state that ultimately succeeded in creating a German nation.

German nationalism was for some time more of an intellectual and artistic force than a political one. It appeared in Herder's romantic search for the cultural unity of the German *volk,* in the Grimm brothers' rediscovery of German mythology, in poetry and drama and music. In 1810 the philosopher Johann Fichte gave his famous *Addresses to the German Nation,* in which he offered various historical evidence to prove the superiority of the German race and culture. In the work of Hegel, this growing nationalistic mystique became the dominant theme of an entire philosophical system.

Hegel in his youth had admired the radical revolutionaries of France, and later he was awed by the power of Napoleon. He was a professor at the University of Jena, the town where Napoleon's forces achieved a major victory over the Prussian army, and he wrote: "I saw the Emperor, that world-soul, riding through the city to reconnoiter. It is in truth a strange feeling to see such an individual before one, who here, from this point, as he rides his horse, is reaching over the world, and remoulding it." Later he was a professor at Heidelberg, and in 1818 he went to the new university in Berlin, the capital of Prussia. He remained at Berlin until his death in 1831, and became an enormously influential figure in German intellectual life, one of the great ornaments of the Prussian state that he so faithfully supported.

Hegel's voluminous works ranged over a wide variety of subjects, but the keystone of the whole system was a philosophy of history. History became, for Hegel, a method of unifying religion, politics, and science: history was the unfolding of divine will, the means by which the underlying principles of human actions could be understood. Although Hegel's work predated that of Darwin, it dealt with a certain kind of evolution—the continuing change and progress of societies. The "dialectic" was the intellectual apparatus that Hegel devised for understanding this progress. In the dialectic, every tendency or line of historical development is seen as creating an opposite or antithetical tendency; the two forces come into conflict, and out of this emerges a synthesis or new line of development, which in its turn creates a new conflict leading to a still higher level of development.

The new conservative movement of which Hegel was a part used the dialectical method as a logic of reaction. The revolutionary surge of the eighteenth century had represented one trend of history; now the rediscovery of ancient and deep cultural traditions was moving into conflict with that trend, attempting to conquer it and produce a higher level of consciousness. And whenever Hegel looked at historical developments, he saw the unfolding of a wisdom far beyond that of mere individual human beings; he used such terms as the Idea, ultimate self, universal mind, and, frequently, God. The state, he said, was "the march of God in the world." Obviously, individuals were of little importance in such a perspective, except insofar as they could realize themselves by falling into step with a great historical process.

"Political genius," Hegel once said, "consists in identifying yourself with a principle." Thus, it becomes clear how, even after he became anti-Napoleonic, Hegel could still see Napoleon as a "world-soul," a kind of embodiment of history, and it is also understandable why Hegel felt a bond with Machiavelli's dream of a great leader who would forge Italy into nationhood. He called Machiavelli's *The Prince* "the great and true conception of a real political genius with the highest and noblest purpose." In the sixteenth century, Machiavelli had seen conventional morality as a kind of personal luxury, which might have to be sacrificed in the interests of national unity. In the nineteenth century, Hegel subordinated all personal interests to national sovereignty and also argued that states, being sovereign, could not be expected to be bound by international law in their relations with one another.

Hegel's system assigned a momentous role to Germany in the march of world history. Just as an individual could attain greatness by discovering a role in history, so could a state embody a greater historical process. Hegel conceived of history in terms of stages of development of human consciousness and human freedom; at each stage, progress

was manifest in certain "world-historical" nations. He identified the major "realms" of history as the Oriental, the
Greek, the Roman, and the Germanic. During the Germanic
realm, which began with the rise of Christianity, humanity
passed through three stages: the first culminated in the
secular-spiritual unity of Christendom; the second, which
occurred during the Middle Ages, brought the beginnings
of the nation-states and the secularization of the church;
the third saw the state achieve full realization of itself as
the will of God and the actualization of the rational mind.

Hegel viewed the emergence of the modern nation-state
as the highest attainment of personal freedom, but it must
be understood that his concept of freedom was far different
from the liberal interpretation. Political theorists generally
define this difference in terms of "negative" and "positive"
senses of freedom. Isaiah Berlin has described negative freedom as being involved in the answer to the question: "What
is the area within which the subject—a person or group
of persons—is or should be left to do or be what he is
able to do or be, without interference from other persons?"
Positive freedom is involved in the answer to another question: "What, or who, is the source of control or interference
that can determine someone to do, or be, this rather than
that?"[32]

The positive sense of freedom is generally associated
with philosophers such as Rousseau, who saw society as
an organism that united its individual members into a whole
greater than themselves; most of all, it is associated with
Hegel:

*Few political theorists have attributed to the concept and idea of
freedom the centrality which it possesses in Hegel's political system
and in his theory of history. Indeed, according to Hegel, the history
of the world must be understood in terms of its progress toward
freedom. Although Hegel sometimes uses the concept in a way which
commends it to the liberal tradition, the real meaning of the concept
is precisely antithetical to the liberal's use. Freedom, according to
Hegel, does not consist merely in the absence of external restraints
and coercion. It does not mean merely the freedom that an individual
may have to do what he wills with his own faculties and his
own possessions; it means rather that the individual is obliged by
virtue of the fundamental laws of his own nature and existence
to develop those moral and intellectual and spiritual powers which
are his by nature.*[33]

For Hegel, true personal development—and hence true
freedom—was only possible in relation to the state, which
was the highest manifestation of the rational mind and, in
fact, the will of God. Citizenship in the nation-state was
a form of personal salvation.

Although it is not clear exactly what aspirations Hegel
had for the future of Germany, it is obvious that much
of the history of that nation in the nineteenth and twentieth
centuries has moved in a Hegelian spirit of predestination
for world greatness.

The emergence of Germany was one of the most remarkable transformations in European history. There had
been more than 300 German states at the time of the French
Revolution, but few of the small entities could withstand
the Napoleonic wars, the growing popular spirit of nationalism, and the efforts of the great monarchies to become still
greater. The number of German states was down into the
thirties by 1815, and consolidation proceeded more rapidly
after a war between Austria and Prussia settled the question
of who would dominate the new Germany; the Prussian
military machine quickly subdued Austrian forces in the
so-called Seven Weeks' War, and out of the peace settlement
emerged a new North German Confederation, dominated
by Prussia. A few years later France was defeated in the
Franco-Prussian war, and the states of Bavaria, Württemberg,
Baden, and Hesse-Darmstadt also became parts of the powerful new German nation. In 1871 the King of Prussia, Wilhelm I, was crowned Emperor of Germany. Industrialization
proceeded with amazing speed in Germany during the later
part of the century, adding another element of strength to
Germany's nationalistic spirit and military might. It took
two World Wars and the industrial resources of the United
States to prevent Germany from controlling most of Europe.

Hegelian philosophy, which was extremely pervasive
in the German academic world, made an important contribution to the spirit of German nationalism: it gave nationalism
a broad and impressive intellectual foundation. Many people

---

[32] Isaiah Berlin, *Four Essays on Liberty* (London: Oxford University Press,
1969), pp. 121–22.

[33] Joseph S. Murphy, *Political Theory: A Conceptual Analysis* (Homewood, Ill:
Dorsey, 1968), p. 160.

have argued that Hegelian philosophy performed a similar favor for fascism. "Though garbed in high-sounding philosophical terms," William Ebenstein writes, "Hegel's political theory . . . contains all essential elements of fascism: racialism, nationalism, the leadership principle, government by authority rather than consent, and, above all, the idolization of power as the supreme test of human values."[34] Others, such as Herbert Marcuse, have argued that Hegel's philosophy was of a different order—that its conservative respect for established institutions, legitimate authority, and gradual change were antithetical to the revolutionary pseudo-democracy of fascism.[35]

Hegel himself believed that his philosophical system and the nationalistic political ideas he derived by it were an integral whole. But the history of philosophy has its ironies: Not long after Hegel's death one young student of his philosophy, Karl Marx, took the Hegelian dialectic and turned it into a logic of international communist revolution.

G. W. F. HEGEL ON THE STATE

The state in and by itself is the ethical whole, the actualization of freedom; and it is an absolute end of reason that freedom should be actual. The state is mind on earth and consciously realizing itself there. The march of God in the world, that is what the state is.

How often we talk of the wisdom of God in nature! But we must not assume that the physical world of nature is a loftier thing than the world of mind; and as high as mind stands above nature, so high does the state stand above physical life. Man must therefore venerate the state as a secular diety and observe that if it is difficult to comprehend nature, it is infinitely harder to comprehend the state. Nowadays we have gained an intuition into the state in general and have been much engaged in discussing and making constitutions, but we have not

[34] William Ebenstein, op cit., p. 573.

[35] Herbert Marcuse, *Reason and Revolution: Hegel and the Rise of Social Theory* (Boston: Beacon Press, 1960).

G. W. F. Hegel, *The Philosophy of Right*, trans. T. M. Knox. (London: Oxford University Press, 1942) © 1942 Oxford University Press. By permission of the Clarendon Press, Oxford. [Edited and Abridged.]

yet settled everything. It is necessary to look for the reason which underlies our intuition, to know what the real essence of the matter is, and to realize that the obvious is not always the essential.

The question, "Who is to frame the constitution?" seems clear at first, but closer inspection shows that it is meaningless; it presupposes that there is no constitution already in existence, only an agglomeration of individuals. But if we realize that a constitution already exists, then the question becomes one of altering it—and the existence of a constitution implies that alteration may come about only by constitutional means. In any case it is absolutely essential that the constitution should not be regarded as something *made,* even though it may have come into existence at some specific time; it must be treated as something divine and constant, which exists in and by itself and is exalted above the sphere of things that are made.

The state is the actuality of ethical mind manifest and revealed to itself, knowing and thinking itself, accomplishing what it knows; it is absolutely rational, and its unity is an absolute end in itself, in which freedom comes into its supreme right. And this final end has supreme right against the individual, whose supreme duty is to be a member of the state.

In duty the individual finds his liberation—liberation from dependence on mere natural impulse and liberation from the subjectivity which, never reaching reality, remains self-enclosed and devoid of actuality. In duty the individual acquires his substantive freedom.

Virtue is the ethical order reflected in the individual character; when virtue displays itself as the individual's conformity with the duties of the station to which he belongs, it is rectitude.

The nation-state is mind in its substantive rationality and immediate actuality and is, therefore, the absolute power on earth. It follows that every state is sovereign and autonomous against its neighbors.

If states disagree and their particular wills cannot be harmonized, the matter can only be settled by war. A state through its subjects has widespread connections and many-sided interests, and these may be readily injured. A state may regard its infinity and honor as at stake in each of its concerns, however minute, and is more susceptible to injury when it is impelled as a result of long domestic peace to seek and create a sphere of activity abroad.

At one time there was much discussion of the opposition between morals and politics, and it was demanded that the latter should conform to the former. But the welfare of a state has claims to recognition totally different from those of the welfare of the individual; the doctrine of a clash between morals and politics rests on superficial ideas about morality and the nature of the state.

The fundamental proposition of international law is that treaties, as the ground of obligations between states, ought to be kept. But since the sovereignty of a state is the fundamental principle of its relations to others, states are actually in a state of nature in relation to each other. Their rights are actualized only in their own wills, not in any universal will with constitutional powers over them. International law is therefore only an ought-to-be, and what actually happens is that international relations based on treaty alter when relations between states are severed; the actuality of international law depends on different wills, each of which is sovereign.

War is the state of affairs which deals in earnest with the vanity of temporal goods and concerns. War has the higher significance that by its agency the ethical health of peoples is preserved in their indifference to the stabilization of finite institutions; just as the blowing of the winds preserves the sea from the foulness which would be the result of a prolonged calm, so also corruption in nations would be the product of prolonged peace. Sacrifice on behalf of the state is the substantial tie between the state and all its members and so is a universal duty. The intrinsic worth of courage is to be found in the final end, the sovereignty of the state; the work of courage is to actualize this end, and the means to this end is the sacrifice of personal actuality.

Karl Marx

When Karl Marx came to the University of Berlin in 1836, he was expected to concentrate on the study of jurisprudence and become a lawyer like his prosperous middle-class father. But Marx was fascinated by philosophy, and to study philosophy in Berlin meant to become steeped in the works of Hegel, who had died a few years earlier but whose works were still read, taken apart, and endlessly argued. Marx fell in with the "Young Hegelians," as the followers of the late master styled themselves, and the Hegelian philosophical system had important influences on the political theories that Marx developed in his years of radical political activity.

In the nineteenth century, Europe was being transformed by the Industrial Revolution. Changing techniques of production and distribution brought both new wealth and new poverty, altered the social and political structures of nations, and forced statesmen and theorists to pay greater attention than ever before to the economic aspects of human interaction. In the confusion of the ideologies with which thinkers tried to grapple with the enormous new energies unleashed by industrialization, we can distinguish at least five important lines of thought: (1) reformist liberalism, which sought to improve the state of the working classes through establishing public health care and universal education, regulating factory conditions, and curbing such abuses as child labor; (2) traditional conservatism, which stressed institutional continuity and gradual change; (3) economic individualism—best expressed by Herbert Spencer[36]—which stressed the freedom of contract between parties and argued that the state should leave the economy alone to produce fully, reward the creative, and weed out the unfit; (4) utopian socialism, proposed by such men as Charles Fourier and Robert Owen, who envisioned communities of workers cooperating in the administration of production; and (5) revolutionism, which viewed government as the ally of greedy capitalist oppressors and believed that the workers would have to gain control of the state before they could expect to gain any control over their own labor and its products. Among the members of the fifth group were Louis August Blanqui, one of the first advocates of a revolution in which the working classes, or proletarians, would take over the government, and Pierre Joseph Proudhon. By the mid-nineteenth century the most famous and powerful theorist of proletarian revolution was Karl Marx.

---

[36] See Herbert Spencer, *Social Statics*, 1851.

Marx's early political ideas were highly critical of the rigidly authoritarian Prussian government, and during the 1840s, while he was writing for—and then editing—a radical newspaper in the Rhineland, his opinions brought about the suppression of the paper and Marx went into exile in France. He had already become interested in socialist thought, and in Paris he met Proudhon, revolutionary anarchist Mikhail Bakunin, and Friedrich Engels, who became his close friend and collaborator. Engels was the son of a wealthy German textile manufacturer who had business interests in England; sent by his father to Manchester to gain business experience, young Engels was converted to socialism by his firsthand observation of factory life. He wrote a book, *Condition of the Working Class in England,* which vividly described the misery of the workers and the wealth and luxury enjoyed by their capitalist employers; the book and its author influenced Marx's own thinking and made him particularly interested in England as the place where industrialization was most advanced and most easily studied.

It was apparent, during the years when Marx and Engels were formulating their new socialistic theories, that the organized reaction of the European monarchies against the French Revolution and Napoleon had not, after all, succeeded in returning the world to a prerevolutionary *status quo.* There was unrest throughout Europe, new threats from the middle classes, and increasing fears that members of the growing working classes might succeed in organizing themselves into some kind of a political movement. Marx and Engels were convinced that the working class was the key to the future.

In conceptualizing his view of human history as a process of human growth and development, Marx borrowed heavily from Hegel. The Hegelian dialectic of the historical conflict of civilizations was transformed into a Marxian dialectic of conflict of classes. Where Hegel had seen certain nations, at certain points in time, as embodying the course of human history, Marx saw certain classes as performing a similar function. Members of the bourgeoisie—the manufacturing and merchandising class—had once been revolutionary and had carried all of mankind forward with them, but now their time had ended, and the proletariat was destined to lead the way toward the next stage.

Obviously, the kinds of conclusions that Marx reached by applying the Hegelian dialectic were far different from the conclusions of Hegel. Marx liked to say that he had taken Hegel, turned him upside down, and stood him on his feet: Where Hegel had seen *mind* as the determining force in human history that shaped the unfolding of all the external forms of society, Marx saw *matter*. The production of things, and the ways people organized themselves economically, shaped human life and thought:

In the social production which men carry on they enter into definite relations that are indispensable and independent of their will; these relations of production correspond to a definite stage of development of their material powers of production. The sum total of these relations of production constitutes the economic structure of society—the real foundation, on which correspond definite forms of social consciousness. The mode of production in material life determines the general character of the social, political and spiritual processes of life. It is not the consciousness of men that determines their existence, but, on the contrary, their social existence determines their consciousness.[37]

Because Marx took economic organization to be the determinant of all other social institutions, it naturally followed that he believed the way to transform society—indeed, to transform mankind—was to change the economic system. This was the goal of all Marxist revolutionary thought and action.

The belief that this revolutionary change would come about was a fundamental part of the Marxist historical dialectic. In this sense, Marxism seems to be almost a religious faith, although Marx himself was convinced that the dialectic was a rigid scientific system and that the revolution was an inevitable consequence of observable historical developments.

The revolution was inevitable because the previous revolution—the Industrial Revolution that had elevated the bourgeoisie—had also created the conditions for the next step: the growth of industry, which increased the number of workers and brought them together. Fluctuations of wages were forcing workers to form unions. Improvements in communication, created by industry, were helping workers in different areas to maintain contact. In these and other

[37] Karl Marx, *A Contribution to the Critique of Political Economy,* trans. N. I. Stone (1904).

ways, Marx and Engels argued, the bourgeois in their moment of triumph were setting the stage for their ultimate defeat.

Marx and Engels wanted the proletarians, as the next "world-historical" class, to become aware of their historical destiny, and the *Communist Manifesto* (the document composed by Marx and Engels and published by the Communist League in 1848) was not merely a statement of ideas—it was an exhortation. Its closing words were:

Let the ruling classes tremble at a communistic revolution. The proletarians have nothing to lose but their chains. They have a world to win.

WORKINGMEN OF ALL COUNTRIES, UNITE!

One curious aspect of Marx's historical dialectic was his conviction that, in history, the triumph of the proletariat would be more than just a stage leading to still another revolutionary change. Rather, it would be the beginning of a posthistorical era in which the conditions for future conflict would be eliminated; the common ownership of the means of production would end the class distinctions that were the source of conflict. Political power itself would gradually become unnecessary—being mainly an instrument of class oppression—and in time the state itself would wither away. In its place would be a world-wide community, a free brotherhood of mankind.

Freedom was a central concern in Marxist writings; he and Engels viewed revolutionary communism as a means of emancipating the workers from the kind of slavery imposed on them by the capitalist system. One such dehumanizing restriction was the division of labor itself:

The division of labor offers us the first example of how . . . man's own deed becomes an alien power opposed to him, which enslaves him instead of being controlled by him. For as soon as labor is distributed, each man has a particular, exclusive sphere of activity which is forced upon him and from which he cannot escape.[38]

Alienation—a forced estrangement from the joy and satisfaction of work itself—was the lot of the worker under capitalism:

In what does this alienation consist? First that the work is external to the worker, that it is not a part of his nature, that consequently he does not fulfill himself in his work but denies himself, has a feeling of misery, not of well-being, does not develop freely a physical and mental energy, but is physically exhausted and mentally debased. The worker, therefore, feels himself at home only during his leisure, whereas at work he feels homeless. His work is not voluntary but imposed, forced labor. *It is not the satisfaction of a need, but only a* means *for satisfying other needs. Its alien character is clearly shown by the fact that as soon as there is no physical or other compulsion it is avoided like the plague. Finally, the alienated character of work for the worker appears in the fact that it is not his work but work for someone else, that in work he does not belong to himself but to another person.*[39]

The revolution, then, would be an emancipation from such alienation:

Every emancipation is a restoration of the human world and of human relationships to man himself. Human emancipation will only be complete when the real, individual man has absorbed in himself the abstract citizen, when as an individual man, in his everyday life, in his work, and in his relationships, he has become a social being *and when he has recognized and organized his own powers.*[40]

Ultimately, under communism, people would be freed from the division of labor:

In communist society, where nobody has one exclusive sphere of activity but each can become accomplished in any branch he wishes, society regulates the general production and thus makes it possible for me to do one thing today and another tomorrow . . .[41]

This concern with alienation, with the economic character of society, was fundamental to the Marxist view of politics. The state itself was, first of all, a means of class

---

[38] Marx and Engels, *The German Ideology*. trans. R. Pascal (New York: International Publishers, 1947), p. 22.

[39] Marx, *Economic and Philosophical Manuscripts*, in *Collected Works of Marx and Engels*, (Moscow: Foreign Languages Publishing House, 1955) p. 41.

[40] Marx and Engels, *The Jewish Question*, in *Collected Works*, p. 175.

[41] Marx and Engels, *The German Ideology*, p. 49

oppression, "an organization of the possessing class for its protection against the non-possessing class."[42] The state was also a form of occupational specialization, "a special organism separated from society through the division of labor."[43] Marx had a great deal of contempt for democracy, as he saw it in capitalist countries, and for the kind of freedom it claimed to offer its citizens. "The modern representative state," he argued, "is an instrument of exploitation of wage labor by capital,"[44] and there could be no true freedom for the workers as long as they were mere commodities controlled by economic interests.

Marx was especially critical of the democratic process in America. "Nowhere," he wrote, "do politicians form a more separate and powerful section of the nation. . . . It is precisely in America that we see best how there takes place this process of the state power making itself independent in relation to society, whose mere instrument it was originally intended to be."[45]

Because he saw the democratic system as essentially a tool of the ruling classes, a reflection of the underlying realities of the economic system, Marx did not think that communism could be achieved through electoral politics. The bourgeoisie would never willingly relinquish its control, and the working classes would have to seize power forcibly and then establish a "dictatorship of the proletariat," which would wield the power of the state until such time as the workings of the new economic system would bring about the free, classless society.

This belief in the ultimate end of political power was the great justification for the use of all forms of power—including violence—in bringing about the change. As Robert Nisbet put it:

If men are convinced of the inevitable disappearance of power, once the proper economic and social conditions have been brought about, why should not every possible technique of centralization and consolidation of power be employed during the revolution and the period immediately following it? And, if political power is indeed only the reflection of a dominant class in a class-torn society, then how

can there be a problem of power in a society leveled of class (and all other social) distinctions?[46]

Thus, Marxist philosophy, which is fundamentally about freedom, has provided a justification for other forms of coercion: enforced loyalty to class, the discipline of revolutionary movements—and, in our own time, the vast and dreary bureaucracy of industrialized communist nations. Marxism has provided us with valuable insights into the relationship between economic processes and political power, and it offers a critique of the effects of the industrial revolution that cannot be ignored. But it has not yet yielded the key to the ancient question of why human beings are not truly free in human societies.

KARL MARX AND FRIEDRICH ENGELS ON THE PROLETARIAN REVOLUTION

The history of all hitherto existing society is the history of class struggles.

Free man and slave, patrician and plebian, lord and serf, guild master and journeyman—in a word, oppressor and oppressed,—stood in constant opposition to one another, carried on an uninterrupted, now hidden, now open fight, a fight that each time ended either in a revolutionary reconstitution of society at large or in the common ruin of the contending classes.

Our epoch, the epoch of the bourgeoisie, has simplified the class antagonisms. Society as a whole is splitting up into two great hostile camps, into two great classes directly facing each other: bourgeoisie and proletariat.

The modern bourgeois society has sprouted from the ruins of feudal society. The discovery of America, the rounding of the Cape opened up fresh ground for the rising bourgeoisie. The new markets, trade with the colonies, the increase in the means of exchange and in commodities generally, gave to commerce, to navigation, to industry an impulse never before known.

The feudal system of industry, under which indus-

---

[42] Engels, *The Origin of the Family, Private Property and the State Collected Works.* p. 102.

[43] Marx and Engels, *A Critique of the Gotha Program. Collected Works.* p. 267.

[44] Engels, *Origin of the Family, Collected Works,* p. 91.

[45] Marx, *The Civil War in France, Collected Works,* p. 316.

[46] Nisbet, *The Sociological Tradition,* pp. 132-33.

From *The Communist Manifesto.* (Edited and abridged.)

trial production was monopolized by closed guilds, no longer sufficed. The manufacturing system took its place. The guild masters were pushed aside by the manufacturing middle class; division of labor between the different guilds was replaced by division of labor in each workshop.

Meantime the markets kept ever growing, the demand ever rising. Thereupon steam and machinery revolutionized industrial production. The place of manufacture was taken by the giant, modern industry, the place of the industrial middle class by industrial millionaires, the leaders of whole industrial armies, the modern bourgeois. We see, therefore, how the modern bourgeoisie is itself the product of a long course of development, of a series of revolutions in the modes of production and exchange.

Each step in the development of the bourgeoisie was accompanied by a corresponding political advance of that class. The bourgeoisie has at last conquered for itself, in the modern representative state, exclusive political sway. The executive of the modern state is but a committee for managing the common affairs of the whole bourgeoisie.

The bourgeoisie, historically, has played a most revolutionary part.

The bourgeoisie cannot exist without constantly revolutionizing the instruments of production, and thereby the relations of production, and with them the whole relations of society. Uninterrupted disturbance of all social conditions, everlasting uncertainty, and agitation distinguish the bourgeois epoch from all earlier ones. All fixed relations, with their train of ancient and venerable prejudices and opinions, are swept away, all new-formed ones become antiquated before they can ossify. All that is solid melts into air, all that is holy is profaned, and man is at last compelled to face with sober senses his real conditions of life.

The need of a constantly expanding market for its products chases the bourgeoisie over the whole surface of the globe, and gives a cosmopolitan character to production and consumption in every country. All old-established national industries are dislodged by new industries, whose products are consumed not only at home, but in every quarter of the globe. In place of the old wants, satisfied by the production of the country, we find new wants, requiring the products of distant lands and climes.

The bourgeoisie, by the rapid improvement of all instruments of production, by the immensely facilitated means of communication, draws all, even the most barbarian, nations into civilization. It compels all nations, on pain of extinction, to adopt the bourgeois mode of production; it compels them to introduce what it calls civilization into their midst, i.e., to become bourgeois themselves. It creates a world after its own image. Just as it has made the country dependent on the towns, so it has made barbarian and semi-barbarian countries dependent on the civilized ones, nations of peasants on nations of bourgeois, the East on the West.

Modern bourgeois society with its relations of production, of exchange, and of property, a society that has conjured up such gigantic means of production and exchange, is like a sorcerer who is no longer able to control the powers of the nether world whom he has called up by his spells. The bourgeoisie has forged the weapons that bring death to itself; it has also called into existence the men who are to wield those weapons—the modern working class—the proletarians.

In proportion as the bourgeoisie, i.e., capital, is developed, in the same proportion is the proletariat, the modern working class, developed—a class of laborers, who live only so long as they find work, and who find work only so long as their labor increases capital. These laborers, who must sell themselves piecemeal, are a commodity, like every other article of commerce, and are constantly exposed to all the vicissitudes of competition, to all the fluctuations of the market.

Modern industry has converted the little workshop of the patriarchal master into the great factory of the industrial capitalist. Masses of laborers, crowded into the factory, are organized like soldiers. As privates of the industrial army they are placed under the command of a perfect hierarchy of officers and sergeants. Not only are they slaves of the bourgeois class, and of the bourgeois state; they are daily and hourly enslaved by the machine, by the overlooker, and by the manufacturer himself.

No sooner is the exploitation of the laborer by the

manufacturer over, to the extent that he receives his wages in cash, than he is set upon by the other portions of the bourgeoisie: the landlord, the shopkeeper, the pawnbroker, etc.

The lower strata of the middle class sink gradually into the proletariat, partly because their diminutive capital does not suffice for the scale on which modern industry is carried on, and is swamped in the competition with the large capitalists, partly because their specialized skill is rendered worthless by new methods of production. Thus the proletariat is recruited from all classes of the population.

All previous historical movements were movements of minorities, or in the interest of minorities. The proletarian movement is the self-conscious, independent movement of the immense majority, in the interests of the immense majority. The proletariat, the lowest stratum of our present society, cannot stir, cannot raise itself up, without the whole superincumbent strata of official society being sprung into the air.

In what relation do the communists stand to the proletarians as a whole?

The communists are the most advanced and resolute section of the working-class parties of every country, that section which pushes forward all others; they have over the great mass of the proletariat the advantage of clearly understanding the line of march, the conditions, and the ultimate general results of the proletarian movement.

The immediate aim of the communists is the same as that of all the other proletarian parties: formation of the proletariat into a class, overthrow of the bourgeois supremacy, conquest of political power by the proletariat.

The distinguishing feature of communism is not the abolition of property generally, but the abolition of bourgeois property. But modern bourgeois private property is the final expression of the system of producing and appropriating products that is based on class antagonisms, on the exploitation of the many by the few.

In this sense the theory of the communists may be summed up in a single sentence: Abolition of private property.

You are horrified at our intending to do away with private property. But in your existing society private property is already done away with for nine-tenths of the population; its existence for the few is solely due to its nonexistence in the hands of those nine-tenths.

Communism deprives no man of the power to appropriate the products of society; all that it does is to deprive him of the power to subjugate the labor of others by means of such appropriation.

The communists are further reproached with desiring to abolish countries and nationality.

The workingmen have no country. We cannot take from them what they have not got. Since the proletariat must first of all acquire political supremacy, must rise to be the leading class of the nation, must constitute itself *the* nation, it is itself national, though not in the bourgeois sense of the word.

National differences and antagonisms between peoples are daily more and more vanishing, owing to the development of the bourgeoisie, to freedom of commerce, to the world market, to uniformity in the mode of production and in the conditions of life corresponding thereto.

The supremacy of the proletariat will cause them to vanish still faster. United action, of the leading civilized countries at least, is one of the first conditions for the emancipation of the proletariat.

In proportion as the exploitation of one individual by another is put to an end, the exploitation of one nation by another will also be put to an end. In proportion as the antagonism between classes within the nation vanishes, the hostility of one nation to another will come to an end.

When, in the course of development, class distinctions have disappeared and all production has been concentrated in the hands of a vast association of the whole nation, the public power will lose its political character. Political power, properly so called, is merely the organized power of one class for oppressing another. If the proletariat during its contest with the bourgeoisie is compelled, by the force of circumstances, to organize itself as a class, if, by means of a revolution, it makes itself the ruling class and, as such, sweeps away by force the old conditions of production, then it will have swept

away the conditions for the existence of class antagonisms and of classes generally, and will thereby have
abolished its own supremacy as a class.

In place of the old bourgeois society, with its classes
and class antagonisms, we shall have an association in
which the free development of each is the condition
for the free development of all.

Max Weber

Political thought often boils down to a way of looking
at history. In considering the emergence of modern nation-
states, for example, Tocqueville saw a process of equalization,
Hegel saw the unfolding of divine wisdom, and Marx saw
a series of class conflicts. Max Weber, one of the earliest
and greatest European political sociologists, saw a progressive
rationalization of government—that is, an increasing rou-
tinization and organization of the state (and, in fact, of
all institutions), which was transforming civilization into
a kind of social machine. He borrowed from the poet Schiller
the phrase "disenchantment of the world," to describe the
process whereby people traded magic and symbols for rules
and efficiency.

Weber, born in 1864, was raised in Berlin; his father
was a politician and a member of the *Reichstag* during the
years that Chancellor Otto von Bismarck was unifying Germany under Prussian leadership and turning the once-frag-
mented nation into an industrialized, imperialistic world
power. Germany made no advances in the direction of
democracy, but it was far ahead of other European nations
in social legislation: Bismarck's chief strategy against the
threat of socialism was a massive governmental program of
workmen's insurance, old-age pensions, and public education.
One of the consequences of these programs was the development of a gigantic civilian bureaucracy, which rivaled the
Prussian military machine and the great industrial corporations in size, organization, and efficiency.

Weber was a member of a dueling fraternity during
his student days at Heidelberg; he held a commission in
the Prussian Army, served in World War I, and remained
a strong German nationalist until his death in 1920. Yet
his political views—he was an outspoken "political professor,"
actively involved in the issues of his time—underwent several

shifts in the direction of liberalism. Even during his years
of loyalty to the institution of monarchy, he had been critical
of the monarch himself (he called Kaiser Wilhelm II a
"crowned dilettante"), and by 1918 he was a professed believer in democracy. But this, too, was a highly qualified
loyalty. He was deeply suspicious of phrase-making about
the rights of man, and he turned toward democracy as a
system that might possibly achieve a higher level of efficiency
and responsible leadership.[47]

Although Weber perceived the need for efficiency and
responsibility in government, he also remained aware of the
other human values that might be sacrificed in the process
of achieving efficiency and responsibility. In this respect he
has some similarity to Tocqueville, who had detected in the
course of history a process toward egalitarian democracy,
had mourned the human qualities that were being lost, and
had set himself to studying the realities of democracy in
order that its future course might be charted with greater
wisdom. Weber, who saw the same kind of inexorability
in the increase of organized rationality in society, was as
much a critic of the development as an advocate of it. His
hope was for a system that would somehow balance the
corruption of democratic politics—he had visited America—
against the rigidity and stratification of authoritarian bureaucracy as he saw it in operation in Europe. Robert Nisbet
writes:

*He perceived the functional relation between democracy and bureau-
cracy, each feeding on the common enemy, inherited privilege. [He]
could see also that, however related the two forces might be in
functional terms, the time must come when the moral objective
of democracy—rule by the people—could no longer be maintained,
given the increasing centrality of the instrument of that rule: the
bureaucracy. The robot would turn upon its master. This was
the mode of dehumanization that became, for Weber, the increasing
preoccupation of his apprehension.*[48]

In his attempt to understand this historical process
toward bureaucratization, Weber became a student—
although not a disciple—of Marx. He agreed with Marx's
belief that the masses of workers were alienated from their

[47] H. H. Gerth and C. Wright Mills, *From Max Weber: Essays in Sociology*
(New York: Oxford University Press, 1946), p. 38.

[48] Nisbet, op. cit., p. 148.

own productivity in the capitalistic system, but he did not agree with Marx's emphasis on economic factors above all else, and he did not see the plight of the workers as significantly different from that of other members of modern society. Gerth and Mills have written:

Marx's emphasis upon the wage worker as being "separated" from the means of production becomes, in Weber's perspective, merely one special case of a universal trend. The modern soldier is equally "separated" from the means of violence; the scientist from the means of enquiry, and the civil servant from the means of administration. Weber thus tries to relativize Marx's work by placing it into a more generalized context and showing that Marx's conclusions rest upon observations drawn from a dramatized "special case" which is better seen as one case in a broad series of similar cases. The series as a whole exemplifies the comprehensive underlying trend of bureaucratization. Socialist class struggles are merely a vehicle implementing the trend.

Weber thus identifies bureaucracy with rationality, and the process of rationalization with mechanism, depersonalization, and oppressive routine. Rationality, in this context, is seen as adverse to personal freedom. Accordingly, Weber is a nostalgic liberal, feeling himself on the defensive. He deplores the type of man that the mechanization and the routine of bureaucracy selects and forms. The narrowed professional, publicly certified and examined, and ready for tenure and career. His craving for security is balanced by his moderate ambitions and he is rewarded by the honor of official status. This type of man Weber deplored as a petty routine creature, lacking in heroism, human spontaneity, and inventiveness. . . .[49]

As a balancing concept, a way of explaining certain human urges away from rationalization, Weber introduced the term "charisma." This was the quality possessed by such leaders as Napoleon—men who, out of their own personal ambition, their own needs, and their own vision of the world's possibilities, broke through the web of convention and, communicating to others on an intensely personal level, generally were able to take a host of followers with them on whatever they conceived their world mission to be. Weber saw this as the direct opposite of impersonal bureaucratic leadership:

In contrast to any kind of bureaucratic organization of offices, the charismatic structure knows nothing of a form or of an ordered procedure of appointment and dismissal. It knows no regulated "career," "advancement," "salary". . . . Charisma knows only inner determination and inner restraint. The holder of charisma seizes the task that is adequate for him and demands obedience and a following by virtue of his mission.[50]

Charisma was for Weber a concept of personal freedom—the wild human spirit's escape—but it was also a concept of authority. He defined the state as a "monopoly of the legitimate use of physical force within a given territory" and itemized three main "inner justifications" that compelled obedience, thus providing control over the state's power:

First, the authority of the "eternal yesterday," i.e., of the mores sanctified through the unimaginably ancient recognition and habitual orientation to conform. This is "traditional" domination exercised by the patriarch and the patrimonial prince of yore.

There is the authority of the extraordinary and personal gift of grace (charisma), the absolutely personal devotion and personal confidence in revelation, heroism, or other qualities of individual leadership. This is "charismatic" domination, as exercised by the prophet or—in the field of politics—by the elected war lord, the plebiscitarian ruler, the great demagogue, or the political party leader.

Finally, there is domination by virtue of "legality," by virtue of the belief in the validity of legal statute and functional "competence" based on rationally created rules. In this case, obedience is expected in discharging statutory obligations. This is domination as exercised by the modern "servant of the state" and by all those bearers of power who in this respect resemble him.[51]

Of these three forms of leadership the bureaucratic was, as Weber saw it, clearly on the rise. And although new charismatic movements might emerge at any time, there was a natural tendency for them to eventually become "routinized" into traditional or bureaucratic structures, which would carry the message onward with greater organizational precision and a good deal less emotional fervor.

Another important contribution of Weber's toward a

---

[49] Gerth and Mills, op. cit., p. 50.

[50] Weber, *Wirtschaft und Gesellschaft*, in Gerth and Mills, *From Max Weber: Essays in Sociology* (New York: Oxford University Press, 1946), p. 246.

[51] *Politics as a Vocation*, in Gerth and Mills, op. cit., pp. 78-9.

critique of modern industrial society was his book *The Protestant Ethic and the Spirit of Capitalism*. In this work Weber set out to explain *why* modern capitalism had emerged. Such a system, he reasoned, required a certain type of person, and the question was: What kinds of psychological conditions would produce the right kind of person? His conclusion was that the values inculcated by Protestantism—especially of the Calvinist or Puritan variety—were the perfect preparation for modern rationalized capitalism; thus, the Protestant Reformation and the Industrial Revolution could be viewed as different facets of one long historical development.

The values necessary for capitalism, according to Weber, were not simply greed or ambition or the desire for material wealth; these, he said, were as old as humanity. What was new in Protestantism was not hedonism but precisely its opposite—an ethic of personal self-denial, which allowed people to manipulate wealth so long as they imposed on themselves a strict discipline of work and thrift.

In Calvinist doctrine every person was predestined, from birth, to a certain after-life. An individual who was not one of the "elect" could do nothing about it, but worldly success was interpreted as a sign that one was favored by God. In this climate of uncertainty, every person naturally strove to succeed in work. A new reverence for work grew up: A person's occupation became a "vocation," a calling. But because self-denial was fundamental to the Protestant ethic, it was natural for wealth to be channeled back into business rather than dissipated on personal luxury—the idea of "stewardship" grew, and business property was increasingly separated from personal property. And because Calvinists were not allowed to believe that they could find salvation in the company of others—life was, rather, a matter between oneself and God—individualism and competition flourished. "The Puritan outlook," Weber concluded, " . . . favored the development of a rational bourgeois economic life; it was the most important, and above all the only consistent influence in the development of that life. It stood at the cradle of the modern economic man."[52]

Weber saw the Protestant ethic as a generative force, which was especially influential in the emergence of modern capitalism in England, Scotland, and the New England states.[53] He did not argue that the ethic was still operative in its original form, and, in fact, he believed that it had degenerated in his own time to a justification for immense personal wealth and consumption.

Thus, the transformation of Protestant values into capitalist values provided, for Weber, one instance of the enormous historical process wherein personal wealth became separated from corporate wealth, and industry became the rationalized, bureaucratized operation of large and impersonal institutions.

Weber's work contained many suggestions that the massive new organizations that were taking the place of the old aristocratic social structures were in turn producing new aristocracies. This idea was developed by Weber's friend Robert Michels, who studied the bureaucracy of the world's largest Marxist political party, the Social Democratic Party of Germany, and found that this organization of the working people was creating within its own ranks a new elite. From this Michels formulated what he called the "iron law of oligarchy":

It is organization which gives birth to the domination of the elected over the electors, of the mandatories over the mandators, of the delegates over the delegators. Who says organization says oligarchy.[54]

Implicit in this evaluation of the elitist tendencies of large organizations—including large democratic organizations—is another kind of "disenchantment of the world," a disenchantment with the belief that revolutions bring an end to inequality, that democracy brings the rule of the people. Michels wrote:

[53] "Without doubt, in the country of Benjamin Franklin's birth (Massachusetts), the spirit of capitalism (in the sense we have attached to it) was present before the capitalistic order. There were complaints of a peculiarly calculating sort of profit-seeking in New England, as distinguished from other parts of America, as early as 1632. It is further undoubted that capitalism remained far less developed in some of the neighboring colonies, the later Southern States of the United States of America, in spite of the fact that these latter were founded by large capitalists for business motives, while the New England colonies were founded by preachers and seminary graduates with the help of small bourgeois, craftsmen and yeomen, for religious reasons." Weber, in Gerth and Mills, op. cit., pp. 55-56.

[54] Robert Michels, *Political Parties*. trans. Eden and Cedar Paul (New York: Collier Books, 1962), p. 365.

[52] Weber, *The Protestant Ethic and the Spirit of Capitalism*. trans. Talcott Parsons (New York: Scribner's, 1958), p. 174.

The democratic currents of history resemble successive waves. They break ever on the same shoal. They are ever renewed. The enduring spectacle is simultaneously encouraging and depressing. When democracies have gained a certain stage of development, they undergo a gradual transformation, adopting the aristocratic spirit, and in many cases also the aristocratic forms, against which at the outset they struggled so fiercely. Now new accusers arise to denounce the traitors; after an era of glorious combats and of inglorious power, they end by fusing with the old dominant class; whereupon once more they are in their turn attacked by fresh opponents who appeal to the name of democracy. It is probable that this cruel game will continue without end.[55]

MAX WEBER
ON LEGITIMATE AUTHORITY

Conduct, especially social conduct, and more particularly a social relationship, can be oriented on the part of the individuals to what constitutes their "idea" of the existence of a *legitimate authority*. The probability that such orientation actually occurs shall be called the "validity" of the authority in question.

1. That an authority assumes "validity" must therefore mean more than the mere regularity of social conduct as determined by custom or self-interest. The fact that furniture-movers advertise their services regularly about the time that leases expire is caused quite clearly by their desire to exploit an opportunity in their self-interest. The fact that a peddler regularly visits a certain customer on a certain day of the week or month is either the result of long habit or of self-interest (e.g. the turnover in his district). When a civil servant shows up at his office every day at the same time, it may be determined not only by custom or self-interest, since he can hold to that as he pleases, but it may be partly the result of his abiding by the office regulations which impose certain duties on him and which he may loath to violate, since such conduct would not only be disadvantageous to him but may be also abhorrent to his "sense of duty," which, to a greater or lesser extent, represents for him

[55] Ibid., p. 371.

an absolute value.

2. Only then will the content of a social relationship represent "authority," if its conduct can be oriented approximately toward certain recognizable axioms. Only then will such authority acquire "validity," if the orientation toward these axioms includes at least the recognition that they are binding on the individual or the corresponding behavior constitutes a model worthy of imitation. Indeed, conduct may be oriented toward an authority for a variety of motives. But the fact that along with other motives the authority is also held by at least some of the other individuals as being worthy of imitation or binding naturally increases to a very considerable degree the probability that conduct will in fact conform to it. An authority which is obeyed for the sole reason of expedience is generally much less stable than one which is upheld on a purely customary basis. The latter attitude toward authority is much the most common one. But even more stable is the type of conduct oriented toward custom, which enjoys the prestige of being considered exemplary or binding, or possesses what is known as "legitimacy." Of course, the transition from a goal- or tradition-oriented conduct to one motivated by a belief in its legitimacy is extremely gradual.

3. There can be orientation toward valid authority even where its meaning (as generally understood) is not necessarily obeyed. The probability that the authority is to some extent held as a valid norm can also have its effect on behavior even where its meaning is evaded or deliberately violated. This may be true at first even on the basis of sheer expediency. Thus the thief's behavior exemplifies the validity of the criminal law merely by the fact that he tries to conceal his conduct. The very fact that an authority is valid within a particular group makes it necessary for him to practice concealment. This is, of course, a marginal case and frequently the authority is violated partially only in one or another respect or its violation is sought to be passed off as legitimate with a varying measure of good faith. Or there may really coexist various interpretations of the meaning of authority alongside of each other. In that case the sociologist will regard each one as valid exactly insofar as it actually shapes the course of behavior. It is no great difficulty for the sociologist to recognize

within the same social group the existence of several, possibly mutually contradictory, valid systems of authority. Indeed it is possible even for the same individual to orient his behavior to mutually contradictory systems of authority. This can take place not only in short succession, as can be observed daily, but even in the case of the same conduct. A person who engages in a duel orients his behavior toward the observance of the honor code; but he also orients his conduct toward the criminal law by keeping the duel a secret or, conversely, by voluntarily appearing in court. Where, however, evasion or violation of the system of authority in its generally understood meaning has become the rule, such authority can be said to be "valid" only in a limited sense or has ceased to be valid altogether. For the jurist a system of authority is either valid or it is not; for the sociologist no such choice exists. Rather, there is a gradual transition between the two extremes of validity and non-validity and it is possible for mutually contradictory systems of authority to coexist validly. Each one is valid precisely in proportion to the probability that behavior will be actually oriented toward it.

A system of authority can legitimately assume validity in the eyes of those subject to it in a variety of ways:

a) by tradition: that which has always existed is valid.

b) by virtue of emotional attachment, legitimizing the validity of what has been newly proclaimed or is considered worthy of imitation.

c) by virtue of a rational belief in its absolute value: what has been revealed as being absolutely valid *is* valid.

d) because of a form of positive proclamation whose legality is recognized as being beyond questioning. Such legality can be regarded as legitimate either 1) because it has been agreed to voluntarily by all those concerned, or 2) because it has been imposed on the basis of what is held to be a legitimate authority by some people over others and therefore exercises a corresponding claim to their obedience.

* * *

1. The oldest and most universally held legitimacy of authority is based on the sacredness of tradition. Fear ot magical penalties strengthens the psychological inhibitions regarding changes in customary modes of behavior. At the same time a system of authority continues as valid because of the many vested interests which arise with respect to its perpetuation.

2. Conscious creations of new authorities were originally almost entirely the result of prophetic oracles or at least of revelations enjoying the nimbus of prophecy, as was true as late as the statutes of the Hellenic Aisymnetes. Compliance then depended upon the faith in the legitimacy of the prophet. In periods of strict traditionalism no new system of authority would thus arise without new revelations being proclaimed in this way, unless the new system of authority was not really looked upon as new but was regarded instead as a truth that had already been valid but temporarily obscured and which was now being restored to its rightful place.

3. The archetype of absolutely value-related legitimacy is found in the idea of "natural law." The influence of its logically developed positions upon actual behavior may not always be in accord with its ideal claims, but it cannot be denied that its influence has been far from negligible; these ideal claims therefore must be clearly distinguished from those of revealed, enacted, or traditional law.

4. Today, the most common form of legitimacy is the *belief* in *legality*, i.e., the compliance with enactments which are formally correct and which have been imposed by an accustomed procedure. The contrast between voluntarily agreed-upon rules and those which are imposed from without is strictly relative. In the past, for an authority to be treated as legitimate it was often necessary for it to have been accepted unanimously. Today, however, it frequently happens that an authority is accepted by a majority of the members of a group with the minority, which holds different opinions, merely acquiescing. In such cases the authority is actually imposed by the majority on the minority. Very frequent also is the case of a violent, ruthless or simply energetic minority imposing an authority which eventually comes to be regarded as legitimate by those who originally opposed it. Where voting is the legal method of creating or changing a system of authority, it happens frequently that the will of the minority achieves a formal majority

to which the real majority acquiesces: in this case "majority rule" becomes mere sham. The belief in a contractual system of authority can be traced to fairly ancient times and can also be found among so-called primitive peoples, but in such cases it is almost always supplemented by the authority of oracles.

5. Compliance with authority imposed by any one man or several, insofar as it does not depend on mere fear or is derived from motives of expediency, always presupposes a belief in the legitimate authority of the source imposing it.

6. As a rule, compliance with authority is almost invariably determined by a combination of motives, such as a self-interest, or a mixture composed of adherence to tradition and a belief in legality, unless it is a case of entirely new principles. Very often those who comply thus with authority are not even aware of whether they do so because of custom, convention, or law.

SUMMARY

Most of the events that have occurred throughout the world during our own lifetimes have represented a tremendous acceleration of a certain trend that has been taking shape in the Western world for the past two centuries—the emergence of mass democracy. Today, despite all the cultural and political variety that continues to exist in the world, most nations show some or all of the characteristics of what we consider to be the typical modern mass-democratic state. Among these characteristics are:

1. A political system that pays homage to democratic ideology—that is, it either chooses, or sanctifies the choice of, leaders in public elections.
2. A wide (and usually widening) electorate. In England this was brought about by the series of Reform Bills, in the United States by the gradual abandonment of property qualifications and the addition of the Fifteenth, Nineteenth, and Twenty-sixth Amendments to the Constitution.
3. A rapidly growing population. In terms of "doubling time," it took approximately one million years for world population to double prior to 6000 B.C., two hundred years for it to double between 1650 and 1850. The present world population doubling time is about

37 years.[56]

4. A written constitution, embodying some principle of separation of powers.
5. One or more organized political parties.
6. A corps of professional civil servants, distinct from elected "political" officials.
7. A mechanized, professionalized, and bureaucratized military.
8. An urbanized population.
9. Increasing industrialization, with further industrial "progress" and a steady increase in gross national product as primary governmental goals.
10. A mass-production and mass-distribution economy, with an orientation toward consumer goods and with every citizen socialized into a role as consumer.
11. A mass communications system.
12. A concept of national sovereignty vis-à-vis other nations or internal political subgroups—provinces, tribes, etc.
13. A revolutionary heritage.

The transformation of world society into a complex of industrialized, democratized, mass nation-states has not rendered obsolete or irrelevant the ancient preoccupations of the political philosophers: Community, justice, and freedom, are still as dominant in our minds, and are still as elusive, as they ever were. What has taken place in this century is a great change in the context within which we perceive these needs, the emergence of some new concepts— such as change and alienation—and, above all, a new preoccupation with method, with the *way* in which knowledge and understanding is to be sought after.

When one says "method," in contemporary political discourse, one usually means scientific method. There is a fundamental conviction among modern political scholars, a conviction almost religious in its tenacity, that the intellectual techniques of the physical sciences are applicable to the problems of human societies. This is not entirely new, either: A certain notion of science was basic to Plato's political inquiries, as it was to those of Aristotle; Machiavelli employed one kind of scientific approach in his work, and so did Hobbes. But, from the time of Newton's remarkable discoveries in physics, Locke's attempt to translate his techniques to political questions, and Voltaire's enthusiastic pro-

[56] Paul Ehrlich, *The Population Bomb* (New York: Ballantine, 1968), p. 18.

pagandizing on behalf of them both, it has generally been understood that anything genuinely scientific is based on the physical sciences—on observation, experimentation and verification, and the search for general laws based on empirical findings. The Enlightenment was a rediscovery of the physical sciences by political thinkers. The so-called scientism that became a controversy in American academic circles early in this century was another such rediscovery, and the "behavioral revolution" of the 1950s and 1960s was still another.

The social sciences, as we know them today, are of fairly recent origin. In American universities the separation into clearly identified departments took place in the 1890s, and, with the founding of the various professional societies at about the same time, there emerged a fairly well-defined set of disciplines—anthropology, economics, political science, psychology, sociology.

The discipline of political science represents, basically, an organized attempt on the part of Western—primarily American—scholars to observe and analyze the workings of mass democracy, in the search for general laws of political behavior.

In the first section of this book, we have examined work that was done prior to the emergence of political science as an academic discipline. In the next section, we will consider the contributions of some modern political scientists.

Part Two
Science and Mass Democracy

The ambition to construct a science of mass democracy lies deeply entrenched at the core of contemporary political inquiry. With an almost romantic enthusiasm, American political scientists have sought to apply the values, assumptions, and precise methods of science, in their attempts to bring about an all-encompassing and objective explanation of the realities of mass democracy.

Although some scholars have viewed this extension of the scientific method into the realm of human behavior as a "grand adventure" and a trend that is historically inevitable, others have taken the view that the trend devalues man to the role of just another observed and manipulated object of scientific experimentation.

When the power of science to unlock the mysteries of the physical universe first became obvious, many observers of the social scene became convinced that, by applying the techniques that had been used in the physical sciences by Galileo, Newton, and Descartes to the explanation of human behavior, man could acquire the power to control his social order. The vision of an accumulative and experimentally verifiable explanation of human behavior, which in time could be used to construct truly utopian human communities, captured the imagination and intellect of many, perhaps most, twentieth-century social scientists (including political scientists). If man could use scientific methods to explain and predict political, economic, and social behavior, then this knowledge could be applied in constructing new social orders—an achievement unprecedented in human history.

Perhaps the brightness of the vision partially blinded some of its proponents to the full implications of pursuing a model based on scientific presuppositions in analyzing man's behavior. There are many such implications, but we will take up in this text only the two that are most closely related to our concerns.

Scientific knowledge is the accumulation of observed and verified relationships among real events. Knowledge, in this view, is much like a large picture puzzle. Each scientist, acting as an observer of a particular portion of reality, rigorously verifies the relationship among the events that take place in his section of the puzzle. An explanation of reality is gradually accumulated, through the collecting of efforts made separately by experts. Knowledge is the information being accumulated by and communicated among scientists, but few of them have any grasp of its total dimensions. This perspective leads inevitably to an ever-greater reliance on the expertise of specialists and to a genuine and almost compulsive concern for the rigor and accuracy with which the picture of reality is constructed. There is apparently a great deal less concern with what the picture looks like or with whether the average person can see and understand it at all. Thus, man becomes alienated from his own understanding of the world, and the explanation of reality becomes the objective world agreed on by experts. Knowledge no longer consists of what any individual has derived from his personal experiences and his subjective understanding; the average citizen no longer participates in knowing about his world. In the process of being made objective, knowledge has become de-personalized and separated from the people.

This view of knowledge and information does little to reassure those who hold to notions of the "good society," as it is prescribed by classical democratic theory. It was perhaps the central prescription of this theory that the good society encourages its citizenry to become educated and informed about events in their world, so they can become rational and effective participants in their own governance.

The implication of science for mass democracy is clear. The average citizen no longer knows or understands much about the world. He depends on experts and scientists to provide him with explanations of what is going on about him. And often these explanations are provided in highly technical jargon, which overwhelms the average person with its complexity. The citizen, caught amid this tumble of technical terms and esoteric knowledge, with a certain relief bows to the judgments of the experts. He may decide to

"let the generals run the war," or "let the President do what is best for the national interest." The experts become the mediators of information and opinion and, finally, the decision makers for the society. How can man participate in making decisions about the future of his society, when he can no longer participate in understanding the realities on which those decisions are based?

Another implication that is relevant to our evaluation of mass democracy is the definition of the term "evaluation." The commitment to the scientific mode of analysis has coincidentally, if not necessarily profoundly, influenced the way political scientists have evaluated mass democracy. Evaluation, in the scientific mode of analysis, is the testing of the theories that have been constructed to explain what is going on in reality. The concern is with the "goodness of fit" of the theory to the actuality of human events. Evaluation, then, is focused on the accuracy of the theory rather than the adequacy of the reality.

But evaluation also has an alternative meaning. It can be concerned with assessing political realities, to see to what extent these realities are consistent with theoretical notions about how people can live better lives. Rather than being concerned with the "goodness of fit" of the theory to reality, evaluation can be concerned with the "goodness of life" under those political realities. This alternative notion of evaluation places emphasis on changing the political realities to more closely approximate the theory of the good society, rather than changing the theory to more accurately reflect the political realities. In this sense, evaluation is the attempt to assess political conditions as to their likelihood of generating conditions that promote human happiness and development. This kind of evaluation is not so much concerned with the accuracy used in describing political realities as it is with the adequacy of those realities in contributing to the fulfillment of human needs.

In this part of the text, we focus on the evaluation of mass democracy in the context of modern political analysis. What we have somewhat arbitrarily chosen to call "modern political analysis" did not suddenly make an appearance in American universities in the latter part of the nineteenth century. As indicated in Part I, the practices of modern political scientists are deeply embedded in the thought and events of Western culture. From this viewpoint, the concern with science and mass democracy that has continued within the discipline of political science in this century is not modern at all.

Part II is a survey and critique of the way American political scientists, as members of an organized discipline of inquiry, have sought to analyze and evaluate the politics of mass democracy. Much of the discussion will focus on events that have occurred in the discipline since 1950. But generally, what we refer to as modern political analysis coincides with the development of a formal discipline of research and teaching in American universities, which began just prior to the twentieth century.

Our survey is not so much directed toward the widely diverse fields of political analysis as it is toward the impact that science has had on the analysis and evaluation of mass democracy. In Chapters 5 and 6, we trace the development of the behavioral paradigm, which emphasizes scientific analysis. We see early signs of this model in the work of Bentley and, later, Merriam, as well as in the continuing debate over the propriety of analyzing political behavior scientifically. We will detail the procedures of science and will describe some of the research that has grown out of the behavioral paradigm. We then turn to a survey of the major concepts that have been frequently associated with modern political analysis. It will become clear, in this survey of the "classics" of contemporary political theory, that the scientific orientation has had substantial impact on the discipline.

In the last two chapters of Part II, we assess the impact of the behavioral paradigm on the way contemporary political scientists have chosen to analyze and evaluate some of the turbulent events in this century. We focus on events in political science that have resulted in a growing distrust of the principles and practice of liberal democratic doctrine. We describe the construction of a scientific theory of democracy that is more consistent with the realities of politics in a mass industrial society. And we argue that the scientific theory has been associated with a widely shared, if not widely discussed, ideology. This "invisible" ideology values the capability of organizations and systems more than it does the capability of individuals; it values consensus and stability more than conflict and debate; it values people fitting systems rather than systems fitting the needs of people; and, finally, it values change that takes place within a system rather than change that results in a different system.

In the last chapter of Part II, we survey research in two major areas of political analysis and seek to assess the impact of the behavioral paradigm, with its invisible ideology, on how political scientists have analyzed both people and change in democratic political systems.

If much that is discussed in this second section of the book appears to be a critical assessment of modern political science, it is because we feel that such an assessment is necessary at this time, when so much depends on the understanding that new students of politics apply in their attempts to cope with the problems of contemporary society. The critical nature of the assessment necessarily requires that we move toward the question of designing alternative paradigms of analysis and evaluation.

5/Behavioralism: The Emerging Paradigm

American political science as an organized discipline has gradually, although not gently, evolved a paradigm for the analysis of politics that has influenced the present-day understanding and evaluation of mass democracy. The paradigm rests heavily and none too securely on an inconsistency: the desire to carry out research scientifically, while holding a very unscientific preference for democratic political systems.

The term paradigm needs clarification. Its use here is clearly distinguishable from, but is similar to, Thomas Kuhn's usage in his genuinely thoughtful analysis, *The Structure of Scientific Revolutions*. Kuhn characterizes a paradigm as an intellectual achievement that eventually defines the proper scope and methods for a field of research. He suggests that this paradigm comes about because it was " . . . sufficiently unprecedented to attract an enduring group of adherents away from competing modes of scientific activity. Simultaneously, it was sufficiently open-ended to leave all sorts of problems for the redefined group of practitioners to resolve."[1] The term paradigm connotes believing rather than achieving; otherwise, the use here follows Kuhn's definition.

The paradigm of political analysis has evolved from two fundamental beliefs about what is "good." First, the belief that scientific methods are the best way to understand and the only way to explain politics. Second, the belief that mass democracy as it operates in this country is the best political arrangement for achieving the good society.

These two beliefs underlie a set of orientations to be detailed later, which were persuasive enough to inspire a consuming intellectual debate that has continued from the earliest years of the discipline to the present. The paradigm has attracted many (perhaps presently most) political scientists as adherents, while leaving them innumerable provocative problems to work out. Not the least of these was the reconciliation between being scientific, which entails being objectively value-free, and believing in our system of democracy, which is a subjective value judgment.

It is not the intent here to argue that most political scientists accept the elements in this paradigm, but it will be proposed that the paradigm has had a controlling impact on the subject matter, theories, thought, and research of contemporary political science.

PAST AND PRESENT DEVELOPMENT OF THE PARADIGM

Albert Somit and Joseph Tanenhaus have organized their survey of the development of American political science around three objectives, which reflect the historical aspects that most directly affect the present state of the discipline.[2] They examine the rise of political science as a professional association, the way the profession has defined its responsibilities and goals, and the way that political scientists have viewed the scope and methods of analysis.[3]

Although Somit and Tanenhaus thoroughly document the spectacular growth of political science since its establish-

[1] Thomas S. Kuhn, *The Structure of Scientific Revolutions* (Chicago: University of Chicago Press, 1962), p. 10.

[2] Albert Somit and Joseph Tanenhaus, *The Development of Political Science: From Burgess to Behavioralism* (Boston: Allyn and Bacon, 1967).

[3] Ibid, p. 1.

ment as an academic discipline in the late 1800s, they rather surprisingly conclude that the evolution of political science has involved continuity more often than dramatic change. They suggest that from its very beginnings, the discipline was caught up in the debate about whether politics could or should be scientifically analyzed. Further, the responsibilities of the professional political scientist toward the system he sought to analyze and understand was debated.

Somit and Tanenhaus believe that, even though these debates are still unresolved, there have been indications of the outcome concerning the use of science. They suggest that the trend within political science, at the point of their analysis during the mid 1960s, was toward a continuing and expanding commitment not only to the possibility but also to the preferability of applying scientific methods in the study of politics.[4] Also of interest is their conclusion that the debate concerning the responsibilities of professionals has revolved around the question of whether or not political scientists should become actively involved in public affairs on the national, state, and local levels. Some have taken the position that, as a professional, the analyst should remain aloof, objective, and devoted to the development of a "pure science" of politics. Others have argued that the development of political understanding is useful only in that it contributes to an understanding of public policy as it applies to real political issues and problems. Notice that the debate has not been about the role of professionals in evaluating democracy, in assessing whether or not the political system itself is adequate to the challenges of the modern world; the question has been whether professionals should function as pure or practical scientists in attempting to analyze the political system.

Clearly, the profession of political science could have defined its role as including the responsibility to assess and evaluate the adequacy of mass democracy in providing people with the good life and a good society. It is also clear that the profession as a whole has evidently assumed that mass democracy has already been evaluated as adequate, and that the only question left to be resolved is whether it is better to participate in that system or to remain aloof from its workings.

This is not to suggest that all professional political

scientists have been apologists for democratic systems. But the nature of the debate—including the kinds of analysis, activities, and arguments carried out by professionals—indicates an orientation that is clearly reformist rather than radical: most political scientists express preferences in the liberal vein of refining and perfecting what is generally thought to be a fundamentally sound political instrument, rather than taking a radical view that would call for more dramatic and revolutionary departures from the existing political system.

Somit and Tanenhaus point out that some of the advocates of the paradigm that has come to predominate in political science were heard early in the development of the discipline. The foremost early proponent was Arthur Bentley, who presented his analysis, *The Process of Government,* in 1908. Bentley's aspiration (if not his achievement) in this book was not only to argue for the construction of a science of politics but, in addition, to provide the basic raw materials from which such a science could be pursued.

Bentley suggested leaving behind the traditional concern with what he referred to as the "soul stuff" of political analysis, and concentrating instead on the actions of individuals in the political process. Actions such as verbal and overt behavior can be observed and quantified; therefore, they can become the data for a scientific analysis of politics. In addition, Bentley proposed that such activity could best be analyzed in the context of group behavior:

All phenomena of government are phenomena of groups pressing one another, forming one another, and pushing out new groups and group representatives (the organs or agencies of government) to mediate the adjustments.[5]

Bentley saw the actions of men to be the raw material of political analysis. He was convinced that their thoughts, emotions, and values (that is, "soul stuff") were not the ingredients of a science, which must rest on that which can be directly observed. Specifically, he was concerned with observing the actions of men as members of groups, which made attempts to control other groups in the process of affecting public policies consistent with their own interests. Said Bentley:

[4] Ibid., pp. 207–211

[5] Arthur F. Bentley, *The Process of Government* (San Antonio, Tex.: Principia Press, 1949. Originally published 1908.), p. 269.

When the groups are adequately stated, everything is stated. When I say everything I mean everything. The complete description will mean the complete science, in the study of social phenomena, as in any other field.[6]

The major thrust of Bentley's argument may have fallen on relatively deaf ears in those early years, for the discipline at that time was devoted to the legal, descriptive, historical, and speculative philosophical analysis of politics. But there is no doubt that his ideas have had major impact on political science in the years that have followed.

The next major landmark in the development of the paradigm is associated with the work of Charles Merriam at the University of Chicago during the 1920s and 1930s. Merriam's influence cannot be overestimated; nearly all the leading advocates of the movement toward science, in the next generation of scholars, were at one time or another associated with him.

In his presidential address to the American Political Science Association in 1925, Merriam said, "Some day we may take another angle of approach than the formal, as other sciences do, and begin to look at political behavior as one of the essential objects of inquiry."[7] Merriam and his associates moved the discipline yet another step toward the scientific analysis of human behavior in politics.

Although these early voices were a small minority in the profession of political science during the first 30 or 40 years of this century, the aspirations they expressed were evidently shared by many students. By the 1950s the entire discipline was caught up in an impassioned debate about the scientific study of politics, a debate that was often more caustic than enlightening. The controversy went to the very core of the discipline's views of man, society, and understanding; individual scholars, and sometimes whole departments of political science, took sides. The paradigm now had become a movement within the discipline, and it was usually identified by the adjective "behavioral." By the end of the 1950s, behavioralists had become a major influence in political science.

[6] Ibid., pp. 208–209.

[7] Charles E. Merriam, "Progress in Political Research," *American Political Science Review*, (February, 1926), 20, 7, quoted in David B. Truman, "The Implications of Political Behavior Research," *Items* (Social Science Research Council, December, 1951), p. 37.

In 1961, Robert Dahl presented to the Fifth World Congress of the International Political Science Association a prophetically entitled paper, "The Behavioral Approach in Political Science: Epitaph for a Monument to a Successful Protest." Dahl's paper reflected his concern with specifying the factors that had served to generate the behavioral approach, described what he thought this approach was all about, and included suggestions on how it could be integrated into the more traditional concerns of the discipline.

The brief selection adapted from Dahl's paper for presentation here outlines the views of the behavioralists, as seen from the perspective of a leading proponent of the approach.

WHAT IS THE BEHAVIORAL APPROACH?

ROBERT A. DAHL

Historically speaking, the behavioral approach was a protest movement within political science. Through usage by partisans, partly as an epithet, terms like political behavior and the behavioral approach came to be associated with a number of political scientists. Mainly Americans, these scholars shared a strong sense of dissatisfaction with the achievements of conventional political science, particularly through historical, philosophical, and the descriptive-institutional approaches. They believed additional methods and approaches either existed or could be developed to provide political science with empirical propositions and theories of a systematic sort, which could be tested by closer, more direct and more rigorously controlled observations of political events.

At a minimum, then, those who were sometimes called "Behaviorists" or "Behavioralists" shared a mood: a mood of skepticism about the current intellectual attainments of political science, a mood of sympathy toward "scientific" modes of investigation and analysis, a mood of optimism about the possibilities of improving the study of politics.

* * *

Adapted from Robert A. Dahl, "The Behavioral Approach in Political Science: Epitaph for a Monument to a Successful Protest," *American Political Science Review*, (December, 1961), 55, 763–772. Reprinted by permission of the American Political Science Association and the author.

If we consider the behavioral approach in political science as simply an attempt to make the empirical component of the discipline more scientific, as that term is generally understood in the empirical sciences, much of the history that I have referred to falls into place. In a wise, judicious, and until very recently neglected essay entitled "The Implications of Political Behavior Research," David Truman, writing in 1951, set out the fruits of a seminar on political behavior research held at the University of Chicago in the summer of 1951. I think it is not misleading to say that the views Truman set forth in 1951 have been shared in the years since then by the members of the Committee on Political Behavior.

Roughly defined, [he wrote] the term political behavior comprehends those actions and interactions of men and groups which are involved in the process of governing . . . At the maximum this conception brings under the rubric of political behavior any human activities which can be said to be a part of governing.

Properly speaking, political behavior is not a "field" of social science; it is not even a "field" of political science. . . . Political behavior is not and should not be a specialty, for it represents rather an orientation or a point of view which aims at stating all the phenomena of government in terms of the observed and observable behavior of men. *To treat it as a "field" coordinate with (and presumably isolated from) public law, state and local government, international relations, and so on, would be to defeat its major aim. That aim includes an eventual reworking and extension of most of the conventional "fields" of political science. . . .*

The developments underlying the current interest in political behavior imply two basic requirements for adequate research. In the first place, research must be systematic. . . This means that research must grow out of a precise statement of hypotheses and a rigorous ordering of evidence . . . In the second place, research in political behavior must place primary emphasis upon empirical methods . . . Crude empiricism, unguided by adequate theory, is almost certain to be sterile. Equally fruitless is speculation which is not or cannot be put to empirical test.

. . . the ultimate goal of the student of political behavior is the development of a science of the political process . . . [1]

Truman called attention to the advantages of drawing on the other social sciences and cautioned against indiscriminate borrowings. He argued that the "political behavior orientation . . . necessarily aims at being quantitative wherever possible. But . . . the student of political behavior . . . deals with the political institution and he is obliged to perform his task in *quantitative terms if he can and in qualitative terms if he must.*" (Emphasis added.) Truman agreed that "inquiry into how men *ought* to act is not a concern of research in political behavior" but insisted on the importance of studying values as "obviously important determinants of men's behavior."

Moreover, in political behavior research, as in the natural sciences, the values of the investigator are important in the selection of the objects and lines of inquiry. . . . A major reason for any inquiry into political behavior is to discover uniformities, and through discovering them to be better able to indicate the consequences of such patterns and of public policy, existing or proposed, for the maintenance or development of a preferred system of political values.

Truman denied that "the political behavior orientation implies a rejection of historical knowledge. . . . Historical knowledge is likely to be an essential supplement to contemporary observation of political behavior." Finally, while suggesting that the conventional graduate training of political scientists needed to be supplemented and modified, Truman emphatically opposed the notion that the behavioral approach required "the elimination of . . . traditional training."

Any new departure in an established discipline must build upon the accomplishments of the past. Although much of the existing literature of politics may be impressionistic, it is extensive and rich in insights. Without a command of the significant portions of that literature, behavioral research . . . is likely to be naive and unproductive . . . Many attempts made by persons not familiar with the unsystematized facts [have been] substantively naive even when they may have been methodologically sound.

I have cited Truman's views at length for several reasons: because I wholeheartedly agree with them; because they were expressed a decade ago when the advocates of the behavioral approach were still searching for acceptance and self-definition; because they have been neglected; and because I believe that if the partisans and critics of "political behavior" and "the behavioral approach" had read them, understood them, and accepted them as a proper statement of objectives, much of the irrelevant, fruitless, and ill-formed debate over the behavioral approach over the past decade need never have occurred—or at any rate might have been conducted on a rather higher level of intellectual sophistication.

* * *

Notes

[1] Social Science Research Council, *Items* (December, 1951), pp. 37–39. (Emphasis added.)

Although Dahl's characterization of the "behavioral approach" was widely shared, it was not necessarily widely accepted. And if Dahl had meant to signal the end of the consuming debate between "traditionalists" and "behavioralists," his energies were in vain. In 1962 an anthology of essays criticizing the behavioral paradigm was published under the title *Essays on the Scientific Study of Politics.*[8] In these essays, several spokesmen for the traditional approach presented their views of problems and disadvantages of behavioral research and its underlying paradigm.

In an epilogue to the essays, Leo Strauss leveled a clear and irreverent critique of the behavioral paradigm. The adaptation from this piece presented here gives some of the flavor, if not all of the substance, of the arguments with which traditionalists attacked the behavioral approach.

Strauss aims his argument at the most revered element in the paradigm of the behavioralists—their belief in a "value-free" science of politics. By value-free, behavioralists meant that a science cannot answer questions having to do

[8] Herbert J. Storing (ed.), *Essays on the Scientific Study of Politics* (New York: Holt, Rinehart & Winston, 1962).

with "what should be," but must be content to generate research that will answer the questions of "what is." In other words, the scientific investigation of any subject can only pursue the explanation of what is going on; the evaluation of whether that is good or bad must be left to moralists.

THE NEW POLITICAL SCIENCE

LEO STRAUSS

There is more than a mysterious preestablished harmony between the new political science and a particular version of liberal democracy. The alleged value-free analysis of political phenomena is controlled by an unavowed commitment built into the new political science to that version of liberal democracy. That version of liberal democracy is not discussed openly and impartially, with full consideration of all relevant pros and cons. We call this characteristic of the new political science its democratism. The new political science looks for laws of human behavior to be discovered by means of data supplied through certain techniques of research which are believed to guarantee the maximum of objectivity; it therefore puts a premium on the study of things which occur frequently now in democratic societies: neither those in their graves nor those behind the Curtains can respond to questionnaires or to interviews. Democracy is then the tacit presupposition of the data; it does not have to become a theme: it can easily be forgotten: the wood is forgotten for the trees: the laws of human behavior are in fact laws of the behavior of human beings more or less molded by democracy; man is tacitly identified with democratic man. . . . While the new political science becomes ever less able to see democracy or to hold a mirror to democracy, it ever more reflects the most dangerous proclivities of democracy. . . . By teaching the equality of all values, by denying that there are things which are intrinsically high and others which are intrinsically low as well as by denying that there is an essential difference between men and brutes, it unwittingly contributes to the victory of the gutter. . . .

Adapted from Leo Strauss, "An Epilogue," in Herbert J. Storing, Ed. *Essays on the Scientific Study of Politics,* (New York: Rinehart Press, 1962), pp. 307–327. Reprinted by permission of the publisher.

But it succeeded in reconciling those doubts with the unfaltering commitment to liberal democracy by the simple device of declaring that no value judgments, including those supporting liberal democracy, are rational, and hence that an iron-clad argument in favor of liberal democracy ought in reason not even to be expected. The very complex pros and cons regarding liberal democracy have thus become entirely obliterated by the poorest formalism. The crisis of liberal democracy has become concealed by a ritual which calls itself methodology or logic. . . .

Only a great fool would call the new political science diabolic: it has no attributes peculiar to fallen angels. It is not even Machiavellian, for Machiavelli's teaching was graceful, subtle, and colorful. Nor is it Neronian. Nevertheless one may say of it that it fiddles while Rome burns. It is excused by two facts: it does not know that it fiddles, and it does not know that Rome burns.

To Strauss, the new political science was oriented toward subject matter that he could accept, but with a scientific posture that he could not accept. This emphasis, he argued, precluded from the analysis of politics much of that which is significant for political understanding. He felt that behavioralists, with their value-free analysis, run the risk of concluding that all values are relative to their time and space, and that there are no universal criteria for the evaluation of "good" and "bad" in politics. Strauss concluded that this risk does not justify the gain of being scientific.

ELEMENTS IN THE BEHAVIORAL PARADIGM

The following characterization of the behavioral paradigm results from sifting out the major statements of both its proponents and opponents. To begin with, the behavioral paradigm rests on the aim of analyzing politics scientifically. In using scientific methods, the analyst must search for regularities in observable political behavior, such as what people do and say in political situations and at political events. He must also be concerned with identifying the variables associated with these regularities in human actions. Having identified the variables, he must analyze the relationships among them and arrive at explanations and theories. Finally, the explanations and theorized relationships must be tested against the realities of the political arena.

The testing of theorized relationships among variables involves the forming of predictions, or hypotheses, that are based on known preconditions. Once the scientist has formed a hypothesis about what he expects to be the consequence of a set of preconditions, then he can observe similar preconditions in the real world and find whether or not his expected outcome occurs. Prediction permits the researcher to test his theory and to establish it as either a reliable and valid explanation of political activities, or as a working hypothesis that must be reformulated and tested again.

A second and overlapping element in the behavioral paradigm is the belief that political analysis should be concerned primarily with human behavior. Behavioralists focus on that which is observable, and on what people do and say. The behavioralist may be interested in how individuals or aggregates of individuals are affected by history, laws, institutions, ideas, and values, but he places primary emphasis on the behavior of the individuals and groups as a consequence of these factors, not on the factors per se.

A third element of the behavioral paradigm is its emphasis on research methods, techniques, and concepts that permit the quantification and measurement of data. If events and activities in politics can be quantified, then it is possible to specify the relationships and regularities that are observed. This emphasis has led to an extensive literature, which describes the uses of research designs, computers, and statistical analysis in the collection and analysis of data.

Still another facet of the behavioral paradigm is that it draws on other social sciences for both theoretical and empirical resources, in explaining political phenomena. Because behavioralists assume that there are regularities in the ways people behave, whether in political situations or other social contexts, the findings of other social sciences are useful in developing explanations about what is going on in politics.

The most debated element in the behavioral paradigm is the use of political theory and the meaning given to it. In traditional political analysis, "theory" normally referred to attempts to prescribe moral solutions and statements about what *should* be occurring in the political processes of the society. In the behavioral approach, theory is a tool to help explain what is going on, rather than a set of universal criteria for evaluation. Thus, the behavioralist does not view theory as either universal truth or even as one man's view of universal truth, but as a tool for examining reality. Behavioralists find this tool useful, to the extent that it aids in explaining and ordering political events. Theory in this sense may be confirmed or rejected, but it is not an evaluation to be debated from the viewpoint of different value perspectives. It is a general statement about how variables are ordered in the real world, a statement that has utility rather than intrinsic truth or falsity.

The behavioralist's goal is that analysis should be value-free. He attempts to keep his own values and biases from affecting his research findings and generalizations. Although behavioralists obviously have personal values, their responsibility as scientists is to separate these values from the conduct of their research and to emphasize objectivity. Behavioralists argue that the positive or negative features of such notions as democracy, freedom, and justice cannot be established by scientific procedures; therefore, they are necessarily beyond the scope of political analysis. The concern of behavioral analysts is with the evaluation of methods of analysis, rather than with the substantive evaluation of politics in terms of its adequacy or inadequacy to provide the good life for people. The ultimate objective of the behavioral approach is to develop broad generalizations that will accurately describe and interrelate political phenomena, using methods similar to those that physicists have applied in developing laws and generalizations that order the physical world.

A final characteristic of the behavioral paradigm is not mentioned by its advocates but is repeatedly pointed out by its critics: behavioralists, like most political scientists, tend to assume that liberal democracy as practiced in this country is, indeed, the best of all practical political worlds. This element of the paradigm arises partly because behavioralists, having declared themselves free of values and value analysis, have in fact declared themselves in support of whatever status quo exists. As Strauss suggested in the excerpt presented previously, stating that political science should no longer be concerned with values is one way of ignoring the problems that are associated with the evaluation of mass democracy as a form of society. If no evaluation is attempted or even expected, then whatever exists may be assumed to be as good as any other possible combinations of political institutions.

With these components of the paradigm in mind, it is obvious why the argument presented here concludes that the paradigm that has come to dominate the discipline of political science rests on two deeply held, if conflicting, convictions: that the scientific method is the best approach to studying man and society, and that democracy as practiced in our political system is the best form of human society.

Although behavioralism has dominated much of contemporary political science, it has not received unanimous support. The major criticisms that have been directed toward this approach are presented in the following section.

THE BEHAVIORAL PARADIGM AND ITS CRITICS

Behavioralists have been criticized for their attempt to develop general theories and laws that will explain political behavior in various historical and cultural situations. The criticism is based on the rather common finding that much that is observed in any given culture or historical period is a result of conditions unique to that situation; therefore, it is logically inconsistent to seek general explanations that would serve to explain all situations.

Behavioralists respond that the level of generality a researcher achieves depends more on what he looks for than on what he sees. Generalizations can be made about the relationship between leaders and followers in any society or historical period, as long as it is understood that it is the relationship that is important, rather than the specific actions of leaders or followers. For example, relationships might be termed "autocratic" in situations involving a tribal chief and warriors, a general and his army, or the chairman and members of a committee formed to support a candidate for public office.

Another criticism is that behavioralists attempt to use scientific procedures in order to predict human behavior, yet people who are aware of such attempts at prediction can act either to confirm or deny the prediction. For example, people may vote differently after they become aware that public opinion polls indicate a particular candidate is leading in the campaign.

Behavioralists answer that, even though the general public is probably unaware of most of the research being done by political scientists, it is indeed true that awareness could influence political behavior. Such a possibility must be considered and controlled by the researcher, when he analyzes and interprets his data.

Another less easily answered criticism is that if behavioralists are able to develop data that permit them to predict how people will behave under known conditions, then such knowledge could be used to manipulate and to control. For instance, if it becomes known that voters will respond favorably to a certain kind of political appeal, then politicians could conceal their true beliefs on an issue behind a screen of appealing rhetoric.

Many behavioralists would respond that such criticism assumes that people are acting as free agents. Behavioralists, however, feel that people's choices are largely determined by economic, political, social, geographic, and psychological variables—whether those who choose are aware of the variables or not. When people become aware of how they are influenced by such factors, then they have a broader choice. They can either go along with a known prediction or defy it. If they are not aware of the factors that help to determine their choices, however, then they have no choice except that of responding unthinkingly and automatically.

Behavioralists have been criticized as being so involved in being objective in their analyses, and so technique-oriented, that they overlook the important purposes of understanding politics. They have been accused of neglecting the questions significant for political analysis, in their attempts to develop better techniques.

The behavioralist might respond that good methodology and significant research are not necessarily incompatible. If emphasis has been distorted, this can be corrected. But, regardless of the significance of an issue, it cannot be understood until there are adequate methodologies for analysis.

A few critics of the trend toward scientific methodology have persisted in arguing that members of the discipline have become too involved in the objective observation of politics and too fascinated by techniques. These critics believe that the discipline is losing sight of such goals as evaluating what is good and bad for people in terms of political processes and institutions, that research has become largely a matter of developing ever more sophisticated techniques, and that the development of these techniques has become a goal in itself. As a goal, methodology is often unrelated to what many see as the primary task of political analysis: to gain a better understanding of the political process in relationship to its ability to facilitate a better life for people in a given society.

In a real sense, these critics are arguing that the pursuit of objectivity and scientific techniques for observation and quantification of data have led political scientists astray from the kind of problems they should be attempting to understand. The real purpose of analysis, from this perspective, is to evaluate both social goals and the means of reaching such goals. Yet political analysts are often so caught up in the attempt to justify research by its precision and objectivity that the more fundamental question of whether or not such research contributes to the goal of understanding man's relationship to the good life and to society has been forgotten. The striving for objectivity and scientific rigor has tended to separate many researchers from the task of understanding the people, problems, and politics of their society. This focus has tended to diminish the awareness of individual significance, needs, feelings, and values.

Many people defer to scientists, technicians, and other experts, assuming that people who are sophisticated in collecting and analyzing data scientifically are also adept at making decisions. Too often, those who have information about issues that require decisions have also been given the responsibility and power to make those decisions. Our society tends to leave judgments about policy priorities to those who have information.

But just because a military general has a great deal of information about how to fight a war and about the probabilities of military success, it does not necessarily follow that he has good judgment about whether the war should be fought, or what goals it will or will not achieve. Similarly, medical technicians and doctors can inform people of the effects that cigarette smoking is likely to have on their health, but this does not mean that they should also have the power to stop people from smoking cigarettes. Individuals have the right to make their own choices in such matters. The expert's contribution to individual choice ends when he has made people aware of the causes and consequences of a certain action or policy. The expert has no special insight into whether an individual should act in one way or another. How, then, do people come to believe that experts are better able to make value judgments than are other individuals?

Somehow, many people seem to conclude that whatever

is possible is also preferable. If it is possible to go to the moon, to fight wars all over the world, to produce enough material goods to exhaust the world's resources, then they feel that all of these things should be done. They fail to distinguish between something that can be done and something that should be done. Experts can tell people a great deal about what is possible and about the capabilities inherent in a given matter, but they cannot give anyone a better sense of what he, personally, should do about the matter. Information is necessary in making choices, but people also need to have the right to use that information for their own purposes. Judgments properly belong to individuals in the society, even though information about the consequences of those judgments is usually provided by experts.

Experts have gained a great deal of prestige and power in our society. Many people merely act out in their lives the behaviors that some set of experts say is best for them. In so doing, individuals are relieved of the responsibility for making their own choices as well as the possibility of becoming self-valuing and accepting people. Simply put, many people in our society have come to believe that they no longer know what is good for them, and they are waiting for some scientist, expert, or technician to tell them what to do. They have become servants of the very science that has been created to provide more control over the human future. Instead of using the information and know-how provided by scientists in making informed and moral choices, they have delegated to scientists the power to make the decisions for society. As a result, many people no longer believe that they can evaluate for themselves what is good, just, and necessary for survival. This deference to the role of science and expertise has resulted in the devaluation of people as significant individuals who are able to make both moral and political choices to control their own and society's future.

Perhaps some of this skepticism about the influence of the paradigm is unwarranted. However, it is necessary to examine what some believe is the most profound criticism of the dominating trend in political analysis.

THE PARADIGM IN PRACTICE: THE PROCESS OF SCIENCE

When a person observes a street corner fist-fight, he may use his observations as the basis for a generalization about such situations. The generalization allows him better understanding of how he will relate to such a situation in the future. Common sense, which is based on observed events, becomes an important factor in how an individual understands, decides, and behaves in the world he lives in.

One of the basic problems with the common sense approach to understanding is knowing whether or not the observations and generalizations are valid. Scientific procedure is designed to resolve this problem and to produce data and generalizations that are more likely to be valid than invalid.

What are the procedures that make the difference between common sense observation and scientific analysis? First, the scientist identifies the problem in terms of variables, which are related to one another and are clearly part of the problem to be investigated. Second, he theorizes about the relationship among these variables. Finally, he makes systematic and controlled observations to test his theory against the realities of the situation.

The identification of the problem begins when the researcher defines the problem situation by asking questions about the relationship between two or more events or conditions. A scientist looking at the problem of how people will vote in a given election might identify the problem in terms of the variables that affect voting behavior.

A variable is an event or condition that can be measured along a given scale, in terms of higher or lower. For example, personal income may influence whether an individual votes for a Republican or a Democrat. The problem defined, then, is: What is the relationship between the amount of personal income and the way an individual votes in a given election? Both factors can be determined by asking the person to supply the relevant information. Thus, the problem situation has been identified, and the variable conditions within the problem have been specified.

Next, the scientist develops a theoretical explanation of what kind of relationship he expects to find between the two variables, amount of income and voter preference. He may theorize that the person who has a high income will probably try to protect it, by supporting programs and politicians that do not threaten to reduce his income. Therefore, he would be more likely to vote in favor of a candidate who asks for reductions in government spending and taxes.

Because the Republican party is most often associated with the policy of reducing government spending, it might be expected that voters with higher income would vote Republican. Similarly, a voter with a lower income might be expected to want government programs, which would provide services that are beyond his income. He might vote for Democratic candidates, who normally support government spending as a solution to social problems.

To this point, the researcher has identified a problem by considering the relationship between amount of income and voter preference. The theoretical guess that has been made about the relationship between these variables can be stated in the form of a hypothesis: The higher an individual's income, the more likely he will be to vote for a Republican party candidate. The next step is to test this hypothesis, by means of systematic and controlled observations. But how does one observe in a systematic and controlled fashion?

The logic of control, in any scientific research, is to demonstrate that the effect of one variable condition on another is caused only by the single condition specified in the hypothesis, and not by any other extraneous variable. This kind of control requires setting up the research in such a way that variation in income—and only variation in income—is the factor that will affect how the person actually votes. Controls make sure that such differences as religion, education, family organization, and other factors do not affect voting behavior. Many methods of control are available to the researcher. In all cases the logic is the same; he seeks to demonstrate that the variable he has identified in his hypothesis, and not some other variable, is effecting the impact he is trying to understand. The following brief essay by Samuel Stouffer clarifies the various methods of control available to researchers.

Now, what does it mean to observe "systematically"? First, the researcher must observe a representative cross-section of events and activities, rather than merely those he happens upon by chance. Systematic observation is based on the researcher's attempt to obtain a representative set of observations from those events or activities that compose his problem situation.

If the researcher were simply to observe variation of voting behavior among people with very high incomes, he might find little difference in voter preference. It is necessary to observe a representative cross-section of people with widely varying incomes, making sure that there are people with very low incomes as well as people with medium and higher incomes. Once he has acquired a sample representing all income levels, the researcher can find out if his hypothesis concerning the relationship of income and voter preference is actually true for the real world.

The scientific method can be defined as a process in which problems are identified in terms of the relationship among variables, hypotheses are formed to explain the relationship among the variable conditions, and hypotheses are tested against real world events observed in a controlled and systematic way. Scientific analysis differs substantially, therefore, from what people do when they make "common sense" generalizations that are based on haphazard personal observations.

Samuel Stouffer presents the basic logic of scientific research design, showing how social scientists in particular have varied the design of experiments in order to carry out their research. Each of the variations he describes departs from the controlled and systematic observation that we have been discussing, yet the research designs indicate how political analyses may be carried out in ways that closely approximate scientific methods of analysis.

SOME OBSERVATIONS ON STUDY DESIGN

SAMUEL A. STOUFFER

As a youth I read a series of vigorous essays in the *Century Magazine* by its editor, the late Glenn Frank. His theme was that the natural sciences had remade the face of the earth; now had arrived the age of the social sciences. The same techniques which had worked their miracles in physics, chemistry, and biology should, in competent hands, achieve equally dazzling miracles in economics, political science, and sociology. That was a long time ago. The disconcerting fact is that people are writing essays just like that today. Of course, the last two decades have seen considerable progress in social science—in theory, in technique, and in the accumulation of data. It is true that the number of practitioners is

From Samuel A. Stouffer, "Some Observations on Study Design," *American Journal of Sociology,* vol. 55, no. 4, pp. 355–61. Published by the University of Chicago Press.

pitifully few; only a few hundred research studies are reported annually in sociology, for example, as compared with more than twenty thousand studies summarized annually in *Biological Abstracts*. But the bright promise of the period when Frank was writing has not been fulfilled.

Two of the most common reasons alleged for slow progress are cogent, indeed.

The data of social science are awfully complex, it is said. And they involve values which sometimes put a strain on the objectivity of the investigator even when they do not incur resistance from the vested interests of our society. However, an important part of the trouble has very little to do with the subject matter of social science as such but, rather, is a product of our own bad work habits. That is why this paper on the subject of study design may be relevant. So much has been spoken and written on this topic that I make no pretense to originality. But in the course of a little experience, especially in an effort during the war to apply social psychology to military problems, and in an undertaking to nurture a new program of research in my university, I have encountered some frustrations which perhaps can be examined with profit.

A basic problem—perhaps *the* basic problem—lies deeply imbedded in the thoughtways of our culture. This is the implicit assumption that anybody with a little common sense and a few facts can come up at once with the correct answer on any subject. Thus the newspaper editor or columnist, faced with a column of empty space to fill with readable English in an hour, can speak with finality and authority on any social topic, however complex. He might not attempt to diagnose what is wrong with his sick cat; he would call a veterinarian. But he knows precisely what is wrong with any social institution and the remedies.

In a society which rewards quick and confident answers and does not worry about how the answers are arrived at, the social scientist is hardly to be blamed if he conforms to the norms. Hence, much social science is merely rather dull and obscure journalism; a few data and a lot of "interpretation." The fact that the so-called "interpretation" bears little or no relation to the data is often obscured by academic jargon. If the stuff is hard to read, it has a chance of being acclaimed as profound. The rewards are for the answers, however tediously expressed, and not for rigorously marshaled evidence.

In the army no one would think of adopting a new type of weapon without trying it out exhaustively on the firing range. But a new idea about handling personnel fared very differently. The last thing anybody ever thought about was trying out the idea experimentally. I recall several times when we had schemes for running an experimental tryout of an idea in the sociopsychological field. Usually one of two things would happen: the idea would be rejected as stupid without a tryout (it may have been stupid, too) or it would be seized on and applied generally and at once. . . .

* * *

To alter the folkways, social science itself must take the initiative. We must be clear in our own minds what proof consists of, and we must, if possible, provide dramatic examples of the advantages of relying on something more than plausibility. And the heart of our problem lies in study design *in advance,* such that the evidence is not capable of a dozen alternative interpretations.

Basically, I think it is essential that we always keep in mind the model of a controlled experiment, even if in practice we may have to deviate from an ideal model. Take the simple accompanying diagram. The test of whether a difference d is attributable to what we think it is attributable to is whether d is significantly larger than d'.

	Before	After	After — Before
Experimental group	x_1	x_2	$d = x_2 - x_1$
Control group	x'_1	x'_2	$d' = x'_2 - x'_1$

We used this model over and over again during the war to measure the effectiveness of orientation films in changing soldiers' attitudes. . . .

One of the troubles with using this careful design was that the effectiveness of a single film when thus measured turned out to be so slight. If, instead of using the complete experimental design, we simply took an unselected sample of men and compared the attitudes of those who said they had seen á film with those who said they had not, we got much more impressive differences. This was more rewarding to us, too, for the management wanted to believe the films were powerful medicine. The gimmick was the selective fallibility of memory. Men who correctly remembered seeing the films were likely to be those most sensitized to their message. Men who were bored or indifferent may have actually seen them but slept through them or just forgot.

Most of the time we are not able or not patient enough to design studies containing all four cells as in the diagram above. Sometimes we have only the top two cells, as in the accompanying diagram. In this situa-

$$\boxed{\begin{array}{|c|c|} x_1 & x_2 \end{array}} \quad d = x_2 - x_1$$

tion we have two observations of the same individuals or groups taken at different times. This is often a very useful design. In the army, for example, we would take a group of recruits, ascertain their attitudes, and restudy the same men later. From this we could tell whose attitudes changed and in what direction (it was almost always for the worse, which did not endear us to the army!). But exactly what factors in the early training period were most responsible for deterioration of attitudes could only be inferred indirectly.

The panel design described above is usually more informative than a more frequent design, which might be pictured thus:

Here at one point in time we have one sample, and at a later point in time we have another sample. We observe that our measure, say, the mean, is greater for the recent sample than for the earlier one. But we are precluded from observing which men or what type of

men shifted. Moreover, there is always the disturbing possibility that the populations in our two samples were initially different; hence the differences might not be attributable to conditions taking place in the time interval between the two observations. Thus we would study a group of soldiers in the United States and later ask the same questions of a group of soldiers overseas. Having matched the two groups of men carefully by branch of service, length of time in the army, rank, etc., we hoped that the results of the study would approximate what would be found if the same men could have been studied twice. But this could be no more than a hope. Some important factors could not be adequately controlled; for example, physical conditions. Men who went overseas were initially in better shape on the average than men who had been kept behind; but, if the follow-up study was in the tropics, there was a chance that unfavorable climate already had begun to take its toll. And so it went. How much men overseas changed called for a panel study as a minimum if we were to have much confidence in the findings.

A very common attempt to get the results of a controlled experiment without paying the price is with the design that might be as shown in the accompanying diagram. This is usually what we get with correlation

analysis. We have two or more groups of men whom we study at the same point in time. Thus we have men in the infantry and men in the air corps and compare their attitudes. How much of the difference between x_2' and x_2 we can attribute to experience in a given branch of service and how much is a function of attributes of the men selected for each branch we cannot know assuredly. True, we can try to rule out various possibilities by matching; we can compare men from the two branches with the same age and education, for example. But there is all too often a wide-open gate through which other uncontrolled variables can march.

Sometimes, believe it or not, we have only one cell:

$$\boxed{x_2}$$

When this happens, we do not know much of anything. But we can still fill pages of social science journals with "brilliant analysis" if we use plausible conjecture in supplying missing cells from our imagination. Thus we may find that the adolescent today has wild ideas and conclude that society is going to the dogs. We fill in the dotted cell representing our own yesterdays with hypo-

thetical data, where x_1 represents us and x_2 our offspring. The tragicomic part is that most of the public, including, I fear, many social scientists, are so acculturated that they ask for no better data.

I do not intend to disparage all research not conforming to the canons of the controlled experiment. I think that we will see more of full experimental design in sociology and social psychology in the future than in the past. But I am well aware of the practical difficulties of its execution, and I know that there are numberless important situations in which it is not feasible at all. What I am arguing for is awareness of the limitations of a design in which crucial cells are missing.

* * *

OTHER RESEARCH STRATEGIES

Although there has been a great deal of debate in the discipline of political science about whether or not research should be conducted in a scientific manner, a general consensus underlies this debate: that researchers, "scientific" or not, will generally maintain an *empirical orientation* to their analyses. This means that they will conduct research that is primarily oriented toward data and information that can be observed and, therefore, communicated to other scholars. Empirical orientation has been the bedrock of most research strategies in political science, whether they have been scientific, comparative, historical, or case studies. Scientific investigations are only one manifestation of the empirical methods that are common to most political analysis.

What other research strategies have been used by political scientists, aside from experimental or scientific analysis? The reality of research in the discipline indicates that there have been very few experimental studies and that most research is empirical but not scientific.

Generally, research begins with the identification of a problem, a review of the existing information and research findings that others have contributed to the understanding of the problem, the gathering of data and information on the specific aspects under investigation, and the analysis of the collected data for purposes of interpretation and explanation.

The researcher selects the strategy that seems most appropriate to the specific problem chosen for study. Some problems are more amenable to one strategy than to another, or perhaps the researcher does not have the time, money, or commitment for a demanding strategy and must be content to conduct his research expediently. No single research strategy is necessarily more valuable than another, however. Scientific or experimental research may be the preferred way to collect data about a specific problem, but it may be either too costly or too time-consuming to justify its application to the problem under analysis.

The researcher may choose, then, to use a comparative research strategy rather than an experimental one. In such a research design, he is essentially comparing two or more political situations to gain some understanding of their differences and similarities. Comparative analysis, too, is relatively demanding of time and resources.

The scholar may decide to do an intensive analysis of the particular dynamics of a single situation, in order that similar political situations may be better understood. This form of analysis is usually called a case study.

Finally, the analyst may choose to survey historical situations, which may give insight into a particular kind of political problem. In this kind of a study, he relies on the records that have been kept about the situation in the past and on descriptions of the situation provided in memoirs, biographical material, or novels.

There are many different strategies for analysis. The important point to be kept in mind is that the research design is selected according to the researcher's goals as well as the nature of the problem. The problem is the important issue, which must be resolved and understood. The design of research is secondary in importance to the attempt to find out what is going on in the situation.

BEHAVIORAL RESEARCH ON POLITICAL INSTITUTIONS

A systematic survey of how the behavioral mode of political analysis is being applied would require an extensive textbook in itself. To illustrate the impact of the behavioral paradigm on a single research area—political institutions—three different studies have been selected. The research deals with the United States Senate, the relationship between Congress and its constituency, and the two major political parties.

As each of these studies is discussed, attention is directed to how the research has been influenced by the elements of the behavioral paradigm, which emphasizes the observation of human behavior. Rather than focusing on institutions as structures in and of themselves, the research analyzes how those institutions affected, and were affected by, the actions of the people who operated within them. Another component of the paradigm is the emphasis on methodology that permits more precise observation, measurement, and analysis of political behavior within institutions. The development of such methodologies has, in turn, permitted the verification and replication necessary for scientific procedure. The studies presented here illustrate how behavioral research has attempted to conform to these norms.

THE SENATE

Traditionally, research on major institutions of government has tended to concentrate on the legal mechanics of their operations. Typical studies have described the organizational structure of the two branches of Congress, including their committee systems and their internal rules of conduct, and have traced the development of the Senate as a major instrument of the constitutional powers set forth in the Constitution. Case studies have described the actual working of the Senate as it processes bills into laws.

Donald Matthews broke with tradition, in carrying out a most extensive behavioral analysis of the United States Senate. He chose to analyze the Senate as a group of people who, like members of any other group, were greatly affected by the norms of conduct evolved within the group to preserve and direct the activities of its members. He hypothesized that the behavior of particular senators would be affected by their conformity to these norms, which he called the "folkways" of the Senate.

Matthews' analysis involved in-depth interviews, in which he gathered empirical data by asking members of the Senate what they did as senators. From these data, Matthews discerned a pattern of norms, which could be related to the effectiveness of senators in getting their bills passed.

Matthews then developed indexes that enabled him to quantify the data collected in the interviews. His indexes of "effectiveness" and "specialization" are good examples of how such techniques are developed. Finally, Matthews' analysis shows the relationship between his quantification of the norms existing in the Senate and his observation of the effectiveness of senators in their jobs. Matthews' general conclusion was that the closer senators came to conformity to the folkways of the Senate, the more likely they were to be effective in that body.

FOLKWAYS OF THE SENATE

DONALD R. MATTHEWS

The Senate of the United States, just as any other group of human beings, has its unwritten rules of the game, its norms of conduct, its approved manner of behavior. Some things are just not done; others are met with widespread approval. "There is great pressure for conformity in the Senate," one of its influential members said. "It's just like living in a small town."

What are the standards to which the senators are expected to conform? What, specifically, do these unwritten rules of behavior say? Why do they exist? In what ways do they influence the senators? How, concretely, are they enforced? What kinds of senators obey the folkways? Which ones do not, and why?

* * *

From Donald R. Matthews, *U.S. Senators and Their World,* (North Carolina: University of North Carolina Press.) pp. 92–117. (Edited and Abridged.)

APPRENTICESHIP

The first rule of Senate behavior, and the one most widely recognized off the Hill, is that new members are expected to serve a proper apprenticeship.

The freshman senator's subordinate status is impressed upon him in many ways. He receives the committee assignments the other senators do not want. The same is true of his office suite and his seat in the chamber. In committee rooms he is assigned to the end of the table. He is expected to do more than his share of the thankless and boring tasks of the Senate, such as presiding over the floor debate or serving on his party's Calendar Committee. According to the folkways of the Senate, the freshman is expected to accept such treatment as a matter of course.

Moreover, the new senator is expected to keep his mouth shut, not to take the lead in floor fights, to listen and to learn. "Like children," one freshman said, "we should be seen and not heard." Just how long this often painful silence must be maintained is not clear, but it is certainly wiser for a freshman to postpone his maiden efforts on the floor too long than to appear overly aggressive. Perhaps, ideally, he should wait until pushed reluctantly to the fore. . . .

Freshmen are also expected to show respect for their elders ("You may think you are smarter than the older fellows, but after a time you find that this is not true") and to seek their advice ("'Keep on asking for advice, boy,' the committee chairman told me. 'That's the way to get ahead around here'"). They are encouraged to concentrate on developing an acquaintanceship in the Senate. ("Young senators should make a point of getting to know the other senators. This isn't very hard: there are only ninety-nine of them. And if the other senators know and like you, it increases your effectiveness.")

The freshman who does not accept his lot as a temporary but very real second-class senator is met with thinly veiled hostility. . . .

Even so, the veterans in the Senate remark, rather wistfully, that the practice of serving an apprenticeship is on the way out, and, to some extent, they are undoubtedly correct. The practice seems to have begun well before the popular election of senators and the exigencies of the popularly elected official have placed it under considerable strain. . . .

This judgment is also colored by the tendency in any group for the old-timers to feel that the younger generation is going to hell in a handbasket. To the present-day freshmen in the Senate, the period of apprenticeship is very real and very confining. . . .

LEGISLATIVE WORK

"There are two kinds of Congressmen—show horses and work horses. If you want to get your name in the papers, be a show horse. If you want to gain the respect of your colleagues, keep quiet and be a work horse." Senator Carl Hayden of Arizona remembers being told this when he first came to the Congress many years ago. It is still true.

The great bulk of the Senate's work is highly detailed, dull, and politically unrewarding. According to the folkways of the Senate, it is to those tasks that a senator *ought* to devote a major share of his time, energy, and thought. Those who follow this rule are the senators most respected by their colleagues. Those who do not carry their share of the legislative burden or who appear to subordinate this responsibility to a quest for publicity and personal advancement are held in disdain.

This results, at first, in a puzzling disparity between the prestige of senators inside and outside the Senate. Some of the men most highly respected by their colleagues are quite unknown except on the Hill and in their own states; others whose names are household words are thought to be second-raters and slackers.[1] . . .

But this does not mean that all publicity is undesirable. It takes publicity to get, and stay, elected. This publicity, as long as it does not interfere with the performance of legislative duties, is considered necessary and desirable. Nor is there any objection to publicity calculated to further the cause of a program or policy or to publicity which flows from a senator's position or performance. But the Senate folkways do prescribe that a senator give first priority to being a legislator. Everything else, including his understandable desire for personal and political publicity, must be secondary to this aspect of his job.

SPECIALIZATION

According to the folkways of the Senate, a senator should not try to know something about every bill that comes before the chamber nor try to be active on a wide variety of measures. Rather, he ought to specialize, to focus his energy and attention on the relatively few matters that come before his committees or that directly and immediately affect his state. . . .

In part, at least, senators ought to specialize because they must: "Thousands of bills come before the Senate each Congress. If some senator knows the fine details of more than half a dozen of them, I've never heard of him." Even when a senator restricts his attention to his committee work, the job is more than one man can do. . . .

The relatively few senators who have refused to specialize agree. One of these, a relatively young man of awesome energy, says, "I'll be perfectly frank with you. Being active on as wide a range of issues as I have been is a man-killing job. In a few years I suspect that I will be active on many fewer issues. I came down here a young man and I'm gradually petering out." The limit of human endurance is not, however, the only reason for a senator to specialize. By restricting his attention to matters concerning his committee work and his home state, the senator is concentrating on the two things he should know best. Only through specialization can he know more about a subject than his colleagues and thus make a positive contribution to the operation of the chamber.

Moreover, speaking too much tends to decrease a senator's legislative impact. "Look at——," one of them said. "He came in here with his mouth open and he hasn't closed it yet. After a while, people stop listening." Furthermore, a senator who is too active outside his specialty may destroy his influence within his area of special competence. "When——, one of my best friends in the Senate, came here he was known as an expert on——, and they used to listen to him as such. But then he began talking on many other issues as well. As a result, he lost some of his effectiveness on——matters

as well as on the other issues to which he addressed himself."

Almost all the senators are agreed that: "The really effective senators are those who speak only on the subjects they have been dealing with at close quarters, not those who are on their feet on almost every subject all the time."[2] Why this pressure for specialization? Why does this folkway exist? There would seem to be a number of reasons.

The formal rules of the Senate provide for what amounts to unlimited debate. Even with the folkways limiting the activity of freshmen, discouraging "playing to the galleries," and encouraging specialization, the Senate moves with glacial speed. If many more senators took full advantage of their opportunities for debate and discussion, the tempo of action would be further slowed. The specialization folkway helps make it possible for the Senate to devote less time to talking and more to action.

Moreover, modern legislation is complex and technical, and it comes before the Senate in a crushing quantity. The committee system and specialization—in a word, a division of labor within the chamber—increase skill and decrease the average senator's work load to something approaching manageable proportions. When a senator refuses to "go along" with specialization, he not only challenges the existing power structure but also decreases the expert attention which legislative measures receive.

COURTESY

The Senate of the United States exists to solve problems, to grapple with conflicts. Sooner or later, the hot, emotion-laden issues of our time come before it. Senators as a group are ambitious and egocentric men, chosen through an electoral battle in which a talent for invective, righteous indignation, "mud-slinging," and "engaging in personalities" are often assets. Under these circumstances, one might reasonably expect a great deal of manifest conflict and competition in the Senate. Such conflict does exist, but its sharp edges are blunted by the felt need—expressed in the Senate folkways—for courtesy.

A cardinal rule of Senate behavior is that political disagreements should not influence personal feelings. This is not an easy task; for, as one senator said, "It's hard not to call a man a liar when you know that he is one."

Fortunately, a number of the chamber's formal rules and conventions make it possible for him to approximate this ideal—at least so far as overt behavior is concerned. The selection of committee members and chairmen on the basis of their seniority neatly bypasses a potential cause of grave dissention in the Senate. The rules prohibit the questioning of a colleague's motives or the criticism of another state. All remarks made on the floor are, technically, addressed to the presiding officer, and this formality serves as a psychological barrier between antagonists. Senators are expected to address each other not by name but by title—Earle C. Clements does not disagree with Irving M. Ives, but rather the Senior Senator from Kentucky disagrees with the Senior Senator from New York.

* * *

Few opportunities to praise publicly a colleague are missed in the Senate. Senators habitually refer to each other as "The distinguished Senator from——" or"The able Senator from——." Birthdays, anniversaries, re-election or retirement from the Senate, and the approach of adjournment are seized as opportunities for the swapping of praise. Sometimes, on these occasions, the sentiment is as thick as Senate bean soup. . . .

* * *

This kind of behavior—avoiding personal attacks on colleagues, striving for impersonality by divorcing the self from the office, "buttering-up" the opposition by extending unsolicited compliments—is thought by the senators to pay off in legislative results.[3] Personal attacks, unnecessary unpleasantness, and pursuing a line of thought or action that might embarrass a colleague needlessly are all thought to be self-defeating—"After all, your enemies on one issue may be your friends on the next." Similar considerations also suggest the un-

desirability of excessive partisanship. "I want to be able to pick up votes from the other side of the aisle," one Republican said. "I hope that a majority of the Republicans will vote for anything I sponsor. But always some of them are going to have special problems that impel them to vote against the party." They also suggest, despite partisan differences, that one senator should hesitate to campaign against another. "The fellows who go around the country demagoging and calling their fellow senators names are likely to be ineffective senators. It's just human nature that the other senators will not cooperate with them unless they have to."

In private, senators are frequently cynical regarding this courtesy. They say that "it doesn't mean a thing," that it is "every man for himself in the Senate," that some of their colleagues "no more should be senators than I should be Pope," that it is "just custom." Senator Barkley's advice to the freshman senator—if you think a colleague stupid, refer to him as "the able, learned and distinguished senator," but if you *know* he is stupid, refer to him as "the *very* able, learned and distinguished senator"—is often quoted.[4] Despite its blatant hypocrisy, the practice persists, and after serving in the Senate for a period of years most senators grow to appreciate it. . . .

Courtesy, far from being a meaningless custom as some senators seem to think it is, permits competitors to cooperate. The chaos which ensues when this folkway is ignored testifies to its vital function.

RECIPROCITY

Every senator, at one time or another, is in a position to help out a colleague. The folkways of the Senate hold that a senator should provide this assistance and that he be repaid in kind. The most important aspect of this pattern of reciprocity is, no doubt, the trading of votes. Occasionally this is done quite openly in the course of public debate. . . .

* * *

Usually, however, this kind of bargain is either made by implication or in private. Senator Douglas of

Illinois, who tried unsuccessfully to combat this system, has analyzed the way in which a public works appropriation bill is passed.

... This bill is built up out of a whole system of mutual accommodations in which the favors are widely distributed, with the implicit promise that no one will kick over the apple cart; that if Senators do not object to the bill as a whole, they will "get theirs." It is a process, if I may use an inelegant expression, of mutual backscratching and mutual logrolling.

Any member who tries to buck the system is only confronted with an impossible amount of work in trying to ascertain the relative merits of a given project; and any member who does ascertain them, and who feels convinced that he is correct, is unable to get an individual project turned down because the senators from the State in which the project is located, and thus is benefiting, naturally will oppose any objection to the project; and the other members of the Senate will feel that they must support the Senators in question, because if they do not do so, similar appropriations for their own States at some time likely will be called into question.[5]

Of course, *all* bills are not passed as the result of such implicit or explicit "deals."

On the other hand, this kind of bargaining (or "logrolling" or "backscratching" or "trading off," phrases whose invidious connotations indicate the public's attitude toward these practices) is not confined just to the trading of votes. Indeed, it is not an exaggeration to say that reciprocity is a way of life in the Senate. "My boss," one highly experienced administrative assistant says, "will—if it doesn't mean anything to him—do a favor for any other Senator. It doesn't matter *who* he is. It's not a matter of friendship, it's just a matter of I won't be an S.O.B. if you won't be one."

It is this implicit bargaining that explains much of the behavior of senators. Each of them has vast power under the chamber's rules. A single senator, for example, can slow the Senate almost to a halt by systematically objecting to all unanimous consent requests. A few, by exercising their right to filibuster, can block the passage of all bills. Or a single senator could sneak almost any piece of legislation through the chamber by acting when floor attendance is sparse and by taking advantage of the looseness of the chamber rules. While these and other similar powers always exist as a potential threat, the amazing thing is that they are rarely utilized. The spirit of reciprocity results in much, if not most, of the senators' actual power not being exercised. If a senator *does* push his formal powers to the limit, he has broken the implicit bargain and can expect, not cooperation from his colleagues, but only retaliation in kind. "A man in the Senate," one senator says, "has just as much power as he has the sense to use. For this very reason he has to be careful to use it properly or else he will incur the wrath of his colleagues."

To play this game properly and effectively requires tolerance and an understanding of the often unique problems and divergent views of the other senators. "No man," one highly placed staff assistant says, "can really be successful in the Senate until he has adopted a *national* point of view. Learning what the other senators' problems are and working within this framework to pass legislation gives him this outlook. If he assumes that everyone thinks and feels the same way he and his constituents do, he will be an ineffective legislator." It demands, too, an ability to calculate how much "credit" a senator builds up with a colleague by doing him a favor or "going along." If a senator expects too little in return, he has sold himself and his constituents short. If he expects too much, he will soon find that to ask the impossible is fruitless and that "there are some things a senator just can't do in return for help from you." Finally, this mode of procedure requires that a senator live up to his end of the bargain, no matter how implicit the bargain may have been. "You don't *have* to make these commitments," one senator said, "and if you keep your mouth shut you are often better off, but if you *do* make them, you had better live up to them."

These are subtle skills. Some men do not have them in sufficient quantity to be successful at this sort of bargaining. A few take the view that these practices are immoral and refuse, with some display of righteous indignation, to play the game that way. But these men are the exceptions, the nonconformists to the Senate folkways.

INSTITUTIONAL PATRIOTISM

Most institutions demand an emotional investment from their members. The Senate of the United States is no exception. Senators are expected to believe that they belong to the greatest legislative and deliberative body in the world. They are expected to be a bit suspicious of the President and the bureaucrats and just a little disdainful of the House. They are expected to revere the Senate's personnel, organization, and folkways and to champion them to the outside world.

* * *

A senator whose emotional commitment to Senate ways appears to be less than total is suspect. One who brings the Senate as an institution or senators as a class into public disrepute invites his own destruction as an effective legislator. One who seems to be using the Senate for the purposes of self-advertisement and advancement obviously does not belong. Senators are, as a group, fiercely protective of, and highly patriotic in regard to, the Senate.

* * *

CONFORMITY AND "EFFECTIVENESS"

All this would be very "interesting" but not particularly important to serious students of politics if the Senate folkways did not influence the distribution of power within the chamber.

The senators believe, either rightly or wrongly, that without the respect and confidence of their colleagues they can have little influence in the Senate. "You can't be effective," they said over and over again, "unless you are respected—on both sides of the aisle." The safest way to obtain this respect is to conform to the folkways, to become a "real Senate man." Those who do not run a serious risk. "In the Senate, if you don't conform, you don't get many favors for your state. You are never told that, but you soon learn."

In order to test this hypothesis, a crude index of "Legislative Effectiveness" was constructed for the

Eighty-third and Eighty-fourth Congresses by calculating the proportion of all public bills and resolutions introduced by each senator that were passed by the Senate. While such an index does not pretend to measure the overall power or influence of a senator, it does seem to reflect his efficiency as a legislator, narrowly defined. To the extent that the concept as used on Capitol Hill has any distinct meaning, "effectiveness" seems to mean the ability to get one's bills passed.

The "effectiveness" of the conforming and nonconforming senators is presented in Table 44. The less a senator talks on the Senate floor, and the narrower a senator's area of legislative interest and activity, the greater is his "effectiveness." Conformity to the Senate folkways does, therefore, seem to "pay off" in concrete legislative results.[6]

Table 44
FLOOR SPEAKING, INDEX OF SPECIALIZATION, AND LEGISLATIVE EFFECTIVENESS
83rd and 84th Congresses

Level of Floor Speaking	Index of Legislative Effectiveness			
	High	Medium	Low	
High	0%	33%	67%	100% (9)
Medium	3%	68%	29%	100% (31)
Low	15%	59%	26%	100% (39)
Index of Specialization				
High	23%	69%	8%	100% (13)
Medium	10%	62%	28%	100% (29)
Low	8%	51%	41%	100% (39)

There are unwritten rules of behavior, which we have called folkways, in the Senate. These rules are normative, that is, they define how a senator ought to behave. Nonconformity is met with moral condemnation, while senators who conform to the folkways are rewarded with high esteem by their colleagues. Partly because of this fact, they tend to be the most influential and effective members of the Senate.

These folkways, we have suggested, are highly functional to the Senate social system since they provide motivation for the performance of vital duties and essential modes of behavior which, otherwise, would go unrewarded. They discourage frequent and lengthy speech-making in a chamber without any other effective limitation on debate, encourage the development of expertness and a division of labor in a group of overworked laymen facing unbelievably complex problems, soften the inevitable personal conflicts of a problem-solving body, and encourage bargaining and the cautious use of awesome formal powers. Without these folkways, the Senate could hardly operate with its present organization and rules.

Nonetheless, the folkways are no more perfectly obeyed than the nation's traffic laws. Men who come to the Senate relatively late in life, toward the close of a distinguished career either in or out of politics, have a more difficult time fitting in than the others. So do those elected to the Senate with little prior political experience. The senators who aspire to the presidency find it hard to reconcile the expectations of their Senate colleagues with their desire to build a national following. Finally, all senators belong to, or identify with, many other groups beside the Senate, and the expectations and demands of these groups sometimes conflict with the folkways. This seems to happen most often with the liberals from large, urban two-party states. When confronted with such a conflict situation, a senator must choose between conforming to the folkways, and thus appearing to "sell out," or gaining popularity back home at the expense of goodwill, esteem, and effectiveness in the Senate, a course which diminishes his long-run ability to achieve what his followers demand. For this reason, conflicts between the demands of constituents and legislative peers are by no means automatically resolved in favor of constituents.

It would be a mistake to assume that the folkways of the Senate are unchangeable. Their origins are obscure, but sparse evidence scattered throughout senatorial memoirs suggests that they have changed very little since the nineteenth century. Certainly the chamber's small membership and gradual turnover is conducive to the transmission of such rules virtually unchanged from one generation to the next. Yet the trend in American politics seems to be toward more competitive two-party politics; a greater political role for the mass media of communications and those skilled in their political use;

larger, more urban constituencies. All these are factors which presently encourage departure from the norms of Senate behavior. In all likelihood, therefore, nonconformity to the folkways will increase in the future if the folkways remain as they are today. Moreover, the major forces which presently push senators toward nonconformity tend to converge upon a relatively small group of senators. Certainly, this is a more unstable situation than the random distribution of such influences—and, hence, of nonconforming behavior—among the entire membership of the Senate.

Notes

[1] Cf. Harry S. Truman's comments. "I learned [upon entering the Senate] . . . that the estimates of the various members which I formed in advance were not always accurate. I soon found that, among my ninety-five colleagues the real business of the Senate was carried on by unassuming and conscientious men, not by those who managed to get the most publicity." *New York Times,* October 3, 1955.

[2] *Providence* (R.I.) *Evening Journal,* February 8, 1956.

[3] For example, witness the following exchange from the *Congressional Record* (Daily Edition), June 11, 1956, p. 8990. *Mr. Hill.* Mr. President, although I greatly love the Senator from Illinois and although he has been very generous toward me in his remarks on the bill,— *Mr. Douglas.* I had hoped I would soften up the Senator from Alabama. (Laughter).

[4] Alben W. Barkley, *That Reminds Me,* (Garden City: Doubleday and Co., 1954) p. 255.

[5] Congressional Record (Daily Edition). June 13, 1956, p. 9153.

[6] It should be pointed out, as one friendly critic remarked after reading a draft of this analysis, that it is possible that "concentration and silence may be a product of legislative effectiveness, rather than the other way around." Statistical analysis is unable to tell us which came first. However, our Capitol Hill informants *overwhelmingly* argued that conformity leads to effectiveness and not the other way around. Until such time as a more refined analysis is possible, this seems to be the best evidence we have upon which to determine which is cause and which is effect.

[7] "Should the new legislator wish to be heard, the way to command the attention of the House," George Washington wrote to his favorite nephew, Bushrod, upon Bushrod's election to the Virginia House of Delegates in 1787, "is to speak seldom, but to important subjects, except such as relate to your constituents and, in the former case, make yourself perfectly master of the subject. Never exceed a decent warmth, and submit your sentiments with diffidence. A dictatorial style, though it may carry conviction, is always accompanied with disgust." J. A. Carroll and M. W. Ashworth [continuing D. S. Freeman's biography], *George Washington* (New York: C. Scribner's Sons, 1957), VII, 591. At least some of the folkways are very old and not restricted to the Senate of the United States!

CONGRESS AND CONSTITUENTS

Some of the earliest contributions of behavioralists to the analysis of American politics were made in the area of voting behavior. This area has since been researched as thoroughly as any. Largely as a result of survey techniques and computer technology, it has become possible to interview large random samples of the American electorate and to predict with great accuracy their actual vote, based on their attitudes and opinions about major issues and candidates, and on their socio-economic background.

One of the most extensive analyses of American voting behavior has been conducted by the Survey Research Center of the University of Michigan; the article adapted here for illustration is drawn from data collected and interpreted by two leading political scientists at the center, Warren F. Miller and Donald F. Stokes.

The research analyzes the relationship between the opinions of the American electorate and the opinions and votes of the congressmen who represent them in the United States House of Representatives. The researchers examined the extent to which the constituency has control over the actual performance of a congressman, on several critical issues.

In this analysis, a highly complex research design draws on different kinds of data. Specifically, the data include the opinions of constituents in a random sample of Congressional districts, interviews with congressmen, interviews with their nonincumbent opponents, and the actual roll call votes of congressmen on specific bills.

The investigators have attempted to identify the relationship between different conceptions of the role of the representative and the behavior of representatives in Congress. First they identify three optional roles for a legislator: he can operate independently of his constituents, and risk losing their support in the next election; he can vote for what he believes to be their opinion consistently; or he can vote with the program that his party has supported. The researchers' conclusions suggest that all three of these roles are important in the actual operation of the Congress and that the choice of role depends in large part on the type of issue.

Clearly, the researchers are not intent on evaluating whether such a situation is good or bad; they are attempting to establish what is actually happening. They use sophisticat-ed methodology in the examination of their research questions. All of these things are consistent with the norms of the behavioral paradigm.

Miller and Stokes rely extensively on the "correlation coefficient" in this analysis, and a brief description of that statistical device may prove useful in understanding their research. Correlation coefficients measure the relationship between two variables, by means of numbers that vary from +1.0, through 0.0, to −1.0. A positive correlation of +1.0 indicates that the events being observed always occur together; if A occurs, B will also occur, and an increase in A will be associated with an increase in B. A negative, or inverse, correlation of −1.0 indicates that if A occurs, B will not occur, and that as A increases, B tends to decrease. Most coefficients lie somewhere between +1.0 and −1.0, rather than at the extremes of the scale. A zero correlation indicates that the two variables simply do not relate in any discernible pattern.

In the research described here, the correlation coefficient has been used to assess the relationship between such variables as the opinion of the constituency, the legislator's perception of that opinion, the personal opinion of the legislator, and the actual vote of the legislator.

CONSTITUENCY INFLUENCE IN CONGRESS

WARREN E. MILLER AND DONALD E. STOKES

Substantial constituency influence over the lower house of Congress is commonly thought to be both a normative principle and a factual truth of American government. From their draft constitution we may assume the Founding Fathers expected it, and many political scientists feel, regretfully, that the Framers' wish has come all too true.[1] Nevertheless, much of the evidence of constituency control rests on inference. The fact that our House of Representatives, especially by comparison with the House of Commons, has irregular party voting does not of itself indicate that Congressmen deviate from party in response to local pressure. And even more, the

Adapted from Warren E. Miller and Donald E. Stokes, "Constituency Influence in Congress," *American Political Science Review*, LVII, 45–56. Reprinted by permission of the American Political Science Review and the author.

fact that many Congressmen *feel* pressure from home does not of itself establish that the local constituency is performing any of the acts that a reasonable definition of control would imply.

CONSTITUENCY CONTROL IN THE NORMATIVE THEORY OF REPRESENTATION

Control by the local constituency is at one pole of *both* the great normative controversies about representation that have arisen in modern times. It is generally recognized that constituency control is opposite to the conception of representation associated with Edmund Burke. Burke wanted the representative to serve the constituency's *interest* but not its *will,* and the extent to which the representative should be compelled by electoral sanctions to follow the "mandate" of his constituents has been at the heart of the ensuing controversy as it has continued for a century and a half.[2]

Constituency control also is opposite to the conception of government by responsible national parties. This is widely seen, yet the point is rarely connected with normative discussions of representation. Indeed, it is remarkable how little attention has been given to the model of representation implicit in the doctrine of a "responsible two-party system." . . .

The conception of representation implicit in the doctrine of responsible parties shares the idea of popular control with the instructed-delegate model. Both are versions of popular sovereignty. But "the people" of the responsible two-party system are conceived in terms of a national rather than a local constituency. Candidates for legislative office appeal to the electorate in terms of a *national* party program and leadership, to which, if elected, they will be committed. Expressions of policy preference by the local district are reduced to endorsements of one or another of these programs, and the local district retains only the arithmetical significance that whichever party can rally to its program the greater number of supporters in the district will control its legislative seat.

No one tradition of representation has entirely dominated American practice. Elements of the Burkean, instructed-delegate, and responsible party models can all be found in our political life. . . .

AN EMPIRICAL STUDY OF REPRESENTATION

To extend what we know of representation in the American Congress the Survey Research Center of The University of Michigan interviewed the incumbent Congressman, his nonincumbent opponent (if any), and a sample of constituents in each of 116 congressional districts, which were themselves a probability sample of all districts. These interviews, conducted immediately after the congressional election of 1958, explored a wide range of attitudes and perceptions held by the individuals who play the reciprocal roles of the representative relation in national government. The distinguishing feature of this research is, of course, that it sought direct information from both constituent and legislator (actual and aspiring). To this fund of comparative interview data has been added information about the roll call votes of our sample of Congressmen and the political and social characteristics of the districts they represent.

* * *

In view of the electorate's scanty information about government it was not at all clear in advance that such a comparison could be made. Some of the more buoyant advocates of popular sovereignty have regarded the citizen as a kind of kibitzer who looks over the shoulder of his representative at the legislative game. Kibitzer and player may disagree as to which card should be played, but they were at least thought to share a common understanding of what the alternatives are.

No one familiar with the findings of research on mass electorates could accept this view of the citizen. Far from looking over the shoulder of their Congressmen at the legislative game, most Americans are almost totally uninformed about legislative issues in Washington. At best the average citizen may be said to have some general ideas about how the country should be run, which he is able to use in responding to particular questions about what the government ought to do. For example, survey studies have shown that most people have a general (though differing) conception of how far government should go to achieve social and economic welfare objectives and that these convictions fix their response to various particular questions about actions government might take.[3]

What makes it possible to compare the policy preferences of constituents and Representatives despite the public's low awareness of legislative affairs is the fact that Congressmen themselves respond to many issues in terms of fairly broad evaluative dimensions. Undoubtedly policy alternatives are judged in the executive agencies and the specialized committees of the Congress by criteria that are relatively complex and specific to the policies at issue. But a good deal of evidence goes to show that when proposals come before the House as a whole they are judged on the basis of more general evaluative dimensions.[4] For example, most Congressmen, too, seem to have a general conception of how far government should go in the area of domestic social and economic welfare, and these general positions apparently orient their roll call votes on a number of particular social welfare issues.

It follows that such a broad evaluative dimension can be used to compare the policy preferences of constituents and Representatives despite the low state of the public's information about politics. In this study three such dimensions have been drawn from our voter interviews and from congressional interviews and roll call records. As suggested above, one of these has to do with approval of government action in the social welfare field, the primary domestic issue of the New Deal-Fair Deal (and New Frontier) Eras. A second dimension has to do with support for American involvement in foreign affairs, a latter-day version of the isolationist-internationalist continuum. A third dimension has to do with approval of federal action to protect the civil rights of Negroes.[5]

* * *

THE CONDITIONS
OF CONSTITUENCY INFLUENCE

Broadly speaking, the constituency can control the policy actions of the Representative in two alternative ways. The first of these is for the district to choose a Representative who so shares its views that in following his own convictions he does his constituents' will. In this case district opinion and the Congressman's actions are connected through the Representative's own policy attitudes. The second means of constituency control is for the Congressman to follow his (at least tolerably accurate) perceptions of district attitude in order to win re-election. In this case constituency opinion and the Congressman's actions are connected through his perception of what the district wants.[6]

These two paths of constituency control are presented schematically in Figure 1. As the figure suggests, each path has two steps, one connecting the constituency's attitude with an "intervening" attitude or perception, the other connecting this attitude or perception with the Representative's roll call behavior. Out of respect for the processes by which the human actor achieves cognitive congruence we have also drawn arrows between the two intervening factors, since the Congressman probably tends to see his district as having the same opinion as his own and also tends, over time, to bring his own opinion into line with the district's. The inclusion of these arrows calls attention to two other possible influence paths, each consisting of *three* steps, although these additional paths will turn out to be of relatively slight importance empirically.

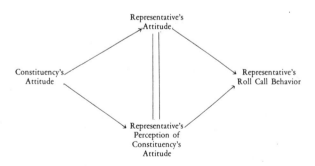

FIGURE 1.
CONNECTIONS BETWEEN A CONSTITUENCY'S ATTITUDE AND ITS REPRESENTATIVE'S ROLL CALL BEHAVIOR

Neither of the main influence paths of Figure 1 will connect the final roll call vote to the constituency's views if either of its steps is blocked. From this, two necessary conditions of constituency influence can be stated: *first,* the Representative's votes in the House must agree substantially with his own policy views or his perceptions of the district's views, and not be determined entirely by other influences to which the Congressman is exposed; and, *second,* the attitudes or perceptions governing the Representative's acts must correspond, at least imperfectly, to the district's actual opinions. It would be difficult to describe the relation of constituency to Representative as one of control unless these conditions are met.[7]

Yet these two requirements are not sufficient to assure control. A *third* condition must also be satisfied: the constituency must in some measure take the policy views of candidates into account in choosing a Representative. If it does not, agreement between district and Congressman may arise for reasons that cannot rationally be brought within the idea of control. For example, such agreement may simply reflect the fact that a Representative drawn from a given area is likely, by pure statistical probability, to share its dominant values, without his acceptance or rejection of these ever having been a matter of consequence to his electors.

EVIDENCE OF CONTROL: CONGRESSIONAL ATTITUDES AND PERCEPTIONS

How well are these conditions met in the relation of American Congressmen to their constituents? There is little question that the first is substantially satisfied; the evidence of our research indicates that members of the House do in fact vote both their own policy views and their perceptions of their constituents' views, at least on issues of social welfare, foreign involvement, and civil rights. If these two intervening factors are used to predict roll call votes, the prediction is quite successful. Their multiple correlation with roll call position is 0.7 for social welfare, 0.6 for foreign involvement, and 0.9 for civil rights; the last figure is especially persuasive. What is more, both the Congressman's own convictions and his perceptions of district opinion make a distinct contribution to his roll call behavior. In each of the three domains the prediction of roll call votes

is surer if it is made from both factors rather than from either alone.

* * *

The connections of congressional attitudes and perceptions with actual constituency opinion are weaker. If policy agreement between district and Representative is moderate and variable across the policy domains, as it is, this is to be explained much more in terms of the second condition of constituency control than the first. The Representative's attitudes and perceptions most nearly match true opinion in his district on the issues of Negro rights. Reflecting the charged and polarized nature of this area, the correlation of actual district opinion with perceived opinion is greater than 0.6, and the correlation of district attitude with the Representative's own attitude is nearly 0.4, as shown by Table 1. But the comparable correlations for foreign involvement are much smaller—indeed almost negligible. And the coefficients for social welfare are also smaller, although a detailed presentation of findings in this area would show that the Representative's perceptions and attitudes are more strongly associated with the attitude of his electoral *majority* than they are with the attitudes of the constituency as a whole.

Table 1
CORRELATIONS OF CONSTITUENCY ATTITUDES

Policy Domain	Correlation of Constituency Attitude With	
	Representative's Perception of Constituency Attitude	Representative's Own Attitude
Social welfare	.17	.21
Foreign involvement	.19	.06
Civil rights	.63	.39

Knowing this much about the various paths that may lead, directly or indirectly, from constituency attitude to roll call vote, we can assess their relative importance. Since the alternative influence chains have links of unequal strength, the full chains will not in general be equally strong, and these differences are of great importance in the relation of Representative to constituency. For the domain of civil rights Figure 2 assembles all the intercorrelations of the variables of our system. As the figure shows, the root correlation of constituency attitude with roll call behavior in this domain is 0.57. How much of this policy congruence can be accounted for by the influence path involving the Representative's attitude? And how much by the path involving his perception of constituency opinion? When the intercorrelations of the system are interpreted in the light of what we assume its causal structure to be, it is influence passing through the Congressman's perception of the district's views that is found to be preeminently important. Under the least favorable assumption as to its importance, this path is found to account for more than twice as much of the variance of roll call behavior as the paths involving the Representative's own attitude. However, when this same procedure is applied to our social welfare data, the results suggest that the direct connection of constituency and roll call through the Congressman's own attitude is the most important of the alternative paths. The reversal of the relative importance of the two paths as we move from civil rights to social welfare is one of the most striking findings of this analysis.

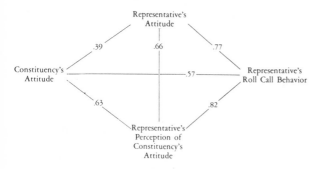

Civil Rights: Intercorrelations

FIGURE 2.
INTERCORRELATIONS OF VARIABLES PERTAINING TO CIVIL RIGHTS

EVIDENCE OF CONTROL: ELECTORAL BEHAVIOR

Of the three conditions of constituency influence, the requirement that the electorate take account of the policy positions of the candidates is the hardest to match with empirical evidence. Indeed, given the limited information the average voter carries to the polls, the public might be thought incompetent to perform any task of appraisal. Of constituents living in congressional districts where there was a contest between a Republican and a Democrat in 1958, less than one in five said they had read or heard something about both candidates, and well over half conceded they had read or heard nothing about either. And these proportions are not much better when they are based only on the part of the sample, not much more than half, that reported voting for Congress in 1958. The extent of awareness of the candidates among voters is indicated in Table 2. As the table shows, even of the portion of the public that was sufficiently interested to vote, almost half had read or heard nothing about either candidate.

Table 2
AWARENESS OF CONGRESSIONAL CANDIDATES
AMONG VOTERS, 1958

Read or Heard Something About Non-Incumbent	Read or Heard Something About Incumbent[a]		
	Yes	No	
Yes	24	5	29
No	25	46	71
	49	51	100%

[a]In order to include all districts where the House seat was contested in this table retains ten constituencies in which the incumbent Congressman did not seek re-election. Candidates of the retiring incumbent's party in these districts are treated here as if they were incumbents. Were these figures to be calculated only for constituencies in which an incumbent sought re-election, no entry in this four-fold table would differ from that given by more than two percent.

* * *

This evidence that the behavior of the electorate is largely unaffected by knowledge of the policy positions of the candidates is complemented by evidence about the forces that *do* shape the voters' choices among congressional candidates. The primary basis of voting in American congressional elections is identification with party. In 1958 only one vote in twenty was cast by persons without any sort of party loyalty. And among those who did have a party identification, only one in ten voted against their party. As a result, something like 84 percent of the vote that year was cast by party identifiers voting their usual party line. What is more, traditional party voting is seldom connected with current legislative issues. As the party loyalists in a nation-wide sample of voters told us what they liked and disliked about the parties in 1958, only a small fraction of the comments (about 15 percent) dealt with current issues of public policy.[8]

Yet the idea of reward or punishment at the polls for legislative stands is familiar to members of Congress, who feel that they and their records are quite visible to their constituents. Of our sample of Congressmen who were opposed for re-election in 1958, more than four-fifths said the outcome in their districts had been strongly influenced by the electorate's response to their records and personal standing. Indeed, this belief is clear enough to present a notable contradiction: Congressmen feel that their individual legislative actions may have considerable impact on the electorate, yet some simple facts about the Representative's salience to his constituents imply that this could hardly be true.

In some measure this contradiction is to be explained by the tendency of Congressmen to overestimate their visibility to the local public, a tendency that reflects the difficulties of the Representative in forming a correct judgment of constituent opinion. The communication most Congressmen have with their districts inevitably puts them in touch with organized groups and with individuals who are relatively well informed about politics. The Representative knows his constituents mostly from dealing with people who *do* write letters, who *will* attend meetings, who *have* an interest in his legislative stands. As a result, his sample of contacts with a constituency of several hundred thousand people is heavily biased: even the contacts he apparently makes at random are likely to be with people who grossly overrepresent the degree of political information and interest in the constituency as a whole.

But the contradiction is also to be explained by several aspects of the Representative's electoral situation that are of great importance to the question of constituency influence. The first of these is implicit in what has already been said. Because of the pervasive effects of party loyalties, no candidate for Congress starts from scratch in putting together an electoral majority. The Congressman is a dealer in increments and margins. He starts with a stratum of hardened party voters, and if the stratum is broad enough he can have a measurable influence on his chance of survival simply by attracting a small additional element of the electorate—or by not losing a larger one. Therefore, his record may have a very real bearing on his electoral success or failure without most of his constituents ever knowing what that record is.

Second, the relation of Congressman to voter is not a simple bilateral one but is complicated by the presence of all manner of intermediaries: the local party, economic interests, the news media, racial and nationality organizations, and so forth. Such is the lore of American politics, as it is known to any political scientist. Very often the Representative reaches the mass public through these mediating agencies, and the information about himself and his record may be considerably transformed as it diffuses out to the electorate in two or more stages. As a result, the public—or parts of it—may get simple positive or negative cues about the Congressman which were provoked by his legislative actions but which no longer have a recognizable issue content.

Third, for most Congressmen most of the time the electorate's sanctions are potential rather than actual. Particularly the Representative from a safe district may feel his proper legislative strategy is to avoid giving opponents in his own party or outside of it material they can use against him. As the Congressman pursues this strategy he may write a legislative record that never becomes very well known to his constituents; if it doesn't win votes, neither will it lose any. This is clearly the situation of most southern Congressmen in dealing with the issue of Negro rights. By voting correctly on this issue they are unlikely to increase their visibility to constituents. Nevertheless, the fact of constituency influence, backed by potential sanctions at the polls, is real enough.

* * *

CONCLUSION

Therefore, although the conditions of constituency influence are not equally satisfied, they are met well enough to give the local constituency a measure of control over the actions of its Representatives. Best satisfied is the requirement about motivational influences on the Congressman: our evidence shows that the Representative's roll call behavior is strongly influenced by his own policy preferences and by his perception of preferences held by the constituency. However, the conditions of influence that presuppose effective communication between Congressman and district are much less well met. The Representative has very imperfect information about the issue preferences of his constituency, and the constituency's awareness of the policy stands of the Representative ordinarily is slight.

The findings of this analysis heavily underscore the fact that no single tradition of representation fully accords with the realities of American legislative politics. The American system *is* a mixture, to which the Burkean, instructed-delegate, and responsible-party models all can be said to have contributed elements. Moreover, variations in the representative relation are most likely to occur as we move from one policy domain to another. No single, generalized configuration of attitudes and perceptions links Representative with constituency but rather several distinct patterns, and which of them is invoked depends very much on the issue involved.

The issue domain in which the relation of Congressman to constituency most nearly conforms to the instructed-delegate model is that of civil rights. This conclusion is supported by the importance of the influence-path passing through the Representative's perception of district opinion, although even in this domain the sense in which the constituency may be said to take the position of the candidate into account in reaching its electoral judgment should be carefully qualified.

The representative relation conforms most closely to the responsible-party model in the domain of social welfare. In this issue area, the arena of partisan conflict for a generation, the party symbol helps both constituency and Representative in the difficult process of communication between them. On the one hand, because

Republican and Democratic voters tend to differ in what they would have government do, the Representative has some guide to district opinion simply by looking at the partisan division of the vote. On the other hand, because the two parties tend to recruit candidates who differ on the social welfare role of government, the constituency can infer the candidates' position with more than random accuracy from their party affiliation, even though what the constituency has learned directly about these stands is almost nothing. How faithful the representation of social welfare views is to the responsible-party model should not be exaggerated. Even in this policy domain, American practice departs widely from an ideal conception of party government.[9] But in this domain, more than any other, political conflict has become a conflict of national parties in which constituency and Representative are known to each other primarily by their party association.

It would be too pat to say that the domain of foreign involvement conforms to the third model of representation, the conception promoted by Edmund Burke. Clearly it does in the sense that the Congressman looks elsewhere than to his district in making up his mind on foreign issues. However, the reliance he puts on the President and the Administration suggests that the calculation of where the public interest lies is often passed to the Executive on matters of foreign policy. Ironically, legislative initiative in foreign affairs has fallen victim to the very difficulties of gathering and appraising information that led Burke to argue that Parliament rather than the public ought to hold the power of decision. The background information and predictive skills that Burke thought the people lacked are held primarily by the modern Executive. As a result, the present role of the legislature in foreign affairs bears some resemblance to the role that Burke had in mind for the elitist, highly restricted *electorate* of his own day.

Notes

[1] To be sure, the work of the Federal Convention has been supplemented in two critical respects. The first of these is the practice, virtually universal since the mid-19th Century, of choosing Representatives from single-member districts of limited geographic area. The second is the practice, which has also become virtually universal in our own century, of selecting party nominees for the House by direct primary election.

[2] In the language of Eulau, Wahlke, *et al.*, we speak here of the "style," not the "focus," of representation. See their "The Role of the Representative: Some Empirical Observations on the Theory of Edmund Burke," *American Political Science Review*, Vol. 53 (September, 1959), pp. 742–756. An excellent review of the mandate-independence controversy is given by Hanna Fenichel Pitkin, "The Theory of Representation" (unpublished doctoral dissertation, University of California, Berkeley, 1961). For other contemporary discussions of representation, see Alfred de Grazia, *Public and Republic* (New York, 1951), and John A. Fairlie, "The Nature of Political Representation," *American Political Science Review*, Vol. 34 (April–June, 1940), pp. 236–48, 456–66.

[3] See Angus Campbell, Philip E. Converse, Warren E. Miller, and Donald E. Stokes, *The American Voter* (New York, 1960), pp. 194–209.

[4] This conclusion, fully supported by our own work for later Congresses, is one of the main findings to be drawn from the work of Duncan MacRae on roll call voting in the House of Representatives. See his *Dimensions of Congressional Voting: A Statistical Study of the House of Representatives in the Eighty-First Congress* (Berkeley and Los Angeles: University of California Press, 1958).

[5] The content of the three issue domains may be suggested by some of the roll call and interview items used. In the area of social welfare these included the issues of public housing, public power, aid to education, and government's role in maintaining full employment. In the area of foreign involvement the items included the issues of foreign economic aid, military aid, sending troops abroad, and aid to neutrals. In the area of civil rights the items included the issues of school desegregation, fair employment, and the protection of Negro voting rights.

[6] A third type of connection, excluded here, might obtain between district and Congressman if the Representative accedes to what he thinks the district wants because he believes that to be what a representative *ought* to do, whether or not it is necessary for re-election. We leave this type of connection out of our account here because we conceive an influence relation as one in which control is not voluntarily accepted or rejected by someone subject to it. Of course, this possible connection between district and Representative is not any the less interesting because it falls outside our definition of influence or control, and we have given a good deal of attention to it in the broader study of which this analysis is part.

[7] It scarcely needs to be said that demonstrating *some* constituency influence would not imply that the Representative's behavior is *wholly* determined by constituency pressures. The legislator acts in a complex institutional setting in which he is subject to a wide variety of influences. The constituency can exercise a genuine measure of control without driving all other influences from the Representative's life space.

[8] For a more extended analysis of forces on the congressional vote, see Donald E. Stokes and Warren E. Miller, "Party Government and the Saliency of Congress," *Public Opinion Quarterly*, Vol. 26 (Winter, 1962), pp. 531–546.

[9] The factors in American electoral behavior that encourage such a departure are discussed in Stokes and Miller, loc cit.

POLITICAL PARTIES

A third area in which behavioralists have made a significant research contribution is that of political parties. Traditional analyses of political parties have focused on their historical development, the platforms or programs they have supported, their internal organizational structure, and the legal requirements for their operation. The behavioral contribution has been the addition of a great deal of data concerning what the members of political parties believe and what they actually do.

In the research described here, the investigators have attempted to discover whether or not there are major differences between the two major political parties in this country, as well as the extent to which any differences might be reflected among leaders and followers within these parties.

The data were drawn from questionnaires sent to participants in the two presidential nominating conventions, who were assumed to represent the opinions of the leadership in both parties. Questionnaires were also distributed through the American Institute of Public Opinion ("Gallup poll") to a random sample of voters in the American electorate.

Some of the most significant conclusions of this study are 1) that opinion among the leaders of the two parties concerning the major issues differs more widely than previously suspected; 2) that the followers of the two different parties agree on a great many issues; and 3) that the followers of both parties appear to be closer to the leadership of the Democratic party than to the leadership of the Republican party.

ISSUE CONFLICT AND CONSENSUS IN POLITICAL PARTIES

HERBERT MC CLOSKY, PAUL J. HOFFMAN,
AND ROSEMARY O'HARA

American political parties are often regarded as "brokerage" organizations, weak in principle, devoid of ideology, and inclined to differ chiefly over unimportant

Adapted from Herbert McClosky, *et. al.*, "Issue Conflict and Consensus Among Party Leaders and Followers," *American Political Science Review*, LIV, 405–27. Reprinted by permission of the American Political Science Association and the authors. [footnotes abridged.]

questions. In contrast to the "ideological" parties of Europe—which supposedly appeal to their followers through sharply defined, coherent, and logically related doctrines—the American parties are thought to fit their convictions to the changing demands of the political contest. According to this view, each set of American party leaders is satisfied to play Tweedledee to the other's Tweedledum.

* * *

The research reported here was designed not to refute these observations but to test the accuracy of the claim that they are sufficient to prevent differences in outlook from taking root in the American party system. We believed that the homogenizing tendencies referred to are strongly offset by contrary influences, and that voters are preponderantly led to support the party whose opinions they share. We further thought that the competition for office, though giving rise to similarities between the parties, also impels them to diverge from each other in order to sharpen their respective appeals. For this and other reasons, we expected to find that the leaders of the two parties, instead of ignoring differences alleged to exist within the electorate, would differ on issues more sharply than their followers would. We believed further that even in a brokerage system the parties would serve as independent reference groups, developing norms, values, and self-images to which their supporters could readily respond. Their influence, we felt, would frequently exceed that of ethnic, occupational, residential and other reference groups. In sum, we proceeded on the belief that the parties are not simply spokesmen for other interest groups, but are in their own right agencies for formulating, transmitting, and anchoring political opinions, that they attract adherents who in general share those opinions, and that through a feedback process of mutual reinforcement between the organization and its typical supporters, the parties develop integrated and stable political tendencies. Other hypotheses will be specified as we present and analyze our findings.

PROCEDURES

* * *

For our samples of party "leaders" we turned to the Democratic and Republican national conventions, largely because they are the leading and most representative of the party organs, their delegates coming from every part of the United States and from every level of party and government activity. Our samples ranged from governors, senators, and national committeemen at the one end to precinct workers and local officials at the other. In the absence of comprehensive information about the characteristics of the party élites in America, no one can say how closely the convention delegates mirror the total party leadership. We felt it fair to assume, nevertheless, that the delegates represented as faithful a cross section of American party leadership as could be had without an extraordinary expenditure of money and labor. . . . Of the 6,848 delegates and alternates available to be sampled, 3,193 actually participated; 3,020 (1,788 Democrats and 1,232 Republicans) completed and returned questionnaires that were usable in all respects.[1] The proportion of returns was roughly equivalent for both sets of party leaders.

The rank and file sample, which we wanted both for its intrinsic value and for its utility as a control group, was obtained by special arrangement with the American Institute of Public Opinion. In January 1958, Gallup interviewers personally distributed our questionnaire to 2,917 adult voters in two successive national cross-section surveys. Some 1,610 questionnaires were filled out and returned, of which 1,484 were completely usable. This sample closely matched the national population on such characteristics as sex, age, region, size of city, and party affiliation, and, though it somewhat oversampled the upper educational levels, we considered it sufficiently large and representative for most of our purposes. Of the 1,484 respondents, 821 were Democratic supporters (629 "pure" Democrats, plus 192 whom we classified as "independent" Democrats) and 623 were Republican supporters (479 "pure" Republicans, plus 144 "independent" Republicans). Forty respondents could not be identified as adherents of either party.

*   *   *

The questions most relevant for the present article were those which asked each respondent to express his attitudes toward 24 important national issues, and to state whether he believed support for each issue should be "increased," "decreased," or "remain as is." The list of issues and the responses of each sample will be found in Tables II-A through II-E, where for convenience of analysis, the issues have been grouped under five broad headings: Public Ownership, Government Regulation of the Economy, Equalitarianism and Human Welfare, Tax Policy and Foreign Policy.

In tabulating the results, we first scored each individual on each issue and then computed aggregate scores for all the members of a given sample. To begin with, percentages were used to show the proportion who favored increasing, decreasing, or retaining the existing level of support on each issue. But as it was clumsy to handle three figures for each issue, we constructed a single index or "ratio of support" which would simultaneously take account of all three scores. The index was built by assigning a weight of 1.0 to each "increase" response in the sample, of 0 to each "decrease" response, and of .50 to each "remain as is" (or "same") response. Thus the ratio-of-support score shown for any given sample is in effect a mean score with a possible range of 0 to 1.0, in which support for an issue increases as the scores approach 1.0 and decreases as they approach 0. In general, the scores can be taken to approximate the following overall positions: .0 to .25—strongly wish to reduce support; .26 to .45—wish to reduce support; .46 to .55—satisfied with the *status quo*; .56 to .75—wish to increase support; and .76 to 1.00—strongly wish to increase support. Note that the differences in degree suggested by these categories refer not to the *strength of feeling* exhibited by individuals toward an issue but rather to the *numbers of people* in a sample who hold points of view favoring or opposing that issue.

*   *   *

FINDINGS: COMPARISONS BETWEEN LEADERS

No more conclusive findings emerge from our study of party issues than those growing out of the comparisons between the two sets of party leaders. Despite the brokerage tendency of the American parties, their active members are obviously separated by large and important differences. The differences, moreover, conform with the popular image in which the Democratic party is seen as the more "progressive" or "radical," the Republican as the more "moderate" or "conservative" of the two.[2] In addition, the disagreements are remarkably consistent, a function not of chance but of systematic points of view, whereby the responses to any one of the issues could reasonably have been predicted from knowledge of the responses to the other issues.

Examination of Tables II-A through E shows that the leaders differ significantly on 23 of the 24 issues listed and that they are separated on 15 of these issues by .18 or more ratio points—in short, by differences that are in absolute magnitude very large. The two samples are furthest apart in their attitudes toward public ownership and are especially divided on the question of government ownership of natural resources, the Democrats strongly favoring it, the Republicans just as strongly wanting it cut back. The difference of .39 in the ratio scores is the largest for any of the issues tested. In percentages, the differences are 58 per cent (D) vs. 13 per cent (R) in favor of increasing support, and 19 per cent (D) vs. 52 per cent (R) in favor of decreasing support. Both parties preponderantly support public control and development of atomic energy, but the Democrats do so more uniformly.

V. O. Key, among others, has observed that the Republican party is especially responsive to the "financial and manufacturing community," reflecting the view that government should intervene as little as possible to burden or restrain prevailing business interests. The validity of this observation is evident throughout all our data, and is most clearly seen in the responses to the issues listed under Government Regulation of the Economy, Equalitarianism and Human Welfare, Tax Policy. Democratic leaders are far more eager than Republican leaders to strengthen enforcement of antimonopoly laws and to increase regulation of public utilities and business. . . .

The two sets of leaders are also far apart on the farm issue, the Democrats preferring slightly to increase farm supports, the Republicans wanting strongly to reduce them. . . . The Republican desire to reduce government expenditures and to promote independence from

"government handouts" prevails on the farm question as it does on other issues, while the Democratic preference for a more regulated economy in which government intervenes to reduce economic risk and to stabilize prosperity is equally evident on the other side. Party attitudes on this issue appear to be determined as much by ideological tendencies as by deliberate calculation of

Table I
AVERAGE DIFFERENCE IN THE RATIO-OF-SUPPORT SCORES AMONG PARTY LEADERS AND FOLLOWERS FOR THE FIVE CATEGORIES OF ISSUES

Category of Issues	Democratic Leaders vs. Republican Leaders	Democratic Followers vs. Republican Followers	Democratic Leaders vs. Democratic Followers	Republican Leaders vs. Republican Followers	Democratic Leaders vs. Republican Followers	Republican Leaders vs. Democratic Followers
a. Public ownership of resources	.28	.04	.06	.18	.10	.22
b. Government regulation of the economy	.22	.06	.08	.10	.12	.16
c. Equalitarianism, human welfare	.22	.05	.08	.21	.06	.25
d. Tax policy	.20	.06	.06	.20	.04	.26
e. Foreign policy	.15	.02	.05	.08	.07	.10
Average differences in ratio score for all categories	.21	.04	.07	.15	.08	.20

Sample sizes: Democratic leaders, 1,788; Republican leaders, 1,232; Democratic followers, 821; Republican followers 623.

Table II-A
COMPARISON OF PARTY LEADERS AND FOLLOWERS ON "PUBLIC OWNERSHIP" ISSUES, BY PERCENTAGES AND RATIOS OF SUPPORT

| Issues | Leaders | | Followers | |
	Democratic N = 1,788	Republican N = 1,232	Democratic N = 821	Republican N = 623
		(%s down)		
Public ownership of natural resources, % favoring				
Increase	57.5	12.9	35.3	31.1
Decrease	18.6	51.9	15.0	19.9
Same, n.c.*	23.8	35.2	49.7	49.0
Support ratio	.69	.30	.60	.56
Public control of atomic energy % favoring				
Increase	73.2	45.0	64.2	59.4
Decrease	7.2	15.3	7.1	10.0
Same, n.c.	19.6	39.7	28.7	30.6
Support ratio	.83	.65	.79	.75
Mean support ratios for the public ownership category	.76	.48	.70	.66

*n.c. = no code.

the political advantages to be gained by favoring or opposing subsidies to farmers. . . .

Having implied that agriculture policies partly result from principle, we must note that on three other issues in this category (trade unions, credit, and tariffs),

principle seems to be overweighed by old-fashioned economic considerations. In spite of their distaste for government interference in economic affairs, the Republicans almost unanimously favor greater regulation of trade unions and they are more strongly disposed than

Table II-B

COMPARISON OF PARTY LEADERS AND FOLLOWERS ON "GOVERNMENT REGULATION OF THE ECONOMY" ISSUES, BY PERCENTAGES AND RATIOS OF SUPPORT

	Leaders		Followers	
	Democratic N = 1,788	Republican N = 1,232	Democratic N = 821	Republican N = 623
Issues		(%s down)		
Level of farm price supports, % favoring:				
Increase	43.4	6.7	39.0	23.0
Decrease	28.1	67.4	27.6	40.3
Same, n.c.	28.5	25.8	33.4	36.7
Support ratio	.58	.20	.56	.41
Government regulation of business, % favoring:				
Increase	20.2	0.6	18.6	7.4
Decrease	38.5	84.1	33.4	46.2
Same, n.c.	41.3	15.3	48.0	46.4
Support ratio	.41	.08	.43	.31
Regulation of public utilities, % favoring:				
Increase	59.0	17.9	39.3	26.0
Decrease	6.4	17.6	11.1	12.0
Same, n.c.	34.6	64.5	49.6	62.0
Support ratio	.76	.50	.64	.57
Enforcement of anti-monopoly laws, % favoring:				
Increase	78.0	44.9	53.2	51.0
Decease	2.9	9.0	7.9	6.6
Same, n.c.	19.1	46.1	38.9	42.4
Support ratio	.88	.68	.73	.72
Regulation of trade unions, % favoring:				
Increase	59.3	86.4	46.6	57.8
Decrease	12.4	4.5	8.9	10.6
Same, n.c.	28.3	9.2	44.5	31.6
Support ratio	.73	.91	.69	.74
Level of tariffs, % favoring:				
Increase	13.0	19.2	16.6	15.2
Decrease	43.0	26.3	25.3	21.3
Same, n.c.	43.9	54.5	58.1	63.4
Support ratio	.35	.46	.46	.47
Restrictions on credit, % favoring:				
Increase	24.8	20.6	26.1	25.7
Decrease	39.9	20.6	22.2	23.8
Same, n.c.	35.9	58.8	51.8	50.5
Support ratio	.43	.50	.52	.51
Mean support ratios for "government regulation of the economy" category	.59	.48	.58	.53

the Democrats toward government intervention to restrict credit and to raise tariffs. Of course, party cleavages over the credit and tariff issues have a long history, which may by now have endowed them with ideological force beyond immediate economic considerations. The preponderant Democratic preference for greater regulation of trade unions is doubtless a response to recent "exposures" of corrupt labor practices, though it may also signify that the party's perspective toward the trade unions is shifting somewhat.

The closer Republican identification with business, free enterprise, and economic conservatism in general, and the friendlier Democratic attitude toward labor and toward government regulation of the economy, are easily observed in the data from other parts of our questionnaire. . . . The key to the explanation has to be sought in the symbolic and reference group identifications of the two parties, and in their underlying values.

Table II-C

COMPARISON OF PARTY LEADERS AND FOLLOWERS ON "EQUALITARIAN AND HUMAN WELFARE" ISSUES, BY PERCENTAGES AND RATIOS OF SUPPORT

	Leaders		Followers	
	Democratic N = 1,788	Republican N = 1,232	Democratic N = 821	Republican N = 623
Issues		(%s down)		
Federal aid to education, % favoring:				
Increase	66.2	22.3	74.9	64.8
Decrease	13.4	43.2	5.6	8.3
Same, n.c.	20.4	34.5	19.5	26.8
Support ratio	.76	.40	.85	.78
Slum clearance and public housing, % favoring:				
Increase	78.4	40.1	79.5	72.5
Decrease	5.6	21.6	5.8	7.9
Same, n.c.	16.0	38.3	14.6	19.6
Support ratio	.86	.59	.87	.82
Social security benefits, % favoring:				
Increase	60.0	22.5	69.4	57.0
Decrease	3.9	13.1	3.0	3.8
Same, n.c.	36.1	64.4	27.5	39.2
Support ratio	.78	.55	.83	.77
Minimum wages, % favoring:				
Increase	50.0	15.5	59.0	43.5
Decrease	4.7	12.5	2.9	5.0
Same, n.c.	45.2	72.0	38.1	51.5
Support ratio	.73	.52	.78	.69
Enforcement of integration, % favoring:				
Increase	43.8	25.5	41.9	40.8
Decrease	26.6	31.7	27.4	23.6
Same, n.c.	29.5	42.8	30.7	35.6
Support ratio	.59	.47	.57	.59
Immigration into United States, % favoring:				
Increase	36.1	18.4	10.4	8.0
Decrease	27.0	29.9	52.0	44.6
Same, n.c.	36.9	51.7	37.6	47.4
Support ratio	.54	.44	.29	.32
Mean support ratios for "equalitarian and human welfare" category	.71	.50	.70	.66

Nowhere do we see this more clearly than in the responses to the Equalitarian and Human Welfare issues. The mean difference in the ratio scores for the category as a whole is .22, a very large difference and one that results from differences in the expected direction on all six issues that make up the category. On four of these issues—federal aid to education, slum clearance and public housing, social security, and minimum wages—the leaders of the two parties are widely separated, the differences in their ratio scores ranging from .36 to .21. The percentages showing the proportions who favor increased support for these issues are even more striking. In every instance the Democratic percentages are consid-

erably higher: 66 *vs.* 22 per cent (education); 78 *vs.* 40 per cent (slum clearance and housing); 60 *vs.* 23 per cent (social security); and 50 *vs.* 16 per cent (minimum wages). The Democratic leaders also are better disposed than the Republican leaders toward immigration; twice as many of them (36 per cent *vs.* 18 per cent) favor a change in policy to permit more immigrants to enter. The overall inclination of both party élites, however, is to accept the present levels of immigration, the Democratic ratio score falling slightly above, and the Republicans slightly below, the midpoint.

More surprising are the differences on the segregation issue, for, despite strong Southern influence, the

Table II-D

COMPARISON OF PARTY LEADERS AND FOLLOWERS ON "TAX POLICY" ISSUES,
BY PERCENTAGES AND RATIOS OF SUPPORT

	Leaders		Followers	
	Democratic N = 1,788	Republican N = 1,232	Democratic N = 821	Republican N = 623
Issues	(%s down)			
Corporate income tax, % favoring:				
Increase	32.3	4.0	32.0	23.3
Decrease	23.3	61.5	20.5	25.7
Same, n.c.	44.4	34.5	47.5	51.0
Support ratio	.54	.21	.56	.49
Tax on large incomes, % favoring:				
Increase	27.0	5.4	46.6	34.7
Decrease	23.1	56.9	13.8	21.7
Same, n.c.	49.9	37.7	39.6	43.6
Support ratio	.52	.24	.66	.56
Tax on business, % favoring:				
Increase	12.6	1.0	24.6	15.9
Decrease	38.3	71.1	24.1	32.6
Same, n.c.	49.1	27.8	51.3	51.5
Support ratio	.37	.15	.50	.42
Tax on middle incomes, % favoring:				
Increase	2.7	0.8	4.5	3.0
Decrease	50.2	63.9	49.3	44.3
Same, n.c.	47.1	35.3	46.2	52.6
Support ratio	.26	.18	.28	.29
Tax on small incomes, % favoring:				
Increase	1.4	2.9	1.6	2.1
Decrease	79.2	65.0	77.5	69.6
Same, n.c.	19.4	32.1	20.9	28.3
Support ratio	.11	.19	.12	.16
Mean support ratios for "tax policy" category	.36	.19	.42	.38

Democratic leaders express significantly more support for enforcing integration than the Republicans do. Moreover, the difference between the two parties rises from .12 for the national samples as a whole to a difference of .18 when the southern leaders are excluded. . . .

Examination of the actual magnitude of the ratio scores in this category reveals that the Republicans want not so much to abrogate existing social welfare or equalitarian measures as to keep them from being broadened. The Democrats, by comparison, are shown to be the party of social equality and reform, more willing than their opponents to employ legislation for the benefit of the underprivileged. . . .

The self-images and reference group identifications of the two parties also should be noted in this connection. For example, many more Democratic than Republi-

can leaders call themselves liberal and state that they would be most likely to take advice from liberal reform organizations, the Farmers' Union, and (as we have seen) from the trade unions; only a small number consider themselves conservative or would seek advice from conservative reform organizations, the National Association of Manufacturers, or the Farm Bureau Federation. The Republicans have in almost all instances the reverse identifications: only a handful regard themselves as liberal or would seek counsel from liberal organizations, while more than 42 per cent call themselves conservative and would look to the NAM or to conservative reform organizations for advice. Almost two-thirds of the Republicans (compared with 29 per cent of the Democrats) regard the Chamber of Commerce as an important source of advice. Businessmen are listed as having "too much power" by 42 per cent of the Democrats but by only

Table II-E

COMPARISON OF PARTY LEADERS AND FOLLOWERS ON "FOREIGN POLICY" ISSUES, BY PERCENTAGES AND RATIOS OF SUPPORT

Issues	Leaders		Followers	
	Democratic N = 1,788	Republican N = 1,232	Democratic N = 821	Republican N = 623
		(%s down)		
Reliance on the United Nations, % favoring:				
Increase	48.9	24.4	34.7	33.4
Decrease	17.6	34.8	17.3	19.3
Same, n.c.	33.5	40.7	48.0	47.3
Support ratio	.66	.45	.59	.57
American participation in military alliances, % favoring:				
Increase	41.5	22.7	39.1	32.3
Decrease	17.6	25.7	14.0	15.4
Same, n.c.	40.9	51.6	46.9	52.3
Support ratio	.62	.48	.62	.58
Foreign aid, % favoring:				
Increase	17.8	7.6	10.1	10.1
Decrease	51.0	61.7	58.6	57.3
Same, n.c.	31.1	30.7	31.3	32.6
Support ratio	.33	.23	.26	.26
Defense spending, % favoring:				
Increase	20.7	13.6	50.5	45.7
Decrease	34.4	33.6	16.4	15.4
Same, n.c.	44.8	52.8	33.0	38.8
Support ratio	.43	.40	.67	.65
Mean support ratios for "foreign policy" category (excl. defense spending)	.54	.39	.49	.47

9 per cent of the Republicans. The Democrats are also significantly more inclined than the Republicans to consider Catholics, Jews, and the foreign born as having "too little power." While self-descriptions and reference group identifications often correspond poorly with actual beliefs—among the general population they scarcely correspond at all, in fact—we are dealing, in the case of the leaders, with a politically informed and highly articulate set of people who have little difficulty connecting the beliefs they hold and the groups that promote or obstruct those beliefs.

Our fourth category, Tax Policy, divides the parties almost as severely as do the other categories. The mean difference for the category as a whole is .20, and it would doubtless have been larger but for the universal unpopularity of proposals to increase taxes on small and middle income groups. Table II-D shows that the differences between the parties on the tax issues follow the patterns previously observed and that tax policy is for the Democrats a device for redistributing income and promoting social equality. Neither party, however, is keen about raising taxes for *any* group: even the Democrats have little enthusiasm for new taxes on upper income groups or on business and corporate enterprises. The Republican leaders are overwhelmingly opposed to increased taxes for *any* group, rich *or* poor. This can be seen in their low ratio scores on the tax issues, which range from only .15 to .24. But while they are far more eager than the Democratic leaders to cut taxes on corporate and private wealth, they are less willing to reduce taxes on the lower income groups. These differences, it should be remarked, are not primarily a function of differences in the income of the two samples. Although there are more people with high incomes among the Republican leaders, the disproportion between the two samples is not nearly great enough to account for the dissimilarities in their tax views.

Of the five categories considered, Foreign Policy shows the smallest average difference, but even on these issues the divergence between Democratic and Republican leader attitudes is significant. Except for defense spending the Democrats turn out to be more internationalist than the Republicans, as evidenced in their greater commitment to the United Nations and to

American participation in international military alliances like NATO. Twice as many Democrats as Republicans want the United States to rely more heavily upon such organizations, while many more Republicans want to reduce our international involvements. Both parties are predominantly in favor of cutting back foreign aid—a somewhat surprising finding in light of Democratic public pronouncements on this subject—but more Republicans feel strongly on the subject. Our data thus furnish little support for the claim that the parties hold the same views on foreign policy or that their seeming differences are merely a response to the demands of political competition. . . .

Notice that the issues commonly thought to be most divisive do not always evoke the greatest cleavage between the parties. Immigration, tariffs, civil rights, monopoly control, and credit regulation fall toward the lower end of the rank order, while farm supports, federal aid to education, slum clearance, social security, minimum wages, public housing, and issues dealing with the regulation and taxation of business fall toward the upper end. Though by no means uniformly, the older, more traditional issues appear to have been superseded as sources of controversy by issues that have come into prominence chiefly during the New Deal and Fair Deal.

COMPARISONS BETWEEN FOLLOWERS

So far we have addressed ourselves to the differences between Democratic and Republican *leaders*. In each of the tables presented, however, data are included from which the two sets of party *followers* may also be compared.

The observation most clearly warranted from these data is that the rank and file members of the two parties are far less divided than their leaders. Not only do they diverge significantly on fewer issues—seven as compared with 23 for the leader samples—but the magnitudes of the differences in their ratio scores are substantially smaller for every one of the 24 issues. . . . Insofar as they differ at all, however, the followers tend to divide in a pattern similar to that shown by the leaders, the correlation between their rank orders being .72. All the issues on which the followers significantly disagree are of the "bread and butter" variety, the more symbolic issues being so remotely experienced and so vaguely grasped that rank and file voters are often unable to identify them with either party. Policies affecting farm prices, business regulation, taxes, or minimum wages, by contrast, are quickly felt by the groups to whom they are addressed and are therefore more capable of arousing partisan identifications. It should also be noted that while the average differences are small for all five categories, they are smallest of all for foreign policy—the most removed and least well understood group of issues in the entire array.

Democratic and Republican followers were also compared on a number of scales and reference group questions. The results, while generally consistent with the differences between the leaders, show the followers to be far more united than their leaders on these measures as well. . . . The average Democrat is slightly more willing than the average Republican to label himself a liberal or to seek advice from liberal organizations; the contrary is true when it comes to adopting conservative identifications. Only in the differential trust they express toward business and labor are the two sets of followers widely separated.

These findings give little support to the claim that the "natural divisions" of the electorate are being smothered by party leaders. Not only do the leaders disagree more sharply than their respective followers, but the level of consensus among the electorate (with or without regard to party) is fairly high. Inspection of the "increase" and "decrease" percentage scores (Tables II-A-E) shows that substantial differences of opinion exist among the electorate on only five of the 24 issues (credit restrictions, farm supports, segregation, and corporate and business taxes). Of course, voters may divide more sharply on issues at election time, since campaigns intensify party feeling and may also intensify opinions on issues. . . .

LEADERS VERSUS FOLLOWERS

In comparing each party elite with its own followers we were mainly interested in seeing how closely each body of supporters shared the point of view of its lead-

ers, in order to test the hypothesis that party affiliation, even for the rank and file, is a function of ideological agreement. In predicting that the parties would tend to attract supporters who share their beliefs, we expected, of course, to find exceptions. We knew that many voters pay little attention to the ideological aspects of politics and that, in Gabriel Almond's phrase, a party's more "esoteric doctrines" are not always known to its followers.[3] Nevertheless we were not prepared for the findings turned up by this phase of the inquiry, for the differences between leaders and followers—among the Republicans at least—are beyond anything we had expected. Indeed, the conclusion is inescapable that the views of the Republican rank and file are, on the whole, much closer to those of the Democratic leaders than to those of the Republican leaders. Although conflicts in outlook also exist between Democratic leaders and followers, they are less frequent or severe. . . .

In short, whereas Republican leaders hold to the tenets of business ideology and remain faithful to the spirit and intellectual mood of leaders like Robert A. Taft, the rank and file Republican supporters have embraced, along with their Democratic brethren, the regulatory and social reform measures of the Roosevelt and Truman administrations. This inference receives further support from the scores on our Party Ideology scale where, on a variety of attitudes and values which characteristically distinguish the leaders of the two parties, the Republican followers fall closer to the Democratic than to the Republican side of the continuum. Thus, in addition to being the preferred party of the more numerous classes, the Democrats also enjoy the advantage over their opponents of holding views that are more widely shared throughout the country.

Assuming the findings are valid, we were obviously wrong to expect that party differentiation among followers would depend heavily upon ideological considerations.[4] Evidently, party attachment is so much a function of other factors (e.g. class and primary group memberships, religious affiliation, place of residence, mass media, etc.) that many voters can maintain their party loyalties comfortably even while holding views that contradict the beliefs of their own leaders.

Still, we are not entitled to conclude that issue

outlook has no effect on the party affiliation of ordinary members. It is conceivable, for example, that the Republican party has come to be the minority party partly because the opinions of its spokesmen are uncongenial to a majority of the voters. We have no way of knowing from our data—collected at only a single point in time—how many "normally" Republican voters, if any, have defected to the Democrats or fled into independency because they disapprove of Republican beliefs. . . .

SUMMARY AND CONCLUSIONS

. . . From the data yielded by this inquiry, the following inferences seem most warranted:

1. Although it has received wide currency, especially among Europeans, the belief that the two American parties are identical in principle and doctrine has little foundation in fact. Examination of the opinions of Democratic and Republican leaders shows them to be distinct communities of cobelievers who diverge sharply on many important issues. . . . The unpopularity of many of the positions held by Republican leaders suggests also that the parties submit to the demands of their constituents less slavishly than is commonly supposed.

2. Republican and Democratic leaders stand furthest apart on the issues that grow out of their group identification and support—out of the managerial, proprietary, and high-status connections of the one, and the labor, minority, low-status, and intellectual connections of the other. The opinions of each party élite are linked less by chance than by membership in a common ideological domain. . . .

3. Whereas the leaders of the two parties diverge strongly, their followers differ only moderately in their attitudes toward issues. The hypothesis that party beliefs unite adherents and bring them into the party ranks may hold for the more active members of a mass party but not for its rank and file supporters. Republican followers, in fact, disagree far more with their own leaders than with the leaders of the Democratic party. Little support was found for the belief that deep cleavages exist among the electorate but are ignored by the leaders. One might, indeed, more accurately assert the contrary, to wit: that the natural cleavages between the leaders are largely ignored by the voters. . . .

4. Except for their desire to ingratiate themselves with as many voters as possible, the leaders of the two parties have more reason than their followers to hold sharply opposing views on the important political questions of the day. Compared with the great mass of supporters, they are articulate, informed, highly partisan, and involved; they comprise a smaller and more tightly knit group which is closer to the wellsprings of party opinion, more accessible for indoctrination, more easily rewarded or punished for conformity or deviation, and far more affected, politically and psychologically, by engagement in the party struggle for office. . . .

5. Finding that party leaders hold contrary beliefs does not prove that they *act* upon those beliefs or that the two parties are, in practice, governed by different outlooks. . . . Until further inquiries are conducted, however, it seems reasonable to assume that the views held privately by party leaders can never be entirely suppressed but are bound to crop out in hundreds of large and small ways—in campaign speeches, discussions at party meetings, private communications to friends and sympathizers, statements to the press by party officials and candidates, legislative debates, and public discussions on innumerable national, state, and local questions. If, in other words, the opinions of party leaders are as we have described them, there is every chance that they are expressed and acted upon to some extent. . . .

6. The parties are internally united on some issues, divided on others. In general, Republican leaders achieve greatest homogeneity on issues that grow out of their party's identification with business, Democratic leaders on issues that reflect their connection with liberal and lower-income groups. We find no support for the hypothesis that the parties achieve greatest internal consensus on the issues which principally divide them from their opponents. . . .

. . . The parties must be considered not merely as spokesmen for other interest groups but as reference groups in their own right, helping to formulate, to sustain, and to speak for a recognizable point of view.

Notes

[1] This gratifyingly large number of returns of so lengthy and detailed a questionnaire was attained through a number of follow-up mailings and special letters. These and other procedures designed to check the adequacy of the sample will be fully described in the volume containing the report of the overall study. The difference in the number of returns from the two parties was largely a result of the greater number of Democratic delegates to begin with.

[2] Conservatism is here used not in the classical but in the more popular sense, in which it refers to negative attitudes toward government ownership, intervention, and regulation of the economy; resistance to measures for promoting equalitarianism and social welfare through government action; identification with property, wealth, and business enterprise; etc.

[3] Gabriel Almond, *The Appeals of Communism* (Princeton, 1954), pp. 5-6, and ch. 3.

[4] See the discussion bearing on this conclusion in Campbell *et al.*, op. cit., ch. 8 and 9. Also, Avery Leiserson, *Parties and Politics: An Institutional and Behavioral Approach* (New York, 1958), pp. 162-166.

The thesis of this chapter is that behavioralism, the emerging paradigm in political science, has exerted a controlling influence on contemporary political analysis. The task in the balance of Part II will be to examine this thesis and its implications further.

In Chapter 6 the impact of the behavioral paradigm on theory will be examined. In Chapter 7 the presentation will analyze how the paradigm's seeming inconsistency in valuing both science and democratic political systems has been resolved, through the construction of a "scientific" theory of democratic systems. This scientific theory of democracy has been consistent with an "invisible" ideology and has served to bring about consensus among contemporary political scientists. The influence of the invisible ideology will be further examined in the context of two significant developments in current political analysis. Chapter 8 will investigate the ideology's influence on the areas of political socialization and the analysis of change. The chapter suggests that the goal of socialization studies has been to understand how people learn the attitudes, values, and norms necessary to fit the requirements of a democratic political system, and that the analyses of change in political science have been directed toward understanding change *within* democratic political systems rather than toward change from what exists to other social orders.

6/The Paradigm and Modern Political Theory

Nowhere is the behavioral paradigm's impact on political science more visible than in the contributions that have been made toward the development of a modern political theory. This chapter surveys some of these theoretical developments, which range from concepts widely used in political analysis—such as power and role—to more general theoretical offerings that seek to define approaches to the analysis of factors such as groups and systems.

There are two purposes for including such a survey here. First, it provides an overview of thoughts and activities that have consumed an inordinate proportion of the intellectual energies of professional political scientists. The overview clarifies (although it does not unify) the diversity that characterizes contemporary political analysis. Second, surveying these theoretical developments permits additional examination of the extent to which the behavioral paradigm has influenced the discipline.

If any single theoretical approach to politics dominated present-day analyses, a survey would be unnecessary. But political science, more than most other disciplines, has resisted unified definition of what is to be studied and how. For students and teachers alike, this state of affairs is a source of vitality and, more often than not, of confusion.

On the positive side, it is clear that the lack of a single definition of either scope or methods has permitted an open-mindedness toward different ways of understanding and researching political events. The discipline has been free to draw on related areas of social science for concepts, data, and analysis. In general, political science remains committed to intellectual debate about subject matter and methodology. This, in turn, has created an environment for teaching and

research that more clearly meets the criteria of liberal education than have those of other more well-defined disciplines.

The negative side of the inability to agree is that political scientists have been unable to concentrate their energies toward the accumulation of information and understanding that could be applied to the practical problems that presently overwhelm our society. There is still little agreement about what should be studied or taught.

Although different faculties at different universities have chosen to emphasize one field of analysis over another, there are some fields of subject matter that continue to be central to most political science curricula. A brief listing of courses illustrates the diversity that is political science. Larger departments offer a variety of courses dealing with the internal aspects of political systems, focusing primarily on the American political experience. These courses include constitutional law, federal and state and local courts, judicial behavior, Congress and state legislatures, executive roles (usually the Presidency) and leadership, public administration in bureaucracies and large organizations, political parties, pressure groups, community politics, public opinion and voting behavior, political socialization, and public policy and issues. Additionally, curricula may include courses that are concerned with relationships among political systems, such as comparative governments and/or politics, area studies (for example, Southeast Asia or Latin America), and international relations and organizations.

Differences of opinion are reflected in political theory, as it is taught in political science departments today. In some cases, courses called "political theory" survey the philosophical and often highly value-oriented contributions of "classic" political works, from the early Greeks to the nineteenth century. In other courses taught under the same name, subject matter includes such material as systems analysis, application of role models, groups theory, and game theory.

The theoretical developments surveyed here further expose some of the impacts of behavioralism. Because one component of the paradigm is its interdisciplinary focus, the conceptualizations surveyed have been based on developments in such widely diverse disciplines as biology, sociology, anthropology, psychology, and economics. A second component of the paradigm, its emphasis on observable human actions as basic raw material, is also obvious in the theoretical concepts surveyed. In most cases, the concept is directed toward the actions of—or relationships among—people in political situations. Finally, the survey indicates that modern political analysts usually resist the temptation to make value judgments.

A SURVEY OF THEORETICAL DEVELOPMENTS

George E. G. Catlin once defined politics as the study of the act of control in society. Few political scientists today would argue with this generalized statement about the major focus of political analysis. There is little doubt that the study of politics is based on the attempt to understand how people are controlled and how they control others in society.

The primary concept that has been used to examine control is power. One esteemed political scientist, V. O. Key, Jr., has argued that "politics as power consists fundamentally of relationships of superordination-subordination, of dominance and submission, of the governors and the governed."[1] Key's view—that politics can be defined as the relationship between those in society who control and those who are controlled—has been widely accepted by political scientists. But some theorists have urged that researchers approach the analysis of politics by conceptualizing it as a "system" of interrelated power relationships among aggregates of people. Others view power as a relationship between individuals rather than aggregates of people, and they tend to stress the concept of "role."

[1] V. O. Key, Jr., *Politics, Parties, and Pressure Groups*, 4th Ed. (New York: Thomas Y. Crowell, 1958), p. 5.

Power can also be examined in terms of how it is distributed and used in society. Researchers in group theory and elite analysis have directed attention to those in society who have power, and how they get what they want by using and maintaining their power. Other investigators view power relationships as being dependent on communications among people; they interpret political events as part of a communication system. Theories of conflict and games are efforts to analyze characteristics of the groups and individuals that use power to achieve strategic objectives. Finally, the concept of political culture has been offered, for analysis of how the masses of people in society perceive and respond to power relationships.

POWER

Although political scientists in general agree that the concept of power is central to practically every area of research in political analysis, notions of how power is to be understood and how it is used differ widely.

The theorists usually referred to as "power elitists" argue that power accrues to those who have resources that are associated with the control of human behavior. For these theorists, power is assumed to be held by those who have wealth, status, prestige, or other social or economic resources at their disposal; these theorists define the power structure of a society or community by identifying those who have the most of what there is to get. Although to some extent the reasoning is circular, it is nonetheless persuasive to many: Those who have power have used it in their own self-interest, to gain what is of value in the community; therefore, they can be assumed to have power to affect decisions about the allocation of other advantages among people. In such a logic, it is less important to demonstrate how the power elite affect the decisions made than to demonstrate that elites with the resources to affect those decisions do exist. For example, if a small group of people can be demonstrated to have wealth and status in a community, it can be assumed that they got their positions in that community by being powerful, and that they will use their position to remain powerful, continuing to accrue more wealth and other values.

The other basic concept of power, which is supported by theorists who have been called "pluralists," is that the power must be demonstrated to have impact on public policy. Pluralists view power as a relationship among people, in which some are able to get others to concede to their desires in decisions affecting all the members of the community. In this theory, power is not a possession, but a relationship between those who command and those who obey. In this form of analysis, it is not enough to find that groups have resources with which they might command others in the society to obey; it must also be shown that they have actually used such power to satisfy their own preferences in public decision making.

The opposing positions of power elitists and pluralists have greatly influenced the analysis of political events. For the power elitists, it is enough to prove that there are those in the community who have the resources with which to manipulate the behavior of others for their own self-interests. For the pluralists, it is more important to focus on how decisions that affect the distribution of values in the community are made and influenced; they argue that although elites have the potential to command, they do not necessarily use that power to influence the decisions made in the community.

The debate between those who argue that power is a possession and those who argue that it is a relationship is evaluated in the first paper presented in this chapter. Bachrach and Baratz conclude that power is a relationship among people. As they develop the argument, they are careful to note the conditions under which the relationship exists. It is not as simple as saying there are those who have power and those who don't; as they point out, power occurs only under specified conditions.

POWER RELATIONSHIPS

PETER BACHRACH AND MORTON S. BARATZ

It is customary to say that this or that person or group "has power," the implication being that power, like wealth, is a possession which enables its owner to secure some apparent future Good.[1] Another way of expressing the same point of view is to say that power is a "simple property . . . which can belong to a person or group considered in itself."[2]

From *Power and Poverty: Theory and Practice* by Peter Bachrach and Morton S. Baratz, pp. 17–27. Copyright © 1970 by Oxford University Press, Inc. (Footnotes abridged.) Reprinted by permission.

For at least three reasons this usage is unacceptable. First, it fails to distinguish clearly between power over people and power over matter; and "power in the political [or economic or social] sense cannot be conceived as the ability to produce intended effects in general, but only such effects as involve other persons. . . ."[3] Second, the view that a person's power is measured by the total number of desires that he achieves is erroneous; one cannot have power in a vacuum, but only in relation to someone else. Third and most important, the common conception of the phenomenon mistakenly implies that possession of (what appear to be) the instruments of power is tantamount to possession of power itself. Such a notion is false because it ignores the fundamental relational attribute of power: that it cannot be possessed; that, to the contrary, the successful exercise of power is dependent upon the relative importance of conflicting values *in the mind of the recipient* in the power relationship.

A few illustrations should clarify and enlarge our position. Imagine, first, an armed military sentry who is approached by an unarmed man in uniform. The sentry levels his gun at the intruder and calls out, "Halt or I'll shoot!" The order is promptly obeyed. Did the sentry therefore have power and exercise it? So it would seem; but appearances could be deceiving. Suppose that the intruder obeyed, not because he felt compelled to do so in the face of the threatened sanction, but because he was himself a trained soldier for whom prompt obedience to a sentry's order was part of a system of values he fully accepted. If that was the case, there was no conflict of goals or interests between the two principals; the sentry's threatened sanction was irrelevant, and the result would have been the same if he, and not the intruder, had been unarmed. Because the soldier put obedience to a sentry's order at the top of his schedule of values, the threat of severe deprivations had no bearing on his behavior. In such circumstances it cannot be said that the guard exerted power.

Let us now suppose that a second man approaches the sentry and, like the first, is ordered to stop or be shot. The second stranger ignores the order, attempts to smash through the gate, and is forthwith fatally wounded. If we assume that the intruder's intention was to sabotage the military installation, we can have no doubt that his and the sentry's values were in direct conflict. Even so, the sentry's fatal shot did *not* constitute an exercise of power. For it did not bring about compliance to his order—and it did not because, apparently, the intruder valued entry to the base more highly than either obedience to the sentry's order or his own well-being.

Suppose, finally, that a third man approaches the sentry box, a man who wants to die but cannot bring himself to the act of self-destruction. He therefore deliberately ignores the sentry's command and is duly shot to death. Did someone in this situation have power and exercise it? As we see it, the "victim" did—for it was he, cognizant of the conflict of values between himself and the guard, who utilized the latter's supposed sanction to achieve his own objective.

We reiterate that power is relational, as opposed to possessive or substantive. Its relational characteristics are threefold. First, in order for a power relationship to exist there must be a conflict of interests or values between two or more persons or groups. Such a divergence is a necessary condition of power because, as we have suggested, if A and B are in agreement as to ends, B will freely assent to A's preferred course of action; in which case the situation will involve authority rather than power. Second, a power relationship exists only if B actually bows to A's wishes. A conflict of interests is an insufficient condition, since A may not be able to prevail upon B to change his behavior. And if B does not comply, A's policy will either become a dead letter or will be effectuated through the exercise of force rather than through power. Third, a power relationship can exist only if one of the parties can threaten to invoke sanctions: power is "the process of affecting policies of others with the help of (. . . threatened) severe deprivations for nonconformity with the policies intended."[1] It must be stressed, however, that while the availability of sanctions—that is, of any promised reward or penalty by which an actor can maintain effective control over policy—is a necessary condition of power, it is not sufficient. It is necessary simply because the threat of sanctions is what differentiates power from influence; it is insufficient because the availability of a sanction endows

A with power over B only if the following conditions are met:

(a) The person threatened is aware of what is expected of him. In a power situation there must be clear communication between the person who initiates policy and the person who must comply. If our imaginary sentry challenges a man who understands no English or is perhaps deaf, the sentry has—at least at the moment he issues his order—no power. In other words, power has a rational attribute: for it to exist, the person threatened must comprehend the alternatives which face him in choosing between compliance and noncompliance.

(b) The threatened sanction is *actually* regarded as a deprivation by the person who is so threatened. A threat by the President to "purge" a Congressman for failure to support the Administration's legislative program would be to no avail if the Congressman reckoned that his chances for re-election would be increased rather than reduced by Presidential intervention.

(c) The person threatened has greater esteem for the value which would be sacrificed should he disobey than for another value which would be foregone should he comply. Fear of physical injury did not deter those Southern Negro "sitters-in" who put greater store by the righteousness of their cause. It is worth noting at this stage that threatened deprivations are often ineffectual because the policy-initiator, in deciding what sanction to invoke, mistakenly projects his own values into the minds of his subjects.

(d) The person threatened is persuaded that the threat against him is not idle, that his antagonist would not hesitate *in fine* actually to impose sanctions. To illustrate, if a famous general calculates that the President lacks the will or the popular support to employ his Constitutional prerogatives, he may ignore—even defy—the President's policy instructions. Or, again, the success of a resistance movement based on the principle of nonviolence rests in large measure upon the assumption that those who can invoke sanctions will refrain from doing so, that value conflicts within A will prevent him from carrying out his threat against B. In point are the Indians who sat on the railroad tracks in defiance of the British and got away with it because (as the Indians well knew) the British put a higher value on human life than on obedience to their orders.

We can now draw together the several elements of our conception of power. A power relationship exists when (a) there is a conflict over values or course of action between A and B; (b) B complies with A's wishes; and (c) B does so because he is fearful that A will deprive him of a value or values which he regards more highly than those which would have been achieved by non-compliance.

Several points must be made in reference to this definition. First, in speaking of power relations, one must take care not to overstate the case by saying that A has power over B merely because B, anxious to avoid sanctions, complies with a given policy proclaimed by A. This could well be an inaccurate description of their relationship, since A's power with respect to B may be extremely limited in scope, that is, in range of values affected. Thus, the power of a traffic policeman over a citizen may be confined to the latter's activities as a motorist—and no more than that. Moreover, in appraising power relationships account must be taken of the weight of power, i.e. the degree to which values are affected, and of its domain, i.e. the number of persons affected. For example, the power of the chairman of the House Committee on Ways and Means is limited mainly to fiscal affairs; but within this scope he wields immense power in the determination of Federal tax and expenditure policies (weight), which affect a vast number of persons—up to and including at times the President himself (domain).

Furthermore, account must be taken of what Friedrich has dubbed the "rule of anticipated reactions."[5] The problem posed by this phenomenon is that an investigation might reveal that, though B regularly accedes to A's preferred courses of action, A in fact lacks power over B because A just as regularly tailors his demands upon B to dimensions he thinks B will accept. As an illustration, if the President submits to the Congress only those bills likely to be palatable to a majority of lawmakers, he can hardly be said to have power over the Congress simply because all his proposals are enacted into law.

There is an additional dimension to anticipated reactions. It is often inferred that because a group is unorganized, inarticulate, and lacks effective access to key centers of decision-making, it is totally powerless in every sense of the word. The inference could be incorrect. An investigation might well reveal that decision-makers alter their policy choices out of deference to the supposedly powerless group, in anticipation that failure to do so would bring on severe deprivations, e.g. riots, boycotts, and so on. Here is a situation in which policy-makers' recognition of the possibility of future sanctions *(potential* power) results in "exercise" of power in the present. Potential power, that is, becomes actual power, even in circumstances where those who "threaten" the sanctions have not actually invoked them.

We must also take note of *latent* power. It is commonly supposed that anyone who possesses what appear to be important instruments for exercising power, such as wealth, high social rank, or a well-stocked military arsenal, necessarily puts them to work. C. Wright Mills, for example, has argued that the "power elite" in America is made up of those persons who command the major institutions—great corporations, the military establishment, and the political bureaucracy. In his words, "Not all power . . . is anchored in and exercised by means of such institutions, but only within and through them can power be more or less continuous and important."[6] Although his point has merit, Mills and others tend to overlook that those who have the means for threatening sanctions may and often do abstain from doing so. Their power is *latent*, rather than real. We must mention, however, that the existence of latent power can result in its actual, if unintended, exercise. For instance, the managing director of a community's largest business firm may choose to abstain from exercising power in the resolution of local political issues. Yet the resources at his disposal are so great—that is, he has so much latent power—that others in the locality may regularly defer to his (real or imagined) preferences. In cases like this, B is the recipient in a power relationship with A, even though A did not "exercise" power in Lasswell and Kaplan's sense of participation in decision-making with respect to policies that affect B.

* * *

Notes

[1] Thomas Hobbes, as paraphrased by C. J. Friedrich, *Constitutional Government and Politics* (New York, 1937), p. 12.

[2] Harold D. Lasswell and Abraham Kaplan, *Power and Society* (New Haven, 1950), p. 75, draw this implication from the definition of power, that is, "the production of intended effects," in Bertrand Russell, *Power: A New Social Analysis* (New York, 1938), p. 35.

[3] Lasswell and Kaplan, loc. cit.

[4] Lasswell and Kaplan, op. cit., p. 76. We have deleted "actual or" from the parenthetical expression because *actual* deprivation for nonconformity is a property of force, rather than power. . . .

[5] Friedrich, op. cit. pp. 17–18.

[6] C. Wright Mills, *The Power Elite* (New York, 1954), p. 9.

Whether power is viewed as a position in society or as a relationship among people, there is agreement that power itself is relatively limited. For the power elitists, power is finite, in the sense that it can only accrue to those who have resources, which are relatively finite. There is just so much power in any community, and small elites have most of it. In order to change the society and use power to bring about new and different policies in society, the mass of people must seize power from the elite. This is the common logic of revolution.

To pluralists, however, power is a quantity that is not necessarily finite. It can be increased or decreased, depending on the numbers of people who relate to the one who is using the power. When power is viewed as a relationship, it may be considered as a quantity that varies according to the awareness of people that a problem exists. Therefore, power expands when large numbers of people are aware of conflict resulting from some shared problem, and it contracts when people perceive that the conflict has been resolved and their interests are no longer affected.

The notion of expanding and contracting power is most important in relation to political conflict. As people seek to bring about changes in society—in ways that favor either their own or the public interest—they attempt to increase individual awareness of a need for change. This awareness makes a greater number of people more willing to share a power relationship with the leader who articulates a commonly shared demand on the political system. In this manner, the politics of a society expands as power increases, and those who have not previously had power can expand the scope of the political arena and, thus, can influence public policy. They do not take power from the elite. They create their own power in pursuit of their interests.

Correspondingly, the elite in power, who are interested in maintaining their positions, define public issues according to their personal interests. They may define the issue in such a way that the problem is solved and the power in the system contracts, leaving them with more power than before. Or they may define the issue, making sure that the power in the system expands in such a manner that they can control both its expansion and its eventual contraction. Thus, the elite may have to make concessions in the political arena, in order to prevent an escalation of conflict and power that would demolish their control.

POLITICAL SYSTEMS AND DECISION MAKING

Most political scientists have adopted the position that power is a relationship. Thus, the obvious question is how to conceptualize and identify power relationships as distinct from all the other kinds of human relationships in the society. David Easton has been the leading proponent of the view that the major conceptualizations required for this purpose are political systems and decision making.[2]

Easton sides with those who argue that power is an interdependent set of actions among people who are in the process of making decisions about how a society's valuables are to be distributed. If people value wealth, then decisions are made about who will have advantages in the seeking of wealth. Who will get tax breaks? Who will get government subsidies that further their interests? Who will pay for tax loopholes and subsidies? Finally, when these decisions are accepted by most people in the society as the way things ought to be, then an "authoritative allocation of values" has taken place.[3] For Easton, the decision making in which values are authoritatively allocated is the political process, and power relationships can be observed among people as they attempt to use their power to get more of what they value.

In the sequence of decision making, the political system can be thought of as a point in time and activity. At any particular moment in time, decisions are made that bind

[2] David Easton, "An Approach to the Analysis of Political Systems," *World Politics* (1956–57), pp. 9, 383–400.

[3] *Ibid.*, p. 383.

everyone in the society to a particular distribution of valuables.

Easton describes the political system as having certain internal characteristics, as well as inputs and outputs. This system model has been a most influential conceptualization in contemporary political science. It is necessary to understand that the system Easton describes is not a static model, it is a continuing process in which political demands and supports are fed into the collection of power relationships that constitute the political system, in order to produce the public policies, or laws, that authoritatively allocate the things that are valued in the society. Once enacted, these policies provide "feedback" that affects the amount and kind of support and demands, which are once again fed into the political system.

AN APPROACH
TO THE ANALYSIS
OF POLITICAL SYSTEMS

DAVID EASTON

*   *   *

Once we begin to speak of political life as a system of activity, certain consequences follow for the way in which we can undertake to analyze the working of a system. The very idea of a system suggests that we can separate political life from the rest of social activity, at least for analytical purposes, and examine it as though for the moment it were a self-contained entity surrounded by, but clearly distinguishable from, the environment or setting in which it operates. In much the same way, astronomers consider the solar system a complex of events isolated for certain purposes from the rest of the universe.

Furthermore, if we hold the system of political actions as a unit before our mind's eye, as it were, we can see that what keeps the system going are inputs of various kinds. These inputs are converted by the processes of the system into outputs and these, in turn,

David Easton, "An Approach to the Analysis of Political Systems," 9 *World Politics* no. 3, pp. 383–400. Copyright © 1957 by Princeton University Press, edited and abridged. The point of view described here is fully elaborated in D. Easton, *A Systems Analysis of Political Life* (Wiley, 1965).

have consequences both for the system and for the environment in which the system exists. The formula here is very simple but, as I hope to show, also very illuminating: inputs—political system or processes—outputs. These relationships are shown diagrammatically in Figure 1. This diagram represents a very primitive "model" . . . for approaching the study of political life.

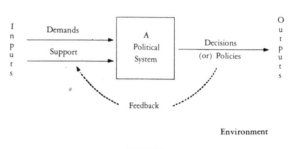

FIGURE I

Political systems have certain properties because they are systems. To present an overall view of the whole approach, let me identify the major attributes, say a little about each, and then treat one of these properties at somewhat greater length, even though still inadequately.

(1) Properties of Identification

To distinguish a political system from other social systems, we must be able to identify it by describing its fundamental units and establishing the boundaries that demarcate it from units outside the system.

(a) Units of a Political System
The units are the elements of which we say a system is composed. In the case of a political system, they are political actions. Normally it is useful to look at these as they structure themselves in political roles and political groups.

(b) Boundaries
Some of the most significant questions with regard to the operation of political systems can be answered

only if we bear in mind the obvious fact that a system does not exist in a vacuum. It is always immersed in a specific setting or environment. The way in which a system works will be in part a function of its response to the total social, biological, and physical environment . . . The boundary of a political system is defined by all those actions more or less directly related to the making of binding decisions for a society; every social action that does not partake of this characteristic will be excluded from the system and thereby will automatically be viewed as an external variable in the environment.

(2) Inputs and Outputs

Presumably, if we select political systems for special study, we do so because we believe that they have characteristically important consequences for society, namely, authoritative decisions. These consequences I shall call the outputs. If we judged that political systems did not have important outputs for society, we would probably not be interested in them.

. . . Without inputs the system can do no work; without outputs we cannot identify the work done by the system. The specific research tasks in this connection would be to identify the inputs and the forces that shape and change them, to trace the processes through which they are transformed into outputs, to describe the general conditions under which such processes can be maintained, and to establish the relationship between outputs and succeeding inputs of the system.

From this point of view, much light can be shed on the working of a political system if we take into account the fact that much of what happens within a system has its birth in the efforts of the members of the system to cope with the changing environment. We can appreciate this point if we consider a familiar biological system such as the human organism. It is subject to constant stress from its surroundings to which it must adapt in one way or another if it is not to be completely destroyed. In part, of course, the way in which the body works represents responses to needs that are generated by the very organization of its anatomy and functions; but in large part, in order to understand both the struc-

ture and the working of the body, we must also be very sensitive to the inputs from the environment.

* * *

(3) Differentiation Within a System

As we shall see in a moment, from the environment come both energy to activate a system and information with regard to which the system uses this energy. In this way a system is able to do work. It has some sort of output that is different from the input that enters from the environment. We can take it as a useful hypothesis that if a political system is to perform some work for anything but a limited interval of time, a minimal amount of differentiation in its structure must occur. . . . The members of a system engage in at least some minimal division of labor that provides a structure within which action takes place.

(4) Integration of a System

This fact of differentiation opens up a major area of inquiry with regard to political systems. Structural differentiation sets in motion forces that are potentially disintegrative in their results for the system. If two or more units are performing different kinds of activity at the same time, how are these activities to be brought into the minimal degree of articulation necessary if the members of the system are not to end up in utter disorganization with regard to the production of the outputs of interest to us? We can hypothesize that if a structured system is to maintain itself, it must provide mechanisms whereby its members are integrated or induced to cooperate in some minimal degree so that they can make authoritative decisions. . . .

Among inputs of a political system there are two basic kinds: demands and support. These inputs give a political system its dynamic character. They furnish it both with the raw material or information that the system is called upon to process and with the energy to keep it going.

The reason why a political system emerges in a society at all—that is, why men engage in political activity—is that demands are being made by persons or groups in the society that cannot all be fully satisfied. In all societies one fact dominates political life: scarcity prevails with regard to most of the valued things. Some of the claims for these relatively scarce things never find their way into the political system but are satisfied through the private negotiations of or settlements by the persons involved. Demands for prestige may find satisfaction through the status relations of society; claims for wealth are met in part through the economic system; aspirations for power find expression in educational, fraternal, labor, and similar private organizations. Only where wants require some special organized effort on the part of society to settle them authoritatively may we say that they have become inputs of the political system.

Systematic research would require us to address ourselves to several key questions with regard to these demands.

(1) How do demands arise and assume their particular character in a society? In answer to this question, we can point out that demands have their birth in two sectors of experience: either in the environment of a system or within the system itself. We shall call these the external and internal demands, respectively.

Let us look at the external demands first. I find it useful to see the environment not as an undifferentiated mass of events but rather as systems clearly distinguishable from one another and from the political system. In the environment we have such systems as the ecology, economy, culture, personality, social structure, and demography. Each of these constitutes a major set of variables in the setting that helps to shape the kind of demands entering a political system. For purposes of illustrating what I mean, I shall say a few words about culture.

The members of every society act within the framework of an ongoing culture that shapes their general goals, specific objectives, and the procedures that the members feel ought to be used. Every culture derives part of its unique quality from the fact that it emphasizes one or more special aspects of behavior and this strategic emphasis serves to differentiate it from other cultures with respect to the demands that it generates. As far as the mass of the people is concerned, some cultures, such as our own, are weighted heavily on the side of economic wants, success, privacy, leisure activity, and rational efficiency. Others, such as that of the Fox Indians, strive toward the maintenance of harmony, even if in the process the goals of efficiency and rationality may be sacrificed. Still others, such as the Kachins of highland Burma, stress the pursuit of power and prestige. . . . The typical demands that will find their way into the political process will concern the matters in conflict that are labeled important by the culture. . . .

But not all demands originate or have their major locus in the environment. Important types stem from situations occurring within a political system itself. Typically, in every on-going system, demands may emerge for alterations in the political relationships of the members themselves, as the result of dissatisfaction stemming from these relationships. For example, in a political system based upon representation, in which equal representation is an important political norm, demands may arise for equalizing representation between urban and rural voting districts. . . .

(2) How are demands transformed into issues? What determines whether a demand becomes a matter for serious political discussion or remains something to be resolved privately among the members of society? The occurrence of a demand, whether internal or external, does not thereby automatically convert it into a political *issue*. Many demands die at birth or linger on with the support of an insignificant fraction of the society and are never raised to the level of possible political decision. Others become issues, an issue being a demand that the members of a political system are prepared to deal with as a significant item for discussion through the recognized channels in the system.

The distinction between demands and issues raises a number of questions about which we need data if we are to understand the processes through which claims typically become transformed into issues. For example, we would need to know something about the relationship between a demand and the location of its initiators or supporters in the power structures of the society, the importance of secrecy as compared with publicity in presenting demands, the matter of timing of demands, the possession of political skills or know-how, access to channels of communication, the attitudes and states of mind of possible publics, and the images held by the initiators of demands with regard to the way in which things get done in the particular political system. . . .

*   *   *

Inputs of demands alone are not enough to keep a political system operating. They are only the raw material out of which finished products called decisions are manufactured. Energy in the form of actions or orientations promoting and resisting a political system, the demands arising in it, and the decisions issuing from it must also be put into the system to keep it running. This input I shall call support. Without support, demands could not be satisfied or conflicts in goals composed. . . .

What do we mean by support? We can say that A supports B either when A acts on behalf of or when he orients himself favorably toward B's goals, interests, and actions. Supportive behavior may thus be of two kinds. It may consist of actions promoting the goals, interests, and actions of another person. We may vote for a political candidate, or defend a decision by the highest court of the land. In these cases, support manifests itself through overt action.

On the other hand, supportive behavior may involve not external observable acts, but those internal forms of behavior we call orientations or states of mind. As I use the phrase, a supportive state of mind is a deep-seated set of attitudes or predispositions, or a readiness to act on behalf of some other person. It exists when we say that a man is loyal to his party, attached to democracy, or infused with patriotism. What such phrases as these have in common is the fact that they refer to a state of feelings on the part of a person. No overt action is involved at this level of description, although the implication is that the individual will pursue a course of action consistent with his attitudes. . . .

(1) THE DOMAIN OF SUPPORT

Support is fed into the political system in relation to three objects: the community, the regime, and the government. . . .

(a) The Political Community

No political system can continue to operate unless its members are willing to support the existence of a group that seeks to settle differences or promote decisions through peaceful action in common. . . . To refer to this phenomenon we can speak of the political community. . . .

(b) The Regime

Support for a second major part of a political system helps to supply the energy to keep the system running. This aspect of the system I shall call the regime. It consists of all those arrangements that regulate the way in which the demands put into the system are settled and the way in which decisions are put into effect. They are the so-called rules of the game. . . .

(c) The Government

If a political system is going to be able to handle the conflicting demands put into it, not only must the members of the system be prepared to support the settlement of these conflicts in common and possess some consensus with regard to the rules governing the mode of settlement; they must also be ready to support a government as it undertakes the concrete tasks involved in negotiating such settlements.

*   *   *

(2) QUANTITY AND SCOPE OF SUPPORT

How much support needs to be put into a system and how many of its members need to contribute such support if the system is to be able to do the job of converting demands to decisions? . . .

Under certain circumstances very few members need to support a system at any level. The members might be dull and apathetic, indifferent to the general operations of the system, its progress or decisions. In a loosely connected system such as India has had, this might well be the state of mind of by far the largest segment of the membership. . . .

Alternatively, we may find that all the members of a system are putting in support, but the amount may be so low as to place one or all aspects of the system in jeopardy. Modern France is perhaps a classic illustration. . . . for a variety of historical and contemporary reasons, there is considerable doubt as to whether the members of the French political system are putting in anything but a low order of support to the regime or any particular government. . . .

* * *

. . . I have suggested that no political system can yield the important outputs we call authoritative decisions unless, in addition to demands, support finds its way into the system. . . . We are now ready to turn to the main question raised by our attention to support as a crucial input: how do systems typically manage to maintain a steady flow of support? Without it a system will not absorb sufficient energy from its members to be able to convert demands to decisions.

* * *

A society generates support for a political system in two ways: through outputs that meet the demands of the members of society; and through the processes of politicization. Let us look at outputs first.

(1) OUTPUTS AS A MECHANISM OF SUPPORT

An output of a political system, it will be recalled, is a political decision or policy. One of the major ways of strengthening the ties of the members to their system is through providing decisions that tend to satisfy the day-to-day demands of these members. Fundamentally this is the truth that lies in the aphorism that one can

fool some of the people some of the time but not all of them all of the time. Without some minimal satisfaction of demands, the ardor of all but the most fanatical patriot is sure to cool. The outputs, consisting of political decisions, constitute a body of specific inducements for the members of a system to support that system.

Inducements of this kind may be positive or negative. Where negative, they threaten the members of the system with various kinds of sanctions ranging from a small monetary fine to physical detention, ostracism, or loss of life, as in our own system with regard to the case of legally defined treason. In every system support stems in part from fear of sanctions or compulsion; in autocratic systems the proportion of coerced support is at a maximum. . . .

. . . It is clear that to obtain the support of the members of a system through positive incentives, a government need not meet all the demands of even its most influential and ardent supporters. Most governments, or groups such as political parties that seek to control governments, succeed in building up a reserve of support. This reserve will carry the government along even though it offends its followers, so long as over the extended short run these followers perceive the particular government as one that is in general favorable to their interests. One form that this reserve support takes in Western society is that of party loyalty, since the party is the typical instrument in a mass industrialized society for mobilizing and maintaining support for a government. . . .

Thus a system need not meet *all the demands* of its members so long as it has stored up a reserve of support over the years. Nor need it satisfy even *some of the demands* of all its members. . . .

(2) POLITICIZATION AS A MECHANISM OF SUPPORT

It would be wrong to consider that the level of support available to a system is a function exclusively of the outputs in the form of either sanctions or rewards. If we did so conclude, we could scarcely account for the maintenance of numerous political systems in which satisfaction of demands has been manifestly low, in which public coercion is limited, and yet which have endured for epochs. Alternately, it might be difficult to explain how political systems could endure and yet manage to flout or thwart urgent demands, failing thereby to render sufficient *quid pro quo* for the input of support. The fact is that whatever reserve of support has been accumulated through past decisions is increased and reinforced by a complicated method for steadily manufacturing support through what I shall call the process of politicization. It is an awkward term, but nevertheless an appropriately descriptive one.

As each person grows up the other members of society communicate to and instill in him the various institutionalized goals and norms. This is well known as the process of socialization. Through its operation a person learns to play his various social roles. Part of these goals and norms relate to political life. The ways in which these political patterns are learned by the members of society constitute what I call the process of politicization. In stable systems the support that accrues through these means adds to the reservoir of support being accumulated on a day to-day basis through the outputs of decisions. . . .

When the basic political attachments become deeply rooted or institutionalized, we say that the system has become accepted as legitimate. Politicization therefore effectively sums up the way in which legitimacy is created and transmitted in a political system. And it is an empirical observation that in those instances where political systems have survived the longest, support has been nourished by an ingrained belief in the legitimacy of the relevant governments and regimes.

* * *

POLITICAL ROLES

The primary concept used in analyzing power relationships at the individual level is the notion of political role. Stated simply, political roles are the expectations that people have about behavior that is appropriate in decision-making situations. In society, political roles are generally shared expectations about how public officials, political leaders, and

their followers should interact in the political system. The voter has a role in making decisions about who will be elected as a public official. The positions of legislators, the President, cabinet members, and campaign managers are all political roles, in which people share expectations about behavior. Clearly, then, roles describe relationships among people, and are ways of conceptualizing how individuals with power relate to others.

Heinz Eulau proposes role as the basic unit of analysis for political scientists, arguing that role is useful in analyzing personality, interaction on the social level, and cultural patterns that support the political system.

POLITICAL ROLE AS A UNIT OF ANALYSIS

HEINZ EULAU

* * *

The concept of role is familiar to most people. We speak of the father's role, the teacher's role, the minister's role, the judge's role, and so on. What we mean in all of these instances is that a person is identified by his role and that, in interpersonal relations activating the role, he behaves, will behave, or should behave in certain ways. In looking at man's social behavior or judging it, we do so in a frame of reference in which his role is critical. If we do not know a person's role, his behavior appears to be enigmatic. But a child ringing a doorbell is unlikely to be mistaken for a political "doorbell ringer." Political behavior, then, is always conduct in the performance of a political role.

* * *

Role can be used as a conceptual tool on all three levels of behavioral analysis: the social, the cultural, and the personal. . . . On the social level, it invites inquiry into the structure of the interaction, connection, or bond that constitutes a relationship. On the cultural level, it calls attention to the norms, expectations, rights, and

From *The Behavioral Persuasion in Politics*, by Heinz Eulau, pp. 38–45. Copyright © 1963 by Random House, Inc. Reprinted by permission of the publisher.

duties that sanction the maintenance of the relationship and attendant behavioral patterns. And on the personal level, it alerts research to the idiosyncratic definitions of the role held by different actors in the relationship. . . .

On the social level, many of the most immediate interactions can be analyzed in terms of polar roles: husband implies wife; student implies teacher; priest implies communicant; leader implies follower; representative implies constituent, and so on. The behavior of one actor in the relationship is meaningful only insofar as it affects the behavior of the other actor or is in response to the other's behavior. Whatever other acts a representative may perform, for instance, only those in the performance of his constituent relationships are of immediate interest in political behavior analysis. I say of immediate interest because, in actuality, no single relationship is isolated from other social relationships in which the partners to the focal relationship are likely to be involved.

Many relationships are not structured by unipolar roles alone. In most cases, a role is at the core of several other roles, making for a network of roles that can be very complex. A legislator is "colleague" to his fellow legislators, "representative" to his constituents, "friend" (or "enemy") to lobbyists, "follower" to his party leaders, "informant" to the press, and so on. Whatever role is taken, simultaneously or seriatim, what emerges is a very intricate structure of relations in which one role is implicated in several other roles.

A role may be implicated in several networks. For example, the mayor of a city is not only a chief executive, a role that implicates him in several other role relationships related to his position, but he is also involved in many other relationships of more or less direct relevance to his political roles. He may be a husband and father, an alumnus of the local college, a member of the Rotary Club, a lawyer, a churchgoer, an investor in a local business, and so on. Depending on circumstances, these roles may complement each other, be mutually exclusive, or conflict. A network of roles reflects the complexity of social and political behavior patterns and warns against treating any one role as if it were exclusive.

Analytically, each network of roles can be thought of as a "role system." This has two corollaries. First, some roles are more directly related to each other than are other roles. For instance, the roles of husband and father or legislator and representative are intimately connected. Other roles may be less so. . . . The legislator's role as a lawmaker is less likely to be related to his role as a parent than it is to his occupational role as, say, an insurance agent. This does not mean that the parent role is altogether irrelevant in his legislative behavior. A legislator with children attending public schools is probably more interested in school problems than a legislator who is a bachelor. . . .

The second corollary of role system implies that a change in one role may have consequences for the actor's other roles and therefore, for the relationships in which he is involved by virtue of his roles. (This must not be confused with a change in position. When a Senator becomes President, his Senatorial role is terminated. His new position will make for new roles that greatly affect his other role relationships). As an example of role change, take the representative who finds it impossible to accept instructions from his constituents and increasingly relies on his own judgment. In the technical language of role analysis, this is a change from the "delegate" to the "trustee" role. It is likely that this change in the representational role will have consequences for the legislator's party-relevant roles. He might change from a partisan follower into an independent.

The structure of role relationships is not only patterned but also fluid. One source of change in role is a change in the expectations of others in the role system. Another source may be an actor's own redefinition of his role. These possibilities suggest the importance of treating role concepts from a cultural and personal standpoint as well as a social one.

On the cultural level, role refers to those expectations of a normative sort that actors in a relationship entertain concerning each other's behavior. These are the rights and duties that give both form and content to the relationship. A relationship can be maintained only as long as the participants are in agreement as to what each actor must or must not do in the performance of his role. . . .

Expectations which define roles and give direction to the behavior of actors in a role relationship are cultural in two ways. People do not continuously define and redefine their mutual relations and expectations. If a relationship had to be defined anew with each interaction, or if expectations had to be elaborated with every new encounter, stable social life would be impossible. In fact, most of the crucial role relationships are well defined. They are well defined because expectations are widely shared and transmitted through time. There is, then, a broad cultural consensus as to what the rights and duties pertaining to social roles are, and there is consensus on the sanctions available to participants in a relationship if behavior should violate agreed-on norms.

* * *

Precisely because role expectations may be widely shared and relatively permanent, they give stability to the relationship. Role relationships thus make for stable patterns of behavior and minimize what would otherwise have to be considered arbitrary behavior. Understanding a role means that we know how a person should behave and what he should do in the performance of a role. . . .

* * *

Actors do bring idiosyncratic perceptions of the interpersonal situation, attitudes, and motivations to a role. Role analysis does not preclude, but may require, investigation of role conceptions from the point of view of the actor's personality. An actor's capacity to take certain roles is predicated on the possession of certain personality characteristics. . . .

Role conflict may stem from various conditions, but two are noteworthy. These may actually be divergent expectations of a person's behavior. A city councilman may expect the city manager to guide and direct the council's legislative business, while another councilman may expect him to abstain from policy recommendations. Or there may be disagreement between others' expectations and an actor's own conceptions of his role.

Moreover, the demands made from one role system to another may be so intense.that behavior in the performance of various roles cannot satisfy role requirements. For example, involvement in the life of the Senate may so absorb a member's time that he cannot meet his obligations as a representative of his state. In all of these cases, role conflict is likely to have dysfunctional consequences of either a social or a personal sort. On the social level, certain functionally necessary roles may not be taken. For instance, conflicting expectations concerning the democratic politician's role may deprive a group of strong leadership. On the personal level, role conflict may so disorganize behavior that it becomes highly erratic, irregular, and even irrational.

Study of how role conflict is avoided or resolved suggests a number of possibilities. I shall only list them. First, some roles are more pervasive than others and conflict is resolved in their favor. Second, some roles are more clearly defined than others, which again aids the resolution of conflict in their favor. Third, some roles are more institutionalized than others, leaving the actor relatively little choice. Finally, roles are more or less segmentalized so that, depending on circumstances, even potentially conflicting roles can be taken.

* * *

ELITES AND CLASSES

The concepts of elite, group, and class have been used by political scientists in their attempts to identify those who use power to bring about public policies that implement their interests and values within a society. The concept of "political elite" is exceedingly simple. Harold Lasswell defines a political elite as those who have most of what there is to get in a society. The "mass" of people includes everyone else.[4]

From the perspective of analysts, the identification of elites and the means and skills that elites use in gaining and maintaining power to control the mass are critical elements in understanding politics. Elites have most of what others want, and they try to keep what they have. Counter-

[4] *Politics: Who Gets What, When and How?* (Cleveland and New York: Meridian Books, 1958), p. 13.

elites emerging from the mass of people seek to redistribute what is valued in society, so that they can acquire a greater share. From the view of elite theorists, this confrontation between elites and counter-elites makes up the substance of politics.

Although the notion that people are divided into classes of elite and mass is somewhat repugnant to members of a society that has an ideology of equality and democracy, political scientists no longer debate whether or not classes exist. The central questions now are: To what extent are there chances for mobility between classes? And does the existence of classes affect political outcomes?

Most researchers who have used the concept of political class have studied local communities rather than the national scene. Some political analysts argue that the class structure defines the flow of political control and influence in society. The flow is from top to bottom, with the top getting what there is to get and the bottom paying for it. Others who view society as less stratified and structured argue that there is a great deal of mobility among classes, and that the upper class is not necessarily the ruling class.

There are difficulties with the use of the concept of class. Is a class structure to be demonstrated simply by identifying the fact that some people have more wealth, status, and power than others? Or do members of a class have to know that they are members, before one can talk about a class structure? Is a person "middle class" because he is found in the census to have earned a particular amount of money last year, or because he identifies with the values, life styles, and opportunities held by the middle class? Is a person who earns less money but has middle-class values a member of the lower class or the middle class? These are the difficult questions which have not yet been resolved.

The concepts of class and elites are useful in identifying the basic ingredients in a political situation. For some political scientists, then, the upper social classes are also the ruling class in the society. For others, the upper class is a less well-defined group that is neither closed to upward mobility nor synonymous with the ruling class.

Whether the elite are good or bad, and whether they are liked or not, they are the reality of politics in any kind of political system—democratic or totalitarian. The important elements for political analysts are the conditions associated with elite control and the conditions under which counter-

elites can capture and redistribute the advantages resulting from that control. Other questions that become relevant to this form of analysis are: Are new members recruited to existing elites on the basis of wealth and status? Are there other paths to becoming a member? Do elites operate to the advantage of the public, or do they operate only to their own private gain? How can elites manipulate the mass of people so that the mass accepts its rule?

Lasswell's study attempts to identify the major characteristics of elites and the skills they must have to gain or maintain their position in the society.

The analysis suggests that regardless of the kind of society one is studying, its political structure can best be understood by identifying the elites, the mass, and the methods used by elites and counter-elites in maintaining or adjusting the status quo.

ELITE

HAROLD LASSWELL

The study of politics is the study of influence and the influential. The science of politics states conditions; the philosophy of politics justifies preferences. This essay, restricted to political analysis, declares no preferences. It states conditions.

The influential are those who get the most of what there is to get. Available values may be classified as *deference, income, safety.* Those who get the most are *elite;* the rest are *mass.*

The distribution of deference is relatively clear in a formal hierarchy. The peak of the Roman Catholic pyramid is occupied by a comparatively small number of officials. There are one Pope, 55 cardinals, 22 apostolic delegates, 256 vicars apostolic, 245 archbishops, 1,578 bishops. The Communist party in the Soviet Union comes to a sharp head in the Political Committee of nine or ten members. The looser structure of government in the United States none the less confers special influence upon the Supreme Court of nine, the Presidency of one, and the Congress of a few hundred. . . .

The distribution of safety is usually less inequitable than the distribution of deference, and may often show a negative relationship to it. Thus one study showed that 31.9 per cent of a series of 423 monarchs of different countries and different periods died by violence. Forty per cent of the presidents of the Republic of Bolivia came to a violent end. Such figures may be put in rough perspective by recalling that deaths by violence (including suicide) in the United States were 7.2 per cent of the whole number of deaths in 1921; 12.1 per cent of the presidents of the United States and of France, and 9 per cent of the Catholic popes, died by violence. The relative safety of whole populations varies from epoch to epoch. . . .

In countries of Western European civilization wealth and income are inequitably distributed. In 1928 . . . the national income of the United States was $541 per capita, which was two and a half times the figure for France or Germany. . . . In 1913, just before the World War, the figure had been $368 per capita in the United States. In the interim the United States snowed the largest absolute increase among the major powers, but the sharpest relative advance was made by Japan, whose per capita rose from $22 in 1913 to $53 in 1925. The United Kingdom, next to the United States in absolute numbers, stood at $250 in 1911 and $293 in 1928. Russia rose from $52 in 1914 to $96 in 1928, which was greater than the relative gain of France or Germany. Italy dropped from $108 in 1914 to $96 in 1928.

There are sharp differences in the apportionment of income within given communities. Ten per cent of the population of the United States took one-third of the money income of the nation in the years between 1918 and 1926.

The values of deference, safety, and income which have just been singled out are representative and not exclusive values. Political analysis could make use of other combinations, and the resulting elite comparisons would differ. The findings of political analysis also vary when different characteristics of the influential are chosen for emphasis. One form of analysis considers the division of values according to *skill*.

Fighting skill is plainly one of the most direct ways by which men have come to the top, whether the fighting be done in the name of god, nation, or class. Mustafa Kemal Pasha fought in the Turco-Italian War in 1911, and commanded the northern section of the Turkish army in Gallipoli in 1915, and elsewhere. Mussolini and Hitler got their baptism of fire in the World War. Several men at the helm in the Soviet Union made their way mainly by illegal, rather than legal, violence. Josef Stalin was first arrested in 1901 by the authorities, and thereafter went into hiding, worked in the revolutionary movement, and ran constant risks. . . .

* * *

Skill in political organization is traditionally represented in the American Cabinet by the postmaster general. Skill in organization was indispensable to the elimination of Trotsky by Communist party secretary Stalin. Hitler was a notable combination of oratory and organization; Mussolini, of oratory, journalism, and organization; Masaryk, of oratory, journalism, scholarship, and organization. . . .

Skill in handling persons by means of significant symbols involves the use of such media as the oration, the polemical article, the news story, the legal brief, the theological argument, the novel with a purpose, and the philosophical system. The opportunities for men to live by manipulating symbols have grown apace with the complication of our material environment through the expansion of technology. . . .

* * *

Elites may be compared in terms of *class* as well as skill. A class is a major social group of similar function, status, and outlook. The principal class formations in recent world politics have been aristocracy, plutocracy, middle class, and manual toilers.

* * *

The concentration of landownership in the hands of a small aristocratic coterie is especially noteworthy in Chile, where it has been officially estimated that 2,500 individuals hold 50,000,000 acres of the 57,000,000 acres in private possession. In prewar Hungary properties of 1,300 acres or more, comprising only one tenth of one per cent of the total number of holdings in the country, included 17.5 per cent of the total area. So large were the holdings of the aristocracy in the Baltic provinces of the former Russian Empire that a new state like Estonia found at the beginning of its national life that 1,149 large estates occupied 58 per cent of its total area. . . .

Great plutocracies have arisen from commerce, industry, and finance, as capitalistic society developed through its several phases. Typical of the merchant capitalist period was the fortune of John Jacob Astor, which aggregated $20,000,000 and was derived from the Oriental and fur trade, and from speculation in New York real estate. Industrial fortunes rose later. Cornelius Vanderbilt left $100,000,000 from speculations in railroads. Cyrus McCormick built on the basis of agricultural machinery, Andrew Carnegie on steel, John D. Rockefeller on oil, and J. Pierpont Morgan on investment banking. By 1929 there were 504 persons in America whose incomes were in excess of $1,000,000 . . .

* * *

The lesser middle class is composed of those who exercise skills which are requited by modest money returns. Hence the class comprises small farmers, small businessmen, low-salaried professional people, skilled workers and craftsmen. The manual workers are those who have acquired little skill; they are the true proletariat. The line between plutocracy, lesser bourgeoisie, and proletariat is a matter of acrimonious debate in practical politics, and of great uncertainty among scientists. . . .

* * *

The distribution of values may be considered with reference to *personality* in addition to skill and class. What is the relative success of all the forms of personality known to clinical and cultural psychologists? What is the varying fortune of the masochists, the sadists, the detached, the hysterical, the obsessive, the compulsive?

From this standpoint the march of time ceases to pivot exclusively around the cavalcade of classes and skills; it becomes a succession of personality forms.

Special interest attaches to personality forms which are predisposed by nature and by early nurture to find satisfaction in playing particular roles on the stage of politics. The agitator is such a type: he is set off from his fellows by the intensity of his craving for prompt and excited deference from his contemporaries. Hence he is emotionally disposed to cultivate such skills of mass appeal as oratory and polemical journalism. Men with less need for emotional responsiveness may be less spectacular organizers. The agitator comes into his own during the fiery intensity of crises; the organizer is favored by the intercrisis periods. . . .

During the initial phases of crisis, personalities may forge ahead who are benevolent as well as firm, and more considerate than ruthless. The stern cloud of approaching war or revolution generates profound anxieties among the masses. The need for reassurance may favor the gentle Lincoln over the flaming Seward on the very eve of disaster.

There are forms of personality easily addicted to imperious violence. They have often learned to cow their environment by the sheer intensity of their willfulness. They have succeeded in control by externalizing their rages against deprivation. Such are the men of Napoleonic mold, prone to break themselves or others.

Whatever the special form of political expression, the common trait of the political personality type is emphatic demand for deference. . . .

The true political personality is a complex achievement. When infants are born, they are unequipped with language of reference to environment, immediate or remote. Their impulses are first organized toward an immediate intimate circle. The symbols of reference to the world of affairs are endowed with meaning in this primary situation, and the true politician learns to use the world of public objects as a means of alleviating the stresses of his intimate environment. Cravings for deference, frustrated or overindulged in the intimate circle, find expression in the secondary environment. This displacement is legitimized in the name of plausible symbols. He does not act for the sake of action; he implies that he strives for the glory of God, the sanctity of the Home, the independence of the Nation, the emancipation of the Class. In the extreme case, the politician is bound to no specific objects in his environment. He is not preoccupied with the routines of nature, discernible in science, art, technology; he is concerned only with the deference meaning of objects for his ego.

Besides skill, classes, and personality groups, we may examine the distribution of values among *attitude groups*. The world is divided among those who are influential on the basis of shared symbols of loyalty to nation, class, occupation, person. Some rise to eminence in the name of militant or conciliatory methods; in the name of demands for a vast gamut of policies; in the name of optimistic visions of the future. Quite different personality types may be united in loyalty to nation or class, method, policy, outlook. Thus attitude groups cut across personality classifications, even as they cut across skill or class. At any given time the members of a skill or class group may not have risen to full skill or class consciousness. . . .

At this point it may be convenient to cast a glance backward over the ground which has been covered. The term politics has been used to mean the study of influence and the influential. It is plain, however, that no simple index can be profitably used to measure influence and the influential. One aspect of influence is the relative sharing of values. Different results can be obtained by using different values. *An* elite of deference is not necessarily *an* elite of safety. More values may be added to the present list of three (deference, safety, income). Whatever the list, the items may be differently combined, thus reaching different results to correspond to varying judgments of *the* elite. New results may be obtained by defining influence in other terms than relative share of values. The term may be used to indicate a judgment of how values *might* be influenced if there were conflicts about them. Thus financial capitalists may be judged to be stronger or weaker than industrial capitalists in case of a hypothetical collision.

From analysis, then, we can expect no static certainty. It is a constant process of reexamination which brings new aspects of the world into the focus of critical attention. The unifying frame of reference for the special student of politics is the rich and variable meaning of "influence and the influential," "power and the powerful."

* * *

POLITICAL GROUPS

The notion of groups—political groups, interest groups, or pressure groups, as they are variously called—has been central to political analysis for a long time. Indeed, many theorists propose to explain all politics within the framework of the group. They define the term in different ways, but the definition that is most frequently emphasized is that a group involves members who share interests as well as activities carried out in the pursuit of these interests. When groups attempt to control others in order to enhance their own shared interests, they become political groups.

Accordingly, group theorists view politics as being composed of a multitude of groups that are attempting to impose their own particular interests on the public. Such groups come into conflict because of different and often incompatible interests; so groups with differing amounts and kinds of resources compete in trying to influence public decisions.

A group's resources determine its effectiveness. Because of the variability of effectiveness, political groups are forced to negotiate and bargain with one another. Any group finds that it must necessarily compromise with other groups, if it is to gain their support in achieving some part of its own goals. Groups bargain with one another to enhance their own positions in society, and analysts study the characteristics that make some groups more (or less) effective than others.

The importance of pressure groups is familiar to most observers of the political scene. Such groups as the American Medical Association, labor unions, and the National Association of Manufacturers engage in obvious attempts to influence government policy. But these easily recognized political groups form only part of what group theorists consider to be the basic fabric of politics. Government itself is composed of groups that pursue shared interests and attempt to affect public policy. All politics, ultimately, can be reduced to varying kinds of groups.

The general proposition offered by group theorists is that the greater the group's access to decision making, the more likely it is to dominate its competition. Given this proposition, government groups, which are part of the actual decision-making apparatus, are the ones most likely to have their interests made into public law. Vast associational groups, such as labor unions and corporations, may be well organized, but they are at least one step removed from the actual decision-making process; they must use their organization and power to influence that process rather than being directly involved in it. The impact of associational groups on public policy is usually gained through the assistance of groups within the government, which attempt to win votes, loyalty, and support by making laws that are consistent with the demands of the associational groups.

Group theorists may make rough predictions about the outcome of particular conflicts in the political process, by assessing the groups involved in the competition, their differing resources, and their relative strengths. A short selection from David Truman's *The Governmental Process* provides a clear statement of the basic conceptual material of the group approach to political analysis, as seen by a leading spokesman for this approach.

INTEREST GROUP POLITICS

DAVID B. TRUMAN

* * *

Many interest groups, probably an increasing proportion in the United States, are politicized. That is, either from the outset or from time to time in the course of their development they make their claims through or upon the institutions of government. Both the forms and functions of government in turn are a reflection of the activities and claims of such groups. The constitution-writing proclivities of Americans clearly reveal the influence of demands from such sources, and the statutory creation of new functions reflects their continuing operation. Many of these forms and functions have re-

From *The Governmental Process*, by David B. Truman, pp. 501–513. Copyright 1951 by Alfred A. Knopf, Inc. Reprinted by permission of the publisher.

ceived such widespread acceptance from the start or in the course of time that they appear to be independent of the overt activities of organized interest groups. The judiciary is such a form. The building of city streets and the control of vehicular traffic are examples of such a function. However, if the judiciary or a segment of it operates in a fashion sharply contrary to the expectations of an appreciable portion of the community or if its role is strongly attacked, the group basis of its structure and powers is likely to become apparent. Similarly, if street construction greatly increases tax rates or if the control of traffic unneccessarily inconveniences either pedestrians or motorists, the exposure of these functions to the demands of competing interests will not be obscure. Interests that are widely held in the society may be reflected in government without their being organized in groups. They are what we have called potential groups. If the claims implied by the interests of these potential groups are quickly and adequately represented, interaction among those people who share the underlying interests or attitudes is unnecessary. But the interest base of accepted governmental forms and functions and their potential involvement in overt group activities are ever present even when not patently operative.

The institutions of government are centers of interest-based power; their connections with interest groups may be latent or overt and their activities range in political character from the routinized and widely accepted to the unstable and highly controversial. In order to make claims, political interest groups will seek access to the key points of decision within these institutions. Such points are scattered throughout the structure, including not only the formally established branches of government but also the political parties in their various forms and the relationships between governmental units and other interest groups.

The extent to which a group achieves effective access to the institutions of government is the resultant of a complex of interdependent factors. For the sake of simplicity these may be classified in three somewhat overlapping categories: (1) factors relating to a group's strategic position in the society; (2) factors associated with the internal characteristics of the group; and (3) factors peculiar to the governmental institutions themselves. In the first category are: the group's status or prestige in the society, affecting the ease with which it commands deference from those outside its bounds; the standing it and its activities have when measured against the widely held but largely unorganized interests or "rules of the game;" the extent to which government officials are formally or informally "members" of the group; and the usefulness of the group as a source of technical and political knowledge. The second category includes: the degree and appropriateness of the group's organization; the degree of cohesion it can achieve in a given situation, especially in the light of competing group demands upon its membership; the skills of the leadership; and the group's resources in numbers and money. In the third category, are: the operating structure of the government institutions, since such established features involve relatively fixed advantages and handicaps; and the effects of the group life of particular units or branches of the government.

* * *

. . . in any society, and especially a complex one, no single group affiliation accounts for all of the attitudes or interests of any individual except a fanatic or a compulsive neurotic. No tolerably normal person is totally absorbed in any group in which he participates. The diversity of an individual's activities and his attendant interests involve him in a variety of actual and potential groups. Moreover, the fact that the genetic experiences of no two individuals are identical and the consequent fact that the spectra of their attitudes are in varying degrees dissimilar means that the members of a single group will perceive the group's claims in terms of a diversity of frames of reference. Such heterogeneity may be of little significance until such time as these multiple memberships conflict. Then the cohesion and influence of the affected group depend upon the incorporation or accommodation of the conflicting loyalties of any significant segment of the group, an accommodation that may result in altering the original claims. Thus the leaders of a Parent-Teacher Association must take some account of the fact that their proposals must be acceptable to members who also belong to the local taxpayers' league, to the local chamber of commerce, and to the Catholic Church.

The notion of overlapping membership bears directly upon the problems allegedly created by the appearance of a multiplicity of interest groups. . . . Multiple membership is more important as a restraint upon the activities of organized groups than the rarely aroused protests of chronic nonparticipants.

Organized interest groups are never solid and monolithic, though the consequences of their overlapping memberships may be handled with sufficient skill to give the organizations a maximum of cohesion. It is the competing claims of other groups *within* a given interest group that threaten its cohesion and force it to reconcile its claims with those of other groups active on the political scene. The claims within the American Medical Association of specialists and teaching doctors who support group practice, compulsory health insurance, and preventive medicine offer an illustration. The presence within the American Legion of public-housing enthusiasts and labor unionists as well as private homebuilders and labor opponents provides another example. Potential conflicts within the Farm Bureau between farmers who must buy supplementary feed and those who produce excess feed grains for the market, between soybean growers and dairymen, even between traditional Republicans and loyal Democrats, create serious political problems for the interest group. Instances of the way in which such cleavages impose restraints upon an organized group's activities are infinitely numerous, almost as numerous as cases of multiple membership. Given the problems of cohesion and internal group politics that result from overlapping membership, the emergence of a multiplicity of interest groups in itself contains no dangers for the political system, especially since such overlapping affects not only private but also governmental "members" of the organized group.

But multiple membership in organized groups is not sufficiently extensive to obviate the possibility of irreconcilable conflict. There is little overlapping in the memberships of the National Association of Manufacturers and the United Steelworkers of America, or of the American Farm Bureau Federation and the United

Automobile Workers. Overlapping membership among relatively cohesive organized interest groups provides an insufficient basis upon which to account for the relative stability of an operating political system. . . .

We cannot account for an established American political system without the second crucial element in our conception of the political process, the concept of the unorganized interest, or potential interest group. Despite the tremendous number of interest groups existing in the United States, not all interests are organized. If we recall the definition of an interest as a shared attitude, it becomes obvious that continuing interaction resulting in claims upon other groups does not take place on the basis of all such attitudes. One of the commonest interest group forms, the association, emerges out of severe or prolonged disturbances in the expected relationships of individuals in similar institutionalized groups. An association continues to function as long as it succeeds in ordering these disturbed relationships, as a labor union orders the relationships between management and workers. Not all such expected relationships are simultaneously or in a given short period sufficiently disturbed to produce organization. Therefore only a portion of the interests or attitudes involved in such expectations are represented by organized groups. Similarly, many organized groups—families, businesses, or churches, for example—do not operate continuously as interest groups or as political interest groups.

Any mutual interest, however, any shared attitude, is a potential group. A disturbance in established relationships and expectations anywhere in the society may produce new patterns of interaction aimed at restricting or eliminating the disturbance. Sometimes it may be this possibility of organization that alone gives the potential group a minimum of influence in the political process. Thus Key notes that the Delta planters in Mississippi "must speak for their Negroes in such programs as health and education," although the latter are virtually unorganized and are denied the means of active political participation.[1] It is in this sense that Bentley speaks of a difference in degree between the politics of despotism and that of other "forms" of government. He notes that there is "a process of representation in despotisms which is inevitable in all democracies, and which may be distinguished by quantities and by elaboration of technique, but not in any deeper 'qualititative' way." He speaks of the despot as "representative of his own class, and to a smaller, but none the less real, extent of the ruled class as well."[2] Obstacles to the development of organized groups from potential ones may be presented by inertia or by the activities of opposed groups, but the possibility that severe disturbances will be created if these submerged, potential interests should organize necessitates some recognition of the existence of these interests and gives them at least a minimum of influence.

More important for present purposes than the potential groups representing separate minority elements are those interests or expectations that are so widely held in the society and are so reflected in the behavior of almost all citizens that they are, so to speak, taken for granted. Such "majority" interests are significant not only because they may become the basis for organized interest groups but also because the "membership" of such potential groups overlaps extensively the memberships of the various organized interest groups. The resolution of conflicts between the claims of such unorganized interests and those of organized interest groups must grant recognition to the former not only because affected individuals may feel strongly attached to them but even more certainly because these interests are widely shared and are a part of many established patterns of behavior the disturbance of which would be difficult and painful. They are likely to be highly valued.

These widely held but unorganized interests are what we have previously called the "rules of the game." . . . Each of these interests (attitudes) may be wide or narrow, general or detailed. For the mass of the population they may be loose and ambiguous, though more precise and articulated at the leadership level. In any case the "rules of the game" are interests the serious disturbance of which will result in organized interaction and the assertion of fairly explicit claims for conformity. In the American system the "rules" would include the value generally attached to the dignity of the individual human being, loosely expressed in terms of "fair dealing" or more explicitly verbalized in formulations such as the Bill of Rights. They would embrace what . . . we [have] called "the democratic mold,"

that is, the approval of forms for broad mass participation in the designation of leaders and in the selection
of policies in all social groups and institutions. They
would also comprehend certain semi-egalitarian notions
of material welfare. This is an illustrative, not an exhaus-
tive, list of such interests.

The widely held, unorganized interests are reflected
in the major institutions of the society, including the
political. The political structure of the United States,
as we have seen, has adopted characteristic legislative,
executive, and judicial forms through the efforts of organized interest groups. Once these forms have been
accepted and have been largely routinized, the supporting organized interest groups cease to operate as such
and revert to the potential stage. As embodied in these
institutional forms and in accepted verbal formulations,
such as those of legal and constitutional theory, the
interests of these potential groups are established expectations concerning not only *what* the governmental institutions shall do, but more particularly *how* they shall
operate. To the extent that these established processes
remain noncontroversial, they may appear to have no
foundation in interests. Nevertheless, the widespread
expectations will receive tacit or explicit deference from
most organized interest groups in consequence of the
overlapping of their memberships with these potential
groups.[3] Violation of the "rules of the game" normally
will weaken a group's cohesion, reduce its status in the
community, and expose it to the claims of other
groups. . . .

* * *

Notes

[1] Key: *Southern Politics*, pp. 235 and *passim*.

[2] Bentley: *The Process of Government*, pp. 314–5. Copyright 1908 by
and used with the permission of Arthur F. Bentley.

[3] Cf. Bentley: *The Process of Government*, p. 397, and MacIver: *The Web
of Government*, p. 79.

POLITICAL CULTURE

The concept of political culture, which has become
a part of political analysis in recent years, includes the attitudes, values, and orientations that people hold regarding
the political system in their society. In this sense, then, the
political culture is the mental aspect of the total configuration of political control. The political system is supported
(or undermined) in large part by what people in the society
think about the appropriateness or legitimacy of the power
relationships in the political system. It is becoming increasingly apparent that there is a significant relationship between
the political culture and the political system; to understand
the political behavior of people, it is necessary to understand
their attitudes.

Gabriel Almond and Sydney Verba, in their research
on five different political cultures, set forth the basic concept
and a typology of political cultures. The most significant point
is that political analysis is not concerned only with a system
of behavior in which people attempt to control one another,
but also with the internalized thought processes that predis-
pose people to act in particular ways within the political
system.

TYPES OF
POLITICAL CULTURE

GABRIEL ALMOND AND SYDNEY VERBA

* * *

TYPES OF POLITICAL CULTURE

. . . We speak of the "political culture" of a nation
rather than the "national character" or "modal personality," and of "political socialization" rather than of child
development or child rearing in general terms. This is
not because we reject the psychological and anthropological theories that relate political attitudes to other components of personality, or because we reject those
theories that stress the relationship between child development in general terms and the induction of the child
into his adult political roles and attitudes. . . .

We employ the term political culture for two reasons. First, if we are to ascertain the relations between
political and nonpolitical attitudes and developmental

Selections from Gabriel A. Almond and Sidney Verba, *The Civic Culture:
Political Attitudes and Democracy in Five Nations.* Copyright © 1963 by Princeton
University Press; Little Brown and Company, Inc. © 1965, pp. 12–21.

patterns, we have to separate the former from the latter even though the boundary between them is not as sharp as our terminology would suggest. The term political culture thus refers to the specifically political orientations—attitudes toward the political system and its various parts, and attitudes toward the role of the self in the system. We speak of a political culture just as we can speak of an economic culture or a religious culture. It is a set of orientations toward a special set of social objects and processes.

But we also choose political *culture,* rather than some other special concept, because it enables us to utilize the conceptual frameworks and approaches of anthropology, sociology, and psychology. Our thinking is enriched when we employ, for example, such categories of anthropology and psychology as socialization, culture conflict, and acculturation. Similarly, our capacity to understand the emergence and transformation of political systems grows when we draw upon the body of theory and speculation concerned with the general phenomena of social structure and process.

We appreciate the fact that anthropologists use the term culture in a variety of ways, and that by bringing it into the conceptual vocabulary of political science we are in danger of importing its ambiguities as well as its advantages. Here we can only stress that we employ the concept of culture in only one of its many meanings: that of *psychological orientation toward social objects.* When we speak of the political culture of a society, we refer to the political system as internalized in the cognitions, feelings, and evaluations of its population. People are inducted into it just as they are socialized into nonpolitical roles and social systems. Conflicts of political cultures have much in common with other culture conflicts, and political acculturative processes are more understandable if we view them in terms of the resistances and the fusional and incorporative tendencies of cultural change in general.

Thus the concept of political culture helps us to escape from the diffuseness of such general anthropological terms as cultural ethos and from the assumption of homogeneity that the concept implies. It enables us to formulate hypotheses about relationships among the different components of culture and to test these

hypotheses empirically. With the concept of political socialization we can go beyond the rather simple assumptions of the psychocultural school regarding relationships between general child development patterns and adult political attitudes. We can relate specific adult political attitudes and behavioral propensities to the manifest and latent political socialization experiences of childhood.

The political culture of a nation is the particular distribution of patterns of orientation toward political objects among the members of the nation. . . . Orientation refers to the internalized aspects of objects and relationships. It includes (1) "cognitive orientation," that is, knowledge of and belief about the political system, its roles and the incumbents of these roles, its inputs, and its outputs; (2) "affective orientation," or feelings about the political system, its roles, personnel, and performance, and (3) "evaluational orientation," the judgments and opinions about political objects that typically involve the combination of value standards and criteria with information and feelings.

In classifying objects of political orientation, we start with the "general" political system. We deal here with the system as a whole and include such feelings as patriotism or alienation, such cognitions and evaluations of the nation as "large" or "small," "strong" or "weak," and of the polity as "democratic," "constitutional," or "socialistic." At the other extreme we distinguish orientations toward the "self" as political actor; the content and quality of norms of personal political obligation, and the content and quality of the sense of personal competence vis-à-vis the political system. In treating the component parts of the political system we distinguish, first, three broad classes of objects; (1) specific *roles* or *structures,* such as legislative bodies, executives, or bureaucracies; (2) *incumbents* of roles, such as particular monarchs, legislators, and administrators, and (3) particular public *policies, decisions,* or *enforcements* of decisions. These structures, incumbents, and decisions may in turn be classified broadly by whether they are involved either in the political or "input" process or in the administrative or "output" process. By political or input process we refer to the flow of demands from the society into the polity and the conversion of these demands into authoritative policies. Some structures that are predominantly involved in the input process are political parties, interest groups, and the media of communication. By the administrative or output process we refer to that process by which authoritative policies are applied or enforced. Structures predominantly involved in this process would include bureaucracies and courts.

We realize that any such distinction does violence to the actual continuity of the political process and to the multifunctionality of political structures. Much broad policy is made in bureaucracies and by courts; and structures that we label as input, such as interest groups and political parties, are often concerned with the details of administration and enforcement. What we are referring to is a difference in emphasis, and one that is of great importance in the classification of political cultures. The distinction we draw between participant and subject political cultures turns in part on the presence or absence of orientation toward specialized input structures. For our classification of political cultures it is not of great importance that these specialized input structures are also involved in the performance of enforcement functions and that the specialized administrative ones are involved in the performance of input functions. The important thing for our classification is what political objects individuals are oriented to, how they are oriented to them, and whether these objects are predominantly involved in the "upward" flow of policy making or in the "downward" flow of policy enforcement. We shall treat this problem in greater detail when we define the major classes of political culture.

FIGURE 1
DIMENSIONS OF POLITICAL ORIENTATION

	1. System as General Object	2. Input Objects	3. Output Objects	4. Self as Object
Cognition				
Affect				
Evaluation				

We can consolidate what we have thus far said about individual orientations toward the polity in a sim-

ple 3 x 4 matrix. Figure 1 tells us that the political orientation of an individual can be tapped systematically if we explore the following:

1. What knowledge does he have of his nation and of his political system in general terms, its history, size, location power, "constitutional" characteristics, and the like? What are his feelings toward these systemic characteristics? What are his more or less considered opinions and judgments of them?

2. What knowledge does he have of the structures and roles of the various political elites, and the policy proposals that are involved in the upward flow of policy making? What are his feelings and opinions about these structures, leaders, and policy proposals?

3. What knowledge does he have of the downward flow of policy enforcement, the structures, individuals, and decisions involved in these processes? What are his feelings and opinions of them?

4. How does he perceive of himself as a member of his political system? What knowledge does he have of his rights, powers, obligations, and of strategies of access to influence? How does he feel about his capabilities? What norms of participation or of performance does he acknowledge and employ in formulating political judgments, or in arriving at opinions?

Characterizing the political culture of a nation means, in effect, filling in such a matrix for a valid sample of its population. The political culture becomes the frequency of different kinds of cognitive, affective, and evaluative orientation toward the political system in general, its input and output aspects, and the self as political actor.

Parochial Political Culture

When this frequency of orientations to specialized political objects of the four kinds specified in Table 1.2 approaches zero, we can speak of the political culture as a parochial one. The political cultures of African tribal societies and autonomous local communities referred to by Coleman[1] would fall into this category. In these societies there are no specialized political roles: headmanship, chieftainship, "shamanship" are diffuse political—economic—religious roles, and for members of these

Table I.2
TYPES OF POLITICAL CULTURE

	System as general object	Input objects	Output objects	Self as active participant
Parochial	0	0	0	0
Subject	1	0	1	0
Participant	1	1	1	1

societies the political orientations to these roles are not separated from their religious and social orientations. A parochial orientation also implies the comparative absence of expectations of change initiated by the political system. The parochial expects nothing from the political system. . . .

The Subject Political Culture

The second major type of political culture listed in Table 1.2 is the subject culture. Here there is a high frequency of orientations toward a differentiated political system and toward the output aspects of the system, but orientations toward specifically input objects, and toward the self as an active participant, approach zero. The subject is aware of specialized governmental authority; he is affectively oriented to it, perhaps taking pride in it, perhaps disliking it; and he evaluates it either as legitimate or as not. But the relationship is toward the system on the general level, and toward the output, administrative, or "downward flow" side of the political system; it is essentially a passive relationship . . .

Again we are speaking of the pure subject orientation that is likely to exist in a society in which there is no differentiated input structure. The subject orientation in political systems that have developed democratic institutions is likely to be affective and normative rather than cognitive. Thus a French royalist is aware of democratic institutions; he simply does not accord legitimacy to them.

The Participant Political Culture

The third major type of political culture, the parti-

cipant culture, is one in which the members of the society tend to be explicitly oriented to the system as a whole and to both the political and administrative structures and processes: in other words, to both the input and output aspects of the political system. Individual members of the participant polity may be favorably or unfavorably oriented to the various classes of political objects. They tend to be oriented toward an "activist" role of the self in the polity, though their feelings and evaluations of such a role may vary from acceptance to rejection . . .

This threefold classification of political cultures does not assume that one orientation replaces the others. The subject culture does not eliminate diffuse orientations to the primary and intimate structures of community. To the diffuse orientations to lineage groups, religious community, and village it adds a specialized subject orientation to the governmental institutions. Similarly, the participant culture does not supplant the subject and parochial patterns of orientation. The participant culture is an additional stratum that may be added to and combined with the subject and parochial cultures. Thus the citizen of a participant polity is not only oriented toward active participation in politics, but is also subject to law and authority and is a member of more diffuse primary groups.

To be sure, adding participant orientations to subject and parochial orientations does not leave these "earlier" orientations unchanged. The parochial orientations must adapt when new and more specialized orientations enter into the picture, just as both parochial and subject orientations change when participant orientations are acquired. . . .

Another caution is necessary. Our classification does not imply homogeneity or uniformity of political cultures. Thus political systems with predominantly participant cultures will, even in the limiting case, include both subjects and parochials. The imperfections of the processes of political socialization, personal preferences, and limitations in intelligence or in opportunities to learn will continue to produce subjects and parochials, even in well-established and stable democracies. Similarly, parochials will continue to exist even in "high" subject cultures.

Thus there are two aspects of cultural heterogeneity or cultural "mix." The "citizen" is a particular mix of participant, subject, and parochial orientations, and the civic culture is a particular mix of citizens, subjects, and parochials. For the citizen we need concepts of proportions, thresholds, and congruence to handle the ways in which his constellation of participant, subject, and parochial attitudes is related to effective performance. For the civic culture . . . we need the same concepts of proportions, thresholds, and congruence to handle the problem of what "mix" of citizens, subjects, and parochials is related to the effective performance of democratic systems. . . .

* * *

Notes

[1] Almond and Coleman, *Politics of the Developing Areas*, p. 254.

CONFLICT AND GAMES

From earliest Greek thought to the present, it has been clear that some theorists view the politics of society as essentially a cooperative and consensual process, and others view politics as basically a process of conflict. The debate between the two positions is relatively easy to clarify, but it has been impossible to resolve.

Theorists who view society as cooperative and consensual argue that the essential ingredient in society is the norms or values its people share. In this perspective, political leaders hold positions of power because they are viewed as the appropriate spokesmen for the values shared by most people in the society. Systems theories and role analysis have been greatly influenced by the view that politics is basically a cooperative and consensual process.

The conflict theorists argue that leadership falls to those who can accumulate the power to maintain such positions in the society. The power of elites does not come from their acceptance by the mass of people in society, but from their ability to apply power and coercion to prevent others from removing them from their elite position. It is clear that the conflict perspective has contributed a great deal to contemporary political analysis.

A specific development in the category of conflict theory

has been the use of game analysis to understand political conflicts. Through gaining an understanding of the events taking place in simple situations, analysts can sometimes better understand more complex phenomena. The theory of games, which was borrowed from the discipline of economics, has important impact in political science, and the game vocabulary has become a part of this discipline's analytic language. The analysis of games includes the concept of "players," who are interested in using their resources to maximize their chances of gaining "payoffs," under conditions of uncertainty about what other players are doing or what the outcome will be. Each player forms a "strategy" about how to maximize his chances, given his resources and preferred payoff.

The game called the "prisoners' dilemma" is a good example of the type of game situation that many political analysts see as comparable to conflict situations within and between countries. Essentially, the prisoners' dilemma is that the authority in the game has a weak case against two individuals who have been accused of a crime. The prosecuting attorney admits that his evidence is incomplete, and he gives each of the accused the choice of confessing or not confessing to the crime. The rules establish that if both individuals confess, their sentences will be the same (for instance, five years each), and if neither confesses they both get one year. If one confesses and the other does not, the one who confesses gets the lighter sentence of only six months for helping solve the case. The other is given a ten-year sentence for committing the crime.

As the game proceeds the prisoners are separated, so that each must make a decision without consulting the other. The possible payoffs for the players in this dilemma illustrate some interesting conclusions about the nature of conflict situations. The reasonable prisoner considers the following alternatives: He can confess or not confess. If the other prisoner does not confess, then he is better off confessing, because a six-month sentence is better than the one-year sentence given if both confess. The interesting point is that the individual is better off confessing even if the other prisoner also confesses. In this situation, his confession gets them both five years rather than the ten he would get if he did not confess and the other did. If both prisoners act as rational, self-interested parties with little information or trust, they both receive heavier sentences than they would have received if they had been more cooperative.

Political analysts use such games as this in laboratory situations, to gain a better understanding of much more complex political situations. In international relations, for example, countries must decide whether or not to escalate their stockpiling of arms, without having either complete information or trust of another country. Much of the arms race between the Soviet Union and the United States can be seen as a form of the prisoners' dilemma, in which both sides make rational decisions to escalate; these decisions, in turn, work against their own interests by using resources that could be put to other purposes. Spying, forming alliances and treaties, diplomacy, and revising attitudes are obvious ways of increasing information about or gaining more trust of another country. Decisions could then be based on more complete information or on mutual cooperation.

Kenneth Boulding has contributed a great deal to the theoretical development of game theory in political analysis. The selection here spells out the basic vocabulary and methods of analysis, and generally illustrates the game theory approach.

THE CONTRIBUTION
OF GAME THEORY

KENNETH BOULDING

* * *

The basic concept of game theory is that of the payoff matrix. A *game* is a situation in which we have a certain number of parties each of which is capable of assuming one out of a given number of positions or choices (a finite number in the case of a finite game and an infinite number in the case of an infinite game). The *outcome* or the *payoff* of the game is the set of rewards or penalties accruing to each party at each combination of positions of all the parties. This outcome is expressed in the payoff matrix, illustrated in Fig. 3.1 for the simplest possible case of two parties, A and B, with two choices or positions each: A can choose either

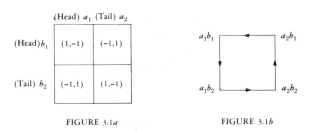

FIGURE 3.1a   FIGURE 3.1b

A_1 or A_2 and B can choose either B_1 or B_2. We can think of these positions either as simple choices or as complex *strategies;* a strategy is simply a rule of choice that is complex enough to take care of all possible eventualities. It makes no difference to the analysis how a position is defined: all that is necessary is that there be more than one position and the ability to choose one position among those available. In the boxes of the matrix, we write the outcomes; we adopt the convention that the first symbol represents the outcome to A, the second the outcome to B. To fix ideas, we may suppose that the matrix in Fig. 3.1a shows the outcomes of a game of matching pennies, with position 1 as head and position 2 as tail. Then we draw up the rules of the game, which is the payoff matrix: if both choices are heads (a_1b_1) or both tails (a_2b_2) B pays a penny to A, so that A's outcome is $+1$ and B's is -1; if a head and a tail come up (a_1b_2 or a_2b_1), A pays a penny to B, so that A's outcome is -1 and B's is $+1$. In Fig. 3.1b, we show a simplified pattern of the matrix expressed as what is called a *directed graph.* The dots (*nodes*) at the corners of the square represent the boxes of the matrix, and the dynamics of the system is expressed by arrows between the nodes. The dynamics of the system depends, of course, on the assumptions that are made. Suppose we assume that, if one party knows what the other is going to do, that party will move to the higher payoff for itself. Thus, suppose that A knows that B is going to adopt position b_1. Then, A will adopt position a_1; if A were already at a_2, he would move to a_1. This is the meaning of the arrow between a_2b_1 and a_1b_1 in Fig. 3.1b; the direction of the arrow shows that, for A, a_1b_1 dominates a_2b_1. Likewise, for A, a_2b_2 dominates a_1b_2. Similarly, for B, a_1b_2 dominates a_2b_2. It will be observed that the horizontal arrows represent A's potential shifts of choice, or dominances, whereas the vertical arrows refer to B.

It will be observed that, in Fig. 3.1b, the arrows chase each other endlessly around the square; there is no position of equilibrium. If A chooses a_1 and sticks to it, B will move to b_2; whereupon it will pay A to move to a_2, and then it will pay B to move to b_1, and then it will pay A to move to a_1, whence we repeat the circle indefinitely. We shall return to this case later. Meanwhile, consider the slightly different pattern of Fig. 3.2a. Here we suppose different rules: if two heads or

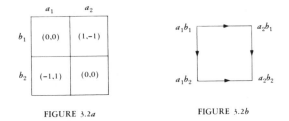

FIGURE 3.2a FIGURE 3.2b

two tails turn up, nobody gets anything; if B plays head and A tail, B pays A a penny; if A plays head and B tail, A pays B a penny. In Fig. 3.2b, we draw the corresponding directed graph, and we see that there is now an equilibrium position at a_2b_2. If A starts at a_1, B will go to b_2, and then A will go to a_2; if B starts at b_1, A will go to a_2, and then B will go to b_2. Once the parties have arrived at a_2b_2, it pays neither party to change his position even if he knows that the other party will continue in his present position. This type of equilibrium position . . . may be called the short-sighted equilibrium. It is the result of a dynamics that assumes that each party simply supposes that the other party's behaviour will continue indefinitely, and reacts accordingly, and does not, therefore, consider the effect of the other party's reaction. . . .

The payoff matrices of Figs. 3.1 and 3.2 have one thing in common; the sum of the payoffs in each box of the matrix is zero. They belong, therefore, to an important category of games known as *zero-sum* games, in which what any one party gains the other loses (or the others taken collectively lose if there is more than one party). Such a game neither requires any subsidy from nor pays any tax to the outside: its payoffs are internal to the game and involve a simple redistribution

of some initial good among the players. Adding (or subtracting) a fixed amount to each payoff of a zero-sum game produces a *constant-sum* game, in which the sum of the payoffs in each box of the matrix is constant. The dynamics of a constant-sum game is identical with that of the zero-sum game from which it is derived. By contrast, the *variable-sum* game is one in which the sum of the payoffs in each box is not constant. This, as we shall see, has many properties different from the constant-sum game. The constant-sum game may be regarded as an interaction process of pure conflict, for any increase in the gain to one party must result in an equal decrease in the gain to the other. Variable-sum games may involve both conflict and cooperation. In a *positive-sum* game, there is at least one position in which both parties can be better off than if the game were not played. In a *negative-sum* game, there is no such position.

In constant-sum games, the payoff matrix for one party can be derived immediately from that of the other by subtracting each figure from the constant sum. Thus, in Figs. 3.1 and 3.2, B's payoff is always minus A's payoff. Frequently, only the payoffs of one party are shown in the boxes, as those of the other can immediately be derived. In a constant-sum game, it can be shown that the shortsighted equilibrium point always occurs at a point in the matrix that has the properties of a *minimax*, or *saddle point*, that is, which is both a maximum of a row and a minimum of a column. This is illustrated in Fig. 3.3. Here we suppose a three-by-three matrix, with each party having three choices, 1, 2, and 3. (It should be noticed that a payoff matrix does not have to be symmetrical; it would be quite possible, for instance, for one party to have three choices and the other two, in which case we would have a three-by-two matrix.) In Fig. 3.3a, we show the directed graphs of the shortsighted equilibrium, the equilibrium position being at a_2b_2, in the center of the figure. We place it in the center merely to illustrate the principle; it could just as well, of course, be at an edge or corner. Here, the vertical arrows indicate B's movements and the horizontal arrows A's movements. Thus, in the figure, we know that B's payoff at a_1b_2 is greater than B's payoff at a_1b_1. If this is a constant-sum game, howev-

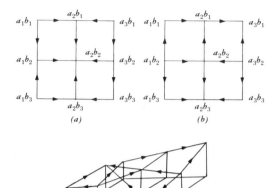

FIGURE 3.3

er, this means that A's payoff at a_1b_1 is greater than A's payoff at a_1b_2, as A's payoff is the constant sum less B's payoff. Thus, suppose B's payoffs at a_1b_1 and a_1b_2 were 7 and 4 respectively and the constant sum were 10; A's payoffs would be $10 - 7 = 3$ and $10 - 4 = 6$. In Fig. 3.3b, then, we reverse the direction of the vertical arrows, leaving the horizontal arrows unchanged; this gives us the directed graph of A's payoff matrix, where, in each case, the arrow points from the smaller to the larger payoff. These arrows, it should be observed, have the opposite sense to the usual "greater than" or "less than" signs; it seems best, however, to preserve the arrowhead convention as indicating the potential dynamics of the system: we always go toward the larger payoff. An arrow, that is, always points uphill. We now see that, because the equilibrium point a_2b_2 in Fig. 3.3a has four arrows pointing in toward it, the same point in Fig. 3.3b has two horizontal arrows pointing in toward it, indicating that the point is a maximum along the horizontal line a_1b_2, a_2b_2, a_3b_2, but it has two vertical arrows pointing away from it, indicating that it is a minimum on the line a_2b_1, a_2b_2, a_2b_3. This, then, is a minimax. If we plot the payoffs vertically, as in Fig. 3.3c, we see that the point a_2b_2 is a saddle point; it is like the top of a mountain pass, which is the highest point going over the pass from a_1b_2 to a_3b_2 and the lowest point going along the ridge from a_2b_3 to a_2b_1.

If there is only a single minimax point in the payoff matrix, it can be shown that, if both parties choose their positions according to the principle of choosing the best of the worst, or the *maximin*, they will settle down right away at the minimax. This again is illustrated in Fig. 3.3. We suppose here that the payoff matrix is known to each party (not usually a very realistic assumption) but that neither knows which position the other will choose. We suppose, then, that A looks over the matrix. If he chooses a_1, the worst thing that can happen to him (looking down the column) is that B chooses b_2; if he chooses a_2, the worst thing that can happen to him is a_2b_2; if he chooses a_3, the worst is a_3b_3. The best of these worsts is a_2b_2, which is the minimax. A's worst from any choice can be worse than the payoffs along the mountain pass, but they cannot be better, or else the mountain-pass values become the worst. Hence, the value at the top of the mountain pass must be the maximin, or the best of the worst. Similarly, remembering that B's payoffs are minus A's payoffs, we show that B's maximin must be at the trough of the ridge, a_2b_1 to a_2b_3, which is also at the minimax a_2b_2.

The minimax equilibrium has been criticized on the grounds that the maximin is an unrealistic rule of choice, that, in particular, it is too conservative and pessimistic, and that people are more likely to choose the position that gives them the chance of the highest gain (the maximax) or, if the probabilities of the other parties' choices are known, will choose the position that gives them the highest expected value of gain, or something of this kind. These criticisms of the rule of behavior may be entirely valid, and yet they do not necessarily upset the concept of the minimax as the shortsighted equilibrium. The minimax is, in general, the only position in which knowledge of the intentions of the other party will not change the policy of either. Its claim to be an equilibrium position, therefore, rests on the assumption that, if one party adopts a position that is not at the minimax and sticks to it, the other party will find this out by observation and will move its position and a succession of such moves must eventually bring us to the minimax. In the case of the constant-sum game, the minimax, therefore, has strong claims to be a true equilibrium position, even though inertia or ignorance may act like friction to prevent the system from attaining it.

* * *

COMMUNICATION AND INFORMATION

Communications theory, too, has added a new vocabulary to political analysis. The new language includes such terms as the "transmission" and "reception" of the "message" or "information bit." Theorists consider such variables as "distortion" of the message by the "transmitter" and the "capacity" of the "receiver" to receive messages.

Communication analysis is another attempt to use simple analogs of complex behavior to gain a better understanding of what is occurring in reality. The analog in this case is a computer. The assumption is that for any relationship, including power relationships, to exist, there must be communication among people. From this perspective, it is the communicating act or relationship that is considered to be the most appropriate focus for understanding political events and situations.

Karl Deutsch is one of the leading proponents of the communications approach to political analysis. His position, greatly simplified here, is that a nation can exist only when communication takes place among people. To the extent that the communication processes among people are efficient transactors of information within the community, and only to that extent, can one conceptualize a nation, society, or community. Deutsch spells out some of the basic elements and relationships associated with the analysis of political decisions in terms of a communications model.

COMMUNICATION MODELS
AND
POLITICAL DECISIONS

KARL W. DEUTSCH

* * *

The recent models of communication and control may make us more sensitive to some aspects of politics

Edited and abridged with permission of Macmillan Publishing Co., Inc., from *The Nerves of Government* by Karl W. Deutsch, pp. 145–62. Copyright © The Free Press, a Division of The Macmillan Company 1966.

that have often been overlooked or slighted in the past. This, as we know, is a major function of models in their early stages. Well before they permit quantitative inferences, they may already aid in adding new criteria of relevance: What kinds of facts are now interesting for us, since we have acquired a new intellectual context for them?

This chapter will deal with such possible areas of relevance. It will survey a few of the concepts, and suggest a few of the questions that could be asked in political research, once we are willing to entertain the proposition that governments and parties—that is, political systems or networks of decision and control—are dependent on processes of communication and that they resemble certain aspects of man-made communication equipment to a sufficient degree to arouse our interest.

The first major point of resemblance is the dependence of all governments, as of all communication systems, upon the processing of information.

[The concept of information is central to the distinction made by theorists like Norbert Wiener] . . . between communication engineering and power engineering. Power engineering . . . transfers energy which then may produce gross changes at its place of arrival. In the case of power engineering, these changes are in some sense roughly proportionate to the amount of energy delivered. Communication engineering transfers extremely small amounts of energy in relatively intricate patterns. It can produce sometimes very large changes at the point of arrival, or in the "receiver" of the "message," but these changes need in no way be proportionate to the amount of energy that carried the signal, much as the force of a gun shot need not be proportionate to the amount of pressure needed to set off the trigger.

Power, we might say, produces changes; information triggers them off in a suitable receiver. In the example just given, the most important thing was not the amount of pressure on the trigger, once it had reached the required threshold, but rather the fact that it was delivered at the trigger, that is, at one particular point of the gun. Similarly, the information required for turning the gun to a particular target need not be carried by any amount of energy proportionate to the energy delivered to the target by the gun. The important thing about information is thus not the amount of energy needed to carry the signal, but the *pattern* carried by the signal, and its relationship to the set of patterns stored in the receiver.

Generally, *information* can be defined as a patterned distribution, or a *patterned relationship between events*. Thus the distribution of lights and shadows in a landscape may be matched by the distribution of a set of electric impulses in a television cable, by the distribution of light and dark spots on a photographic plate, or on a television set, or by the distribution of a set of numbers if a mathematician had chosen to assign coordinates to each image point. In the case of photography or television the processes carrying this information are quite different from each other: sunlight, the emulsion on the photographic plate, the electric impulses in the cable, the television waves, the surface of the receiving screen. Yet each of these processes is brought into a state that is similar in significant respects to the state of the other physical processes that carried the image to it.

A sequence of such processes forms a *channel of communication*, and information is that aspect of the state description of each stage of the channel that has remained invariant from one stage to another. That part of the state description of the first stage of the channel that reappears invariant at the last stage is then the information that has been transmitted through the channel as a whole.

THE RECEPTION OF INFORMATION

The effectiveness of information at the receiver depends on two classes of conditions. First of all, *at least some parts of the receiving system must be in highly unstable equilibrium*, so that the very small amount of energy carrying the signal will be sufficient to start off a much larger process of change. Without such disequilibrium already existing in the receiver, information would produce no significant effects.

This obvious technical relationship might have some parallels in politics. The extent of the effect of the introduction of new information into a political or economic system might well be related, among other things, to the extent of the instabilities that already exist there. A crude empirical expression of this problem is found in the perennial debate concerning the relative share of "domestic instabilities" versus "foreign agitators" in strikes or political disturbances. On a somewhat more sophisticated level, the problem reappears as the question of the role of ideas in inducing or prompting social change, and it has relevance for studies of the conditions favoring political reform or technological innovations in different countries. In all such cases a search for "promising instabilities," that is, instabilities relevant for possible innovation, should be rewarding.

RICHNESS OF INFORMATION AND SELECTIVITY OF RECEPTION

The second class of conditions involves the *selectivity* of the receiver. What patterns are already stored in the receiver, and how specific must be the pattern of the incoming signal in order to produce results? A simple example of this problem is furnished by the relationship of lock and key. How many tumblers and notches have been built, let us say, into a particular Yale lock, and what restrictions do they impose upon the distribution of notches on any key that is to turn it? Clearly, the effectiveness of any key in turning a particular lock depends only slightly on the energy with which it is turned (beyond a minimum threshold), and far more on the correspondence of the configuration of its notches with the configuration of the tumblers in the lock.

* * *

THE MEASUREMENT OF INFORMATION AND THE FIDELITY OF CHANNELS

The upshot of all this work has been the emergence of information as a quantitative concept. Information can be measured and counted, and the performance of communication channels in transmitting or distorting information can be evaluated in quantitative terms. Some of these measurements in electrical engineering have reached high levels of mathematical sophistication.[1]

* * *

The fact that social scientists may have to use some of the cruder rather than the more refined methods for measuring the amounts of stored or transmitted information should not obscure the importance of being able to measure it at all. . . .

INFORMATION AND SOCIAL COHESION

If we can measure information, no matter how crudely, then we can also measure the cohesion of organizations or societies in terms of their ability to transmit information with smaller or larger losses or distortions in transmission. The smaller the losses or distortions, and the less the admixture of irrelevant information (or "noise"), the more efficient is a given communications channel, or a given chain of command.

If we think of an ethnic or cultural community as a network of communication channels, and of a state or a political system as a network of such channels and of chains of command, we can measure the "integration" of individuals in a people by their ability to receive and transmit information on wide ranges of different topics with relatively little delay or loss of relevant detail.[2]

Similarly, we can measure the speed and accuracy with which political information or commands are transmitted, and the extent to which the patterns contained in the command are still recognizable in the patterns of the action that are supposed to form its execution.

The difference between a cohesive community or a cohesive political system, on the one hand, and a specialized professional group—such as a congress of mathematicians—on the other hand, consists in the multiplicity of topics about which efficient communication is possible. The wider this range of topics, the more broadly integrated, in terms of communications, is the community, or the "body politic." In traditional societies this range of topics may be broad, but limited to topics and problems well within the traditional culture; the ability to communicate widely and effectively on nontraditional topics may be relevant for the cohesion and learning capacity of peoples and political systems in countries undergoing rapid industrialization.

* * *

FACE-TO-FACE COMMUNICATION NETWORKS AND LEGITIMACY SYMBOLS

If many studies of politics have stressed *power*, or enforcement, it should now be added that information precedes compulsion. It is impossible to enforce any command unless the enforcing agency knows against whom the enforcement is to be directed—a truism that has given much delight to readers of detective stories. The problem becomes more serious where enforcement is to be directed against a significant number of personally unknown members of an uncooperative population, as in situations of conspiracy, political "underground activities," resistance to military occupation, or guerrilla warfare.

Similarly, information must precede compliance. It is impossible for anyone to comply with a command unless he knows what the command is. In this sense, a "legitimacy myth," discussed by some writers, is an effective set of interrelated memories that identify more or less clearly those classes of commands, and sources of commands, that are to be given preferential attention, compliance, and support, and that are to be so treated on grounds connecting them with some of the general value patterns prevailing in the culture of the society, and with important aspects of the personality structures of its members. Yet, even where such legitimacy beliefs are effectively held in the minds of a large part of the population, its members must have ways of receiving the commands rapidly and accurately if they are to act on them. Governments-in-exile or leaders of underground movements during World War II not only had the task of maintaining their status as legitimate but also the task of maintaining an actual network of communication channels to carry the essential two-way flow of information.

In evaluating the political significance of this fact, two mistakes may easily be made. The first mistake consists in overestimating the importance of impersonal media of communication, such as radio broadcasts and newspapers, and underestimating the incomparably greater significance of face-to-face contacts. . . .

The second mistake might consist in considering legitimacy myths or symbols in isolation from the actual communications networks, and from the human networks—often called "organizations," "machines," "apparatus," or "bureaucracy"—by which they are carried and selectively disseminated. . . .

Without widespread and favorable legitimacy beliefs, a face-to-face communications network is exceedingly hard to build, as, for example, the failure of the Quisling group in Norway has demonstrated. Without effective control of the bulk of the actual face-to-face communication networks, on tne other hand, the nominal holders of the legitimacy symbols may become relatively helpless vis-à-vis those groups that do have this control. The Polish government-in-exile, as well as the group of President Benes of Czechoslovakia, found themselves with far less power at the end of the war than their symbolic status of legitimacy would have suggested.

Perhaps we may suspect, accordingly, that it is rather in the more or less far-reaching *coincidence* between legitimacy beliefs and social communication channels that political power can be found. Thus, when we speak loosely of the "manipulation of political symbols" we might do well to distinguish sharply between their manipulation in a speech or book, and the manipulation of those human and institutional chains of communication that must carry and disseminate these symbols and all other information and that are crucial for the functioning of political power.

The frequent superiority of networks of face-to-face contacts over either isolated legitimacy symbols or even impersonal media of mass communication can be illustrated by two examples. The Democratic party in the big cities in the United States has shown persistent electoral strength despite the fact that it is notoriously weak in newspaper support; however, it is relatively strong in face-to-face contacts on the ward level. The second example was demonstrated to television viewers in the United States during the presidential campaign of 1952:

the discrepancy between the amount of publicity and symbolic reputation attracted by Senator Estes Kefauver in his campaign for the Democratic presidential nomination, and his inability either to overcome the coldness or hostility of the "insiders" and "machines" of the Democratic party or to attract really substantial support without their aid.

As these examples indicate, the discrepancy between the "newspaper strength" of a leader or candidate and his real strength, not at the "grass roots" but *at the decisive middle level of communication and decision*, may be a promising field for comparative political research.

THE "MIDDLE LEVEL" OF COMMUNICATIONS AND COMMAND

The strategic "middle level" can perhaps be defined somewhat more closely. It is that level of communication and command that is "vertically" close enough to the large mass of consumers, citizens, or common soldiers to forestall any continuing and effective direct communication between them and the "highest echelons"; and it must be far enough above the level of the large numbers of the rank and file to permit effective "horizontal" communication and organization among a sufficiently large portion of the men or units on its own level. . . .

The "middle-level" concept permits perhaps a relatively simple approach to the short-run analysis of governments, parties, or political decision systems, where time and resources for research are limited. In all such systems we might look for the crucial middle-level group—or rather upper-middle-level group—of between fifty and five hundred persons without whose cooperation or consent (or, of course, replacement) very little can be done in the decision system. In the army these are the colonels; in the government, perhaps the permanent undersecretaries in the ministries, and the heads of personnel departments . . . In part, these persons may be expected to reflect the influence of others who put them into their positions. In part, they will themselves be agents shaping the course of events in terms of their desires. Their crucial characteristics are two: (1) Without them, taken all together, little can be done, and particularly, little can be changed. (2) Each of them must count with the group of his peers, with whose support he can win easily but against whom he is nearly powerless. Together, they form a small universe of political possibilities that can be studied intensively or that can perhaps be scanned by listing the "middle-level" jobs and men, and selecting a random sample of one-half or one-fifth or one-tenth for intensive investigation. . . .

It should be noted that the persons on this strategic "upper-middle-level" usually receive very little publicity. They are the "men behind the scenes" in the sense that they are the "men who do the work" of making, permitting, and executing the largest number of strategic decisions. To investigate this group systematically by structure and personnel requires us once again to supplement the study of symbols and publicity, or of general "elites," by the study of samples of an unpublicized but crucial set of persons.[3]

* * *

THE INTERNAL INTELLIGENCE FUNCTION AND CONTINUING LEADERSHIP

If politics requires a machinery of enforcement, and a set of habits of compliance, then politics is impossible without a flow of information to those who are expected to comply with the commands. These two streams of information can be taken for granted in what has been called "normal" politics, that is, in politics in a Western European state during the late nineteenth century, in times of peace, with no immediate danger of war or domestic political upheaval. Under these conditions, common beliefs about legitimacy would be sufficiently widely held to identify clearly most laws and most lawbreakers, and to ensure cohesion within the law-enforcing agencies.

A large part of politics during the last fifty years, however, has not occurred in such "normal" situations, but rather under conditions of crisis, emergency, revolution, war, and extreme factional conflict. Under such conditions it has sometimes been very difficult for enforcing agencies to know against whom to direct their force, or to know the consequences of particular commands given, or the consequences of attempts to enforce them.

Indeed, under such conditions it has often been difficult for an enforcing agency to know which members of its staff, or which of its subsidiary organizations, were still reliable. Purges in dictatorships and "loyalty tests" in democracies are attempts to obtain and verify such information when reliability is no longer taken for granted. At this stage the enforcing agencies believe that they can rely on the loyalty of individuals who carry out the investigations essential for the purges or the tests. History is replete with instances, however, where the armies, police forces, totalitarian parties, or secret police organizations have themselves become unreliable. . . .

In such situations of unrest, governments face not only a substantive problem of ensuring the retention of desirable loyalties or values by their officials but also a technical problem of obtaining a continuous flow of accurate information about their behavior. Up to a point, the question "Who watches the watchmen?" is answered by "Their peers, and the population at large, as long as both are sufficiently motivated by established legitimacy beliefs." If this problem arises, however, in a society in which most persons are political opportunists who care little about legitimacy, and rather wish to rush to the assistance of the victor, the problem turns into a calculation as to how many men may change their political alignments to what extent within a given time. In a country or period in which legitimacy beliefs are weak, the time element in political realignments, conspiracies, and purges may thus be most important. Even where legitimacy beliefs are well established, potentially insubordinate subleaders may have to be demoted slowly and by honorific stages—as has at times been done in the Soviet Union—so as to give their followers time to disassociate themselves from them with the least loss in their own status.

In addition to the failure of the enforcement agency to keep itself informed about the probable behavior of its own officials or subsidiary organizations, political enforcement may fail because of a failure to predict correctly the reaction of the population to it. Under this aspect, the history of revolutions appears to a significant extent as the history of internal intelligence failures in the governments that were overthrown. Thus between 1789 and 1792 the King of France seems to have misjudged or disregarded the probable reaction of almost every major element of the French population. He misjudged the reaction of his creditors who refused to lend him more money; the reaction of the Paris Parliament that refused to register his new tax decrees; the reaction of the French nobles who refused to pay their share of taxes; the reaction of the representatives of the Third Estate who defied his command by their Tennis Court Oath; the reaction of his troops who proved unreliable against the Parisians; the reaction of the Parisians who stormed the Bastille; and the reaction of the population of the little town of Varennes who stopped his flight and forced him to return to the custody of the Legislative Assembly. Perhaps most fatally of all, he misjudged the reaction of the French people to the defeat of their armies in a foreign war: instead of surrendering to the Duke of Brunswick, many Frenchmen supported the Revolution more strongly, even to the beheading of their monarch.

What occurred dramatically in the French Revolution occurs less spectacularly every day in politics. Everywhere political decisions depend for their effectiveness on the correctness with which the relevant reactions to them have been predicted. Lacking such information, they are apt to produce results quite different from those intended, and all attempts at enforcement are then apt to make the danger of an eventual breakdown worse.

Detailed studies of leadership are indicating the very large extent to which the emergence of a leader and his continuance in that role depend on his ability to anticipate correctly the likes and dislikes of his followers, and hence their probable reactions. The most important single function a leader must perform, according to these studies, is to "maintain his acceptability with the group." This maintenance of acceptability is bound up primarily, at least in most situations, with the ability to anticipate explicitly or intuitively the configuration of their reactions as a group: Will this or that policy unite them, or will it split the group and drive out some of its members?

Leadership in the group, as well as in the state, thus depends to a very significant extent upon something that we may call the "internal intelligence function." Even in warfare the first thing a general must know is not the numbers and capabilities and intentions of the enemy, but the numbers, capabilities, and reliability of his own troops. To misjudge the strength and intentions of an enemy may be very serious, but to order into battle nonexistent armies, or armies in rebellion, is apt to be fatal.

The channels and institutions by means of which a government or a party obtains and uses information concerning its own constituency and personnel, and the efficiency with which such information is collected, applied, and perhaps stored for future use in records, or in the memories of men, are all promising objects of comparative political studies. In democracies, such studies may deal with the comparative effectiveness of hearings, opinion polls, "grass-roots" politics, pressure-group activities, and the like. In dictatorships, or under conditions of war or near war, such studies may throw some light on the ability of particular political regimes or organizations to appraise their own internal resources and obstacles, and to steer their own behavior accordingly.

VOLUNTARY IMITATION AND MORALE: THE CONCEPT OF MIMESIS

A counterpart to the ability of leaders or rulers to get and use information from the populace is the willingness of the population to accept information and suggestions, rather than mere commands, from its rulers. This problem touches upon the general setting of the political process.

In estimating the political capabilities of a government, we often ask: Does the population accept messages and orders from the government? Do they follow such orders with little or no supervision, and do they lend them active support above and beyond mere compliance?

Now, however, we can add a further question, asked by some social scientists: Are the rulers accepted as models or reference groups by the ruled? This question has been applied to the breakdown of empires by

A. J. Toynbee: Does the population *imitate voluntarily* the behavior patterns demonstrated or suggested by its rulers? . . .

Questions about voluntary imitation and compliance have a clear bearing on politics, and they make it possible to use the very considerable literature on morale studies,[4] both as to methods and results, for studies of the behavior of political systems.

DECISION SYSTEMS AND INFORMATION-CARRYING CAPACITY

Another line of research interest might deal with the ability of decision-makers to predict the kind and intensity of the reactions to their decisions, both by possible opponents and by supposed passive bystanders, or supposed supporters or subordinates. We cannot find out, of course, except after the event, how well a politician or ruler has anticipated such reactions, but we can find out well in advance of the event what efforts were made to collect the relevant information, through what channels it was brought to the point of decision, and what chance the decision-makers had to consider it at all.

In this sense we may be able to identify political decision systems that are equipped with adequate facilities for the collection of external and internal information as well as for its transmission to the points of decision-making, and reasonably well equipped for its screening and evaluation before the decisions are made. Such systems will by no means be infallible, but they will have at least a chance to use the information they need. On the other hand, we may be able to identify decision systems where this is not the case, and where either the collection, or the transmission, or the screening and evaluation of the information has broken down, or has never been adequately developed. Such systems perform well on occasion, but in the long run the odds should be heavily against them.

More generally, this line of thought suggests that *communication overload* or *decision overload* may be a major factor in the breakdown of states and governments.[5] Similarly, attention overload may be an element in the troubles of our driven and often shallow mass culture with its spot news, capsule reviews, and book digests. Again, attention and communication overload may force a frantic search for a privileged status for their own messages upon many people in a prosperous and economically equalitarian democracy. Unless its citizens turn into "status seekers," they must fear that they will lack the social status—that is, the priority accorded in the social system to the messages they send—and that their attractive, interesting, or influential contemporaries will simply have no time to pay attention to them. If this is true, an economic democracy may turn into a jungle of frustrated snobs, starved for individual attention. The concept of communication overload may then be a key to the understanding of this cruel reversal of democratic hopes, and eventually to the amelioration of the underlying maladjustment.

Notes

[1] Y. W. Lee, *Statistical Theory of Communication* (New York: Wiley, 1960).

[2] K. W. Deutsch, *Nationalism and Social Communication*, (Cambridge-New York: M.I.T. Press-Wiley, 1953), pp. 70–74.

[3] For efforts to include some data on elite attitudes and personnel at this middle level, see K. W. Deutsch and L. J. Edinger, *Germany Rejoins the Powers: Mass Opinion, Interest Groups, and Elites in Contemporary German Foreign Policy* (Stanford: Stanford University Press, 1959), pp. 60–144, 195–216. On this broad problem of political communication, see also Gabriel A. Almond, "A Functional Approach to Comparative Politics," in G. A. Almond and J. S. Coleman, eds., *The Politics of the Developing Areas* (Princeton: Princeton University Press, 1960), pp. 3–64, particularly pp. 45–52. Cf. also Charles Y. Glock, "The Comparative Study of Communication and Opinion Formation," in Schramm, op. cit., pp. 469–79, and particularly the section on "Informal Channels of Communication," pp. 474–76. For the general elite problem, see also G. A. Almond, *The American People and Foreign Policy* (New York: Praeger, 1960), xxiv and pp. 57.

[4] For an outstanding example, see E. A. Shils and M. Janowitz, "Cohesion and Disintegration in the Wehrmacht in World War II" in Schramm, op. cit., pp. 501–16.

[5] For an extremely informative summary of recent research on communications overload in biological systems and in small groups, see the forthcoming book by James Grier Miller, *Living Systems* (Ann Arbor: Mental Health Research Institute, 1962), preprint, Chapter 4.

7/A Scientific Theory of Mass Democracy and the Invisible Ideology

Although the contribution of the behavioral paradigm to modern political analysis has been considerable, this development is seriously rivaled for significance by the behavioralists' accomplishment of redefining the classical theory of liberal democracy. In Chapter 5 it was noted that the behavioral paradigm rests on two central but contradictory values: the value for science as a method for political analysis, and the value for democracy as the best of all practical political worlds. The reasoning involved in that argument requires further exploration here.

Scientific evaluation involves measuring what is thought to be true against what is actually going on in the real world. Scientists do not evaluate by measuring reality against a set of moral prescriptions; nothing is good or bad, it is merely described validly or invalidly. The unwillingness of behavioral political scientists to entertain moral questions is debated by few, but the reasons behind this unwillingness are open to speculation. Behavioralists are the first to claim that, as scientists, they neither value nor devalue any political systems but attempt only to describe them accurately.

A few critics of this amoral approach continue to point out that whatever reasons behavioralists have for not raising moral concerns, the effect is that they stand tacitly in favor of the status quo. This argument assumes that to be uncritical is to be satisfied, that not to be in opposition is to be in favor, that everyone—including behavioralists—must be either for the system or against it. Obviously, it is imperative to clarify the position taken here.

The thesis of this chapter is that the continuing and controlling influence of the behavioral paradigm in American political science can be accounted for, at least in part, by its ability to permit American political scientists to value their political system on the firm ground of science, rather than on the less secure bases of sentiment and morality. The behavioral paradigm has reconciled a widely shared value for scientific analysis and a just as widely shared value for American mass democracy. The forging of this new consensus among political scientists who hold diverse views on practically everything else has taken two forms. The first form is a scientific theory of democracy, and the second is a supporting but invisible ideology.

The reconciliation of these widely accepted values has been brought about by the construction of a scientific theory of democratic political systems, which has become (with a perhaps unconscious sleight of hand) more than just a scientific description of what exists. The intellectual shift among behavioralists—from a scientific theory explaining the American political system to an ideology justifying that system as the best of all practical political worlds—can be accounted for by positing the values for democracy and science as part of the behavioral paradigm.

The development of a scientific theory of democratic political systems and the invisible ideology came about in large part because of the success of what appears to have been an all-out intellectual attack on the view of man and society that was basic to classical democratic theory. Rightly or wrongly, the classical doctrine was judged by many political scientists to be an inadequate theory of democracy. A new and more acceptable theory of democratic practice was developed, which greatly influenced the evaluation of democracy within contemporary political science. This chapter traces the developments that gave rise to the new theory and the invisible ideology, describes the values that were a part of a new view of democracy, and assesses the influence of these developments on contemporary political science and the evaluation of democracy. All political scientists did not concur in the movement, and some of the critical argument will be surveyed in the final part of the chapter.

CLASSICAL DEMOCRATIC THEORY UNDER ATTACK

When Abraham Lincoln characterized classical democratic theory as "government of the people, for the people, and by the people," he captured with clarity and elegance the essence of the classical conception of man, society, and government.

The basis of classical democratic governance is the assumption that man is a rational being who can understand his own wants, needs, and interests; who can assess political priorities, policies, and candidates on the criterion of his interest; who can choose those political options most closely representing his interest in the making of public decisions for the society. The government of a democratic society should reflect what the people in that society need, want, and perceive to be their individual interests and desires.

In this view, the politics of the society should be constructed in a way that will maximize individual will and active participation in the political decisions that bind the future course of events in the society. The purpose of politics is to liberate the individual from the social, economic, intellectual, and political constraints that conflict with his inherent right to pursue a definition of the good life for himself.

Because making decisions in the political arena requires accurate information concerning alternative public policies, the classical democratic theory assumes that there will be a free flow of information, ideas, thought, and criticism. Dissent, criticism, and deliberation are prerequisite to enlightened public participation in decision making for the society. Without deliberation and without toleration of diverse positions on issues, it would be impossible for individuals to rationally calculate the relationship of their own interests to political choices.

It is further assumed, in the classic view, that every man has certain unalienable rights, and that no interference with those rights can be tolerated. Man has such rights not because they were given by government, but because they are inherent in the human condition. They cannot legitimately be taken away, and for a government to take them away illegitimately is grounds for dissolving the contract with that government through revolution.

These notions served as a basis for constructing political institutions that would realize stated ideals in the practice of government. The two major devices used were majority rule and representative government.

Even if one assumes that all men are reasonable, it is difficult to maintain that they will always agree. Under majority rule, the criterion for judging that a policy is in the best interest of a society is when most of its members support that policy.

It is also clear that all people cannot directly participate in making decisions for the society, so the notion of political representation of the majority was the solution. Individuals in the society calculate their own best self-interest, and elect representatives who work toward transforming their interests into public policy. On the next election day, the representative's adequacy in presenting the interests of his constituency would then be evaluated. In this manner, a majority of the people elected representatives to carry out their will, or elected others if those representatives had not done the job.

Such a set of institutions was a practical compromise with the ideals of democratic governance. Not everyone's individual interests could be realized, but the opinion of the majority of the people would be acted on. At the same time, the inherent rights of every individual, whether he was a member of the majority or of a dissenting minority, was guaranteed. The majority could not make public policy to remove the rights of any individual or group to continue to work to realize their own beliefs; the minority was permitted the opportunity to convince others, and was given the hope that in time, its position could become the majority position.

Lane Davis summarizes these notions in the following characterization of classical democratic theory.

This theory posits the existence of rational and active citizens who seek to realize a generally recognized common good through the collective initiation, discussion, and decision of policy questions concerning public affairs, and who delegate authority to agents (elected

*government officials) to carry through the broad decisions reached
by the people through majority vote.*[1]

What happened to the commitment to these ideals,
which had so greatly influenced both the American Revolution and the construction of American government? Many
events that occurred during the earlier parts of this century
were to cast real doubt on the theory's interpretation of
man's relationship to society and the good life. Intellectual
developments, research into the workings of American government, and historical realities appeared to conspire in eroding the beliefs that political scientists had shared in their
classical definition of democracy.

Skepticism is a process rather than a product. It is
impossible to point to any specific event or intellectual
break-through that caused political scientists to begin to
doubt the classical theory of democratic governance. Instead,
there were multiple causes for the skepticism that infiltrated
the discipline. Two very important intellectual developments
stimulated criticism. These developments were associated
with the growth of the disciplines of psychology and sociology and were heavily influenced by the works of European
scholars. The theories of Sigmund Freud and the rise of
the psychoanalytic movement were of major significance.
Freud's work had implications for all of the social sciences,
but none was more critical for liberal political theories than
his proposal that man was not a rational agent. Freud's
theory left little basis for the assumption that humans are
purposeful, conscious, and rational agents who determine
their own destinies. Man, in Freud's view, was largely the
product of unconscious and irrational forces that lead him
to his overt behavior. Although all scholars may not have
been persuaded, Freud's views made it impossible to naïvely
continue to assume that all men operated in society as rational individuals.

Early-day sociologists dealt another blow to the concept
of individuality. Their idea was simply that man functions
more often as a member of groups than as an individual.
Most of what had been thought of as individual behavior
was, in sociological analysis, a product of participation in
groups, which included everybody from family to friends to
working associates and social peers. In the "new" sociology,

these group and class associations, rather than individual
internal forces, were the major determinants of man's behavior. Thus, as psychology turned away from man as a rational
agent, sociology turned away from man as an individual.
The combined effect of these reformulations of basic conceptions of man was devastating to any intellectual defense of
a rational individual, as prescribed in liberal democratic
theory.

These intellectual and theoretical developments were
in many ways compatible with the pragmatic and practical
orientation of American academics. By the end of the nineteenth century, American scholars were earnestly in pursuit
of a more "realistic" understanding of man, society, and politics. Some of the early scholars in American political science
were already examining what was "really" going on in politics and were searching for theory and data that would more
clearly meet the requirements for a science of human behavior. From their perspective, classical democratic theory was
not so much "idealistic" as it was mystical and unpractical.
They sought for theory that would explain the hard realities
of politics, rather than for prescriptions describing how people and governments should ideally behave. These men wanted to get away from such "soul stuff" as motivations and
morality, and get on with the empirical task of explaining
democratic practice.

Combined with these early events in the intellectual
realm of social science were the realities of historical change
in the twentieth century: World War I, the Great Depres-
sion, World War II, the collapse of the democratic government in Germany, the emergence of fascist movements in
Japan and Italy and Germany, and the phenomena of totalitarian government produced by revolutions in developing
countries (particularly the Soviet Union). All gave serious
cause for doubting the ability of either liberal theory to
explain—or democratic government to survive—in the rapidly
changing circumstances of a modern industrial world. Many
political scientists turned toward a more realistic appraisal
of our own society and its government. Assumptions about
man and government that had long gone unquestioned became the target of renewed concern and thought.

These new developments generated a great deal of research and analysis, because scholars suddenly became more
interested in observing what was actually going on in a
specific society than in describing ideal societies. At about

---

[1] Lane Davis, "The Cost of the New Realism," in Henry S. Kariel, *The Frontiers
of Democratic Theory* (New York: Random House, 1970), p. 214.

the same time that Arthur F. Bentley was arguing the importance of groups and their use of power to gain their own ends,[2] sociologist Robert Michels proposed that elites within any group are the basic movers of politics and social organization. Michels derived an "Iron Law of Oligarchy" from his study of socialist movements in Europe.[3] Even in these socialistic organizations, with their avowed goals of mass participation in decision making, the tendency for an elite to emerge was evident. Michels' study suggested not only that elites were likely to develop in any organization, but that they were irresistible in gaining control over the other members of the group. He saw it as inevitable that elites would emerge and use organizations for their own purposes.

Another type of study that contributed to the general disillusionment with democratic theory was the investigation of voting behavior. Some of the earliest and most sophisticated behavioral methodologies were applied to the analysis of public opinion and voting behavior for the stated purpose of testing democratic theory, or, as one of these researchers put it, ". . . empirical research can help to clarify the standards and correct the empirical presuppositions of normative theory."[4] These studies sought to examine the "reality" of the assumptions and conceptions involved in the classical theory of democracy. The accumulated finding of many of the voting studies was that voters failed to satisfy the requirements of the classical theory of democracy. They tended to be uninformed, uninvolved, unprincipled, lacking in interest, or totally apathetic and irrational.[5]

Studies done by sociologists and political scientists during the first three decades of the twentieth century led to the accumulation of data suggesting that powerful political groups and elites were very significant, if not the determinant factor, in politics. Such findings left the classical theory of democracy in a precarious position. It was becoming more difficult, as time and study passed, to dismiss the evidence.

Lane Davis concisely states the "indictment" that was leveled against classical liberal theory by behavioralists:

The indictment brought against this version of political democracy is a sweeping one. The theory has been asserted to be logically unsatisfactory. It fails to provide clear definitions of such terms as "rule" and "people" which are obviously central to a conception of government by rule of the people. It posits a substantive common good as "the beacon light of policy" but fails to develop a consistent explanation of the nature of such a common good or how men may come to recognize it. It lacks a satisfactory treatment of the problems raised by the simultaneous affirmation of majority rule and minority rights. Finally, the theory defines democracy in ideal terms rather than by reference to existing political reality. . . .

The departures of classical theory from reality also have been pointed out in detail. Classical democracy, it is asserted, rests on untenable or radically incomplete conceptions of man and politics. Democratic man is neither as rational, as disinterested, as informed, nor as active in public affairs as he is assumed to be. The roles of organized groups, leadership, and emotion in political affairs are either ignored, underplayed, or simply condemned. The highly technical and complex process of policy making is oversimplified and misunderstood.[6]

In a major work of political theory published in 1942, Joseph Schumpeter concluded a devastating review of the problems in liberal democratic theory with the scathing statement that "the pillars of classical liberal doctrine inevitably crumble into dust."[7] So the attention of our discipline was once again focused on the need for a more thorough examination, understanding, and evaluation of the classical theory of democratic government.

To these diverse sources of skepticism, political scientists have responded that there is really nothing wrong with the practice of democracy in this country. That is, our society does operate as a democratic system. The problem is that we do not have adequate theory to explain how the government operates. The practice is all right, but the classical theory is in need of basic reformulation.

[2] Arthur F. Bentley, *The Process of Government* (Chicago: University of Chicago Press, 1908).

[3] Robert Michels, *Political Parties*, trans. Eden and Cedor Paul (New York: Dover, 1959; first published 1915).

[4] Bernard Berelson et al., *Voting* (Chicago: University of Chicago Press, 1954), p. 306.

[5] See particularly Berelson, op. cit., Campbell et al., *The Voter Decides* (Evanston: Row, Peterson, 1954); Campbell, et al., *The American Voter* (New York: Wiley & Sons, 1960).

[6] Lane Davis, "The Cost of New Realism," op. cit., p. 215.

[7] Joseph A. Schumpeter, *Capitalism, Socialism, and Democracy*, (3rd ed.; New York: Harper, 1942), p. 269.

CHANGING THE CLASSICAL THEORY TO FIT THE MODERN PRACTICE: THE SCIENTIFIC THEORY OF DEMOCRACY

Because much debate about the alleged inadequacies of the theory of liberal democracy has occurred in the last three or so decades, this review of theories that have attempted to reformulate liberal doctrines begins with the work of Joseph Schumpeter.

Schumpeter expressed both the emergent skepticism about liberal doctrine and the outlines of an alternative that assumes that the existing practice of our political institutions has been democratic, even if they don't fit the ideals of liberal theory. Schumpeter stated:

I think that most students of politics have by now come to accept the criticisms leveled at the classical doctrine of democracy. . . . I also think that most of them agree, or will agree before long, in accepting another theory which is much truer to life and at the same time salvages much of what sponsors of the democratic method really mean by this term. Like the classical theory, it may be put into the nutshell of a definition.

It will be remembered that our chief troubles about the classical theory centered in the proposition that "the people" hold a definite and rational opinion about every individual question and that they give effect to this opinion—in a democracy—by electing "representatives" who will see to it that the opinion is carried out. Thus the selection of the representatives is made secondary to the primary purpose of the democratic arrangement which is to vest the power of deciding political issues in the electorate. Suppose we reverse the roles of these two elements and make the deciding of issues by the electorate secondary to the election of the men who are to do the deciding. To put it differently, we now take the view that the role of the people is to produce a government or else an intermediate body which in turn will produce a national executive or government. And we define: the democratic method is that institutional arrangement for arriving at political decisions in which individuals acquire the power to decide by means of a competitive struggle for the people's vote.[8]

The emphasis added in this quotation underlines two purposes of Schumpeter's reformulation. It was to be more

[8] Joseph A. Schumpeter, *Capitalism, Socialism, and Democracy*, 3rd ed. (New York: Harper & Row, 1942), p. 269.

"realistic" (that is, scientific) and at the same time to "salvage much of what sponsors of the democratic method really mean." This brief statement of politics as a competitive struggle for power among contending individuals, groups, or elites became the predominant view within political science. Schumpeter and many political analysts who followed argued that if we understand democracy as a method of government in which people have the basic right to choose the government rather than the right to make decisions and policy, we can "salvage" the belief that our government is in practice democratic. They argue that, although people do choose a government on election day, they have little control over the major issues and the actual decisions made by their government. One way of dealing with these political realities is to redefine democracy. For these theorists, then, democracy is no longer a system in which people affect public policy by electing representatives to do their will; instead, it is a system in which people choose a particular group or political elite to be their government, which in turn makes decisions for them.

Schumpeter further refined this notion by suggesting that the choice of government takes place in an arena in which there is "a competitive struggle for the people's vote." This competitive struggle is among powerful groups and elites, which contend to gain control of the society. As they compete with one another for the votes of a majority, they attempt to formulate policy and programs that will attract the largest following in the electorate.

Actually, there is little here that is new to democratic thought. The notion that an elite should make policy as they understand the alternatives, free from the interference of the mass of people (at least until election day) was clearly and persuasively argued in Edmund Burke's *Reflections upon the French Revolution,* more than a hundred years before. Schumpeter takes this conservative notion of representative government and adds the thought that there is a mechanism built into this selection of a ruling elite that makes it more responsive to majority will. That mechanism is the competition among contending groups for support of the voters in the electorate. The elite in society is not a monolithic group but is composed of many different elites, which have varying resources. Elites do rule and make policy for the total society. But they are checked in this process by competition with other powerful groups, and they are, by their own attempts to stay in power, forced to appeal to the majority of voters.

Here is the basic theme that was to be sounded, with many variations, for the next 30 or so years in political science. This is the basis of what later came to be called a "pluralist" conception of democracy.

David Truman's *The Governmental Process,* a modern classic in political science, was published in 1959.[9] In this work a political scientist summarized the findings of earlier studies about the power of groups to determine public policy, through the kind of "competitive struggle" that Schumpeter described. Truman's book is a statement of a group theory of politics that was a forerunner of the pluralist conception of democracy. Truman's book suggests a full reformulation of a theory of democratic governance, while at the same time it betrays an uneasiness as to just how democratic "group politics" really is. Truman has contributed some rather significant variations to the theme sounded by Schumpeter. Among other things, he was trying to counter the fears that groups in competition with one another would seek to perpetuate their own interests rather than reflecting the interests of a majority of people.

Truman offered several reasons why these competing groups are responsive to the interests of the majority. First is his notion of "overlapping" membership; people hold membership in several different groups at the same time. Therefore, in order to maintain the loyalty of its own members who are also members of the other groups, the leadership of any particular group is required to compromise and bargain with other groups.

Truman also noted "potential" groups, which are possible new groups that might organize around the reaction to some decision made by an existing group. Potential groups act as a constraint in the decision-making process; Truman argues that in order to avoid dealing with the activation of potential groups, existing groups will take the interests of potential groups into consideration in the formulation of policy. In this way the interests of many people in the society are represented.

Finally, Truman pointed out still another major constraint on the policy-making activities of interest groups: the "democratic mold," or basic values that he believes are shared by the leadership of the interest groups. These values are supportive of the democratic process of government and are a part of the belief system of each member of the groups as well as the leaders. Powerful groups, then, have democratic values that constrain them from acting in totally self-interested ways.

These basic ideas, introduced by Truman in his analysis of the governmental process, became the dominant formulation of the "group theory" of politics—which still survives as one major explanation of democratic government.

Still other theorists rendered other formulations of democratic theory, which in their view were more consistent with the democratic practice of our political institutions. Anthony Downs' book, *An Economic Theory of Democracy,* appeared in 1957. Downs characterized democracy in now-familiar terms: "A *democratic* government is one chosen periodically by means of popular elections in which two or more parties compete for the vote of all adults."[10] Downs "avoids ethical premises" and describes democracy as a set of conditions that must prevail in the society. The conditions are:

1. A single party (or coalition of parties) is chosen by popular election to run the governing apparatus.
2. Such elections are held within periodic intervals, the duration of which cannot be altered by the party in power acting alone.
3. All adults who are permanent residents of the society, are sane, and abide by the laws of the land are eligible to vote in each such election.
4. Each voter may cast one and only one vote in each election.
5. Any party (or coalition) receiving the support of a majority of those voting is entitled to take over the powers of government until the next election.
6. The losing parties in an election never try by force or any illegal means to prevent the winning party (or parties) from taking office.
7. The party in power never attempts to restrict the political activities of any citizens or other parties as long as they make no attempt to overthrow the government by force.
8. There are two or more parties competing for control

---

[9] David Truman, *The Governmental Process* (New York: Knopf, 1959), pp. 501–516.

[10] Anthony Downs, *An Economic Theory of Democracy* (New York: Harper and Row, 1957), p. 34.

of the governing apparatus.[11]

Clearly, Downs attempted to avoid valuing democratic theory and tried to accurately describe what is really going on in "democratic" societies. His assumption was that our society has a democratic system.

In 1960 another classic attempt to reformulate the theory of democratic practice was published, in *The Semi-Sovereign People*, by E. E. Schattschneider. The basic thesis of this work is that government is the major institution through which a society manages and resolves conflict among the competing groups and organizations that seek their own interests. Schattschneider argued that all politics involves expanding and contracting the "scope of conflict" in society, and that government attempts to deal with conflict by ensuring that it can take place in such a way that competing organizations are able to define alternatives and to mobilize support for those alternatives in becoming the ruling power in the society.

Schattschneider argued that, "At the nub of politics are, first, the way in which the public participates in the spread of the conflict and, second, the processes by which the unstable relation of the public to the conflict is controlled."[12] In a later chapter of his book he sounded the familiar theme in his definition: "Democracy is a competitive political system in which competing leaders and organizations define the alternatives of public policy in such a way that the public can participate in the decision-making process."[13] He continued:

The initiative in this political system is to be found largely in the government or in the opposition. The people profit by this system, but they cannot, by themselves, do the work of the system. We have already had a great deal of experience with this kind of system. Is it not about time that we begin to recognize its democratic implications?

. . . The advantage of this definition over the traditional definition is that it is operational, it describes something that actually happens. It describes something feasible. It does not make impossible demands on the public. Moreover, it describes a going

democratic concern whose achievements are tremendous.[14]

Schattschneider contributed an additional notion to the familiar theme of competing groups in the political arena. Groups are always attempting to mobilize mass support by expanding the scope of conflict in the society, through defining public policy alternatives in such a way as to gain popular support in their struggle with other groups. The result of this expanding conflict is that people are significant in the formation of alternative programs: They either are attracted to supporting such policy or they are not. They do not directly affect the policy, but in this "semi-sovereign" way they do have impact on policy becoming the law of the land.

Both Downs and Schattschneider departed significantly from tradition, in developing the pluralist theory of democracy that had been forecast by Schumpeter. Downs developed his model in an attempt to demonstrate the importance of the rational individual voter as an agent who could choose among competing political parties for the governance of the nation. His emphasis of the linkage between the mass and elite is essentially one of popular elections; in such elections, individuals influence public policy as they choose which programs they will support and which they will not. For Schattschneider, the relationship between mass and elite was established in the attempt of leaders and organizations to develop alternatives and to mobilize popular support for these alternative policies. His theory of democracy fulfills two purposes for its author. First, "it describes something that actually happens," and "it describes a going democratic concern whose achievements are tremendous." This says explicitly that the theory recognizes the aspiration to be scientific and in addition retains the value for American democracy.

The development of a pluralist theory of democracy was already in the final stages of construction as the works of Downs and Schattschneider were being read and criticized. Robert Dahl and his students at Yale University were then carrying out a community study that was published in 1961 as *Who Governs?*[15] This study clearly articulates the pluralist theory of democratic practice.

Truman's work, *The Governmental Process*, had largely

[11] Ibid., pp. 23-24.

[12] E. E. Schattschneider, *The Semi-Sovereign People* (New York: Holt, Rinehart & Winston, 1960), p. 3.

[13] Ibid., p. 141.

[14] Ibid., p. 141. (Emphasis added.)

[15] Robert A. Dahl, *Who Governs?* (New Haven: Yale University Press, 1961).

ignored the question of powerful elites in the attempt to analyze politics in terms of competing groups. Truman argued that elites could not continue to lead a group unless they were in large part representative of its membership. Dahl, like other political scientists, was dissatisfied with the notion of the group as the basic unit of analysis and he chose to emphasize the nature of competing elites rather than competing groups. His analysis of *Who Governs?* expanded on the now well-developed notion of competition among groups, leaders, and organizations in the struggle for power, by emphasizing the power of elites in this competition.

Instead of assuming that elites were those who have wealth and status, Dahl made a careful distinction between real and potential power in the struggle to affect decisions about public policy. Dahl and his students argued that elites vary in the amount of power that they can bring to bear on any particular issue. The pluralist theory states that the competition among contending elites defines alternatives, which in part reflect the general interests of those with values similar to those of contending elites. Dahl characterizes politics as a system of "dispersed inequalities in political resources," and argues that

This system of dispersed inequalities is, I believe, marked by the following six characteristics:

1. Many different kinds of resources for influencing officials are available to different citizens.
2. With few exceptions, these resources are unequally distributed.
3. Individuals best off in their access to one kind of resource are often badly off with respect to many other resources.
4. No one influence resource dominates all the others in all or even in most key decisions.
5. With some exceptions, an influence resource is effective in some issue-areas or in some specific decisions but not in all.
6. Virtually no one, and certainly no group of more than a few individuals, is entirely lacking in some influence resources.[16]

Another key concept in Dahl's analysis is the notion of "slack in the system," which is an attempt to refine Truman's notion of a potential group. The slack in the

[16] Ibid., p. 227.

system refers to those in the political system who are not involved in issues or policy making, but who could enter the elite arena, if their interests were severely threatened by the actions of existing elites. Further, Dahl refines Truman's notion of the democratic mold in his "democratic creed," which is the value structure shared by those within and without the elite structure of the decision-making process. Those values that are sympathetic to democratic practices aid in molding the actions of elites, making them more consistent with the behavior expected in a democratic society. Finally, the firm outline of a new scientific theory of democratic practice had emerged.

This scientific theory of democracy has the following major tenets. Public decisions are made by elites in a bargaining and compromising process, rather than by the direct participation of the mass of people. Power in society is diffused. There are many different elites with differing interests and resources, who enter the political arena when issues affect their particular interests. Elites are operative both within and without governmental institutions; elites outside the government have power with which to affect governmental decisions. These governing and private elites are accountable, in several ways: Elections create new political elites, the interests of many people in society are reflected in the interests of competing elites, existing elites are wary of activating the slack in the system and compromise on policies in ways that are consistent with the needs of others, and elites basically hold democratic values about their actions in the public arena. According to this model of democracy, the mass of people do not rule, but they do have considerable access to the elite structure of society that does make decisions. This access and the elite values about democratic practice make the system responsive to the public interests.

A DEBATE: THE PLURALISTS VS. THE POWER ELITISTS

As these final guidelines of the scientific theory of democracy were gaining widespread attention within the discipline, a dissenting view to this pluralist conception was also heard. It is of more than passing interest that the dissent was voiced primarily by sociologists rather than political scientists. These dissenters were to become known as the "power elite" theorists. The review of this alternative begins with a work of sociologist Floyd Hunter, *The Community Power Structure*, published in 1953. Hunter proposed a different concept of the power structure in his analysis of a Southern American community.[17] His analysis led him to conclude that, rather than a multiplicity of groups competing to define public policy, there was a monolithic and omnipotent elite at the top of the socio-economic hierarchy, which dominated the decisions made in the community. The power elite was a small group of influential and economically powerful individuals who ran the community he studied.

Following closely on this analysis by Hunter was the work of C. Wright Mills, which stated the power elite position most clearly. Mills argued that the entire country, not just a particular community, is ruled by a power elite made up of industrial, military, and political cliques. He proposed that a small cadre of corporate, military, and political leaders manipulate the public to accept as its own the selfish interests of its rulers. No one can more clearly state Mills' basic argument than he himself:

The power to make decisions of national and international consequence is now so clearly seated in political, military, and economic institutions that other areas of society seem off to the side and, on occasion, readily subordinated to these . . . Behind this fact there is all the push and drive of a fabulous technology; for these three institutional orders have incorporated this technology and now guide it, even as it shapes and paces their development. . . .

There is no longer, on the one hand, an economy, and, on the other, a political order, containing a military establishment unimportant to politics and to money-making. There is a political economy numerously linked with military order and decision. This triangle of power is now a structural fact, and it is the key to any understanding of the higher circles in America today. For as each of these domains has coincided with the others, as decisions in each have become broader, the leading men of each—the high military, the corporation executives, the political directorate—have tended to come together to form the power elite of America.[18]

Further on in this essay, Mills directly confronted the

arguments put forth by the pluralists concerning the existence of multiple and competitive elites compromising with one another to determine public policy. He did not completely reject this type of analysis, but he clearly argued that it only applies to what he terms "middle levels" of power. And he concluded that this middle level of power is not to be confused with the top levels, which truly rule the society or with the bottom levels, which are truly excluded from ruling their own lives.

There are of course other interpretations of the American system of power. The most usual is that it is a moving balance of many competing interests. . . .

I believe that the balance and the compromise in American society—the "countervailing powers" and the "veto groups," of parties and associations, of strata and unions—must now be seen as having mainly to do with the middle levels of power. It is these middle levels that the political journalists and the scholars of politics are most likely to understand and to write about—if only because, being mainly middle class themselves, they are closer to them. Moreover these levels provide the noisy content of most "political" news and gossip; the images of these levels are more or less in accord with the folklore of how democracy works; and, if the master-image of balance is accepted, many intellectuals, especially in their current patrioteering, are readily able to satisfy such political optimism as they wish to feel. Accordingly, liberal interpretations of what is happening in the United States are now virtually the only interpretations that are widely distributed.

But to believe that the power system reflects a balancing society is, I think, to confuse the present era with earlier times, and to confuse its top and bottom with its middle levels.[19]

Mills presents an entirely different concept of the practice of American democracy than that offered by the pluralists. In his analysis, power is assumed to be highly structured in society and to be directly related to the economic resources of people. So those with wealth tend to maintain their wealth, status, and power regardless of the decisions being made in the public arena. The power elites tend to be in agreement about the basic policies they must follow to perpetuate their own interests. And there is a clear separation of the elites, who have most of what there is to get, and those who do not have these valuables. The dominant elites

[17] Floyd Hunter, *Community Power Structure* (Chapel Hill: University of North Carolina Press, 1953).

[18] C. Wright Mills, "The Structure of Power in American Society," in *American Society, Inc.*, ed. Maurice Zeitlin (Chicago: Markham, 1970), p. 343.

[19] Ibid., pp. 346–47.

rule without fear of intervention or influence by the masses of people. There may be some disagreement among these elites, but for the most part their interests are consistent and dominant.

Mills' position is a clear formulation of the alternative conception that the *theory* of democracy contained in liberal doctrine has not failed, but that political institutions have failed to live up to the ideals of liberal democracy in practice. For Mills and those who follow this argument, it is not necessary to reformulate the basic doctrine of liberal democracy. The people should have a voice in affecting their own destiny. The problem is to change, reform, and render the practice of our political institutions more consistent with those original goals of the classical theory.

CONTRASTING THE INVISIBLE IDEOLOGY AND CLASSICAL DEMOCRATIC THEORY

Many theorists have accepted the behavioral paradigm described in Chapter 5, but the influence of the paradigm on the discipline does not seem to be explained by simply saying that it has many adherents. To account for its influence, it is necessary to evaluate its contribution to political analysis.

Notwithstanding the debate between the power elitists and the pluralists who argue for competitive multiple elites, the new competitive elite theory of democracy has evolved to a point where it has received virtually total acceptance among the ranks of political scientists. This was possible because the new scientific theory was consistent with widely shared, if invisible, values. With few exceptions, the implications and impacts of this invisible ideology have not been thoroughly compared with the ideals of liberal democracy.[20] The following is an attempt to contrast the basic values of the invisible ideology with the values of the classical theory of democracy. Basically, the invisible ideology departs significantly from traditional democratic doctrine in four ways:

1. *The value for organizational and system performance rather than individual preferences and potentiality:* The invisible ideology values the capability of institutions, organizations, and systems, while the classical doctrine values the worth of individuals and their potential for growth and development as human beings. Central to the development of a theory of democratic political systems that involve competition among elites is the preference for systems and organizations of multiple elites, which do the work of a democratic government that individuals are thought not to be able to do.

The behavioralists in their research have examined the ideals of classical democratic theory against the realities of behavior in political processes, and have found these ideals to be too much for individuals to live up to. Simply stated, the masses involved in politics were not performing as the ideals of classical doctrine prescribed that they should.

It might be argued that the classical theory was an attempt to provide people with goals and guidelines for achieving the good society and the good life. It was never intended to be an accurate description of what people were doing in politics but was meant to be a set of ideals.

In any case, the analysis of actual behavior led many behavioralists to conclude that the masses simply could not live up to these demanding expectations. These theorists appear to have held a static conception of human nature rather than a developmental perspective; they observed how people behaved, and found this behavior wanting in view of the goals of classical theory. Rather than concluding from this that people have the potential for developing and becoming more like the kind of citizen prescribed in classical theory, behavioralists assumed that their findings described a condition of man that was static and unchanging. This assumption gave them little hope of improving the lot of individuals. To them it made more sense to focus on the capabilities of the total system to operate as a democratic process rather than to focus on how individuals might be educated and liberated to become the informed and active citizens required in a truly democratic society.

Behavioralists evidently saw no need to be concerned about the development of individuals, because the total system seemed to be operating democratically without such development. Their theory of multiple competing elites permitted political analysts to value the system of democracy as a process of governance, without evaluating its ability as a political mechanism to encourage people to become more involved and better-informed citizens.

[20] Many of these exceptions are contained in an anthology edited by Henry S. Kariel, *The Frontiers of Democratic Theory* (New York: Random House, 1970), particularly the articles by Hield, Gouldner, Bottomore, Kariel, Bay, Duncan and Lukes, Davis, and Walker.

Bernard Berelson, one of the first of the behavioral researchers to study voting behavior, states this element in the following way:

The system of democracy does meet certain requirements of a going political organization. The individuals may not meet all standards, but the whole nevertheless survives and grows. This suggests that where the classical theory is defective is in its concentration on the individual citizen.[21]

E. E. Schattschneider points out the same element in the invisible ideology when he says, "The people profit by this system, but they cannot by themselves do the work of the system."[22] Later on, he states, "It [the democratic system] does not make impossible demands upon the public." Or, as Robert Dahl writes,

Nevertheless, what we call democracy—that is, a system of decision-making in which the leaders are more or less responsive to the preferences of non-leaders—does seem to operate with a relatively low level of citizen participation. Hence, it is inaccurate to say that one of the necessary conditions of democracy is extensive citizen participation.[23]

Given this central notion that systems, organizations, and institutions can operate democratically even though individuals cannot, it becomes clearer how the other elements of the invisible ideology have developed.

2. *The value for stabilizing and maintaining the functioning of the system rather than enjoining ideological conflicts and debates about critical issues that would inform, involve and educate citizens:* The second element in the invisible ideology is that stabilizing the functioning of the system is more important than attempting to bring about a genuine consensus among people concerning their interests and their understanding of critical issues in the society. Ideology, from this perspective, is not only insignificant; it is also an extra burden on the operation of the system. The process of the democratic system produces democratic policy, and any conflicts and debates involving the public at large interfere in smooth functioning and the stability of the system. Ideological debate, conflict, dissent, and public deliberation of issues are "dysfunctional" to the working of the democratic political system.

Although all of these factors are necessary in the classical view of democracy, in which people are involved and enlightened by the public deliberation of issues, they are also obvious sources of instability within the system. The invisible ideology prefers stability to conflict, at any cost. From the perspective of the invisible ideology, conflict is unnecessary to the purpose of creating public policy that approximates the best interests of all people. The substance of issues and the effects of decisions on the lives of people in society is secondary to maintaining a smoothly functioning process.

If the system is functioning, then it must be producing what is best for people, so there need be little concern for the content of the issues or their impact on the masses. Some adherents to this invisible ideology suggest that apathy is a sign of popular satisfaction with the system, rather than a sign that the system is failing to educate and involve its citizens in their rightful role as valuing and valuable individuals in a democratic society.

3. *The value for fitting people into systems rather than changing systems to meet needs of people:* Given this element in the invisible ideology, one of the central tasks of research has become to understand how people come to accept the norms and shared values that support the system of democracy, rather than to understand how they develop their own individual potentialities and preferences. The impact of the invisible ideology was to lead researchers to examine how to fit people into the democratic political system instead of attempting to understand how that system might be reconstructed to liberate and generate the individual development of human beings. The reasoning was that if the system is operating democratically in spite of the individuals in it, then it is more important to find out how to get the individual to accept the norms of the system than it is to understand the individuals themselves.

In terms of actual research, this impact has been evidenced in studies that sought to understand how people are socialized (that is, how they learn) to hold the values

---

[21] Bernard Berelson, Quoted in Graeme Duncan and Steven Lukes, "Democracy Restated," in Kariel, op. cit., p. 203.

[22] E. E. Schattschneider, *The Semi-Sovereign People* (New York: Holt, Rinehart & Winston, 1960), p. 141.

[23] Robert A. Dahl, Quoted in Graeme Duncan and Steven Lukes, in Kariel, op. cit., p. 196. (Emphasis added.)

that are shared by most others in the political system. The family, schools, work place, peer groups, and reference groups were studied, to see how these groups and institutions taught people to value the norms of the system. People were also studied, to see what conditions led them to deviate from the norms of the democratic system. The focus has been on the study of authoritarian personalities and alienation, as they affected the ability of people to accept and accommodate to the social system. With this emphasis on fitting people into systems rather than fitting systems to people, the next element of the invisible ideology makes a great deal of sense.

4. *The value for change within the system rather than change of the system:* This final component of the invisible ideology is the one most commonly referred to in political rhetoric and speeches. The value is for change within the existing procedures of the democratic system rather than reconstruction of the total system. Given the reasoning reviewed in the above analysis, it makes a great deal of sense to urge the preservation of the democratic system. For change to take place, it must be change that is incremental, that is gradually evolved through the processes and procedures of the democratic system. Dramatic or revolutionary change is likely to throw the system out of equilibrium and to be dysfunctional to its capability to produce democratic public policy.

Change is not viewed in terms of how people can reconstruct their government and its institutions to more nearly meet their self-defined goals and needs. It is viewed as how people work within the system to bring about outcomes that are compatible with the functioning of the system.

Classical democratic theory was very specific in urging that when government was no longer meeting the needs of the people in the society, it was their duty and right to revolt against that government. The contract that bound them and their government was not to be violated by either party to the agreement. Government could coerce to preserve its powers under the social contract, and people could rebel to preserve their rights under the contract. Change had a revolutionary nature, in the classical doctrine of democracy. In the invisible ideology, change takes on a much different light: It is acceptable only to the extent that it does no harm to the functioning of the democratic system.

The commonly heard assertion that people should work within the system is a very central part of the invisible ideology of democratic political systems. To basically change the structure of the democratic system is to take a risk that the adherent of this view is unwilling to take. He feels that it is better to stay with a smoothly functioning system, which produces a "close approximation" to democratic public policy, than to take the risks involved in reconstructing the system that more nearly meets the criteria of the liberal theory of democracy. From this perspective, it is hard to improve on what we have; and, because people are assumed to be capable of no more than they presently demonstrate, it would be foolhardy to put the system in jeopardy on the chance of improving the lot of the individuals in it.

IMPACTS OF THE INVISIBLE IDEOLOGY

There is virtual consensus among political scientists on the basic components of the invisible ideology. In recent years, two articles that have been widely cited by political scientists serve to illustrate this impact. The first selection presented here is from Charles E. Lindblom's "The Science of Muddling Through." The author compares two different ways of making decisions in the administration of public policy. The article has become a classic in its own time, largely because it argues for a decision-making process in public administration that in many ways reflects the values of the invisible ideology, and it is consistent with the scientific theory of democracy.

Lindblom does not explicitly discuss classical democratic theory or the theory of competitive political elites as such. He compares the advantages of what he calls "root theory" and "branch theories" in the analysis and making of public decisions. It can be readily seen that root theories are those that urge the making of public policy that is consistent with the basic values of the classical democratic theory. Public policy should be substantively judged against the prescriptions for "good" policy contained in the classical theory; to the extent that the policy meets such criterion of the root theory, it is considered good policy. Presumably, theorists who urge the use of root theory believe that it should be used to implement both the development and implementation of public policy.

Lindblom argues that such a procedure of evaluation

of public policy is neither possible nor practical. To evaluate public policy in terms of such criteria as are contained in classical democratic theory is beyond the capability of actual administration, according to Lindblom. He prefers a "branch theory" approach.

Branch theory is not so much a theory as a "method of successive comparisons," which Lindblom describes in the following terms, "Policy-making is a process of successive approximations to some desired objective in which what is desired itself continues to change under reconsideration."[24] Later he argues:

A wise policy-maker consequently expects that his policies will achieve only part of what he hopes and at the same time will produce unanticipated consequences he would have preferred to avoid. If he proceeds through a succession of incremental changes, he avoids serious lasting mistakes in several ways.[25]

Underlying Lindblom's analysis of decision making in public administration is a preference for avoiding the evaluation of policy in terms of its relationship to the ideals of a root theory such as democratic doctrine. His preference is for the operation of the system as a reality in decision making. This reality is an incremental policy process, in which the pattern of policy making fits in with the multiple pressure activities described in a competitive elite theory of democracy. Thus, policy decisions are to be evaluated by the extent to which they are incremental changes in existing policy, reflecting the interests of competing elites that seek to redefine the existing policy.

The "muddling through" that Lindblom describes is, in reality, the scientific theory of democratic political systems. It involves multiple and competing elites attempting to reconstruct public policy consistent with their interests. Lindblom argues that this is the reality of public policy making, and any attempt to evaluate public policy in other ways is simply not going to work. In this way the status quo becomes the preference. The scientific theory becomes the ideology.

THE SCIENCE OF "MUDDLING THROUGH"

● CHARLES F. LINDBLOM

Suppose an administrator is given responsibility for formulating policy with respect to inflation. He might start by trying to list all related values in order of importance, e.g., full employment, reasonable business profit, protection of small savings, prevention of a stock market crash. Then all possible policy outcomes could be rated as more or less efficient in attaining a maximum of these values. This would of course require a prodigious inquiry into values held by members of society and an equally prodigious set of calculations on how much of each value is equal to how much of each other value. He could then proceed to outline all possible policy alternatives. In a third step, he would undertake systematic comparison of his multitude of alternatives to determine which attains the greatest amount of values.

In comparing policies, he would take advantage of any theory available that generalized about classes of policies. In considering inflation, for example, he would compare all policies in the light of the theory of prices. Since no alternatives are beyond his investigation, he would consider strict central control and the abolition of all prices and markets on the one hand and elimination of all public controls with reliance completely on the free market on the other, both in the light of whatever theoretical generalizations he could find on such hypothetical economies.

Finally, he would try to make the choice that would in fact maximize his values.

An alternative line of attack would be to set as his principal objective, either explicitly or without conscious thought, the relatively simple goal of keeping prices level. This objective might be compromised or complicated by only a few other goals, such as full employment. He would in fact disregard most other social values as beyond his present interest, and he would for the moment not even attempt to rank the few values

Adapted from Charles E. Lindblom, "The Science of "Muddling Through", *The Public Administration Review*, (1959) p. 19, 79–88. Reprinted by permission. (edited and abridged.)

[24] See this chapter, p. 207.
[25] Ibid, p. 207.

that he regarded as immediately relevant. Were he pressed, he would quickly admit that he was ignoring many related values and many possible important consequences of his policies.

As a second step, he would outline those relatively few policy alternatives that occurred to him. He would then compare them. In comparing his limited number of alternatives, most of them familiar from past controversies, he would not ordinarily find a body of theory precise enough to carry him through a comparison of their respective consequences. Instead he would rely heavily on the record of past experience with small policy steps to predict the consequences of similar steps extended into the future.

Moreover, he would find that the policy alternatives combined objectives or values in different ways. For example, one policy might offer price level stability at the cost of some risk of unemployment; another might offer less price stability but also less risk of unemployment. Hence, the next step in his approach—the final selection—would combine into one the choice among values and the choice among instruments for reaching values. It would not, as in the first method of policy-making, approximate a more mechanical process of choosing the means that best satisfied goals that were previously clarified and ranked. Because practitioners of the second approach expect to achieve their goals only partially, they would expect to repeat endlessly the sequence just described, as conditions and aspirations changed and as accuracy of prediction improved.

BY ROOT OR BY BRANCH

For complex problems, the first of these two approaches is of course impossible. Although such an approach can be described, it cannot be practiced except for relatively simple problems and even then only in a somewhat modified form. It assumes intellectual capacities and sources of information that men simply do not possess, and it is even more absurd as an approach to policy when the time and money that can be allocated to a policy problem is limited, as is always the case. Of particular importance to public administrators is the fact that public agencies are in effect usually instructed not to practice the first method. That is to say, their prescribed functions and constraints—the politically or legally possible—restrict their attention to relatively few values and relatively few alternative policies among the countless alternatives that might be imagined. It is the second method that is practiced. . . .

. . . I propose in this paper to clarify and formalize the second method, much neglected in the literature. This might be described as the method of *successive limited comparisons*. I will contrast it with the first approach, which might be called the rational-comprehensive method.[1] More impressionistically and briefly—and therefore generally used in this article—they could be characterized as the branch method and root method, the former continually building out from the current situation, step-by-step and by small degrees; the latter starting from fundamentals anew each time, building on the past only as experience is embodied in a theory, and always prepared to start completely from the ground up.

Let us put the characteristics of the two methods side by side in simplest terms. [See table on page 203.]

* * *

INTERTWINING EVALUATION AND EMPIRICAL ANALYSIS (1B)

The quickest way to understand how values are handled in the method of successive limited comparisons is to see how the root method often breaks down in *its* handling of values or objectives. The idea that values should be clarified, and in advance of the examination of alternative policies, is appealing. But what happens when we attempt it for complex social problems? The first difficulty is that on many critical values or objectives, citizens disagree, congressmen disagree, and public administrators disagree. Even where a fairly specific objective is prescribed for the administrator, there remains considerable room for disagreement on subobjectives. . . .

Administrators cannot escape these conflicts by ascertaining the majority's preference, for preferences have not been registered on most issues; indeed, there often *are* no preferences in the absence of public discussion sufficient to bring an issue to the attention of the electorate. Furthermore, there is a question of whether intensity of feeling should be considered as well as the number of persons preferring each alternative. By the impossibility of doing otherwise, administrators often are reduced to deciding policy without clarifying objectives first.

Even when an administrator resolves to follow his own values as a criterion for decisions, he often will not know how to rank them when they conflict with one another, as they usually do. . . .

How does one state even to himself the relative importance of these partially conflicting values? A simple ranking of them is not enough; one needs ideally to know how much of one value is worth sacrificing for some of another value. The answer is that typically the administrator chooses—and must choose—directly among policies in which these values are combined in different ways. He cannot first clarify his values and then choose among policies.

A more subtle third point underlies both the first two. Social objectives do not always have the same relative values. One objective may be highly prized in one circumstance, another in another circumstance. . . .

The value problem is . . . always a problem of adjustments at a margin. But there is no practicable way to state marginal objectives or values except in terms of particular policies. That one value is preferred to another in one decision situation does not mean that it will be preferred in another decision situation in which it can be had only at great sacrifice of another value. Attempts to rank or order values in general and abstract terms so that they do not shift from decision to decision end up by ignoring the relevant marginal preferences. The significance of this third point thus goes very far. Even if all administrators had at hand an agreed set of values, objectives, and constraints, and an agreed ranking of these values, objectives, and constraints, their marginal values in actual choice situations would be impossible to formulate.

Unable consequently to formulate the relevant values first and then choose among policies to achieve them, administrators must choose directly among alternative policies that offer different marginal combinations of values. Somewhat paradoxically, the only practicable way to disclose one's relevant marginal values even to oneself is to describe the policy one chooses to achieve them. Except roughly and vaguely, I know of no way to describe—or even to understand—what my relative evaluations are for, say, freedom and security, speed and

RATIONAL-COMPREHENSIVE (ROOT)	SUCCESSIVE LIMITED COMPARISONS (BRANCH)
1a. Clarification of values or objectives distinct from and usually prerequisite to empirical analysis of alternative policies.	1b. Selection of value goals and empirical analysis of the needed action are not distinct from one another but are closely intertwined.
2a. Policy-formulation is therefore approached through means-end analysis: First the ends are isolated, then the means to achieve them are sought.	2b. Since means and ends are not distinct, means-end analysis is often inappropriate or limited.
3a. The test of a "good" policy is that it can be shown to be the most appropriate means to desired ends.	3b. The test of a "good" policy is typically that various analysts find themselves directly agreeing on a policy (without their agreeing that it is the most appropriate means to an agreed objective).
4a. Analysis is comprehensive; every important relevant factor is taken into account.	4b. Analysis is drastically limited: i) Important possible outcomes are neglected. ii) Important alternative potential policies are neglected. iii) Important affected values are neglected.
5a. Theory is often heavily relied upon.	5b. A succession of comparisons greatly reduces or eliminates reliance on theory.

accuracy in governmental decisions, or low taxes and better schools than to describe my preferences among specific policy choices that might be made between the alternatives in each of the pairs.

In summary, two aspects of the process by which values are actually handled can be distinguished. The first is clear: evaluation and empirical analysis are intertwined; that is, one chooses among values and among policies at one and the same time. Put a little more elaborately, one simultaneously chooses a policy to attain certain objectives and chooses the objectives themselves. The second aspect is related but distinct: the administrator focuses his attention on marginal or incremental values. Whether he is aware of it or not, he does not find general formulations of objectives very helpful and in fact makes specific marginal or incremental comparisons. . . .

As to whether the attempt to clarify objectives in advance of policy selection is more or less rational than the close intertwining of marginal evaluation and empirical analysis, the principal difference established is that for complex problems the first is impossible and irrelevant, and the second is both possible and relevant. The second is possible because the administrator need not try to analyze any values except the values by which alternative policies differ and need not be concerned with them except as they differ marginally. His need for information on values or objectives is drastically reduced as compared with the root method; and his capacity for grasping, comprehending, and relating values to one another is not strained beyond the breaking point.

RELATIONS BETWEEN MEANS AND ENDS (2B)

Decision-making is ordinarily formalized as a means-end relationship: means are conceived to be evaluated and chosen in the light of ends finally selected independently of and prior to the choice of means. This is the means-ends relationship of the root method. But it follows from all that has just been said that such a means-ends relationship is possible only to the extent that values are agreed upon, are reconcilable, and are stable at the margin. Typically, therefore, such a means-

end relationship is absent from the branch method, where means and ends are simultaneously chosen.

Yet any departure from the means-ends relationship of the root method will strike some readers as inconceivable. For it will appear to them that only in such a relationship is it possible to determine whether one policy choice is better or worse than another. How can an administrator know whether he has made a wise or foolish decision if he is without prior values or objectives by which to judge his decisions? The answer to this question calls up the third distinctive difference between root and branch methods: how to decide the best policy.

THE TEST OF "GOOD" POLICY (3B)

In the root method, a decision is "correct," "good," or "rational" if it can be shown to attain some specified objective, where the objective can be specified without simply describing the decision itself. Where objectives are defined only through the marginal or incremental approach to values described above, it is still sometimes possible to test whether a policy does in fact attain the desired objectives; but a precise statement of the objectives takes the form of a description of the policy chosen or some alternative to it. To show that a policy is mistaken one cannot offer an abstract argument that important objectives are not achieved; one must instead argue that another policy is more to be preferred.

So far, the departure from customary ways of looking at problem-solving is not troublesome, for many administrators will be quick to agree that the most effective discussion of the correctness of policy does take the form of comparison with other policies that might have been chosen. But what of the situation in which administrators cannot agree on values or objectives, either abstractly or in marginal terms? What then is the test of "good" policy? For the root method, there is no test. Agreement on objectives failing, there is no standard of "correctness." For the method of successive limited comparisons, the test is agreement on policy itself, which remains possible even when agreement on values is not.

It has been suggested that continuing agreement

in Congress on the desirability of extending old age insurance stems from liberal desires to strengthen the welfare programs of the federal government and from conservative desires to reduce union demands for private pension plans. If so, this is an excellent demonstration of the ease with which individuals of different ideologies often can agree on concrete policy. Labor mediators report a similar phenomenon: the contestants cannot agree on criteria for settling their disputes but can agree on specific proposals. Similarly, when one administrator's objective turns out to be another's means, they often can agree on policy.

Agreement on policy thus becomes the only practicable test of the policy's correctness. And for one administrator to seek to win the other over to agreement on ends as well would accomplish nothing and create quite unnecessary controversy.

If agreement directly on policy as a test for "best" policy seems a poor substitute for testing the policy against its objectives, it ought to be remembered that objectives themselves have no ultimate validity other than that they are agreed upon. Hence agreement is the test of "best" policy in both methods. But where the root method requires agreement on what elements in the decision constitute objectives and on which of these objectives should be sought, the branch method falls back on agreement wherever it can be found.

In an important sense, therefore, it is not irrational for an administrator to defend a policy as good without being able to specify what it is good for.

NONCOMPREHENSIVE ANALYSIS (4B)

Ideally, rational-comprehensive analysis leaves out nothing important. But it is impossible to take everything important into consideration unless "important" is so narrowly defined that analysis is in fact quite limited. Limits on human intellectual capacities and on available information set definite limits to man's capacity to be comprehensive. In actual fact, therefore, no one can practice the rational-comprehensive method for really complex problems, and every administrator faced with a sufficiently complex problem must find ways drastically to simplify.

* * *

In the method of successive limited comparisons, simplification is systematically achieved in two principal ways. First, it is achieved through limitation of policy comparisons to those policies that differ in relatively small degree from policies presently in effect. Such a limitation immediately reduces the number of alternatives to be investigated and also drastically simplifies the character of the investigation of each. For it is not necessary to undertake fundamental inquiry into an alternative and its consequences; it is necessary only to study those respects in which the proposed alternative and its consequences differ from the status quo. The empirical comparison of marginal differences among alternative policies that differ only marginally is, of course, a counterpart to the incremental or marginal comparison of values discussed above.

Relevance As Well As Realism

It is a matter of common observation that in Western democracies public administrators and policy analysts in general do largely limit their analyses to incremental or marginal differences in policies that are chosen to differ only incrementally. They do not do so, however, solely because they desperately need some way to simplify their problems; they also do so in order to be relevant. Democracies change their policies almost entirely through incremental adjustments. Policy does not move in leaps and bounds.

The incremental character of political change in the United States has often been remarked. The two major political parties agree on fundamentals; they offer alternative policies to the voters only on relatively small points of difference. Both parties favor full employment, but they define it somewhat differently; both favor the development of water power resources, but in slightly different ways; and both favor unemployment compensation, but not the same level of benefits. Similarly, shifts of policy within a party take place largely through a series of relatively small changes, as can be seen in their only gradual acceptance of the idea of governmental responsibility for support of the unemployed, a change

in party positions beginning in the early 30's and cul-
minating in a sense in the Employment Act of 1946.

Party behavior is in turn rooted in public attitudes,
and political theorists cannot conceive of democracy's
surviving in the United States in the absence of fundamental agreement on potentially disruptive issues,
with consequent limitation of policy debates to relatively
small differences in policy.

Since the policies ignored by the administrator are
politically impossible and so irrelevant, the simplification of analysis achieved by concentrating on policies
that differ only incrementally is not a capricious kind
of simplification. In addition, it can be argued that,
given the limits on knowledge within which policy-makers are confined, simplifying by limiting the focus
to small variations from present policy makes the most
of available knowledge. Because policies being considered are like present and past policies, the administrator
can obtain information and claim some insight. Non-
incremental policy proposals are therefore typically not
only politically irrelevant but also unpredictable in their
consequences.

The second method of simplification of analysis is
the practice of ignoring important possible consequences
of possible policies, as well as the values attached to
the neglected consequences. If this appears to disclose
a shocking shortcoming of successive limited comparisons, it can be replied that, even if the exclusions are
random, policies may nevertheless be more intelligently
formulated than through futile attempts to achieve a
comprehensiveness beyond human capacity. Actually,
however, the exclusions, seeming arbitrary or random
from one point of view, need be neither.

Achieving a Degree of Comprehensiveness

Suppose that each value neglected by one policy-making agency were a major concern of at least one
other agency. In that case, a helpful division of labor
would be achieved, and no agency need find its task
beyond its capacities. The shortcomings of such a system
would be that one agency might destroy a value either
before another agency could be activated to safeguard
it or in spite of another agency's efforts. But the possibility that important values may be lost is present in any
form of organization, even where agencies attempt to
comprehend in planning more than is humanly possible.

The virtue of such a hypothetical division of labor
is that every important interest or value has its watchdog. And these watchdogs can protect the interests in
their jurisdiction in two quite different ways: first, by
redressing damages done by other agencies; and, second,
by anticipating and heading off injury before it occurs.

In a society like that of the United States in which
individuals are free to combine to pursue almost any
possible common interest they might have and in which
government agencies are sensitive to the pressures of
these groups, the system described is approximated. Almost every interest has its watchdog. Without claiming
that every interest has a sufficiently powerful watchdog,
it can be argued that our system often can assure a more
comprehensive regard for the values of the whole society
than any attempt at intellectual comprehensiveness.

* * *

Mutual adjustment is more pervasive than the explicit forms it takes in negotiation between groups; it
persists through the mutual impacts of groups upon each
other even where they are not in communication. For
all the imperfections and latent dangers in this ubiqui-
tous process of mutual adjustment, it will often accomplish an adaptation of policies to a wider range of interests than could be done by one group centrally.

Note, too, how the incremental pattern of policy-making fits with the multiple pressure pattern. For
when decisions are only incremental—closely related to
known policies, it is easier for one group to anticipate
the kind of moves another might make and easier too
for it to make correction for injury already accomplished.

Even partisanship and narrowness, to use pejorative
terms, will sometimes be assets to rational decision-making, for they can doubly insure that what one agency
neglects, another will not; they specialize personnel to
distinct points of view. The claim is valid that effective
rational coordination of the federal administration, if
possible to achieve at all, would require an agreed set

of values[2]—if "rational" is defined as the practice of the root method of decision-making. But a high degree of administrative coordination occurs as each agency adjusts its policies to the concerns of the other agencies in the process of fragmented decision-making I have just described.

For all the apparent shortcomings of the incremental approach to policy alternatives with its arbitrary exclusion coupled with fragmentation, when compared to the root method, the branch method often looks far superior. In the root method, the inevitable exclusion of factors is accidental, unsystematic, and not defensible by any argument so far developed, while in the branch method the exclusions are deliberate, systematic, and defensible. Ideally, of course, the root method does not exclude; in practice it must.

Nor does the branch method necessarily neglect long-run considerations and objectives. It is clear that important values must be omitted in considering policy, and sometimes the only way long-run objectives can be given adequate attention is through the neglect of short-run considerations. But the values omitted can be either long-run or short-run.

SUCCESSION OF COMPARISONS (5B)

The final distinctive element in the branch method is that the comparisons, together with the policy choice, proceed in a chronological series. Policy is not made once and for all; it is made and remade endlessly. Policy-making is a process of successive approximation to some desired objectives in which what is desired itself continues to change under reconsideration.

Making policy is at best a very rough process. Neither social scientists, nor politicians, nor public administrators yet know enough about the social world to avoid repeated error in predicting the consequences of policy moves. A wise policy-maker consequently expects that his policies will achieve only part of what he hopes and at the same time will produce unanticipated consequences he would have preferred to avoid. If he proceeds through a *succession* of incremental changes, he avoids serious lasting mistakes in several ways.

In the first place, past sequences of policy steps have given him knowledge about the probable consequences of further similar steps. Second, he need not attempt big jumps toward his goals that would require predictions beyond his or anyone else's knowledge, because he never expects his policy to be a final resolution of a problem. His decision is only one step, one that if successful can quickly be followed by another. Third, he is in effect able to test his previous predictions as he moves on to each further step. Lastly, he often can remedy a past error fairly quickly—more quickly than if policy proceeded through more distinct steps widely spaced in time.

Compare this comparative analysis of incremental changes with the aspiration to employ theory in the root method. Man cannot think without classifying, without subsuming one experience under a more general category of experiences. The attempt to push categorization as far as possible and to find general propositions which can be applied to specific situations is what I refer to with the word "theory." Where root analysis often leans heavily on theory in this sense, the branch method does not.

The assumption of root analysis is that theory is the most systematic and economical way to bring relevant knowledge to bear on a specific problem. Granting the assumption, an unhappy fact is that we do not have adequate theory to apply to problems in any policy area, although theory is more adequate in some areas—monetary policy, for example—than in others. Comparative analysis, as in the branch method, is sometimes a systematic alternative to theory.

Suppose an administrator must choose among a small group of policies that differ only incrementally from each other and from present policy. He might aspire to "understand" each of the alternatives—for example, to know all the consequences of each aspect of each policy. If so, he would indeed require theory. In fact, however, he would usually decide that, *for policy-making purposes*, he need know, as explained above, only the consequences of each of those aspects of the policies in which they differed from one another. For this much more modest aspiration, he requires no theory (although it might be helpful, if available), for he can proceed to isolate probable differences by examining the differences in consequences associated with past differences in policies, a feasible program because he can take his observations from a long sequence of incremental changes.

* * *

SUCCESSIVE COMPARISON AS A SYSTEM

Successive limited comparisons is, then, indeed a method or system; it is not a failure of method for which administrators ought to apologize. None the less, its imperfections, which have not been explored in this paper, are many For example, the method is without a built-in safeguard for all relevant values, and it also may lead the decision-maker to overlook excellent policies for no other reason than that they are not suggested by the chain of successive policy steps leading up to the present. Hence, it ought to be said that under this method, as well as under some of the most sophisticated variants of the root method—operations research, for example—policies will continue to be as foolish as they are wise.

Why then bother to describe the method in all the above detail? Because it is in fact a common method of policy formulation, and is, for complex problems, the principal reliance of administrators as well as of other policy analysts. And because it will be superior to any other decision-making method available for complex problems in many circumstances, certainly superior to a futile attempt at superhuman comprehensiveness. The reaction of the public administrator to the exposition of method doubtless will be less a discovery of a new method than a better acquaintance with an old. But by becoming more conscious of their practice of this method, administrators might practice it with more skill and know when to extend or constrict its use. (That they sometimes practice it effectively and sometimes not may explain the extremes of opinion on "muddling through," which is both praised as a highly sophisticated form of problem-solving and denounced as no method at all. For I suspect that in so far as there is a system in what is known as "muddling through," this method is it.) . . .

Notes

[1] I am assuming that administrators often make policy and advise in the making of policy and am treating decision-making and policy-making as synonymous for purposes of this paper.

[2] Herbert Simon, Donald W. Smithburg, and Victor A. Thompson, *Public Administration* (Alfred A. Knopf, 1950), p. 434.

The second article selected to illustrate consensus on the invisible ideology evolved from a conference held in Milan, Italy, in September of 1955. Among the participants were many of the leading political analysts of this country, including Seymour M. Lipset, whose paper "The End of Ideology?" identifies the major thrust of the conclusions reached in this conference.

This particular argument has been referred to as the "end-of-ideology debate," in the literature of political science. According to Lipset, the thinking of the people at that conference is that although ideology (that is, classical democratic theory) may have been important during the historical development of our society—and although it may still be important in the "under-developed" countries of the world—it is no longer important in the context of our present affluent and highly industrialized society.

Although Lipset does not suggest that conflict has disappeared from democratic political systems, he believes that there is a basic value consensus, which defines the significant issues. Conflicts tend to be about how much, rather than whether, and are still class-based; there is conflict in terms of how much of the pie groups and individuals will get, but they are no longer concerned with whether or not pie is a good thing. There is no longer any need to evaluate whether the system is doing its job according to the values of classical democratic theory, according to these analysts, for it is doing the job well. Thus, they argue that ideology itself is ended. And more importantly, that the politics of a society have been largely usurped as an ongoing process. For, if politics is understood to be the allocation of values for the society and a consensus already has been established about these values, then the process of politics itself is ended. What is left to understand is not what the values will be, but how they will be allocated. Ideology, in the sense of preferences or values, is dead. In this fashion, many political analysts have come to the conclusion that the democratic political system functions to the best interest of everyone, and that there is no longer reason to evaluate the system by the criterion of whether it is a good society or not. It clearly is good, in their view.

THE END OF IDEOLOGY?

SEYMOUR MARTIN LIPSET

A basic premise of this essay is that democracy is not only or even primarily a means through which different groups can attain their ends or seek the good society; it is the good society itself in operation. Only the give-and-take of a free society's internal struggles offers some guarantee that the products of the society will not accumulate in the hands of a few power-holders, and that men may develop and bring up their children without fear of persecution. And, as we have seen, democracy requires institutions which support conflict and disagreement as well as those which sustain legitimacy and consensus. In recent years, however, democracy in the Western world has been undergoing some important changes as serious intellectual conflicts among groups representing different values have declined sharply.

* * *

The fact that the differences between the left and the right in the Western democracies are no longer profound does not mean that there is no room for party controversy. But as the editor of one of the leading Swedish newspapers once said to me, "Politics is now boring. The only issues are whether the metal workers should get a nickel more an hour, the price of milk should be raised, or old-age pensions extended." These are important matters, the very stuff of the internal struggle within stable democracies, but they are hardly matters to excite intellectuals or stimulate young people who seek in politics a way to express their dreams.

This change in Western political life reflects the fact that the fundamental political problems of the industrial revolution have been solved: the workers have achieved industrial and political citizenship; the conserv-

atives have accepted the welfare state; and the democratic left has recognized that an increase in over-all state power carries with it more dangers to freedom than solutions for economic problems. This very triumph of the democratic social revolution in the West ends domestic politics for those intellectuals who must have ideologies or utopias to motivate them to political action.

* * *

. . . A large number of surveys of the American population made from the 1930s to the 1950s report that most people believe that the Republicans do more for the wealthy and for business and professional people and the Democrats do more for the poor and for skilled and unskilled workers.[1] Similar findings have been reported for Great Britain.

These opinions do not simply represent the arguments of partisans, since supporters of both the left and the right agree on the classes each party basically represents—which does not mean the acceptance of a bitter class struggle but rather an agreement on the representation functions of the political parties similar to the general agreement that trade-unions represent workers, and the Chamber of Commerce, businessmen. Continued class cleavage does not imply any destructive consequences for the system; . . . a stable democracy requires consensus on the nature of the political struggle, and this includes the assumption that different groups are best served by different parties.

The predictions of the end of class politics in the "affluent society" ignore the relative character of any class system. The decline of objective deprivation—low income, insecurity, malnutrition—does reduce the potential tension level of a society, as we have seen. But as long as some men are rewarded more than others by the prestige or status structure of society, men will feel *relatively* deprived. The United States is the wealthiest country in the world, and its working class lives on a scale to which most of the middle classes in the rest of the world aspire; yet a detailed report on the findings of various American opinion surveys states: "The dominant opinion on polls before, during, and after the war is that the salaries of corporation executives are too high and should be limited by the government." And this sentiment, prevalent even among prosperous people, finds increasing support as one moves down the economic ladder.

The democratic class struggle will continue, but it will be a fight without ideologies, without red flags, without May Day parades. This naturally upsets many intellectuals who can participate only as ideologists or major critics of the *status quo*. . . .

The decline of political ideology in America has affected many intellectuals who . . . must function as critics of the society to fulfill their self-image. And since domestic politics, even liberal and socialist politics, can no longer serve as the arena for serious criticism from the left, many intellectuals have turned from a basic concern with the political and economic systems to criticism of other sections of the basic culture of American society, particularly of elements which cannot be dealt with politically. . . .

Yet many of the disagreeable aspects of American society which are now regarded as the results of an affluent and bureaucratic society may be recurring elements inherent in an equalitarian and democratic society. Those aspects of both American and socialist ideology which have always been most thoroughly expressed in the United States make a concern with status and conformity constant features of the society.

* * *

Although the pressures toward conformity within democratic and bureaucratic society are an appropriate source of serious concern for Western intellectuals, my reading of the historical evidence suggests that the problem is less acute or threatening today than it has been in the past, if we limit our analysis to domestic threats to the system. There is reason to expect that stable democratic institutions in which individual political freedom is great and even increasing (as it is, say, in Britain or Sweden) will continue to characterize the mature industrialized Western societies.

The controversies about cultural creativity and conformity reflect the general trend . . . the shift away from

ideology towards sociology. The very growth of sociology as an intellectual force outside the academy in many Western nations is a tribute, not primarily to the power of sociological analysis but to the loss of interest in political inquiry. It may seem curious, therefore, for a sociologist to end on a note of concern about this trend. But I believe that there is still a real need for political analysis, ideology, and controversy within the world community, if not within the Western democracies. In a larger sense, the domestic controversies within the advanced democratic countries have become comparable to struggles within American party primary elections. Like all nomination contests, they are fought to determine who will lead the party, in this case the democratic camp, in the larger political struggle in the world as a whole with its marginal constituencies, the underdeveloped states. The horizon of intellectual political concerns must turn from the new version of local elections—those which determine who will run national administrations—to this larger contest.

This larger fight makes politics much more complex in the various underdeveloped countries than it appears within Western democracies. In these states there is still a need for intense political controversy and ideology. The problems of industrialization, of the place of religion, of the character of political institutions are still unsettled, and the arguments about them have become intertwined with the international struggle. The past political relations between former colonial countries and the West, between colored and white peoples, make the task even more difficult. It is necessary for us to recognize that our allies in the underdeveloped countries must be radicals, probably socialists, because only parties which promise to improve the situation of the masses through widespread reform, and which are transvaluational and equalitarian, can hope to compete with the Communists. Asian and African socialist movements, even where they are committed to political democracy (and unfortunately not all of them are, or can be even if they want to), must often express hostility to many of the economic, political, and religious institutions of the West.

* * *

This . . . concern with making explicit the conditions of the democratic order reflects my perhaps overrationalistic belief that a fuller understanding of the various conditions under which democracy has existed may help men to develop it where it does not now exist. Although we have concluded that Aristotle's basic hypothesis of the relationship of democracy to a class structure bulging toward the middle is still valid, this does not encourage political optimism, since it implies that political activity should be directed primarily toward assuring economic development. Yet we must not be unduly pessimistic. Democracy has existed in a variety of circumstances, even if it is most commonly sustained by a limited set of conditions. It cannot be achieved by acts of will alone, of course, but men's wills expressed in action can shape institutions and events in directions that reduce or increase the chances for democracy's development and survival. Ideology and passion may no longer be necessary to sustain the class struggle within stable and affluent democracies, but they are clearly needed in the international effort to develop free political and economic institutions in the rest of the world. It is only the ideological class struggle within the West which is ending. Ideological conflicts linked to levels and problems of economic development and of appropriate political institutions among different nations will last far beyond our lifetime, and men committed to democracy can abstain from them only at their peril. To aid men's actions in furthering democracy in then absolutist Europe was in some measure Tocqueville's purpose in studying the operation of American society in 1830. To clarify the operation of Western democracy in the mid-twentieth century may contribute to the political battle in Asia and Africa.

Notes

1 See Harold Orlans, *Opinion Polls on National Leaders* (Philadelphia: Institute for Research in Human Relations, 1953), pp. 70–73. This monograph contains a detailed report on various surveys conducted by the different American polling agencies from 1935–53.

Indications of consensus in a discipline can be found in the basic textbooks that are chosen to introduce the subject matter to students. One of the most popular Ameri-can government texts of recent years has been *The Irony of Democracy*, by Thomas R. Dye and L. Harmon Zeigler. This book, which was widely adopted, was unprecedented among textbooks in its argument that "challenges the prevailing pluralistic ideology and interprets American politics from the perspective of elite theory." The interesting point about the book is that the authors adopt the power elite analysis of American politics, yet they disagree considerably with the conclusions of theorists that this power elite in America is eroding the ideals of liberal democracy. Instead, Dye and Zeigler conclude (in a logical extension of the invisible ideology) that

The future of American democracy depends on the wisdom, responsibility, and resourcefulness of the nation's elite. Although it is customary in a book on American government to conclude that the nation's future depends on an enlightened citizenry, this reflects the symbols, rather than the realities of American politics. It is the irony of democracy that the responsibility for the survival of liberal democratic values depends upon elites, not masses.[26]

The analysis of these authors disagrees with the analysis of our political system as a competitive elite model. But it certainly concurs with the invisible ideology of democratic political systems, rather than with the values of classical democratic theory.

This chapter has argued that the invisible ideology has become the reigning ideology of political analysis, whether it is associated with multiple or with monolithic elite analysis. Its influence is real and is largely unchallenged. As long as its impact remains unexamined, it will continue to dominate the discipline. The analysis here is an attempt to critically assess both the scientific theory and the invisible ideology.

26 Thomas R. Dye and L. Harmon Zeigler, *The Irony of Democracy* (Belmont, Calif.. Wadsworth, 1970), p. 339.

8/People and Change in Democratic Political Systems

The Declaration of Independence, in just three sentences, prescribed the relationship of people to their government and to society, and the form of political change necessary if this relationship should falter:

We hold these truths to be self-evident, that all men are created equal, that they are endowed by their Creator with certain unalienable Rights, that among these are Life, Liberty and the pursuit of Happiness. That to secure these rights, Governments are instituted among Men, deriving their just powers from the consent of the governed. That whenever any Form of Government becomes destructive of these ends, it is the Right of the People to alter or to abolish it, and to institute new Government, laying its foundation on such principles and organizing its powers in such form, as to them shall seem most likely to effect their Safety and Happiness.

The classical theory of democracy, formed in this American manifesto of revolt from Great Britain, clearly prescribed that governments were to be instituted as contracts between people and society. Governments existed for the purpose of fulfilling the needs, wants, demands, and rights of the people. It was also clear in the classical doctrine that if governments failed in these purposes, it was the right and duty of citizens to "alter or abolish" that government. From the perspective of classical democratic theory, society exists to serve the people, and political change is their means of altering a government that no longer pursues this objective.

Where classical democratic theory explicitly viewed the relationship between individuals and society as one in which the society and its government should serve the needs of people, the invisible ideology views the relationship as one in which people must adjust to the operation of the democratic political system. Where classical democratic theory viewed political change as revolution against a government that had failed in its obligation to support individual rights and needs, the invisible ideology conceptualizes change as being restricted to the framework of the democratic political system.

Four points of contrast between the invisible ideology and the classical theory of democracy were discussed in the previous chapter: 1) The invisible ideology's value of organizational capability rather than individual development and preferences and 2) its value of system maintenance rather than ideological confrontations. This chapter turns to the impact of the last two aspects of the invisible ideology: 3) the value for fitting people into functioning democratic systems, and 4) the definition of change to mean change *within the system* rather than *of the system*.

How have modern political scientists analyzed the individual's relationship to his government and society? Most research that has been carried out on this traditional question clearly illustrates the influence of the invisible ideology. Even the rubric "political socialization," which is used to describe this research, suggests the value of fitting people into a system. The emphasis is on creating a socially conforming individual who meets the norms required by the system.

SOCIALIZATION FOR THE STABILITY OF THE SYSTEM

Since the early 1930s, political scientists have investigated the role of citizens in a democratic society, always with the underlying assumption that our existing socio-political system was basically sound or at least perfectible. Consequently, the analysis of the relationship of the individual to that system has taken two forms: How individuals are socialized to conform to the socio-political norms of our society, and how people deviate from these norms. Even though they may hold differing values about the nature of the political order, many researchers are still agreed that the essential questions deal with the conditions under which people can be taught to conform, and the conditions under which they learn to deviate. With such understanding, it then becomes possible to engineer ways to achieve greater conformity and less deviance, which produces greater stability; this, in turn, maintains the existing or perfected political structures. Such an approach has dominated the study of political socialization.

Research emphasizing conformity, deviance, and stabilizing social systems is not simply a product of the invisible ideology's value of systems rather than individuals. This analysis has also been heavily influenced by the kinds of theoretical models that are available to researchers who attempt to understand the individual in relationship to the state. Two basic models of man have influenced the analysis of the relationship of human behavior to the social structure.

The first of these models is derived from the work of Freud and later psychoanalysts in psychology. Although the following discussion is brief and simplified, it reveals the theoretical consequences for the analysis of man's relationship to society and politics.

From the psychoanalytic perspective, the individual is driven by the instinctual and largely antisocial drives of the "id." These instinctive impulses are detrimental to the requirements of the social order and must be repressed, if social disorder is to be avoided. It is necessary for the individual to internalize the social norms that are necessary for order, by developing a "superego," which is largely derived from the moral training of childhood. The child's id impulses are inhibited by the commands of the parents, which become internalized in the child's superego. The child's "ego" acts to adjust behavior, effecting a compromise between the id impulses and the realities of social order that are internalized in the superego. Clearly, the assumption here is that man is antisocial by nature, and that successful repression of his anti-social instincts is necessary for civilization to continue.

The social implications of the Freudian model are pessimistic, indeed. The significance of this theory for studies of socialization was twofold. First, it directed a great deal of attention to child-rearing patterns in society, for it argued that the early childhood years were critical in the resolution of the conflicts between id and superego, and in the development of the ego. Second, Freudianism tended to emphasize the necessity of understanding how to adjust individuals and their antisocial tendencies to the social order, which, at best, was one in which people did not destroy themselves through acting out their instinctual urges.

The second theoretical model that has influenced the political analysis of individuals in relationship to society has been that of behaviorist psychology. Behaviorist models of man tend to stress external rather than internal sources in the development of human personality. Behaviorists argue that man is for the most part a "blank slate," and that his actions and values are the product of society's imprint on him. Man and his personality become a function of social situations and conditions.

The theory that life for the individual is a function of perfecting the social environment is well expressed in *Beyond Freedom and Dignity,* by B. F. Skinner, the leading advocate of the behaviorist model of man, who calls for a "technology of behavior." Skinner's book is a direct attack on the humanistic perspective, which values an autonomous man who with dignity searches for freedom. Skinner suggests explicitly that the very concept of an autonomous individual works against the discovery and utilization of basic principles of "operant conditioning," a technique that permits man to better fit into the necessary social conditions required for his welfare.

From Skinner's perspective, the concept of freedom is no more than the escape from unpleasant conditions in the environment. Freedom is not the capacity for becoming a better person but an effort to avoid negative conditions in the social structure.

Skinner advocates doing away with such concepts as autonomous man, freedom, and dignity, and openly admitting that man, like any other organism, is a function of his environment. Both his magnificence and tragedy are brought about by the society. Researchers should not assume that man has the potentiality for development; they should strive to understand the determining conditions that make man what he is. According to Skinner, it is not that people need no control, it is that they need better and more control:

The picture that emerges from a scientific analysis is not of a body with a person inside but of a body that is a person in the sense that it displays a complex repertoire of behavior. . . .

To man qua man we readily say good riddance. Only by dispossessing autonomous man can we turn to the real causes of human behavior—from the inferred to the observed, from the miraculous to the natural, from the inaccessible to the manipulable.[1]

The implications of behaviorism are clear. The individual is little more than a product of his social environment, and that environment can be engineered and manipulated. Therefore, research is directed toward a better understanding of the conditions and social institutions that produce the well-adjusted individual.

Both the psychoanalytic and the behaviorist models of man emphasize the socializing of individuals to fit the social order. The psychoanalytic perspective directs attention to early family life and the repression of antisocial drives, and the behaviorist dogma focuses on various social institutions as determinants of human behavior. As a result, the primary variables in the study of political socialization have been the impacts of family, schools, work place, peers, and authority relationships. The value is in the stabilizing social system by adjusting people to fit its requirements.

"The Child's Image of Government," by David Easton and Jack Dennis, reflects many of these impacts. The article is an attempt to understand how early childhood learning affects later adult behavior in the political system. These researchers are primarily interested in insuring the persistence of the political system, even as it changes.

---

[1] B. F. Skinner, *Beyond Freedom and Dignity* (New York; Knopf, 1971). These quotes were taken from a condensation in *Psychology Today* (August, 1971), p. 78.

THE CHILD'S IMAGE OF GOVERNMENT

DAVID EASTON AND JACK DENNIS

Political socialization refers to the way in which a society transmits political orientations—knowledge, attitudes or norms, and values—from generation to generation. Without such socialization across the generations, each new member of the system, whether a child newly born into it or an immigrant newly arrived, would have to seek an entirely fresh adjustment in the political sphere. But for the fact that each new generation is able to learn a body of political orientations from its predecessors, no given political system would be able to persist. Fundamentally, the theoretical significance of the study of socializing processes in political life resides in its contribution to our understanding of the way in which political systems are able to persist[1] even as they change, for more than one generation.

THE THEORETICAL SETTING

A society transmits many political orientations across the generations, from the most trivial to the most profound. One of the major tasks of research is to formulate criteria by which we may distinguish the significant from the less important. Once we posit the relationship between socialization and system persistence, this compels us to recognize that among many theoretical issues thereby raised, a critical one pertains to the way in which a society manages or fails to arouse support for any political system, generation after generation. In part, it may, of course, rely on force or perception of self-interest. But no political system has been able to persist on these bases alone. In all cases, as children in society mature, they learn through a series of complicated processes to address themselves more or less favorably to the existence of some kind of political life.

* * *

Reprinted from "The Child's Image of Government," pp. 40-57, by David Easton and Jack Dennis in volume no. 361 of The Annals of The American Academy of Political and Social Science. Copyright 1965 The American Academy of Political and Social Science.

This paper seeks to illuminate one of the numerous ways in which the processes of socialization in a single political system, that of the United States, manages to generate support for limited aspects of two political objects: the regime and the government (authorities). . . . generalize about the processes through which members learn to become attached to or disillusioned with all the basic objects of a system.

Within this broad theoretical context our specific problems for this paper can be simply stated: How does each generation born into the American political system come to accept (or reject) the authorities and regime? As the child matures from infancy, at what stage does he begin to acquire the political knowledge and attitudes related to this question? Do important changes take place even during childhood, a time when folklore has it that a person is innocent of things political? If so, can these changes be described in a systematic way?

GOVERNMENT AS A LINKAGE POINT

* * *

For the American democratic system, preliminary interviewing led us to conclude that there are two kinds of initial points of contact between the child and the political system in its broadest sense. One of these is quite specific. The child shows a capacity, with increasing age, to identify and hold opinions about such well-defined and concrete units among the political authorities as the President, policeman, Congress, and Supreme Court. But we also found that simultaneously another and much more general and amorphous point of contact is available. This consists of the conglomeration of institutions, practices, and outcomes that adults generically symbolize in the concept "government." Through the idea of government itself the child seems able to reach out and at a very early age to establish contact both with the authorities and with certain aspects of the regime. In a mass society where the personnel among the authorities changes and often remains obscure for the average person, the utility of so generalized and ill-defined a term as "the government" can be readily appreciated. The very richness and variability of its meaning

converts it into a useful point of contact between the child and the system.

* * *

OUR DATA

The children whom we have surveyed concerning what they think and feel about government, as well as about a number of other political orientations (which we will report elsewhere), are for the most part children in large metropolitan areas of the United States. They are, with few exceptions, white, public school children, in grades two through eight, and were selected from both middle-class and working-class neighborhoods. We have conducted many individual interviews and administered a series of pencil-and-paper questionnaires. The latter we read out to the children in their regular classrooms while they individually marked their answers.

* * *

PREVIEW OF FINDINGS

The findings which grew out of this analysis will, perhaps, surprise those readers who are accustomed to think of children as innocent of political thought. For not only does the child quite early begin to orient himself to the rather remote and mystical world of politics, but he even forms notions about its most abstract parts—such as government in general. Our data at least suggest this. The political marks on the *tabula rasa* are entered early and are continually refurbished thereafter.

We will, perhaps, disappoint as well those readers who are accustomed to think of the American as one who is brought up on the raw meat of rugged individualism, which supposedly nourishes our national frame. We find that the small child sees a vision of holiness when he chances to glance in the direction of government—a sanctity and rightness of the demigoddess who dispenses the milk of human kindness. The government protects us, helps us, is good, and cares for us when we are in need, answers the child.

When the child emerges from his state of nature, therefore, he finds himself a part of a going political concern which he ordinarily adopts immediately as a source of nurturance and protection. His early experience of government is, therefore, analogous to his early experience of the family in that it involves an initial context of highly acceptable dependency. Against this strongly positive affective background the child devises and revises his cognitive image of government. Let us first turn to some empirical evidence bearing upon this cognition.

THE CHILD'S EARLY RECOGNITION OF GOVERNMENT

In earlier studies of the child's growing awareness of political objects and relationships, it was found that the President of the United States and the policeman were among the first figures of political authority that the child recognized.[2] In part, at least, we would expect that attitudes towards political authority would begin to take shape in relationship to these objects. They are clearly the first contact points in the child's perception of wider external authority. . . .

We can, however, now raise a question which takes us beyond these findings. Does the child also establish some early perceptual contact with the more amorphous, intangible abstraction of government itself, that is, with the more general category of political authority among whose instances are counted presidents and policemen? Is the child's cognitive development such that he is likely to work immediately from a few instances to the general class of objects? This would then put him in a position to apply his concept to new instances, as well as to refurbish it as the experiences of its instances grow. If this is so, we can anticipate that, in addition to such points of contact as the policeman and the President, in the American political system the child will also be able to orient himself to political life through perceptions of and attitudes towards the more generalized and diffuse object that we call "the government."

The Crystallization of the Concept

When do our respondents first begin to recognize the general category of things labeled "government?"

One simple way of exploring this is to see whether the child himself thinks he knows what the word "government" means, even if no verbalization of his understanding is called for. On this simple test we would contend that even the seven- or eight-year-old child is likely to feel that he has attained some rudimentary grasp of this general concept. This test is met in a question we asked on our final questionnaire which read as follows: "Some of you may not be sure what the word *government* means. If you are not sure what government means, put an X in the box below." The changing pattern of response to this question over the grades is shown in Table 1.

* * *

Table 1
DEVELOPMENT OF A SENSE OF CONFIDENCE IN
UNDERSTANDING THE CONCEPT OF GOVERNMENT
(RESPONSES OF CHILDREN BY GRADE LEVEL)[a]

Grade	%	N
2	27.29	1,655
3	19.01	1,678
4	17.61	1,749
5	11.15	1,803
6	12.41	1,749
7	8.36	1,723
8	9.79	1,695

[a]The questionnaire which contained this item was administered to a purposively selected group of 12,052 white, public school children in regular classrooms in eight large metropolitan areas (100,000 and over) in four major geographic regions (South, Northeast, Midwest, and Far West) in late 1961 and early 1962. The children were in grades two through eight and from both middle- and working-class areas. We will refer to this questionnaire hereinafter as simply "CA-9," which is our code name for Citizenship Attitude Questionnaire #9. This question is item #55, page 12. [Page number refers to original article.]

Symbolic Associations of the Concept "Government"

Since it appears that the child is rather likely to develop some working conception of government in these early years, we can move on to ask: Is there any specific content to this concept, especially of a kind that is political in character? We might well expect that because of the inherent ambiguity and generality of the term, even for adults, considerable differences and disjunctiveness would characterize this concept for aggregates of children. Our findings do, in part, support this expectation. Yet there are clear patterns of "dominance" in these collective conceptions, and these patterns vary to a large degree with the age and grade level of the children.

One way we have devised for getting fairly directly at which patterns are dominant in this period and at how these patterns change involves a pictorial presentation of ten symbols of government. These are symbols which appeared strongly in our extensive pretest data when children were asked either to define *government* or to "free associate" with a list of words, one of which was government.

What we asked in our final instrument was the following: "Here are some pictures that show what our government is. Pick the *two* pictures that show best what our government is." This instruction was then followed for the balance of the page by ten pictures plus a blank box for "I don't know." Each of the ten pictures represented a salient symbol of the United States government and was accompanied by its printed title underneath the picture. The options in order were: (1) Policeman; (2) George Washington; (3) Uncle Sam; (4) Voting; (5) Supreme Court; (6) Capitol; (7) Congress; (8) Flag; (9) Statue of Liberty; (10) President (Kennedy); (11) I don't know. The pattern of response to these ten symbols of government is shown in Table 2.

Several interesting facts emerge from this table. If we take 20 per cent as a rough guide to what we might expect purely by chance as a maximum level of response to each of the ten symbol options (for two-answer format), we see that only four of these pictures were chosen with a frequency greater than chance. These four are George Washington, Voting, Congress, and President Kennedy. These four are considerably more dominant than any of the others, but this dominance varies by grade level. For the youngest children, the two most popular options are the two Presidents, Washington and Kennedy. But these choices drop in the later grades. In Figure 1, the developmental curves for the four dominant options are plotted over the grade span in order to interpret more easily the major changes that are taking place.

It would appear that, in terms of these symbols, the youngest child's perception of government is quite likely to be framed by the few personal figures of high governmental authority that cross his cognitive horizon, probably both in the school . . . and outside. The young child focuses most directly upon personal or perhaps "charismatic" aspects of political authority for his interpretation of what government is. But as he moves into the middle years, there is a greater likelihood that

Table 2

DEVELOPMENT OF A COGNITIVE IMAGE OF GOVERNMENT: SYMBOLIC ASSOCIATIONS
(PER CENT OF CHILDREN AND TEACHERS RESPONDING)[a]

GRADE	Police-man	George Wash-ington	Uncle Sam	Voting	Supreme Court	Capitol	Congress	Flag	Statue of Liberty	President Kennedy	I Don't Know	N Respond-ing	N Not Respond-ing
2	8.15	39.47	15.63	4.32	4.51	13.65	5.93	15.75	12.11	46.26	15.69	1,619	36
3	4.09	26.77	19.01	8.36	6.38	16.13	12.94	16.49	14.26	46.81	12.94	1,662	16
4	5.74	14.19	18.02	10.83	10.25	16.57	28.97	13.33	12.92	37.25	13.15	1,726	23
5	2.74	6.93	19.40	19.23	16.77	11.57	49.08	11.57	11.18	38.51	4.86	1,789	14
6	2.36	4.94	16.78	27.99	16.84	9.94	49.66	11.38	17.07	30.52	4.66	1,740	9
7	3.03	3.44	18.26	39.44	13.54	9.39	44.22	12.84	18.61	27.89	2.98	1,714	9
8	1.66	1.72	16.40	46.77	15.87	6.93	49.14	11.78	19.60	22.91	1.54	1,689	6
TEACHERS	1.00	1.00	5.00	72.00	13.00	5.00	71.00	6.00	8.00	15.00	1.00	390	1

[a](1) Percentages should add to 200 due to the two-answer format, but do not, because of the failure of some children to make two choices. This is especially the case for those answering "I don't know." (2) 113 children failed to respond to this question. Thus the N at each grade are those responding and the percentages are of that number. (3) We have added, at the bottom, the responses of the teachers of these children, for the sake of comparison. The teachers were given a similar questionnaire at the time of administration of the children's questionnaire.

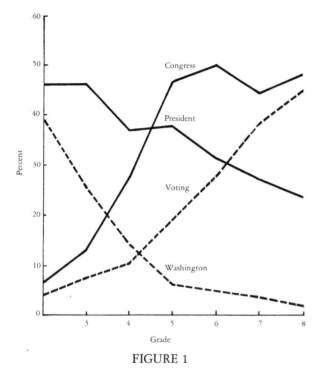

FIGURE 1

DEVELOPMENT OF A COGNITIVE IMAGE OF GOVERNMENT:
THE FOUR DOMINANT SYMBOLIC ASSOCIATIONS (THE NUMBER
OF CHILDREN RESPONDING AT EACH GRADE LEVEL VARIES
FROM 1,619 TO 1,789).

his attention will be turned to rather different, prominent aspects of the authorities.

First, he revises his notions to include the Congress
and drops George Washington—who suffers a precipi-
tous decline after his initial showing. Undoubtedly, the
growing adoption of Congress reflects an awareness of
several things, and these are supported by various other
data. First, the older children become more aware of
the group character of government rather than simply
identifying it with single persons. Second, the more frequent choice of Congress probably also reflects a greater
awareness of governmental institutions—particularly the
ongoing organizations engaged in *law-making* (as suggested undoubtedly in the beginning social studies, history, or civics texts). . . .

Third, children appear to reflect a greater awareness
of the representative character of these institutions. . . .
This conclusion is borne out to some degree by the third

marked shift which occurs—that concerning the older
child's greater tendency to pick "voting" as the best
picture of our government. Thus, by grade eight nearly
half the children choose voting. This suggests some beginning awareness of the regime rules associated with
popular democracy and the role of ordinary people in
it.

The child's conception of government is, therefore,
brought in stages from far to near, from one small set
of persons to many people, from a personalistic to an
impersonalized form of authority, and toward an awareness of the institutionalization in our system of such
regime norms as are embodied in the idea of a representative, popular democracy. . . .

Generally, therefore, in these data about the cognitive development of this rather abstract category of the
individual's political thought, we detect more than a
mere glimmering of a concept. Furthermore, the emergent conception in this instance seemingly reflects some
fairly wide and regularly changing comprehension for
aggregates of children.

This suggests that considerable societal efforts are
probably being made to transmit a concept deemed appropriate in the American political system. If we compare children with their teachers, for example, we find
that the latter most roundly endorse the two options
dominant for the eighth-grade children. . . .

The Concept of Government
and the Law-Making Function

A supporting piece of evidence which is connected
to the above, but supplements it from the standpoint
of governmental functions (rather than from the structural aspects of the concept alone), has to do with the
child's changing awareness of the chief law-makers in
our system of government. One thing we find is the
fact that, of the various kinds of political or other functions that the child most readily associates with government, the making of laws is very prominent. That is,
when the child is asked, "What does the government
do?" he is quite likely to answer that he, it, or they
make the laws.

A questionnaire item that we presented in this con-

Table 3

DEVELOPMENT OF AN AWARENESS OF THE CHIEF LAW-MAKER (PER CENT OF CHILDREN AND TEACHERS RESPONDING)[a]

GRADE	Congress	President	Supreme Court	I Don't Know	N Responding	N Not Responding
2	4.79	75.55	11.49	8.17	1,627	28
3	11.41	66.14	16.93	5.52	1,648	30
4	27.51	44.11	21.07	7.31	1,723	26
5	57.39	19.35	19.85	3.40	1,793	10
6	65.06	13.25	18.30	3.38	1,743	6
7	72.14	8.88	16.41	2.57	1,712	11
8	85.33	5.44	7.87	1.36	1,690	5
TEACHERS	96.00	1.00	3.00	0.00	339	5

[a]CA-9, item 33.

nection reads as follows: "Who makes the laws? Put an X next to the *one* who does the most to make the laws." The options were: (1) Congress, (2) President, (3) Supreme Court, (4) I don't know. The same pictures as before were used. In Table 3, we see the patterns of change over the grade span for this aspect of the child's understanding.

Here the President's early dominance is apparent, but Congress gradually supplants him by grade five. Thus, by the middle grades the child is both increasingly prone to identify Congress as the chief source of law-making as well as a more representative symbol of our government than the President.

* * *

All of these findings converge with our data as far as the developmental trends are concerned. . . . Our respondents tend over the grades toward the adoption of a vision of government which puts great emphasis upon Congress as the center of government, upon law as its most visible product, and upon benign, helpful, protective, and responsive qualities as those most appropriately describing its manner of operation. The latter, more affective image will be discussed shortly after we present some further findings concerning cognitive development.

Differentiation of the Public Sector

Even though the children tested assert a growing awareness of government as an idea and object, are they, in fact, able to distinguish it as a sphere separate from other areas of social life? If attitudes towards the authorities as an object are to have relevance for later ties to the system, we need some evidence indicating that even in their earliest years children are, in fact, able to recognize some minimal difference between that which is governmental and that which is not. Only under such conditions could we infer that attitudes towards government—to which we shall turn in a moment—refer to distinctively political bonds.

To discover whether the child's declared knowledge of what government means includes a capacity to discriminate governmental from nongovernmental objects, we chose to test his awareness of the difference between what we normally view as the public and private sectors of life. . . .

What we asked was very simple. Taking various occupations—milkman, policeman, soldier, judge, postman, and teacher—we said: "Here are some people. Which ones work for the government?" Then followed six questions with an appropriate picture for each such as: "Does the MILKMAN work for the government?" The options were: (1) Yes, (2) No. What we found is shown in Table 4.

Only the first of these people was considered by us to be clearly outside the governmental system as determined by his occupation. Of the rest, two were more directly local government workers—the policeman and the teacher; two were clearly national government workers—the soldier and the postman; and one was indeterminate as among levels—the judge.

Several things are apparent from the table. Of these

Table 4
DEVELOPMENT OF AN AWARENESS OF THE PUBLIC AND PRIVATE SECTORS
(PER CENT OF CHILDREN AND TEACHERS RESPONDING)[a]

GRADE	Milkman	Policeman	Soldier	Judge	Postman	Teacher	N Responding (varies by item)
2	29.12	86.04	68.33	86.42	56.87	48.01	1,601–1,626
3	30.77	89.11	79.16	88.35	62.74	54.95	1,627–1,656
4	28.03	90.98	83.17	88.70	71.35	58.29	1,702–1,730
5	20.54	88.99	90.18	90.45	80.02	62.65	1,778–1,792
6	16.24	87.84	93.28	91.70	85.53	64.48	1,730–1,747
7	12.85	82.47	95.52	94.16	89.02	64.03	1,697–1,718
8	8.38	80.95	98.11	93.72	93.20	59.31	1,681–1,692
TEACHERS	1.00	77.00	100.00	91.00	99.00	45.00	330–341

[a]CA-9, items 49–54.

workers, the milkman is the one (as we would expect) who is least often identified as a member of the public sector. Around 70 per cent of the youngest children were able to make an accurate assessment of his non-governmental status. From grade four on, this proportion steadily increased so that by grade eight, less than 10 per cent were in error.

For the rest, the policeman and the judge are most easily recognized as belonging in the governmental system by the youngest children. Then come the soldier, postman, and teacher in that order. Both the soldier and postman—the more nearly exclusively national government workers—increase in the proportions of children endorsing them at successively higher grade levels until, by grade eight, they are the ones who, with the judge, get the greatest governmental identification.

* * *

In general, the child in his elementary years attains the capacity to differentiate the governmental system of behavior from nongovernmental systems. . . .

There is thus sufficient content in the child's perception of government for us to have some confidence that when we now come to talk about his attitudes toward this object, it will reflect affect towards a genuinely political (that is, public) authority. It will also prove significant for our interpretation that there is even a tendency to think of government at the national rather than at the local level.

Summary of Findings on the Child's Developing Cognitive Image of Government

As a possible object toward which affect might be directed, the idea of government undergoes far-reaching changes in the cognitive development of the child as represented in our test group. As he passes through grades two to eight, he begins with a rudimentary notion in which government is personal in character, represented by a few high-ranking and visible leaders. But as he grows older, the child sees government in less personal terms. He becomes increasingly aware of its group character and its major institutions; he learns something about the norms (voting) of a representative and popular democracy. In addition, it is crucial that the child proves increasingly able to identify government as something that is different from the private sector of life, however the latter may be defined in different epochs of society. All of these things suggest that, aside from any feelings that may be associated with government, the efforts by society to convey an adequate representation of this abstract object are by no means in vain.

THE CHILD'S AFFECTIVE RESPONSE
TO GOVERNMENT

Although analytically we are able to separate the cognitive aspects of the image of government from accompanying feelings towards it, empirically they go hand in hand. For an understanding of the way in which the American political system stimulates diffuse support for the political authorities, it is critical to appreciate the fact that from the very beginning of his awareness—at its conceptually most rudimentary stage—the child interprets government as something provided to further his welfare and that of the people around him. The benevolent, protective, helpful, and otherwise good qualities of government constitute the first and continuing overall context of evaluation. Even at the end of this period—when the child is thirteen or fourteen years of age, and government and individual authorities, such as the President and the policeman, are beginning to be seen more realistically and less ideally—the child still regards them as great blessings, if slightly mixed ones.

The child thus continues to endorse government even though what he understands it to be is changing. Having started off his evaluation in highly positive terms, he seems reluctant to give it up. In this we see, perhaps, the early formation of a bond that it is hard to loosen. . . .

The Child's Approval of Government's Role

In our pilot data, we found such a uniformly favorable affective image of government, from the earliest grades onward, that we felt no special large-scale effort was necessary to deal with this in our final instrument. Yet we do have some data from our eight cities which bear upon the question. First, however, we shall present a few examples of our considerable body of pilot data

in order to show how highly consensual our young children's approval of government is over the whole grade range.

In an instrument administered to children in the Chicago area, we proposed that the children either agree or disagree with statements such as these:

1. The government is getting too big for America.
2. The government meddles too much in our private lives.
3. The government has too much power.
4. The United States government usually knows what is best for the people.
5. The government ought to give money and food to people out of work.
6. The government should have more power over the people.

. . . The patterns of response to these statements are shown in Table 5.

What we see is that children at all of these grade levels roundly approve of government. They reject, at a fairly high level of agreement (75 per cent or more), the first three statements about the scope of government becoming too large. Statements 4 and 5, on the other hand, reflect approval of the role of government in guiding and caring for the people, and these statements elicit a high level of agreement. Only for the last statement do we see any impetus toward restricting the role of government; that is, the children like it the way it is.

The over-all response is one which is better characterized as collectivist endorsement than individualistic disapproval of government. In spite of the great myth

Table 5
ATTITUDES TOWARD THE ROLE OF GOVERNMENT

GRADE	1. "The government is getting too big for America." % Agree	N	2. "The government meddles too much in our private lives." % Agree	N	3. "The government has too much power." % Agree	N	4. "The government usually knows what is best for the people." % Agree	N	5. "The government ought to give money and food to people out of work." % Agree	N	6. "The government should have more power over the people." % Agree	N
3	16	113	28	108	36	116	80	69	70	69	22	69
4	14	125	21	118	19	122	77	119	84	119	33	120
5	10	118	17	116	22	118	87	117	80	117	24	117
6	7	146	19	145	10	146	84	145	78	143	13	145
7	13	143	19	139	12	139	91	139	71	139	20	138
8	11	149	14	148	15	147	84	147	77	145	19	145

of rugged individualism which is supposed to pervade the American consciousness, these children, at least, seem to be inclined toward the opposite kind of feeling about government. Thus the child begins as something of a natural collectivist, and whatever individualistic tendencies he may exhibit are developed later on.

The sixth item suggests, moreover, that the child is likely to be a "conservative collectivist" in that he is not much in favor of extending the scope of government beyond its present limits. He is rather happy with government as it stands and would not give it "more power over the people." Thus, the child's early contentment with government is fairly complete, and it is one which exhibits the characteristics of a high acceptance of government as a given, necessary part of the natural environment. If the child is to develop discontent and a desire for change, it is undoubtedly yet to be learned. It thus will be overlaid upon an early base of high regard for the government.

The Child's Rating Of Government's Qualities

The early positive regard for the government is shown, as well, over a larger group of respondents in some ratings of the government in our final "eight cities" questionnaire. Using five role attributes and qualities of government as descriptions, we asked the child to "think of the Government as it really is." . . .

We asked for these ratings at grades four to eight. The results are shown in Table 6, page 224.

Over-all, on these five ratings approval of government is high across the grades. There is some decline for two of these ratings, however, and an increase on three. The most apparently affectively loaded item, "would want to help me if I needed it," for example, shows a greater tendency of the older child to rate the government's willingness to help him "almost always" or "usually" rather than "always." And the same is true for the somewhat affectively loaded item "makes mistakes." The more cognitively directed, role-relevant items show steady increases in the more positive categories although the perception of government's capacity to punish is seemingly never as high as the other two— "makes important decisions" and "knows more than

other people."

Perhaps the most interesting observation is that the most directly affective item, "would want to help me if I needed it," elicits a high regard for government over the whole span of grades, with a small drop of this support for the older children.

Summary of the Child's Affective Response to Government

The child's affect in this context begins high but diminishes somewhat as he learns more about the political world. He begins with deep sympathy for government, and this early aura of approval is likely to remain at the base of this acceptance of the government, whatever later modifications and limitations he puts on his trust and approval. These limited data, at least, suggest that he certainly begins with highly supportive feelings.

* * *

Notes

[1] For the idea that persistence includes change, see D. Easton, *A Framework for Political Analysis* (Englewood Cliffs, N.J.: Prentice-Hall, 1965) and *A Systems Analysis of Political Life* (New York: John Wiley & Sons, 1965).

[2] David Easton, with R. D. Hess, "The Child's Changing Image of the President," 24 *Public Opinion Quarterly*, pp. 632–644; "Youth and the Political Systems," *Culture and Social Character*, ed. S. M. Lipset and L. Lowenthal (New York: Free Press of Glencoe, 1961); and "The Child's Political World," 6 *Midwest Journal of Political Science* (1962), pp. 229–246.

The Easton and Dennis essay illustrates the conformity of the individual in relationship to the political system. In an attempt to understand how people learn to adjust to the norms required of a democratic society, researchers who use this mode of analysis have tended to concentrate on specific attitudes and values, particularly those that are oriented toward government and politics. The logic here is simple: The system is relatively democratic, and certain attitudes and values are required to support that system. Therefore, the question is: How do people learn these norms?

Typical research in the other major kind of investigation, the analysis of deviance, has emphasized the total personality. The classic research in this area of analysis, *The*

Table 6
RATINGS OF THE QUALITIES OF GOVERNMENT (PER CENT OF CHILDREN RESPONDING)

1. "Makes mistakes"

GRADE	1. Almost Never	2. Rarely	3. Sometimes	4. Often	5. Usually	6. Almost Always	Mean Rating	N Responding	N Not Responding
4	29.75	42.70	25.02	1.13	.87	.53	2.02	1,499	250
5	23.95	45.72	27.87	1.90	.39	.17	2.10	1,787	16
6	22.18	47.93	27.18	1.67	40	.63	2.12	1,740	9
7	16.78	48.89	31.59	2.21	.12	.41	2.21	1,716	7
8	13.44	45.51	38.25	2.26	.18	.36	2.31	1,681	14

2. "Would want to help me if I needed it"

GRADE	1. Always	2. Almost Always	3. Usually	4. Sometimes	5. Seldom	6. Not Usually	Mean Rating	N Responding	N Not Responding
4	25.27	31.72	23.92	11.63	5.17	2.28	2.47	1,488	261
5	16.60	31.01	27.80	16.26	5.29	2.98	2.72	1,777	26
6	16.60	31.12	28.36	16.43	4.50	3.00	2.70	1,735	14
7	15.64	29.00	30.92	15.99	5.72	2.74	2.75	1,714	9
8	13.66	28.82	32.34	15.93	6.26	2.98	2.81	1,676	19

3. "Makes important decisions"

GRADE	1. All the Time	2. A Lot of the Time	3. Sometimes	4. Seldom	5. Almost Never	6. Never	Mean Rating	N Responding	N Not Responding
4	35.01	47.93	13.92	2.21	.54	.40	1.87	1,494	255
5	38.75	46.89	12.00	1.63	.45	.28	1.79	1,783	20
6	47.70	40.39	9.78	1.32	.35	.46	1.68	1,738	11
7	54.32	35.06	8.75	1.46	.06	.35	1.59	1,714	9
8	57.81	35.16	5.72	.83	.18	.30	1.51	1,678	17

4. "Can punish"

GRADE	1. Anyone	2. Almost Anyone	3. Many People	4. Some People	5. A Few People	6. No One	Mean Rating	N Responding	N Not Responding
4	13.90	29.28	24.11	19.01	9.13	4.57	2.94	1,489	260
5	13.68	33.67	25.45	16.61	6.53	4.05	2.81	1,776	27
6	19.83	31.82	23.29	14.47	6.22	4.38	2.69	1,735	14
7	22.46	31.79	23.75	13.43	5.34	3.23	2.57	1,705	18
8	26.44	30.58	21.28	12.83	5.52	3.36	2.50	1,668	27

5. "Knows"

GRADE	1. More Than Anyone	2. More Than Most People	3. More Than Many People	4. Less Than Many People	5. Less Than Most	6. Less Than Anyone	Mean Rating	N Responding	N Not Responding
4	13.68	44.67	36.35	2.88	1.41	1.01	2.37	1,491	258
5	11.35	52.11	33.56	1.46	.79	.73	2.30	1,779	24
6	14.02	52.05	29.95	2.25	.75	.98	2.27	1,733	16
7	16.05	54.09	27.34	1.65	.53	.35	2.18	1,701	22
8	15.34	58.24	23.83	1.56	.60	.42	2.15	1,662	33

Authoritarian Personality, was published in 1950. The authors of this research report began by saying:

The research to be reported in this volume was guided by the following major hypothesis; that the political, economic, and social convictions of an individual often form a broad and coherent pattern, as if bound together by a "mentality" or "spirit," and that this pattern is an expression of deep-lying trends in his personality.[2]

The study of the authoritarian personality arose from a deep concern among social scientists about the events that had occurred in fascist countries, in particular the rise of the Nazi movement in Germany. They had witnessed the destruction of the Weimar republic and its conversion to a fascist regime that encouraged barbarism as a national goal for the German people. The problem for these social scientists was to discover if there were attributes of human personality that led people to become susceptible to such appeals by their leaders.

Max Horkheimer, in a preface to the research report, claimed that the researchers had focused on a new type of man. He says:

The central theme of the work is a relatively new concept—the rise of an "anthropological" species we call the authoritarian type of man. In contrast to the bigot of the older style he seems to combine the ideas and skills which are typical of a highly industrialized society with irrational or anti-rational beliefs. He is at the same time enlightened and superstitious, proud to be an individualist and in constant fear of not being like all the others, jealous of his independence and inclined to submit blindly to power and authority.[3]

Although the thesis generated a great deal of debate, the controversy primarily concerned the methods of research rather than the findings. It is not possible to review all of the subsequent literature here, but it is possible to derive some generalizations.

Three questions will help to organize these generalizations concerning the non-democratic personality. First,

what does the non-democratic person think and feel about himself? Second, how does such a person relate to others? Finally, how does this person conceptualize society in general?

There is considerable agreement among researchers about what the non-democratic personality thinks and feels about himself: Usually, he does not like himself. Researchers have referred to this basic self-dislike as low self-esteem, low ego-strength, lack of self-acceptance, or weak self-identity. Research suggests that such personalities, in relating to others, tend to divide the world as "we" and "they." Such people can be accepting and submissive toward those who are considered to be "we," but at the same time may be aggressive and hostile toward those who are "they." The non-democratic person tends to like power and toughness in others; he has trouble trusting others and forming relationships with them unless the relationship involves submission.

Finally, how does the non-democratic person think about society? Here, the research suggests that because the person does not like himself and has difficulty in relating to others, he tends to dislike society as well. Although he dislikes and mistrusts society generally, he seems predisposed to adhere rigidly to the conventional norms and traditions of the society. In his attempt to escape his fear of others, he conforms to generally shared expectations.

In all, the sketch of the non-democratic personality presents a dismal view of a person who dislikes himself to such an extent that he projects his own fears to others, and hates them. What he finds within himself is not acceptable, so he turns to some other definition of self, which can be provided by authoritative sources such as a social movement or socially defined success roles. He trades his non-acceptable self for a more acceptable social image provided by some authoritative source. This analysis suggests that the personality of the non-democratic man is, indeed, a source of major instability and non-support of a democratic social order.

Research concerned with the non-democratic personality has greatly outweighed the research on democratic individuals. Generally, the findings about democratic people are much more speculative, and there is less agreement. The democratic person tends to have an accurate and acceptable self-image. He usually likes himself. Because he does not have internal emotional problems that would cause him to project his fears to others, he can have more honest and

[2] T. W. Adorno *et al., The Authoritarian Personality* (New York: Harper & Row, 1950), p. 1.

[3] Ibid., p. ix.

open relationships with others. As a result he can be more trusting of others and, in turn, more trusting of the society as a whole.

In the following article, Fred Greenstein reviews the literature on these types of personalities and suggests some research questions that may help to understand how people can be taught to live in a democratic social order.

PERSONALITY AND POLITICAL SOCIALIZATION

FRED I. GREENSTEIN

The socialization experiences which culminate in adult citizenship can be divided into two rough categories: that learning which is specifically about government and politics, and non-political personal development which affects political behavior. My concern here is with a particularly controversial, but intriguing, portion of the topics arising in the second category—the notions of "authoritarian" and "democratic" character. In addition to reviewing theory and research on these character types, I will discuss briefly several of the problems involved in untangling the complex connections among personal character, political beliefs, political action, and the functioning of political and other social institutions. . . .

Put bluntly, the questions which concern us are: "Can we distinguish types of individuals whose personal make-up—apart from their specifically political beliefs—disposes them to act in a democratic or an authoritarian manner?" "What socialization practices produce such individuals?" "What can be said about the circumstances under which the actual behavior of such individuals will be democratic or authoritarian, and about the aggregate effects which individuals with democratic or authoritarian dispositions may have on the functioning of political institutions?"

Reprinted from "Personality and Political Socialization: The Theories of Authoritarian and Democratic Character." pp. 81–95, in volume no. 361 of The Annals of The American Academy of Political and Social Sciences. Copyright 1965 by The American Academy of Political and Social Sciences.

THE STUDY OF AUTHORITARIAN AND DEMOCRATIC CHARACTER

There is, by far, more literature on authoritarian than on democratic character. One of the wonders of recent social science scholarship has been the profusion of "Authoritarianism" research in the past decade and a half. An admittedly selective review of writings on the topic through 1956 contained 260 bibliographical references.[1] . . .

The main immediate stimulus for this explosion of research was the publication in 1950 of a 990-page volume by T. W. Adorno, Else Frenkel-Brunswik, Nevitt Sanford, and Daniel J. Levinson, entitled *The Authoritarian Personality*,[2] which reported the fruits of several years of investigation into the psychology of anti-Semitism. On the basis of a rich but bewilderingly varied and uneven assortment of research procedures, the authors of this work reached a striking conclusion about the psychology of hostility to Jews and other minority groups. Such prejudiced attitudes, they argued, were not simply beliefs which people happened to have acquired. Rather, one could identify what might be called a "bigot personality,"[3] a type of individual with deep-seated psychological needs which manifested themselves in a variety of ways over and beyond ethnic prejudice. *The Authoritarian Personality* is a book dealing more with prejudice than with the problem suggested by its title—psychological dispositions toward authority . . .

* * *

There is, of course, nothing new in the awareness that some people are more deferential toward authority than others and that the same people often are harsh to their subordinates. . . .

What *is* new in the twentieth-century literature on authoritarianism is the specification of a constellation of psychological correlates of this tendency and the elaboration of a theory of its psychodynamics and genesis. . . . Underlying all of these discussions was what still is probably the most revolutionary facet of twentieth-century social science—psychoanalysis—and, particularly, several overlapping elements in Freud's thought:

the notion of the anal character, his analyses of obsessional neuroses and of paranoia, and his delineation of the mechanism of projection. (The dependence of the conception of authoritarianism upon a personality theory that places such a great emphasis on the significance of childhood experience makes authoritarianism a particularly strong candidate for discussion in a symposium on political socialization.)

The Authoritarian Personality, therefore, served to focus attention on hypotheses which had been in the air for some time, rather than to suggest completely new hypotheses. But it did something more—and this seems to have been especially important in spurring the subsequent research. The section of the book devoted to "measurement of ideological trends" provided a number of "ready-made tests that had already been taken through many of the technical procedures of validation which every [psychological] test must pass,"[4] the most notable and widely used of these being the F- (fascism) scale. . . .

In contrast to the several paragraphs required simply to make peremptory reference to the intellectual history of authoritarian personality study, the state of investigation into democratic personality can be briefly stated. There has been some theorizing on this topic and virtually no research. No one, to my knowledge, has attempted to devise and use a D- (democratic) scale. . . . I shall concentrate mainly on what seems to me to be an especially interesting discussion of the topic, an essay by Harold Lasswell which, I think, has not received the attention it merits.[5]

*   *   *

AUTHORITARIAN CHARACTER

Three general distinctions appropriate for setting forth a typology of personality are: phenomenology, dynamics, and genesis. In other words, first we may take note of all of the psychological characteristics composing the type which, with a minimum of inferential interpretation, are readily observable. Then we summarize our hypotheses about the processes underlying the observables. How are the observed features related to

each other? What ties them together? Finally, we assemble the hypotheses which are most relevant to the present essay: What accounts for the development of this type of individual? How does he arise in the socialization process?

*   *   *

Phenomenology of the Authoritarian

. . . Most central for our purposes is the pair of traits labeled "authoritarian aggression" and "authoritarian submission"—the dominance-submissiveness tendencies of the authoritarian. . . . "German folklore," Adorno relates, "has a drastic symbol for this"— bicyclist's personality *(Radfahrernaturen):* "Above they bow, below they kick."[6]

Also politically relevant is the tendency of such individuals to *think* in power terms, to be acutely sensitive to questions of who dominates whom. Only at a slightly further remove from politics is the pervasive rigidity in the authoritarian's manner of confronting the world. He is, in Else Frenkel-Brunswik's phrase, "intolerant of ambiguity."[7] He likes order and is made uncomfortable by disorder: where the phenomena he is exposed to are complex and subtle, he imposes his own tight categories upon them, ignoring their nuances. His thinking therefore makes more than the usual use of stereotypes. Another of the traits composing the character type is "conventionalism." The authoritarian, much like Riesman's "radar-controlled" other-directed personality,[8] is described as being particularly sensitive to "external agencies" and, especially, to the prevailing standards of his own social group.

The foregoing authoritarian traits, all of which can be seen to have some rather immediate potential bearing on behavior in the political arena, hang together in a fashion which puts little strain on our common sense: dominance of subordinates; deference toward superiors; sensitivity to power relationships; need to perceive the world in a highly structured fashion; excessive use of stereotypes; and adherence to whatever values are conventional in one's setting. . . . But what is perhaps most intriguing about the authoritarian syndrome is that several further, less obvious, traits are found as a part of the presenting symptoms.

These rather exotic additional concomitants lead us beyond phenomenology to the psychoanalytically based theory of dynamics. For example, the authoritarian is described as being superstitious. (One of the items of the F-scale is: "Although many people may scoff, it may yet be shown that astrology can explain a lot of things.") He is preoccupied with virility, tending toward "exaggerated assertion of strength and toughness." (While this trait might be juxtaposed with the authoritarian's interest in power, there is the added element here of being hard-boiled and rugged. The equivalent trait in the less well-developed typology of female authoritarianism is "pseudo-femininity"—a preoccupation with being "feminine and soft.") The authoritarian assumptions about human nature are generally pessimistic, and he tends to be cynical about the motives of others. He is disposed to believe that "wild and dangerous things go on in the world"—that "the world is a jungle." He shows a puritanical preoccupation with sex—a "concern with sexual 'goings on'" and "a strong inclination to punish violators of sex mores." And, finally, he shows a trait of which much is made in the theoretical explanation of this pattern—"anti-intraception." This is "an attitude of impatience with and opposition to the subjective and the tender-minded." One of its more conspicuous forms is an inability to introspect, to acknowledge one's own feelings and fantasies.

* * *

Dynamics of Authoritarianism

. . . The authoritarian, it is argued, is an individual with strong, but ambivalent, dispositions toward figures of authority. Denial of the negative side of these feelings is central to such an individual's functioning. The authoritarian is able to conceal from himself his rage toward those in authority only by the massive defense procedure reaction formation, involving a total repression of critical and other unacceptable impulses toward authority and a bending over backwards in excessive praise of it.[9] But repression has its costs and side-effects, and

repressed impulses seek alternative outlets. Hostility not only is rechanneled toward whoever is perceived as weak and unauthoritative, but also has a more diffuse effect on the authoritarian's generally negative views of man and his works, as well as contributing to his need to scan his environment for signs of authority relationships, his tendency (via projection) to see the world as full of dangerous things and people, and his desire to punish others, for example, sex offenders, who have surrendered to their impulses. Feelings of personal weakness are covered by a façade of toughness. A side-effect of channeling enormous energy into repression and reaction formation is that the authoritarian's emotional capacities and even certain of his cognitive capacities are stunted. He is unable to face the prospect of canvassing his own psyche—for fear of what such introspection may yield—and therefore becomes highly dependent upon external sources of guidance.[10]

This general theis about authoritarian dynamics might be called the ego-defensive theory of authoritarianism. After the fashion of classical psychoanalysis, the theory places great emphasis on irrationality—on how the self, in seeking to maintain inner equilibrium (that is, to defend against impulses and conscience), is flawed in its perception of and response to the environment. Since the empirical standing of psychoanalysis continues to be controversial, it is not difficult to understand why this aspect of authoritarian theory is less settled than the question of phenomenology.[11]

It is quite possible to accept the phenomenological typology of authoritarianism and reject the ego-defensive thesis of its dynamics. This, in effect, has been done by several commentators who present what might be called a *cognitive* theory of authoritarianism. The cognitive theory holds that the patterns of expression and behavior that have been characterized as authoritarian are based upon simple learning of the conceptions of reality prevalent in one's culture or subculture, and that these patterns also may to some extent be accurate reflections of the actual conditions of adult life faced by some individuals, rather than having the labyrinthine roots in reaction formation suggested by the ego-defensive theory.[12] . . .

The Genesis of Authoritarianism

* * *

The Authoritarian Personality . . . concentrates on elucidating the childhood antecedents of ego-defensive authoritarianism. The typical early determinants of this pattern come as no surprise in the light of the theory of underlying dynamics.

When we consider the childhood situation . . . we find reports of a tendency toward rigid discipline on the part of the parents, with affection which is conditional rather than unconditional, i.e., dependent upon approved behavior on the part of the child. Related to this is a tendency . . . to base [family] interrelationships in rather clearly defined roles of dominance and submission . . . Forced into a surface submission to parental authority, the child develops hostility and aggression which are poorly channelized. The displacement of a repressed antagonism toward authority may be one of the sources, and perhaps the principal source, of his antagonism toward outgroups.[13]

The authors derived these and similar conclusions about how ego-defensive authoritarianism arises in the socialization process partly from their subjects' retrospective reports of childhood experiences, but also from direct studies by Frenkel-Brunswik of ethnically prejudiced and unprejudiced children. The studies of children suggested that "warmer, closer and more affectionate interpersonal relationships prevail in the homes of the unprejudiced children" and that prejudice was associated with "strictness, rigidity, punitiveness, rejection vs. acceptance of the child."

. . . It is the Freudian emphasis on early childhood socialization that occupies most of the discussion in *The Authoritarian Personality* of how authoritarianism is socialized. But occasionally a Marxian explanation of the genesis of authoritarianism appears, as in the final paragraph of the volume where the authors remark that "people are continuously molded from above because they must be molded if the overall economic pattern is to be maintained."[14] The point being made here is evidently that of Fromm, who in *Escape from Freedom*

develops, *inter alia*, a conception of "social character" as that which "internalizes external necessities and thus harnesses human energy for the task of a given economic and social system;" a conception of the authoritarian character as the energy source in the development of Western capitalism (in contrast to Weber's Protestant Ethic); and a conception of the family as, in effect, mainly a transmission belt providing the system the type of personality it "requires."[15] Apart from whatever merit there may be in Fromm's specific historical argument, we have here a further class of explanatory factors—overlapping the references to culture in the cognitive model—which may be introduced to explain the genesis of authoritarianism, namely, social structure and social role requirements.[16]

* * *

DEMOCRATIC CHARACTER

Lasswell's essay "Democratic Character," like the discussion which has just preceded, is essentially typological. In effect, he elaborates a hypothetical construct, in part from the existing research on the antidemocratic character, in part by deductions from an analysis of the role requirements of democratic society. The main general features of the psychological typology are a "self-system" (the individual's conscious orientations, which consist of his cognitive assumptions, his preferences, and his identifications), an "energy-system" (roughly equivalent to the Freudian unconscious, composed of conscience, ego ideals, and drives), and a special definition of the term "character," as "the self-system of the person, together with the degree of support, opposition or nonsupport received from the unconscious parts of the personality." "Character" therefore acquires the dimension of strength and weakness, much as in lay usage. "When we say that a man is of steadfast character it is implied that he has sufficient command of the resources of the whole personality to maintain the self-system despite environing conditions which are adverse."[17]

At the cognitive level, the democratic character believes in the benevolent potentialities of mankind, rejecting the authoritarian's more Hobbesian conception of human nature. The democrat's preferences are consistent with the role requirements in the model of the democratic social system—that is, he *wants* to behave in the ways he should behave, if the functioning of the democratic system is to be successful. Furthermore, he is a "multi-valued" moderate who can weigh alternative goals against each other, rather than an absolutist in pursuit of a single value who, because of his inability to compromise, might endanger the stability of the system. And it is especially important that the democratic character be free of the pursuit of power as a single end-in-itself. In addition, the democrat's identifications are broad and comprehensive—Lasswell speaks of the "open ego"—unlike the good guys-bad guys pattern of the authoritarian.

This pattern of conscious perspectives, Lasswell points out, might well be found among individuals who at the unconscious level had antidemocratic inclinations and, particularly, destructive, power-seeking, or self-punishing tendencies. Referring, in effect, to the curiously labeled "rigid low scorer" of the authoritarian studies, Lasswell acknowledges that

democratic responses often arise from motivations which are incompatible with . . . [democracy], and signify that the individual has achieved part of his democratic outlook by 'reaction formation' against tendencies of an opposite kind. Many democrats appear to develop in opposition to anti-democratic parents, for example.

While he grants that "the destructive energies of a person may be directed against enemies of the democratic community," he nevertheless excludes the democrat-by-reaction formation from his typology, since "from the point of view of modern personality research, the characters which are achieved by a complex process of balanced defense are viewed as constituting less enduring formations than those which evolve more directly."[18] On the matter of socialization, Lasswell comments that "there is reason to believe that in some cultures the possibility of developing an outgoing democratic character is excluded at an early period. The prevailing patterns of child care appear to induce early despair that profound gratifications can emanate from other human beings."[19] The concluding sections of the essay are directly addressed to the problem of how to socialize democratic characters.

* * *

Notes

[1] Richard Christie and Peggy Cook, "A Guide to Published Literature Relating to the Authoritarian Personality through 1956," *The Journal of Psychology*, Vol. 45 (April 1958), pp. 171–199.

[2] T. W. Adorno *et al.*, *The Authoritarian Personality* (New York: Harper, 1950), hereafter cited as *AP*.

[3] A phrase used in a prepublication report of the study to the general public: Jerome Himelhoch, "Is There a Bigot Personality?" *Commentary*, Vol. 3 (March 1947), pp. 277–284.

[4] Nathan Glazer, "New Light on 'The Authoritarian Personality,'" *Commentary*, Vol. 17 (March 1954), p. 290.

[5] Harold D. Lasswell, "Democratic Character," in *The Political Writings of Harold D. Lasswell* (Glencoe, Ill.: Free Press, 1951), pp. 465–525, hereafter cited as *DC*. Also see Karl Mannheim, *Freedom, Power and Democratic Planning* (London: Oxford University Press, 1950), pp. 228–245; Christian Bay, *The Structure of Freedom* (Stanford, Calif.: Stanford University Press, 1958), pp. 155–239; Alex Inkeles, "National Character and Modern Political Systems," *Psychological Anthropology*, ed. Francis Hsu (Homewood, Ill.: Dorsey Press, 1961), pp. 172–209; Robert E. Lane, *Political Ideology* (New York: Free Press of Glencoe, 1962), pp. 400–412.

[6] T. W. Adorno, "Freudian Theory and the Pattern of Fascist Propaganda." *Psychoanalysis and the Social Sciences*. ed. Géza Róheim, Vol. VII (New York, 1951), p. 291n. My discussion of authoritarian traits is based on *AP*, chap. 7 and *passim* and the Sanford discussion referred to in note 4. The latter is perhaps the single most concise and comprehensive exposition by an *AP* contributor.

[7] Else Frenkel-Brunswik, "Intolerance of Ambiguity as an Emotional and Perceptual Personality Variable," *Journal of Personality*, Vol. 18 (September 1949), pp. 108–143.

[8] David Riesman, with Nathan Glazer and Reuel Denney, *The Lonely Crowd* (New Haven: Yale University Press, 1950).

[9] The authoritarian type is described as having repressed sexual as well as hostile impulses, but the significance of repressed sexuality in authoritarianism does not seem to have been fully explicated. At points in the *AP*, the implication seems to be simply that the authoritarian has acceded to parental taboos concerning sexuality. At other points (for example, p. 798), the implication is that the repressed sexual impulses are toward the parents and particularly the father. The latter, more classically psychoanalytic construction, is developed in some detail by Fromm in the work cited in note 9 (pp. 77–135, English abstract, pp. 908–911). See especially his discussion of sado-masochism.

[10] Dependence upon external guidance provides the common element in several of the surface manifestations of authoritarianism, which at first glance seem not to be related to each other: conventionality (accepting the prevailing values in one's environment); stereotypy (accepting the prevailing descriptive categories); superstition (belief that we are controlled from without by mysteri-

ous agencies); intolerance of ambiguity and use of rigid categories (discomfort when the environment provides few guideposts for thought and action).

[11] For two recent discussions designed to reduce polemic and seek empirical clarification of the issues underlying the controversial status of psychoanalysis, see B. A. Farrell, "The Status of Psychoanalytic Theory," *Inquiry*, Vol. 7 (Spring 1964), pp. 104–123; Peter Madison, *Freud's Concept of Repression and Defense: Its Theoretical and Observational Language* (Minneapolis: University of Minnesota Press, 1961). A number of interesting investigations based on the ego-defensive theory of authoritarian dynamics have been reported. For example, Herbert C. Schulberg, "Insight, Authoritarianism and Tendency to Agree," *Journal of Nervous and Mental Disease*, Vol. 135 (December 1962), pp. 481–488.

[12] See the essay by Hyman and Sheatsley in *SSMAP* (esp., p. 91 ff: Herbert H. Hyman, *Political Socialization* (Glencoe, Ill.: Free Press, 1959), p. 47; S. M. Miller and Frank Riessmann, "'Working-Class Authoritarianism:, A Critique of Lipset," *British Journal of Sociology*, Vol. 12 (September 1961), pp. 263–276. I take the ego-defensive versus cognitive distinction from the recent literature on the functions served by opinions for the personality: M. Brewster Smith *et al.*, *Opinions and Personality* (New York: John Wiley & Sons, 1956), chap. 3; Daniel Katz, "The Functional Approach to the Study of Attitudes," *Public Opinion Quarterly*, Vol. 24 (Summer 1960), pp. 163–204.

[13] Adorno op. cit., pp. 482–483.

[14] Ibid., p. 976.

[15] See especially the appendix to *Escape from Freedom* on "Character and the Social Process," pp. 277–299.

[16] There is, of course, nothing incompatible between explanations of authoritarianism in terms of family socialization and explanations in terms of social structure. Nor need the latter be exclusively in economic terms. Evidence of the effects of the socioeconomic organization of a society on its members' personality characteristics is now becoming available from a study of personality differences between farmers and herders in four East African tribes. Two preliminary reports are Walter Goldschmidt, "Theory and Strategy in the Study of Cultural Adaptability," *American Anthropologist*, Vol. 67 (April 1965), pp. 402–408 and Robert B. Edgerton, "'Cultural' vs. 'Ecological' Factors in the Expression of Values, Attitudes, and Personality Characteristics," Ibid., pp. 442–447.

[17] Lasswell, op. cit., p. 428.

[18] Ibid., pp. 506–507

[19] Ibid., p. 497.

The material surveyed to this point has considered how the mass of people in society can be socialized to accept the norms and values that support and stabilize society. Whether the literature focuses on specific attitudes and values or on the underlying personality of the individual, the basic assumption appears to be that the social order itself is acceptable and that the most serious problem is how to adjust people to fit that social order.

Another kind of literature concerning the relationship of individuals to mass society, drawn largely from disciplines other than political science, has examined the nature of social structures that contribute to the development of *unhealthy* people. Rather than assuming the soundness or perfectibility of society, these researchers propose that society is often a source of human problems rather than a cure.

LEARNING TO CHANGE

Researchers who have been influenced by humanistic sociology and psychology have recently begun to consider how people learn to change, rather than how they learn to conform. Clearly, the assumptions of this research have been that social and political structures must be fitted to human needs, and that people should not be adjusted to the imperatives of any social, political, or economic structure.

This attack on the basic integrity of our system has resulted largely from analyses of human alienation, by sociologists, and of human potential, by humanistic psychologists. These analyses have taken their most concrete form in the argument that mass democracy as a social, political, and economic structure requires adjustments from individuals that amount to mass neurosis. Presumably, then, those people who have successfully adjusted to the social system have become neurotic in the process. The norm is neurosis rather than individual health. Erich Fromm articulates this position clearly in his book *The Sane Society*:

To speak of a whole society as lacking in mental health implies a controversial assumption contrary to the position of sociological relativism held by most social scientists today. They postulate that each society is normal inasmuch as it functions, and that pathology can be defined only in terms of the individual's lack of adjustment to the ways of life in his society.

To speak of a "sane society" implies a premise different from sociological relativism. It makes sense only if we assume that there can be a society which is not sane, and this assumption, in turn, implies that there are universal criteria for mental health which are valid for the human race as such, and according to which the state of health of each society can be judged.[4]

This thought suggests that the emphasis for research should be placed on how people relate to social structures that are constantly changing to meet the needs and wants

[4] Erich Fromm, *The Sane Society* (Greenwich, Conn.: Fawcett, 1965), p. 21.

of people, instead of on either conformity or deviance.

A view that tends to emphasize the social order as being either facilitative, or inhibitive, of individual development and health represents a profound contrast to the notion that social structure is the source of the good life for individuals. As long as individuals are being adjusted to any social order, they are not really dealing with their own needs and motivations. There is a trend, then, to see social structure as a source of neurosis rather than of health in individuals.

The studies of socialization reviewed previously tended toward psychoanalytic and behavioristic viewpoints, while the literature considered here has been influenced primarily by studies in humanistic psychology. It is not as easy to identify these influences with a particular set of integrated theoretical positions, but there are central arguments that have been generally associated with this position.

One of the leading spokesmen for humanistic psychology is Fromm, and we can do no better than to quote him directly. Much of his basic viewpoint is contained in the following passage:

> . . . that mental health cannot be defined in terms of the "adjustment" of the individual to his society, but, on the contrary, that it must be defined in terms of the adjustment of society to the needs of man, of its role in furthering or hindering the development of mental health. Whether or not the individual is healthy, is primarily not an individual matter, but depends on the structure of his society. A healthy society furthers man's capacity to love his fellow men, to work creatively, to develop his reason and objectivity, to have a sense of self which is based on the experience of his own productive powers. An unhealthy society is one which creates mutual hostility, distrust, which transforms man into an instrument of use and exploitation for others, which deprives him of a sense of self, except inasmuch as he submits to others or becomes an automaton.[5]

This set of assumptions and theoretical perspectives has directed researchers' attention to different kinds of questions. Rather than attempting to discover the roots of stability and adjustment in the family, schools, and work place or among peers and authorities, analysts have investigated the sources that develop human potentiality and change society. This research leads to a specific question: To what extent do particular social structures and conditions facilitate or inhibit human development? Researchers guided by this perspective have analyzed different central problems. They have analyzed the impact on people of the social imperatives that are required for the continuation of the social order. The research has focused on analysis of the human needs and motivations that are required for the development of healthy people, regardless of the social context in which they live. What is there about the mass, technological society that leads many theorists to fear that postindustrial society has become a breeding ground for human degradation rather than human development and health?

Various social philosophers have attempted to characterize the problems. Among the major works are Jacques Ellul's *The Technological Society*, Herbert Marcuse's *One-Dimensional Man*, and John Kenneth Galbraith's *The New Industrial State*. There appears to be a common theme to these descriptions of modern society: *that technology has become the goal of social development rather than the means of bringing about human development.* Modern industrial societies have acquired a set of social values that are imperative for the continuation of those societies: The development and expansion of technology is no longer a means of producing the good life for individuals in the society, but has become the goal of existence in the society itself. Robert Merton, in a preface to Ellul's book, summarizes this thesis: " . . . every part of a technical civilization responds to the social needs generated by technique itself. Progress then consists in progressive de-humanization—a busy, pointless, and, in the end, suicidal submission to technique."[6]

John Kenneth Galbraith has helped to clarify this argument by showing how it applies to the economics of a technological society.[7] He notes that, because corporations invest large amounts of time, talent, and capital in the preparation of a mass-produced product, they by necessity become deeply involved in planning and controlling the consumption of the item as well as its production. Such corporations cannot tolerate the risks of the traditional marketplace.

The marketplace, in traditional economics, required the producer to take the risk that his product might not appeal

---

[5] Ibid., p. 71.

[6] Robert Merton, "Preface," in Jacques Ellul, *The Technological Society* trans. (New York: Vintage Books, translated by John Wilkinson 1969; first published 1959), p. viii.

[7] J. K, Galbraith, *The New Industrial State* (New York: Signet Books, 1967).

to the consumer. High profits were the incentive for taking such risks. But large corporations, having spent vast sums in the preparation of an item, cannot be expected to take such risks if they are to survive. A single loss would be so great as to nearly destroy the corporation. Therefore, corporations are not so much interested in maximizing profits as they are in minimizing losses. They can better minimize their losses by controlling the processes of production and consumption.

A corporation may gain substantial control of the resources required to produce its product, thus reducing variations in the price of raw materials. It may also attempt to control the outlets for its products, thus reducing competition and stabilizing the retail price of the product. Another strategy is to acquire a government subsidy for the development, production, and consumption of products. Defense contracting, for example, permits manufacturers to develop highly complex weapon systems under government-financed contracts, and then sell these weapons to the government for profit. Still another strategy is to use the mass media to advertise products in such a way that consumers will feel that they need them.

If one accepts this analysis of the economic process as being motivated primarily by attempts to minimize loss rather than to maximize profits, there emerges a very different notion of the relationship of corporations to the marketplace of individual consumers. No longer are corporations motivated to produce items that appeal to consumer needs. They are motivated to produce items that have a predictable market and can be sold regardless of needs. It is in their interest to determine what the consumer needs to the extent that this is possible.

One clear outcome of this analysis, for individuals, is that corporations in a society are now motivated by the goals of expanding their operations and control rather than producing items that meet human needs. They have become oriented totally to the goals and techniques necessary for the survival of the organization.

Individuals do not have any need for corporations to become larger, for manufacturers to tool their plants for making weapons that are outdated before they are produced, or for the tons of gadgets that flow from the giant production-consumption process. Indeed, there seems to be a direct incompatibility between the goals of corporations and the needs of individuals in the society. How is it that individuals adjust themselves to accept the goals of these organizations as their own human needs? Why do people join the ever-expanding consumption-production process, when so much of what is being produced and consumed is irrelevant to their real needs?

Philip Slater's *The Pursuit of Loneliness* provides persuasive answers to these questions.[8] Slater's argument is that society has maintained the consumption-production orientation by relying on a "scarcity culture," in which children are raised to believe that whatever is gratifying to their needs is scarce. Instead of being given acceptance, security, and love, children are taught to pursue the scarcities: wealth, status, and material goods. The combination of these factors creates people who are willing to strive endlessly in the consumption-production process, as both workers and consumers, while at the same time the needs for affection and support that they were deprived of as children are never really satisfied. They become perpetual-motion machines, which propel the society but do little to develop human potentiality. Society, in this view, has become one in which organizational goals and requirements have been substituted for individual needs and motivations.

Another reason for this situation is that individuals in our society have little or no understanding of what their own human needs really are. Thus, it becomes easier to accept the expectations of society as a means of individual fulfillment. Adopting the social expectations of pursuing wealth, status, and power in order to become successful becomes more likely, in a context where people have little self-awareness of what they really need to do to become better human beings.

More than anyone else, Abraham Maslow has contributed to the theoretical understanding of the need structure of individuals.[9] Without attempting to go into great detail about his general argument, it is possible to clarify what Maslow refers to as a "need hierarchy" in individuals. He suggests that there are five basic categories of human needs: 1) physiological needs, for food, water, shelter, sex, and sleep;

[8] Philip Slater, *The Pursuit of Loneliness* (Boston: Beacon Press, 1970), particularly pp. 81–95.

[9] Abraham H. Maslow, "A Theory of Metamotivation," in *The Age of Protest*, edited by Walt Anderson (Pacific Palisades, Calif.: Goodyear Publishing, 1969) pp. 246–254.

2) safety needs, for order and stability; 3) belongingness and love needs; 4) esteem needs, for self-respect and the respect of others; and 5) self-actualization needs.

According to Maslow, the human is a biological organism that must strive to satiate each level of need in the order of its occurrence in the need hierarchy. As the person satisfies the first category of needs, he is motivated to satisfy the next level. Maslow considers the lower needs that must be satisfied as being "deficiency" needs and the higher levels of needs as "metamotivations." Both kinds of needs are biologically rooted and are necessary for human survival and growth. Regardless of whether one accepts the particular categories that Maslow suggests, the idea that there is a biological necessity involved in the actions of individuals to actualize themselves, in the same sense that there is a biological need to eat, is provocative. In this view, needs to belong, to associate with others, and to have self esteem are not altruistic desires of individuals, but requirements that they as biological organisms must satisfy in order to survive.

Putney and Putney, in *The Adjusted American,* help to clarify some of this analysis of human needs.[10] They divide individual needs into physical and self needs. (This is similar to Maslow's distinction between deficiency needs and metamotivations.) Putney and Putney argue that neurosis develops in our society largely because people do not have an accurate understanding of their needs, which leads them to behavior that does little to satisfy those needs, and this creates anxiety from constant deprivation.

THE ANALYSIS OF CHANGE

It is more than a little curious that, as one surveys the literature dealing with political change, it becomes clear that the bulk of this analysis focuses on historical situations or on the so-called underdeveloped countries of Latin America, Africa, or Asia. What this emphasis indicates is that change is apparently not considered to be a relevant concept in understanding industrially developed mass democracy. Change is relevant only to how this country developed into its present stage and to countries that are "less developed" than our own. Thus, analysts seek to understand the conditions that will permit underdeveloped societies to become

more like our own society.

As a preface to the discussion of the analysis of change in contemporary political science, the following brief essay by Lucien W. Pye evidences the influence of the invisible ideology.

DEMOCRACY AND POLITICAL DEVELOPMENT

LUCIAN W. PYE

* * *

. . . constitutional democracy is a peculiarly Western institution, and few questions relating to contemporary public affairs are more puzzling and more fundamentally disturbing than that of whether Western political forms and ideals are appropriate or even relevant for the new states of Africa and Asia. Is it reasonable to ask impatient new states, anxious to speed up all the processes of economic and social development, to rely upon democratic institutions and procedures? What is the best way of achieving the modernization of old societies? And is there any relationship between modernization and democracy, and between democracy and nation-building? And finally that most fundamental and disturbing question: Is a commitment to liberal democratic values likely to be a major handicap in nation-building? Doesn't the situation call for hardheaded and singleminded leadership?

DEMOCRACY AND THE NEED FOR ECONOMIC GROWTH

It may be useful to begin our discussion of democracy and political development by frankly confronting the basic argument that new states cannot "afford" democracy because they must place a prior value on economic growth. The assumption behind this point of view is that rapid economic development is likely to be retarded by a pluralistic political system. More specifi-

---

[10] Snell Putney and Gail J. Putney, *The Adjusted American* (New York: Harper & Row, 1964), particularly pp. 12-36.

Abridged from *Aspects of Political Development,* Lucian W. Pye, pp. 71-88. Copyright © 1966 by Little Brown and Company (Inc.). Reprinted by permission.

cally, the widespread belief is that efficiency in the allocation of resources and the necessary discipline in controlling current consumption in order to create the needed savings are more likely in one-party systems where there is a minimum of competitive politics. Presumably partisan politicians in competing for electorial support will cater to the people and will not demand of them the sacrifices and postponements of gratifications necessary for national development. And this is believed to be particularly likely with an illiterate and inexperienced electorate. This point of view classifies democracy as a luxury which can best be afforded only after the big push for development. This is also the argument which Indians frequently make when picturing themselves as taking on the tremendous task of raising the standards of living under the handicap of democratic methods.

It has been our contention . . . that most transitional societies will realize more effective administration only if they broaden and more explicitly organize the non-bureaucratic components of the political process. We are prepared to recognize that under certain very special and limited conditions there may be some advantages in highly centralized authoritarian methods. . . . In general, however, these conditions do not obtain in most transitional societies, and, as we have observed, the fear of many elites about divisive forces often stems from threats to their own monopoly of power and not to the basic unity of the country. On the contrary, it can be argued that at present in most situations rapid economic growth is more likely to be stimulated by a reduction in authoritarian practices and an increase in popular participation in the nation-building process. It should be remembered that the history of most backward societies is that of authoritarian rule.

The argument for a one-party system and for administrative rule tends greatly to oversimplify the problem of economic development by assuming that development hinges largely on a more rational allocation of resources. In any society the political system must cope with a wide range of demands. Even a one-party system must expend energy and resources in dealing with such demands. It is significant, however, most demands do not entail issues about allocation of material resources. Just the process of participation in a pluralistic system

can satisfy the search for identity of large numbers of people and thereby reduce the number of demands which might involve economically relevant resources. On the other hand, a one-party system, oriented primarily to economic development, may find that it can take care of demands only by decisions affecting the use of economic resources. Under such conditions many groups within the society may translate their aspirations into economic terms and thus place an excessive strain on the limited resources of the country.

The goal of economic development can often be better realized if the functional requirements of the political system for integration and for adjustment are met by participation in competitive politics. When the gratification of the goals of economic development becomes also the prime means for realizing the functions of integration and adaptation, the result is likely to be a less efficient approach to the objective of development.

It is of course a part of the democratic ethos to believe that somehow the democratic method is less efficient than authoritarian means. . . .

No useful purpose is served in minimizing the very great difficulties which confront the transitional societies in their efforts to modernize. . . . To a disturbing degree the strange idea has been spread within many transitional societies that democracy is linked with inefficiency, muddled actions, and corrupt practices, while authoritarian ways are identified with clear thinking, purposeful action, and firm dedication. . . . The basic point is that competent democratic leadership by inspiring popular participation can, in fact, mobilize greater involvement in the tasks of economic development than is possible with autocratic, but unpopular, leaders.

THE FUNDAMENTAL ISSUE OF INSTABILITY AND ORDER

A second major reason for doubting the validity of democratic values in transitional societies is an appreciation of how weak public order is in many of these states. The contention is that, aside from the inherently optimistic view of the importance of achieving economic development before worrying about the luxuries of democracy, there is the pessimistic prospect that many of these societies may fall into a state of disorder in which all progress will become impossible. In this view the problem of mere political survival must dominate all considerations.

At first blush there is much to this argument, for at the heart of the acculturation process in all transitional societies lies an inherent conflict between the need for order and the need for continuing change.[1] The diffusion of the world culture is fundamentally disruptive of all traditional forms of social organization. At the same time, however, the process of diffusion demands that societies achieve a new level of order. The state of equilibrium between order and change is thus critical in determining the political condition in any transitional society at any particular moment.

In this context, however, we would note first that the essence of political stability is the ability to realize purposeful change, since stability connotes adaptiveness in the face of changing conditions. In direct contrast, political instability connotes a public policy either too rigid and inflexible to accommodate the changing balance of values in the society or too vacillating and unsure to be able to advance any objectives. Thus political stability can be associated with change that is rationally directed toward satisfying the social needs of the maximum possible proportion of the population, while instability is associated with change that fails to gratify the social demands of the people and leaves an increasing proportion frustrated.

Second, we would note that democratic practices in the new states are often threatened by the mood of frustration so common when there is an excessive gap between aspiration and reality. The dynamic factor in creating such tensions has generally been the uneven and discontinuous process of social change in the direction of greater urbanization, for it seems that in transitional societies the rate of urban growth tends to outstrip the rate of industrial and economic development which is the functional basis of the modern city. People have chosen the life of the city even when they cannot find there the activities usually associated with a modern city, a development which demonstrates that individuals can become acculturated to a modern way of life far more readily than societies can be reorganized.

* * *

The great difference between the pace at which individuals can be acculturated to the modern world and that at which societies can be reconstructed is the source of the great human tragedy of the underdeveloped areas. . . .

When we look beyond the individual we see that most transitional societies lack two of the essential prerequisites for a stable system of representative government. The first is a social mechanism whereby it becomes possible to determine and clarify continuously the pattern of values and interests within the society and relate these to the pattern of power through an aggregating and bargaining process. The second is the availability of appropriate instruments for carrying out public policy once the society has expressed its relative values and interests—that is, an efficient bureaucracy which is not just a domineering power group.

Although the lack of these prerequisites in a transitional society constitutes a basic weakness, it is possible for the society to avoid excessive tensions if those who have political aspirations can be recruited into the elite society and accept its outlook. Indeed, some such form of political tutelage is essential if a traditional society is to adopt a more modern form of political life. The danger always exists, however, that the current elite will strive to maintain its administrative and political monopoly and not permit the development of the autonomous roles of the administrator and the politician. When this occurs, the resulting rise in authoritarianism is reinforced by the fact that the elite is becoming even more isolated from the masses.

The lack of those who can perform the full role of the politician is also a major reason why the gap between aspiration and reality becomes a source of general frustration in many transitional societies. An important but often overlooked function of open and competitive political articulation is that of creating in the minds of the public a better appreciation of the distinction between the plausible and the possible.

* * *

To summarize and to return to our attempt to identify the central cause of political instability in transitional societies, we would point to the lack of an effective relation between the ruling elites and their peoples. We see that in some instances political instability is directly connected with the fact that sudden and sharp changes in intra-elite relations are possible because the key members of the elite do not have any firm commitments to the interests of particular segments of the public and so are free to act according to their personal interpretations of what is advantageous in the limited sphere of intra-elite relations. Consequently their behavior often tends to be essentially opportunistic. We see that in other instances the elite may remain united but project to the public only its own views of what is socially and politically desirable. Even though they may believe themselves to be sympathetic to the aspirations of the people they may be in fact isolated in their own world. It is clear that when for any reason the gap between elite and public is excessive there is both opportunity and temptation for any set of would-be leaders, with or without valid qualifications, to attempt to fill it—a situation almost inevitably fatal to hopes for political stability.

DEMOCRACY AND THE FUSION
OF THE UNIVERSAL AND THE PAROCHIAL

We may return now to our original questions about the applicability of Western institutions, and particularly of democratic practices, for the process of nation-building in the new states. It should be apparent from our analysis that we are dealing with a problem that is on the one hand deeply grounded in the context of our particular period of history, but which on the other hand is of such tremendous significance for the development of world history that it does seem to constitute a universal problem above all particularistic considerations of time and place.

The fundamental problem of nation-building at this stage of history in most of the new states is that of finding a satisfactory reconciliation between the universalistic dimensions of the world culture and the parochial expressions of the local culture. A modern nation-state represents not only the political applications of all the technologies, attitudes, and knowledge basic to what we have called the world culture but also a unique expression of the local and special interests of a distinctive community of people. The essence of nation-building in the new states is the search for a new sense of collective identity for an entire people—a sense of identity which will be built around a command of all the potentialities inherent in the universal and cosmopolitan culture of the modern world, and a full expression of self-respect for all that is distinctive in one's own heritage.

During the first stages when the world culture is being introduced into a transitional society the process can be greatly facilitated by the application of authoritarian means. . . .

. . . there appear to be three inherent limitations of authoritarian methods in introducing the world culture. First, harsh and apparently unfriendly agents of acculturation may strengthen a people's feeling that the world culture is essentially foreign and hence a threat to the self. The result may be psychological counterreactions and a subsequent rejection of the new imposed patterns. Second, authoritarian methods often increase the tendencies toward fragmentation rather than toward fusion. Acculturation is likely to occur only in limited spheres, and sharp divisions may later appear between those so acculturated and those who have not been so directly acculturated. Finally, authoritarian methods appear to be of value only in creating the role of the administrator and hence of formal government, and not in strengthening the role of the politician and hence of the political process. Consequently, excessively authoritarian methods in first introducing the elements of the world culture can produce a profound imbalance between government and politics, impeding complete nation-building.

At a second stage of nation-building the need is for bringing together the universal and the parochial. This stage requires a more intimate relation between the government and the masses. This is the delicate stage when the particularistic sentiments and the real interests of the people must be brought into the political process without disrupting the requirements of the state apparatus. The merging of the cosmopolitan and the parochial can appear to be done through populist movements and enunciation of nationalist ideologies, but in the main these turn out to be synthetic attempts. For only rarely in human history has it been possible for a creative individual to give expression to the sense of identity of an entire people, and under conditions of rapid social change this is particularly difficult.

* * *

It is at this point that the basic functions of representative government become critical in the nation-building process. If these new societies are going to achieve a new level of integration, they must find methods for giving representation to both cosmopolitan and parochial forces. Out of the interplay of representative politics it is possible for a society to realize a fundamental fusion of elements of the world culture and the indigenous traditions. This is because competitive politics forces people to classify their real interests, to seek a rational relationship between ends and means in their social life, and to distinguish between the realms of private and public policies—precisely the problem of identity which often plagues people in transitional societies. With competitive politics both individuals and a society can fuse elements of the modern cosmopolitan world with their own historic sense of individuality. This process of blending lies at the heart of the modernization process; and it is this fact which justifies our faith that there is a close association between democratization and modernization.

THE PROBLEM OF INTEREST ARTICULATION AND AGGREGATION

What we have been suggesting is that the concern over the fate of democracy in the new states can be inspired not just by appreciating the basic values of a democratic society but also by understanding the nature of politics as a process by which conflicting interests can be brought out into the open and then adjustments can be made which will maximize the interests of all parties. For this to take place there must be an open process by which interests are articulated and then aggregated into public policies. A basic function of the representative politician is precisely to articulate such interests.

Unfortunately, however, it is often peculiarly difficult in transitional societies for politicians to perform such a role. In most transitional countries the processes of modernization and industrial growth have not as yet proceeded to the stage in which the social structure is sufficiently differentiated and the population adequately specialized to create a wide range of specific interests with quite definite but still limited political objectives. . . .

National leaders in such situations are compelled to speak to an essentially undifferentiated audience.[2] Without ready means at hand for measuring the distribution of any specific interests, such leaders may feel that they have no alternative but that of striving to appeal to all by reaching for the broadest common denominator. Hence the propensity to avoid in public discussions the specific treatment of concrete issues and to indulge in emotional and more diffusely nationalistic appeals.

The sum effect of the inadequate processes for articulating particular interests is to weaken the possibilities for a rationally based system of interest aggregation. When leaders are unsure of the distribution of particular interests they cannot follow strategies of systematically calculating the relative appeal of different policies in support of different combinations of very specific concerns. Under such conditions public discussion tends to drift away from the hard realities of social conflicts and to become mired in vague generalities.

This tendency may not have serious consequences for the development of a modern democratic polity if there is open competition among all who might wish to engage in such forms of political articulation. Indeed, the continuous exposure of a citizenry to the exaggerated language, the substanceless promises, and the emotion-tapping appeals of politicians who are avoiding hard realities and disciplined reasoning can produce the widespread sense of skepticism about the potentialities of politics which is a first requirement of a responsible and democratic electorate. Once a people have learned to discount and distrust the pie-in-the-sky language of shallow politicians and to see through the superficial idealism of easy prophets, they have entered the world of modern, sober politics. It is this possibility of immunity through exposure which caused the philosopher T. V. Smith to observe, "They also serve who only articulate."

In most transitional societies the public experience in learning to discount the exaggerated language of politics fails to take place because there is little open competition among politicians. Instead of different themes and different combinations of policies competing for public attention, those engaged in political articulation tend to present a common front. . . . The lack of competition means that for the public the trend is not toward choosing and selecting with a skeptical mind but the more extreme consequence of either becoming completely distrustful and contemptuous of the realm of politics or abandoning any attempt at rational judgment and seeking satisfactions from emotionally identifying with the only ones who speak with power.

The purpose of political articulation is not just the training of a critical and questioning electorate. For transitional societies it might be argued that a more basic purpose of political articulation is that of instilling in people new values and new outlooks. . . .

The test, however, must be a pragmatic one. . . . When politicians talk about radical programs of change but fail to produce substantive results, the consequence can only be a general debasement of standards throughout the society.

The dilemma of the modernizing politician is that he must strive to bring about in a people a fusion of emotions and skills, a desire for the novel but also a respect for the self. The articulating politician must call both for change according to the ways of the modern and hence foreign world and for loyalty to the sense of historical identity of a people. . . . What tends to happen is that the articulating politician must generalize his discussion of the parochial and parochialize his treatment of the universal. Unsure of what are the parochial interests in his society, he is driven to creating an idealized and abstracted version of a traditional pattern. At the same time he must present the universal that is at the heart of the modern culture as being merely the values and interests of one apparently parochial segment

of the society, albeit this is usually the elite segment. In short, the modernizing politician can easily appear to be cast in the role of wanting to advance only the particular interests of a small elite when he speaks of the goals of modernization, and not being able to understand the values of the specific interests when he talks of the traditional and the unique in his society.

These problems, combined with numerous others, tend to weaken the sense of assurance of political leaders. The very concepts of political representation and of responsible leadership are confused as those with power become anxious about their capability to manage a modern political system. . . .

The sum effect of these various difficulties is confusion over expected standards of performance throughout the society. . . . The responsibility of the popular politician is to facilitate the transformation of an inchoate political community into a civil society. There is thus a direct link between the ways in which leaders perform the function of political articulation and the possibilities for the emergence of elements throughout the societies which have a sense of competence and which are dedicated to raising the level of society.

STANDARDS OF DEMOCRACY

The question of realistic standards becomes peculiarly difficult with respect to democratic performance because of the almost universal tendency to discuss democracy in ideal, if not idealistic, terms. For most people it is the pureness of democracy which counts, and not so much the practical realities of democratic accommodation to an imperfect world. The tendency to treat democracy in abstract terms greatly complicates the problems of strengthening democratic development in the new states. The difficulty is that leaders are often unsure of what might reasonably constitute democratic behavior in their troubled settings but they are sure they have not achieved the ideals of democracy. Thus they not only often have a deep sense of failure but also may conclude that it is impossible even to aspire to building democratic institutions.

In most transitional societies there is a concreteness about almost all modern political roles except that of the popular politician, who is the critical key to democracy. . . .

. . . The colonial authorities not only were hesitant in sharing power, but often possessed little understanding of the practical realities of democratic politics, for most colonial officials entered their overseas careers immediately upon completion of college and thus had little more than a textbook understanding of democracy in their own countries. These relatively innocent officials in turn tended to pass on to the Asians and Africans a textbook version of democracy in the mother country. . . .

What has been missing in the efforts to instill democracy in the public life of the new states is a realistic understanding of what democratic politics actually involves in, say, the comparably unsettled life of the early and rapid urban development in Europe and America. The story of how American democracy grew and flourished out of the rough and tumble of the old city machines and of the disciplined ward heelers who inducted generations of immigrant Americans into a public life. . . .

In short, while searching for the proper standards for democratic behavior in the new states it is necessary to look beyond the ideals and to ask what are the tasks that must be performed if there is to be in time a greater growth of democracy. These tasks include not only leadership but the development of citizens who recognize that their relationship to government involves inputs on their side of effort, sacrifice and loyalty, and not just the receiving of services and outputs of governmental policies.

In the light of all these considerations we are led to the conclusion that it will be a slow and difficult process to achieve the substance of democratic life in most of the new states. There is much truth in the often cynically advanced generalization that these societies are "unprepared" for democracy. This is a disturbing conclusion for many people in the West who share a basic sympathy for the struggles of the new states because personally they are committed to the democratic spirit and are naturally inclined to identify with the weak, the poor, and the disadvantaged.

At the same time our analysis suggests a ray of hope for people who do have faith in the powers of democracy, for we have noted that advances in the direction of more democratic practices can produce strength. The advantages do not lie with totalitarian or authoritarian methods. The more political development occurs, the more the advantages of democracy will become apparent. For once people have a greater stake in their society and come to believe that progress is possible, they are more likely to appreciate the rewards of living in more open societies.

The problem of working toward a more open society is above all a test of statecraft. To simply open the door to the ever-wider popular participation in politics of illiterate and insecure citizens can easily destroy any possibility for orderly government. In the developing areas there is a genuine problem of establishing effective administrations and as shown in later chapters, the threats of insurgency and revolutionary violence are endemic in many transitional societies. There is a need for firm rule if societies are going to advance toward definite goals.

The argument [here] . . . is that firm rule and efficient administration need not be seen as the opposite of democratic development, but rather authority and participation must go hand in hand in the building of modern states. We have sought to stress somewhat the practical advantage of expanding democratic participation through strengthening the role of the popular politician because in recent years there has been so much discussion of the presumed practical liabilities of democracy. It would, however, be unrealistic to carry this argument to the extreme of suggesting that the problems of popular participation should assume top priority at all times in the nation-building problem. As the discussion of the crises of development indicated, we must recognize that matters of administration and governmental rule which come under the crises of integration, penetration, and distribution are quite as important in building effective modern states.

Thus, in the last analysis, democratic development involves more than just the successful dealing with problems of popular participation. To have democratic government it is necessary to have government and ordered authority.

Notes

[1] The remaining paragraphs in this section first appeared in Lucian W. Pye, "Democracy, Modernization, and Nation Building," in J. Roland Pennock, ed., *Self-government in Modernizing Nations.* © 1964. By permission of Prentice-Hall, Inc., Englewood Cliffs, N.J.

[2] The remaining paragraphs in this section are adapted from Lucian W. Pye, ed., *Communications and Political Development* (Princeton: Princeton University Press, 1963), and are being reproduced with the kind permission of the Princeton University Press.

The implications of the values of the invisible ideology for system maintenance, stability, and change within the systems is clear in this literature. The assumption of most political scientists is that stability is the significant condition for analysis of the relationships within the social order. Change is considered as a rare event that can be accounted for simply, as a deviation from the "natural" order of stability.

There are those theorists who assume that the origins of change lie within the individual, that an understanding of psychology and human nature is essential to understanding the collective behavioral change in societies. In a simple sense, society is a collection of individuals, and it is necessary to understand how an individual changes in order to understand how collections of people change. In opposition to this is the view that the structures of the institutions and processes that surround individuals are the important elements in the analysis of political change. Thus, it is considered more important to understand how collectivities of people—classes, institutions, groups, organizations, or societies—relate to change, and how changes in structure affect changes in individuals.

It is useful to distinguish between change as a descriptive phenomena and change as a normative concept. As a descriptive concept, change refers to differences occurring between two points in time, and it closely resembles the common-sense idea of "growth." In this sense of change, a person grows from childhood to adulthood. Certain differences in his or her physical and psychological makeup can be observed over the period of time in which the growth takes place.

Changes, in a different sense, may refer to alterations that result from man's intentional intervention into a situation in order to bring about some preferred outcome. Change toward a preferred outcome can be thought of as progress rather than growth.

This concept of change, when it occurs between two points in time, is usually considered as "progress" rather than growth.

This distinction between change that is growth and change that is progress is rarely made in the literature, and even when it is, its impact on analysis is often overlooked. In reviewing the literature in this chapter, it may be useful to keep in mind that some theorists are attempting to explain how growth takes place in the political context of the society, and others are talking about progress in reaching political goals.

Assumptions are also made about the directions of change. Some theorists assume that it takes a circular direction, that events return in cycles. "History repeats itself" might be the common notion of this conception.

A different assumption, which is more likely to be used by Western civilization's theorists, is that change is linear. In this view, change travels in a straight line, and events do not repeat themselves. One can assume either that changing events lead toward deterioration and decay of the social structure, as did many of the Greek political theorists, or that society constantly evolves into a better condition. In either case, the underlying notion is that change is not cyclic but constantly moves toward either improvement or decline.

The implications of these two different views of change are clear. If it is assumed that change is cyclical, then the theorists become more concerned with stabilizing events, in order to prevent the eventual return of less preferable social conditions. If it is assumed that change is linear and that it is moving toward the eventual decay and destruction of society, then attempting to again stabilize the society becomes a significant activity. Finally, if it is assumed that change is linear but moving toward some progressive stage of human development, then the notion of facilitating change makes sense. (Indeed, the notion of revolution itself makes sense only if one assumes that the product of change is progress.)

Still another set of distinctions that will be helpful in understanding the literature is that some theorists view change as "evolutionary," or incremental, and others see it as "revolutionary," or dramatic and discontinuous. Those who view change as incremental tend to see it as a gradual process, with small bits and pieces of history fitting together in an accumulation of events that culminate in a differing set of social conditions. This kind of view is commonly reflected in the ideologies of "liberal" political analysts, who argue that changes must occur over time through clearly defined processes, and that the maintenance of procedures for change are more important than the substance of the change itself.

On the other hand, a theorist with a more radical ideology might argue that changes that take place in an incremental manner through orderly procedures are merely illusions, rather than real change. Incremental change is a way of absorbing the energy for change without really changing anything fundamental in the society. Change must be dramatic and revolutionary in nature in order to have any real effect upon the society.

EQUILIBRIUM AND CONFLICT IN THE ANALYSIS OF POLITICAL CHANGE

Ralph Dahrendorf, who has contributed a great deal toward the clarification of the difference between evolutionary and revolutionary change, has traced these two perspectives from a Platonic dialogue between Socrates and Thrasymachus, through the political philosophies of Hobbes and Rousseau, to the present-day debates.

Dahrendorf has summarized the view of Thrasymachus:

In all human societies, there are positions that enable their bearers to exercise power. These positions are endowed with sovereignty—the men who hold them lay down the law for their subjects. Obedience is enforced, for the most important single aspect of power is the control of sanctions. (Sanctions do not always have to be applied; mere anticipation of their effect may suffice to guarantee compliance with the law.) It follows from this notion of power and sanctions that there is always resistance to the exercise of power, and that both the effectiveness and the legitimacy of power—if there is any difference between these two concepts—are precarious. Normally those in power manage to stay in power. Theirs is the stronger group, and society is held together by the exercise of their strength, that is, by constraint.[11]

[11] Ralph Dahrendorf, "In Praise of Thrasymachus," quoted in George A. Kelly and Clifford W. Brown Jr., *Struggles in the State* (New York: Wiley & Sons, 1970), p. 40.

In this view, society is a conflictful and changing process. Intrinsic to any society is an inequality in the distribution of power: Those who have the power tend to run the society in their own best interests; those without power attempt in conflict with those having it to change the distribution of power, and therefore, the society itself. Society can only be understood as a conflict between those who have power and those who do not have power.

Dahrendorf then summarizes the opposing position of Socrates, which represents a different way to view society:

It is true, he says, that power is exercised in human societies, but it is exercised on behalf of societies rather than against them. Positions of power are created to give active expression to a general will that represents the consensus of the society's members. What appears to be obedience is in many ways but an expression of this consensus. The exercise of power is dependent on the support of those who are apparently subject to it. Subjection never involves a renunciation of sovereignty; rather, sovereignty remains with the total body politic, with all the citizens in the society. Any differences and divisions in a society are due to outside interference with a basically legitimate system; such divisive influences are in any case destructive of society. Normally, society is held together by the agreement of all citizens on certain fundamental tenets, to which they then adhere voluntarily as a way of protecting their own interests.[12]

In this perspective, those who hold power are seen as the legitimate spokesmen for the values and interests of the members of that society. Society is held together by the agreement of those in that society, not by the coercion or power of the rulers. The important element for analysis is to understand how such agreements are developed and maintained in society, rather than how conflicts arise and are resolved; the focus is on consensus, legitimacy, stability, and equilibrium, rather than on conflict, coercion, and change.

These two basic postures can be readily identified in contemporary political analysis. Thrasymachus' argument is commonly presented by conflict theorists and power-elite theorists. Equilibrium theorists who develop "structur-

[12] Ibid., p. 40.

al-functional" theories of political systems are present-day advocates of Socrates' position.

To illustrate the uses of equilibrium notions in present-day analysis of change, a selection from Chalmers Johnson's "Revolution and the Social System" is presented below. This work demonstrates the assumptions and analyses of those who see consensus, equilibrium and incremental adjustments as the essential ingredients for the political analysis of change.

REVOLUTION AND THE SOCIAL SYSTEM

CHALMERS JOHNSON

I. THE CAUSES OF REVOLUTION

When Hannah Arendt writes in the first paragraph of *On Revolution*, "For revolutions, however one may be tempted to define them, are not mere changes,"[1] she has indicated at the outset the one thing that all revolutions are: changes. Revolution is a form of change within the social system; not *mere* change, but change nonetheless. Revolution is not a unique social phenomenon; there exist functional equivalents of revolution—namely, other forms of social change—and questions directed at discovering the causes of social change and identifying the level in the social system at which social change occurs are relevant to the problem of the causes of revolution. As a kind of social change, revolution is "the most wasteful, the most expensive, the last to be chosen; but also the most powerful, and therefore always appealed to in what men feel to be a last resort."[2]

And what causes social change? We put this question not because we hope to answer it to everyone's satisfaction, but in order to introduce the series of models and assumptions that will be most helpful as a foundation for the analysis of social change.[3] Our point of departure in analyzing social change is the model

of a functionally integrated social system—a system whose members cooperate with each other by "playing" various "roles" that, taken together, permit the whole system to "function." This basic model is well known in contemporary social science; it is the primary construct upon which "structural-functional" analysis rests.[4] Within the framework of this model, we hope to show that revolution is a form of social change undertaken in response to specific conditions of the social system, and that it occurs at a particular stage in the system's efforts to resolve functional difficulties.

One notoriously misunderstood problem with this model of society is that it portrays the social system in a state of equilibrium; it is supposed that the model is useless (or worse) for analyzing social change because of its static bias.[5] Obviously, a changing system is not one in equilibrium; conversely, there is no place for change in an equilibrium system. But this is not an either/or proposition; "equilibrium" is not a real condition but a concept. An equilibrium social system is an ideal type, and the concept of equilibrium is only a reference point for measuring change. No other interpretation of a system's equilibrium, least of all a normative one, is permissible.[6] Since an equilibrium system is not a changing system, a changing system is one that is out of balance. What puts a social system (as here conceived) out of equilibrium?

We believe that society can best be understood as a functionally integrated system. In such a system, if one of the various component structures does not function in the way that it must in order to maintain equilibrium, then first the affected substructure and then, if no remedial action occurs, the entire system will move out of equilibrium. The condition that causes the disequilibrium, and that demands remedial action in order to restore or to create a new equilibrium, we call *dysfunction*. Dysfunction is a potential condition of any functionally integrated system, and dysfunctional conditions within an imbalanced social system vary in degree of severity over a broad range from slight to mortal. Dysfunctional conditions are caused by pressures (whether they are external or internal is a distinction that is relevant only in an historical case) that compel the members of a substructure to do their work, or view their roles, or imagine their potentialities differently from the way that they did under equilibrium conditions. The pressures that cause dysfunction (e.g., technological discoveries, imperialism, and many others discussed below) we call *sources* of dysfunction. In this context, *social change* is action undertaken to alter the structure of the system for the purpose of relieving the condition of dysfunction (in one or more of the system's substructures or, occasionally, throughout the entire structure).

Dysfunction is the condition that demands the response of social change—and of revolution. But what distinguishes revolutionary change from other forms of social change? Two considerations are relevant here: revolution occurs because non-violent evolution is not occurring, and revolution occurs in response to a distinct condition of the system that we call "multiple dysfunction." With regard to the first point, we note that a distinctive characteristic of revolutionary change is the employment of physical violence to relieve dysfunction. "Revolutionary" changes—in the popular sense of changes of great magnitude—that are not initiated by violent alteration of the system are instances of some other form of social change. Big changes are not necessarily revolutionary changes, or else the word merely means "big change." In specifying why revolutionary change is violent, we must refer to the fact that non-violent change has not previously taken place in the dysfunctional system. Social violence is the appropriate response to intransigent resistance; it occurs because known methods of non-violent change are blocked by the ruling elite. That is to say, revolution is politics continued at the level of a violent physical showdown. It takes two to make a revolution, and one of these two is always the status quo elite. The revolutionaries—those recognizing the dysfunctional situation in the face of elite intransigence—are not necessarily the masses; they may be an intrinsic elite (say, a corps of officers) challenging the socially recognized extrinsic elite. Or they may be the masses. (Whatever damage may have to be done to Leninism or to the flamboyantly cynical "iron law of oligarchy," it is an error to suppose that the masses will never rise without guidance.)[7] Of course, if the elite is not intransigent, simple change

will occur, dysfunction will be relieved, and no revolution will take place. Therefore the target elite must be blocking change in a revolutionary situation. These considerations say nothing about who will emerge victorious when the revolution occurs; that question is related to the condition of one particular subsystem—the army—which will be considered later.

In distinguishing revolutionary change from other, non-violent forms of change in terms of the failure of the latter to relieve dysfunctional conditions, we are oversimplifying actual revolutionary situations. Simple change in response to conditions of dysfunction may be occurring, but it may be an inappropriate or an insufficient response, it may be outrun by spreading dysfunctions or by an accelerator (see below), or it may itself produce other dysfunctions (which may, in turn, produce the "anarchistic" type of revolution, different from the one that simple change sought to forestall). True conservatives may attempt to maintain the continuity of a dysfunctional system (particularly of its integrating myth) by reforming and adjusting the system to changed circumstances. But if they fail to relieve dysfunction to a level at which revolution is inappropriate, or if an accelerator intervenes before such relief is completed, revolution will occur—and it will be directed against them.

It seems hardly necessary to say that dysfunction in the system of elite recruitment is an important element in hastening a revolution. In some instances, a caste-type of elite (e.g., the First and part of the Second Estate) which is no longer the intrinsic elite of the system may, by its actions, promote revolution. In other cases, the elite may be open to rising groups of representatives from the intrinsic elite (even, although rarely, in colonial situations); and such an elite may be implementing policies intended to relieve dysfunction. If only the structure of social mobility within a system is dysfunctional, this can probably be corrected by non-violent change—that is, either by redefining the criteria of the elite or by clipping its powers (e.g., the Lords' Reform). Regardless of the qualities of an elite and of the actions it is taking to relieve dysfunction, if change eventually takes a revolutionary form, the system elite will be attacked violently by the revolutionaries. Such an occurrence is, empirically, a mark of revolution.

The second criterion of revolution we call "multiple dysfunction." At the present stage of knowledge about social systems and social change, it is not possible to measure "amounts" of dysfunctions in a system. If we could, we would be able to describe distinctive conditions of the social system in response to which revolution is the appropriate mode of social change. In lieu of such precision, however, we still require a criterion of "appropriateness." There exists a level of dysfunctional conditions below which revolution (purposive political violence) is not appropriate regardless of how intransigent the elite may be in opposing efforts to relieve it. On the other hand, even if the elite is not intransigent, or is no longer intransigent after a period of initial vacillation, there are levels of dysfunctional conditions that transcend the adjustment capabilities of a system. Revolution will occur in these cases unless the elite acts first and declares its bankruptcy by abdication, resignation, or by otherwise terminating the old order nonviolently. . . .

Social systems may survive extraordinary dislocations without experiencing revolutions so long as certain conditions are met. These conditions are: the existence of the social problems (dysfunctions) must be clearly recognized by the elites as well as by the ordinary members of the system; basic agreement on the need for change must exist; and the sector (substructure) in which the dysfunction prevails must be capable of being isolated within the general context of the social system. If the dysfunction cannot be identified or isolated, it will—like cancer or (as the French Army in Algeria called it) *pourrissement*—metastasize and lead to revolution. It is a people's awareness of the actual, or incipient, metastasis of social ills that causes the "loss of confidence" or "rupture of consensus" that so often presages revolutionary conditions.[8] We suggest as a rule-of-thumb criterion of revolutionary change (in addition to the criterion of elite intransigence in the face of system dysfunction) that dysfunction must "metastasize" beyond one substructure in order for revolution to become appropriate. Generally speaking, no single condition of dysfunction (with the possible exception of agricultural production in certain types of systems) can dis-

integrate a social system; in a revolutionary situation, more than one of the relatively separable substructures of a system is dysfunctional and, in one type of revolution discussed in Part II, dysfunction is systemic, including the integrative myth. Let us emphasize that this is a rule-of-thumb criterion; we are as yet unable to describe, in the macroscopic terms of the model of the functionally integrated social system, precisely what are revolutionary conditions. This point will be explored further in our discussion of an "accelerator"—i.e., the final aggregate of pressure (source of dysfunction) on a system that leads at once to revolution.

Let us summarize the analysis of revolution to this point. Revolution is one form of social change in response to the presence of dysfunction in the social system. Revolution is the preferred method of change when (a) the level of dysfunctions exceeds the capacities of traditional or accepted methods of problem solving; and when (b) the system's elite, in effect, opposes change. (The second point is analytically necessary because it is possible to conceive of a system that is *completely* dysfunctional without being revolutionary. A natural catastrophe, such as a severe earthquake, might produce this condition.) Conversely, a system elite may resolutely oppose changes advocated by special groups within the system, but no revolutionary situation is generated because the system is basically functional. Revolution is the acceptance of violence in order to bring about change.

* * *

Notes

[1] On Revolution (New York, 1963), p. 13.

[2] George Sawyer Pettee, *The Process of Revolution* (New York, 1938), p. 96.

[3] For an excellent critical summary of all the major theories of social change J. A. Ponsioen, *The Analysis of Social Change Reconsidered* (The Hague, 1962).

[4] The standard works are Marion J. Levy, *The Structure of Society* (Princeton, 1952); Robert K. Merton, *Social Theory and Social Structure* (Glencoe, 1949); and the books of Talcott Parsons. For an early statement of the logic of the approach see A. R. Radcliffe-Brown, "On the Concept of Function in Social Science," *American Anthropologist*, N.S., XXXVII (July-September 1935), 394–402. For a recent application of structural-functional method see William C. Mitchell, *The American Polity* (New York, 1962).

[5] Cf. W. E. Moore, "A Reconsideration of Theories of Social Change," *American Sociological Review*, XXV (December 1960), 811.

[6] This point is made ably by Lewis Coser, "Social Conflict and the Theory of Social Change," *British Journal of Sociology*, VII (September 1957), 206–207, n. 22.

[7] Many jacqueries illustrate this point; Eric Hobsbawm's remarks on the Andalusian anarchist movement offer a concrete example: "Spanish anarchism . . . was overwhelmingly a poor men's movement and it is thus not surprising that it reflected the interests and aspirations of the Andalusian *pueblo* with uncanny closeness." *Primitive Rebels* (Manchester, 1959), p. 83.

[8] See, for example, Walter Lippmann's article on the possibility of a Negro rebellion in the United States, *San Francisco Chronicle*, May 28, 1963.

Johnson focuses on the total structure of society, rather than on the individuals in that society. Further, he adopts a "structural-functionalist" view of political dynamics: he sees the structure as involving a system of behaviors in which members cooperate with one another in playing various roles, and the successful acting out of these roles permits the system to function.

Structural-functionalists view the social system as "healthy," or in equilibrium, to the extent that the structure successfully carries out the functions required for the maintenance of the system. When a system suffers "dysfunctions," or no longer effectively performs its functions, then the theorists expect some form of activity in the system to return conditions to a normal equilibrium.

For Johnson, it is the analysis of "multiple dysfunctions" that leads to an understanding of political revolution. Clearly, for this model to make any sense, it is necessary to assume that people act out their roles in the system because they are in basic agreement with the values of the system. Society is understood as basically consensual in nature; because people agree, they cooperate to perform the functions of the system effectively. They do not act because they fear the sanctions of the rulers; they perform because they feel that the system and its rulers are operating the way they should operate. When these agreements between rulers and the ruled break down, the system experiences dysfunctions, and new agreements must be reached so that equilibrium can be restored.

Lewis Coser represents well the views of many conflict theorists, although he is less committed to a pure conflict theory position than are some. He tends to recognize the necessity for understanding both consensus and conflict in analyzing change in society:

Peace and feuding, conflict and order, are correlative. Both the cementing and breaking of the cake of custom constitute part of the dialectic of social life. One is hence ill advised to distinguish sharply a sociology of order from a sociology of conflict, or a harmony model of society from a conflict model. Such attempts can only result in artificial distinctions. The analysis of social conflicts brings to awareness aspects of social reality that may be obscured if analytical attention focuses too exclusively on phenomena of social order; but an exclusive attention to conflict phenomena may obscure the central importance of social order and needs to be corrected by a correlative concern with the ordered aspects of social life. We deal here not with distinct realities, but only with differing aspects of the same reality, so that exclusive emphasis on one or the other is likely to lead the analyst astray.[13]

Coser's analysis does not reject the assumptions and analyses of the equilibrium and conflict theorists. He is arguing that it is necessary to understand conflict as well as consensus in analyzing change. More specifically, Coser proposes that there are changes within a system, or there are changes of systems.[14] To the extent that the social system is flexible enough to tolerate and resolve conflicts within the basic structures of the society, then change can occur within the system. To the extent that the system is too rigid to tolerate inner change, it will suffer changes of the entire system. Revolution, in the common-sense use of the term, results from the inability of the society to accommodate conflicts.

Coser points out that the debate between equilibrium and conflict theorists may be more a matter of emphasis than kind. Where equilibrium theorists value consensus and regard conflict as a mere dysfunction in the system, conflict theorists prefer to see disagreement as an elemental part of any society. Both views contribute a great deal to the understanding of change processes in the social order.

Implicit in the arguments of the equilibrium and conflict theorists is a point that needs to be clarified. Do societies respond to certain functions that are necessary to maintain the well being of the individuals in the collectivity in a more-or-less automatic fashion? Or do societies change as

[13] Lewis A. Coser, "Conflict: Social Aspects," *International Encyclopedia of Social Sciences* (New York: Macmillan, 1966), pp. 235–36.

[14] Lewis A. Coser, "Social Conflict and the Theory of Social Change," in George A. Kelly and Clifford W. Brown Jr., op. cit., pp. 54–69.

a result of conscious efforts by individuals and groups? Is man active, or passive, in the social order?

HUMAN NATURE
AND THE SOCIAL STRUCTURE

There are probably as many different views of human nature as there are people to hold such views. But several basic concepts return time and again to the literature of political change. Some theorists think of man as good in his natural state, when he is unencumbered by social, or learned, attitudes and values. Others tend to see man as having the potential for goodness—if social and environmental factors do not retard his development.

In both cases, man is considered as basically good or as having the potential for goodness. Progress, in such a view, removes the social and environmental constraints that make it difficult for man to fulfill his nature. Many would argue, for example, that poor people are not inherently lazy, shiftless, or ignorant; it is the social conditions of poverty that promote crime, loss of human dignity, and inability to learn, preventing the development of poor people as members of the community. As society removes the conditions of poverty, the poor are able to assume positions of dignity and meaning in society. But man can also be viewed as evil, conniving, and socially destructive. Without the social constraints of law, religion, and traditions, he would act out his innate evilness to the eventual destruction of the entire society.

Is man rational or irrational by nature? For those who assume he is rational, the essential elements in the good society are availability of information and opportunities. Man needs both, if he is to calculate his best advantage and achieve his self-interest. In the Freudian view, however, man is compelled by instinctual forces that he has little ability to control. Man is basically anti-social by nature, and unless his urges are constrained by society, the social order will be destroyed. Still another view of man is that he is nothing more than what society teaches him to be. Environment determines his nature. Man progresses to the extent that social conditions and institutions can be constructed to teach men to be good. Opposed to this view is one that considers man as having certain natural needs, and the social environment as existing to facilitate the satisfaction of those needs.

Finally, is the study of man the best means of understanding society? Or is society a collective unit that has to be analyzed differently than does man as an individual?

Emile Durkheim, the founder of modern sociology, is often quoted to support the position that society must be understood as something quite different from a collection of individuals. Theorists who adopt this view state that the nature of man may be relevant to psychology, but that the dynamics of society are a different order of analysis. These theorists do not seek to understand social change by examining human nature; instead, they concentrate on the institutions and processes of society that are intrinsic to the collectivity of man.

James C. Davies exemplifies those theorists who choose to view political change and revolution as a function of individual changes in people. Davies argues, "Political stability and instability are ultimately dependent upon a state of mind, a mood in society."[15] He believes that as people's needs are met by the political structures in society, their expectations continue to rise. When their rising expectations are not satisfied by the political structure, the society is most susceptible to revolution. Davies proposes that the dynamics of political revolution are tied to the needs and actions of individuals in society.

Davies' analysis has been influential, because he has been successful in logically combining the "poverty thesis" of Marx with the observation of Tocqueville that revolutions tend to occur during periods of rising economic prosperity. Marx's analysis of the dynamics of revolution clearly suggested that as the "haves" in society get more and the "have-nots" get less, the disparity precipitates the class struggle that leads to the eventual overthrow of the capitalists by the working classes. Tocqueville, on the other hand, observed that revolutions tend to occur not when there is widespread poverty in society, but when things seem to be getting better for the mass of people. Davies believes both conditions may coincide. Improved economic situations will generate rising expectations that economic conditions will become even better. If at that point the society is unable to meet these rising expectations, then there is a dramatic drop in the capability of the system, and the people in the society experi-

[15] "Toward a Theory of Revolution," *American Sociological Review*, (February, 1962), 6, 5-19.

ence "relative deprivation." It is not so much that they are actually poor, but that they are psychologically deprived relative to their expectations.

For other theorists,—perhaps the majority—the crucial point of study is how political structures in society facilitate the ability of individuals to live together cooperatively. The predominant view here is consistent with the invisible ideology's preference for the system rather than the individual. Instead of trying to understand political structures and processes as the result of individual needs, these theorists tend to focus on individuals in relationship to political institutions and on the functions of those institutions for the collectivity of people.

For an illustration of this kind of analysis, an article by Samuel Huntington has been selected. Huntington argues well for the importance of understanding the "institutionalization," as he calls it, of the political processes in a developing polity. He defines political development as the institutionalization of the political processes of the society. Generally, Huntington argues that institutions must be adaptable to new situations and demands. To him, the proper focal points, for the analysis of political change are the structures and institutions in politics, not individuals.

POLITICAL DEVELOPMENT AND POLITICAL DECAY

SAMUEL P. HUNTINGTON

. . . Writers on political development emphasize the processes of modernization and the closely related phenomena of social mobilization and increasing political participation. A balanced view of the politics of contemporary Asia, Africa, and Latin America requires more attention to the "art of associating together" and the growth of political institutions. For this purpose, it is useful to distinguish political development from modernization and to identify political development with the institutionalization of political organizations and procedures. Rapid increases in mobilization and participation, the principal political aspects of modernization, undermine political institutions. Rapid moderniza-

From Samuel P. Huntington, "Political Development and Political Decay," *World Politics*, (April, 1965) XVII, p. 386–430. Reprinted by permission of Princeton University Press.

tion, in brief, produces not political development, but political decay. . . .

POLITICAL DEVELOPMENT AS INSTITUTIONALIZATION

There is thus much to be gained (as well as something to be lost) by conceiving of political development as a process independent of, although obviously affected by, the process of modernization. In view of the crucial importance of the relationship between mobilization and participation, on the one hand, and the growth of political organizations, on the other, it is useful for many purposes to define political development as the institutionalization of political organizations and procedures. This concept liberates development from modernization. It can be applied to the analysis of political systems of any sort, not just modern ones. It can be defined in reasonably precise ways which are at least theoretically capable of measurement. As a concept, it does not suggest that movement is likely to be in only one direction: institutions, we know, decay and dissolve as well as grow and mature. Most significantly, it focuses attention on the reciprocal interaction between the on-going social processes of modernization, on the one hand, and the strength, stability, or weakness of political structures, traditional, transitional, or modern, on the other.

The strength of political organizations and procedures varies with their scope of *support* and their *level of institutionalization*. Scope refers simply to the extent to which the political organizations and procedures encompass activity in the society. If only a small upper-class group belongs to political organizations and behaves in terms of a set of procedures, the scope is limited. If, on the other hand, a large segment of the population is politically organized and follows the political procedures, the scope is broad. Institutions are stable, valued, recurring patterns of behavior. Organizations and procedures vary in their degree of institutionalizations Harvard University and the newly opened suburban high school are both organizations, but Harvard is much more of an institution than is the high school. The seniority system in Congress and President Johnson's select press conferences are both procedures, but seniority is much more institutionalized than are Mr. Johnson's methods of dealing with the press. Institutionalization is the process by which organizations and procedures acquire value and stability. The level of institutionalization of any political system can be defined by the adaptability, complexity, autonomy, and coherence of its organizations and procedures. So also, the level of institutionalization of any particular organization or procedure can be measured by its adaptability, complexity, autonomy, and coherence. If these criteria can be identified and measured, political systems can be compared in terms of their levels of institutionalization. Furthermore, it will be possible to measure increases and decreases in the institutionalization of particular organizations and procedures within a political system.

* * *

MOBILIZATION VS. INSTITUTIONALIZATION: PUBLIC INTERESTS, DEGENERATION, AND THE CORRUPT POLITY

Mobilization and Institutionalization

Social mobilization and political participation are rapidly increasing in Asia, Africa, and Latin America. These processes, in turn, are directly responsible for the deterioration of political institutions in these areas. As Kornhauser has conclusively demonstrated for the Western world, rapid industrialization and urbanization create discontinuities which give rise to mass society. "The *rapid* influx of large numbers of people into *newly* developing urban areas invites mass movements."[1] In areas and industries with very rapid industrial growth, the creation and institutionalization of unions lag, and mass movements are likely among the workers. As unions are organized, they are highly vulnerable to outside influences in their early stages. "The rapid influx of large numbers of people into a new organization (as well as a new area) provides opportunities for mass-oriented elites to penetrate the organization. This is particularly true during the formative periods of organizations, for at such times external constraints must carry the burden of social control until the new participants

have come to internalize the values of the organization."[2]

So also in politics. Rapid economic growth breeds political instability.[3] Political mobilization, moreover, does not necessarily require the building of factories or even movement to the cities. It may result simply from increases in communications, which can stimulate major increases in aspirations that may be only partially, if at all, satisfied. The result is a revolution of rising frustrations."[4] Increases in literacy and education may bring more political instability. By Asian standards, Burma, Ceylon, and the Republic of Korea are all highly literate, but no one of them is a model of political stability. Nor does literacy necessarily stimulate democracy: with roughly 75 per cent literacy, Cuba was the fifth most literate country in Latin America (ranking behind Argentina, Uruguay, Chile, and Costa Rica), but the first to go Communist; so also Kerala, with one of the highest literacy rates in India, was the first Indian state to elect a Communist government. Literacy, as Daniel Lerner has suggested, "may be dysfunctional—indeed a serious impediment—to modernization in the societies now seeking (all too rapidly) to transform their institutions."

Increased communication may thus generate demands for more "modernity" than can be delivered. It may also stimulate a reaction against modernity and activate traditional forces. Since the political arena is normally dominated by the more modern groups, it can bring into the arena new, anti-modern groups and break whatever consensus exists among the leading political participants. It may also mobilize minority ethnic groups who had been indifferent to politics but who now acquire a self-consciousness and divide the political system along ethnic lines. Nationalism, it has often been assumed, makes for national integration. But in actuality, nationalism and other forms of ethnic consciousness often stimulate political disintegration, tearing apart the body politic.

Sharp increases in voting and other forms of political participation can also have deleterious effects on political institutions. In Latin America since the 1930's, increases in voting and increases in political instability have gone hand in hand. "Age requirements were lowered, property and literacy requirements were reduced or discarded, and the unscrubbed, unschooled millions on the farms were enfranchised in the name of democracy. They were swept into the political life of the republics so rapidly that existing parties could not absorb many of them, and they learned little about working within the existing political system."[5] The personal identity crises of the elites, caught between traditional and modern cultures, may create additional problems: "In transitional countries the political process often has to bear to an inordinate degree the stresses and strains of people responding to personal needs and seeking solutions to intensely personal problems."[6] Rapid social and economic change calls into question existing values and behavior patterns. It thus often breeds personal corruption. In some circumstances this corruption may play a positive role in the modernizing process, enabling dynamic new groups to get things done which would have been blocked by the existing value system and social structure. At the same time, however, corruption undermines the autonomy and coherence of political institutions. It is hardly accidental that in the 1870's and 1880's a high rate of American economic development coincided with a low point in American governmental integrity.[7]

Institutional decay has become a common phenomenon of the modernizing countries. *Coups d'état* and military interventions in politics are one index of low levels of political institutionalization: they occur where political institutions lack autonomy and coherence. . . .

* * *

The differences which may exist in mobilization and institutionalization suggest four ideal-types of politics (see Table 1). Modern, developed, civic polities (the United States, the Soviet Union) have high levels of

both mobilization and institutionalization. Primitive polities (such as Banfield's backward society) have low levels of both. Contained polities are highly institutionalized but have low levels of mobilization and participation. The dominant political institutions of contained polities may be either traditional (e.g. monarchies) or modern (e.g., political parties). If they are the former, such polities may well confront great difficulties in adjusting to rising levels of social mobilizaion. The traditional institutions may wither or collapse, and the result would be a corrupt polity with a high rate of participation but a low level of institutionalization. In the corrupt society, politics is, in Macaulay's phrase, "all sail and no anchor." This type of polity characterizes much, if not most, of the modernizing world. Many of the more advanced Latin American countries, for instance, have achieved comparatively high indices of literacy, per capita national income and urbanization. But their politics remains notably underdeveloped. Distrust and hatred have produced a continuing low level of political institutionalization. "There is no good faith in America, either among men or among nations," Bolivar once lamented. "Treaties are paper, constitutions books, elections battles, liberty anarchy, and life a torment. The only thing one can do in America is emigrate."[8] Over a century later, the same complaint was heard: "We are not, or do not represent a respectable nation . . . not because we are poor, but because we are disorganized," argued an Ecuadorian newspaper. "With a politics of ambush and of permanent mistrust, one for the other, we . . . cannot properly organize a republic . . . and without organization we cannot merit or attain respect from other nations."[9] So long as a country like Argentina retains a politics of coup and countercoup and a feeble state surrounded by massive social forces, it cannot be considered politically developed, no matter how urbane and prosperous and educated are its citizens.

In reverse fashion, a country may be politically highly developed, with modern political institutions, while still very backward in terms of modernization. India, for instance, is typically held to be the epitome of the underdeveloped society. Judged by the usual criteria of modernization, it was at the bottom of the ladder during the 1950's: per capita GNP of $72, 80 per cent

Table 1

TYPES OF POLITICAL SYSTEMS

SOCIAL MOBILIZATION	POLITICAL INSTITUTIONALIZATION	
	High	*Low*
High	Civic	Corrupt
Low	Contained	Primitive

illiterate, over 80 per cent of the population in rural areas, 70 per cent of the work force in agriculture, a dozen major languages, deep caste and religious differences. Yet in terms of political institutionalization, India was far from backward. Indeed, it ranked high not only in comparison with other modernizing countries in Asia, Africa, and Latin America, but also in comparison with many much more modern European countries. A well-developed political system has strong and distinct institutions to perform both the "input" and the "output" functions of politics. India entered independence with not only two organizations, but two highly developed—adaptable, complex, autonomous, and coherent—institutions ready to assume primary responsibility for these functions. The Congress Party, founded in 1885, was one of the oldest and bestorganized political parties in the world; the Indian Civil Service, dating from the early nineteenth century, has been appropriately hailed as "one of the greatest administrative systems of all time."[10] The stable, effective, and democratic government of India during the first fifteen years of independence rested far more on this institutional inheritance than it did on the charisma of Nehru. In addition, the relatively slow pace of modernization and social mobilization in India did not create demands and strains which the Party and the bureaucracy were unable to handle. So long as these two organizations maintain their institutional strength, it is ridiculous to think of India as politically underdeveloped, no matter how low her per capita income or how high her illiteracy rate.

*   *   *

STRATEGIES OF INSTITUTIONAL DEVELOPMENT

If decay of political institutions is a widespread phenomenon in the "developing" countries and if a major cause of this decay is the high rate of social mobilization, it behooves us, as social scientists, to call a spade a spade and to incorporate these tendencies into any general model of political change which we employ to understand the politics of these areas. If effective political institutions are necessary for stable and eventually

democratic government and if they are also a precondition of sustained economic growth, it behooves us, as policy analysts, to suggest strategies of institutional development. . . .

*   *   *

Given our hypotheses about the relation of social mobilization to institutionalization, there are two obvious methods of furthering institutional development. First, anything which slows social mobilization presumably creates conditions more favorable to the preservation and strengthening of institutions. Secondly, strategies can be developed and applied directly to the problem of institution-building.

Slowing Mobilization

Social mobilization can be moderated in many ways. Three methods are: to increase the complexity of social structure; to limit or reduce communications in society; and to minimize competition among segments of the political elite.[11]

In general, the more highly stratified a society is and the more complicated its social structure, the more gradual is the process of political mobilization. The divisions between class and class, occupation and occupation, rural and urban, constitute a series of breakwaters which divide the society and permit the political mobilization of one group at a time. On the other hand, a highly homogeneous society, or a society which has only a single horizontal line of division between an oligarchy that has everything and a peasantry that has nothing, or a society which is divided not horizontally but vertically into ethnic and communal groups, has more difficulty moderating the process of mobilization. . . .

The communications network of a society is undoubtedly much more subject to governmental influence. Rapid gains in some of the most desired areas of modernization—such as mass media exposure, literacy, and education—may have to be purchased at the price of severe losses in political stability. This is not to argue that political institutionalization as a value should take precedence over all others; if this were the case, modernization would never be good. It is simply to argue that governments must balance the values won through rapid increases in communications against the values jeopardized by losses in political stability. . . .

The uncontrolled mobilization of people into politics is also slowed by minimizing the competition among political elites. Hence mobilization is likely to have less disturbing effects on political institutions in one-party systems than in two-party or multiparty systems. In many new states and modernizing countries, a vast gap exists between the modernized elite and the tradition-oriented mass. If the elite divides against itself, its factions appeal to the masses for support. This produces rapid mobilization of the masses into politics at the same time that it destroys whatever consensus previously existed among the politically active on the need for modernization. Mobilization frequently means the mobilization of tradition; modern politics become the vehicle of traditional purposes. . . .

Creating Institutions

. . . in the contemporary world, political leaders prefer modernization to institution-building, and no matter who leads modernization, the process itself generates conflicting demands and inducements which obstruct the growth of political institutions. Where modernization is undertaken by traditional leaders working through traditional political institutions, the efforts of the traditional leaders to reform can unleash and stimulate social forces which threaten the traditional political institutions. Traditional leaders can modernize and reform their realms, but, where substantial social elements oppose reform, they have yet to demonstrate they can put through reforms without undermining the institutions through which they are working. The problem is: how can the traditional political institutions be adapted to accommodate the social forces unleashed by modernization? . . .

* * *

The Primacy of Party

Charismatic leaders and military chiefs have . . . had little success in building modern political institutions. The reason lies in the nature of modern politics. In the absence of traditional political institutions, the only modern organization which can become a source of authority and which can be effectively institutionalized is the political party. *The importance of the political party in providing legitimacy and stability in a modernizing political system varies inversely with the institutional inheritance of the system from traditional society.* Traditional systems do not have political parties. Unlike bureaucracy, the party is a distinctly modern form of political organization. Where traditional political institutions (such as monarchies and feudal parliaments) are carried over into the modern era, parties play secondary, supplementary roles in the political system. The other institutions are the primary source of continuity and legitimacy. Parties typically originate within the legislatures and then gradually extend themselves into society. They adapt themselves to the existing framework of the political system and typically reflect in their own operations the organizational and procedural principles embodied in that system. They broaden participation in the traditional institutions, thus adapting those institutions to the requirements of the modern polity. They help make the traditional institutions legitimate in terms of popular sovereignty, but they are not themselves a source of legitimacy. Their own legitimacy derives from the contributions they make to the political system.

Where traditional political institutions collapse or are weak or non-existent, the role of the party is entirely different from what it is in those polities with institutional continuity. In such situations, strong party organization is the only long-run alternative to the instability of a corrupt or praetorian or mass society. The party is not just a supplementary organization; it is instead the source of legitimacy and authority. In the absence of traditional sources of legitimacy, legitimacy is sought in ideology, charisma, popular sovereignty. To be lasting, each of these principles of legitimacy must be embodied in a party. Instead of the party reflecting the state, the state becomes the creation of the party and the instrument of the party. The actions of government are legitimate to the extent that they reflect the will of the party. The party is the source of legitimacy because it is the institutional embodiment of national sovereignty, the popular will, or the dictatorship of the proletariat.

Where traditional political institutions are weak or non-existent, the prerequisite of stability is at least one highly institutionalized political party. States with one such party are markedly more stable than states which lack such a party. States with no parties or many weak parties are the least stable. Where traditional political institutions are smashed by revolution, post-revolutionary order depends on the emergence of one strong party: witness the otherwise very different histories of the Chinese, Mexican, Russian, and Turkish revolutions. Where new states emerge from colonialism with one strong party, the problem is to maintain the strength of that party. In many African countries the nationalist party was the single important modern organization to exist before independence. The party "was generally well organized. The conditions of the political struggle and the dedication of the top elite to the party as the prime instrument of political change led the elite to give the major portion of their energies and resources to building a solid, responsive organization capable of disciplined action in response to directives from the top and able to ferret out and exploit feelings of dissatisfaction among the masses for political ends."[12] After independence, however, the dominant political party is often weakened by the many competing demands on organizational resources. A marked dispersion of resources means a decline in the overall level of political institutionalization. "Talents that once were available for the crucial work of party organization," one observer has warned, "may now be preoccupied with running a ministry or government bureau. . . . Unless new sources of loyal organizational and administrative talents can be found immediately, the party's organization—and, therefore, the major link between the regime and the masses—is likely to be weakened."[13]

The need for concentration applies not only to the allocation of resources among types of organizations but also to the scope of organization. In many modernizing countries, the political leaders attempt too much too fast; they try to build mass organizations when they should concentrate on elite organizations. Organizations do not have to be large to be effective and to play a crucial role in the political process.

* * *

Notes

[1] William Kornhauser, *The Politics of Mass Society* (Glencoe 1959), 145.

[2] Ibid., 146.

[3] See Mancur Olson, Jr., "Rapid Growth as a Destabilizing Force," *Journal of Economic History*, XXVII (December 1963), 529–52; and Bert F. Hoselitz and Myron Weiner, "Economic Development and Political Stability in India," *Dissent*, VIII (Spring 1961), 172–79.

[4] See Daniel Lerner, "Toward a Communication Theory of Modernization," in Pye, ed., *Communications and Political Development*, 330ff.

[5] John J. Johnson, *The Military and Society in Latin America* (Stanford 1964), 98–99.

[6] Lucian W. Pye, *Politics, Personality and Nation Building* (New Haven 1962), 4–5.

[7] See, in general, Ronald E. Wraith and Edgar Simpkins, *Corruption in Developing Countries* (London 1963).

[8] Simon Bolivar, quoted in K. H. Silvert, ed., *Expectant Peoples: Nationalism and Development* (New York 1963), 347.

[9] *El Dia*, Quito, November 27, 1943, quoted in Bryce Wood, *The Making of the Good Neighbor Policy* (New York 1961), 318.

[10] Ralph Braibanti, "Public Bureaucracy and Judiciary in Pakistan," in LaPalombara, ed., *Bureaucracy and Political Development*, 373.

[11] These are not, of course, the only ways of slowing mobilization. Myron Weiner, for instance, has suggested that one practical method is "localization": channeling political interests and activity away from the great issues of national politics to the more immediate and concrete problems of the village and community. This is certainly one motive behind both community development programs and "basic democracies."

[12] William J. Foltz, "Building the Newest Nations: Short-Run Strategies and Long-Run Problems," in Deutsch and Foltz, eds., Nation-Building, 121.

[13] Ibid., 123–24.

To this point, our review of the literature associated with the analysis of political change has been devoted primarily to the work of theorists who have a particular theory to grind. It is useful, however, to examine one analysis of political change that did not start with a particular theoretical viewpoint but was the work of a historian who sought to observe and record similarities in several different political revolutions. Crane Brinton's book, *The Anatomy of Revolu-*

tion, has been widely accepted as the most important contemporary analysis of political change and revolution.[16]

Interestingly enough, Brinton posits five similarities that he discerned in four very different political revolutions. These common characteristics of revolutionary situations in many ways confirm aspects of the various theories discussed in the foregoing sections of this chapter. For instance, Brinton found that economic up-turns were a condition of the revolutions he studied, that class conflicts were evident, that the intellectuals in the revolutionary context deserted the established regime and sought new allegiances with different ideas and ideologies, that the political process was ineffective in dealing with social problems, and that the ruling elites lost confidence in their ability to deal with the society's problems.

AN OVERVIEW

Part II began by positing that the emergence of a behavioral paradigm within the discipline of political science has gravely influenced the analysis and evaluation of democracy by contemporary political scientists. Proponents of the paradigm have explicitly sought to be scientific and value free in their analyses, while at the same time they have implicitly placed value on the American political experience.

The impact of the paradigm has been substantial, and its most significant influence has been to effect the reconceptualization of the notion of evaluation. Evaluation in traditional theory meant to compare what is going on with what should be going on, as prescribed by the ideals of a normative theory of governance. Reality was to be evaluated by comparing it with a set of conditions that were preferable, given the prescriptions of the normative theory. Evaluation, under the influence of the behavioral paradigm, became reality testing. No longer were the realities of politics being tested against some preferred state of affairs; rather, theoretical models were being tested against what was going on in the real world. If theories did not match reality, the theory had to be reconstructed, rather than the reality being changed to more clearly fit the prescriptions of the ideal.

This change in emphasis has, in turn, had profound influence on what has been going on in the analysis and evaluation of American democracy. The behavioral paradigm, as traced through its influence on both research and theorizing in political analysis, has resulted in the redefining of the very meaning of democracy. Behavioralists constructed a scientific theory of democracy, viewing it as a process of bargaining among competitive political elites. Democracy now meant the existence of a reality of multiple elites competing for valued advantages, rather than a system of government where the people were sovereign. Thus, the behavioral paradigm generated a widespread consensus in political science around basic values that have here been termed the invisible ideology. This ideology is separate from both the behavioral paradigm and the theory of competitive elites, but it has served to support the influence of these conceptualizations and views of the world.

The invisible ideology values systems over people, it values the functioning of the system over issue conflict, it values fitting people to systems rather than systems to people, and it values change within the system rather than change of the systems. These values have substantially reversed the meaning of democracy, as it was conceptualized in the classic liberal theory of democracy.

The invisible ideology has influenced how people define democracy and how they evaluate its performance. No longer is our political system being evaluated in terms of what it should and might be, but in terms of whether or not it is going to last.

The invisible ideology has been found to influence much that is going on in contemporary political analysis. Particularly, its influence is apparent in research on the individual's relationship to the society and in research on the area of change. Political socialization has focused on fitting people to the functioning of a stable system, and the analysis of change—with a few exceptions—has been viewed as change within a society, rather than as change of the form of the society.

Although these trends do not necessarily represent a total consensus within political science today, they have had a profound influence on the analysis and evaluation of democracy and politics.

[16] Crane Brinton, *The Anatomy of Revolution* (New York: Vintage Books, 1965), pp. 250–64.

Part Three
Toward a Developmental Paradigm of Politics

In Part I of this book we saw how political theories emerged out of such historical phenomena as the collapse of the Greek democracies, the rise and fall of the Roman Empire, the conflict between spiritual and secular authorities, the power of the great nation-states, waves of revolutions, and the·emergence of mass democracy. In Part II we saw how contemporary political scientists have grappled with the phenomenon of mass democracy in the United States, trying to understand how it works, to locate its centers of power, and to find out whether it is, in fact, democratic. We saw, too, how the study of politics in our time has been dominated increasingly by the philosophical values, the ideas about what truth is and how to find it, that characterize our modern scientific-technological culture.

In these final chapters we will be sketching the outlines of a new approach to the science of politics, an approach that we describe as "developmental." This approach is both different from—and similar to—the behavioral approach that has been described in the foregoing chapters. Perhaps it can best be described as a shift of priorities.

The first priority of behavioral political science is accuracy. This may well be its greatest strength, but it has also been the source of its weaknesses. The search for scientific precision has led to excessive quantification, to avoidance of problems that are not readily dealt with in acceptably precise terms, to downgrading of subjective experience, and to a tendency for political science research to be communicated exclusively by, for, and among experts.

The first priority of developmental political science is usefulness—or, to use a more loaded word, relevance. It begins with ideas of the purpose of study; research is conceived not only in terms of *how* (the main question in behavioral methodology) but equally in terms of *why*. It seeks to make explicit the nature of the problem that may be solved by the discovery of new knowledge, to identify and communicate with the people who may be able to use the information.

These two perspectives are not totally exclusive of each other. Political scientists in the behavioral era have always had some degree of concern for the social usefulness of their work, and those who are now moving toward a new orientation are doing so with the intention of making maximum use of the empirical research know-how that has been produced by behavioralists. The difference is largely a matter of priority: The priority of developmental research is to facilitate the growth and well-being of people, and to value scientific accuracy not merely for its own sake but also in terms of its ability to contribute to developmental goals.

When we speak of "development," we do not mean economic or industrial development, but human development. It is obvious that some of the writers included in this section, who are speaking on behalf of a new humanistic/developmental approach to political science, are highly critical of much of the existing "political development" literature. These spokesmen for a new paradigm tend to take as their models for thinking about society the theories of psychologists of personal development, such as Piaget, Erickson, Kohlberg, and Fromm. Even more frequently they cite the work of Abraham Maslow, the father of modern humanistic psychology.

As an introduction to this body of thought we will briefly summarize here some of the key concepts of Maslow's work:

1. *Health.* The starting point of Maslow's innovative work was the conviction that psychology had become preoccupied with mental illness and had failed to address itself to the task of exploring the highest possibilities of health. He said: "It becomes more and more clear that the study of crippled, stunted, immature, and unhealthy specimens can yield only a cripple psychology and a cripple philosophy."[1]

2. *Self-actualization.* In pursuit of greater knowledge about human health, Maslow studied superior, "self-actualiz-

ing" people, those who had achieved "the full use and exploitation of talents, capacities, potentialities, etc. . . . people who have developed or are developing to the full stature of which they are capable."[2] Out of this research with the fortunate and highly endowed few came a hypothesis of more wide and general application: that the drive toward self-actualization is biologically based and species-wide, that all human beings possess an inherent capacity and need for higher levels of personal development.

3. *Need hierarchy.* This basic developmental theory seeks to order human needs into a meaningful pattern. It holds that all human beings are motivated by certain needs, which can be understood in terms of a hierarchical growth pattern. As the most basic needs are satisfied, new and higher needs will tend to emerge and to require the attention of the growing organism. The most basic are physiological needs, such as those for food, shelter, sex, sleep, air. The next are safety needs, then belongingness and love needs, then esteem needs—self-respect and respect from others; the highest are self-actualization needs. The theory says that satisfaction of needs at one level will normally lead to concentration on the next higher set of needs, and that deprivation will block or fix development at any level.

This model does not, of course, ignore economic or industrial development, but it does tend to measure its value in human terms. The satisfaction of needs for food and shelter are recognized as essential starting points for human development; consequently, any technological progress that can effectively contribute toward this basic goal is valuable. However, if technological progress also produces a high degree of alienation and dehumanization—frustration of needs for belongingness, love, and esteem—then it cannot be considered entirely "advanced." In short, economic-industrial development and human development are possibly but not necessarily the same thing.

The difference between the behavioral and developmental approaches can also be stated in terms of different ways of looking at mass democracy. The behavioral paradigm tends to produce mechanistic images of politics; government is seen as a system, a communications net of inputs and

---

[1] *Motivation and Personality* (New York: Harper and Row, 1954), p. 180.

[2] Ibid., p. 200.

outputs and feedback loops, or, in Easton's term, "a huge and complex factory."[3] The mechanistic view of mass democracy reveals vast countervailing forces, which balance, overlap, compete, and feed demands into a political order that periodically disgorges policy outputs, which, in turn, govern the lives of human beings. It is, of course, understood that individuals play a part in all this, but there is a strong preference for dealing with larger units—that is, interest groups—and because of the emphasis on external, verifiable behavior, there is a strong bias toward viewing participation in terms of explicit and measurable demands. Also, there is a tendency to pay more attention to competition than to cooperation.

Traditional or prebehavioral American political science had been committed to classical democratic theory, to the heritage of the constitution-writers and the Enlightenment philosophers. The behavioralists tried to break political science free of this ideological commitment, to show that democracy in practice was far different from democracy in theory. They mobilized powerful evidence against the view of political behavior as rational and reasoned action, against the faith in "natural" rights. They showed that the political order was subject to the power of large interest groups and that the voter, the fundamental unit of classical democracy, was often ignorant and apathetic. These revelations quickly became the basis of a new ideology, an invisible one. It said, in essence, that what we have is not classical democracy, but something better: a more realistic way of dealing with the forces and facts of a massive industrialized society. The pillars of classical liberal doctrine crumbled into dust, as one writer put it, and in its place arose a new democratic doctrine, sometimes described as pluralism or interest-group liberalism.

But the pillars of pluralism are already showing signs of wear. They were severely buffeted by the political upheavals of the past decade, and a variety of searches are now underway for some new way of evaluating mass democracy as a form of human organization. Our aim in these final chapters is to pull together some of these efforts, to show how work along many fronts—in several disciplines and political persuasions, in policy analysis and action research—is contributing toward the creation of a new political paradigm.

If the prevailing image of government under the behavioral paradigm is mechanistic, then what might be the alternative image to emerge from a developmental paradigm? One promising model is that of synergy.

The idea of synergy comes to political science from anthropology, by way of psychology. It originated out of Ruth Benedict's attempts to explain the striking differences in aggression among different cultures. Her findings are quoted in the following passage from an article by Maslow:

The conclusion that emerges is that societies where non-aggression is conspicuous have social orders in which the individual by the same act and at the same time serves his own advantage and that of the group . . . *Non-aggression occurs (in these societies) not because people are unselfish and put social obligations above personal desires, but when social arrangements make these two identical. . . .*

I shall speak of cultures with low synergy where the social structure provides for acts which are mutually opposed and counteractive, and of cultures with high synergy where it provides for acts which are mutually reinforcing. . . . I spoke of societies with high social synergy where their institutions insure mutual advantage from their undertakings, and societies with low synergy where the advantage of one individual becomes a victory over another, and the majority who are not victorious must shift as they can.[4]

To bring the idea of synergy into clearer focus, it is helpful to examine briefly what it is not. One nonsynergistic view of society states that there is a natural and inevitable difference between the needs of a civilized society and the needs of individuals. Sigmund Freud argued this. He said: "It is impossible to overlook the extent to which civilization is built up upon a renunciation of instinct, how much it presupposes precisely the nonsatisfaction. . . . of powerful instincts."[5] This view, that one must pay a certain price of frustration and unhappiness in return for the benefits of civilized life, is widely and deeply embedded in our culture. So is the assumption of scarcity, of limited goods: There is not enough to go around, and so social and political

---

[3] David Easton, *A Systems Analysis of Political Life* (New York: John Wiley and Sons, 1965), p. 72.

[4] Ruth Benedict, quoted in A. H. Maslow, "Synergy in the Society and in the Individual," *Journal of Individual Psychology*, (1964) p. 20, 156.

[5] Sigmund Freud, *Civilization and Its Discontents*, trans. James Strachey (New York: Norton, 1961), p. 44.

interaction can be understood as largely a matter of competition among individuals (or groups), in which there are inevitably winners and losers, "haves" and "have-nots." The study of politics is thus the study of who gets what, when, and how—with the understanding that for everyone who gets, there is somebody else who does not. This picture of how things work usually refers not only to a limited quantity of tangible commodities such as food and housing, but also to intangibles—the items higher on Maslow's need hierarchy, such as love and self-esteem. The concept of synergy suggests the possibility that there may be social structures that do not require that the esteem needs of one segment of society be satisfied only through the deprivation of some other segment.

Although there have been some enthusiastic preliminary discussions about using the concept of synergy in analyzing and evaluating modern institutional structures—one writer calls it "the basis for a scientific description of a good society"[6]—it has so far been used only in the study of primitive cultures.[7] It is introduced here because it appears to be a useful building block for a developmental political science. It enables us to think about political institutions and historical processes in terms of the effects they have upon the growth of individuals, and thus to make wider use of the existing knowledge about personal growth and change.

With a political science firmly grounded in developmental concepts, it would be possible to evaluate the institutions of mass democracy not only in terms of their stability or economic productivity, but also in terms of their ability to facilitate the growth and self-actualization of the people who are affected by them. Also, new—and scientifically valid—ways of understanding how the upheavals of our time have touched the lives of individuals might be discovered.

[6] Frank Goble, *The Third Force* (New York: Pocket Books, 1971), p. 114.

[7] See Ruth Benedict, *Patterns of Culture* (Boston: Houghton Mifflin, 1934). The theory of synergy was developed later, as a way of explaining some of the cultural differences that had been discovered in the earlier studies. See Goble, op. cit., pp. 111-15.

9/Evaluating the Pluralist Ideology

THE CORPORATE STATE: CRITIQUES

The pluralist, political-systems view of mass democracy that emerged from the behavioral revolution still prevails within the discipline. Yet, this view has always had to contend and coexist with its opposition, most notably those views that consider mass democracy as a dangerous concentration of power and wealth in the hands of elites, and today the critics of the pluralist ideology appear to be growing ever more numerous. The dialogue between the defenders and the critics of pluralism is not a contest of abstractions; it is, rather, a vital debate about the quality of our political system and about the quality of life in America in our time.

Not long ago Robert Dahl—who wrote one of the classics of pluralist analysis, *Who Governs?*, and coined the term "polyarchy" to describe the existing system[1]—seemed to have joined the critics. He pointed out three large areas of inequity in the American political order: (1) an inequality of resources—of material wealth, opportunity for personal choice and self-esteem, capacity for political action; (2) a lack of workable democratic controls over business and industry; and (3) the absence of wide effective participation in decision making by the majority of the population.

Although Dahl has pointed out ways in which the American system falls short of ideal democracy and has suggested some rather sweeping changes in it, his reform proposals are for change within the pluralist system. He says:

Although polyarchy shows up badly compared with unrealized ideal forms, it looks very much better when it is compared with other political systems that have actually existed up to the present. In particular, when it is placed alongside rival political forms that have been tried out in this century—waves of the future that swept the people overboard—polyarchy looks to be not only incomparably closer to genuine rule by the people but much more humane, decent, tolerant, benign, and responsive in dealing with its own citizens.

The antique trademark of the state is coercion. And polyarchies have most definitely not eliminated coercion. In dealing with persons who are de jure or de facto excluded from citizenship—foreigners, colonials, people in enemy countries, and, in the United States for a full century after the Civil War, southern blacks—polyarchies have yet to show that they are on the whole superior to the average run of states in the past. Yet polyarchies rarely adopt highly coercive measures (or if they do, rarely enforce them for long) against any group of citizens with recourse to the ballot and other processes of polyarchy. Taken all in all, in comparison with the alternatives cast up by history rather than by imagination, polyarchy must be appraised, I believe, as a superior instrument for achieving a decent government among a very large body of citizens.[2]

Other observers of modern American government, however, criticize not only certain inequities in the system

[1] Polyarchy is used by Dahl to describe "rule by many" as opposed to rule by one or a small group or, at the other extreme, pure democracy. Robert A. Dahl, *Modern Political Analysis* (Englewood Cliffs, N.J.: Prentice-Hall, 1963), p. 73. He now uses the term to mean "'representative democracy as we know it in practice,' that is, systems with broad electorates, extensive opportunities to oppose the government and contest it in elections, competitive political parties, peaceful displacement of officials defeated in honestly conducted elections, and so on." Dahl, *After the Revolution?* (New Haven: Yale University Press, 1970), p. 78.

[2] Ibid., pp. 140–41.

but the system itself—and not only the system, but the pluralist ideology that explains and to some extent justifies the system. We will present selections from two such criticisms in this chapter: Charles Reich's *The Greening of America* and Theodore Lowi's *The End of Liberalism*.

When Reich describes America as a "corporate state," he is presenting a refutation of the pluralist view of mass democracy as a system of countervailing forces, of government as the mediator among the demands of various groups. As he sees it, the public and private sectors flow together, and the power blocs and power elites avoid competition whenever possible: "The various units of the Corporate State no longer appear to be parts of a diverse and pluralistic system in which one kind of power limits another kind of power; the various centers of power do not limit each other, they all weigh in on the same side of the scale, with only the individual on the other side."

The context within which Reich presents his concept of the corporate state—the theory of Consciousness I, II, and III—is an example of one kind of a developmental model, one in which history is seen as evolving successively higher levels of personal consciousness. In this system, Consciousness I represents the political values of early America, the psychology of the rugged individualist; Consciousness II, a more advanced stage of historical growth, can be seen as the mind of the organization man, the role-player within the vast and complex political system; and Consciousness III stands for the emerging revolution of thought and feeling that will render such political systems—indeed, the state itself, as it is presently conceived—obsolete.

Reich, working with a developmental system, characterizes the corporate state as the manifestation of a certain kind of human consciousness. Lowi, working within a more traditional frame of reference, sees the problem as fundamentally one of weaknesses in the "public philosophy." The two approaches agree in their criticism, although Reich operates from a revolutionary perspective and Lowi operates from a conservative one. Reich calls for a transformation of consciousness to carry us beyond the inequities of our present political order. Lowi calls for a return to principles, constitutionality, and the rule of law; the failing of the pluralist system, as Lowi sees it, lies in the abandonment of law for the improvised mediating of interest-group demands.

"Pluralistic government," Lowi writes, "depended upon policy without law." Furthermore, "underlying pluralist political theory provided reasoning for the necessity and the justification of policy without law." Lowi's prescription for eliminating the inequities is to use—really use—our heritage of constitutional democracy and law. His hope for the future is "juridical democracy."

Lowi describes pluralism as an "ideology," and thus his argument has a particular relevance to some of the issues that were raised in Part II of this text. When the underlying assumptions of pluralism are being discussed in these terms, it is an indication that the "invisible ideology" is becoming increasingly visible, that the issues for discussing the future of political science are beginning to be more clearly drawn.

ANATOMY OF THE CORPORATE STATE

CHARLES REICH

* * *

Our present system has gone beyond anything that could properly be called the creation of capitalism or imperialism or a power elite. That, at least, would be a human shape. Of course a power elite does exist and is made rich by the system, but the elite are no longer in control, they are now merely taking advantage of forces that have a life of their own. Nor is our system a purely technological society, although technology has increasingly supplied the basis for our choices and superseded other values. What we have is technology, organization, and administration out of control, running for their own sake, but at the same time subject to manipulation and profiteering by the power interests of our society for their own non-human ends. And we have turned over to this system the control and direction of everything—the natural environment, our minds, our lives. Other societies have had bad systems, but have endured because a part of life went on outside the system. We have turned over everything, rendered ourselves powerless, and thus allowed mindless machinery to become our master.

The American Corporate State today can be thought of as a single vast corporation, with every person as an involuntary member and employee. It consists primarily of large industrial organizations, plus nonprofit institutions such as foundations and the educational system, all related to the whole as divisions to a business corporation. Government is only a part of the state, but government coordinates it and provides a variety of needed services. The Corporate State is a complete reversal of the original American ideal and plan. The State, and not the market or the people or any abstract economic laws, determines what shall be produced, what shall be consumed, and how it shall be allocated. It determines, for example, that railroads shall decay while highways flourish; that coal miners shall be poor and advertising executives rich. Jobs and occupations in the society are rigidly defined and controlled, and arranged in a hierarchy of rewards, status, and authority. An individual can move from one position to another, but he gains little freedom thereby, for in each position he is subject to conditions imposed upon it; individuals have no protected area of liberty, privacy, or individual sovereignty beyond the reach of the State. The State is subject neither to democratic controls, constitutional limits, or legal regulation. Instead, the organizations in the Corporate State are motivated primarily by the demands of technology and of their own internal structure. . . .

*   *   *

. . . we shall attempt to outline the main features of the Corporate State. We shall build our picture out of several elements, but the description is cumulative, for it is the *interrelationship* of the elements that gives the State its extraordinary form. . . .

1. AMALGAMATION AND INTEGRATION

We normally consider the units of the Corporate State, such as the federal government, an automobile company, a private foundation, as if they were separate from each other. This is, however, not the case. In the first place, there is a marked tendency for "separate" units to follow parallel policies, so that an entire industry makes identical decisions as to pricing, kind of product, and method of distribution; the automobile and the air travel industries show this. Second, very different companies are coming under combined management through the device of conglomerates, which place vast and diverse empires under a single unified control. But even more significant is the disappearance of the line between "public" and "private." In the Corporate State, most of the "public" functions of government are actually performed by the "private" sector of the economy. And most "government" functions are services performed for the private sector.

Let us consider first how government operations are "privately" performed. To a substantial degree, this relationship is formalized. The government hires "private" firms to build national defense systems, to supply the space program, to construct the interstate highway system, and sometimes, in the case of the think institutes, to do its "thinking" for it. An enormous portion of the federal budget is spent in simply hiring out government functions. This much is obvious, although many people do not seem to be aware of it. What is less obvious is the "deputizing" system by which a far larger sector of the "private" economy is enlisted in government service.

. . . consider a foundation which receives a special tax-exempt status. The foundation is in this favored position because it is engaged in activities which are of "public benefit." That is, it is the judgment of the government that some types of activities are public services although performed under private auspices. The government itself could do what private foundations now do aid education, sponsor research, and other things which do not command a profit in the commercial sense. It is the government's decision that these same functions are better performed by foundations. It is the same judgment that government makes when it hires Boeing to build bombers, or a private construction firm to build an interstate highway. Public utilities—airlines, railroads, truck carriers, taxicabs, oil pipe lines, the telephone company—all are "deputized" in this fashion. They carry on *public* functions—functions that in other societies might be performed by the government itself.

* * *

Let us now look at the opposite side of the coin: government as the servant of the "private" sector. Once again, sometimes the relationship is formal and obvious. The government spends huge amounts for research and development, and private companies are often able to get the benefits of this. Airports are built at public expense for private airlines to use. Highways are built for private trucking firms to use. The government pays all sorts of subsidies, direct and indirect, to various industries. It supplies credit services and financial aid to homeowners. It grows trees on public forest lands and sells them at cut-rate prices to private lumber companies. It builds roads to aid ski developments.

It is true that government has always existed to serve the society; that police and fire departments help business too; that paving streets helps business, and so do wars that open up new markets—and that is what government is and always has been all about. But today, governmental activity in aid of the private sector is enormously greater, more pervasive, more immediately felt than ever before. The difference between the local public services in 1776 and millions of dollars in subsidies to the shipping industry may be a difference of degree but it is still quite a difference. But the difference is not only one of degree. In the difference between a highly autonomous, localized economy and a highly interdependent one, there is a difference of principle as well as one of degree. Government help today is *essential*, not a luxury. The airlines could not operate without allocation of routes and regulation of landing and take-offs, nor could the television industry. The educational system, elementary school through high school, is essential for the production of people able to work in today's industry. Thus it may be said that everyone who operates "privately" really is aided and subsidized, to one degree or another, by the public; the sturdy, independent rancher rides off into the sunset on land irrigated by government subsidy, past sheep whose grazing is subsidized and crops whose prices are artificially maintained by governmental action; he does not look like a welfare client, but he is on the dole nevertheless.

Regulation itself is a service to industry. The film industry and the professional sports industry have elaborate systems of private regulation, including "commissioners;" a system of laws and government, fines and penalties, all designed to place the industry on the best and most united basis to sell its product. Such "regulation" as is performed by such federal agencies as FCC, SEC, FTC, and CAB, is remarkably similar in general effect, but it is a service rendered at taxpayers' expense. Indeed, there is a constant interchange of personnel between the regulatory agencies and industry; government men leave to take high-paying positions with the corporations they formerly regulated; agency officials are frequently appointed from industry ranks.

This public-private and private-public integration, when added to the inescapable legislative power we have already described, gives us the picture of the State as a single corporation. Once the line between "public" and "private" becomes meaningless and is erased, the various units of the Corporate State no longer appear to be parts of a diverse and pluralistic system in which one kind of power limits another kind of power; the various centers of power do not limit each other, they all weigh in on the same side of the scale, with only the individual on the other side. With public and private merged, we can discern the real monolith of power and realize there is nothing at all within the system to impose checks and balances, to offer competition, to raise even a voice of caution or doubt. We are all involuntary members, and there is no zone of the private to offer a retreat.

* * *

2. THE PRINCIPLE OF ADMINISTRATION AND HIERARCHY

The activities, policies, and decisions of a society might theoretically be carried out by a variety of methods—voluntary cooperation by individuals, the physical coercion of a military tyranny, or the psychological conditioning of B. F. Skinner's *Walden Two*. The Corporate State has chosen to rely on the method of administration and hierarchy. So pervasive, indeed, is the principle of administration that in many ways the Corporate State is in its essence an administrative state. The theory of administration is that the best way to conduct any activity is to subject it to rational control. A framework of organization is provided. Lines of authority, responsibility, and supervision are established as clearly as possible; everyone is arranged in a hierarchy. Rules are drawn for every imaginable contingency, so that individual choice is minimized. Arrangements are made to check on what everyone does, to have reports and permanent records. The random, the irrational, and the alternative ways of doing things are banished.

It is worth recalling how this State derived from classic liberalism, and, more proximately, from the New Deal and the welfare state. Liberalism adopted the basic principle that there is no need for management of society itself; the "unseen hand" is all that is needed. The New Deal modified this by requiring activities to be subject to "the public interest." Gradually this came to mean ever-tightening regulation in directions fixed by the demands of a commercial, technological, mass society. Gradually it came to mean the replacement of a "political" state with an "administrative" state. . . .

* * *

The structure of the administrative state is that of a hierarchy in which every person has a place in a table of organization, a vertical position in which he is subordinate to someone and superior to someone else. This is the structure of any bureaucracy; it represents a "rationalization" of organization ideals. When an entire society is subjected to this principle, it creates a small ruling elite and a large group of workers who play no significant part in the making of decisions. While they continue to vote in political elections, they are offered little choice among the candidates; all the major decisions about what is produced, what is consumed, how resources are allocated, the conditions of work, and so forth, are made administratively.

* * *

Administration seeks to remove decision-making

from the area of politics to the area of "science." It does not accept democratic or popular choice; this is rejected in favor of professionals and experts and a rational weighing of all of the factors. Procedures are set up by which decision-making is channeled, and care is taken to define exactly which institution shall make which decisions. For each type of decision, there is someone "best" qualified to decide it; administration avoids participation in decisions by the less qualified. Its greatest outrage is directed toward a refusal to enter into its procedures—this seems almost a denial of the very principle of administration. If followed, these procedures usually produce a decision that is a compromise or balance which rejects any particular choice in its pure, uncompromised form. Choice takes place within narrow limits. A weighing of all the factors produces a decision somewhere in between, rather than one or another "extreme."

Administration has no values of its own, except for the institutional ones just described. It has no ideas; it is just professional management. Theoretically, it could accept any values. In practice, however, it is strongly conservative. Things go most smoothly when the status quo is maintained, when change is slow, cautious, and evolutionary. The more elaborate the machinery of administration, the less ready it is for new, disquieting values. . . .

* * *

3. THE CORPORATE STATE IS AUTONOMOUS

What controls the amalgamated power of the Corporate State? We usually make at least three reassuring assumptions. One: power is controlled by the people through the democratic process and pluralism in the case of government, and through the market in the case of the "private" sector. Two: power is controlled by the persons who are placed in a position of authority to exercise it. Three: power is subject to the Constitution and the laws. These assumptions stand as a presumed barrier to the state power we have described. We will deal with the first two in this section, and the third in a later section on law.

As machinery for translating popular will into political effect, the American system functions impossibly badly. We can hardly say that our political process makes it possible for voters to enforce their will on such subjects as pollution, the supersonic plane, mass transportation, the arms race, or the Vietnam War. On the contrary, if there are any popularly held views, it is impossible for them to be expressed politically; this was demonstrated for all to see in the 1968 presidential campaign, where both candidates supported the Vietnam War. Even if the political machinery did allow the electorate to express its views, it is difficult for citizens to get the information necessary to form an opinion.

What we have said with respect to the failure of the political process is also true with respect to the "private" economic process which supposedly is governed by a market. There is nothing at all to "stockholder democracy" in the control of corporations; it has long been true that stockholders have no realistic power in the government of corporate affairs. But the more important fact is that producers largely create their own demand for products. . . .

If pure democratic theory fails us in both the public and private spheres, we must nevertheless consider whether a modified version of democracy can permit large competing interests to achieve a balance which represents a rough approximation of what people want; this is the theory of pluralism. Here again, the theory simply does not work out. . . . "Pluralism" represents not interests, but *organized* interests. Thus, "labor" means large labor organizations, but these do not necessarily represent the real interests of individual employees. "Labor" may support heavy defense expenditures, repressive police measures, and emphasis on economic growth, but this may not be at all an expression of the true interests of the industrial worker. Likewise the three major religions may fail to represent the more individual spiritual strivings of persons which might take such forms as resistance to the draft. Indeed, at the organizational level there is far more agreement than difference among the "competing interests," so that they come to represent the same type of cooperation as conglomerate mergers produce among interests in the private sphere. Even if the people had power to give orders, the

orders might have little or no effect. Increasingly, the important part of government is found in the executive departments, which are staffed by career men, experts, professionals, and civil servants who have specialized knowledge of technical fields. These persons are not elected, nor are they subject to removal on political grounds. They are thus immunized from direct democratic control. Congress and the state legislatures, however, have neither the time nor the specialized knowledge to oversee all of these governmental activities. Instead, the legislatures have increasingly resorted to broad delegations of authority. . . .

If the people do not control the Corporate State, is it at least controlled by those who give the orders—the executives and the power elite behind them? Such control might not satisfy those who favor democracy or the rule of law, but it would still be control that had to consider the broad trends of public opinion—still a major difference from no control at all.

Let us focus on an imaginary organization —government or private (an agency or corporation)—and its executive head—the personification of the "power elite." We enter into the paneled executive suite or, in the case of a more sophisticated organization, a suite in the most advanced taste, and there we expect to find an individual or "team" who really do exercise power. But the trappings, from the modern sculpture to the console telephone, do not tell the whole story. Any organization is subject to the demands of technology, of its own organization, and to its own middle-management. The corporation *must* respond to advances in technology. It *must* act in such a way as to preserve and foster its own organization. . . .

If the organization is a private corporation, the power elite must take much else into consideration; the fact that there are financial interests: bondholders, stockholders, banks and bankers, institutional owners (such as pension funds and mutual funds), potential raiders seeking financial control, possible financial control by a system of conglomerate ownership. This is not to suggest that stockholders or bondholders have any significant part in management, that there is any investor democracy, or that conglomerate structure necessarily means guidance of management. But the very existence of these interests creates certain impersonal demands upon the corporation; for example, the demand for profit, for growth, for stability of income. The manager cannot act without an awareness of the constant demand for profits. . . . The business executive is also required to be aware of many different kinds of state and federal law. The corporation is quite likely to be influenced by another set of relationships to government. It may possess valuable government contracts, subsidies, franchises or licenses, any of which can be modified or revoked. It may be the beneficiary of favored tax treatment that can be changed. It must therefore act in such a manner as to preserve whatever special privileges and advantages it has.

Inside a corporation, there is the important influence of the system of decision-making. Most managements consist of a committee rather than a single head; all students of group behavior know how a committee is limited in ways that a single executive is not. Beyond this, management is limited by the many kinds of specialists and experts whose views must be consulted: the experts in marketing, in business management methods, the technicians, the whole class of people who occupy what Galbraith calls the "technostructure." The structure of any large organization is bureaucratic, and all bureaucracies have certain imperatives and rules of their own. The bureaucracy acts to preserve itself and its system, to avoid any personal responsibility, to maintain any policy once set in motion. Decisions become "institutional decisions" that can be identified with no one person, and have the qualities of the group mind. . . .

* * *

From all of this, there emerges the great revelation about the executive suite—the place from which power-hungry men seem to rule our society. The truth is far worse. In the executive suite, there may be a Léger or Braque on the wall, or a collection of African masks, there may be a vast glass-and-metal desk, but there is no one there. No one at all is in the executive suite. What looks like a man is only a representation of a man who does what the organization requires. He (or it) does not run the machine; he *tends* it.

4. THE NEW PROPERTY

If the Corporate State were *merely* autonomous, its effects would be profoundly harmful to human beings; but the State is *worse* than autonomous: its machinery is influenced by private manipulation for power and gain, yet those who use it in this way have no power to influence it in a more positive direction, and ultimately they become captives as well as profiteers. These paradoxical results follow from the development of what we may call the New Property.

With the rise of organization as the governing principle of American life, a change in the nature of private property and wealth necessarily followed. Organizations are not really "owned" by anyone. What formerly constituted ownership was split up into stockholders' rights to share in profits, management's power to set policy, employees' right to status and security, government's right to regulate. Thus older forms of wealth were replaced by new forms. Just as primitive forms of wealth such as beads and blankets gave way to what we familiarly know as property, so "property" gave way to rights growing out of organizations. . . .

* * *

These statuses, public and private, achieve their great importance because they become, for most individuals, the chief goals of life. Instead of seeking happiness in more tangible ways, the Consciousness II person defines happiness in terms of his position in the complex hierarchy of status. A new job, he says, cannot be a mistake as long as it is "a step up," an individual gets satisfaction from "having people under him," a title can compensate for the absence of many other things. The individual feels he must be happy because he has status, as a student or teacher, at a high-class university; if he is "at Yale" he glows with an artificial inward warmth. Statuses involve money, security, convenience, and also power, but these things do not quite express what they mean. They are a substitute self. The organizations of the Corporate State are empowered to confer and take away selfhood, and this fact, perhaps more than any other, explains the State's ability to dominate all of the thinking and activities within it.

*   *   *

Now we can see how the squeeze works against individuals in the Corporate State. In the preceding section of this outline we suggested that the organizations in the Corporate State gain external power as choice is reduced; the individual is compelled to deal with them and belong to them. Statuses apply a different but related kind of compulsion; they erode the individual's basis of independence, his ability and desire to "go it alone." They offer him a reward for compliance; they purchase an abandonment of independence. From the welfare recipient to the licensed physician, from the student with a government scholarship to the man with an executive job, individuals have an *interest* in the compliance which the Corporate State demands. Power is the stick and status-benefits are the carrot; when combined they leave few people with the means or the will to resist what is, after all, designed expressly to be in their "best interests."

*   *   *

The deepest problem concerning statuses has to do with the kind of individual they create. Each person gets increasingly tied to his own status-role. He is forced more and more to *become* that role, as less and less of his private life remains. His thoughts and feelings center on the role. And as a role-person he is incapable of thinking of *general* values, or of assuming responsibility for society. He can do that only in the diminishing area outside his role. Consider an automobile company executive. He can propose public housing as a solution to the urban crisis. But he cannot propose that fewer cars be produced, or that models be kept the same, to save money for public housing. Thus his role prevents him from acting for the community in the one area where he has power to act, and it prevents him from even realizing that his cars are one of the things draining money that should be used for cities. As long as he is in his role, he cannot act or think responsibly within the community. Outside his role, if there is any outside, he is virtually powerless, for his power lies in the role. Thus a nation of people grows up who cannot fight back against the power that presses against them, for each, in his separate status cubicle, is utterly apart from his fellow men.

*   *   *

5. LAW: THE INHUMAN MEDIUM

Law is supposed to be a codification of those lasting human values which a people agree upon. "Thou shalt not kill" is such a law. The Corporate State is a distinctively legalistic society. It utilizes law for every facet of its activity—there has probably never been a society with so much law, where law is so important. Thus it might be expected that law would represent a significant control over the power of the Corporate State, and a source of guidelines for it. But law in the Corporate State is something very different from a codification of values. The State has transformed it.

During the New Deal period the law was gradually changed from a medium which carried traditional values of its own to a value-free medium that could be adapted to serve "public policy," which became the "public interest" of the Corporate State. This produced law that fell into line with the requirements of organization and technology, and that supported the demands of administration rather than protecting the individual. Once law had assumed this role, there began a vast proliferation of laws, statutes, regulations, and decisions. For the law began to be employed to aid all of the work of the Corporate State by compelling obedience to the State's constantly increasing demands.

One area in which this can be demonstrated is the field of constitutional rights. The first point that must be made is that despite the vast growth of corporate power the courts, except in the area of racial discrimination, have failed to hold that corporations are subject to the Bill of Rights. A mere statement of this fact may not seem very significant; corporations, after all, are not supposed to exercise the governmental powers with which the Bill of Rights was concerned. But this has been radically changed by the emergence of the public-private state. Today private institutions do exercise government power; more, indeed, than "government" itself.

They decide what will be produced and what will not be produced; they do our primary economic planning; they are the chief determinants of how resources are allocated. With respect to their own employees, members, or students, they act in an unmistakably governmental fashion; they punish conduct, deprive people of their positions within the organization, or decide on advancement. In a sweeping way they influence the opinions, expression, associations, and behavior of all of us. Hence the fact that the Bill of Rights is inapplicable is of paramount importance; it means that these constitutional safeguards actually apply only to one part (and not the most significant part) of the power of the Corporate State. . . .

But does the Bill of Rights afford protection even where it directly applies? The Supreme Court decisions of the last few decades are not reassuring. In its adjudications the Court gives heavy weight to the "interest of society." It defers to what the legislature-executive-administrators have decided. The commands of the state are to be overturned only if there is no "rational" basis for them or if they contravene an express provision of the Constitution, and that provision is not outweighed by "the interest of society." The result over the years has been that virtually any policy in the field of economics, production, planning, or allocation has been declared constitutional; that all sorts of decisions classifying people in different and unequal statuses for tax or benefit purposes have gone unquestioned; that peace-time selective service has been upheld; that free speech has been severely limited.

A second area where law has been made to serve the state is that of federal regulation of economic activity. Here, if anywhere in the law, one might expect control to be exercised over corporate power. But the story is the same as the story of constitutional law. In the first place, most regulation is either very superficial or does what the regulated industry really wants to be done anyway. Regulation polices the outlaws, prevents unruly competition, limits entry into a field, and in effect rationalizes and stabilizes industry. . . . Food in interstate commerce must be properly labeled, inspected, and not adulterated. Stocks must not be sold in a misleading way. These are regulations with which any industry can

feel comfortable. Moreover, regulation has to a large extent been taken over by personnel representing the thinking and interests of those supposed to be regulated.

Ultimately, what the Corporate State does is to separate man from his sources of meaning and truth. To humans, the cosmos cannot be a source of truth. Nor can an entity such as the state. For human beings, the only truth must be found in their own humanity, in each other, in their relation to the living world. When the Corporate State forces its "public interest" truth as a substitute for man's internal truth—for the truth man creates—it cuts him off from the only reality he can live by. We say a man is mad when he believes he is Napoleon, or kills someone because an outside voice told him to do so. A society is mad when its actions are no longer guided by what will make men healthier and happier, when its power is no longer in the service of life. . . .

THE END OF LIBERALISM: THE INDICTMENT

THEODORE LOWI

The corruption of modern democratic government began with the emergence of interest-group liberalism as the public philosophy. Its corrupting influence takes at least four important forms, four counts, therefore, of an indictment. Also to be indicted, on at least three counts, is the philosophic component of the ideology, pluralism.

SUMMATION I: FOUR COUNTS AGAINST THE IDEOLOGY

(1) Interest-group liberalism as public philosophy corrupts democratic government, because it deranges and confuses expectations about democratic institutions. Liberalism promotes popular decision making but derogates from the decisions so made by misapplying the notion

Reprinted from *The End of Liberalism* by Theodore J. Lowi, pp. 287–97. By permission of W. W. Norton & Company, Inc. Copyright © 1969 by W. W. Norton & Company, Inc.

to the implementation as well as the formulation of policy. It derogates from the processes by treating all values in the process as equivalent interests. It derogates from democratic rights by allowing their exercise in foreign policy, and by assuming they are being exercised when access is provided. Liberal practices reveal a basic disrespect for democracy. Liberal leaders do not wield the authority of democratic government with the resoluteness of men certain of the legitimacy of their positions, the integrity of their institutions, or the justness of the programs they serve.

(2) Interest-group liberalism renders government impotent. Liberal governments cannot plan. Liberals are copious in plans but irresolute in planning. Nineteenth-century liberalism was standards without plans. This was an anachronism in the modern state. But twentieth-century liberalism turned out to be plans without standards. As an anachronism it, too, ought to pass. But doctrines are not organisms. They die only in combat over the minds of men, and no doctrine yet exists capable of doing the job. All the popular alternatives are so very irrelevant, helping to explain the longevity of interest-group liberalism. Barry Goldwater proved the irrelevance of one. The *embourgeoisement* of American unions suggests the irrelevance of others.

The Departments of Agriculture, Commerce, and Labor provide illustrations, but hardly exhaust illustrations, of such impotence. Here clearly one sees how liberalism has become a doctrine whose means are its ends, whose combatants are its clientele, whose standards are not even those of the mob but worse, are those the bargainers can fashion to fit the bargain. Delegation of power has become alienation of public domain—the gift of sovereignty to private satrapies. The political barriers to withdrawal of delegation are high enough. But liberalism reinforces these through the rhetoric of justification and often even permanent legal reinforcement: Public corporations—justified, oddly, as efficient planning instruments— permanently alienate rights of central coordination to the directors and to those who own the corporation bonds. . . .

(3) Interest-group liberalism demoralizes government, because liberal governments cannot achieve justice. The question of justice has engaged the best minds

for almost as long as there have been notions of state and politics, certainly ever since Plato defined the ideal as one in which republic and justice were synonymous. And since that time, philosophers have been unable to agree on what justice is. But outside the ideal, in the realms of actual government and citizenship, the problem is much simpler. We do not have to define justice at all, in order to weigh and assess justice in government, because in the case of liberal policies we are prevented by what the law would call a "jurisdictional fact." In the famous jurisdictional case of *Marbury* v. *Madison*, Chief Justice Marshall held that even if all the Justices hated President Jefferson for refusing to accept Marbury and the other "midnight judges" appointed by Adams, there was nothing they could do. They had no authority to judge President Jefferson's action one way or another, because the Supreme Court did not possess such jurisdiction over the President. In much the same way, there is something about liberalism that prevents us from raising the question of justice at all, no matter what definition of justice is used.

Liberal governments cannot achieve justice because their policies lack the *sine qua non* of justice—that quality without which a consideration of justice cannot even be initiated. Considerations of the justice in or achieved by an action cannot be made unless a deliberate and conscious attempt was made by the actor to derive his action from a general rule or moral principle governing such a class of acts. One can speak personally of good rules and bad rules, but a homily or a sentiment, like liberal legislation, is not a rule at all. The best rule is one which is relevant to the decision or action in question and is general, in the sense that those involved with it have no direct control over its operation. A general rule is, hence, *a priori*. Any governing regime that makes a virtue of avoiding such rules puts itself totally outside the context of justice. . . .

The general rule ought to be a legislative rule, because the United States espouses the ideal of representative democracy. However, that is merely an extrinsic feature of the rule. All that counts is the character of the rule itself. Without the rule, we can only like or dislike the consequences of the governmental action. In the question of whether justice is achieved, a government without good rules, and without acts carefully derived therefrom, is merely a big bull in an immense china shop.

(4) Finally, interest-group liberalism corrupts democratic government in the degree to which it weakens the capacity of governments to live by democratic formalisms. Liberalism weakens democratic institutions by opposing formal procedure with informal bargaining. Liberalism derogates from democracy by derogating from all formality in favor of informality. Formalism is constraining; playing it "by the book" is a role often unpopular in American war films and sports films precisely because it can dramatize personal rigidity and the plight of the individual in collective situations. Because of the impersonality of formal procedures, there is inevitably a separation in the real world between the forms and the realities, and this kind of separation gives rise to cynicism, for informality means that some will escape their collective fate better than others. There has as a consequence always been a certain amount of cynicism toward public objects in the United States, and this may be to the good, since a little cynicism is the father of healthy sophistication. However, when the informal is elevated to a positive virtue, and hard-won access becomes a share of official authority, cynicism becomes distrust. It ends in reluctance to submit one's fate to the governmental process under any condition. Public officials more and more frequently find their fates paradoxical and their treatment at the hands of the public fickle and unjust, when in fact they are only reaping the results of their own behavior, including their direct and informal treatment of the public and the institutions through which they serve the public. The more government operates by the spreading of access, the more that public order seems to suffer. The more public men pursue their constituencies, the more they seem to find their constituencies alienated. Liberalism has promoted concentration of democratic authority but deconcentration of democratic power. Liberalism has opposed privilege in policy formulation only to foster it, quite systematically, in the implementation of policy. Liberalism has consistently failed to recognize, in short, that in a democracy forms are important. In a medieval monarchy, all formalisms were at court. Democracy proves, for better

or worse, that the masses like that sort of thing too. . . .

Democratic forms were supposed to precede and accompany the formulation of policies, so that policies could be implemented authoritatively and firmly. Democracy is indeed a form of absolutism, but ours was fairly well contrived to be an absolutist government under the strong control of consent-building prior to taking authoritative action in law. Interest-group liberalism fights the absolutism of democracy, but succeeds only in taking away its authoritativeness.

SUMMATION II: THREE COUNTS AGAINST THE INTELLECTUAL COMPONENT

It ought to be clear from many sources that liberal leaders operate out of a sincere conviction that what they do constitutes an effort to respond to the stress of their times, in ways best calculated to further the public interest. If the results are contrary to their hopes, it is because their general theory of cause and effect must be wrong. Everyone operates according to some theory, or frame of reference, or paradigm—some generalized map that directs logic and conclusions, given certain facts. The influence of one's paradigm over one's decisions is enormous. It helps define what is important among the multitudes of events (i.e., it "sets one's attention"). And it literally programs one toward certain kinds of conclusions. Men are unpredictable if they do not fully understand their own theory, and no theory is explicit enough on all issues to provide predictable guidance. But no thinking man operates without one. . . .

Interest-group liberals have the pluralist paradigm in common, and its influence on liberal policy and liberal methods of organization has obviously been very large and very consistent. Among the many charges made against pluralism, the following three seem relevant to a final effort at discrediting the entire theoretical apparatus.

(1) The pluralist component has badly served interest-group liberalism, by propagating and perpetuating the faith that a system built primarily upon groups and bargaining is perfectly self-corrective. This is based upon assumptions which are clearly not often, if ever, ful-

filled—assumptions that groups always have other groups to confront them, that "overlapping memberships" will both insure competition and keep competition from becoming too intense, that "membership in potential groups" or "consensus" about the "rules of the game" are natural and inevitable, scientifically verifiable phenomena that channel competition naturally toward a public interest. It is also based on an impossible assumption that when competition does take place it yields ideal results. This is as absurd as a similar assumption of laissez-faire economists about the ideal results of economic competition. One of the major Keynesian criticisms of market theory is that even if pure competition among factors of supply and demand did yield an equilibrium, the equilibrium could be at something far less than the ideal of full employment. Pure pluralist competition, similarly, might produce political equilibrium, but the experience of recent years shows that it occurs at something far below an acceptable level of legitimacy and at a price too large to pay—exclusion of Negroes from most of the benefits of society.

(2) Pluralist theory is outmoded and unrealistic in still another way comparable to the rise and decline of laissez-faire economics. Pluralism has failed to grapple with the problem of oligopoly or imperfect competition as it expresses itself in the political system. When a program is set up in a specialized agency, the number of organized interest groups surrounding it tends to be reduced. Generally it tends to be reduced precisely to those groups and factions to whom the specialization is most salient. That in turn tends to reduce the situation from one of potential competition to potential oligopoly. That is to say, one can observe numerous groups in some kind of competition for agency favors. But competition tends to last only until each group learns the goals of the few other groups. Each adjusts to the others. Real confrontation leads to net loss for all rather than gain for any. Rather than countervailing power there will more than likely be accommodating power.

Galbraith has assumed that each oligopoly will be checked by an oligopsony—an interest from the opposite side of the market rather than a competitor for a share in the same market. This notion of countervailing power—competition between big labor and big industry,

big buyers against big sellers, etc.—was to explain economic and political phenomena. But not only is this new kind of confrontation an unfounded assumption. It was to be created by public policy: " . . . the support of countervailing power has become in modern times perhaps the major peacetime function of the Federal government."[1] Countervailing power, in old or new form, can hardly be much of a theory of the way the industrial state naturally works if it requires central government support. And it hardly warrants government support if its consequences do not produce the felicitous results claimed for them.

(3) Finally, the pluralist paradigm depends upon an idealized and almost totally miscast conception of *the group*. Laissez-faire economics may have idealized the firm and the economic man but never to the degree to which the pluralist thinkers today sentimentalize the group, the group member, and the interests. Note the contrast between the traditional American notion of the group and the modern pluralist definition. Madison in Federalist 10 defined the group ("faction") as "a number of citizens, whether amounting to a majority or minority of the whole, who are united and actuated by some common impulse of passion, or of interest, *adverse to the right of other citizens, or to the permanent and aggregate interests of the community.*" (Emphasis added.) David B. Truman uses Madison's definition but cuts the quotation just before the emphasized part.[2] In such a manner pluralist theory became the complete handmaiden of interest-group liberalism, in a sense much more than laissez-faire economics was ever a handmaiden to big capitalism. The Madisonian, and also to the early twentieth-century progressive, groups were necessary evils much in need of regulation. To the modern pluralist, groups are good; they require accommodation. Immediately following his definition in Federalist 10, Madison went on to say: "The regulation of these various interfering interests forms the principal task of modern legislation. . . . " This is a far cry from Galbraith's "support of countervailing power," or Schlesinger's "hope of harnessing government, business, and labor in a rational partnership . . . ," or the sheer sentimentality behind the notion of "maximum feasible participation," and "group representation in the interior processes of. . . ."

A revived feeling of distrust toward interests and groups would not destroy pluralist theory but would only prevent its remaining a servant of a completely outmoded system of public endeavor. Once sentimentality toward the group is destroyed, it will be possible to see how group interactions might fall short of creating an ideal equilibrium. Such distrust of prevailing theory might then lead to discomfort with the jurisprudence of delegation of power, for it too rests mightily upon an idealized view of how groups make law today. In such a manner the theoretical foundations of interest-group liberalism can be discredited. Some progress will then have been made toward restoration of an independent and legitimate government in the United States. Until that occurs, liberalism will continue to be the enemy rather than the friend of democracy.

Notes

[1] J. K. Galbraith, *American Capitalism* (Boston: Houghton Mifflin, 1962,) p. 136.

[2] David B. Truman, *The Governmental Process* (New York: Alfred A. Knopf, 1951), p. 4.

POLITICS AND DEVELOPMENT

The third reading in this chapter is addressed to another aspect of the pluralist ideology: its emphasis on demands as basic units in the operation of political systems. Christian Bay argues that this tendency to pay attention mainly to the demands of interest groups diverts political science from the greater and more humane challenge of understanding and making clear how political systems meet, or fail to meet, the *needs* of human beings. Politics, in his view, should be an art and science of human development, not a technique of system maintenance. (In making this kind of a recommendation for a new line of political inquiry and suggesting a new conceptual framework for political thought, Bay anticipates some of the things that will be investigated in the final two chapters of this book.)

It is important to note here that Bay's essay is simultaneously an exploration of the developmental paradigm in political science, and also a criticism of the kind of developmental research and theory that modern political science has produced so far. The latter "developmental" approach—

which is used in comparative political analysis—describes political development in terms of industrial development, increased gross national product, technological advancement, and the creation of political systems resembling our own. Bay, surveying its literature, is dismayed by the lack of "even a hint of the possibility that 'political development' ought to be defined relative to *human* development. . . . "

Where Reich's essay is a revolutionary critique of pluralism and Lowi's is a conservative one, Bay's thinking appears to contain elements of both. He pleads for a new and radical commitment to principles of human development as the basis of political inquiry, and also suggests a return to normative thinking, to a concern with human values comparable to that which inspired the works of the earliest political philosophers. We believe that this stance is not self-contradictory: The future political science will and must consist of imaginative scientific research and political innovation based solidly on human values and human needs. It will transcend many of our current categories and habits of thought, and will be at once scientific, normative, and radically creative.

POLITICAL SCIENCE AND THE COMMON GOOD

CHRISTIAN BAY

. . . The end of politics, Aristotle tells us, is the highest good attainable by action. For of all creatures, man alone "has any sense of good and evil, of just and unjust, and the like. . . . Justice is the bond of men in states, for the administration of justice, which is the determination of what is just, is the principle of order in political society." Politics, then, is the master science, for its aim embraces the aims of all other scientific pursuits; the study of politics is the study of how best to promote the common good of the political community.

* * *

But the modern study of politics stands in stark contrast to this classic conception. Increasingly it be-

From *The Dissenting Academy*, edited by Theodore Roszak, pp. 210–30. Copyright © 1968 by Random House, Inc. Reprinted by permission of Pantheon Books, a Division of Random House, Inc.

comes identified with the study of existing patterns of political behavior. And for this study the Aristotelian concept of politics is clearly unsuited, focusing as it does on an assumed state of tension between the actual and the ideal, or between existing realities and the optimal common good. It is, rather, formulations like that of Harold D. Lasswell that now seem more pertinent. "Politics," according to Lasswell's boldest and best-known definition, refers to "who gets what, when, how."[1] Other modern behavioralists like to add a "why" to their conception of politics, by way of relating their definitions not only to "power" but to "authority" or "legitimacy" as well. But the latter terms are invariably intended as descriptive rather than normative: "legitimacy" is established by way of opinion surveys and "authority" by way of communication or decision-making as well as survey research. Neither term has anything to do with justice, inherent rightness, or any other normative concept.[2]

It is not difficult to understand why this capitulation to the status quo has taken place on the part of professional students of politics. "A political science that is mistreated," writes Hans Morgenthau, "is likely to have earned that enmity because it has put its moral commitment to the truth above social convenience and ambition." But a political science that is respected, he continues, helps the powers that be by way of mollifying the conscience of society, justifying existing power relationships, etc. "The relevance of this political science does not lie primarily in the discovery of the truth about politics, but in its contribution to the stability of society."[3]

Conversely, every political philosophy which is concerned with humane ideals and their implications in logically rigorous ways is subversive of every existing order; for it is in the nature of political philosophy, as distinguished from merely linguistic or logical analysis, to contrast existing realities with more ideal alternatives. There is always a strong temptation, then, even for philosophers to adjust to the most basic demands and assumptions of the status quo, for in most societies it is rather uncomfortable to be treated as a subversive. And when political philosophers and other social scientists establish professions and take on public educational

employment, the adjustment of basic philosophical assumptions to the postulates of the established order almost inevitably becomes institutionalized. That is, perspectives on the aims of politics or philosophy or social analysis become transformed from a focus on man's needs and potentialities to a focus on systems maintenance; and most individual recruits to the social science professions are spared the agonizing ethical dilemma of choosing between being true to their role as intellectuals and embarking on comfortable careers. Indeed, they are carefully trained *not* to discover this existential dilemma.

It is not only the average academic student of politics, however, who has become theoretically incapacitated for scientific concern with issues of justice or the common good. In their descriptive studies of the political behavior of the supposedly "developed" American and other Western electorates, political scientists have discovered that the public too appears unconcerned with the Public Interest. Quite correctly, they describe most voters as either apathetic or anxiety-ridden, and as rarely able to see their private and group interests in the perspective of their stake in the public interest. The rule, in short, is what I prefer to call "pseudopolitical" rather than "political" behavior.

By "political," I refer to all activity aimed at improving or protecting conditions for the satisfaction of human needs and demands in a given society according to some universalistic scheme of priorities, implicit or explicit. "Pseudopolitical," on the other hand, refers to activity that *resembles* political activity but is exclusively concerned either with alleviating personal neuroses or with promoting private or interest-group advantage, deterred by no articulate or disinterested conception of what would be just or fair to other groups. Thus, pseudopolitics is the counterfeit of politics.[1]

Now, I am in no way opposed to the study of pseudopolitical behavior. The behavioral literature of our profession is an invaluable source of facts about our political and pseudopolitical life; my plea is for more and better behavioral research. What I ask for is a more comprehensive, more humane, more truly *political* framework of theory for the study of pseudopolitical and political behavior. There should be no excuse for jumping from the fact of prevailing pseudopolitical behavior in our competitive, unjust, anxiety-ridden social order to the enormous conclusion that pseudopolitics is "normal" in a "developed society"—that, in other words, we are doomed to a *permanent* eclipse of genuine politics in the modern democratic world, and that no educational liberation from *Time, U.S. News,* and their intellectual equivalents is ever to reach more than a small minority of our electorate.

I plead, further, for the necessity of liberating our political science literature from the following prevailing assumptions: (1) that political research in America must take the present system for granted, leaving out the study of experiments directed toward radical change; (2) that this nation is "politically developed," even though its electorate behaves by and large pseudopolitically, not politically; (3) that it is either impossible or not worthwhile to develop assumptions about national goals (e.g. reduction of suffering, maximization of justice or of freedom) and to study their empirical implications; and (4) that it is either impossible or not worthwhile to develop and apply psychological models of need priorities as a basis for research into their political implications—i.e., to develop a scientific study of politics founded on the study of basic human needs, as distinct from manifest wants and demands.

One would have hoped that our own profession had maintained a Socratic commitment to the defense of genuine politics, particularly in this age of conspicuous, high-powered, systematic propagation of mindless pseudopolitics. But as we have seen, the tendency has been to conform to the powerful demands on us, much as the autonomous spirit of the university has been replaced by the more pliant stance of the "multiversity." We study expressed wants and demands, often the result of indoctrination from the outside, and are unconcerned about inner needs, or prerequisites for social and individual health. We willingly submit to the deception that our corporation-ridden pluralist order is to be called "democratic" and that our laws are to be judged as democratically enacted and therefore legitimate in more than a descriptive sense of the term. Worst of all, we continue to think of our bailiwick as the study of means-ends relationships, while conveniently claiming that ends cannot be studied "scientifically."

It will, I think, be instructive to examine the way in which one very important mainstream textbook currently influences the professional study of politics. *Comparative Politics: A Developmental Approach,*[5] by Gabriel A. Almond and G. Bingham Powell, Jr., is probably the most widely used textbook today in the field of comparative politics. Professor Almond, the book's senior author, was in 1965–1966 the president of the American Political Science Association, and for many years has been one of the most influential members of the profession. Not only is he undoubtedly the most influential name in the currently important field of comparative politics, but he has also distinguished himself as a scholar in the neighboring social sciences where he has done creative, influential work on a variety of problems. And apart from his own writings, Almond's editorship of the Studies in Political Development series, published by the Princeton University Press, is another monument to his commanding influence.[6]

Almond and Powell acknowledge that "the functional approach" acceptably describes the orientation of their book. They place themselves to this extent in the tradition of the *Federalist Papers,* but contend that their own concept of "system" is more explicit, as they have the advantage of building on modern developments in sociology, anthropology, and communications theory. And let it be stressed here that Almond's and his (present and earlier) collaborators' conceptual contributions to the analysis of political input, output, and conversion processes are most fruitful and have helped to brighten considerably the prospects for future political research. Also, the often judicious and illuminating use of survey data and other empirical materials in the context of conceptual and theoretical discussions in this literature constitutes a real contribution to sociological as well as political knowledge.

My chief objections are to the *uses* made of this knowledge, in Almond and Powell and more generally in the modern comparative politics literature. I object, not to a functional approach, but to a functional approach that has no normative reference beyond the range of data it seeks to order and make use of. The range of data is simply called "the political system." The trouble with this theoretical framework is that it has little bearing on politics as distinct from pseudopolitics; for it has little bearing on the problem of man and his needs, as distinct from, in Herbert Marcuse's phrase, the "one-dimensional man" and his manipulated propensities as consumer of political outputs and contributor of inputs.

Almond and Powell acknowledge some merit in the criticism that has been made of Almond's past work to the effect that it carried static, conservative implications. They contend that their latest book substantially modifies or complements the earlier Almond approach: "We need to take a major analytical step if we are to build political development more explicitly into our approach to the political system. We need to look at political systems as whole entities shaping and being shaped by their environments." But alas, no "major steps" are likely to remedy the problem of conservatism and irrelevancy to humane politics if the *political system* is to remain inviolate as the frame of reference for functional analysis. Far too easily the problem of "system maintenance and adaptation" comes to fill the normative vacuum and becomes the main evaluative standard; indeed, should we expect political scientists who disclaim professional competence with respect to normative issues to be untouched by conventional patriotism, or unconcerned with the defense ("system maintenance and adaptation") of their country and its present institutions?

Almond and Powell's concern with the empirical problems of system maintenance and adaptation is of course legitimate and praiseworthy; these are issues to be faced up to by intelligent political inquiry anywhere. But in the absence of concern with politics in the classical sense, the imagery they evoke is rather frightening in its inescapable normative implications. For example: "For an automobile to perform efficiently on the road, parts must be lubricated, repaired, and replaced. New parts may perform stiffly; they must be broken in. In a political system the incumbents of the various roles (diplomats, military officers, tax officials) must be recruited to these roles and learn how to perform in them. New roles are created and new personnel 'broken in.'"

True, the authors do not go on record as favoring bigger and better automobiles as ends in themselves, regardless of where they would take us. But in so many ways, if by implication rather than explicitly, they testify to their faith in the present pluralist American system as if *it* were an end in itself, regardless of what it does to forestall politics in the classical sense, to prevent human development, or even to destroy human lives at home and abroad. If the virtual absence of effective political dialogue and of control by public opinion on the national level has left the American "military-industrial complex" free to develop a frightful military machine, with feeble brakes and strong accelerators (or "escalators"), these are problems to which Almond and Powell's analysis pays no attention.

Indeed, their tendency is to see all firm political commitments as a developmental stage to be overcome for the good of the political system: "An ideological style emerges when the individual develops a *specific* set of political orientations, but fails to develop the open, bargaining attitudes associated with full secularization." In fairness, their stress on "specific" indicates their chief concern with making a point that I consider valid: that cognitive rigidity associated with ideological politics can create irrational conflicts. My objection is to their clear assumption, in the concluding phrase, that free, entirely flexible bargaining is *and should be* the essence of "developed" politics.

Last year I had my students in a graduate seminar read Frantz Fanon's *The Wretched of the Earth* alongside Almond and Powell's book. The work of Almond and Powell is far superior in its conceptual clarity and sophistication; the romantic revolutionary Fanon is more concerned with exhortation than with analysis. Yet the fact that we inhabit a world filled with desperation and explosive indignation is a manifest reality, eloquently described, perhaps exaggerated, but hardly conjured up by Fanon. Where is this reality accounted for, or even acknowledged, in the Almond-Powell scheme of analysis? It appears as "anomic interest groups"! "Political systems may be marked by a high frequency of such violent and spontaneous group formation (as in France of the Fourth Republic, Italy, and the Arab nations), or notable for its absence." In less than a page the "wretched of the earth" are disposed of; the implied norm appears to be that the more the state is able to monopolize violence the better, while the state of wretchedness is at best a secondary issue. Which is perhaps a suitable value premise for those hardy professionals who wish to justify the American warfare in Vietnam; but it hardly contributes a realistic approach toward understanding the political behavior of such "anomic interest groups" (what an anemic phrase!) as, for example, South Vietnam's National Liberation Front.

In their discussion of the "capabilities of political systems" Almond and Powell quite explicitly confine the universe of their inquiry to the welfare of systems rather than people. Broadly speaking, they write, "elite responses to inputs or demands may take the form of repression, indifference, substitution, or accommodation."[12] For Almond and Powell these four responses appear to exhaust the possibilities. They will not allow that revolutionary leftist or even established communist systems occasionally may at least have *attempted* a fifth kind of response: namely, to *facilitate* the development of political demands. They write as if the four types of response listed are the only possible responses. No midwifery for just causes, no massive relief in response to the often muted longings of the hopelessly oppressed can find even the smallest niche of a category within this particular input-output scheme of analysis.

It is this point that gets to the core of my main objection to the pluralist philosophy, or perhaps I should say "stance": a concern with human needs according to priorities dictated by justice is virtually ruled out, even as a problem for empirical inquiry. The vision of political inquiry is limited to articulated demands, occasionally deplorably "anomic" and violent, but usually neatly promoted by well-behaved (and well-heeled) organizations in pursuit of legitimate private interests. Regimes have a choice of suppressing demands, ignoring them, trying to placate those interests with alternate rewards, or granting the demands—presumably depending on the strength and persistency of the interest groups involved. Granted, this may well be how American and Western governments in fact behave, and possibly communist governments too. But to suggest that this is *all* there can be to "developed" politics is to abdicate all concern with justice or *human* development as the aim of politics, and to sanction, if not sanctify, pluralist pseudopolitics forever.

It bears repetition that Almond's conceptual scheme

for analyzing the processes and capabilities of pluralist political systems, including their developmental potentialities if any, is a most valuable contribution of tools for political inquiry. But what the authors fail to see is how these tools can be, and predominantly are, used for the purpose of celebrating pluralist oppression and stagnation rather than as means for seeking ways toward a politics in the service of human needs. There are myriads of possibilities for empirical study of how specific output and input processes or aspects of processes relate to conditions of human well-being; yet Almond and his collaborators and students have tended to content themselves with studying the development and maintenance of the political systems as the general dependent variable. Pressures and bargaining processes are seen as the important things for elites to be concerned with, not human waste or fulfillment; and "political development" takes the place of a concern with justice and individual freedom for the least privileged.

The implications of Almond's approach, for American domestic as well as foreign policy, show up clearly in the work of one of Almond's former collaborators, Lucian W Pye. With respect to the general population the key elements of political development involve, Pye writes, "a change from widespread subject status to an increasing number of contributing citizens, with an increasing spread of mass participation, a greater sensitivity to the principles of equality, and a wider acceptance of universalistic laws." In the United States, more than half the citizens vote,[13] while possibly still larger numbers participate vicariously in the glories of Vietnam victories as TV viewers and as readers of *Time* and *Life*, have a great sensitivity to the right of equality under the law for General Motors Corporation and the individual worker, and firmly believe in the sanctity of universalistic laws of contract. If American political development might lead to something better some day, Pye is not about to suggest the direction; his chief concern, at least in the fuller discussion in his more recent book, *Aspects of Political Development: An Analytic Study,* is with how the more benighted, still developing countries can come to resemble the Western systems more.

On this occasion Pye reviews ten types of definitions of "political development" but ends up by seeking to establish empirically "the developmental syndrome," seeking "to isolate those characteristics of political development which seem to be most widely held and most fundamental in the general thinking about problems of political development."[14] Widely held among whom? Why, among fellow American political scientists, of course, and especially, it would seem, among those who have served on the Social Science Research Council's Committee on Comparative Politics, whose past chairmen include Almond as well as Pye. By a natural habit of citing primarily each other's work, this school of thought has produced quite an imposing consensus on the meaning of "political development."

What concerns me is that I have yet to find in this literature even a hint of the possibility that "political development" ought to be defined relative to *human* development in some sense; certainly there is no such possibility left open in Pye's work. And this is particularly remarkable in view of the fact that both Pye and Almond belong to that rare species of political scientist who are articulate and well read in dynamic psychology. The most plausible explanation is that Pye, too, has become caught up in the system, i.e., in the fashion of theorizing about political systems in functional terms, in a normative vacuum in which easy patriotism rather than a more complex and less professionally rewarding concern with humanity and justice has come to dictate the underlying value standards.

True, it is hard to do research on genuine human needs as opposed to the neater categories of expressed wants, demands, and the volumes of noise and cash displayed by pluralist interest groups. But needs as distinct from conscious wants do exist, as every clinical psychologist and psychiatrist can testify, and as delinquency experts, penologists, social workers, public health officials, anthropologists, and sociologists increasingly emphasize in their work and in their writings. It is time, I submit, that political scientists also come to recognize this fact and its significance, and in this respect try to catch up with Plato and Aristotle. I am convinced that our profession will never help us to advance from our wasteful, cruel, pluralist pseudopolitics in the direction of justice and humane politics until we replace *political systems* with concepts of *human need* and *human development*

as the ultimate value frameworks for our political analysis. Almond's functional approach to the study of input and output processes would by no means become obsolete by such a change in value perspective. On the contrary, it would become useful.

* * *

Notes

[1] Harold D. Lasswell, *Politics: Who Gets What, When, How?* (New York, McGraw-Hill Book Co., Inc., 1936).

[2] Representative examples are David Easton's definition of political science as the study of "the authoritative allocation of values as it is influenced by the distribution and use of power"; and Robert A. Dahl's formulation, "A political system is any persistent pattern of human relationships that involves, to a significant extent, power, rule, or authority." See Easton, *The Political System* (New York, Alfred A. Knopf, 1953), p. 146; and Dahl, *Modern Political Analysis* (Englewood Cliffs, N.J., Prentice-Hall, Inc., 1963), p. 6.

[3] Hans Morgenthau, "The Purpose of Political Science" in James C. Charlesworth, ed., *A Design for Political Science: Scope, Objectives, Methods* (Philadelphia, American Academy of Political and Social Science, 1966), p. 73.

[4] See my "Politics and Pseudopolitics: A Critical Evaluation of Some Behavioral Literature," in the *American Political Science Review*, vol. 59 (May 1965), pp. 39–51.

[5] Boston, Little, Brown and Company, 1966.

[6] Among Almond's other contributions to comparative politics are Almond and Sidney Verba, *The Civic Culture* (Princeton, Princeton University Press, 1963) and "A Developmental Approach to Political Systems," *World Politics*, Vol. 17 (1965), pp. 183–214. His other studies include *The Appeals of Communism* (Princeton, Princeton University Press, 1954) and his (ed.) *The Struggle for Democracy in Germany* (New York, Russell & Russell Publishers, 1965).

[7] *Comparative Politics*, pp. 13–14.

[8] Ibid., pp. 29–30.

[9] Ibid., p. 61.

[10] New York, Grove Press, Inc., 1966.

[11] Almond and Powell, op. cit., pp. 75–76.

[12] Ibid., pp. 205–6.

[13] But less than 2 percent are politically participative in any other way. See Lester W. Milbrath, *Political Participation* (Chicago, Rand McNally & Co., 1965).

[14] The quotations from Pye come from his *Aspects of Political Development* (Boston, Little, Brown and Company, 1966), p. 45.

10/Developmental Research

POLICY ANALYSIS

Two issues are never far from the center of any discussion about the shape of political analysis, present and future: (1) the issue of political science as science—its proper methodologies, the matter of quantification, and the value and limits of empirical research; and (2) the issue of the proper role of the political scientist—the matter of separating the role of scientist from that of citizen, the relationship to the existing system, and the responsibility of functioning within it or bringing about change in it. Discussion of these issues usually raises questions of values and morality. Some of the more radically scientific of behavioral researchers once hoped to make their work "value-free," but today there seems to be a growing agreement among political scientists that values—principles of choice and rejection, of priority, of personal morality and commitment and responsibility, of right and wrong—must inevitably play a part in the study of politics.

This issue becomes more meaningful when we make a distinction about what political actions are to be studied. In recent years, some political scientists have turned their attention more toward policies. Policy analysts say that political scientists have paid too much attention to the various processes by which political decisions are made—such as elections, legislative behavior, executive behavior, and so forth—and have tended to neglect the study of how policies are actually carried out and what kinds of human consequences they have. Kenneth M. Dolbeare, who speaks for that position here, sees in policy analysis an opportunity to make political science more genuinely relevant to the needs of

the people who are governed by the system. He also sees policy analysis as an area where the techniques of empirical research can be put to use in a way that will make research less vulnerable to the criticism of being remote and irrelevant to human needs. The role of the political scientist, as Dolbeare outlines it, will be to evaluate different policy alternatives and, thus, make the democratic system more effective by putting at the disposal of voters and office-holders better information about what different laws and actions and decisions are, in fact, likely to *do*.

Although Dolbeare does not mention the usefulness of policy analysis as a part of a developmental political science, the connection is there to be made. If, as Christian Bay has suggested, political science is to be concerned with human development, with finding ways to bring about the optimum satisfaction of human needs and the fullest realization of the potentials of all members of a society, then it makes sense that political scientists should apply themselves to the evaluation of policy outcomes, to finding out how governmental processes help (or hinder) the development of the individuals affected by them.

POLICY ANALYSIS

KENNETH M. DOLBEARE

At least since the end of the decade of the thirties, empirically oriented political scientists have concentrat-

Kenneth M. Dolbeare, "Public Policy Analysis," pp. 88–110, from *Power and Community*, edited by Philip Green and Sanford Levinson. Copyright © 1970 by Random House, Inc. Reprinted by permission of Pantheon Books, a Division of Random House, Inc.

ed almost exclusively upon aspects of the political *processes* through which policies are made. Voting behavior, political parties, interest-group activities, decision making in institutions, etc., have all been prominent fields of concentration for those who specialize in American politics. Analysis starts with a claim made for government action of a particular kind and ends when a statute is passed, a decision rendered, or a regulation issued in that subject area. Relatively little attention has been paid to the *content* of the policies produced through these processes or to the *effects* which they may have on the people and problems which are their objects.

The return to a substantive policy focus on the part of some political scientists now is apparently due to the convergence of several disparate factors. Not least among these causes are pressures from our students for us to deal intellectually with the realities that confront them personally. We should frankly acknowledge the substantial debt that we owe them for forcing us to reexamine the nature and purposes of our discipline. Clearly, the pressing nature and unavoidable salience of domestic-policy problems in the United States have also been a major factor. . . . But the great majority of the studies of public policies which are visible in political science today have developed from a very limited extension of the long-established process focus within the discipline. Two very broad characterizations encompass practically all of this recent body of work.[1]

One usage employs policy characteristics (frequently expenditures) as the dependent variable for analysis and seeks to add new dimensions of understanding about the policy-making process by relating such characteristics to process or environmental features such as the competitiveness of the party system or the per capita income of the community. Some recent theoretical extensions of these interests have begun to conceptualize policies in terms of their substance or to create categories based on observers' impressions of the "impact" of policies, but none of these have detached themselves from a primary focus on characteristics of the policy-making process. This primary interest in explanation of the political process, as well as an affinity for quantitative methods, links this category of approaches closely with the mainstream of process-oriented empirical political

science and insulates it against contact with the value components of current policy problems.

A second and even looser category of approaches includes research which takes a policy problem (welfare, urban renewal, the space program, economic growth, medicare) as its focus and analyzes the processes surrounding its making or implementation. Such studies include both national and local (particularly urban) policy problems, and their goals usually are to understand why particular policies were produced at specific times or how implementation has been shaped by political actors and forces. Although the problem area has been selected because of its special importance, analysis is directed primarily at the policy-making processes in which it is embedded rather than at the substance of the policies or their consequences for the problems which inspired them.

Patently, these approaches neither have taken nor will take us very far into the substance of public policy: they ask *why policies have their present form*, and they look for answers exclusively within certain narrow subareas of the visible political process. At no time do they ask *what difference it made* to people or problems that such policies were enacted. . . . In short, what government does is studied chiefly in terms of how it came to be that way, not in terms of whether it was effective or ineffective, better or worse than some other way of solving a problem, or good or bad in the absolute or overall sense.

Thus we come to what has been termed by some a major theme in the "postbehavioral revolution." Nascent within the current movement into the study of public policy is a concern for the substance of policies which takes the form of systematic empirical tracing of the tangible consequences of a policy within the society. Dropping (for the purposes of this research) all concern for why the policy has its present form, such an approach undertakes to spell out precisely what the allocations of burden and benefit actually are—in short, who wins and who loses, and what, by virtue of the policy in question. Components of policies are linked empirically to specific consequences wherever possible, and an effort is made to trace direct and secondary effects on the society and economy as far as they can be identified.

People's reactions are assessed, together with the manner in which their attitudes toward the policy and the government itself are affected. Finally, attention is paid to the way in which one set of policies may affect popular desires for more or less or different policies in the same field and to the way in which unanticipated effects of a policy create new circumstances affecting government action.[2]

Regardless of its sharp contrast to process-focused analysis, this shift involves no dramatic conceptual breakthrough. Such an output-focused approach has long been explicit in the works of major general theorists. More than three decades ago, Harold Lasswell suggested that politics be understood as who gets what, when, and how.[3] More recently, David Easton has stressed output, outcome, feedback, and support as crucial stages of political activity.[4] But the fact is that such areas remain empirically unexplored: we cannot really know *who* gets *what,* or what outputs produce which outcomes or generate what types of feedback, until such questions are studied systematically and empirically. We have left half of the entirety of politics unexamined because of an apparent fascination with the dynamics of the other half, and we have not even explored that side fully. We cannot know what aspects of the policy-making process are really important, for example, until we know what effects specific provisions of a statute or a regulation have actually had. Quite often, the actual consequences of policies may be different from either the hopes or the fears of policy makers, interest-group leaders, newspaper editors, or the general public at the time of enactment. (No study yet shows, for example, that the Supreme Court's much-criticized defendants'-rights decisions have resulted in a lower conviction rate among complying police departments.) Nor can we know to what extent government policies are achieving designed objectives, or what unexpected results they are producing, until such studies are made. Thus, although this movement is no conceptual innovation, it surely implies a major shift in the focus of empirical investigation.

Opening this vast new terrain for careful empirical inquiry may indeed have a profound effect on the scientific understanding of politics. It may render political science considerably more useful in regard to immediate social needs—and it may even justify the label of the "postbehavioral revolution." Clearly, this type of policy analysis is not merely a return to the nonempirical, policy-prescribing days of the prebehavioral or traditional era in the study of politics. It is a synthesis of the newest and best empirical techniques with the worthy substantive concerns of the past. It might well mark a new stage for the discipline—provided, of course, that we avoid the dangers inherent in uncritically extending some of our present approaches. Let us look in depth at the promise and the dangers.

II. OPPORTUNITIES IN THE ANALYSIS OF POLICY CONSEQUENCES

The essential impact of a focus on the consequences of public policies lies in its inescapable reintroduction of the substantive dimension to the concepts and definitions which are central to our understanding of the nature of politics. Americans generally, and American political thinkers (including political scientists) particularly, have always placed heavy emphasis on the procedures by which governmental decisions are made and relatively little emphasis on the concrete substance or results of government actions. . . .

But if we begin to view politics through the eyes of the consumer, to consider the substance and consequences of policies for people and problems within the society, we are in effect greatly expanding the horizons of the political. Procedures and processes are indeed important, we say in effect, but they are not the only things that are meaningful; it is also vital to see what happens and to whom through these processes. . . . Judgments about a policy or a program will take into consideration not just how it happened to be produced, but whether it produces results in keeping with the expressed intentions of policy makers, with the preferences of particular groups or of the people generally, and whether it is rationally responsive to the character of problems. Democracy, for example, becomes not just civil rights and participation, but the consistency of results with the desires of masses of people. . . .

*   *   *

Murray Edelman's hypotheses about the many possible ways in which symbolic issues and satisfactions may structure our politics[3] offer another illustration of possible objects and purposes of evaluation. A focus on the tangible consequences of public policies will shed light on the extent to which reality differs from rhetoric—on the gap between substance and symbol—in American politics. To what degree are Americans deflected from attention to the real actions of their government by the manipulation of symbols? Are policy makers and masses equally attracted to the symbolic rather than the real? On occasion, of course, symbolic goals are the primary stakes and rewards of political activity, and tangible consequences relatively less significant. It is often the case also that what actors and public believe to be true is more significant to the character of their political activity than the actual conditions which exist. But these are hardly reasons for a detached observer to eschew reality when he can find it. Analysis of tangible consequences not only would show clearly the occasions and extent of symbolic deflection but also provide a basis for assessing the relative significance of various actions within the policy-making process.

The *standards* for evaluation may range from the orthodox liberal values perhaps unconsciously preferred by most political scientists to frankly normative, value-justifying standards more characteristic of some activists. Researchers with a concern for scientific evaluation will seek some relatively objective standards, while others may be content to apply standards of their own contrivance to the same findings. *The particular standard employed is less important than that (1) the data and findings be set out comprehensively, and (2) the standards be specified precisely and defended independently of the judgment to which they lead the evaluator.* The inevitable lack of unanimity on judgmental criteria should not deter development of descriptions of policy consequences. Once the descriptive base has been established, debate over criteria and conclusions can be rendered more rational at least, and perhaps the general problem of scholarly evaluation will become more tractable.

Some of the dangers encountered in policy analysis

become visible at this point. An initial objection to the act of evaluation itself may be anticipated from those whose commitment is to "scientific" inquiry and therefore to "value-free" research and presentation of data—and the avoidance of evaluative judgments. It is at least debatable whether the strictest self-discipline could render researchers, unavoidably children of our culture, truly value-free. It seems clear that the choices of what is important enough to research and the interpretation of the meaning of data involve definitions, assumptions, and choices of what is relatively more plausible and logical. Inevitably, these are affected by the heritage and life experience of the researcher. Further, any research findings which are meaningful must support some value-based arguments or assumptions within the polity and refute others.

Thus, we are involved in value realms today, and we have no choice in the matter. Not expressing value judgments does not mean, therefore, that we are not affecting value-laden outcomes or actions. It means only that for the most part our findings are (or may be rendered) supportive of the status quo because we do not say they are at odds with it. Or our findings may be given totally contradictory or erroneous interpretations by contending parties, again, because we have failed to *say* what these findings mean. The only way that research can avoid these prospects is to confine itself to essentially trivial questions or methodological minutiae. This is apparently the route preferred by some political scientists, but they by such self-limitation remove themselves as sources of danger to the useful study of policy consequences. The danger here flows from the pretensions, on the part of those who do relevant research, to value-free scientific standards: not only are these political scientists self-limiting in what they study, but through a misplaced "professionalism" (and perhaps concern for preservation of access and expert status), their contribution becomes either uncritical endorsement of the status quo or just another bit of ammunition for use by various partisan contenders.

But even greater danger may be anticipated from the well-intentioned but uncritical empiricist who offers his services (including his judgmental capacities) in the cause of social improvement. The evaluative standards he is prone to use may serve as an illustration of three interrelated components of what I have previously referred to as the central problem of reviving policy research as a scholarly enterprise: the frame of reference within which research is conducted. The three leading prospects I see for faulty evaluative standards, all reflecting limitations in the contemporary frame of reference of much empirical research, are as follows:

(1) Extra-empirical convictions stemming from liberal ideology or democratic mythology will structure judgments. Because we (as Americans and as political scientists) know from extra-empirical conviction that our political system is just, that it balances the interests of all, and that the United States is a democracy, we lose judgmental perspective on the facts that we find from our research. As a result, we may innocently redefine justice or participation or equality or democracy to fit what we find. What is, is right. Or at least (in the United States), it is the best that is practical under the circumstances. The same phenomenon may develop in regard to stability and change. Stability is necessary because we have had it in the United States in recent decades, and it is definable as what we have experienced. Change should be at the pace that we have experienced it—to proceed faster would be dangerous, impossible, and (no doubt) undesirable.

(2) The only questions asked will be essentially procedural, rather than substantive, despite an ostensible focus on policy substance. Did the officials have authorization to take a particular action? Were established procedures followed, rules of the game observed, familiar forms used? The unstated assumption is . . . that any policy produced without violation of established procedures would be "good" and any requiring new or different procedures would be "bad." This avoids the very strong probability that the procedures themselves are value-laden and favor one set of people or values over others. Nothing in politics—Constitution, laws, rules, and hallowed traditions particularly included—is either neutral or value-free: structures and procedures alike militate toward some ends and to the exclusion of others. Thus, to say that whatever emerges from established procedures is "right" is to beg the important question. Who wins (and who loses) under such conditions is

not just a coincidence.

(3) The values and priorities of policy makers will be accepted without question as "givens" within the context of which analysis must be conducted. If we apply no evaluative standards except those which accept these parameters, we can be no more than skilled propagators of whatever those preferences happen to be. To preserve our position as detached, independent observers and evaluators, we must examine those very premises and priorities, pointing out, if necessary, occasions where they themselves are the prime sources of problems or the inability to solve problems. To do less is to be controlled by the values and assumptions of the policy makers. Thus circumscribed, we may not only obscure the basic causes of problems, but also endorse illusory, minimal, or chiefly rhetorical "solutions," and thus in effect perpetuate the very problems we seek to solve.

A related faulty standard emerges from taking the stated intentions or expressed purposes of policy makers at face value and making assumptions to the effect that policies actually achieve such goals *and were really intended to.* In either case, research and evaluation will be controlled by whatever the policy makers accepted or articulated. Alternative policies, or different value premises or priorities which would lead to alternative policies, may be excluded as part of the evaluative criteria. To evaluate comprehensively what was done, of course, we must consider what other options were available under exactly the same conditions, what *could* have been done (given existing resources and *other* priorities), and what the nature of the *problem* suggests is requisite to solution.

Explicit definition of policy consequences and the incorporation of a substantive dimension into concepts of politics raise the possibility of employing much more revealing and useful standards of evaluation, reflecting a broader and more critical frame of reference. Relatively objective standards might include *(a)* the stated intentions of a statute or regulation, or of its supporters and promoters—or a carefully framed synthesis of the purposes behind such action; *(b)* various possible alternative policies which might have been undertaken under the same perceived circumstances and somewhat variant value premises and priorities; *(c)* the nature of popular preferences where and as determined by survey evidence; and *(d)* widely accepted values generally thought to be applicable within the system, such as equality. Somewhat more speculative and value-justifying standards for evaluation might also be developed, such as *(e)* assessment of the resources and capabilities of the society, and *(f)* definition of the depth and scope of public problems facing the polity, such as racial discrimination and poverty. Any or all of these might in particular circumstances be used as measuring standards against which the tangible consequences of government policies could be evaluated. From such comparisons, we might reasonably expect to build a comprehensive assessment of the desirability of some of our procedures, of whether the needs of citizens are being adequately fulfilled, of whether the government and the economy are performing at the level of their capabilities—in short, whether the American political system is working well or not. (Again, I do not mean that the procedures by which it works are irrelevant, but only that the results of its workings are a necessary and fundamental component of any overall evaluation.) Similarly, the extent and rate of "improvement" in each of these categories would be ascertainable. Various other more prescriptive standards will no doubt suggest themselves to observers, but again, judgment and inevitable controversy may at least proceed from an established set of findings.

In more general terms, several studies of policy consequences might make it possible to begin to define the major values of the political system in operational form. That is, the values and priorities which actually (rather than merely rhetorically) animate the major actors in politics might be inferable from recurring patterns of policy consequences. These patterns, as well as the priorities implicit in their origins, might then be contrasted with the describable problems of the society, the needs and aspirations of various groups within it, and some of the widely celebrated values of the culture, such as equality. It seems clear that there are many ways available to build an empirical base for scholarly judgment about the performance of the American political system.

* * *

. . . Most needed now are several studies of the consequences of various public policies, in which responsibly executed empirical research is set in wide-ranging value frameworks and employed openly for evaluative purposes: if we do our work promptly and well, it may be that the field of policy analysis can be developed into a model of the critical use of politically sophisticated intelligence. Evaluative conclusions will probably not be unaminous, of course, but at least we shall disagree over relatively well-focused value questions. Perhaps this is the ultimate promise: political science could be well satisfied if it provided the evidence about operations of the political order and focused the value questions for decision by the citizenry.

Notes

[1] Summaries of the literature included in this category may be found in Ranney, *Political Science,* and Herbert Jacob and Michael Lipsky, "Outputs, Structure, and Power: An Assessment of Changes in the Study of State and Local Politics" in Marian Irish, ed. *Political Science: Advance of the Discipline* (Englewood Cliffs, N.J., Prentice-Hall, 1968).

[2] See James W. Davis, Jr. and Kenneth M. Dolbeare, *Little Groups of Neighbors: The Selective Service System* (Chicago, Markham Publishing Company, 1968) for further explanation and an attempt to apply these goals in research. In some ways, however, this book is subject to the very criticisms made in this essay.

[3] Harold Lasswell, *Politics: Who Gets What, When, How* (New York, McGraw-Hill Book Company, 1936).

[4] David Easton, *A Systems Analysis of Political Life* (New York, John Wiley & Sons, 1965).

[5] Murray Edelman, *The Symbolic Uses of Politics* (Urbana, The University of Illinois Press, 1964).

ACTION RESEARCH

Another method of political inquiry that operates from the developmental perspective is action research. Action research is concerned with one of the most important issues in the social sciences, that of the proper role of the investigator. In the attempt to follow the lead of the "hard" sciences, behavioral political scientists have evolved a set of role-expectations in which the researcher is to be objective, accurate, impartial, and clearly separate from the topic of research. This means that the political scientist must not go into a political situation with his or her own agenda for change and must not contaminate the study with his or her own political values. "Let us not," one of the leading behavior-alists has said, "confuse our role of responsible citizen with our role of scientist."[1] This set of values is not supposed to prohibit the scholar from being politically active, but only to separate activism from scholarship.

In reality, however, scientism has often forced a choice of one or the other mode of functioning. It has required people either to draw away into a concentration on abstract scientific concepts that are totally removed from immediate social applicability, or it has required them to abandon the values of science and scholarship entirely and plunge into political commitment.

Action research, like policy analysis, attempts to get beyond this dichotomy and to make a clear connection between scholarship and social purposes. In actual practice, action research and policy analysis may well turn out to be the same thing. Whether this is so or not will depend on the approach chosen by the researcher—whether the research is done from a distance, using secondary source material and available statistical data, or from within the milieu being studied.

This brings us to a central problem of scientific theory, which is sometimes called the "principle of uncertainty," a term devised by physicist Werner Heisenberg to deal with the fact that, in studying the movements of subatomic particles, the act of measurement itself has an affect on what is being measured. Similar problems arise in research with human actions. Abraham Kaplan, writing of behavioral science methodology, notes that "The act of observation affects the person being observed, directly or indirectly, and to a degree which is often of the same order of magnitude as the phenomena which the scientist is interested in observing." Furthermore, there is likely to be a reverse process that is even more subtle, in which the scientist is changed by the subject of study: "The more involved he is with his subject matter, the more likely it is that his observations will be affected by the involvement."[2]

The quality of the relationship between the researcher and research subjects must also be considered. Frequently,

the requirements of "good" research methodology demand elaborate techniques for deceiving research subjects about the exact nature of what is going on. This is to some extent true of all questionnaire and field research procedures, and it is especially true of "laboratory" social science research. Much of the most respected existing material on small-group behavior is based on the observed behavior of people who have been placed into contrived situations in which they either did not know about or were deliberately deceived about the exact nature of what was being studied. The action-research model outlined here by Nevitt Sanford holds that the research procedure itself must be favorable to the development of the people affected by it—that is, it must be "favorable to their autonomy, privacy, and self-esteem."

A MODEL FOR ACTION RESEARCH

NEVITT SANFORD

[For Kurt Lewin, in 1947] action research consisted in analysis, fact-finding, conceptualization, planning, execution, more fact-finding or evaluation; and then a repetition of this whole circle of activities; indeed, a spiral of such circles.[1]

Leon Festinger told Alfred Marrow that Lewin's greatest contribution "on the abstract level may have been the idea of studying things through changing them and seeing the effect. This theme—that in order to gain insight into a process one must create a change and then observe its variable effects and new dynamics—runs through all of Lewin's work."[2] This seems very close to common sense. It is the way to solve any practical problem or to learn any skill. Yet for Lewin this kind of involvement with practical problems was a never-failing source of theoretical ideas and knowledge of fundamental social psychological relationships.

My reason for asking what has been the fact of this contribution of Lewin's is not just a fascination with history or a desire to preserve intact the work of an admired figure; I am interested in working out a model, for the integration of action and research, that is adequate for today. . . .

[1] James C. Charlesworth (ed.) *A Design for Political Science: Scope, Objectives and Methods,* (Philadelphia: American Academy of Political and Social Science, 1956), p. 115.

[2] Abraham Kaplan, *The Conduct of Inquiry: Methodology for Behavioral Science* (San Francisco: Chandler, 1964), pp. 136–138.

Nevitt Sanford, "Whatever Happened to Action Research?" *Journal of Social Issues,* (1970) 26, no. 4, 3–23. (Edited and abridged.)

The categorical separation of research from practice has had some serious negative consequences for social science. For one thing, it has cut the academic researcher off from lines of investigation that are necessary to the development of his science, for example, the study of phenomena that cannot be experimented on in the laboratory or the study of social structures that can be understood only through attempts to change them. Again, it has laid the social sciences wide open to the charge of irrelevance, not only by students but by men of affairs. . . .

Much of the trouble comes from the fact that the separation of science from practice raised for academic men—who have a deep interest in the matter—the question of which has the greater status; and, despite the fact that social scientific work on practical problems poses the greater intellectual challenge, the decision went to "pure" science. A result has been that brave new efforts by federal agencies to do something about the problems of society soon become bogged down. For example, when new bureaus or "study sections" on applied social science are set up, their personnel seek to avoid appearing second-class by being just as hard-nosed or "scientific" as their heroes in the academic social sciences—and end up being just as narrow. Or when centers for research and development are set up within universities, academic social scientists, who are needed to lend prestige to the enterprise, seize the opportunity to get funding for what they were doing already, and things go on much as before. . . .

Once science is split off from practice, further splits develop. We have on the one side experts in conceptualization, theoretical model-building, research design, experimentation and on the other side experts in planning, in execution, and in evaluation, each class of whom has more and more difficulty in talking with the others. Training follows the general trend of events in science: separated bureaucratically from research and from action at the funding level, it is mainly in the hands of the segregated experts. Sensitivity training, for example, a proceeding of enormous potential and with some solid achievements to its credit, has been lifted out of its natural context of social structure and social practice and rendered free-floating, apparently on the assumption that its recipients are also free-floating.

Small wonder that social science is having an identity crisis, that social scientists generally seem to be well-heeled but unhappy. We do not want to be "mere technicians" who carry out other people's purposes, as Sherif has so eloquently said;[3] yet, we have so detached ourselves from practical affairs that we do not know how to make decisions in important matters ourselves. There should be a large place for idle curiosity in a civilized community, yet, if we are not doing action research, we find it hard to indulge our curiosity at a time when our basic institutions seem about to fall to pieces. As liberal intellectuals we would like to make social science available to people who need it the most, that is, the poor and the oppressed, but for this the science-engineering model . . . is hopelessly inadequate.

How did we get into this fix? The basic trouble is the fragmentation I have described and this in turn can be understood as an aspect of the general tendency toward specialization in modern science and scholarship. Effective social problem solving calls for multidisciplinary work, yet departmentalism seems everywhere on the increase. . . .

There is, of course, specialization within as well as among the disciplines in consequence of which we have a fantastic proliferation of bitsy and disconnected and essentially unusable researches. Specialization is a natural accompaniment of high levels of development in science, and it has obviously led to some intellectual and practical pay-off in the past, but the compartmentalization of social scientific activities and the scarcity of efforts to pull things together calls for explanation. Like professional practice, social science has been adapting itself to the requirements of an advanced technological society—which demands more and more segregation of functions and the training of experts to perform them.

Just as professionals in health, education, and welfare no longer treat or deal with the whole person but only with particular symptoms or functions, so psychologists in their research and theory-making focus more and more on part-functions without bothering to connect them with central structures in the person. Indeed, the very concept of the person, downgraded and ignored, seems about to disappear from the literature.

I have elsewhere, and more than once, pointed to what seem to me to be the serious consequences of this.[1] Not only have we contributed to the dehumanization of our research subjects by reducing them to "respondents" for the sake of enterprises that never yield any benefit to them, and to the dehumanization of ourselves by encouraging self-definition in terms of narrow specialties; we have also been disseminating a more unfortunate image of man. What is for the social scientist now researchable, an aggregate of meaningless "behaviors," becomes for great masses of our people a conception of the self as fragmented and externalized: one *is* what one can present to others in a particular situation.

It is understandable that social science, like most other human activities in our society, should accommodate itself to inexorable social and historical processes. But more than other disciplines and professions it must bear responsibility for what has happened, for it has had the knowledge and the values to permit it to see what was happening. In any case it is certainly up to the social scientists, particularly those who work in universities, to oppose the current trend. . . .

What is needed is a contemporary model for action research or, as I prefer to say, research-action. [This new model] contains the main features of Lewin's model—that is, analysis, fact findings, planning, execution, and evaluation. There is, however, more emphasis here on research as the action, and less emphasis on the effort to solve particular problems or induce particular changes in behavior. The aim, rather, is to promote liberation and growth and these are considered to be favored by the processes of the research and by the model the researchers present as they carry out their work.

Let us consider some of the main features of the model in turn.

Analysis

Analysis determines what kinds of questions are to be asked. These should be practical, although somewhat general and open-ended. . . . Most social-science questions, in my view, should be of this general kind: how to arrange the environment, institution, or the social setting in such a way as to promote the development of all the individuals concerned.

Fact Finding

The aim of promoting individual development has several important implications.

1. It is necessary to have a conceptualization of the person and theory concerning how he actually develops. Here, it seems to me, we must go far beyond the highly abstract formulations of Kurt Lewin, filling in a scheme such as his, with particular kinds of needs, dispositions, values, conflicts, and so forth.

2. An approach that is concerned with individual development must be comprehensive and field theoretical. An interest in changing one aspect of the person or of his behavior must take into account the implications of such change for the total person. And to understand the person we must see him in his total setting. This means that research-action is properly multidisciplinary—and in my view it is only a focus on problems, ultimately problems of human development or human welfare, that will bring about collaboration among the academic disciplines.

3. The concern with human development, of which I speak, is a concern with development now rather than in the future. It means that we must behave toward our subjects in a way that is favorable to development. For example, favorable to their autonomy, privacy, and self-esteem. We go contrary to this value if we use our subjects as means to some other end, including the end of their own well-being in the remote future. Research must, in other words, serve the purposes of its subjects. This does not mean that the researcher must sacrifice his own values. It does mean that he will probably have to say what they are and work out as much agreement with his subjects as possible.

The subject is the client, and reporting to him is an action. Lewin considered that his action research would favor the purposes of "social management as well as the self management of groups." I think it was easier during World War II, and in the years shortly thereafter, than it is now to assume that "management" would use social science knowledge in the interest of all concerned. For surely there was much more agreement about large national purposes than there is now. . . .

Planning

Planning, or "planning ahead," does not have such an important role in the present model as in the action research of the past. There is no point in planning for people who will upset all such plans as soon as they find out that they have not been permitted to take part in the planning. To arrange things in such a way that the "natives" (students, faculty, poor people, ethnic minorities, and so on) can and do take part in the planning readily becomes a goal that supersedes the model of planning from above by experts.

Notes

[1] Kurt Lewin, "Group Decision and Social Change," in T. M. Newcomb and E. L. Hartley (eds.) *Readings in Social Psychology* (New York: Holt, Rinehart, and Winston, 1947).

[2] A. J. Marrow, *The Practical Theorist: The Life and Work of Kurt Lewin* (New York: Basic Books, 1969), p. 235.

[3] M. Sherif, "If the Social Scientist is to be More than a Mere Technician," *Journal of Social Issues,* 1968, 24(1), 41–62.

[4] N. Sanford, "I Know How It Is Done but I Just Can't Do It: Discussion of Rollo May's Paper," in R. B. McLeod (ed.) *William James: Unfinished Business* (Washington, D. C.: American Psychological Association, 1968); N. Sanford, "The Decline of Individualism," *Public Health Reports,* 1970, 85, 213–19.

PERSONAL DEVELOPMENT AND POLITICAL BEHAVIOR

Policy analysis and action research are two examples of research procedures that are compatible with a developmental approach to political science. The following paper provides an example of how such an approach may also result in different findings, in basically different ways of understanding and explaining what goes on in politics. It also illustrates another approach to the problem of reconciling a concern about values and morality with a concern for scientific method.

Charles Hampden-Turner and Phillip Whitten confront the subject of personal morality directly and attempt to bring it within the realm of science. Morality, in the theory of human development that they sketch, is one facet of the level of psycho-social development that a person has attained. Higher levels of human development manifest higher orders of reasoning about moral questions, and also manifest different kinds of political behavior. Like Reich, Hampden-Turner and Whitten are trying to use consciousness as a key variable in political analysis.

This is a revolutionary endeavor. It seeks to supplant such concepts as social class and group or economic self-interest, which are commonly held to be fundamental to thinking about political behavior; it also suggests that there may be heretofore undiscovered limitations to the empirical study of human behavior. The authors assert that the higher levels of psycho-social development are simply not comprehensible to individuals who have not themselves achieved fairly high development; they will misunderstand the meaning that principled behavior has for the people who are performing it, but the actual nature of the action will be invisible.

In another work, Hampden-Turner argues that, because of a built-in inability to understand principled behavior, the modern social scientist also is victim to a built-in conservatism: "While life processes face forwards towards greater complexity, variety, and higher synthesis, the vast majority of social scientists face backwards, searching for the causes of present behavior in a myriad of separate incidents, group affiliations, economic conditions, and occupational roles. . . . Their conservatism is unaware, nonideological, unowned, and is latent in the tools they employ. It comes about less by valuing conservatively than by the 'value-free' selection of the less than human."[3] Thus, Hampden-Turner calls for a new way of looking at human behavior—again, we are pushing at the limits of the existing paradigm—which will provide a new perspective on radical action and political change.

[3] Charles Hampden-Turner, *Radical Man* (Boston: Schenkman, 1970), pp. 12, 16.

A THEORY
OF POLITICAL MORALITY

CHARLES HAMPDEN-TURNER AND PHILLIP WHITTEN

All responsible law-abiding citizens resemble one another; every outlaw is responsible in his own fashion. In the past decade the wanted poster replaced the campaign poster as the official portrait of the American hero. Test cases turned the courtroom into a forum for national issues; members of conspiracies received more attention than members of Congress. Henry David Thoreau was a household word, along with his doctrine of civil disobedience. Commitment was defined by one's willingness to be arrested, political experience by the length of one's police record. The "Group W Bench" (those selected for prosecution by the State) included such diverse figures as Martin Luther King and Abbie Hoffman, Dr. Spock and Bobby Seale.

The national campaign for law and order has since produced a new dictionary of household words, and a new American hero. Those who take the brunt charge political repression, claiming that blind enforcement of the legal code threatens an important and legitimate source of social change. It has become critical that we understand the fashions of responsible outlaws, as well as those of ordinary citizens, in terms that will allow their politics to remain constructive. We cannot accept the simple analysis of an Agnew speech or a Weatherman bomb threat.

Recent research indicates that the polarization of Americans into political camps—left-wing vs. right-wing, militant vs. pacifist, the movement vs. the system—can be traced to the levels of moral development that guide individuals through most of their daily activity. Certain moral perspectives impel "radical" thinking, while certain other moral perspectives impel "conservative" interpretations of reality.

Studies comparing the moral judgments made by political conservatives, liberals and radicals have confirmed some of the sterotypes each group uses to describe the others as well as those they use to describe

Charles Hampden-Turner and Phillip Whitten, "Morals Left and Right," Reprinted from *Psychology Today* Magazine, pp. 39–76, April 1971. Copyright © Communications/Research/Machines, Inc.

themselves. There is evidence to support the conservative's notion that the radical movement consists of starry-eyed idealists "infiltrated" by Machiavellian opportunists. The same evidence, however, also justifies the radical's claim of moral superiority over both liberals and conservatives.

There are also indications that the confrontation tactics developed by the radical movement, and so violently condemned by law-and-order advocates, can actually increase the moral awareness of the young. Not surprisingly, these tactics are less effective with older generations. Radical education tends to accelerate the polarization of Americans into political camps—the armed camps of the revolution.

Research conducted in the San Francisco Bay Area and Boston offers four keys to an understanding of the recent political and cultural turmoil in the United States.

1. Different levels of moral judgment tend to discriminate radicals from liberals—at least among middle-class Americans.
2. College activists typically are found at the highest and lowest stages of moral development.
3. A person seldom can comprehend judgments more than one level above the one in which he usually is found.
4. Growth in the capacity for moral judgment can be induced by creating conflicts between two or more stages and by dramatizing the issues.

This research incorporates the model of sequential stages of moral growth developed by Lawrence Kohlberg of the Harvard Graduate School of Education. He found that moral perspective progresses through as many as six stages during a person's life. To determine a subject's stage of development Kohlberg would ask him to explain his solutions to a variety of moral dilemmas that had no "right" answers. For example, a subject might be asked to imagine that his wife will die of a disease unless she takes a certain drug. The sole supplier of the drug demands so great a profit that the subject cannot find the money. The typical solution in this case is theft, but the justifications offered by subjects vary according to their levels of moral development.

Moral value in the first two preconventional states is defined in terms of self-centered needs. At Stage 1, the individual is primarily motivated by desire to avoid punishment by a superior power: *God would punish me if I let my wife die. My father-in-law would make trouble for me.*

At Stage 2, concern has shifted to the satisfaction of quasi-physical needs. The individual develops an awareness of the relative value of each person's needs as his own drives are frustrated by demands for exchange and reciprocity: *I have a right to the services of my wife, and naturally this is more important than whatever rights the druggist may claim. No one is going to look out for my interest or my wife's unless I do.*

The conventional orientation of Stages 3 and 4 involves conformity to traditional role expectations and maintenance of existing social and legal order. The Stage-3 individual is motivated to avoid social disapproval for nonconformity and would like to be judged by his intentions: *I'd do what any half-decent husband would do—save his family and carry out his protective function.*

The Stage-4 person understands how his role fits into larger constellations of roles, the institutions approved by others. He seeks to perform his duty—to meet the expectations of society: *My wife and I submitted ourselves to a higher law, the institution of marriage. The fabric of our society is held together by this institution. I know my lawful duty when I see it.*

The two postconventional stages represent the most advanced levels of moral development. Decisions are based on consideration of shared values rather than on self-centered interests or blind conformity to external standards. The Stage-5 individual perceives his duty in terms of a social contract, recognizing the arbitrary nature of rules made for the sake of agreement. He avoids infringing on the rights of others, or violating the welfare of the majority: *My wife and I promised to love and help one another whatever the circumstances. We chose to make this commitment and in our daily lives together it is constantly renewed. I am therefore committed to saving her.*

The Stage-6 person relies heavily on his own conscience and the mutual respect of others. He recognizes the universal principles that underlie social commitments and seeks to apply them as consistent principles

of moral judgment: *No contract, law, obligation, private gain or fear of punishment should impede any man from saving those he loves. For the sake of my wife I will steal the drug; for the sake of others who might share my experience, I will steal the drug publicly, so that society may cease to sacrifice human relationships to the profit motive.*

People progress from stage to stage, but most never advance beyond Stages 3 and 4. It is primarily college-educated, middle-class youth who have attained high levels of moral judgment in recent years. And even they are inclined, when their formal education has been completed, to backslide on the scale.

At each level, the person takes into consideration the logic of each of the lower steps, with the highest level taking precedence. The Stage-6 man is aware of the demands made upon him in a situation by role laws and previous commitments—and he may undergo much agony if these considerations conflict with his conscience.

We found in the research that young adults who thought of themselves as political conservatives consistently referred to law, order, authority maintenance (Stage 4) and conformity to stereotyped roles (Stage 3) in making their moral judgments. Self-professed liberals and moderates tended to make Stage-5 judgments. Radicals, however, showed an interesting division. Although most radicals had Stage-6 consciences and principle orientation, a large minority made egocentric Stage-2 judgments.

These findings correspond to the image of a fairly homogenous silent majority of conservative Americans confronting a disparate array of left-of-center idealists (Stage 6) and opportunists (Stage 2). Between these poles are the Stage-5 liberals, desperately urging the two groups at least to agree on the methods of disagreement.

If the U.S. faced dilemmas no more complex than whether or not poor men should steal drugs to save their wives, most political partisans would probably agree. The levels of rationale used to arrive at a solution to the problem would then concern only philosophers. Unfortunately, it is not that simple.

Conservatives, liberals and radicals use moral judgments to justify actions that affect the lives of millions. Different levels of moral development are intimately associated with different political positions on such issues as race relations and the Vietnam war. For instance, radicals attack Asian policy on grounds of conscience (Stage 6), or on grounds that it is detrimental to the personal economic or domestic interests of American citizens (Stage 2). Conservatives in Stages 3 and 4 defend the war. They praise "our boys" for meeting role expectations so well, especially by comparison with "campus bums." They exhort patriotic citizens to support the lawful authority of the Commander in Chief, who knows much more about the situation than those who try to legislate in the streets. This polarity tears apart the moral hierarchy and discourages commitment to a rational dialogue.

The cleavages between stages of development can be understood on a deeper level by using Silvan Tomkin's distinction between left-wing and right-wing ideology. Tomkins asks:

"Is man the measure, an end in himself, an active, creative, thinking, desiring, loving force in nature (Left)? or, must man realize himself, attain his full stature, only through struggle towards, participation in, conformity to, a norm, a measure, an ideal essence, basically independent of man (Right)?"

The Stage-6 man whose conscience shrieks at the barbarity of the Vietnam war perceives *himself* as an "active, creative, thinking, desiring, loving" arbiter of right and wrong. He is undaunted by charges of treason or unAmericanism because he has an ideal of a nobler America yet to be created by people like him. At a more primitive level, the Stage-2 radical objects to the war because it threatens to delay satisfaction of his own personal needs and impulses. The war constrains and frustrates him in a dozen different ways and confronts him with obligations beyond his will and, perhaps, beyond his ability to fulfill.

Conservatives express concern that the war is eroding patriotism and respect for authority (Stages 3 and 4). They fear that disrespect for authorities and the breaking down of order are tarnishing America's reputation and undermining its position in the world. Duty, honor, patriotism, loyalty, the flag, the free world and our national mission help define our proper roles (Stage 3) and constitute the symbolic fabric of lawful authority

(Stage 4).

The Stage-5 liberal objects to the war because it disregards social contracts of negotiation and agreement. He believes, however, that democratic politics and academic freedom can survive only if dissenters and authorities respect implied agreements on the limits of dissent, the need to work for change within the system by peaceful means, and the necessity for rational dialogue. As a result the liberal regards virtually no act by those in authority as base enough to merit opposition that violates the social contract. When Robert McNamara went to Harvard to speak as Secretary of Defense, the academic community apparently was more shocked by the students who shouted him down than they were by the saturation bombing and killing of civilians that his policy brought about. These Harvard liberals wanted polite discussion of wholesale slaughter confined to the question-and-answer period.

The race issue also has polarized conservatives and radicals at their different levels of moral judgment. Law and order (Stage 4) has, of course, become a rallying cry for resistance to black demands. But the cultural stereotypes typical of Stage-3 thinking—Miss America, the Wild West, our boys, red-blooded Americans, etc.—are more subtly racist. The images are those of the dominant culture, a culture ostensibly dedicated to individualism, but actually demanding a conformity some can never achieve. Those who are already several laps behind in the Great American Race are absurdly handicapped, while those who maintain the system with their own preferences in mind have a distinct advantage.

Radicals and many liberals have become convinced that the black and the poor must be given the right to define their own needs and shape their own institutions and norms. This can happen only in a society that permits the disadvantaged to create and implement Stage-6 judgments and Stage-5 contracts, which in turn can become laws (Stage 4), roles (Stage 3), and instrumentalities (Stage 2) infused with their creators' consciousness. In short, the disadvantaged can never "catch up." They must instead be encouraged to *originate*.

Young people have been forced to create a counterculture in order to transcend cultural values that are dominated by the conservative, rule-centered Stages 3 and 4 and to move through Stage 5 into the fully person-centered Stage 6. The old culture's external symbols of virtue—status, high income, private property, good grades, winning the ball game—were amenable to relatively precise measurement and linear ordering. A man was only as good as his credit rating. Now virtue is being attributed to the self. This sort of virtue must be uncovered and shaped from a thousand jumbled ideas and feelings deep within the person. The quest for self may require many of the things conservatives abhor: permissiveness, experimentation, incompleteness, frankness about previously taboo topics, criticism of and skepticism toward the inherited truths, and the recognition of contradictions.

Growth beyond Stage 4 requires the creation of voluntary commitments to others as well as acts of conscience in which *authenticity* is crucial to communication and agreement. Those who deviate from well-worn roles and traditions risk total alienation, unless their humanity and sensitivity can evoke others' humanity to create new bonds.

For those at Stages 3 and 4, authenticity is at best a qualified good. They see the self as lacking intrinsic worth, able to achieve value only by conformity to a norm, a measure, an ideal essence, basically independent of man. Conservative Americans believe that the self-centered strivings typical of Stage-2 behavior must be harnessed and controlled by imposed roles (Stage 3) and due respect for authority (Stage 4). It is considered safer, and indeed more civilized, to make a calculated impact or good impression. The well-groomed, self-conscious, respectable aspects of the personality should be revealed to others selectively. President Nixon embodies this type of control; having learned that his temper gets him into trouble, he will be silent for days—even months—after a setback before he counterattacks with carefully rehearsed indignation. Although people at Stages 5 and 6 may regard this attribute as unauthentic, those at Stages 3 and 4 regard it as essentially civilized. The President checks himself, keeps himself in control, and personifies the lawful restraint of potentially dangerous impulses.

An individual must like and trust his unvarnished self before he can give authenticity a free rein. Unbridled and confident, kids let their hair fly free, their beards grow wild and their bodies go unsupported. Their love is expressed openly; their indignation is combustible. Their quest for self-discovery frustrates and provokes the authorities determined to squeeze the young into conservative molds. The old culture believes that the spontaneous self betrays the individual, causes trouble, impedes the installation of new technology, weakens moral imperatives, undermines social control, and is bad for business.

The people of the conservative old culture (Stages 3 and 4) live with perpetual psychological scarcity—the assumption that there is never enough, materially or spiritually, to satisfy everyone's needs. There is always a shortage—of status, authority, wealth, property and school marks that are ordered hierarchically for purposes of envious competition and comparison. Profiteers push their ideals safely beyond the reach of most persons, and those who fall just short in an atmosphere of contrived scarcity never feel adequate to question those ideals.

Radicals and liberals are perplexed by the contradictions of the old culture. They know there is enough to go around. They attack the system that the old culture designed to protect the resources—a system that maintains itself at the cost of abandoning millions of its own citizens to malnutrition, infant mortality and death from easily preventable diseases.

It is significant that the radical counterculture originated among some of the brightest students at the best universities. Having won the glittering prizes, these students denounced the whole rat race as worthless and unjust. They formed an uncertain alliance with those who rejected the race because they missed the shining prizes by a mile. Both groups increasingly reject marks, hierarchies and competitiveness, as they insist on sharing and communal festivals of life, and are determined to create an abundance of sights, sounds, experiences and the necessities of life.

The drawback to a morality that adheres to cultural stereotypes and law and order is that such guidelines are national rather than international. In the absence of international law and order such moral judgments steer rival nations into collision courses.

Paradoxically, the only way to create international

law-and-order and world-citizen stereotypes is through the preliminary exercise of conscience (Stage 6) and contracts between nations (Stage 5). These initially would conflict with the patriotic structure of each nation. In the absence of world authority or roles by which Stage-3 and Stage-4 persons can be guided, we are stuck in an international jungle where our national authority and our boys struggle for dominion.

The crucial flaw in the radical morality can be seen in the Janus-faced character of college protest movements. Studies by Norma Haan and her associates at the University of California at Berkeley and Irvin Doress in Boston have found that both the highly moral Stage 6 and the essentially premoral Stage 2 were heavily represented in the radical population, along with a few Stage-5 allies.

Researchers who compared persons in these highest and lowest groups found that they are outwardly very similar. Many members of both groups had interrupted their college careers, moved off-campus, disagreed with their parents and involved themselves intensely in politics, assumed the dress and speech of the counterculture, and begun to pursue creative and artistic endeavors.

Highly moral radicals, however, valued sensitivity, empathy and altruism far more than did the premoral subjects, who prided themselves on being aloof, reserved, stubborn and uncompromising. Whereas the Stage-6 radicals seem capable of replacing outdated structures by pouring in their creative energies and capacities and building anew, Stage-2 radicals are essentially adolescents who mimic, misinterpret and misrepresent the principled thinkers.

Elliot Turiel's recent discovery of "Temporary 2s" complicates any neat distinction between 6s and 2s. Unlike the typical premoral individual, the Temporary 2 comprehends higher levels of judgment but refuses to use them. This could be interpreted as a regression in the service of the ego, or it might be that such students do not oppose roles or authorities in general, but merely the particular roles and the particular authorities they are confronting. It could also mean, however, that the transition from Stage 4 to the more person-centered Stages 5 and 6 has miscarried, with the result that the individual slips back into premoral judgment.

These findings suggest that the characteristics commonly regarded as symptoms of person-centered growth—the communal, experiential trappings of the counterculture—might equally well be interpreted as a regression to an egocentric state. Indeed, there is some evidence that hippies and street people are mostly 2s with some stereotyped beautiful 3s. Radicalism became fashionable, a local convention, and many adopted the style of the revolution without the awareness of the revolutionary. The harsh truth is that crime spreads and drug addiction reaches epidemic proportions as the constituency of conscience grows. Chase N. Peterson, Harvard's Dean of Admissions, speaks of "kids, searching earnestly for a magical mystery tour as they share despair, hope, marijuana and gonorrhea."

Given this ambiguity in which those who are moral run in harness with those who are amoral, we can begin to understand the conspiracy theories so prevalent on the American Right. The Right accuses radicals of putting up an idealistic front of wishy-washy, starry-eyed, bleeding-heart do-gooders and dupes, behind which all manner of sinister and criminal elements gnaw at the nation's moral fiber.

To many conservatives the Left seems conspiratorial and treacherous for yet another reason. Practitioners of Stage-3 and Stage-4 judgments can easily understand the rationale of Stage-2 leftists, but they cannot comprehend the judgments of Stage-6 radicals. Kohlberg found that people cannot generally comprehend more than one level above their own. Conservatives know that conscience is somehow good. The liberal (Stage-5) media may frequently have stressed how high-minded was the disobedience of such men as Daniel and Philip Berrigan, William Sloane Coffin and Martin Luther King, but individuals at Stages 3 and 4 can never accept the wisdom or sincerity of such men. Rather, it sounds to them like typical liberal rhetoric that covers the advance of dangerous elements whose Stage-2 behavior conservatives recognize clearly.

One of the more predictive items on the California F Scale, which discriminates between conservative and liberal tendencies, is the statement that *young people sometimes get rebellious ideas, but as they grow up they ought to get over them and settle down.* The statement describes precisely the experiences of Stage-3 and Stage-4 individuals who have grown out of the self-assertive, premoral Stage 2.

Both the Left and the Right, therefore, have good reason to see each other in terms of their own immoral pasts. While conservatives at Stages 3 and 4 see the Stage-2 radical as occupying a level morally beneath them, Stage-6 radicals and Stage-5 liberals see conservatives as being in a condition from which they have emancipated themselves. Each partisan feels that in attacking the other he is burning the effigy of his own moral infancy.

Finally, we come to the difficult problem of how maturity might best be induced in moral judgment. One hypothesis, implicit in Kohlberg's model of moral development, holds that congruence between the different levels will enhance growth. For example, if authorities are fair-minded, then persons will swiftly pass through the law-and-order orientation to share the conscience of the authorities themselves. Research indicates that children with Stage-6 mothers reach and transcend Stage 4 at a relatively early age, suggesting that conservative and radical levels of judgment are potentially synergistic.

But a second hypothesis, also supported by research, suggests another conclusion. When disputes are dramatized in a classroom and higher-level judgments clash with lower-level ones in dialectic, students learn to prefer the higher-level judgments. From this we might infer that the shortcomings of lower-level judgments must be demonstrated before they are discarded.

Our two hypotheses are, perhaps, reconcilable. Growth is enhanced by congruence between the different levels of judgment. For example, Kenneth Keniston found that young radicals are oriented to conscience and commitment, partly because fairminded parents explained rules to them when they were children. This kind of progress is blocked, however, when the different levels move *out* of harmony, when there is a credibility gap between the explanations of the authorities and the perceptions of the young. At this point growth proceeds from conflict rather than from cooperation.

This pattern parallels many college uprisings in the late '60s. Students seized buildings on issues of conscience (Stage 6). Administrators responded with law-and-order arguments (Stage 4). Liberal faculties desperately tried to mediate (Stage 5).

Persons who witnessed police violence were shocked away from conventional thinking, either rising to Stage 5, Stage 6, or backsliding to Stage 2.

Such confrontations can promote moral growth by dramatizing the conflict between higher and lower stages of development. Even when the conflict fails to produce immediate reform, it gathers more recruits for what promises to be a long and continuing struggle.

In any society the Stage-6 individuals, and to a lesser extent the Stage-5 ones, are the experimenters, the innovators, the dynamic segment of society. But the conventional elements in society, represented by Stages 4 and 3, function to salvage the conventional social system when experimental morality miscarries.

POLITICAL POWER AND HUMAN GROWTH

At several points in this book, the pluralist ideology has been characterized as a revision or refutation of classical democratic theory. In particular we have noted that where traditional concepts of democracy had a great faith in the necessity and value of a high degree of participation by citizens in political processes, the new ideology that emerged from behavioral research argued that (a) vigorous citizen participation does not in fact exist in a modern mass democracy, and (b) the system works quite well without it. Developmental considerations now require us to re-open the argument, to take another look at the actions of individual citizens, to evaluate democracy from a slightly different perspective.

The question that is now being raised is not whether the failure of citizens to participate has some adverse effect on the political system, but whether it has some adverse effect on the citizens themselves. Daniel Goldrich and Joseph A. Kremers, authors of the following paper, ask:

Have we been too insensitive to the disintegrating effects of modern hierarchical authority structures . . . on human potential? Have we been too unwilling to rethink our assumptions about the link between social structures and potential human development? Have we been too confident in the self-renewing capabilities of a society dominated by large, complex, impersonal and formal groups?

Clearly, a political science capable of dealing with such questions would have different disciplinary boundaries from those that are currently recognized. The applicability of the growth psychologies and Benedict's anthropologically derived concept of synergy have already been mentioned, and a later paper will explore the biological foundations of political science. This boundary-widening process also includes economics, which has always been strongly influential in American political science. Goldrich and Kremers, for example, see one way in which economic processes might be considered from a developmental perspective. They are concerned with how the imperatives of economic/industrial organization touch the lives of individuals. When they talk about factories and businesses they are—in a way that illustrates common humanistic/developmental concerns—talking about work as *experience*. The focus is not solely on what work produces or even on what it pays, but on what kinds of opportunities the working milieu provides for individuals to live out their daily lives, relate to others, influence their surroundings, and explore their own potentials. And the value premise that is basic to their discussion is the belief that passivity, lack of power, lack of involvement—whether in the work place or the political system—tend to diminish and weaken the human drive toward self-actualization.

The content of the paper is highly activist, going well beyond the action research model presented by Nevitt Sanford. The authors present, as a unit, both a program for research and a program for social change that would reform institutions. Reform proposals are not particularly unusual in political science, but it is unusual for a set of reform proposals to be based entirely on concepts of human development.

THE DEVELOPMENTAL COMMUNITY

DANIEL GOLDRICH AND JOSEPH A. KREMERS

* * *

Decisions in . . . organizations [of the corporate state] are becoming ever more closed to public scrutiny,

Daniel Goldrich and Joseph A. Kremers, "From the Corporate State through Vietnam to the Developmental Community," paper presented at the 1972 Annual Meeting of the American Political Science Association. Washington, D.C. (Edited and abridged.)

while life within them, for those not of top rank, grows ever more specialized, isolated and artificial. As time goes on, each of us has less and less experience with broad responsibility, with having to think through the links between our acts and the wider consequences of those acts for others.[1] Paradoxically, many of these large organizations are, in effect, highly dependent on the fragmented technical skill of their employees below top levels. These middle and even low level specialists have the information and know-how which enable them to see through the official deceptions worked on the general public. This know-how and skill are misused, and the middle range people know it. They are the "insiders" without whose courage the public would continue to be duped, in many cases, by public relations pap and obfuscation. It is these "cogs" who have become the focus of much of the moral tension within these organizations. The middle range expert finds that to assume responsibility for the consequences of the larger entity violates the terms (generally implicit, but at times explicit) of employment and the cultural norms of an organization-dominated society.[2] The presumptuous person who raises such issues becomes vulnerable to the powerful range of sanctions available to the organization and quite possibly to the organizations interdependent with it. So, most of us lie low,[3] even those of us uneasy about the ways in which the organizations frustrate our common interests, or even our own personal development.

Consciousness of mass murder, of pollution, of physically dangerous industrial practices, of the waste of tax monies by public agencies in collusion with effectively unaccountable "private" corporations have led a handful of people to act on their own sense of responsibility. Having first tried the "proper channels," and having been told, in effect, they were operating outside their organizational and moral sphere . . . these few have finally "blown the whistle." Some of them have forced temporary change in policy; but most have failed. Operating as lone figures, they have been abruptly and severely sanctioned, losing their jobs and perhaps their chance for equivalent employment, becoming pariahs, thrust outside the corporate state system that embraces an expanding amount of the material and psychic rewards of modern life.

Granted that all this is so, that dissenters within the corporate state are finding new and frightening constraints on their efforts to speak out, what has this to do with "community power studies"?

Since the early power studies were written, we have come to believe that they all suffered from some critical lacks. These lacks have meant that the studies, like much of what academic social science did in the sixties, missed the various signals in the social environment that times were "a-changin." In simple form, we did not anticipate the growing presence of the concentrations of power we have called "the corporate state." We did not fathom its penetrative power nor its subtlety. . . .

THE LACK OF A POLITICAL-ECONOMIC FOCUS

The first major failing in those studies was the lack of perception of the interpenetration between major segments of the economy and the political system, and the vital importance of that interpenetration in any understanding of "who rules" in American communities. We failed to identify the links between the two major sections, political and economic, and we did not comprehend the factor of sheer size in the equation. We now can see that all the fundamental groups of American life have been drawn into the purview of the "corporate state," to a greater or lesser degree. The latter seems to operate more and more according to technical or organizational imperatives, and less and less in response to constituent-consumer or general public interests. The political-economic perspective leads one to investigate the relationships between all sources of allocated societal values, formally governmental or not, and thereby to a more adequate comprehension of the vital forces in the American exercise of power.

The political-economic perspective has a fairly long history within American social science, but not many political scientists can be found among its adherents. Of the more recent people who have maintained an ongoing concern with the anomalies yielded by this perspective, Peter Bachrach has had perhaps the steadiest influence. Recently, he and his colleagues have stimulated debate by revealing the elitist bias of American political theory, by examining the threat of corporate unac-

countability to democratic theory, by exploring the "two faces" of public-affecting power, and by tracing the implications of all these things for the exercise of power in an American community setting.[1]

Bachrach has helped us see that systems have *biases,* that democracy is not simply method, but is shaped and formed and used by men with conflicting values. He has helped us to detect the ability of a system to deflect, coopt, smother or simply prevent, without overt action, significant efforts to use it and change it. He has alerted us to the power of "the smooth system," the ever more faceless strength to blunt conflict over values at their source. Bachrach's work has been constant and lucid on these issues; it appears that time will continue to enhance the retrospective value of what he has done. As the saying goes "he was there first." Acknowledged or not, the discipline is in his debt.

J. K. Galbraith's *The New Industrial State*[2] examined the new complexity and size of the system from an economist's viewpoint. He sees new social structural forces at work in modern business, challenging our heretofore accepted descriptions of the dynamic elements of corporate power. Power is divided in an as yet imperfectly understood way between managers, technicians and corporate state leadership. One thing is clear in Galbraith's vision, however, and that is that far from being related in the classical adversary manner, modern corporations and government agencies have developed an extensive symbiosis along several fronts. These fundamental changes in corporate-state relationships have shrunk our understanding and our controls over public-affecting activities of both groups.

The political-economic perspective, i.e., the heightened attention to the interconnections between economic and political forms of public-affecting power and the pattern of benefits resulting from related decisions, must force itself on any new "community power studies."[3] Researchers must learn methods of measuring the new patterns of power and payoff. Formerly used definitions must be recast. Whatever "community" we study now, we must realize that the salient power links extend above and beyond the local territorial-geographic boundaries of, for example, a municipality. The allocating power of the corporate state is now so great that it penetrates from the national congress to the small town, here and abroad, and laterally at each level in between. No doubt this approach will make power more difficult to find and therefore to measure. But the answers to the questions of who rules any particular community are so important that we must begin the development of a proper methodology. We have measured the wrong thing only too accurately in the past. We must find ways of revealing the "other face" of power spoken of by Bachrach and Baratz. We must bring into our analyses those voices which are being raised in unorthodox or "anomic" ways. We must seriously entertain the proposition that decisions found in the public "sites" or arenas may be only the tip of the power iceberg, and that the greatest part is more shadowy, less distinct than the visible top. We must be tuned into not only observable power and influence, but also covert power, preemptive power, cooptative power, and power linked to technological and organizational imperatives.

THE LACK OF A HUMAN DEVELOPMENTAL FOCUS

The second major lack in community studies, and in American social investigations in general, is the failure to set forth some explicit ideas or criteria of what constitutes human development, within individuals and within groups. The original power studies which detected a healthy pluralism in America implicitly held a view of human potential which was rather pessimistic. That is, they usually felt that general apathy was normal and even desirable, that participation among common people in power decisions could not be broadened or deepened without unacceptable risks, and that the elitist forms of plural rule were a permanent and stabilizing force in American politics. The fulfilled life for most people was seen as lying outside public involvement, in material consumer pursuits or social involvement within the family or church or elsewhere.

The turbulence of the 'sixties has caused challenges to those assumptions to be raised. Within social science, many are saying that perhaps an apathy that was once comforting has turned into a deepening frustration which now seems clearly linked to the structures of power and control in the political economy. Again, Peter Bachrach must be noted as one of the prescient thinkers. In his work on American pluralist theory, he assailed the dominant orthodoxy for not seriously considering the possibility that "classical" democratic theories, which emphasize the importance of human development through participant power-sharing, are not only viable, but necessary in the modern democracy.

Carole Pateman, in a short work entitled "Participation and Democratic Theory," has also spoken out against the neglect of the "educative" and psychological benefits of citizen participation.[8] Pateman looks to the Yugoslav experiment in worker control for evidence that the institutions of political, economic and citizen-worker power can be blended if we could divorce ourselves from our present theoretical and normative biases.

In the last concern Pateman is joined by Robert Dahl. In *After the Revolution?* he considers the problem of accountability inhering in "The Corporate Leviathan."[9] He praises the Yugoslav experiment and laments the fact that Americans, in being blind to one half of the possible methods for effective but personally fulfilling social control, betray their often-denied love for the ideological approach to problems. Dahl, after warning that these problems cannot be solved until a much greater equalization of resources occurs in the USA, suggests that we follow these two principles:

1. If a matter is best dealt with by a democratic association seek always to have it dealt with by the smallest associations which can handle it satisfactorily.
2. In considering whether a larger association might not be more satisfactory, always consider the extra costs of the larger, including the possibility that the sense of individual powerlessness will increase.[10]

Dahl's guidelines reflect a new concern with the quality of political participation, with the opportunity to grow by engaging in the political arena, to learn by attempting to reconcile one's personal goals with those of others and to pursue commonly held goals. This new urgency is the fruit of work by psychologists, social psychologists, and political scientists with an interest in the psychological implications of various forms of societal organization and change.[11] Many of these scholars feel that the always-present tension between the need for security and group belonging and the need to achieve one's maximum development as an autonomous individual is in danger of being resolved in modern industrial society in favor of the former needs. Just as there appear to be factors operant in the economic sphere which are smoothing out formerly vitalizing conflicts and cleavages, so too our social and political lives are in danger of becoming excessively conflict-avoiding and are thereby resulting in the stunting of human growth and maturity.

Christian Bay has urged that we affirm the first political goal to be the maximizing of individual freedom, "psychological, social and potential."[12] Bay adopts a straightforward normative commitment to freedom, but does not do so in an empirical vacuum. His work is based in part on that of A. H. Maslow, who argues that there is great usefulness in positing among all men of all cultures a "hierarchy" of values, attenuated but not totally changed by cultural and social variables. Other researchers and theorists have also posited developmental stages and have begun investigating the effects of cultural and social institutions on the possibilities of achieving the highest levels. A recent work using this approach is *Radical Man* by Charles Hampden-Turner. He attempts to blend humanist psychology and radical politics, asserting that the rebellious young of the sixties in the U.S. and elsewhere may be the nearest thing we have to a group of "self-actualizing" individuals, who, by their rebellion, are signalling that the institutions of which they are members are preventing both personal and social development.

Sociologist Philip Slater has written a devastating description of "American culture at the breaking point."[14] What he paints is essentially a picture of a society "stuck" at the lower levels of the developmental "ladder" posited by the psychologists. Our culture is characterized by avoidance of others to the maximum extent, excessive dependence on gratification by material objects, a sick individualism, passive acceptance of technological penetration of moral choice situations, and an antiquated adherence to scarcity assumptions.

Charles Reich has analyzed the American culture and concluded that out of the furor of the sixties has emerged a new "consciousness" which is spreading through the nation's young and inevitably will foster a true social revolution within all the institutions of the corporate state.[15] Reich's description of that state is somewhat the same as Slater's, but he does not dwell at any length, as does Slater, on the political side of the revolution. Rather, he opts for a transcendent, creeping cultural revolution which may or may not partake of violence.

Whether or not we agree with any of these descriptions or prescriptions, it must be clear that they are driving at the same points, trying to untie the same political-social-cultural knots.

These works, some merely (but powerfully) critical, some explicitly but more implicitly offering suggestions of possible definitions of human development, have stirred people concerned with American power. What they cry out for is *some* way of judging whether or not a particular power arrangement is developmental or not.

For our part, we feel that a beginning is being made, in these works and others, to cope with this lack. This beginning can be seen in the asking of questions like these: have we been too comfortable in the belief that men cannot respond to participatory power-sharing in ways that make acceptable any loss in system reliability and stability? Have we been too insensitive to the disintegrating effects of modern hierarchical authority structures, even within a nominally democratic pluralist society, on human potential? Have we been too unwilling to rethink our assumptions about the link between social structures and potential human development? Have we been too confident in the self-renewing capabilities of a society dominated by large, complex, impersonal and formal groups? . . .

Part of future efforts in power studies involves the use of the word "community." We suggest two things. First, methodologically we must broaden "community" to include all the important elements of any societal value-allocating process. This means seeing where and in what ways the corporate state is present in the "community." Secondly, we would ask that some thinking and research begin on what a truly human-developmental "community" might look like in the future. That is, let us begin to posit some alternate ideas of power-sharing which will be "communal" in the sense of making possible the growth, in a positive direction, of individuals and groups. This will involve considerations of optimal *size* of groups which allocate societal values. It means taking seriously the abundant research in existence on the educative and developmental benefits of broadly shared power. It means extending these insights beyond what is now thought of as "political" to functional areas of social organization such as the work-place or the bureau which administers societal goods. In short, it means seeing all forms of power for what they are and where they are found, as potentially developmental sites for human interactions.

In this paper we wish to contribute to these efforts by describing some of the major components of the corporate state structure and by considering some ways of building counter-organizations and mobilizing related political resources to sustain and promote a citizenship capable of transcending present limits in the movement toward a more humane society.

To begin with, we must study those who seem to be rising above the stifling atmosphere of the corporate state, risking its sanctions to point out its nature to us all. By so doing we hope to begin the corrective efforts in meeting the two vital lacks of past works.

Among the most important of those who are placing themselves in personally precarious positions to alert us to the realities of corporate state power are the "whistle-blowers." In the tragedies of these cases we can see the two major lacks in earlier power studies being made manifest. These are men who have reacted to the isolation of modern industrial specialization, to the depersonalization and moral sterility of "citizenship" within the giant corporation or bureaucracy. They are dramatizing the fact that the system is biased in such a way that our lives are shaped by technological and organizational imperatives, not rational choice rooted in articulated values which have been publically validated. They are saying that as individuals and as members of a common society, they are being held down at a level of moral development which frustrates them. They are being encouraged or forced to ignore their moral responsibilities to their fellow men, to accept being less

than full, actualized people. The "other face of power" seems to them to dictate a purely functional rationality for all below the top rank of decision-makers. They are to concern themselves only with the means of carrying out an already ratified plan, to produce a product whose usefulness and value has already been affirmed "somewhere." In these cases we see "little people" who somehow rise above the prevailing model of apathetic, selfish man and take a stand in the name of interests commonly held with fellow citizens. Through these men we get a glimpse both of the spectre of unaccountable public-affecting power and of the dehumanizing lives being forced on many by the giant structures we have evolved.

We aim in studying "whistle-blowers" and similar examples of a "new citizenship," at reducing the presently prohibitive costs of active, responsible citizenship for the minority of people motivated in that direction. We expect that action by such an unshackled minority would move some of the remaining majority to become more tentative about acceptance of authority and more disposed to consider the moral legitimacy of entering a conflict with authority over political values.

SUPPORTING THE WHISTLE-BLOWERS; THE DEVELOPMENTAL FUNCTION OF CONFLICT

Although more and more whistle-blowers and presumptuous citizens are appearing, most are abruptly sanctioned and removed from employment, whether or not they are ultimately successful, whether or not they continue to make their effort. It is extremely important to work toward the creation of their right to keep their jobs (at least until a determination is made of the public interest substance of their demands, grievances, etc.), while the issues in the case are being developed. Short of this, it is extremely important to sustain their effort, even if job maintenance cannot be won. A clear reason for this is that job-loss is probably the most severe sanction operating in the corporate state. The creation of a right to make a case as an employee in behalf of the public interest (and this would include employee grievances about dehumanizing work, since such work limits or reduces the human development of those involved, depriving society of this fundamental good) would structurally reduce or limit access to this major sanction by corporate state agency managers, thereby lowering the cost of exercising citizenship. The creation of this right alone would be expected to augment the ranks of active citizens beyond the present "superman" category of severe sanction defiers.

But an equally far-reaching reason for keeping the whistle-blower on the job or at least sustained in his struggle concerns the developmental function of conflict. A theme throughout much recent theoretical and empirical work in developmental, cognitive, and humanistic psychology is the positive and necessary function of conflict in promoting moral judgment and action. But the structure and culture of the corporate state smother conflict within the organization, thereby limiting an important condition for human development.

This dimension of our society has received considerable acute attention recently. The narrow delimitation of the scope of responsibility of the individual in large-scale bureaucracies has already been mentioned. A related general structural variable suggested by the work of Galbraith among others is that the size and scope of operation and technological complexity of the major economic units are so great that a premium is placed on predictability regarding each element of the system. This means that "unexpected" conflicts arising from within the organization are highly undesirable. What we propose in this paper would clearly mean higher costs in time "lost" through conflict and the processing of new concerns (functioning ecologically in the public interest, giving employees' representatives a voice in policy, intra-organizational debate about whether anti-personnel bombs should be produced by the company, etc.).

One cultural dimension is the prevailing shrug ("I only work here") about any demand that a corporate state can take cognizance of and act to ameliorate a whole human problem and not just the bureaucratizable bit.[16] Slater also analyzes the predisposition not to deal directly, personally with social problems but to consign them psychologically over to others, especially institutional agencies. He calls this the "Toilet Assumption," that removing difficulties from our presence rids us of the difficulties. Richard Sennett shows how the historical trend toward affluence supports the value that life should be conflictless, by giving increasing numbers of people the financial capacity to buy out of social problems by moving to residential areas that filter out conflict-causing factors (racial homogeneity, for example). "The desire of people beyond the line of economic scarcity is to live in a functionally separated, internally homogeneous environment . . ."[17] Both Sennett and Slater suggest that that which causes or is identified with problems and loss of control is felt as disruptive, bad. And diversity (issues, different types of people) comes to partake of the disruptive, the uncontrolled, the conflict-producing. The drive is toward purified existence, the denial of divergence, the minimization of interpersonal conflict.

The matter becomes particularly pointed within the organizational context, where loyalty and teamwork are deeply prized, so that whistle-blowing raises most serious kinds of conflict—treason against the organization and disloyalty to superiors and colleagues with whom one may have close personal ties.[18] The opinion of such practices by an important corporate state manager, General Motors chairman James M. Roche, is indicated in the following:

Having pitted consumer against producer, some critics are now busy eroding another support of free enterprise, the loyalty of a management team, with its unifying values of cooperative work. Some of the enemies of business now encourage an employee to be disloyal to the enterprise. They want to create suspicion and disharmony, and pry into the proprietary interests of the business. However this is labeled—industrial sabotage, whistle-blowing, or professional responsibility—it is another tactic for spreading disunity and creating conflict.[19]

But active problem-solving in the context of conflict seems a requisite for personal maturity and the development of moral judgment. The central recent work on moral development is that of the psychologist Lawrence Kohlberg. He has worked out a six-stage model of moral development, based on extensive, longitudinal, and cross-cultural study of children, adolescents, and young adults.[20] His stages, ranging from simplest to most complex, are labeled (1) obedience and punishment orientation, (2) instrumental relativism, (3) personal concordance, or "good-boy" orientation, (4) law and order, (5) social contract, and (6) individual principles, or orientation to conscience and mutual respect or trust. The first two stages may be considered pre-conventional, the second two conventional, and the last two post-conventional, and attained by only a minority of post-adolescents in any society. Experimentally, "growth in the capacity for moral judgment can be induced by creating conflicts between two or more stages and by dramatizing the issues."[21]

Reviewing a series of studies of activist youth and other young people, Norma Haan concludes that considerable disagreement and conflict occurred in the families of morally principled young activists, but that the differences were negotiated with basic respect, as the families redefined themselves to include the emerging independence of the adolescent, whereas little disturbance and continuing moral dependence on parents characterized the family experience of conventionally moral non-activist youth.[22] Analyzing a mass of studies of youthful opposition, Kenneth Keniston claims that:

. . . there is much current evidence that individuals who attain high levels of complexity in feeling, thinking, and judging do so as a result of conflict, not in its absence. Students of cognitive development, like observers of personality development, find that disequilibrium, tension, and imbalance tend to produce growth.[23]

Citing two psychological studies, Charles Hampden-Turner points out that those who do stand up in morally challenging situations to protest inhumane conditions or to take a stand in the name of conscience, no matter what the issue, often act as catalysts for others who hold back from such acts. One experiment tested the willingness of a subject to stand by his own perceptions when all others purposely misrepresented what they saw in an attempt to produce conformity pressure. Another experiment was a variant of the famous Milgram experiment, where the subjects' willingness to participate in the (apparent) torture of another person is tested. In the former test, the man who stood by his own feeling or perception in the face of conformity

pressures often caused others to follow him. In the latter "torture" experiment, when the pain was administered by a group instead of by an individual, a single dissenter refusing to torture was followed in most cases by about ninety per cent of the others.[24]

How does all of this concern active citizenship in the corporate state? If the dissenter can't be flushed, if the whistle-blower can be kept on the job or at least sustained in his struggle in the community and in the attention of his colleagues or coworkers, then they will be much more likely than at present to have to deal with the situation, to become parties to the conflict. There is the greater chance that they will have to entertain different positions on a moral issue and be called on to help resolve it. What we cannot yet know, because so little relevant research has been carried on with adults in real life situations, is what degree of development in moral judgment and action can occur at this stage and life situation. But it is hard to imagine that having to take responsibility for helping to resolve such conflicts would not have some positive consequence for citizenship, such as the generation of competence, the stimulus of engagement in the solving of a serious problem, the capacity to weigh the claims of expertise and authority, the disposition to consider the relation between organizational commitments and the human condition.

LIVING WITH CONFLICT: CONSTITUENCIES FOR ACTIVE CITIZENSHIP

Conflict may be a requisite of human development, but what would lead us to be willing to live with it, especially since our society seems so afraid of it?

One factor is the increasing awareness of the structure and consequences of the society, a matter of changing consciousness, which has received much attention by contemporary observers such as Charles Reich, Philip Slater, Robert Lifton, and Kenneth Keniston. Reacting to and further contributing to this development is the action of Ralph Nader and people associated with efforts such as his, Daniel Ellsberg, the Berrigans, and others. The conflict between people of varying consciousness seems to cut right through the social structure, from the level of executive branch professionals and corporate insiders to white and blue collar workers, Vietnam veterans and students. Although the dynamics of consciousness change have not been very effectively theorized about, with the partial exception of the student movement, Philip Slater has suggested that the overwhelming emphasis on personal uninvolvement in this society has rendered life so dull and demeaning as to have created an antithetical desire for engagement; he further states that the balance between drives for withdrawal and engagement is extremely precarious, a point at which much conversion and change or defensive retrogression become likely.[25]

For the anti-war movement, Vietnam has been the driving factor, bringing on a fresh and much-widened consideration of Nuremburg principles. Evidence that this is not a narrow, academic hang-up (though still minoritarian) is the astounding one-third of the public polled on the Calley case, who thought that war crimes had been committed for which high American officials should be held accountable.[26]

For those caught up in the onerous labor of the industrial plant, the increasing "rationality" of production tends to force a shift in consciousness. The supermodern Vega plant at Lordstown is exemplary of a type now, in that the very rapid assembly line pace requiring only the simplest repetitive physical contributions from the workers under rigid, highly authoritarian supervision has apparently created a profound welling up of alienation. The issue for the workers has nothing to do with pay or benefits: it is, nakedly, dehumanization. Some among the younger labor force cannot give over its daily life to mere consumer payoffs. And so conflict is forced on a really tough, fundamental issue—worker control over the conditions and design of work.[27]

Ecological consciousness has also been demonstrated at the work place, surprising both management and social scientists. A Jones and Laughlin steel mill employee refuses to obey orders to (illegally) dump oil pollutants into the legendary Cuyahoga River, and in the ensuing conflict, gains the support of his coworkers and finally influential community elements.[28]

These cases suggest that blue collar workers' politics is considerably more complex and dynamic than the image of a rather primitive backlash mentality purveyed in the popular press or the scholarly extrapolations from studies made before the turmoil that developed in the 1960s.[29] With relative affluence and the manifold impetus to change in consciousness there have emerged demonstrations in their actions and thinking that some workers are full, complex people—not just producer-consumers, but active or potentially active citizens, valuers of nature, etc. . . . .

*　*　*

The professional-technician sector is moving into conflict with the corporate state along two dimensions. One of these relates to the aforementioned student movement, a growing number of the graduates of which are now young professionals. Accustomed to conflict through family and university experiences, they bring to their professional functioning an awareness of the contradiction between the technological possibility of meeting men's material needs while freeing them for the pursuit of higher values, and the incapacity of this society as structured either to actualize this possibility or to provide cultural directions appropriate to the potentialities of the future. Reviewing the efforts by young people in medicine, law, social work, teaching, and academia to recast policy and perspectives, Richard Flacks finds this countermovement having two basic goals:

First, they challenge the structure of power, prestige, and decision-making within the institutions and professions—so as to promote cooperative work relations, to increase the workers' autonomy and voice in the "product." Second, they challenge the domination of the institutions and professions by corporate, militarist, or conservative interests and ideological perspectives, and instead compel the institutions to serve the interests of the people as a whole.[30]

*　*　*

Closer to the core of the corporate state, in the goods-producing sector and the federal government, the professional or technical employee finds professional norms increasingly under a different kind of pressure.

As a consequence of the growing complexity and inter-dependence of corporate state structures, commitments to fulfill a particular component of a job require adherence to a tight time schedule. Problems occurring at any point tend increasingly to be swept under the rug because a thorough treatment of them would seriously delay the process and create hassles with other units of the system, and the costs of the deceptions, hidden mistakes, etc. can be shoved off on the consumer or taxpayer. Conflict arises because the professional or technician sees that it is his work, his research that is fudged, rewritten, or "adjusted" in the reports that accompany the product along to the next step in the process. Hence he is aware that his skill, bound by professional ethic to be used in the public interest, is being perverted, and that he is a direct or acquiescent accomplice in it.

* * *

There are additional potential constituencies for the effort to sustain active citizenship and to move away from the social distortions of the corporate state. Those who are now caught up in, processed, and rejected by the inhumane rationality of the corporate state may be disposed to enter the fray, if leadership for it is nurtured and the costs of active citizenship are lowered in ways this paper suggests. At present there are effectively no institutional ways whereby the technologically unemployed and those facing the obsolescence of their skills can find new productive places in the society; they face the social dislocation on their own. There are no ways whereby those still doing brute labor that machines could do can participate in devising a mode to bring the machines and find themselves more humane work. They wait in fear, low-paid, exploited and wasted, for the pink slip, as have the Boeing employees, where company planning seems to have demonstrated a certain deficiency from the human point of view.

A most interesting potential constituency in behalf of active citizenship and the transformation of the corporate state may be a minority sector of corporate management itself. . . . Affluent parents are affected by their children's changes in consciousness; this is apparent from the number of cases involving offspring impacts on

U.S. congressmen and senators regarding the war. The politics of the family has become much more complex whenever the youth of the family explore new political issues linked to the problems of moral development. This happens more typically among children of the professional class. However, it occurs relatively frequently in general among upper middle class offspring.[31] This being the case, we can expect some dissonance to be generated among those executives with activist children or with children who undergo any substantial alteration of consciousness over the salient issues.

* * *

There is a growing incidence of experiments regarding *internal* reorganization of corporations. T-groups and non-hierarchical task organization are two approaches to humanizing the corporate environment. Reports on these innovations do not, however, include much information about their impact on the participants' political commitments and orientations, especially in regard to corporate policy or the relation between the corporation and society.[32] It seems plausible to expect, however, that some employees and executives involved in such experiments would be impelled to push toward greater freedom from unaccountable authority, more organizational rights of citizenship, and even refocusing the organization to produce goods and services in a way that enhances humanity.

* * *

POWER FOR CITIZENSHIP

Most people need sustenance to engage in the sort of active citizenship we have called for to transform the corporate state. By sustenance we mean the range of resources required to counter the highly concentrated, interdependent, and flexible power available to the management of the corporate state. We see three types of required, mutually reinforcing counter-organizations: one representing the employees of individual organizational units of the corporate state; another, a sub-organization within professional or other occupational associations; and finally, community citizenship foundations.

We assume that financing for the first two would have to be provided by the employees and professionals involved, following traditional lines for such associations. But the third represents the most novel of the organizational innovations, with the most diffusely defined constituency, so that its financing and general support would be the most problematic.

We envisage these organizations providing legal, media, research, political mobilizational, and necessary income supports for active citizenship. As ongoing associations, they would be able, for example, to monitor the cases of whistle-blowers over time, to reduce the likelihood that sanctions originally countered would simply be delayed and used effectively in the future against a citizen at such subtle and sensitive points as those involving promotion or job reassignment. For those who now survive in their initial attempts to hold corporate state institutions accountable to the law in the public interest, it is these stages of the process where they can be effectively sanctioned, after whatever originally mobilized publicity and support have died down.

We assume that at any one time such organizations would only be able to offer the full range of supports in a few cases, selected because of their strategic significance, and after a rigorous initial reconnaissance of applications for support. Given the amount of power involved in the corporate state, the recency and shakiness of the tradition of whistle-blowing, the range and subtlety of sanctions, and above all, the difficulty in the electronic age of ascertaining who really is trying to apply sanctions, when, how, etc., it is to be expected that activist citizens seeking to enlist the special support of these organizations may exhibit what looks like and may be paranoia. The structural reasons for fear in the situation, however, are sufficient to err on the side of initial investigation of the proposed complaint and action.

The Corporate State Unit Organization

The potential community of interest here is the employees of a corporation or state agency. The idea is to create a counter-organization, which in addition to the political functions generally referred to earlier would acquire, analyze and disseminate information on company planning, policy, impacts, significance of a particular mode of accounting, etc. so that the employees can have a basis for understanding the total operation. From this a conception of alternatives might emerge regarding such problem areas as ecology, military to civil transition, and the costs of citizenship institutions within the corporation or agency. The cruciality of the occupational tie to a particular large-scale corporation or agency in contemporary America makes this form of counter-organization an especially important one. If employees come to the point of being able to experiment with citizenship-sustaining efforts here, we could expect enormous changes in the functioning of the corporate state.

The Professional Association

The facts that the profession is a basic point of self-identity and that professional skills are employed throughout the corporate state, cross-cutting particular institutional hierarchies, give the professional association a special significance as a counter-organization. The demands of the profession may come into conflict—on a public interest issue basis—with those of the employing organization, and the professional association's relative independence is a potential basis for the building of support for public interest action. Given the high degree of specialization of occupational function and the general isolation of employees in one corporate state unit from the others, the professional association can also serve as a link, a point of communication and education about public service issues, and support. For example, it is possible to conceive a future time when a national association of accountants would have become a forum for heated discussion and development of issues concerning the special interest vs. public interest consequences of certain accounting practices and policies, and consequently have committed itself to developing and modifying over time a code to guide accountants to perform within public interest limits. When the secrecy and complexity of corporate state accounting is considered (think of ITT at home and in Chile, for instance, with reference to the whole issue of the political consequences of intra-multi-national corporate accounting), the potential consequences of developing even an awareness of the politics of accounting is enormous. Another contemporary issue that a professional association can be expected to promote is the changing relation between basic and applied science, regarding the rapidly decreasing time gap between discovery and application. This makes anticipated concern for possible application a general professional problem.

The realism of this conception of professional association development is indicated by a consideration of contemporary conflicts emerging in the range of professions noted earlier, marking the rise of public interest consciousness broadly in that sector.

Another special aspect of the professional association is its sensitivity to sanctions—and utility in offsetting them, not only by provision of political support but by helping provide alternative employment for those sanctioned in the attempt to exercise active citizenship.

The Community Citizenship Foundation

With the fragmenting of experience in modern society, the special contribution of the community citizenship foundation would be its focus on the whole, a sense of place, or context. Its action would promote understanding of the consequences for the whole community of the activities of any one corporate state entity. Presumably, it could select cases of significance for general problems of developing citizenship, as opposed to the more specialized sort that might be treated by the other, more occupationally-related organizations. It could function to integrate the effort of all such organizations, and to link together a range of community sectors. For example, if it is assumed that the struggle to establish citizenship rights within and against corporate state organizations will be a long one, the community foundation might be expected to mobilize a range of local resources to sustain whistle-blowers—the local bar, university (or community college) teachers and students, church social action groups, etc., keeping the issue alive in the community among their colleagues and neighbors.

This type of foundation, theoretically capable of establishment anywhere, would discourage reliance on others, on outsiders, especially large-scale organizations. The focus would be on local support and solutions, not to promote isolation and a narrow community identity but to build the citizenship experience, through the wrestling with responsibility on the local level. Here is where matters can be dealt with on a human scale, where the consequences of action and inaction, of risk and withdrawal from it are apparent in daily life.

EXISTING SUPPORTS FOR THE PROPOSED CITIZENSHIP ORGANIZATIONS

There already exists a wide range of new political rights, movements, and organizations oriented by the same philosophy of active citizenship and rendering corporate state institutions responsive to human needs. The main difference between the existing organizations and movements and those proposed in this paper is that the latter are designed for the local agency and corporate level (though regional and national level organization based on these is a logical extension) and focus directly on the sanctions available to corporate state managers to constrain responsible citizen initiatives, while the former work toward the same ends but at the national level generally and also generally without taking on the sanction structure so directly. In any event, the proposed citizenship organizations and the existing ones could be expected to be mutually reinforcing, and quite conceivably some of the existing ones could assume the suggested functions.

* * *

PRIORITY RESEARCH QUESTIONS

The problem area formulated here lays open a wide variety of crucial questions, forming a research program, requiring a long-term commitment for careful longitudinal study.

The most central problem area seems to be adult moral development, since existing theory and research are largely based on children, adolescents, and youth.

Very little research has been done on the dynamics of moral judgment and action in real life conflict situations involving adults, though the work on student activists is highly suggestive.

A series of inquiries derives from the focus on the active citizen in the corporate state. How is the life of the active citizen, the whistle-blower, affected by his action? Is such action typically a single shot, or a repeated expression of conscience? Do some value gains offset the losses in anxiety and material situation? Do increased self-respect and respect from primary groups (for example, contemporarily, the respect from one's children) or the support of secondary groups help him adjust to a threatened or actually scaled-down material existence? To what degree, down to what level may reduced income be associated with a greater sense of freedom?

What are the critical occupational stages of the politics of whistle-blowing? What are the determinants of promotion, advancement, reinstatement over time?

What is the impact of whistle-blowing on one's family, colleagues, neighbors, and fellow community members? How does this vary with his ability to stay on his job versus being fired? What is the effect on them of his receiving various kinds and levels of support? What are the effects on the bases of moral judgment and subsequent political life of adults "caught" in conflict situations associated with whistle-blowing?

How does the increasing phenomenon of whistle-blowing itself intrude on the culture of the large-scale organization? How do those with or proximate to formal responsibility for organizational policy accommodate this change in the environment? What retards the tendency to deal with it by attempting to tighten security, as opposed to confronting the fundamental issues?

How do professionals come to terms with the recently vitalized issues of public service and human development? What are the patterns of accommodation, the rationales justifying them, and the psychological dynamics associated with the existential toughness of the issues as they daily present themselves? How does a lawyer, for example, psychologically manage his simultaneous dependence on giant polluting organizations and his involvement in citizen conservation efforts? What unbalances this arrangement? Biographies of such people would be extremely useful here.

What is the relationship between active citizenship on the job (directed at some corporate state agency) and community citizenship? That is, what is the spin-off for community responsibility of one's taking increased responsibility for the employing corporation or agency?

What has been the "adult" experience of the student dissenter generation of the past decade? Do they exhibit a higher incidence of active citizenship, whistle-blowing, etc.? Under what circumstances are high public interest orientation and highly developed moral judgment maintained and implemented? How do age, marital status, children, and changes in general economic opportunity affect this? Do erstwhile university activists tend also to dissent on the job, and try to induce the organization to a manner of functioning compatible with the public interest?

How do the new organizational structures affect the moral development and citizenship of the employees involved? To what degree does involvement in less hierarchical, more task-oriented and "responsive" organizations promote something more from a citizenship perspective than simply greater satisfaction with the job, with given corporate objectives?

. . . How do people adjust to institutionalized conflict over time in an intimate environment like the workplace, and what is their effect on the community over time, and vice versa? Can people work with satisfaction in such a setting over a relatively long time, or does the conflict and external threat take its toll, as with the history of some counter-culture and new politics ventures?

What are the effects of the new humanistic psychological therapies on the participants' long-run patterns of citizenship? Are they adjusive and depoliticizing or radical in effect?

* * *

The approach suggested in this paper draws much on moral development theory and research and philosophically on the human developmentalists. The thrust is developmental: human nature is not given. Conflict can promote growth, communities can be created. For this to begin to occur people need much sense of alternatives and support.

* * *

Our approach to create support for active citizenship to transform the corporate state seeks to conserve much that traditional democrats value: the right to dissent, enhancement of individual responsibility, decentralization of power, holding authority accountable, increasing self-reliance as opposed to authoritarian dependency, and so on. The radical prospect lies in the dynamics of the human development process. If support can be created for thinking about and taking responsibility in a central arena of daily life, one's work, then one may be less likely to play the cipher in his formal role as political community member, and more likely to push himself to monitor, evaluate, and hold to account any formal authorities. (And the more models of responsible adult citizens appear, the more the prevailing moral vacuum will be filled, with a consequent lessening of alienation among youth.)

With what implications regarding the other grave areas of American social problems—transition from growth to ecological imperatives, from giganticism of institutions to those on a human scale, from capitalism to _____, from empire to_____? We don't know. The promotion of active citizenship in the corporate state is an end but also a means. We do not envision yet the whole configuration of end states implied in the previous question, but we believe the transitions will be hard and complicated. In this indeterminate meantime, experiments with responsible citizenship will contribute to the growth of Americans, to the raising of the level of political discourse, and thus to the preparation of people, much more than at present, to deal with the tough transitions. Without this attempt, it is hard to imagine desirable changes at all.

Notes

[1] See John H. Schaar, "Legitimacy in the Modern State," in Philip Green and Sanford Levinson, eds., _Power and Community: Dissenting Essays in Political Science_, New York: Vintage, 1970, pp. 276–327.

[2] See Herbert C. Kelman and Lee H. Lawrence, "American Response to the Trial of Lt. William Calley," _Psychology Today_, 6, June 1972, 41–45, 78–81.

[3] Charles Reich, "The Limits of Duty," _The New Yorker_, June 19, 1971, pp. 52–56.

[4] See Peter Bachrach, _The Theory of Democratic Elitism: A Critique_, Boston: Little, Brown and Co., 1967; "Corporate Authority and Democratic Theory," in _Political Theory and Social Change_, ed. David Spitz, New York: Atherton Press, Inc., 1967; with Morton S. Baratz, "Two Faces of Power," in Charles A. McCoy and John Playford, eds., _Apolitical Politics_, New York: Thomas Y. Crowell, 1967; also with Baratz, _Power and Poverty: Theory and Practice_, New York: Oxford University Press, 1970.

[5] J. K. Galbraith, _The New Industrial State_, New York: New American Library, 1968.

[6] A recent study incorporating this approach is Edward C. Hayes' _Power Structure and Urban Policy: Who Rules in Oakland?_ New York: McGraw-Hill, Inc., 1972.

[7] Bachrach, _The Theory of Democratic Elitism_.

[8] Carole Pateman, _Participation and Democratic Theory_. Cambridge: University of Cambridge Press, 1970.

[9] Robert Dahl, _After the Revolution?_ New Haven: Yale University Press, 1970, pp. 115–129.

[10] Ibid, p. 147.

[11] For a summary of these works see Elizabeth Drews and Leslie Lipson, _Values and Humanity_. New York: St. Martin's Press, 1971.

[12] Christian Bay, _The Structure of Freedom_. New York: Atheneum, 1968.

[13] Charles Hampden-Turner, _Radical Man_. Garden City: Anchor Books, 1971.

[14] Philip Slater, _The Pursuit of Loneliness: American Culture at the Breaking Point_. Boston: Beacon Press, 1970.

[15] Charles Reich, _The Greening of America_. New York: Bantam Books, Inc., 1971.

[16] Slater, op. cit., pp. 12–19.

[17] Richard Sennett, _The Uses of Disorder: Personal Identity in City Life_. New York: Vintage, 1970, p. 70.

[18] See Charles Peters and Taylor Branch, _Blowing the Whistle: Dissent in the Public Interest_. New York: Praeger Publishers, 1972, especially the introduction and sections on the Dodd case, the interview with Ellsberg, and the conclusion.

[19] Quoted by Timothy H. Ingram, "The Corporate Underground," _The Nation_, 213, September 13, 1971, 211.

[20] The fullest account of his work is in his "Stage and Sequence: The Cognitive-Developmental Approach to Socialization," in _Handbook of Socialization Theory and Research_, D. A. Goslin, ed. Chicago: Rand McNally, 1969, pp. 347–480.

[21] Charles Hampden-Turner and P. Whitten, "Morals Left and Right," _Psychology Today_, 4, April 1971, 40, citing Kohlberg's work.

[22] Norma Haan, "Moral Redefinition in Families as the Critical Aspect of the Generational Gap," _Youth and Society_, II, March 1971, 259–283.

[23] Kenneth Keniston, "A Second Look at the Uncommitted," _Social Policy_, 2, July/August 1971, 15.

[24] Hampden-Turner, _Radical Man_, p. 127.

[25] Slater, op. cit., pp. 4, 144–48.

[26] "Judgment at Fort Benning," _Newsweek_, April 12, 1971, p. 28.

[27] See Emma Rothschild, "GM in More Trouble," *New York Review of Books,* XVIII, March 23, 1972, 18–25; Barbara Garson, "Luddites in Lordstown," *Harpers,* 244, June 1972, 68–73; Judson Gooding, "Blue-Collar Blues on the Assembly Line," *Fortune,* LXXXII, July 1970, 69. See also Gooding's "The Fraying White Collar," ibid., December 1970, pp. 78–81.

[28] Barbara and John Ehrenreich, "Conscience of a Steelworker," *The Nation,* 213, September 27, 1971, 268–271. See also Joseph Hill, "Steel: Changing Workplace," *Dissent,* Winter, 1972, pp. 37–46.

[29] See for example R. Lane and M. Lerner, "Why Hard-Hats Hate the Hairs," *Psychology Today,* 4, November 1970, 45–48, 104–105.

[30] Richard Flacks, "Strategies for Radical Social Change," *Social Policy,* 1, March/April 1971, 10.

[31] Kenneth Keniston, op. cit., p. 18.

[32] See C. Hampden-Turner, *Radical Man,* chs. VII, "Rebellion, Growth and Regression in Training Groups," and VIII, "Corporate Radicalism;" Warren Bennis, "Post-Bureaucratic Leadership," *Trans-Action,* 6, July/August 1969, 44–51; and George Berkley, *The Administrative Revolution.* Englewood Cliffs: Prentice-Hall, 1971.

11/Evolutionary Development

SCIENTIFIC PARADIGM CHANGE

Allen Wheelis, in *The End of the Modern Age*, writes:

Since man became a historical being each age has been able to recognize the certainties of the past as mistaken, often as absurd. Eternal verities prove both transient and untrue. We look back and see that they were held by a particular people with unique mores living on a limited segment of earth during a certain period of time, and that whatever apparent validity they had was bound to those circumstances. What was self-evident truth to them is seen by us to be arbitrary, culturally relative, derived from needs and fears.

As historical consciousness lengthens, more layers of the past can be examined and compared. It becomes possible for a certain age, A, to look back to an earlier age, B, and to observe that B, in writing the history of a still earlier age, C, recognizes (correctly, we believe) the cherished beliefs of C as primitive superstitions, whereas B's cherished beliefs are seen by B as enlightened and rational, indeed not as beliefs at all, but as objective findings, self-evident truths. But A, in considering B's beliefs, alleged to be so rational and enlightened, finds them just as mistaken, though perhaps in a different direction, as C's.

Such findings pose a special problem: If at every level of the past, eternal verities are found to be culturally relative, must we not infer likewise for our own?[1]

In the course of Western history, several sets of political verities have emerged in the works of political thinkers, have

[1] Allen Wheelis, *The End of the Modern Age* (New York: Basic Books, 1971), p. 83.

influenced the forms of government, and have been in time supplanted. For example, the concept of the divine right of kings, once a powerful force in national government, was replaced by more democratic ideas about authority, such as the once-revolutionary social contract theory. Later, most of the ideas of classical democratic theory came to be regarded by modern political analysts as unscientific abstractions.

In Part II of this book, we investigated the verities of the contemporary science of politics: its methodology, its theoretical constructs, and its evaluation of mass democracy. These verities, too, now appear to be less than eternal. They are being challenged on many fronts, and the search is underway for new ways of looking at Western society, mass democracy, and human nature.

Modern political science is taught and practiced within a behavioral paradigm. Some of the propositions that identify this paradigm are:

That political science should be modeled on the natural sciences, such as physics, which are more advanced in their development.

That the political scientist should strive to be objective, a detached observer, and should separate private goals and personal feelings from scientific research.

That political processes inevitably involve such things as power, authority, and competition.

That mass democracy can be understood as a system, machine-like in nature and operation, which processes interest group demands into governmental policies.

That the study of this system by political scientists can yield general principles, comparable to the laws of physics, capable of being empirically verified by other observers.

That political systems will inevitably change, but the essential nature of human beings will not.

This last proposition, one of the least visible components of the behavioral paradigm, is also the most important. There can be no point in the search for objective laws of human behavior if human nature itself is undergoing a process of transformation. But this is precisely what Charles Reich, with his concept of Consciousness III, says is happening, and the same idea is central to the two works considered in this final chapter.

In his paper on ·the relationship of political science to human evolution, Thomas Landon Thorson revives—with an entirely modern meaning—the ancient Aristotelian definition of the human species as "the political animal." Thorson argues that the activities we call political are indeed inherent to human nature, but that our awareness of history now gives this definition an entirely new meaning. The human species is—and knows it is—the conscious shaper of world evolution, a "new kind of geological force"; and politics is the effort to make wise use of our new understanding of the evolutionary process and of our vast technological capacities for guiding it.

Because Thorson sees the human species as involved in a continuing process of change, he disagrees with an approach to social science that would, borrowing from other sciences, attempt to find any general laws—comparable to those of Newtonian physics—in the workings of the political system or the political behavior of individuals. In fact the whole "detached observer" perspective that was fundamental to that kind of scientific research is, Thorson contends, obsolete; it is contrary to contemporary human experience.

Although Thorson is arguing against modeling political science on other sciences, he is arguing *for* a new concept of politics—again echoing Aristotle—as the "master science," whose purpose is to give order and direction to our use of technology and to our research in such fields as biology and physics.

POLITICAL SCIENCE IN EVOLUTION

THOMAS LANDON THORSON

* * *

. . . If man's long, violent history points to the overwhelming necessity of brain power, of the creative use of intelligence, then man's most important animal task, that task which is fundamental to biological survival, is what Aristotle said it was long ago: reasoning about political and social organization, that enterprise which we have come to call political science.

While time and experience have made it difficult to assent to the notion that the *polis* is natural to man, we can perhaps say in Aristotle's spirit that along with several other characteristics that differentiate the human species, "Man is by nature a political-scientizing animal." Given the growth of the brain, the decline of instinct, the necessity of cooperation for survival, man as a biological matter has become the animal that deliberates, argues, and plans his social organization.

The distinguished British embryologist C. H. Waddington has argued that man is the animal that "goes in for ethicizing" and his suggestions have much to teach us.[1] The core of Waddington's argument is his description of what he calls the socio-genetic system of information transmission in men. Evolution works through a process of information transmission; the genetic system is nature's way of passing adaptive information from generation to generation. Viewed from this perspective man is unique because in man nature has found a way of transmitting adaptive information *outside* the genes. A system of information transmission is, thus, from an evolutionary point of view what culture is, and Waddington refers to it as a socio-genetic system.

Thus, it is a part of man's fundamental biology that he should be a rule-making and rule-deliberating animal. "To summarize the argument very briefly," Waddington says in his preface,"I shall try to support

Thomas Landon Thorson, "The Biological Foundations of Political Science: Reflections on the Post-Behavioral Era," paper presented at 1970 American Political Science Association Annual Meeting, Los Angeles, Calif. (Edited and abridged.)

the following four points: Firstly, that the human system of social communication functions as such an efficient means of transmitting information from one generation to the next that it has become the mechanism on which human evolution mainly depends. Secondly, that this system of 'socio-genetic' transmission can operate only because the psychological development of man is such that the newborn baby becomes moulded into a creature which is ready to accept transmitted information; and, I shall suggest, it is an empirically observed fact that this acceptance is founded on the formation of 'authority-bearing' systems within the mind which also result in the human individual becoming a creature which goes in for having beliefs of the particular tone that we call ethical. Thirdly, I argue that observation of the world of living things reveals a general evolutionary direction, which has a philosophical status similar to that of healthy growth, in that both are manifestations of the immanent properties of the objective world. Finally, I conclude that any particular set of ethical beliefs, which some individual man may advance, can be meaningfully judged according to their efficacy in furthering this general evolutionary direction."[2]

. . . Waddington could as easily be discussing the biological foundations of "political-scientizing." Indeed his argument might even be more appropriate to "political-scientizing" than it is to "ethicizing." What is perfectly clear is that viewed from a biological, evolutionary standpoint political science is very much a part of man's "species business." Rule making and rule deliberating are fundamental to the human animal and thus political science has a biological foundation . . .

Twentieth-century insights into the nature of human biology may say something useful and informative about the essential humanness of "political-scientizing," but they do not, on their face at least, tell us much about what political science should be concerned with in this latter third of the twentieth century. I . . . [believe] that political science . . . [is] reemerging as the master science and that in so doing it must become *the* interdisciplinary science. . . . But to see the full sense in which it is true we must look further at the twentieth-century's insights into human biology. The notion that I hope to get across is that the intellectual situation

for political science, and for that matter for science in general, during the last 100 to 150 years has been utterly unique. I stretch the period to 150 years because, retrospectively, one can see the trends forming that long ago. In the important sense, however, this utterly new philosophical perspective could only be fully grasped by twentieth-century man. Students of political philosophy in the twentieth century have, however, almost entirely failed to understand this fact and have argued for some sort of restoration of the classics. Likewise, they are inclined to reduce whatever they find appealing in contemporary writings to identity with the teachings of a classical writer. Thus, what we have said here might be understood simply as a sort of recapturing of the man-in-nature perspective of Aristotle. There is, of course, truth in this, but I should like to stress the important difference.

Only in the last hundred years or so could any man have possibly known (1) that man is the product of an evolutionary process stretching back some six billion years, and (2) that man was capable of establishing the detached observer position, of devising modern science and technology, and of creating modern society. Plato, Aristotle, Augustine, and Thomas Aquinas—masters though they were—could not possibly have known of these parameters. Descartes, Hobbes, Locke could see the position of detachment and some of its implications, but by the same token man's connection with the rest of nature had to be rejected and the significance of time could not have been grasped. They were, moreover, too busy creating modern science and modern society to step back and reflect on the implications of the possibility.

Twentieth-century man, however, can see the vastness of time and its overriding significance, man's connection with the natural world through evolution, and the fact of modern culture, its intellectual style and its material product. The recognition of these factors—all of them together—provides a standard, a perspective, utterly unique in human history in terms of which man can decide what he *ought* to do. In this sense a new standard for philosophy and for political philosophy *cum* political science in particular becomes possible. What arises from this perspective is a new understanding of recommendation and justification, a new logic of recommendation and justification, which can only make full sense in the twentieth century.

* * *

We ought now to be able to see that the scientific culture which we in the contemporary West take so much for granted, which in fact we take to be the intellectual standard of the universe is an abnormal and unusual state of affairs, a special case, when viewed against the 16,000 years or so of distinctly human development. The method of science is a set of rules built up over time as a way of checking our natural tendency to overgeneralize. The substance of scientific achievement is intellectual creation (but so are art and metaphysics, and story-telling intellectual creation), but it is intellectual creation limited and checked by rules designed to discover error. Accounts of science which stress verification and those which stress creative imagination are both partly right. They become wrong only when they attempt general characterizations which purport to define science and when they fail to notice that science occurs in time.

We are faced with the fact—not the speculation—that scientific culture, industrial society, and modern politics have developed in the West since 1500 A.D. These phenomena are to be found nowhere else (save by transplantation) and never before. Why? This is the question which no matter how complex and how difficult must be faced even if we do not know enough to give a complete answer. Many signs of caution and an equal number of uncertainties warn us to set ourselves a meaner question; but no less a question will do, and we are obliged, therefore, to be bold.

It has already been suggested in a variety of ways and from a variety of angles that cultural evolution is a matter of information transmission, a socio-genetic system we have called it (following Waddington). Let us take our bold leap at the questions before us from this piece of solid ground. If, then, cultural evolution is a matter of information transmission, then what information is transmitted and in what form it is transmitted ought to be crucially important for cultural change. I mention "what information" is transmitted and "in what form" the information is transmitted as if there were two distinct things involved. The fact, however, is that the content and the form in which it is presented and received are inseparable parts of any transmission of information. . . .

* * *

Lately we have begun to hear a line of argument which stresses the impact of changes in the form and style of the cultural communication process itself.[3] An alteration in the physical environment cannot become culturally significant unless it is in fact reacted to, grasped, and communicated by man—and any understanding and communication of that understanding can only be done through the means of communication available. If we look back over the development of Western man we can discern stages in the development of means of communication. They overlap and merge in various ways, but stages are recognizable nonetheless.

Earliest communication was undoubtedly almost entirely oral, supplemented, of course, by gestures. This oral period is by far the longest, constituting by definition the whole of human prehistory. Then pictographic or ideographic writing developed, first on stone and clay and later on more portable substances. This was presumably an extension of early graphic representations like those which have been discovered in the caves of Spain. For the West the next important step was the development of a phonetic alphabet by the ancient Semites. This, it is interesting to note and it may indeed be profoundly significant, is a step which the Chinese never took. The Greeks grasped the phonetic alphabet, adapted it to their fertile oral tradition, and the West has never been the same since. There follows an extended period in which culture was carried by the copying, recopying, and reading aloud of manuscripts. The portability of written messages and regulations literally made the Roman Empire possible. The fact that Christianity not only survived but conquered the barbarians is closely related to Christianity's control of information through its nearly exclusive possession of the ability to deal with manuscript. And then, at the dawn of the modern era came Gutenberg and the printing press. . . .

That the printing press created the public and the possibility of mass politics is, I think, so obvious that in one sense it scarcely needs discussion. And it certainly has not been discussed at least by social scientists. Western society and its politics—and preeminently that of the United States—grew up with the printed word; but because we have not taken time and cultural evolution seriously, we have built up elaborate accounts of Western politics and then been shocked to discover that they did not apply to the essentially oral cultures of Africa or the manuscript cultures of Asia.

The insights of twentieth-century biology lead us to the notion of information transmission. If the genetic system is one of information transmission, then so also is the socio-genetic system one of information transmission. And if this is the case then the mode and manner of information transmission ought to be of central importance in cultural evolution. From the post-modern twentieth century, armed with a comprehensive evolutionary view, we can look back on the classical and the modern in political science and philosophy.

When we talk in broad categories such as classical and modern, we are, as our earlier discussion has clearly indicated, dealing with all-encompassing matters of perspective, with fundamental modes of thought. My contention, which follows upon the insights of Innis and McLuhan, is simply that the dominant means of information transmission conditions, primarily by its form, the dominant mode of thought. A good many writers on epistemology have accepted the notion of Kant that the human world is defined and delimited by the structure of human thought. What they have not typically noticed, however, is that the structure of human thought has not always been the same, that the very structure of thought is affected by the way in which information moves from person to person.

The culture of the Athens of Socrates, Plato, and Aristotle was essentially oral, or more broadly what McLuhan calls audile-tactile. From the point of view of political theory the center of attention was the polis and the polis was understood as a natural and an oral phenomenon. It was speech (not writing), according to Plato and Aristotle, that opened the possibility of fullest human development. Socrates wrote nothing, Plato pre-

sented his ideas as speech transferred to writing (the dialogue form), and Aristotle's "writings" are said to be notes taken by his students.

Aristotle did not receive information by poring over the printed pages of an Encyclopaedia Britannica. He was not, and could not have been, the detached observer *looking* out at the world through the medium of the printed, and thus wholly visual, proposition. The world was all around him—he heard it, he felt it, he saw it, he smelled it, and all of these at once. Ethnologists of almost every description and opinion stress the unity of nature in the primitive mind, the lack of distinction between subject and object. . . . We must recognize that Plato and Aristotle for all their towering achievement were from an evolutionary point of view just a step or two from the primitive. Should we then be surprised that Plato assumed that because there was a noun "justice" that there must be something in reality that corresponded to it.

You may very well be thinking something like this: "Aristotle was not the only one who had the world all around him. I smell, feel, hear, and touch things as well!" But think a little further. Our whole culture is built upon seeing behind the appearances. We are *taught* and we *learn* to realize that the roar of the automobile is incidental to the chemistry of gasoline combustion and to the physics of the piston rod. Aristotle did not think by holding a printed proposition before his mind and seeing how it relates to reality, but we do. Learning for us simply *is* a matter of mentally taking something apart and seeing how it "works." This does not encompass all that we learn and know, but it is its core. Print and all that goes with it is the dominant form of information transmission for us and it creates the dominant mode of our thinking. . . .

Descartes and Hobbes were men of genius and they caught early the implications of the new way of thinking implicit in the printed, visually dominant, method of information transmission. Descartes and Hobbes responded quickly and began to think *objectively* in a way that only makes sense in the modern world. How can I prove that I exist? What kind of weird question would this be to a man swallowed up in nature? What would man be like in a completely pregovernmental situation, in a state of nature? What sort of strange question would this be for a man to whom man was by nature a political animal?

In this sort of context summation is dangerous, but let me nonetheless attempt a crystallization that will allow us to proceed. Modern society and modern culture—that which began in Europe around 1500 A.D.—is built around the detached observer. It is only the detached observer who can attempt to conceive natural processes as a whole, who can consider a manufacturing-marketing process as a whole with the interworking of all of its parts, and who can conceive the governing of a large number of people over a large territory as a whole problem. Conceiving a political system as a whole and attempting to build one in the style of Hobbes or Madison requires a position of detachment like a man observing an ant colony.

Print, which concentrates information transmission into the visual sense, creates this position of detachment. . . .

Aristotle operating as a man in nature is not bothered by the jump from "some" to "all" involved in the proposition, "Man is by nature a political animal." He hears it, he feels it, he sees it, all at once and thus he *knows* it. We, however, in our detached position hold the *words* before our "mind's eye" and we immediately see the difficulty in moving from "some" to "all." Aristotle was not a fool—he knew the difference between "some" and "all"—but because he understood the world from another perspective the difference did not dominate his whole mode of thinking.

The phenomenon of politics, then, is not something for which we can provide an any-time-any-place definition. It occurs in time. It is rooted in our biological nature and it has evolved as culture has evolved. It involves instinct and natural human inclination, but it also involves creative thought and thought has not always been the same. Neither is it the same throughout the world. . . . We can perhaps begin to make sense of our politics—that is, the politics of we humans and not simply we Westerners—if we tear ourselves loose from print culture science and begin to look at man in the whole sweep of nature.

Teilhard de Chardin once remarked that evolution was not simply a theory, it was an epistemological condition, "a curve that all lines must follow" as he says in another place. This is the spirit of the argument I am attempting to make here. From the perspective of the late twentieth century we can see the biological foundations of political science, not only as the product of an animal who is by nature political-scientizing but as itself an evolving phenomenon moving and changing through time with the development of man's socio-genetic system. In Sir Julian Huxley's phrase man since Darwin has become "evolution become conscious of itself."

It is increasingly clear that behavioralism as we know it in political studies, far from being the wave of the future that some contend, is in fact the last gasp of the detached observer perspective. The heavy stress on the separation of "is" and "ought" and the narrowly verifiable proposition, while unexceptionable detached observer science, is being pushed aside by a generation of students avowedly interested in "values." . . .

The problem of behavioralism in political studies has not been one of the application of scientific method where it did not belong; it has been one of the imperialism of a scientific culture which defines itself in terms of nineteenth-century physics.[4] The push for empirically verifiable generalizations on the model of nineteenth-century physics labels all other investigatory activity sub-scientific and intellectually second class. Political studies develops its own microcosmic variation of Snow's two cultures.

Taking evolution in general and the biological foundations of political science in particular seriously, however, has a profound effect on the two cultures problem. First, the notion of the evolution of society as an extension of natural evolution in its more ordinary sense inevitably sends scientists and humanists looking for one another. When, for example, Talcott Parsons, surely one of the principal inspirers of contemporary scientific social science, takes up the evolution of societies, the footnotes to distinguished humanists abound.[5] Similarly, because they deal with the evolution of man, as Professor Piggott suggests, "archaeologists are among those least likely to feel that they find any essential dichotomy between Snow's *Two Cultures*."[6] For a man who deals one day with ancient verb forms and the next with carbon-14 dating the two cultures problem begins to dissolve, and I suggest that it dissolves under a philosophical-scientific perspective that is evolutionary.

The second effect of taking evolution seriously in political science is the more important. We can now see—although I have no doubt that many will refuse to see—when we understand the implications of the socio-genetic system of information transmission that empiricism as we have known it, the radical is-ought separation, scientism, the two cultures problem, and indeed behavioralism itself in its expansionist, chauvinistic form are not final truths buy by-products of a phase in the evolution of the socio-genetic system. And it is this insight that makes the post-behavioral era . . . the opening of a new intellectual era in which social science will pay less attention to aping the method and style of natural scientists and much more attention to the substantive teachings of natural science itself.

For natural science has paved the way for the recovery of the idea of the natural law which has until recently been the core of the Western political tradition. But it is a natural law with a substantive difference. It is no longer the metaphysically teleological natural law of Aristotle and Thomas Aquinas, it is a statement of cosmic evolution supported by a wealth of empirical evidence which gives substance and detail to vague but powerful phrases like Cicero's "right reason." Contemporary natural law synthesizes the "conform to nature" directive of the classical tradition with the "manipulate nature to human ends" exhortation of the scientific and industrial revolution into a notion well expressed by Francis Bacon, "We cannot command nature except by obeying her."

Man is part of nature, subject to the laws of energy transfer, to the need for food and reproduction, and to the force of gravitation. Man is also apart from nature, and the discovery of the sense of apartness by Descartes and others broke the chains of tradition and made the scientific revolution possible. But the detachment has been overdone, for from another point of view, as biologist Marston Bates suggests, "Mankind can be viewed as a new sort of geological force, reshaping the landscape, favoring some kinds of organisms and destroying others, changing the very composition of the atmosphere

with the smoke of countless chimneys, starting new chains of radioactive decay with atomic explosions."[7]

Political order is not in some separate compartment from this "geological force." On the contrary it controls it, directs it, brings it into and out of being; and thus it is that the operators of political order must come to know what they are doing. We cannot, however, expect them to know unless the scientists of political order make an effort to know and to teach.

Notes

[1] C. H. Waddington, *The Ethical Animal* (London: George Allen and Unwin, 1960).

[2] Waddington, Atheneum edition, New York 1961, p. 7.

[3] See especially Harold A. Innis, *Empire and Communication* (Oxford: Clarendon Press, 1950), *The Bias of Communication* (Toronto: University of Toronto Press, 1951), and Marshall McLuhan, *The Gutenberg Galaxy* (Toronto: University of Toronto Press, 1962).

[4] Cf. Thomas Landon Thorson, *Biopolitics* (New York: Holt, Rinehart and Winston, 1970).

[5] See Parsons, *Societies: An Evolutionary and Comparative Perspective* (Englewood Cliffs: Prentice-Hall 1967).

[6] Stuart Piggott, *Ancient Europe* (Chicago: Aldine, 1965), p. 10.

[7] Marston Bates, *Man in Nature* (Englewood Cliffs, N.J.; Prentice-Hall, 1964), p. 106.

SOCIAL PARADIGM CHANGE

There is no way of separating the paradigm of a science from the paradigm—the world-view, the consciousness, the social values, the culture—of the society in which a science operates. This is true of all sciences, no matter how obscure and specialized their content, and it is particularly true of the sciences that deal with human behavior and human institutions. We cannot think of a change of paradigm in political science simply in terms of new theoretical perspectives that might (or might not) be adopted by a clearly defined and relatively small group of academic experts. We have to think about it in terms of different ways that people evaluate the structure of the social order; and when we do, we realize that new ways of thinking about political processes are themselves historical events, that political-science change and political change are two faces of the same coin.

The issue that has been raised by several of the writers whose work has been presented here is the possibility of a new paradigm of political science. But the greater issue that hovers behind that—which is suggested in different ways by Reich and Thorson, and confronted directly by George Leonard—is the possibility that we may be undergoing something far more momentous than the transformation of an academic discipline, a transformation more comparable to the Renaissance—or even to the emergence of what we now call civilization—than to the behavioral revolution of the 1950s.

Although this idea seems somewhat grandiose, it turns up with surprising frequency, both within and without the social sciences. And it is not exactly brand-new; nearly a decade ago economist Kenneth Boulding wrote:

The twentieth century marks the middle period of a great transition in the state of the human race. It may properly be called the second great transition in the history of mankind.

The first transition was that from precivilized to civilized society which began to take place about five (or ten) thousand years ago. This is a transition that is still going on in some parts of the world, although it can be regarded as almost complete. Precivilized society can now be found only in small and rapidly diminishing pockets in remote areas. It is doubtful whether more than 5 per cent of the world's population could now be classified as living in a genuinely precivilized society.

Even as the first great transition is approaching completion, however, a second great transition is treading on its heels. It may be called the transition from civilized to postcivilized society. We are so accustomed to giving the word civilization a favorable overtone that the words postcivilized or postcivilization may strike us as implying something unfavorable. If, therefore, the word technological or the term developed society is preferred I would have no objection. The word postcivilized, however, does bring out the fact that civilization is an intermediate state of man dividing the million or so years of precivilized society from an equally long or longer period which we may expect to extend into the future postcivilization.[2]

When history is viewed in terms of such transitions, we move naturally toward a different way of looking at science, social change, and political institutions; we may be less likely, in the future, to think of political science as the technology for the care and maintenance of the social machine, and more likely to think of it as the search for the best way human beings can organize themselves to understand and carry out the momentous enterprise of passing through a major phase in the development of the species.

Paradigms change in science after a period of crisis, when research has provided new information that does not fit the existing paradigm. Paradigms change in society in the same way, but the crises are not merely intellectual. In the concluding article, Leonard points to some of the crises that have arisen in modern technologically advanced nation-states—environmental destruction, for example—as signs of a breakdown of one kind of a system, as hints that major change will be forthcoming.

We noted as a weakness in earlier developmental political science that it tended to focus only on certain kinds of societies—usually in Latin America, Africa, or Asia—as "underdeveloped" or "developing." This kind of research and theory contains a number of clearly defined ideas about programs for change in such societies, but it lacks any comparable body of thought about how our own society might develop and change. The following reading deals with just that subject. Undoubtedly many political scientists will find it highly speculative, idealistic, and outside the proper subject-matter of the discipline. We choose to include it here not only because of its inherent value, but to argue that such considerations are and must be the concern of political scientists.

SOCIETY IN TRANSFORMATION

GEORGE B. LEONARD

* * *

Western science operates within strict if often unacknowledged boundaries. It concerns itself with the limitation and control of variables. It seeks, in its own terms, verification. This discipline, these limitations, make it possible at the least for us to discuss underlying

---

[2] Kenneth E. Boulding, *The Meaning of the Twentieth Century: The Great Transition* (New York: Harper & Row, 1965), pp. 1–2. Volume 34 of World Perspectives Series, planned and edited by Ruth Nanda Ashen.

Abridged from *The Transformation* by George B. Leonard, pp. 127–41, 187–207. Copyright © 1972 by George B. Leonard. Reprinted by permission of the publisher, Delacorte Press.

assumptions, to isolate the paradigms that shape perception and action, and to see how science itself evolves through paradigm shift.

No such clarity is possible for human affairs in general. A social system derives from a staggering number of variables, and we can rarely discover which are most important. Nor can we readily get our hands on the levers of stability or change. B. F. Skinner says that history generally makes bad experiments, and we cannot fail to note a slipshod, hit-and-miss quality in social and cultural change. . . . Life has its own urges and only so much patience with the status quo. Sooner or later the vibrancy of existence combines in some new way that utterly confounds all plans and predictions, demonstrating perhaps that the step-by-step, logical mode of analysis is in the long run the most fruitless of all. Nevertheless, within these limitations we still may be able to perceive something like paradigm shift in the process of social and cultural evolution.

To do so, we have to step back and view a rather large time scale. The various "periods" and "ages" generally isolated out of a certain cultural lineage—Renaissance, Reformation, Enlightenment, and the like—are useful to historians. But they follow too rapidly one upon the other, overlap and blur, and thus fail to provide distinct patterns of information that rise above the background noise. The Renaissance ideal may differ from the feudal ideal, but both fall within the range that defines Civilization. By choosing to view human change in terms of what we can call anthropological time. . . . we may see different human beings operating under the sway of different and incommensurable paradigms, looking at each other across consciousness gaps that can be bridged only by destruction of a way of life. Thus, the hunter and gatherer exists only through total, moment-by-moment joining with the flux and flow of nature. When [the Indian] Smohalla cried out against the sin of agriculture, the wounding and ripping of the earth, he was not speaking of differences in food-gaining techniques but of differences in reality. Regularized farming tears not just the earth but the very fabric of existence. The primitive hunter and the tribal farmer exist in different worlds. For his part, the tribal farmer, though he wounds and tears the earth, still mediates

every human transaction through the web of kinship. And he ties his religion directly to nature. The paradigm of kinship and immediate personal relationship with the supernatural is totally incommensurable with Civilization. The primacy of kinship must be destroyed for a civilized state to exist. Religion must be tied to the state rather than to nature, or simply deprived of its secular sanctions. When Civilization reaches a tribal village—for example, through the building of a road as in Joyce Cary's novel *Mr. Johnson*—the tribal way of life is doomed. Those who cannot accept the paradigm of Civilization become the flotsam of humanity. Indians on reservations are like the outcast scientists who have never yielded to relativity and quantum theory.

Human societies, like scientific movements, cannot exist without paradigms. Without some consensual shaping, life itself would be, in William James's well-known phrase, a "blooming, buzzing confusion." We may find paradigmatic clues in a society's literature or its oral epics, in its archetypes and its choice of heroes, in its dreams and nursery rhymes. A society's paradigm may be seen most clearly of all in its myths. . . .

* * *

A myth, in fact, *is* a paradigm, pure and simple. But it is an operative paradigm only so long as it is taken as somehow true—in other words, only when it is not considered a myth.

Today, library shelves are crowded with books about the myths of almost every society discovered to have existed on this planet. These myths not only define particular societies but seem also to contain underlying material that is common to all humankind. . . .

* * *

What we are seeking here, however, is the particular and limited paradigm of Civilization and the incommensurables that must shift upon the arrival of a new epoch. In this search, we must keep reminding ourselves that the myths on the library shelves are, by the very fact of being there, dead or dying. They are, for the most part, no longer operative paradigms. The forces that most decisively control our lives, as Marshall McLuhan has pointed out, are "environmental," that is, pervasive and unremarkable. They are nothing that we can analyze, classify, consciously manipulate or, often, even see.

The key elements in a paradigm are generally marked by their ordinariness. It is doubtful that astronomers before Copernicus spent much time discussing the marvelous fact that the earth was a stationary platform around which all the heavenly bodies moved. And yet this assumption dominated their work. How much more the invisible paradigm of existence affects every human life! As with the geocentric universe, the simple awareness of any controlling human paradigm may spell the beginning of its end. When Lewis Mumford, in his recent two-volume work *The Myth of the Machine*, brought into sharp focus one of the controlling paradigms of the Civilized Epoch, he was actually giving notice that the Epoch is over.

Mumford theorizes . . . that the modern megamachine had its birth at the very beginning of Civilization, when the "divine" rulers of the great cities of the Fertile Crescent fashioned giant mechanisms using human beings instead of pistons and cogs. From that time until the present, according to Mumford, men have put their greatest faith in and perhaps sold their souls for technics, not realizing the negative consequences that went along with the gains. Though the warnings came earlier, in Faust and Frankenstein and science fiction, it is only recently that the monster has materialized clearly before our eyes. The time of anomaly and crisis is indeed upon us. What we did not realize until Mumford is how far back the myth of mechanistic manipulation reached and how drastically it has shaped all of the works and will of Civilization, and the consciousness of its people.

A time of anomaly and crisis, and of awakening. Before long, all the stuff of the paradigm of Civilization will take shape before our eyes, and we will be moved to outrage, laughter and horror. And then to understanding, for it obviously could not have been otherwise.

* * *

. . . For now, we may simply bring to mind some of the operative folk beliefs of the old paradigm that are now emerging to our consciousness. Start with the more obvious ones:

The Myth of Growth. More is better. Bigger is better. The largest pyramid, the largest ship, the largest city, the largest empire. . . . Civilization, dealing primarily in gross matter and ordinary physical energy, has at last carried the Myth of Growth to the point of anomaly and crisis. . . .

The Myth of Fertility is a corollary to the Myth of Growth but has consequences of its own. All types of societies have valued fertility, and the production of numerous progeny as an aid to the state may create even more sexual pressures in Civilization. . . . When woman is cherished for the crop she produces, a rigid, bilateral definition of sex is inevitable. We think of bilateral sex as being as permanent and stable as Ptolemy's stationary earth; yet we may be sure, now that unabated procreation threatens the existence of the planet, that it is not. . . . The problems of woman and man cannot be solved in terms of present definitions of woman and man.

The Myth of the Limited Good. Civilized man, dealing primarily in matter and ordinary energy, is doomed to come up against the problem of short supply. And since he finds that matter and energy are limited, he comes to believe that other aspects of life—love and friendship, health, respect, security, even spiritual well-being—are also limited. Thus it seems that when one person or family or political group gains, others must necessarily lose. . . . The idea of limited good is indeed a dangerous one, for it lies behind every model of human conflict. As long as humankind remains preoccupied with matter and energy, and until all people's minimum needs in this respect are satisfied, limited good will continue to pose a problem. But when the human race turns its primary attention to human transformation, it may well be that "good" can be perceived as unlimited.

The Myth of Inevitable Competition developed relatively late in the Civilized Epoch and is a corollary of the Myth of Limited Good. Along with aggression and acquisition, inevitable competition has become not only a given of the mercantile-capitalist society but also has come to define the very essence of existence for many men of our world. . . . All the recent talk about the danger of the United States becoming a "second-rate power" actually concerns the nation's ability to wage war and to dominate more than its share of the world's physical resources. When pundits speak of every movement away from aggressiveness and dominance as a possible "loss of nerve," they are speaking strictly in terms of the old view of the universe. They cannot conceive of how much nerve, courage, and imagination it will take to strike out in the direction of a new quality of existence in which neither grubbing for economic supremacy nor building extravagant armaments to guard it will consume the major part of our energy.

The Myth of Societal Unintentionality. We do not have to look to science fiction for the "group mind." Every social body has a consciousness of sorts. A society, in fact, is probably more "conscious" than are the individuals within it. The individuals are just not privy to the group consciousness. Society certainly possesses will and purpose, however veiled. Transformation entails not the *creation* of a group mind, but awareness and improvement of it.

The Myth of Separate Species. Separation and classification of the various earthly organisms provides us an interesting exercise and defines one way of looking at existence. But making these sharp distinctions blocks an even more important vision. In a very real sense, there is only one species on this planet and its name is Life on Earth. Ecologists acknowledge this fact with their discussions of the biomass. We are beginning to realize that the extinction of what we now refer to as a species is some sort of amputation within the larger species of which we are a part. . . .

The Myth of the Separate Ego. The idea of individuals as separate and discrete egos, pinpricks through the fine skin of existence reached its zenith in the Western branch of Civilization. . . . The Western ego is a construct in the process of collapsing; we know now that accepting the construct means accepting eventual alienation. Increased contact with Eastern philosophy and religion weakens the Western concept of separate ego even as the process of Westernization spreads throughout the underdeveloped nations. The old paradigm struggles mightily before giving up. But it is increasingly clear

that consciousness has no skin.

* * *

The Myth of Glory, Honor and Duty. That a man will suffer pain and deprivation or even give up his life for something as abstract as a flag is good evidence that a social body has intentionality. Otherwise how could it manipulate the individual to behave so strenuously and mindlessly against his own self-interest and in the interest of societal glory, honor and duty? B. F. Skinner provides the clearest picture of this process when he points out that society usually honors an individual in direct proportion to the time that elapses between action and reinforcement. (For the man who dies for glory, that time is infinite.) Every great human enterprise requires some delay of reinforcement. But for the person who has learned to flow with the rhythm of existence the delay is only apparent. Such a person lives in the always vibrant present, and the need for societal glory which is earned through delayed reinforcement becomes clearly a myth.

There may be nothing surprising in the above material. My guess is that most readers already have unmasked those folk beliefs. If so, it is another sign of how far the Transformation has proceeded. There are other assumptions in the civilized paradigm that are more difficult to unmask. . . .

The Myth of Law. No one who lives in civilized society can expect any measure of personal security and social stability without the rule of law. But simply to assume that this will always be the case may blind us to new possibilities in social organization. We may well remind ourselves that formal law is a relatively recent development in the history of humankind, coming into being only with the rise of the first civilized states. Without policemen, judges, prisons, legal codes and lawyers, we would need a drastically altered mode of human relationship—which is a good reason for considering such an eventuality.

The Myth of Matter, Time and Space. Throughout this book are suggestions that the old consensus of matter, time and space as discrete and fixed entities is false and misleading. This is only to echo the by-now venerable concepts of relativity physics and quantum mechanics. When a more fluid feeling about the basic matrices of reality comes to our literature, our journalism and our everyday life (as it already has to our science), we'll find it much easier to deal with other aspects of the emerging paradigm.

The Myth of Illusion. Speaking from the cockpit of nineteenth-century America, Sylvester Graham stated that dreams, imagination, and even mental pictures are dangerous illusions. On the other hand, primitive societies and some early civilized societies gave more weight to dreams and visions than to waking reality. What is to be termed "illusion" as opposed to "reality" has always been a decision of the society, and has always limited the potential of the individual to participate in the fullness of the vibrancy. We may find it possible to consider *all* perceptions as having relevance, each type evoking its own appropriate response.

* * *

The paradigm of Civilization is strong and pervasive. Considering how indomitably it held sway in the nineteenth and early twentieth centuries, we may wonder at how swiftly it is now being unmasked. We might have expected Civilization with its ever-increasing manipulations of humanity and nature to have lasted for centuries longer. The earth is large and for thousands of years it endured the wars and crusades, the building and digging of civilized men, patiently transforming every scar to dust or greenery. But then in the seventeenth century human history took an unexpected turn. Within the civilized paradigm a flood change occurred, out of which emerged the magical means that have swept us, all in a rush, to Civilization's end and the dawn of Transformation.

The Transformation eventually will touch all that is human. It is possible that within fifty years many present-day fields, specialties, institutions will barely be recognizable or will no longer exist as such. It is not my purpose here to provide a compendium of institutional change; I believe such prediction to be impossible. All I can do is suggest a few possible signposts on a journey that is uncertain at every given point but inevitable in the whole.

Politics. We can read the grotesque condition of our dying Civilization in the political arena almost as unmistakably as on the gridiron. I have written elsewhere that doing the things now deemed necessary to achieve high office makes a man unworthy of that office.[2] The candidate schemes, manipulates, lies, veils his true sentiments, appeals to friendship and loyalty for ulterior ends. Upon taking office, he assures himself, he will change. That he rarely if ever does is becoming clear to increasing numbers of voters. What has been termed the Credibility Gap has widened to include not just the politician's words but his very being. We begin to disbelieve the existence of the human being behind the campaign poster. It is probably a testimonial to our awakening perceptions that those smiling faces look more and more like Halloween masks.

The coming years may well bring about reforms in political structure. The Center for the Study of Democratic Institutions, for example, has been working for several years on a tentative new national Constitution. But the first omen of a transformed politics may simply be the emergence of a new breed of political candidate. Some, in fact, already have been elected to state and local offices. Such a politician is dedicated to a kind of openness and honesty that is quite inconceivable to the traditional office seeker. He is clear and aboveboard, not just in verbal statements, but in the deeper matters of feeling, sensing and being. This may seem quite traditional, but actually, in this culture, just to get in touch with real feeling is a radical act. The new politician recognizes that whether he wills it or not he is an exemplar and that the way he leads his life will affect the electorate. He may take it as one of his functions to articulate a new social vision and to help guide his constituency through the difficulties and joys of social and personal change.

The election of large numbers of this breed—not really so unlikely in view of the growing public revulsion against traditional politicians—could create a more significant and lasting political revolution than could a new Constitution. It might also result in real changes *within* formal political structures.

To illustrate, the idea of inevitable winners and

equally inevitable losers may be rather easily modified. The pervasive debate-adversary mode of politics cracks reality down the middle. It is as if every issue must have two sides and every decision must leave a disgruntled minority, with its members muttering, "Just wait until next time." But hardly any question really has only two sides. When legislative or administrative bodies give up the sole notion of victory, they may also avoid the inevitability of defeat. Assuming some sort of eventual agreement, the members would not debate but would explore possibilities. They would make every effort to avoid complete defeat for any faction. This would mean moving towards pluralistic decisions in many cases. Sociologist Herbert Gans points out that, contrary to present practice, we can provide minority groups with maximum choice: "Instead of forcing three minorities to shoehorn themselves into a majority in favor of policy A, let's provide three policies, A, B and C, and let people choose their own best alternative." Such diversity is not always possible, but it applies more often than we might imagine.

The Transformation may also bring changes in the politician's attitude towards power. Though we often hear the traditional warnings against its corrosive effects, political power of the most outrageous stripe still evokes widespread fascination and admiration. The cult of the present-day, overblown United States Presidency, for example, includes many journalists and scholars who should know better. The grasp for more and more power results not just from the increasing size and complexity of our society but also from increasing fear and personal emptiness among the men involved. Modern Western man, essentially alone against the world and deprived of the natural satisfactions of the body and senses, is especially susceptible to the desire for external dominance over others. Political scientist Harold Lasswell argues that the power seeker "pursues power as a means of compensation against deprivation. *Power is expected to overcome low estimates of the self.*"

*   *   *

We have our latter-day, individualized President, a man who controls more deadly power than any king or emperor, a man glamourized for his seat at "the lonely pinnacle of power," glorified for making such statements as "The buck stops here," nurtured by crisis, melodramatic in his "command decisions"—and utterly ravaged by the power he has spent a lifetime seeking. The Presidency sets the style for every other public office, and in every legislative and administrative hall you can smell the decay of humanity as the predators and scavengers gather. Whether he is a United States senator or an assemblyman in a small state, the politician's eyes glint towards something *not here.* So long as he is holding the floor—making speeches, manipulating people or blocs of people, establishing positions—he is likely to be charming, dynamic, and possibly charismatic. But when the situation turns to dialogue, to the candid interchange of thoughts and feelings, the great man begins to fade before your eyes. He becomes restless, preoccupied. Time drags. Each new moment seems to weary him.

The desire for surplus power, the capability to dominate as many people and as many things as possible, is at its height in our society. It is also diminishing. The two tendencies exist simultaneously on either side of a consciousness gap. The new breed of politician may emerge from those who are less deprived personally and thus have less need for dominance. The new politician will seek new power relationships. . . . Whatever his office, the politician and the political groups of the Transformation will do everything they can to share, not amass, political and personal power. That would be revolution enough.

Revolution in the conventional sense is, in fact, an aspect of Civilization, not of Transformation. Surely we have seen enough of those armed overthrows that replace one set of bosses with another set that holds a different doctrine but possesses the same consciousness, the same mode of personal being. Without transformation of the person, there is only the endless chain of injustice and revenge for injustice. The new politician, with his or her being as well as with actions, helps break the chain.

*   *   *

Race. Even before the coming of Civilization, human beings had developed us-versus-them as a mechanism of social cohesion and control. Group prejudice probably predated racial prejudice. But now race stands out in high definition, a symbol of our hates and fears, a metaphor of the centrifugal forces that oppose joining and ecstasy. To the mind of Civilization, racial prejudice appears as a problem, an obstacle to change. It may also be viewed as an opportunity, as one of the most direct, if painful and abrasive, routes towards Transformation. The United States, in fact, has moved further into the Transformation than other countries partially because of its large black population—the crisis it has created, the behavior and consciousness it has changed.

Each time a person of one race confronts one of another, he may consider it an opportunity for self-examination. The loathing, rage, frustration, anxiety and guilt normally lodged deep within rise to the surface, tend to focus on the member of the other race. In 1967, Dr. Price Cobbs and I led the first marathon racial confrontation group. Since then, I have co-led several more; Dr. Cobbs, a black psychiatrist, has gone on to lead or supervise some three hundred racial confrontations and has carried out follow-up studies on the people involved. Cobbs and his colleagues have found no white without prejudice, no black without anger, and no person entirely free of self-decption. Race provides a powerful searchlight. It penetrates to the dark core of the civilized sickness. It illuminates individual neuroses. It makes obscure dialectics as sharp and clear as black and white. If the opportunity for confrontation is taken, what was hidden begins to become visible. What was numbed begins to hurt. The oppressed can turn his anger upon his oppressor rather than inward to poison himself. The oppressor can express his guilt and fear of retaliation. He can recognize, through the oppressed, the spontaneity, the joy, even the ability to perceive reality that he has had to hide somewhere in the sterile suburb of his senses. Through pain and recognition, the most profound learning—that is, significant human change—can take place. In breaking through the many barriers made explicit by race, you break through all barriers to some extent.

* * *

A bold and imaginative national leadership with a vision of human transformation could help speed the process. Just to give an example: If every high school and college in the nation spent the first month of next term doing nothing but confronting the matter of race, the amount of learning would far exceed anything now generally considered possible. What is more, the nation would be joined, at last, in a sense of common purpose that does not involve war and killing. Tremendous difficulties are involved in all plans of this scope and daring. Perhaps such things are simply impossible. But we will never know until we find leaders with vision enough to propose them seriously.

Man and Woman. . . . Sex—the word itself probably derives from the Latin verb *secare,* "to cut or sever"—may seem to highlight separateness. But, optimally, man and woman, taken together, help us to perceive the distance between what we are and what we could be. Sex provides our poor eyes a safe glimpse of the ultimate unity, still too bright for us to bear.

And yet, in the Transformation, we shall probably relinquish "man" and "woman," those caricatures of sexuality that have developed during the reign of Civilization. The proponents of Women's Liberation are right. The traditional construct of man as hard, unfeeling, aggressive and conceptualizing, and woman as soft, yielding, nurturing and intuitive, insults male as well as female. Many of the reformers recognize that "liberation" will mean something quite different for both. Unfortunately, however, much of the society's reward system still works on the basis of competition, aggression and unfeelingness, and we are sometimes presented with the sad spectacle of "liberated" women becoming more like present-day males. Women today are even making inroads into the crime field, once an almost exclusive male territory; since 1960, the number of arrests of women has increased at a rate three times that of men.

Transcending our present, limiting sex roles may seem almost impossible, but it is no more difficult than simply living with our mates for as long as seven straight days with any assurance of harmony and personal growth. The problem of the man-woman relationship, about which so much has been theorized and so little understood, continues to resist rational solution. . . .

We may at last have to admit that there is no satisfactory answer to the man-woman puzzle in the present paradigm. The answer most likely lies somewhere beyond "man" and "woman." This means just what it says. It means dispensing with what now seems most indispensable. It means peeling off layer after layer of the man-ness and woman-ness wrapped around us by Civilization until we discover the essential humanity at the core. What, then, will we have lost?

In our distant past, our life in the wilds may have required lasting pair-bonding to assure care for our slow-maturing young. Agriculture increased the need for fast breeding and large families. Now these tendencies work against us, creating overpopulation and a tight little vacuum-packed family. We need fewer children and bigger, less well-defined families. We need groups of friends and neighbors who are willing and able to share the strongest feelings, to share responsibility for all the children in the group.

During the Civilized Epoch with its wars and empires and physical frontiers, we needed men who would not yield, would not feel, would not weep. But it has turned out that we have no more Vietnams or Lake Eries to spare for the John Wayne-type male.

In a world of work and human components, we needed to hold erotic impulses on a short leash, thus helping to create the dis-ease so necessary for the central tasks of Civilization. But now this work is coming to an end and we must learn to play. . . .

* * *

War. Civilization is impossible without major war. Because of nuclear weapons, major war is impossible. Ergo, Civilization is impossible.

The syllogism may leave room for argument. But do not leave it quickly.

We cannot talk about the end of war without first singing its praises. That war is a necessary element in civilized society, a prime organizing device of the state, need not be argued here. (Among other books, *Report from Iron Mountain*, purporting to be the proceedings of a high-level secret strategy meeting, makes an ironic and chilling exposition of the many social and cultural functions served by civilized warfare.[3]) War is a social necessity. It is also something more. For a citizenry numbed of sense and deprived of emotion, war provides a blessed opportunity to hope, to fear, to exult, to suffer—for God's sake—to *feel*. When the war alarms go out, young men and old are drawn to the stirring of a lost memory. *What is it I've forgotten? Ah, now I remember, My own existence.* The real promise of war is not that we may gain some glorious prize but that we may lose everything. Our lives, our honor. Our flag in the mud, our city in ashes, our women raped. In what other circumstances can we truly do our best, give our all for friends, for others we do not know, for a noble cause?

And without war how can we have those epic movies? (Beneath his helmet, John Wayne's eyes are slits. His mouth is a slit. "Gentlemen, we didn't come all this way to sit on our tails. We're movin' up that road. Tonight.") Without war, the memory of war and the anticipation of war, a good third of our literature would lose its meaning entirely. The obligatory prebattle scene (the common soldiers solemn-faced, grasping their relics, talking of home; the officers heavy with decision, quietly philosophical) is hardly a cinematic invention. The script is etched in our brain, going back in our direct lineage through Shakespeare at least to Homer. It is not something we can easily relinquish.

In war Civilization thrives. Sometimes, in fact, the numbness of dis-ease is scrubbed away and we exist for a moment in the clean vibrancy, not just during the great battles but all around the edges of danger. . . .

* * *

. . . In the end, war is always ugly and dirty and painful and obscene. But we tend to forget that for a majority of people in a nation a great war has usually provided a heightening of experience, a punctuation mark of drama in a lifetime of routine numbness, an occasion for renewing our epic sense.

The Vietnam War has been different. It has become a powerful antidote to glory and perhaps an inoculation against war itself, coming just at a time of widespread awakening of consciousness in this country. The length and futility of this misadventure has helped focus our attention on the ugliness. We may also find a sign of some human transformation, some increase in our sensitivity, in the fact that certain practices not so much condoned as simply ignored in previous conflicts now rise to outrage us. And the sensibility that perceives a war correspondent's detachment as grotesque is by no means a conventional civilized sensibility.

But in spite of the inoculation provided by Vietnam, in spite of increasing national sensitivity to war's horrors, in spite of the fact that all-out war is now "impossible," war and the threat of war continue to hang over our lives. War takes precedence over domestic problems for underdeveloped nations in which millions starve to death every year. War remains as a major option for our own national leaders, supported by an enormous establishment that commands vast resources of money, material, energy and information. These men have tough-minded, practical objections to peacefulness. What would happen, they ask, if we let our guard down and the *others* didn't? They argue that if we do not continue urging our young men, in effect, towards criminal behavior, then those *other* yellow-black-brown-red criminals will come over in hordes and destroy us. Their fear is not entirely paranoid. We would be fooling ourselves to discount aggressive impulses in other civilized states. But it is clear that our own aggressiveness does much to fan the flames.

If a deeply felt, positive will towards peacefulness were present in our national leadership, this nation—master of the most powerful machine of destruction in the history of the planet—could do much to end war. It could make its will known to the world through the usual diplomatic, treaty-making channels. In addition, it could act unilaterally through various imaginative and dramatic means. Not the least of these would be treating every move towards disarmament—dismantling a major foreign base, closing an ABM site, retiring a warship—as an occasion for celebration. These celebrations would be truly festive events, to which representatives of all nations would be invited, accompanied by music and dancing and the best of the arts, described

to all the world through every possible medium of communications. The moral force of such celebrations, if a true expression of our own leadership, would be considerable.

Unfortunately, such occasions would seem funerals rather than festivals to far too many of the men who lead us. To help end war, our leaders would have to *want* to give up war, to give up their esoteric underground war rooms, their secret briefings, their hands on the pulse of destructive power, the possibility of great sacrifice and great achievement through violence, and the attendant renewal of their sense of existence. We must face it. Within the framework of Civilization and in the light of our present unambitious, uninspiring goals, there is nothing to take war's place. Pro football is not the moral equivalent of war, even if the President himself can call the plays.

Opposing war by writing letters, signing petitions, voting for the present breed of peace candidates, engaging in marches, and committing civil disobedience can be quite useful. But it is doubtful that a momentous surge towards true peacefulness can occur until some great enterprise not involving war becomes clear to us. The transformation of the social order into new forms and the commensurate transformation of human beings into what amounts to a higher species certainly constitute such an enterprise. The tingling sense of aliveness that would be sanctioned and inculcated by a transformed society would make it unnecessary for us to remember existence through the memory, anticipation or actuality of battle. And the sweeping reforms implied in the search for a new human nature would make war seem less than epic. To empty our prisons, create a new education and a new politics, end racism, provide a decent minimum living standard for every inhabitant, open the possibilities of meaning and joy for old people, make every city a festival and the entire country a garden is, for a start, enough to engage our energy and aspiration, our enormous unused capability.

*   *   *

Index

•